A HISTORY OF
ENGLISH FURNITURE

Frontispiece (See page 70). Oak Court Cupboard. Height, 7 feet 4 inches; length, 5 feet; depth, 1 foot 9 inches. Property of Sir George Donaldson.

A HISTORY OF
ENGLISH FURNITURE

INCLUDING
THE AGE OF OAK
THE AGE OF WALNUT
THE AGE OF MAHOGANY
THE AGE OF SATINWOOD

BY

PERCY MACQUOID, R.I.

BRACKEN BOOKS
LONDON

Originally published in 1904-1908 by
Lawrence & Bullen Ltd, London W.C.
This edition is published in 1988 by
Bracken Books, a division of
Bestseller Publications Ltd.,
Princess House, 50 Eastcastle Street,
London W1N 7AP
England

Publisher's Note
The text of A History of English Furniture *has been*
reprinted without alteration. The publishers would like to
make it clear that the ownership attributed to all the furniture
and clocks illustrated in the text was that at the time of first
publication in 1904-1908

ISBN 1 85170 080 3

Printed in Hungary

CONTENTS

INTRODUCTION
by Jerome Phillips

ERCY MACQUOID's four-volume *A History of English Furniture* published in 1904–8 is still rightly regarded as the first serious study of the subject. For this very reason, many of the ideas put forward have been revised in the course of the following eighty years, and the issue of this reprint is a useful opportunity to assess Macquoid's book in the light of the 1980s.

Macquoid was the first to recognize the importance of provenance; he used many documentary sources such as letters of the period and, above all, he discovered the original invoices for some furniture supplied by Thomas Chippendale. While many of the pieces illustrated, especially those with heavy carving or elaborately painted decoration, would not be regarded as authentic today, he also illustrated pieces with a fully documented provenance, many of which are still regarded as being among the most important examples of English furniture. Even the 'wrong' illustrations are interesting for the view of the state of furniture studies in the early years of this century.

Although Macquoid divided *A History of English Furniture* into four 'ages', those of oak, walnut, mahogany and satinwood, we now know that there was a considerable overlap between them: for example, mahogany was used as early as 1725, but some very high-quality pieces were being made of walnut as late as the 1760s. Right through his ages of walnut, mahogany and satinwood, Macquoid himself recognized that oak was being used for furniture in the country districts. During his 'Age of Satinwood', rosewood and mahogany were more common than satinwood. None the less, with these reservations, we can accept the broad concept of 'ages' as being reasonably valid, although new artistic influences were sometimes just as important as a new wood in introducing a new style.

Macquoid tended to attribute too many pieces to a handful of well-known makers, such as Thomas Chippendale or, indeed, George Hepplewhite (whose widow published an important book of designs, but who has no definitely documented piece of furniture to her name), but he did not do so as much as later critics have maintained, nor as much as previous writers had. He has since been teased for attributing a 'shellback' chair circa 1735 (Fig. 548) to Thomas Chippendale, who would have then been only seventeen! Nevertheless, he did identify correctly some of Thomas Chippendale's most important pieces for the houses where he worked. Since Macquoid's time much new information has come to light, revealing many significant makers contemporary with Chippendale, such as Cobb, Vile, Hallett and others, although many would still regard Chippendale as the greatest single maker. Furniture historians today tend to describe a piece as 'George III period, circa 1765' rather than 'Chippendale period', and this is more accurate, although the concept of a 'Chippendale period' has some value, provided of course that this does not mean that the piece in question is considered to be by Chippendale himself.

Although Macquoid continued *A History of English Furniture* up to 1820, he clearly had little enthusiasm for the Regency: it was not until Margaret Jourdain's work in the 1930s that any real interest was taken in this period, and it is only in the last few years that collectors have tended to go later than 1830.

While Macquoid is best known for his *History*, he later undertook the catalogue of the Lady Lever Collection and he wrote the first edition of the *Dictionary of English Furniture* in conjunction with Ralph Edwards, who completed the project after Macquoid's death in 1925.

In the next generation, Robert Symonds extended our practical understanding of furniture, while Margaret Jourdain and Ralph Edwards added enormously to our knowledge of individual cabinet makers and their work. Yet without Macquoid's pioneering work, furniture studies would never have reached their present state. Although clearly much more is known now about the construction of furniture and the role of various makers, many of our present ideas may well have to be revised in the years to come. In the field of antique furniture, there is always more to be learned.

PREFACE

N the arrangement of this work, it will be found that the subject has been divided into four periods. The first, dating from 1500 to 1600, comprising furniture that can be attributed to the Renaissance and its evolution from the Gothic, may be termed 'The Age of Oak'. The second, from 1660 to 1720, where the change is varied by the Restoration and Dutch influence, followed by a distinctly assertive English spirit, may be called 'The Age of Walnut'. The third period, where the introduction from France of fresh ideas in design clearly marked another change, lasting from 1720 to 1770, which we call 'The Age of Mahogany'; and the fourth, from 1770 to 1820, inspired by an affectation for all things classical, combined with a curiously unbalanced taste, can best be described as 'The Age of Satinwood'.

It is proposed to deal with the history, development, and evolution of English furniture only, but as the sources of its inspiration can so frequently be traced to foreign origin, it will be necessary to introduce occasionally some of these examples, in order to more clearly explain the different types and their close analogy. The comparison will be useful also for defining where the English craftsman at certain periods departed from his foreign model and struck into an original path.

Inception of design in architecture and its dependent offspring, furniture, was in the Middle Ages wholly due to ecclesiastical influence; and as the more gifted members of religious confraternities were moved from country to country to gain knowledge as well as to impart it, it is impossible to determine now how far design in art of this early period was really indigenous to this country. As long as the monastic architect and his pupils were the originators of furniture, it was natural that such objects should be ecclesiastical and severe in character, for the manners and customs of all periods have had the strongest imprint on design; there was also a practical necessity for its solidity, as a man armed cap-à-pie must have required a very heavily constructed seat. It was therefore reserved for the artist, or a craftsman with strong artistic perception (and it must be remembered that a so-called company of cabinetmakers existed as early as 1480), to evolve from these solid and almost barbaric forms the lighter and more elegant creations that we are accustomed to-day to associate with the word Furniture. For a long period the craftsman was entirely influenced by the architecture that surrounded him, and, being unimaginative, he borrowed all required detail for his decoration from either structure, metal work or textiles. These being all designed, if not actually carried out, by foreigners, may account for the reason why early English furniture lacks the contemporary taste found in France, Germany and Italy, for art feeling in England was neither inborn nor spontaneous. Indeed, until the end of the fifteenth century, the English were far behind those other nations in the luxury and artistic appointments of their great houses; the simultaneous spread of novelty in foreign countries was greatly facilitated by the journeyman who travelled from city to city with his designs, and who perpetually had the opportunity of accumulating the knowledge and fresh inspirations of the countries through which he passed. Patronage and interest were both limited in England, and the sea was such a formidable obstacle, that tastes and fashions do not appear to have been accepted in this country until firmly established on the Continent. When Richard II married the young Princess Isobel of France, he was much condemned by his English subjects for the unnecessary and unprecedented luxury of his palaces; on the other hand, the young bride excited the greatest pity and sympathy from her fellow-countrymen at being torn from the comforts of her own home and transplanted to what they considered the rough and rude surroundings of an English palace.

About 1480 a sudden stride in domestic civilisation took place in England, and decorative furniture was for the first time gradually introduced into private houses. Previous to this it had been confined to the royal and episcopal palaces, monasteries, and the castles of the great nobles, while burghers, merchants and citizens had been content with the most severely simple necessities, for we find no early individual instance of cultivated taste amongst this class, such as Jean van Arteveldt of Flanders, Cosimo di Medici of Italy, or Jacques Cœur of France. At this period detail in the decoration of architecture lost its large simplicity in the effort to produce a lighter and more romantic effect. This change, known as flamboyant, had doubtless much to do with the origin of beauty of detail in wood-carving, the proportion and ornamentation introduced lending themselves to reproduction on articles of furniture, while the much desired and welcomed peace, brought about by the union of the houses of York and Lancaster, consolidated trade, and encouraged the demand for all manner of crafts in England, until by degrees the finer furniture, which had been all imported from abroad, began to be manufactured in this country. At first these were but coarse copies of foreign examples, and though beds, chairs, tables and coffers were no doubt largely made here, it is not till the middle of the sixteenth century that the movement succeeded in creating a distinctive and national taste in sufficient quantity to enable us to obtain existing examples of its style. All very early English furniture that has come down to us is of oak. Deal and chestnut were rare, valuable woods in those days; what was made of beech and elm has perished, and walnut was not grown for its wood in England till about 1500. As an instance of the estimation in which deal was held, we find that Henry VIII had a room panelled in this wood at Nonesuch, 'by which he set great store'. Preference was also given to oak as the representative wood of this country, and for its unquestionable durability. The carting about of furniture over rough roads, when a great personage moved from one of his castles to another in order 'that the same might sweeten', must have demanded great strength in both material and construction, and these periodical removals of personal furniture, from the beds downwards, prove that the supply of such necessities was extremely limited.

THE AGE OF OAK

CHAPTER I

T will be best to subdivide this 'Age of Oak' into three periods: Gothic, Elizabethan and Jacobean.

GOTHIC   That rooms were bare and provided with but few forms of furniture in the Middle Ages is clearly proved by the artists who illustrated the horæ, histories and romances of those times in this country. There is no reason to doubt these representations being correct in their general impression, and they are our only guide to the arrangement and utility of individual objects. In these MS miniatures the furniture is invariably coloured, and from the traces of paint that still remain on some existing ecclesiastical pieces, we may conclude that domestic furniture was frequently painted, and in very bright colours. As these colours were mostly rendered in some form of tempera or wax, it is easy to understand how in time the paint completely disappeared, leaving only the somewhat clumsy forms; the early furniture was evidently also much ornamented by hangings, and dressed up with valances and cushions of bright and rich materials. Of this plain but painted furniture, little or nothing survives, the armoires or livery cupboards, shown in Figs. 1, 2 and 3, would have been

FIG. 1. *Oak Gothic Cupboard.* Height, 4 feet; length, 4 feet 4½ inches; depth, 1 foot 11 inches. Property of C. E. KEMPE, Esq.

FIG. 2. *Armoire or Livery Cupboard.* Oak. Height, 3 feet 10 inches; width, 3 feet 10 inches; depth, 1 foot 6 inches. Property of MORGAN WILLIAMS, Esq.

FIG. 3. *Armoire or Livery Cupboard.* Oak. Height, 3 feet 10 inches; width, 3 feet 2 inches; depth, 1 foot 5 inches. Property of MORGAN WILLIAMS, Esq.

painted with sacred or heraldic subjects, and resemble types of an earlier date. In Fig. 1, of about the date 1500, the front is composed of six panels, two of which form doors, perforated with openings of Gothic tracery cut in the solid for purposes of ventilation, as food, candles, wine and many eatables were kept in such cupboards. The top and base have been reconstructed, otherwise the piece is in its original condition. In Fig. 2, of rather earlier date, the front is made of three oak planks, the centre opening as a door; here there is no attempt at framing, the boards being finished at the edge by a simple channel moulding. The inside is divided into three compartments, and retains the original shelves. In Fig. 3, the openings at the sides take the form of windows, perpendicular in style, those in the door being circular and spiral in motive, with no attempt at mouldings round the decoration. These last two pieces are of Berkshire origin and of about the same date, 1475. With the exception of the hinges, their condition is original throughout.

The panelling and even the wall space above were also frequently painted in colours with varied designs. Original examples of painted panelling are rare, but there is an interesting room in existence in Wiltshire where the stiles and rails are a rich vermilion, and the long Tudor panels olive coloured, on which are stencilled a darker green early sixteenth-century design. Such rooms, with their painted walls and painted furniture, with their rich hangings and tapestries, were on the first floor, and used by the lord and lady of the house as their private apartments; the most important room being a combination of dining and bedroom, with furniture consisting of a table; flanking this against the wall a long bench, with back and canopy, termed a dossier, that could be used as a day-bed or a seat for meals, capable of holding four persons; two buffets, very similar to the foreign credences, for ornamental vessels; another table on which were laid articles connected with the toilet; a standing cupboard or hutch, used as a washstand; a bed, with heavy curtains at the foot, looped up during the day into the form of a long bag; a few stools and a *prie-dieu* completing the room. The floor was strewn with rushes, on which, in the houses of the very rich, were laid small Eastern carpets. Clothes were changed and kept in the Garde-robe, a small room adjoining; the bath was, however, taken in a wooden tub in front of the fireplace, in which probably a fire burnt all the year round, for until the middle of the sixteenth century our ancestors slept naked, and glass in the windows was a great luxury.

The large hall was the general sitting-room, in which the principal meals of the household and all entertaining took place. The furniture here consisted at one end of a long table on a raised portion of the floor, behind which was an important seat with a dossier and overhanging dais or canopy. Chests, forms and benches composed the other seats, and round the large open fireplace were settles and perhaps a couple of chairs; a low side-table for service stood on either side of the principal seat, and a buffet for the silver stood in the centre of the wooden panelled screen, containing two entrances that formed the other end of the room; the portion of the hall cut off in this manner by the screen formed the minstrel gallery, and below it the passage leading to the outer door. One of these low side-tables is given in Fig. 4. Their introduction, late in the fifteenth century, marks an epoch of practical construction in furniture and the invention of the drawer table-top, for hitherto tables had been either trestle, or with fixed tops capable of no enlargement; the piece of furniture in this manner could serve the various purposes of a side serving-table or buffet, a long table for meals, a cupboard for food, or a seat. The two lower leaves that form the extension of the draw-top are in this instance lost, and it has been a little shortened; with these exceptions the buffet is in its original state, and in admirable preservation. It is difficult to realise how this comparatively rude and clumsily constructed piece could be contemporary with the highly finished and beautiful architecture, fabrics, armour, enamels and plate that existed, and it is unlikely that anything better of its kind was made in England, for all relics of this furniture are of the same barbaric quality. Such a side-table would have belonged to some great noble or wealthy prelate; had it been made for royalty, the only difference would have been the introduction of the royal arms, with perhaps elaborate painting and gilding. It stands upon quadrangular legs, bordered on the inside by a rude double channel moulding, forming a finish to the bottom rail; the front is divided into three oblong panels, those on the outside forming doors; they are framed in an unusually bold one-inch moulding, with a deep bevel at bottom: the panels all differ, and are deeply and boldly carved with Gothic tracery of about 1475; the centre panel, which is bevelled out so that the face of the carving is flush with that of the framing, is geometrically centred, contrasting admirably with the eccentric lines of the others. The hinges are original and quite plain; the lock-plates, which have lost their sliding bolts, are also plain, and all of English make; traces of perforated cresting survive on the left-hand plate. The introduction of small panels of checker carving above and below the lock-plates was a favourite Gothic treatment that lasted into the Renaissance; compare Figs. 37 and 38. The sides are decorated with horizontally placed linenfold panels; the colour of the oak is a deep chocolate, having been heavily oiled and varnished at one time. Fig. 5 is another of these rare pieces of furniture, about ten years later in date: it has exceptionally large and bold linenfold decoration throughout; the centre panel forms a door, the lock of which is unfortunately missing, though the plain hinges are still there; the lower rail is cut on the underside into the form of a cusped and depressed arch. These pieces are of Devonshire make. In both specimens, small

FIG. 4. *Oak Buffet*. Height, 2 feet 6 inches; length, 5 feet 6 inches. Property of ERNEST GEORGE, Esq.

FIG. 5. *Oak Buffet*. Height, 2 feet 1 inch; length, 4 feet 5 inches. Property of T. CHARBONNIER, Esq.

projecting brackets or blocks help to support the top.

A more elaborate piece of furniture of this early date is that known as 'Sudbury's Hutch', Plate I, in Louth Church, Lincolnshire. Here the whole structure is more box-like in form, and is almost a coffer on legs; the front opens in two doors, leaving a fixed panel as a centre. It was given to Louth Church by a vicar named Sudbury, who held that office between 1461 and 1504; and documents are in existence, stating that the hutch was repaired in 1586 and 1666, and that it was used for the purposes of keeping coals, candles and money for the poor. The doors are carved with extremely characteristic portraits of Henry VII and Elizabeth of York, framed in classical arches of the Renaissance; the centre panel bears the combined badge of York and Lancaster crowned, with the lion of the Plantagenets and the greyhound of the Tudors as supporters. The lower rail of the hutch is chamfered, suggesting a low Tudor arch; the whole design is bold in style, and shows a fascinating and original sense of proportion. As the King bears his crown and sceptre, and the Queen her crown, with hair long and flowing as at her coronation, one can only presume the hutch was made to commemorate this event; it is at any rate unlikely that any hutch-maker would have suddenly broken out into representations of his King and Queen except at a time connected with some important royal function; but it is more than probable that he would have been commissioned to commemorate the long-deferred coronation of the Queen, which took place in 1487.

The chest or coffer was a most favourite form of furniture, as it could serve the various purposes of bench, armoire, hutch, a dresser and also a travelling-box when changing houses. In the royal bedchambers they were used by the highest personages of the Court; to sit on a chair would have been a breach of etiquette, and constant reference to courtiers seating themselves on coffers in the royal antechambers are to be found in old chronicles. It is not surprising, therefore, how many of these are now in existence, for they were more extensively used by all classes than any other article of furniture. Mr Roe has dealt most ably with these in his work on old chests and coffers, but of the more domestic coffers we give six examples. The first of these, Fig. 6, is of the early part of the fourteenth century; the uprights of the frame are massive, and terminate at the base in winged lions, now almost worn away; the slides slope inwards in the usual fashion of the time. The front is carved in low tracery in the early Gothic taste. This same motive of tracery is found in Fig. 7, of about 1420, although a hundred years of evolution had passed, and it is difficult to imagine a more beautiful sub-division of the arch than this chest front represents. French, no doubt, in inspiration, the execution is undoubtedly English, made at the time when an Englishman was practically King of France. The vessels incised on the uprights are representative of the metal water-pots of the time. Fig. 8 is also early in style, the front being formed of one piece of wood, and the decoration not being divided into panels by a framework of stiles. The date of its manufacture, about 1740, is rather later than its fashion; the outer panels are carved in bold Gothic trefoils, while the other two are what is termed 'chevronny', and probably refer to the coat-armour of the owner.

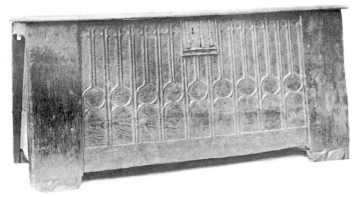

FIG. 6. *Oak Chest.* Property of MORGAN WILLIAMS, Esq.

FIG 7. *Oak Chest.* Property of Messrs. GILL AND REIGATE.

FIG. 8. *Oak Coffer.* Property of A. L. RADFORD, Esq.

FIG. 9. *Oak Coffer.* Property of A. L. RADFORD, Esq.

The original long Gothic lock-plate has been replaced by one that is quite ordinary, beneath which small trefoils in arched compartments are repeated. The legs are spandrelled, which again proves an early type, and the wear on the lid from constant use as a seat is clearly observable. Fig. 9 is a similar chest of rough make and humble origin, probably the work of a village carpenter. These two are fair specimens of the common bench coffer that were universally used by the middle classes, or put into the unimportant rooms of a house. A chest of better workmanship, though of later date, about 1490, is shown in Fig. 10. This is a very simple though perfect specimen of the ordinary clothes and linen chest that continued to be made for two hundred years, until its place was gradually usurped by the chest with drawers. There is a strange sense of flatness in the decoration of the front; the leading lines show thin and cord-like on the surface, a sure sign in art of a period drawing to its close, for with the exhaustion of all variety of its inspiration, every evolution ends more or less as it began. The pattern in this instance is of Flemish origin, no doubt derived from I, the first letter of the word Iησοῦς. Bishop's cords and tassels, with the grape and vine leaf, complete the symbolism of the design. Another very usual mode of decorating chests at this time was by the linenfold or parchment pattern, as in Fig. 11; on these panels, the rod on which the parchment is rolled is introduced. The little strong box, Fig. 12, is of the latter part of the fifteenth century; here the tracery of the panels is cut very deeply and boldly, and the

FIG. 10. *Oak Chest.* Height, 2 feet 7 inches; length, 5 feet 2 inches. Property of A. L. RADFORD, Esq.

FIG. 11. *Oak Chest.* Height, 2 feet 3 inches; length, 4 feet 2 inches.

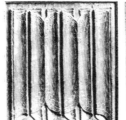

Fig. 13. *Oak Linenfold Panels.*

Fig. 12. *Oak Coffret.* Property of E. A. Barry, Esq.

Fig. 14. *Oak Linenfold Cupboard Door.*

plain surfaces of the stiles and rails, without any mouldings, frame the carving. Such a box was probably used for deeds and other precious papers when travelling. It is banded on all sides with iron, and protected by four locks, which were originally secured by staples, bolted on the inside. It would take a persistent person with a sharp saw-file some time to cut the four thick iron hasps to the lock-plates, and this would be the only way of forcing the box, unless the woodwork was destroyed. These boxes, when larger, were screwed down from the inside to the joists of the floor for extra security, and contained the money, plate and similar treasures of the house. This is proved by wills of this time, as on more than one occasion the strong box is bequeathed, 'but without the papers and valuables contained therein'.

The linenfold pattern, so called from its resemblance to a folded napkin, and emblematical of the chalice veil that covered the host, was a very favourite form of decorating the panels of furniture at the end of the fifteenth and the beginning of the sixteenth centuries. It was first used on the screens of the churches, and although Flemish in its origin, quickly became identified with this country. It was continued well into the century, and is found as late as 1550, forming the lower motive with full Renaissance decoration above. The earlier forms of the pattern had but few folds and were plain, save for fine cut lines representing the embroidery on the edge of the napkin, like Fig. 13. Later the folds were fleur-de-luced, or bunches of grapes and other emblems were introduced, as in the small door of a cupboard, Fig. 14.

Cupboards, or hutches as they were called, were a very usual form of furniture. Fig. 15 is one of these early hutches, opening in two plain doors, hung with hinges of elegant form; these, however, are probably of foreign workmanship, for their size is disproportionate to the doors, and large quantities of foreign locks and hinges were imported into England to complete the furniture manufactured here. The panels on either side of the doors are decorated in plain linen pattern without fold; the cornice is most effective, with its bold Gothic hollow repeated again round the panels. The piece of furniture was originally painted vermilion, which the present owner has removed. In Fig. 16, the bold setting of the door panel in its wide framing, the width of the mouldings, compared with the plain surface of the stiles, and deep splay of the bottom rail, all go to prove that the general character of the piece is that of quite the beginning of the century. The folds of the linen are cusped and left plain; and although the horizontal arrangement of linenfold is frequently found in the lower compartments of this class of furniture, in this particular instance it has probably been added at a later date to form a drawer. The top has also been renewed. The ironwork is in good preservation, and of interesting form. Fig. 17 is another and somewhat larger specimen; it is divided into five panels, four of which form doors; in the top centre panel the linenfold is trefoiled at the points, a very favourite Flemish pattern; but there are so many instances of this variety to be found in England, both on church screens and wall panelling, that the decision as to whether a piece is of English or foreign origin cannot rest upon the actual shape of the fold. The panels forming the upper doors are ordinary in type, and the lines representing the embroidery of the napkin are visible at the top. The lock-plates and hinges are quite plain and

FIG. 15. *Oak Double Hutch.* Height, 3 feet; width, 2 feet 10 inches; depth, 1 foot 6 inches. Property of MORGAN WILLIAMS, Esq.

FIG. 16 (*above right*). *Oak Hutch.* Property of GUY LAKING, Esq.

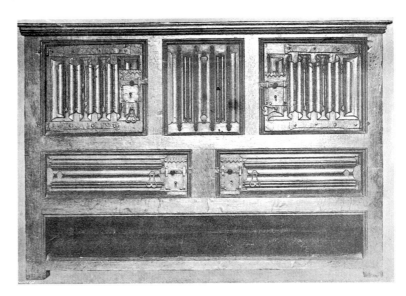

FIG. 17. *Oak Hutch.* Height, 3 feet 4 inches; length, 4 feet 9 inches; depth, 1 foot 11 inches. Property of E. A. BARRY, Esq.

distinctly English; and the mouldings, in which the panels are set, point to a date a few years later than the previous example. Parts of the lower portion of the legs and bottom rail have been renewed. These pieces of furniture, from their shape and height, were often used as washstands; cupboards similar to these are continually found in German prints as serving this purpose in a bedroom.

The dossier and canopied seat to the high table in the great halls often formed part of the structure and wainscot of the wall, and this is probably why no genuine English specimen is in existence; but the lower tier of the choir stalls in the chapel of Henry VII at Westminster Abbey, without their partitions, exactly represent the canopied bench of the fifteenth century, and are given in Fig. 18. Designed for Henry Tudor about 1506, with those of St George's Chapel, and probably by the same architect, they represent a period when Flamboyant Gothic and Perpendicular design were merged into one for the purposes of decoration. The stalls are of oak, and in both tiers measure 2 feet 2 inches across the arms from centre to centre. The small canopy to the lower tier, which forms the book-rest to the upper, is 6 feet 4 inches high, and supported by boldly necked columns that spring from corresponding mouldings of the arm rests. The back of the lower canopy starts from the top rail, divided into two arches to each stall, of open work filled in with a surbase and heading of Gothic trellis, the soffit of this canopy being carved with a fan-shaped and hexagonal decoration, while its upper

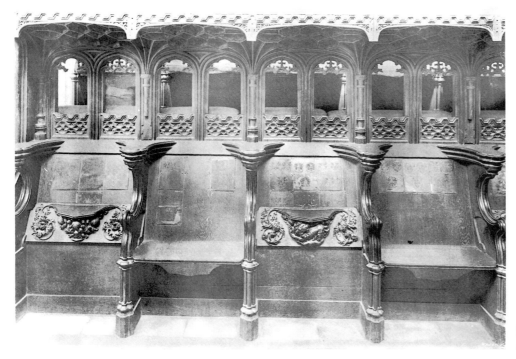

FIG. 18. *Lower Tier of Choir Stalls, Westminster Abbey.*

side finishes in a front rail carved with an engrailed line, and is the above-mentioned book-rest to the higher stalls. The seats are reversible and known as 'miserere', the under part or bracket being carved with tortuous grotesques and sacred emblems in the late Gothic taste (Figs. 19 to 23). The lower series are divided into three portions by steps giving access to the upper row. The newels to each division are plain, but of most original and remarkable form; their edge finishes in a similar moulding to the rest of the seats, surmounted by a seal top finial. The seats and arms of the upper tier corresponds with the lower, but from the arms of these rise columns which support the beautiful, highly decorated canopies that form the culminating feature in the structure (Fig. 24). The shafts of these columns are carved with the well-known Gothic geometrical network or honeycombing, a pattern

FIGS. 19 to 23. *Brackets to Miserere Seats, Westminster Abbey.*

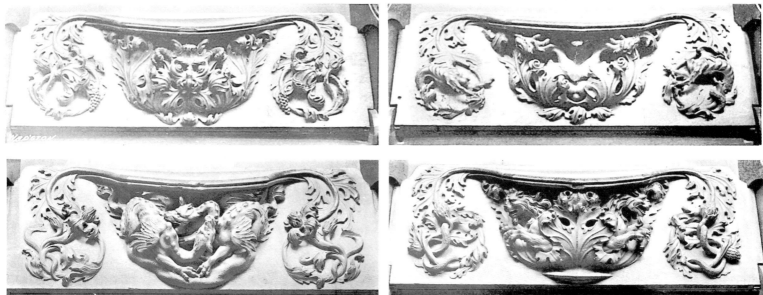

FIG. 24. *Canopies to the Upper Tier of Choir Stalls, Westminster Abbey.*

that may originally have been inspired by the branch of the gorse, on old stems of which can be seen the exact counterpart of this design. The caps are entirely Gothic in sentiment, though the florid and intricate taste of the canopies is tending towards the foreign movement in decoration that was so shortly to make its appearance in this country. This network of tracery in wood-carving is the last effort of a period that had with its various phases practically lasted for over a hundred years. The death of Henry VII found the chapel unfinished, but the stall probably formed part of the original scheme. The contemporary designs by Englishmen for the actual tomb were set aside by his son, who intrusted the work to Pietro Torrigiano; and this tomb marks the first appreciation of the Renaissance taste in England. This Renaissance taste was slow to develop and spread; and owing to the destruction and disappearance of furniture between 1500 and 1550, these steps are difficult to trace. We are therefore obliged to resort to these great ecclesiastical examples of seats which, owing to their position, have been preserved.

A period of design known as transition is far more instructive to the student than the full development of a style; for, apart from any human interest connecting it with important political changes, the adaptation of old ideas with the insertion of the new side by side, explains the cause of form, and enables him to date correctly all differences between these periods; and although the examples of transition are comparatively few in number, it is necessary to pay great attention to them. The choir stalls of Christ Church,

FIG. 25. Choir Stalls, Christ Church, Hampshire.

Hampshire, of about 1528 (Fig. 25), are most interesting to compare with those of Westminster. The divisions between the latter stall are left solid, while in the lower tier of Christ Church the arms are supported on short columns, a method that was adopted a little later for all chairs with arms (Fig. 26); these columns are supported by foliated scrolls, under which pilasters of Italian Renaissance design practically form the legs of the stall. The brackets to the miserere seats (Figs. 27 a, b and c) though coarse in execution, are full of spirit, and very significant of the changing taste. The arms of the upper tier are supported by boldly blocked-out animals in the form of dogs and gryphons (Fig. 28). The panels forming the back, divided by buttressed styles of Gothic character, are headed at the top with eccentric devices in Renaissance design, here and there varied by the introduction of some in purely Gothic taste; above these spring a plain and ribbed canopy, finishing in a trellised balcony front, with pendants and finials all in the Gothic style. It will therefore be seen that no order has been preserved in the introduction of the two styles, and that the Gothic sentiment, which in these transitional examples is usually confined to the base of the structure, is here mingled throughout with that of the Renaissance. Fig. 29 shows some headings of the panels, which although Italian in inspiration, are without any doubt English in execution. The third series of these stalls are those of King's College, Cambridge; and a portion of these, namely the rood-screen, with the complete stalls that are included in its construction, represent the only important example in this country of decorative Renaissance wood-work in its perfection. The most elaborate is the provost's stall (Fig. 30); it is of double size, and resembles the high-backed state seats used in the Italian palaces.

FIG. 26. *Christ Church Stalls, Lower Tier.*

FIGS. 27 a, b and c. *Brackets to Miserere Seats, Christ Church, Hampshire.*

FIG. 28. *Detail of Upper Tier, Christ Church, Hampshire.*

FIG. 29. *Six Panel-headings. Choir Stalls at Christ Church.*

FIG. 31.

The back is carved with the subject of St George and the dragon in medallion, surmounted by the figures of the gods, Mercury and Pluto; below this is the recumbent figure of a woman partially draped and with three children, one of which is being carried off by a lion; the whole panel is crowned by a representation of the Saviour giving a blessing. A most exquisite little frieze runs at the head of the seat, in the centre of which, on an escutcheon, is this monogram (Fig. 31). The initials H. R. and R. A. occur continually and conspiciously in the decoration of the rood-screen and stalls, but only on this one small escutcheon and in one other place almost out of sight, is this other complex monogram to be found, which in English obviously reads 'Henry Rex. Anne. Jane Seymour.', a grim and suggestive witticism on the part of the carver. The dais or canopy surmounting this and

FIG. 30. *Provost's Stall, King's College Chapel, Cambridge.*

the next stall is supported by balustered columns of Raphaelesque design, those to the provost's seat being carved. The newels to the reading-desk are headed by the Tudor greyhound and a lion couchant bearing a shield with the initials H. R. The front of this desk is a marvellous piece of joinery in panels which are three and a half inches below the face of the stiles and rails. The vice-provost's seat and adjacent stalls (Fig 32) resemble the others, but are simpler in their decoration. Fig. 33 is a view of the side stalls, which are in three tiers, the upper being of ordinary type, but with Renaissance mould-ings; the canopy and supports are later seventeenth-century copies from the older portions. The oak throughout was artificially darkened in colour at the date of its erection, but it has never been varnished. There is but little doubt that the rood screen and stalls were designed by some great Italian master or by Holbein; nothing on this subject is really known, though the date of their execution is proved by the perpetual introduction of the initials of Anne Boleyn with those of Henry, which, in his amorous exuberance, he insisted on having showered upon everything he commissioned at the time; and there is every reason to suppose that the construction and much of the carving is of English workmanship, the more important and delicate parts having been left to Italian hands.

This standard of excellence, however, was found too high to be maintained; and this furniture of King's College Chapel, which can hold its own with the finest examples of France and Italy, was mainly instrumental in dealing the final death blow to Gothic taste in this country.

FIG. 32. *Vice-provost's Seat and Adjacent Stalls,*
King's College Chapel, Cambridge.

FIG. 33. *Side Stalls and Miserere Seats, King's*
College Chapel, Cambridge.

CHAPTER II

I N the buffet (Plate II) can be seen a distinct departure from the still traditional Gothic of the Westminster stalls. Next to the canopied seat, the credence or buffet occupied the most important place in the living-room. Originally formed by a chest or coffer mounted on a stand it maintained the characteristics of this particular example throughout the fifteenth century; the cupboards were for the silver cups and wine-flagons, and when in use these were displayed on the top upon an embroidered linen cloth; the upper portion in many of the foreign examples was often elaborately carved, and surmounted by a low panelled back with a canopy. This interesting buffet is of about the date 1520; the front is divided into three plain panels set in a series of fine reed mouldings and flats, such as are found on the French and Italian furniture of the same time, though the whole character of the piece is absolutely English in type; the top rail to the panels is formed of a cornice, roughly carved with a blunt and upright leaf-moulding, the stiles being delicately filled in with the trefoil arrangement generally found in the spandrels of Gothic tracery; the lower rail, in curious contrast to the upper, is composed of a Gothic twist; below this again come the late fifteenth-century cusped and perforated arches joining in a pendant. The columnar supports, in their scaled decoration and baluster form, suggest an Italian origin. It is to be observed that the moulding below the ground-shelf does not run through the legs or supports as in earlier times, but that it dies into the ground, framing a sort of barge boarding, on the centre of which is carved a small cross; the sides present a similar treatment to the front. The oak is light in colour, and cut when the sap was not in the wood. The discovery and preservation of this buffet is due to Mr Seymour Lucas, who found it in the possession of a carpenter in a country town.

For the purposes of comparison, we give in Fig. 34 a French walnut credence of about the same date; being foreign, and therefore more advanced in style, the Gothic sentiment has almost entirely disappeared the panels being carved with pure Renaissance design.

A remarkable difference is to be observed between the front and sides of Fig. 35, which is some ten of fifteen years later in date. The top of this standing cupboard is divided into two compartments; the front is quite plain, the doors being cut flush with the stiles and rails in the usual Gothic manner; these are bordered on either side by narrow upright panels, chamfered and bevelled on the outer and bottom rail and stiles. The cornice mouldings are of early Renaissance type; the uprights, on which the cupboard stands, are flat and coarse in their proportions, yet at the same time give great value to

Fig. 34 *(far left). French Walnut Credence.* Property of Colonel George Kemp.

Fig. 35. *Oak Standing Cupboard.* Height, 4 feet 7 inches; width, 2 feet 8 inches; depth, 1 foot 6 inches. Property of E. A. Barry, Esq.

the rich tracery with which the side panels are decorated; the lower of these has no finishing rail, and it would appear as if this piece of furniture must have occupied a position in which the sides were as much in evidence as the front. Quite close to the ground is a lower shelf with trayed edges, a very unusual feature; the irons at the side are modern additions; those on the door are original. The colour is dark, as the wood must have been varnished in Elizabethan times.

It may be well here to discuss the question of varnish. Furniture was not varnished in this country until the middle of the sixteenth century; wax-polish was no doubt used at times, or the wood slightly oiled, but Gothic oak and early Renaissance furniture were left untouched. As the forms of decoration became rounder, more ornamental, and as simplicity began to disappear, a deep coloured varnish was applied, or the wood was much oiled and then waxed; this oiling accounts for the great amount of dark furniture called black oak. The varnish used abroad was of extremely fine quality, and except for the admixture of colouring matter, probably very similar to that employed on the pictures and musical instruments. This varnish, with constant rubbing, gives the beautiful bronze-like patina of rich chestnut brown colour found on the later Renaissance furniture. Occasionally pieces are to be found which have been merely treated with wax-polish, and therefore have remained light in colour. The varnish employed in England was of coarser quality, and less beautiful in colour; nevertheless, after years of rubbing, the surface presents a metallic appearance impossible to obtain in any other way. Beyond the fact that these varnishes were mixed with oil and not spirit, the secret of their composition is entirely lost, as it has been found impossible to obtain a correct chemical analysis of any old varnish. The original object in applying varnish or wax-polish to furniture was to preserve the wood.

What is called 'figure' in oak was obtained by cutting the wood in the manner of Fig. 36 a as opposed to Fig. 36 b. It is easy to see why wood cut in the former manner was extravagant, waste being entailed in the process. This so-called figure in wood has the appearance of hard diagonal splashes; these not being cellular, do not shrink with age like the rest. It is therefore a certain proof of the antiquity of a piece of oak when, on passing the hand over the surface, the figure appears to be slightly raised; if exposed to the air, unvarnished or merely waxed, it quickly assumes a darker colour than the rest, but if the oak is varnished, an opposite effect is the result. In Fig. 42 the wood has never been darkened or varnished, and the figure splashes are clearly perceptible.

It is not until 1530 to 1535 that the marked change in the decoration of furniture caused by Italian influence really made itself felt. Examples of this invasion in style are easier to find in stone-work than in wood, but in the Christ Church stalls we have seen this transition very clearly taking place, while on the Continent this change had been established over twenty years. The top to a credence of about 1510 (Fig. 37), of Burgundian workmanship, shows distinctly the admixture of the two styles; the framework, the roping of the cornice, the gutter mouldings surrounding the panels and the lock-plates are entirely in the late Gothic taste, whereas the movement and grace in the floriated sprays on the panels, now fat now thin in execution, and the favourite introduction of a male and female head in medallion, all point to the incoming Italian taste. The medallions in this instance are lettered 𝕴𝕳𝕾 and 𝕸𝕒 , i.e. Jesus and Maria, showing that this very usual decoration, which deteriorated into representations of heads of Mars and Venus, and later into portraits of the lord and lady of the house, was originally of religious intention. These new ideas and designs had by 1535 penetrated into every part of England, but in the country Gothic still continued to be introduced in conjunction with such examples of Italian ornament as the craftsman had the opportunity of studying. Fig. 38, of the date 1525, is a hutch or low-standing cupboard in which Renaissance and Gothic sentiment are very equally represented. The heads in medallion that form the doors are in the new taste, while the other panel and those that form the front of the drawers are filled with a well-designed Gothic tracery, perforated for the purposes of ventilation. The arrangement of the little carved spandrels

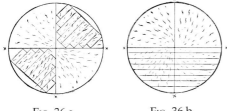

Fig. 36 a.   Fig. 36 b.
Manner of Cutting Oak (Sections).

FIG. 37. *Upper Part of an Oak Credence (Burgundian).* Property of P. MACQUOID, Esq.

above and below the lock-plates is also Gothic, but the two styles are kept totally distinct, and do not affect one another. The sides are carved with a linenfold pattern, and the whole piece is in admirable preservation.

In Fig. 39, a double hutch made in the Eastern Countries, a different motive of construction and decoration is apparent. In this instance the usual heads are replaced by a mullet, the cognisance of the De Veres, and the cornice moulding takes the form of an engrailed cresting. But in reviewing the early oak furniture of country make, it is clear that it possesses no real excellence of workmanship, and only the great charm of simplicity and proportion. This is exemplified very strongly by the buffet given on Plate III, a piece that possesses interest from its heraldic decorations. It was made for John Wynne in 1535, who built Gwydyr Castle at that date, and from which place it has never since been moved. The construction is Gothic, being surmounted by a canopy or dais, the base of which has at one time been cut and reduced. The lower portion opens in three cupboards and two drawers, decorated with armorial bearings and emblems of the Wynne family. The upper right panel bears the arms of John Wynne: Quarterly, 1st and 4th sable, a chevron between three fleur-de-lys argent (Tervan ap Howell, 1399); 2nd and 3rd vert, three eagles displayed in fesse or (Owen Gwynedd, 1169), at the side of which is the so-called leek flower and the initials I. W. The centre panel bears the two royal lions of England crowned passant, above the York and Lancaster Rose, the Wynnes being connected by marriage with the royal House of Tudor. The third panel to the left bears a helm with an eagle rising as crest, with the leek flower and I. W. repeated; the right-hand drawer of the middle compartment bears the Royal Red Dragon of

FIG. 38. *Oak Hutch.* Height, 3 feet; length, 4 feet 5 inches; depth, 1 foot 7 inches. Property of MORGAN WILLIAMS, Esq.

FIG. 39. *Oak Double Hutch.* Property of J. H. A. MAJENDIE, Esq.

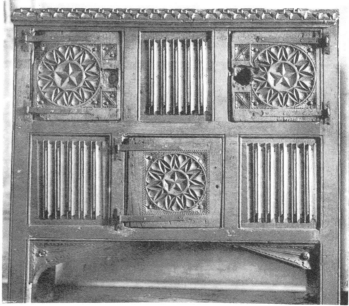

Fig. 40. *Oak Court Cupboard*. Height, 5 feet 7 inches; width, 5 feet; depth, 1 foot 9 inches. Property of Sir CHARLES LAWES-WITTEWRONGE, Bart.

Cadwaladr, the last king of Britain, and a head couped in profile, the other two heads being the corresponding drawer, this being an allusion to the story that during the reign of Llewelyn the Great, Vychan, in the year 1246, defeated the English army who invaded Wales, and having killed three of the principal English officers, brought their heads to the prince, who directed Vychan to bear the arms Three Englishmen's heads couped and proper. On the other panels are the arms of Sorwerth (father of Llewelyn) and his brother Roderic, ancestors of the Wynnes; the arms of John Wynne being again repeated between them. The sides are carved with fine linenfold, which pattern also forms the decoration of the back and soffit of the canopy, the front panels of the latter being carved with the dragon, the royal cognisance of Wales.

The standing, or court cupboard, as it is sometimes called, Fig. 40, is a far more ambitious attempt in art than the preceding specimens, and also inaugurates a new method of construction. The upper portion opens with three doors carved with male and female heroic heads in strapped and laurelled circles, much resembling in treatment the well-known run of panelling (Fig. 41) of the same period, taken from an old house at Waltham. Above the medallions on the cupboard doors is a double dolphin design, varied in one instance by a cherub's head, supporting in its mouth a ball and tassel chord; here the English workmanship is most apparent; the lower portion opens with two doors, each containing four panels, decorated in a similar manner, and the wide centre rail gives great dignity to the surrounding proportions. The whole piece is a deliberate English copy of a foreign cupboard of somewhat earlier date. In both this and the Waltham panelling it is evident that the carver, although dexterous, was trying his hand at something to which he was unaccustomed. Mr Seymour Lucas discovered the cupboard in a cottage near Oxford Castle, Kent, his belief being that it came from the castle, which was originally a bishop's palace; the cottage belonged to quite a poor woman, who could not sell the piece of furniture for some time, as an elder brother claimed a joint interest in it. Both this and Fig. 42 are approximately of the same date, 1530; and although the difference of treatment is very marked, it is but the difference of French and

FIG. 41. *Oak Panelling from a House at Waltham.* VICTORIA AND ALBERT MUSEUM.

FIG. 42. *Upper Part of an Oak Standing Cupboard.* Property of E. A. BARRY, Esq.

Flemish influence on the mind of an English workman, and the difficulty of assigning exact dates is obviously much increased by these contemporary divergences in style. It is divided into two rows of panels, wet in a deep and well-considered series of fillet and flat mouldings; the portrait busts are in very high relief, cut from the solid, with the exception of the faces, for which an extra half-inch of oak has been added; the noses have perished, and give an appearance of age and ugliness to these faces which the healthy developments in the rest of the young woman contradict. The Lombardic letters A. W. on either side of the tun or barrel that are carved on the upper panel of the door accord exactly with the date of the costumes; the mouldings of the cornice, those round the door and the butts to the hinges without flanges, betoken the coming change. Though somewhat rude in construction, the proportions of this piece are well considered, and the strong markings of the figure in the wood adds much to its decoration; in all probability too the lower half, which is missing, possessed features of interest. In 1525 Sir Richard Weston, Under-Treasurer to the King, built Sutton Place, near Guildford, and introduced into the decorations a tun or barrel as a play upon his name, a very usual custom in those days. In 1530 he married his son Francis to his ward Ann, daughter and heiress of Christopher Pickering and there can be but little doubt that this interesting cupboard was once the property of Ann Weston, and probably given to her on her marriage, as the initials A. W. and the two portraits, evidently of husband and wife, would imply that it was a marriage gift, and the whole piece exactly corresponds with the date of the marriage. This young Sir Francis Weston was in 1536, six years after his marriage, tried and executed as one of the lovers of the unfortunate Anne Boleyn. Though perhaps irrelevant matter in a work on furniture, the following extract from Paul Friedman's *Life of Anne Boleyn* may interest the reader as showing what evidence there was against Ann Weston's husband; but it is just these personal and historical links that add so vastly to the interest and possession of any specimen:

'On the 23rd April 1536 the Queen had some private talk with Sir Francis Weston, and upbraided him for making love to Margaret Skelton, her cousin, and for not loving his wife. The young man, knowing the Queen's appetite for flattery, answered that he loved some one in her own house more than either his wife or Margaret Skelton. Anne eagerly asked who it was, and he replied, "It is yourself". She affected to be angry and rebuked him for his boldness; but the reprimand cannot have been very terrible, for Weston continued his talk, and told her that Noreys also came to her chamber, more for her sake than that of Madge, as Margaret Skelton was called. Three weeks after this conversation Sir Francis Weston met his death on Tower Hill. In his speech from the scaffold he said: "I had thought to live in abomination yet this twenty or thirty years and then to have made amends; I little thought I would have come to this." He also left the following letter, the original of

Fig. 43. *Oak Panels*. Property of H. A. Tipping, Esq.

which is at the Record Office: "Father, mother, and wyfe, I shall humbly desyre you for the salvacyon of my sowle to dyschardge me of all my offences that I have done to you, and in especyall my wyfe, whiche I desyre for the love of God to forgyve me and to pray for me, for I beleve prayer wyll do me good. Goddy's blessyng have my chyldrene and meyne, by me a great offender to God." The widow, Ann Weston, made two subsequent marriages, and died in the year 1582.'

Another form of decorating panels of furniture at this time was by cutting out the ground, leaving the rest of the surface for the design; the sunk ground was then filled in with hard coloured composition. The panels (Fig. 43) are either from the top of a long armoire or from the overdoors and overmantel of a room. They were made for Sir William Kingston, Constable of the Tower, who was the gaoler of both Anne Boleyn and Weston. He was created Knight of the Garter, 24 April 1539, and died in 1540, so their date is conclusively fixed by the panel, unfortunately mutilated, bearing his arms, within a garter, Quarterly, 1st and 4th azure, a cross between four leopards' faces argent; 2nd and 3rd ermines, a chevron and in chief a leopard's face. The other arms are those of Lady Kingston, and the remaining panels of this series are decorated with heroic heads and scrolls of conventional ornament. It was solely through the report made by this Sir William Kingston to Cromwell of what Anne Boleyn had during her captivity told Lady Kingston in confidence, that young Sir Francis Weston first became implicated. Fig. 44 is a little gaming or card table; it is rough in execution, and was probably made about 1535. The top opens in two leaves, supported and kept in position by sliding bars; the frame forms a shallow cupboard, in which the cards, chessmen, etc., were kept; the panels are carved with medallioned heads and conventional ornament. A plain shelf, supported on the lion's feet, connects the legs, which are quadrangular and carved with rough acanthus; the whole construction is distinctly Gothic in character. These small gaming-tables were made for the ladies of the house, who at that period were much addicted to cards and other games of chance; they are sometimes found with the tops marked for chess or tric-trac. Mary Tudor, during the time of her semi-captivity, spent much of her time and meagre allowance of money in gambling. A similar table is to be seen in the Long Gallery at Hardwick but the original flap is missing, and some extra shelves have been added.

It has not been thought necessary to point out every individual instance of repair to some of these early specimens. Genuine restorations are often absolutely necessary to prevent very old pieces of furniture from falling into decay, and many of the slight repairs which are clearly visible in the illustrations are of early date, and go to prove that care and interest were taken in the furniture.

Fig. 44. *Oak Game Table*. Height, 2 feet 8½ inches; length, 3 feet. Lord DE LISLE AND DUDLEY.

CHAPTER III

ARLY chairs of English manufacture are extremely rare; the word itself is derived from the Old French *chayre, cheyre* or *cayre*. In Gothic and even later times they fulfilled no common office as they do to-day, but were personal to the Lord and Lady, or Master and Mistress of the house, and were individually as important to them as their silver cups and spoons. The chair originally was probably only devoted to the use of the owner, and carved with his or her initials or some emblem. The number of chairs in use throughout the fifteenth and greater part of the sixteenth centuries cannot have been many; settles, benches, stools and the tops of chests were the most ordinary form of seat, and that the occupation of a chair conferred a considerable amount of authority and caste, is certain. In addition to the personal chairs in a room, it is probable that one or two others were introduced for important guests. One of the first forms was that of a shallow 'X', much on the principle of the modern camp-stool, the upper extremities receiving the rails that formed the arms, and the band that formed the back. The simple excellence of this construction is at once apparent; but when plate armour in addition to the existing mail was worn, the weight of a seated man became so great that a chair of more solid build was found necessary, and we find in the miniatures of the fifteenth century that the principal seat is of box-like form with panelled back and arms; indeed it will be seen that, throughout the whole historical evolution of the chair, the shape was practically governed by the changes that took place in costume. All early chairs had arms to support the heavy hanging sleeves that were in vogue, and would have been much the same form as the fine state seat of 1460, at St Mary's, Coventry, though this can hardly be termed a chair, having once formed part of a series of stalls fixed to a wall. Fig. 45 is a specimen of this solid type, which dates towards the end of the fifteenth century. The seat forms the lid of a box, and has the original flanged hinges; the front, sides and panels to the arms are carved with a decorated linenfold pattern, the uprights in front terminating in finials; the back is panelled with Gothic tracery, which may possibly have been cut down from an original height of four panels, but the alteration, if it took place, must have occurred soon after the chair was made; the oak is unusually light in colour, having never been oiled or varnished. This chair, though exactly resembling the type made in England, is probably Flemish. For decoration, a large piece of rich material was often thrown over this form of chair, completely covering it, and frequently supplemented by loose cushions; it was not until the introduction of the lighter shapes that stuffs commenced to be nailed to the wood.

This solid form of chair continued to be made well into the sixteenth century, the panels being decorated in the same manner as other contemporary furniture, with medallioned heads surmounted by conventional ornament in the Italian manner, and which in this country obtained the name of 'Romayne Work'. Fig. 46 is an English chair decorated with this work, the structure being an evolution from the Gothic type of the previous example, but the linenfold is confined to the back and sides. In the lighter forms of chair that began to make their appearance in 1530, the 'X' shape was again revived. The chair in the sacristy of York Cathedral (Fig. 47) is of this description and period, though an earlier date has frequently been assigned to it. The top extremities finish with embossed metal caps originally gilt, and the whole of the wood-work was left in the rough, showing that it was intended to be covered with material; the back was hung from the spring of the arms to the top with velvet strained on leather, on which was embroidered the arms and cognizances of the owner, and up to 1836 traces of this embroidery still existed. This is the earliest known example of an English upholstered chair. In the portrait of Mary Tudor, Queen of England, by Sir Antonio Moro, she is represented as sitting in a very similar seat. Another chair of this style is (Fig. 48) preserved in Winchester Cathedral, as the seat on the occasion of her marriage with Philip. It is somewhat coarse in

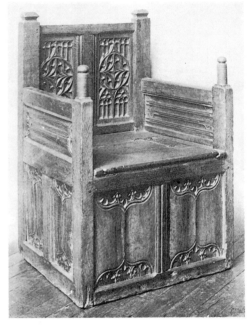

FIG. 45. *Oak Chair, Probably Flemish.* Property of PERCY MACQUOID, Esq.

FIG. 46. *Oak Chair.* Date 1535. Height, 4 feet 2 inches; width, 2 feet 1 inch. Property of MRS BLOOD.

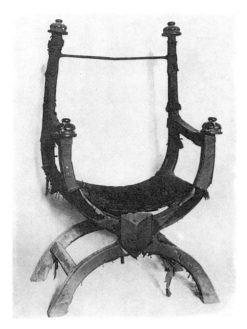

FIG. 47. *Chair in Sacristy of York Cathedral.* Height, 4 feet.

FIG. 48. *Oak Chair, Winchester Cathedral.* Height, 3 feet 1 inch.

FIG. 49. *Walnut Chair.* Property of ALFRED DE PASS, Esq.

FIG. 50. *Walnut Chair.* Property of SIR GEORGE DONALDSON.

form and probably of country make; the two straps at the back show the original foundation on which the piece of embroidered velvet was strained. The Queen travelled to Winchester to receive Philip, who landed at Southampton, and the marriage took place in the Cathedral on 25 July 1554; the date of the chair, however, precedes that of the marriage by a few years. It is a very common error to assign all these 'X' chairs to foreign importation, but Henry VIII had gathered together in this country a small army of French, German, Italian, Flemish and English artificers, with the great artist Holbein, and the architects John of Padua and Antonio Toto del Nunziata at their head, to work on the remarkable building, Nonesuch, that he, the Nebuchadnezzar of the time, was about to set up. Fig. 49 is probably one of a series of 'X' chairs mentioned in a royal inventory of the King's effects, and designed by one of the foreign artists employed on the building. It is of walnut, the curves of the limbs justifying the employment of this wood, which, through universal in France and Italy, was not generally used for furniture here. By tradition, this particular chair was given by Henry VIII to a relation of Anne Boleyn's as a marriage gift, and remained in the possession of the family until 1896. The lines of this chair have a strong Italian feeling, but the carving is without the finish of the foreign craftsman, and the wood is English walnut, light in colour; the parts in relief have been re-gilt, and the leather of the seat and back is comparatively recent. Fig. 50 is another and rather smaller example of this same type; it is also of walnut, and the carving, which is distinctly English, very much resembles in touch that of the preceding chair. The arms are slighter and curve more rapidly upwards, terminating at the top in two ringed knobs; the front, which breaks at its lower extremities into coarsely scrolled crescents, is carved with figures of marine monsters, the centre boss being formed of a boldly carved lion's mask; the leather of the seat and back are not contemporary.

Another movable form of chair very popular at this time in France was that known as a *cacqueteuse* (conversational) or *chaise de femme*, after the manner of Fig. 51, but comparatively few were made here. Plate VI (a) is a cacqueteuse of Devonshire make, found recently in the village of Colyton, and is a very good example of the better class work of the time. The back is tall, slightly fan-shaped, and contains a panel boldly carved with a female bust in the costume of 1535; this portrait is set in lozenge, the heraldic attribute of a woman, and is surmounted and supported by dolphin-shaped scrolls and conventional ornament, terminating at the base in cherubs, all carved in high relief; the arms have angular elbows supported by extra uprights, finishing below the seat in small Gothic pendants. Fig. 52 is the side view of this chair. The upper and under surface of the arms correspond in their shallow but broad mouldings; the seat follows the line of the arms, and its front rail on the lower side is ogeed and cusped; the legs are rectangular, and kept in their position by a broad front rail, an extremly short back rail, and one stretcher. Its preservation is owing to the many coats of black paint with which it was covered; at the back are the initials I. S. in Lombardic letters. As in all Devonshire work, the colour of the oak is very dark. The other chair (b), also given on Plate IV, is from Hornby Castle, the date about 1550. It is made of yew, which adds to its rarity, for up to this time it was practically penal to employ yew-wood for any other purpose than the manufacture of the national weapon; in this instance the wood has become close, hard as steel, and of a beautiful dark amber colour. The design of the back is open work, formed of a double arcade supported on vase-shaped balusters, and the detail of the carving foreshadows that English branch of the Renaissance, later called Elizabethan. Surmounting the chair as a cresting is a coat of arms bearing a lion rampant, with a Tudor rose as a crest, and unicorns backed by pennants as supporters; on the pennants are the initials C. A. in Lombardic and cusped letters. The front of the seat rail is deeply carved with a rich twist between raised diamond-shaped plaques, the seat itself is of oak, the arms are flattened and carved on the upper surface, like those of all early chairs of this type, unless they are inlaid; the back is almost straight, and the whole chair has a barbarous sense of richness and importance.

During the latter part of the reign of Henry VIII, chest fronts partook of the character of that shown in Fig. 53, where the medallion heads have

FIG. 51. *Walnut Cacqueteuse Chair* (French). Property of COLONEL GEORGE KEMP.

FIG. 53. *Chest Front*. Oak. Height, 2 feet 4 inches; length, 4 feet. Property of MESSRS MORANT & Co.

disappeared, giving place to a more spreading decoration of floriated scroll-work with less repetition. In this instance the peg holes for fixing the Gothic mouldings top and bottom are visible, and on the reverse of the front are the grooves to hold the bottom and side panels, proving its original construction as a chest.

Leather-covered chests studded with nails were also used in rooms at this time for furniture as well as for the purposes of travelling. Fig. 54 is an interesting specimen belonging once to Queen Katherine Parr. Having safely outlived her third husband, Henry VIII, she was emboldened immediately to take a fourth, Lord Edward Seymour, brother to the Protector, to whose descendants the chest still belongs. It is of a light wood covered with cow-hide, studded with brass-headed nails in three sizes. On the top (Fig. 55) is a Tudor crown surmounting the letters K. R. (Katherine Regina), with sprays of lilies at the corners. The front opens at the bottom with two drawers, and is covered with an elaborate nail-heading design, into which bunches of grapes are introduced. The clamps, lock-plates, key, and small handles are of iron, and all original. In tracing the evolution of any particular taste and style, it is always difficult to account for sudden change, unless accompanied by some events such as political alterations in government, or a simultaneous growth of original ideas, emanating from men of

FIG. 52. *Side View of English Cacqueteuse Chair*. Oak. Height, 4 feet; width, 1 foot 10 inches. Property of PERCY MACQUOID, Esq.

FIG. 54. *Leather-covered Chest Formerly Belonging to Queen Katherine Parr.* Property of CHARLES R. SEYMOUR,, Esq.

FIG. 55. *Top of Chest Formerly Belonging to Queen Katherine Parr.*

genius. The change that came into furniture and its decoration after the death of Henry VIII in 1547 can be attributed to a combination of these causes; also the occupation of the throne by two women in succession, wielding almost absolute power, brought about an amelioration of manners and a hitherto unknown appreciation of domestic comfort, the unsettled reign of Edward VI being of too brief duration to encourage any noticeable varieties of style. The temporal and artistic powers of Italy were by the middle of the sixteenth century well on their decline; but the art that had poured into England from this source had educated the craftsman to a point that rendered him capable of designing and executing work that could be dignified as both national and distinctive. It is out of this new-born English instinct for originality, grafting itself on to the hard-and-fast lines of classical design, that the style known as Elizabethan sprang into existence. This style, though wanting in simplicity, and often at fault in the arrangement of its heterogeneous ornament, possesses a sense of domesticity and refinement hitherto lacking in the houses and furniture of this country. Sympathy and tolerance for the new religion induced many Flemish and French Huguenots to settle over here permanently (the foreign workmen up to this time having been but birds of passage), and by intermarriage a higher technical skill and truer artistic insight became an inheritance of the Englishman. Literature, through the medium of printing, had begun to create a national school with a very direct and enlightening influence on the manners, entertainments, and life of the people, and as a natural consequence, the barbaric super-fluity, that had hitherto existed among the rich, gave place gradually to a desire for elegance and necessary comforts.

Up to 1550 all inn accomodation was extremely archaic, for till then it was customary for travellers to bring with them their solid provisions and often their feather-beds; all they expected to find at an inn was an indifferent bed, ale and wine. A far more refined state of things is indicated in a diary kept by a Dutch physician, Levinus Lemnius, during his travels in England at the commencement of Elizabeth's reign, and translated into English in 1576:

'The neate cleanliness, the exquisite finenesse, the pleasaunte and delightful furniture in evry poynt for household, wonderfully rejoysed mee, their nosegayes finely entermingled wyth sundry sortes of fragraunte floures in their bedchambers and privy roomes with comfortable smell cheered mee up and entirely delygted all my sences.'

And in an English-Dutch dialogue book for travellers of about the same time, the directions for addressing a chambermaid are as follows:

'TRAVELLER. My shee frinde, is my bed made, is it good?
'CHAMBERMAID. Yea sir, it is a good feder bed, the scheetes be very cleane.
'TRAVELLER. Pull off my hosen and warme my bedde, drawe the curtines and pin them with a pinne. My shee frinde kisse me once and I shall sleape the better. I thanke you, faire mayden.'

Travelling even for the rich was, however, a very serious business. Elizabeth and her Court accomplished their journeys on horseback and in litters, for no kind of light travelling carriage existed in England, and the furniture and personal luggage that accompanied a royal progress often required the employment of six hundred two-wheeled wagons, each drawn by six horses. Civilised society, as we understand it, had nevertheless begun, and smaller houses, designed on the lines of Hampton Court and Nonesuch, sprang up in different parts of the country. Such houses were unfortified in character, their internal plan and arrangements conforming to domestic comforts and requirements. This new growth of luxury was greatly encouraged by a revival of prosperity in trade, which the Wars of the Roses, followed by years by religious controversy, had reduced to so low an ebb; but with the creation of the great merchant companies, who opened up trade with the Baltic, Turkey, Syria and Asia Minor, and the consequent increase of silver specie, which after 1560 poured into this country, a plutocracy was created whose position was quickly recognised, and on whom distinctions were conferred by those in power. This sudden influx of wealth created a certain antagonism between these new rich men and the old-established families, who had hitherto been the only patrons of architecture and furniture, and each tried to go one better than the other; this accounts to some extent for that variety and picturesqueness, which, although chaotic in the redundance of its ornament as a style, and often lacking in true principle, rarely fails in giving richness of effect and individual importance.

The characteristics of the decoration of Elizabethan furniture are a lack of finish in the carving, which usually represents arbesques and strap-work, in combination with figures of human beings, masks, fruit and grotesque animals, all being without the consecutive motive and preciseness of the foreign masters of the same period. These details are varied on the flat surfaces by the introduction of inlaid, coloured and stained woods, a form of decoration that soon became extremely popular.

The writing-cabinet (Plate V) is an example of early marqueterie made in this country by an exceptionally talented craftsman, working out the advantages he had received from association with foreigners and their methods; the small and rather fanciful detail of the inlay, which is additionally decorated with painted lines, suggests a period between 1550 and 1560. Writing-cabinets of this construction originated in Italy; the pattern travelled from there to Spain, where it became universal. It is probable that in this instance the inspiration was Spanish, and that its prototype came over in connection with Philip. The flap is inlaid in four panels in a border of rosewood and other coloured and stained woods; the designs take the form of most delicate floral sprays, springing from vases and baskets; these vases terminate in the head and breasts of a woman, hooded with the cap of 1550, the lip of the vase ingeniously forming the high collar of that date. The rocket-like lines burst into gillyflowers, of divers colours, amongst which birds perch, and below are dogs pursuing rabbits; on two of the panels is a representation of the Tudor rose in the form of an escutcheon, with centres composed of red cedar. Below the flap is one drawer on which the same motive is repeated. The inside of the cabinet, shown in Fig. 56, opens in twelve drawers, their fronts inlaid with the same elegant floriated sprays, in each case springing from a basket. The sides are inlaid with alternate bands of English walnut and rosewood; the frame and finely reeded Renaissance mouldings to the drawers are of walnut; the whole of the internal structure being of English oak. The lock-plate is a perfect example of our iron-work of the time; formed of three balustered columns, one of which forms the hasp (an idea again borrowed from the Spanish taste); these are supported by a strap-work of C scrolls and cocksheaded arabesques; the handles are fat and bold in character, and all this iron-work shows signs of having been originally gilt. It will invariably be found that the iron fittings to furniture are rather earlier in their date than the rest of the construction, as the fashion in metal-work moved more slowly than in wood. This piece of furniture was discovered practically in its present condition in the basement of a house in the country, and used by children as a rabbit-hutch, the baby rabbits being relegated to the smaller compartments.

No architectural construction is attempted in this cabinet, but in the large, important chest (Fig. 57), which is another early example of this new style, it

Fig. 56. *Cabinet Open.* Height, 3 feet; length, 3 feet 6 inches; depth, 1 foot 5 inches. Property of Sir George Donaldson.

will be seen that the Gothic sentiment is entirely excluded, and that the marqueterie and carving decorates a structure of purely classical design. This chest was given in 1556 to the church of St Mary Overie by Hugh Offley, then Lord Mayor of London, and bears his arms and those of his wife, together with his initials and merchant's marks. The design of the front represents the elevation of a building, at the top of which is a frieze of small carved strap-work in cherry-wood in very low relief; below this, the face of the chest is divided into panels, inlaid with the Offley armorial bearings and fine designs of conventional and floral ornaments in stained and coloured woods. Oak, walnut, pear, cherry, box, rosewood, ebony, ash, yew and holly are some of the different woods employed. The panels are framed in flat pilasters, inlaid in the same manner, and to represent the stones, holly knots with their curious marbled grain are employed. The lower compartment of the chest is composed of three drawers (one a restoration) inlaid with architectural views and foliated scrolls, bordered by a marqueterie chain pattern; the side panels of ash are framed by two flat Doric pilasters on inlaid plinths, and have the original iron handles. The whole of this fine chest, owing to the successive and thick coats of varnish with which it has been covered, is now a uniform brown colour, and the different woods can only be discerned by careful examination. Some twenty years only had elapsed between the completion of the King's College Stalls and the gift of this chest to the church, and in that short time this new style had definitely asserted itself. Deprived of its inlay, the structure and mouldings of this

Fig. 57. *Oak Chest Inlaid with Marqueterie.* Height, 3 feet 3 inches; length, 6 feet 6 inches; depth, 2 feet 4 inches. Property of St Saviour's Collegiate Church, Southwark.

piece exactly correspond with the plain Henry II furniture of the time; the vivacity of the marqueterie shows the perception of a taste in which the English eventually excelled, a perception prompted by their skill in needle-work, which for a long period had held the first place in Europe.

As allied to furniture, this needlework was principally employed on the beds of which our early ancestors were so proud. Some of these beds, of which no traces remain, are minutely described in the wills and bequests of the time; for instance, Edmond, Earl of March, in 1380, bequeaths 'One large bed of black satin embroidered with white lions and gold roses, with escutcheons of the arms of Mortimer and Ulster'. In 1932 Richard, Earl of Arundel, leaves to his second wife, Philippa, 'a blue bed marked with my arms and the arms of my late wife, to my son Richard a standing bed called Clove, also a bed of silk, embroidered with the arms of Arundel and Warren'. The custom of giving a bed a name was evidently adopted from the still older habit of naming favourite cups and swords; the somewhat patri-archal arrangement of handing on the bed of one wife to another is also curious. The same will goes on, 'To my dear son Thomas my blue bed of silk embroidered with gryphons, to my daughter Charlton my bed of red silk, to my daughter Margaret my blue bed'. There are very many wills of this description, proving that these elaborate beds were considered most precious property, and that their careful distribution by will was an especial mark of esteem; on the other hand, in Shakespeare's will, the sole bequest to his unfortunate wife is 'Item I give unto my wife my second best bed with the furniture'. The amount of bedding belonging to an important bed must have been stupendous. In an extract from the will of Joane, Lady Bergavenny, in 1437, she devises 'A bed of gold swans with tapetter of green tapestry, two pairs of sheets, a pair of fustians, six pairs of other sheets, six pairs of blankets, six mattresses, six pillows, and the cushions and banncoves that longen to the bed aforesaid'. The banncoves were little benches that were placed at the foot of beds. In addition to all these blankets, mattresses and pillows, constant references can be found to a pane of ermines or other fur, and feather beds. 'Thre feather bedes of hys wife's makin' form the bequest of William Blenkinsopp of Blenkinsopp Castle. Of these feather-beds Frederic, Duke of Wirtemberg, writes in 1591. 'Upon the river Thames there are many swans; these are so tame that you can almost touch them, but it is forbidden on pain of corporal punishment in any way to injure a swan, for Royalty has them plucked every year in order to have their down for feather-beds'. The whole bed, when made up, must have been excessively hot, but the occupants slept naked, and the silk and satin night-gowns, trimmed and lined with fur, that we read of in the middle of the fifteenth century, were probably only a form of dressing-gown for receptions, an audience at the bedside being a daily custom in the houses of the great. There is a vivid description which gives great insight into the arrangements of a bedroom, from a contemporary MS, of a banquet given by Elizabeth Woodville, wife of Edward IV, in 1472, at Windsor, to the Lord of Gruthere, a Burgundian ambassador.

'Then aboute IX of the clocke, the Kinge and the Quene, with her ladies and gentlewomen, brought the sayde Lorde Grautehuse to three Chambres of Plea-sance, all hanged with whyte sylke and lynnen clothe, and all the floures couered with carpettes. There was ordeined a Bedde for hym selue, of as good doune as coulde be gotten, the Shetes of Raynys, also fyne fustyans, the Counterpoynte clothe of golde, furred with armyn, the tester and the celer also shyninge clothe of golde, the Curteyns of whyte sarsenette, as for his headde sute and pillowes, they were of the Quenes owen ordonnance, Item in the third chambre was a other of astate, the whiche was alle whyte. And in the same chambre was made a couche with fether beddes, hanged with a tente, knytt lyke a nette, and there was a cuppborde. Item in the third chambre was ordeined a Bayne or two which were couered with tentes of whyte clothe. And when the Kinge and the Quene, with all her ladyes and gentelwomen, had shewed hym these chambres, they turned againe to their owen chambres, and left the sayde Lorde Grautehuse there accompanied with my Lorde Chamberlein whiche dispoyled hym, and wente bothe together to the Bayne . . . and when they had ben in theire Baynes as longe as was there pleasour, they had grene gynger, divers cyryppes, comfyttes and ipocras and then they wente to bedde'.

We also read in the ordinances of Henry VII, 'that he had a fustian and sheet under his feather bed, over the bed a sheet, then a pane of ermines, a head sheet of raybes (linen of Rennes), and another of ermines over the pillows'. After the ceremony of making this somewhat complicated bed, 'all the esquires, ushers, and others present had bread, ale and wine outside the chamber'.

It is impossible to give an illustration of even a Tudor Gothic bed in its entirety, for though portions of these beds are in existence, they are invariably found adapted and altered. They were composed of a tester of material or wood surmounted by a cornice, and supported on a panelled back, with posts at each corner. After 1550 the back posts were omitted, and in addition to the valance and curtains hung from the tester, other valances reaching to the ground were fixed on to the lower frame, from which the mattresses and bedding were supported on rope-netting. Fig. 58 shows the

Fɪɢ. 58. *Back of Bed*. Oak. Height, 4 feet 4 inches; width, 5 feet 10 inches. Property of J. H. A. Mᴀᴊᴇɴᴅɪᴇ, Esq.

back and side posts of a Tudor bed preserved in Hedingham Castle. The panels are of Renaissance form, carved with grotesque animals, hanaps, scrolls and dolphins, in the usual conventional manner, but a very distinct difference to the earlier work of this style can be remarked in the distribution and relief of the ornament. The design entirely spreads over the face of the panel, and the important points are without emphasis. The interest of the decoration lies in the two panels, the upper bearing the Royal Arms, the Tudor crown, the cup of state with the initials K. E. – the young king, Edward VI, having slept in the bed, the lower panel bears the De Vere arms and crest with their quarterings; both arms are tricked in their tinctures, and all the carving is picked out with gold, which, however, is not the original gilding. The side columns are still Gothic and slight in construction, while the conglomerate ornament and the bulbous growth – a devlopment of Elizabethan taste – is seen in embryo, budding out from the Gothic sticks, so that in this interesting relic we get the rare combination of the three styles, Gothic, Renaissance and Elizabethan. The remaining two posts of this bed are made up into a mantelpiece in another part of the house.

Almost contemporary with this bed is the little joint-stool (Fig. 59), introduced here to explain the evolution of the bulbous form that later developed so strongly on the posts and legs of furniture. It will be observed that on the panels of the bed a Gothic cup and cover in conventional treatment is introduced, and repeated again as a knop on the posts; this occurs in the same manner on the legs of the stool in a slightly more bulbous manner;

Fɪɢ. 59. *Oak Stool*. Height, 1 foot 10 inches; length, 1 foot 4 inches. Property of Sɪʀ Gᴇᴏʀɢᴇ Dᴏɴᴀʟᴅsᴏɴ.

FIG. 60 a. *Gothic Stool.* Property of SEYMOUR LUCAS, Esq.

FIG. 60 b. *Gothic Stool.* Property of SIR CHARLES LAWES-WITTEWRONGE, Bart.

FIG. 61 a. *Oak Stool.* Height, 1 foot 11 inches; length, 1 foot 6 inches. Property of MORGAN WILLIAMS, Esq.

FIG. 61 b. *Oak Stool.* Height, 1 foot 6 inches; length, 2 feet 1 inch. Property of MORGAN WILLIAMS, Esq.

but this cup and cover in its restrained form had but a short life, developing all too rapidly, and at length assuming a circumference wholly disproportionate to its origin.

The legs of this stool are fluted in the Renaissance manner, and finish in bases and caps of a pearled ornament. The frame is studded with bold nail-headings between narrow reed mouldings, and supported by small ogeed brackets; the top is original, and the whole stool is in perfect preservation.

It is only by careful observation of the growth and origin of small details that one is enabled with any degree of certainty to place a piece of furniture in its decade. Characteristic portions of an earlier design may overlap innovations and confuse the student, but a dated piece, such as the bed-back, having on its posts a novelty in ornament in embryo, establishes a period of design that is incontestible. In dating objects like furniture, the tendency generally is to predate them, and tradition connected with an individual piece should always be corroborated by corresponding details in other examples.

Joint or joyned stools were used in every room of a house and always in the bedrooms, where they served the purposes of small tables as well as seats, and before the introduction of the lighter chairs they had been the only portable form of seat. In time of quarrel they were resorted to as offensive and defensive weapons, and in powerful hands could be thrown with deadly effect, for up till the middle of the seventeenth century a fight following a heated discussion was by no means confined to the inn. Fig. 60 shows two of these stools of early date, being entirely of Gothic construction; while those in Fig. 61 are of the date 1535, and decorated on the sides with medallioned heads of the Renaissance. In one of these stools (Fig. 61 b) it will be noticed that the top forms a small coffer, and there are traces on it of the original vermilion with which it was painted. The first light form of chair used in bedrooms was of simple turned work, and often of triangular shape. An extract from an inventory of about 1540 mentions one of these chairs, and well describes the furniture of a bedroom in what is called 'the greate chambre over the perlor':

FIG. 62. *Turned Chair.* Oak. Height, 2 feet 11 inches. Property of MORGAN WILLIAMS, Esq.

'First a hanging all round the room of grene and red saye, paynede. Item, one greate trussing bed with two fether beds, where of one is downe, with two bolsters and two pillows of downe, Item, three blanckets of woolen clothe, a coverlet of verder worke enlyned. Item, a mantill of red. Item, a joined cupborde with a counterfet carpet upon it. Item, a short table joyned with a coaste carpett upon it. Item, two chests, a turneyed chaire. Item, three quysshins. Item, two awndyerns, a fyer pan, a payer of tongs, Item, a chafer of brasse, two basons, two joyned stools.'

Figs. 62 and 63 are two of these turned chairs. Of Byzantine origin, their pattern was introduced by the Varangian guard into Scandinavia, and from there doubtless brought to England by the Normans, they continued to be made until the end of the sixteenth century. The chair in Hereford Cathedral, locally supposed to have been used by King John, is of this type.

Fig. 64 is an example of a state bed that would be used in an important

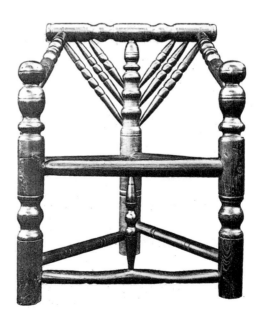

FIG. 63. *Turned Chair.* Oak. Property of A. L. RADFORD, Esq.

FIG. 64 *(left)*. *Oak Bed*. Height, 7 feet 6 inches; width, 6 feet. Property of MORGAN WILLIAMS, Esq.

FIG. 65 *(above)*. *Ceiling of Tester* to FIG. 64.

house. It is of oak, and of about the date 1560. The carving throughout is very large in scale; the cornice moulding is plain, supported by dentals and corbels, beneath which runs a frieze carved in guilloche in low relief. The ceiling of the tester (Fig. 65) is divided into four panels, each bearing a grotesque mask; they are framed in heavy stiles and rails, 15 inches wide and 6 inches deep, which centre in a larger mask, the idea being evidently that from every point a face should look down on the occupant of the bed. This tester and ceiling weighs nearly a quarter of a ton. In the back of the bed are framed the Royal Arms, with the Lion of England and Dragon of Wales as supporters. On either side are the half-length figures of a man and woman in

FIG. 66. *Bed from Sizergh Hall*. VICTORIA AND ALBERT MUSEUM.

FIG. 67. *Oak Bed*. Height, 6 feet 7 inches.
Property of SIR CHARLES LAWES-WITTEWRONGE,
Bart.

the costume of 1560, all carved in extra high relief; above and below runs a frieze of rosace carving, and on the outside are representations of hounds with escutcheons. The posts stand beyond the actual bed, and start from enormous bulbous bases 3 feet high and 3 feet 6 inches in circumference; these are carved with bold gadroons, and are necked top and bottom with a guilloche moulding; the bulbous form is repeated again above, finishing in narrow, graceful columns.

A bed of great purity of style in the classical taste is Fig. 66, which was removed together with the panelling of the room from Sizergh Hall, Westmorland. The date is about 1568; this is shown by the architectural simplicity of construction and the reticence of its ornament, which all bears a strong similarity of taste and treatment to the St Mary Overie chest (Fig. 57). The tester of the bed, 7 feet 6 inches in length, is composed of a cornice and frieze of light-coloured oak, inlaid with an arabesque of holly-wood stained pale green and bog-oak, and is fitted to the pilasters forming part of the panelling; the columns that support this tester are not attached to the actual bed, which lies quite separate within them; they are composite in their order and of walnut, with cups and bases, simple and fine in treatment; the plinths are walnut, panelled with oak. The back is divided into six panels of lime-wood, inlaid with a bold strap-work of walnut, in a framing of oak inlaid with a trellis of holly-wood and bog-oak, on the stiles of which eight terminal figures of classical design are applied. These figures, so constantly found on the backs of beds, represented originally sacred characters, but in later Elizabethan times developed into rudely carved caryatides of warriors and fat goddesses. The embroidered silk curtains, valances, quilts and fringes, together with the carved wood-work of an important Elizabethan bed, very frequently cost the equivalent to £500 of our money to-day, and a sum that would represent more than double that would not have gone very far in the outlay entailed on the elaborate decoration of a state bed. Our ancestors considered the piece of furniture connected with their birth, marriage and death as most important, and emphasised this fact by a corresponding expenditure of money over it. Even the smaller and more domestic specimens, such as Fig. 67, must have been costly; this is a very good representation of the ordinary bed in a well-furnished house of about 1570. It stands low, being about 6 feet 7 inches in height. The frieze to the tester is carved prettily with masks and strap-work, surmounted by a row of dentals, above which runs the favourite acanthus cornice found on most of these beds; this is supported by short columns, springing from the bulbous bases now coming so much into fashion, and lasting as a taste for over fifty years. The bases in this instance are large in proportion to the posts; they measure 2 feet 4 inches in circumference, and stand on plinths of typical Elizabethan design; the panels of the back are in carved and arched compartments, and decorated with vases of flowers, not however of marqueterie, as is usual, but painted in colours, and unfortunately invisible in the reproduction. On the stiles are male and female terms; and grotesque figures playing on pipes take the place of the headposts found in the preceding reigns. The absence of plain surfaces, the restlessness of the perpetual ornament, are very indicative of the ever-changing taste of the time. The 'Great Bed of Ware' is too well known to reproduce. There is an allusion to this celebrated piece of furniture in the Poetical Itinerary of Prince Ludwig of Anhalt-Cothen in 1596, which is anterior to the quotation in *Twelfth Night*. Its dimensions are 10 feet 9 inches in width, 10 feet 9 inches in length, and 7 feet 6½ inches in height. Prince Ludwig states that it held four couples with comfort! Originally at the Crown Inn, Ware, it passed into the possession of Charles Dickens, to find its present resting-place at the Rye House. Fig. 68 exactly resembles this bed in the architectural construction of the columns, but possesses greater elegance of proportion. The carving of the arcades at the back is rich and deep, and the marqueterie inlay of the panels careful in design; the upper mouldings of this arcade are burnt in many places, proving that it was customary to burn a rushlight on the lower edge; the armorial hangings are of the following century, at which date, no doubt, the whole construction was heightened.

All these testered carved oak bedsteads much resemble one another in the general arrangement of their ornament, the differences being marked only by the quality of the carving and form of the posts, the latter as various in their character as the occupants of the bed. Fig. 69, date 1590, shows a

FIG. 68. *Oak Bed.*

FIG. 69. *Oak Bed.* Property of Sir Charles Lawes-Wittewronge, Bart.

THE AGE OF OAK

COLOUR PLATES

PLATE I. *Sudbury's Hutch in St James' Church, Louth, Lincolnshire.* Length, 63 inches; depth, 26½ inches; height, 36½ inches.

PLATE II. *Credence*. Height, 46 inches; length, 57 inches; depth, 24 inches. In the possession of E. A. Barry, Esq. J.P.

PLATE III. *Sir John Wynne's Buffet.* Height, 95 inches; length, 56¾ inches; depth, 23½ inches. In the possession of the Earl of Carrington.

PLATE IV. (a) *Oak Cacqueteuse Chair.* Property of Percy Macquoid, Esq.
(b) *Yew Chair.* Property of the Duke of Leeds.

PLATE V. *Cabinet Inlaid with Marqueterie.* Height, 3 feet; length, 3 feet 6 inches; depth, 1 foot 5 inches. Property of Sir George Donaldson.

PLATE VI. *Writing-cabinet Inlaid with Marqueterie.* Height, 2 feet 3 inches; length, 2 feet 9 inches; depth, 1 foot 3 inches.

PLATE VII. *Walnut and Oak Standing Buffet.* Height, 3 feet 9 inches; length, 4 feet 4 inches; depth, 1 foot 7 inches. Property of Percy Macquoid, Esq.

PLATE VIII. (a) *Oak Chest*. Height, 2 feet 2 inches; length, 3 feet 5 inches; depth, 2 feet. Property of Seymour Lucas, Esq.
(b) *Oak Inlaid Nonesuch Chest*. Height, 1 foot 10 inches; length, 4 feet.

PLATE IX. *Oak Inlaid Chair*. Height, 3 feet 3 inches; depth, 1 foot 3 inches; width of seat, 1 foot 11 inches. Property of Miss Dorothy Chune Fletcher.

PLATE X. *Oak Standing Buffet*. Height, 4 feet 4½ inches; length, 4 feet 3 inches; depth, 1 foot 8 inches. Property of Edward Quilter, Esq.

PLATE XI. *Oak Inlaid Chest.* Height, 2 feet 4½ inches; length, 4 feet 8½ inches; depth, 1 foot 11½ inches. Property of Arthur James, Esq.

PLATE XII. (a) *Oak Inlaid Box*. Height, 9½ inches; length, 2 feet 1 inch; depth, 1 foot 5 inches. Property of Edward Quilter, Esq.
(b) *Oak Inlaid Box*. Height, 2 feet 7 inches; length, 2 feet 9 inches; depth, 1 foot 9 inches. Property of Edward Quilter, Esq.

PLATE XIII. *Oak Cupboard (Welsh)*. Height, 5 feet 2 inches; breadth, 3 feet 10 inches; depth, 1 foot 10½ inches.

PLATE XIV. *Oak Double Chairs* (*Welsh*). (a) Height, 3 feet 6½ inches.
(b) Height, 3 feet 4 inches. Property of H. Clarence Whaite, Esq.

PLATE XV. *Oak Court Cupboard (Tridarn)*. Height, 6 feet 9 inches; length, 2 feet 6½ inches; depth, 2 feet 1 inch. Property of H. Clarence Whaite, Esq.

FIG. 70. *Needlework Tester and Valances.*

further delicacy of proportion in the design of these posts, the lines being inspired by the beautiful French bed-posts of the previous twenty years, though in this particular instance the carving is somewhat coarse. The marqueterie panels of the back, representing the view of a town, are almost obscured by varnish. The soffits of the arches are unusually charming in their simple character, and the four figures on the divisions represent Hope, Charity, Justice and Fortitude, while grotesque figures border the outer stiles; the ceiling and frieze that the columns support are more full of design that the majority of these testers; the pillows and bedding in their proper position should be within six inches of the carved shelf-rail. In these later and smaller examples the hangings were generally of linen, embroidered in crewels, with a pattern of foliage, flowers and birds, the silken and tapestry curtains being used only on the finer beds; a so-called mourning bed draped in black was kept by some families, and lent to different members as occasion required. Paul Hentzner, after travelling here in 1598, writes:

'Their beds are covered with needlework, even those of farmers';

and again in describing the Queen's rooms in Hampton Court:

'In her bedchamber the bed was covered with very costly coverlids of silk. At no great distance from this room we were shown a bed, the tester of which was worked by Anne Boleyn and presented to her husband Henry VIII. In the hall there are curiosities: the bed in which Edward VI is said to have been born, and where his mother, Jane Seymour, died in childbed; numbers of cushions ornamented with gold and silver, many counterpanes and coverlids of beds, lined with ermines; there is also a musical instrument made all of glass except the strings.'

Fig. 70 gives tester valances of English needlework of about 1590, the subject being the allegory of life. They were formerly in Littlecote Wilts, the scene of the strange tradition of the child-murder by William Darrell, in which the hangings of a bed played so prominent a part in the story.

FIG. 71. Set of Elizabethan Cushions. Property of LORD FITZHARDINGE.

Another favourite form of bed-hangings, probably for summer use, were of linen finely embroidered in coloured silks, the quilt, cushion and pillows being made to match. Fig. 71 shows a set of bed-cushions, of about 1580, one unfortunately missing, the largest of which is 2 feet long by 1 foot broad, the others decreasing in the same proportion. They are of the finest linen, embroidered with a border of flowers in white and cherry-coloured silks and silver thread; the centres are plain linen, delicately trellised in a back-stitch of pale yellow silk. These five cushions were used by Queen Elizabeth during a visit to Berkeley Castle, and are preserved there, together with the quilt that matches them on the bed (Fig. 72). Elizabeth was probably the first Queen who paid almost fastidious attention to things connected with her toilet-chamber and the details of her bedroom, where highly favoured visitors were continually received. The following extract from a letter written in 1578 by Gilbert Talbot to his father, the Earl of Shrewsbury, is interesting, showing that night-attire was now worn, and that the Virgin Queen, at the age of forty-five, added to her other charms by leaning out of the window in this costume.

'On May-Day I saw Her Majesty, and it pleased her to speak to me very graciously. In the morning about eight o'clock I happened to walk in the Tiltyard, under the gallery where Her Majesty useth to stand to see the running at tilt, where by chance she was, and looking out of the window my eye was full towards her. She shewed to be greatly ashamed thereof for that she was unready, and in her night-stuff, so when she saw me at after dinner, as she went to walk, she gave me a great fillip on the forehead, and told my Lord Chamberlain who was next to her, how I had seen her that morning and how much ashamed she was.'

The posts of the bed (Fig. 72) stand on architectural canopies supported on four small columns, beneath which are two figures in oak, the large bulbous

FIG. 72. *Oak Bed*. Height, 6 feet 6 inches; width, 5 feet 6 inches; length, 6 feet 10 inches. Property of LORD FITZHARDINGE.

bases to the posts being also carved with human torsos in low relief (an unusual feature), finishing at the top in baluster-shaped columns clothed in raised acanthus. The back contains three panels, the centre of these bears the royal arms of James I, who slept in the bed, those on the sides being painted with the figures of Justice and Mercy. This back is framed in stiles, on which are the four figures, Faith, Hope, Charity and Fortitude; above this runs a band of fine marqueterie, surmounted by a carved frieze. The cornice of the tester is corbelled at intervals with lions' masks, and the carving throughout is picked out rather coarsely with gilding of a recent date.

Although the number of chairs used even in important bedrooms at this time still remained limited, the growth of comfort is shown by an increase in those made for the parlours and withdrawing-rooms. Fig. 73 is a lady's chair of the cacqueteuse type, of Scottish origin. It is of oak, and made during the close relationship that existed between the court of Mary Stuart and France. The back is composed of a raised panel carved with a chain strap-work in very low relief; the uprights framing it are carved in fine line, and the top rail is surmounted by a simple scrolled cresting, terminating in a small finial; the arms are bowed supported on balustered uprights. The front rail of the seat is unusually wide, and on all three sides is on arched compartments, with the same baluster supports. In foreign chairs of this kind, the centre generally finishes in a pendant, and the Scottish workman in introducing a baluster in its place has evidently been at a loss to complete satisfactorily the alteration from the original design; the incised lines on the face of the arches representing bricking are interesting. This chair is contemporary with the murder of Darnley. Fig. 74 is some fifteen years later in date; here the back opens into two arches in the style of Charles IX of France, between which lies

FIG. 73. *Oak Chair*. Height, 3 feet 9 inches; height to seat, 1 foot 4 inches. Property of SIR GEORGE DONALDSON.

FIG. 74. *Oak Chair*. Property of SIR GEORGE DONALDSON.

FIG. 75. *Oak Chair*. Property of SIR GEORGE DONALDSON.

FIG. 76. *Oak Chair*. Height, 3 feet 7 inches. Property of the EARL OF CARRINGTON.

FIG. 77. *End of Table*. Elm. Height, 2 feet 7 inches; length, 9 feet. Property of SIR CHARLES LAWES-WITTEWRONGE, Bart.

a narrow panel of Elizabethan carving. The cresting at the top shows the double scroll that eventually became so typical a finish to all these panel-back chairs; the supports to the arms are tall, like all early chairs of this kind, and their design is repeated on the front legs. These open-back chairs do not appear ever to have become popular; they certainly could not have been conducive to warmth in rooms so draughty that men wore their hats at meals, and drew their chairs so close to open fires, that wicker coverings to fit the legs stood by the hearths to be used as guards against scorched shins. All chairs between 1570 and 1620, except those of 'X' form, had panelled backs, and the well-known type (Fig. 75) continued to be made with slight alterations until the beginning of the eighteenth century, but it is extremely difficult to place them in correct chronological succession. The earlier specimens have no brackets or ears, as they are termed, at the sides of the back panel; the arms are flatter and straighter, and often inlaid or incised, the arm supports are higher, and the seats rather wider than in the later chairs.

The detail of the simple but effective carving on the panel of Fig. 75 very much resembles the decoration and arrangement of the faces on each side of the lunette on the gable dated 1572 over the porch at Kirby Hall; while Fig. 76 is a west country chair of about the same date, the carving exactly corresponding with that of a door at Nailsea Court, Somerset, also built at that time. Here the pattern is formed by sinking the ground and leaving the face of the panel for the design. On the top rail is incised a graceful scroll-work of flowers, originally filled with marqueterie; the introduction of the bold nail-heading marks the period, and at each corner of the rail may be noticed the suggestion of the ear-form that later became so prevalent. The arm supports are high, and of square vase-shaped baluster form, repeated in the legs.

A large and curiously constructed round table top exists in the Castle Hall at Winchester, painted with allusions to King Arthur and his knights, and is shown to tourists as the original piece of furniture connected with the fable, though probably made in the fifteenth century. The disappearance of early tables may be due to the fact that they were of trestle form, the parts being detachable. These trestle tables are represented in the English MSS of the fourteenth and fifteenth centuries as a board laid on two or more crossed supports, often covered with an elaborate embroidered linen cloth. Fig. 77 is about 1520, of elm, and very few of these elm tables exist, owing to the perishable nature of the wood. The frame and stretcher run through the trestle supports, and are kept in position by movable oak pegs. When space was important, these pegs were withdrawn, and the various parts stacked

FIG. 78. *Table.*Oak. Height, 2 feet 8 inches; length, 27 feet; width, 3 feet. Property of LORD DE LISLE AND DUDLEY.

against the wall. Froissart, in speaking of the King of England in 1350, says, 'Quand on eust soupe on lever les tables si demeura le dict roy en la salle'; and again, 'Furent les tables levees et abattues soudainment pour les dames et damouselles estre au large.' An oak table such as Froissart mentions is represented in Fig. 78, and is one of two, standing in the great hall at Penshurst. They are of the beginning of the fifteenth century, and the finest examples in this country of the early trestle table. The top of this table is kept in place by its own weight which is enormous, for it measures 27 feet in length, 3 feet in width, and is composed of four oak planks without any join: although of rude workmanship, the style and proportion is magnificent; and the blocked-out mouldings to the trestle supports relieved by smaller crocketings running up the four sides are most effective. The wood is light in colour and has never been dressed in any way. At the further end of this table the line of the floor dais can be seen, on which another table was placed at right angles for the lord and master of the house, with his family and guests. At this high table the seats were only on one side, the food being served from the other as in classical times; it was therefore easy for those eating to select the food with their fingers from the dishes handed, as the width of these early tables was seldom more than two feet. A wooden trencher or a thick slice of bread served as a plate, the important personages having deep silver saucers or low basins, also a wooden bowl, called a 'voyder', for the portions they did not require: those inferior in station, and seated at the low tables threw what they did not fancy on the floor. The height of these tables averages 2 feet 8 inches – 5 inches higher than the modern dining-table.

With the invention of the draw-top a revolution took place in tables: the solid trestles at the ends were replaced by legs that formed part of the frame, and an outside lower rail or stretcher served the double purpose of a lower tie to the legs and a foot-rest. The top was in three pieces, the lower leaves drawing out and being supported by long armed brackets; the upper leaf dropped into its position, and so the table elongated to double its length – a simple and effective contrivance. The trestle table ceased to be used after the middle of the sixteenth century, and was relegated to the servants' quarters. Fig. 79 is an oak draw-table of 1560, of simple proportion, which originally belonged to the Wadham family of Oxford celebrity. The mouldings are classical, inspired by contemporary French taste; and the legs conform to this style, in no way suggesting the rather bulbous vulgarity of the later fashion. In all early tables of this kind it should be observed that the foot-rail is T-shaped in section; it is not till later that it became four-sided. Fig. 80 is another draw-table of rather later date, the frame and legs made of cherry, a wood highly prized in Tudor times; the top is of oak, and has lost the two lower leaves. The frame is carved on a punched ground in a simple open

FIG. 79. *Table*. Oak. Height, 2 feet 10 inches; length, 7 feet 8 inches. Property of A. L. RADFORD, Esq.

FIG. 80. *Table*. Cherry-wood. Height, 2 feet 6 inches; length, 6 feet 2 inches; width, 2 feet 5 inches. Property of MORGAN WILLIAMS, Esq.

chain of squares and circles, the latter being rosaced; the gadrooning on the bulbous supports is concave, and these finish in a necking of the egg and tongue that preceded the Ionic capitals found on later tables. This cherry-wood furniture is extremely rare; it becomes coffee-colour with age and preserves a most beautiful surface. When not in use for meals, these were often covered with a fine Persian rug, unless the top was inlaid with marque-terie, as in the case of Fig. 82, which is probably the most interesting English table in existence. The top is walnut, composed of three planks, inlaid in a most elaborate manner with musical instruments, armorial bearings, and the properties pertaining to various games of chance: these three lengths of decoration, entirely distinct from each other, are divided by an inlaid cable moulding, an heraldic bordure of the Cavendish family. The upper compart-ment (which can be seen more clearly in the key, Fig. 81) shows the surface inlaid with a cyterrne, lute, viol, rebeck, flutes, sackbuts and shawms; scattered over and amongst them are flowers and fruits inlaid in their proper colours. The centre panel bears the Cavendish, Talbot and Hardwick arms

FIG. 81. *Key* to FIG. 82.

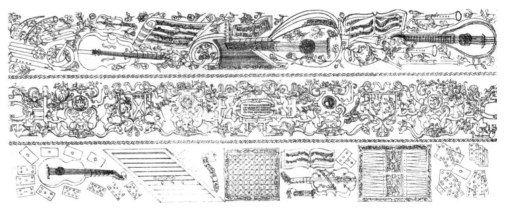

FIG. 82. *Top of Table (Walnut) Inlaid with Marqueterie*. Length, 9 feet 11 inches; width, 4 feet 3 inches. Property of the DUKE OF DEVONSHIRE.

Fɪɢ. 83. *Table (Walnut) Inlaid with Marqueterie.* Same as Fɪɢ. 82. Height, 3 feet. Property of the Dᴜᴋᴇ ᴏꜰ Dᴇᴠᴏɴꜱʜɪʀᴇ.

with their supporters. These bearings are connected with a bold strap-work and garlands of flowers, the centre being occupied by an escutcheon set in strap-work, on which are seated the figures of two nude women, inlaid in many separate pieces, the shadows on the bodies being burned in the wood. The escutcheon bears the inscription:

ᴛʜᴇ . ʀᴇᴅᴏʟᴇɴᴛ . sᴍɪʟᴇ. (smell)
ᴏꜰ . ᴀᴇɢʟᴇɴᴛʏɴᴇ . (sweetbriar)
ᴡᴇ . sᴛᴀɢɢᴇs . (Cavendish & Hardwick) ᴇxᴀᴠᴇᴛ (exault)
ᴛᴏ ᴛʜᴇ ᴅᴇᴠᴇʏɴᴇ . (divine).

On the lower panels are inlaid a cyternne, boards for dice, a violin, and writing materials; the inlay is not laid down in a veneer, but in every instance the cells are cut an eighth of an inch out of the solid walnut to receive the pattern, but it is unfortunately so much damaged that a reference to the key will be found necessary. The frame and legs to this table (Fig. 83) are of oak, the former inlaid with a frieze of classical design, divided by triglyphs, below which are the guttæ; the legs are columns, shaped as inverted cones, with curious little neckings, small capitals, and a very shallow abacus; the shafts are inlaid with rings and festoons, and slips of coloured wood set edgeways to resemble marble in small plaques; the foot-rail is deep, of T-form, inlaid on the outside with a classical frieze, and painted on the inside with an elegant strap-work. This remarkable and beautiful piece of furniture was made for Elizabeth (or Bess) of Hardwick, on the occasion of her marriage to her fourth husband, the Earl of Shrewsbury, in 1568, and the arms represented commemorate, as well as her own marriage, the unions of her son Henry Cavensih and her daughter Mary Cavendish with a son and daughter of Lord Shrewsbury. The stags and stags' heads that so constantly occur all through the decoration of Hardwick are emblems of Cavendish and Hardwick; the Talbot hound of Shrewsbury is also occasionally introduced.

Another ornamental table in the same Great Presence-Chamber at Hardwick is Fig. 84. It is of rather later date, but decorated in a somewhat similar manner. In this instance the entire structure is of walnut, the top being inlaid with a parqueterie of yew, beech, oak and bog-oak, in circles and diamond shapes, surrounded by a border inlaid with a strap-work terminating in cherries; at the four corners is inlaid a playing-card, the five of each suit. The frame of the table (Fig. 85) is inlaid with a classical frieze supported by square Doric columns, the fluting represented by an inlay of yew; the foot-rail is of T-form as in the last table. The woods employed throughout are left in their natural colours and no staining attempted. In both these specimens, and in other furniture of this date at Hardwick, the wood has faded to the colour of pale cinnamon, due to the flood of sunlight that for over three hundred years has poured into its vast rooms, through windows some 20 feet high. In the gallery, which is 167 feet long, 41 feet broad and 26 feet high, the windows are composed of 27,000 panes of glass, the other windows on this same floor being of corresponding proportions. Bess of Hardwick was comprehensive not only in her building but in other matters. Beginning married life at the age of fourteen, she not only managed

Fig. 84. *Top of Table Inlaid with Marqueterie.*
Length, 3 feet 4 inches; width, 3 feet 4
inches. Property of the Duke of Devonshire.

Fig. 85. *Table Inlaid with Marqueterie.*
Same as Fig. 84. Height, 2 feet 10 inches.
Property of the Duke of Devonshire.

to secure large fortunes with each of her husbands, but in the case of the
third, who was by far the richest she managed effectually to fix the inheritance upon herself and her own heirs for fault of issue by him, thereby
excluding his brothers and his own daughter. The originality and power of
this woman's mind is apparent throughout the construction and decoration
of Hardwick; the first Chatsworth and Oldcotes were also results of her
enterprise and genius, and she may well be termed the Master Builder of her
sex. She died on 13 February 1607, aged about eighty-seven.

FIG. 86. *Chest Inlaid with Marqueterie.* Height, 2 feet 10 inches; length, 5 feet 9 inches; width, 2 feet 4 inches. Property of the DUKE OF DEVONSHIRE.

Two other pieces of furniture connected with this lady are Figs. 86 and 87. The first is an oak chest with drawers, much on the lines of the chest (Fig. 57) belonging to St Mary Overie. The front is inlaid and divided into two central panels framed in classical arches, on the keystones of which are the initials G. T. Within these arches the inlay represents views of buildings; the pilasters and panels on either side being also inlaid with floral scrolls and Tudor roses, all in coloured woods; the lower compartment of the chest opens in two drawers, decorated in a similar manner; the panels of the side and top are walnut inlaid in lighter woods, with the arabesque ornament of about 1560 to 1575. This chest was made for Gilbert Talbot, son of the Earl of Shrewsbury, who married in 1568 Mary Cavendish, Bess of Hardwick's daughter by her second husband, and it was probably a marriage coffer. This Gilbert Talbot is he who had the privilege of seeing Queen Elizabeth in her night attire, and who aired his views to his father in the letter already given. Fig. 87 was no doubt originally a long table with six legs cut down to fit a required position. The legs are early in shape and beautiful in proportion, and a comparison with those of the table (Fig. 80) shows a step in the evolution of this form. The great interest, however, of the piece consists in a little iron ring attached to one of the legs, the actual ring to which Bess of Hardwick tied up her little dog.

FIG. 87. *Table, with Ring for Dog.* Property of the DUKE OF DEVONSHIRE.

F𝟣ɢ. 88. *Cabinet and Stand Inlaid with Marqueterie.* V𝟣ᴄᴛᴏʀɪᴀ ᴀɴᴅ Aʟʙᴇʀᴛ Mᴜsᴇᴜᴍ.

The same question of origin with the early carved oak arises again in connection with the highly finished and elaborately inlaid pieces of furniture made between 1560 and the end of the century. The celebrated cabinet and stand (Fig. 88) in the Victoria and Albert Museum is an instance of disputed nationality, though it has been for many years labelled as English. There are so many strong points between the stand of this cabinet and the Sizergh bed, that there can be but little doubt that the stand at any rate is of native workmanship. The inlaid border round the base, composed of portcullis and Tudor rose alternating, the capitals of the columns and their proportions, the inlaid arabesques in the spandrels of the arches, and the frieze into which the fleur-de-lys is introduced, together with the dentals and corbels that support the top, are all distinctly English in their simplicity, and it is these details that have ever raised the hope that the cabinet itself is also of English make; but there is no possible ground for attributing the marvellous little carvings in boxwood on the faces of the drawers, and the skill shown in the portrayal of the human form to this source. The whole design and execution of the façade is South German in feeling, and the costumes of the little figures are foreign in cut, and date the work as that of 1570. The marqueterie both on the open top flap and the inside of the drawers, in its free flowing lines and foreshortened strap-work, the colouring of the stained woods employed and the lock-plates, all strongly suggest foreign taste. The cabinet is decorated on all four sides, showing that it was intended to be placed in the centre of a room. It may very probably have been the work of a foreigner domiciled in this country, and the stand made a few years later by an Englishman, for it will be observed that there is no introduction of the Royal English emblems that are found on the stand on any part of the actual cabinet.

Plate VI of the same type, though much smaller, is entirely English in design and execution. This is evidently a writing-cabinet, as it is full of little secret drawers and cupboards, and implements connected with writing are inlaid on the slide that draws out. All four sides are decorated, showing that it was also intended to stand out in a room. The architectural façade is

English, so are all the woods employed; on the outer doors are representations of warriors on horseback, riding in archaic meadows of green-stained holly, bordered with strap-work panels in a marqueterie of cherry, pear and sycamore woods; the side panels are inlaid in the centre with a falcon, a cognisance of the Boleyns, repeated on the inside of the lid. The drawers are of deal, while in the foreign pieces of this kind, Hungarian ash is almost invariably employed. Inside the top compartment is the little side-box always found in English chests of the time – the handles are all missing. The whole cabinet is of a beautiful golden colour, and there is a close analogy between it and the stand in Fig. 88. It was originally in Hever Castle, but in 1750, after a fire that took place there, when no doubt much of the furniture was hastily removed, it mysteriously passed into the hands of a yeoman farmer in the neighbourhood, and remained in their family until a few years ago. Traces of burning are distinctly visible on one of the doors. It is of the date 1580, and probably belonged to Mary Boleyn or her children, who inherited Hever Castle.

CHAPTER IV

CAREFUL comparison of the St Mary Overie chest (Fig. 57), the Sizergh bed (Fig. 66), the stand to the Victoria and Albert Museum cabinet (Fig. 88), and that from Hever (Plate VI), shows a striking similarity of taste and style. The same passages of colour run throughout the three pieces, and although the causes that constitute charm in marqueterie render its reproduction in black and white very unsatisfactory, the examples on the coloured plates have been chosen with the view of showing distinctly the development of the new taste, which also prompted the many coloured and embroidered clothes, made of small patterned fabrics, more frivolous in design than those of Gothic times.

The almost universal use of wainscot panelling as a wall decoration during Elizabeth's reign demanded more cheerful-looking furniture than the simple oak, which had by this time ceased to be painted and gilded; but all furniture was evidently still expensive and highly treasured, for a German, Samuel Kiechel, travelling here in 1585, wrote: 'The Royal treasures in furniture and tapestries are kept only in that palace in which for the time being the Queen resides; when she moves to another, everything is taken away and only the bare walls remain standing.' Other references to such removals are clearly indicative that the supply of these things, even belonging to royalty, was not yet large.

Many instances are found in inventories, of small and elaborate tables, but few of them appear to have been constructed in this country in the sixteenth century. The beautiful French specimen (Fig. 89) was made from the design of Jacques Androuet Ducereau, and proves how very far behind other countries we were in this matter. Ducerceau, engraver and architect, whose designs for furniture remain to this day pre-eminent in elegance and originality, after a sojourn in Italy, returned to the French Court in 1557, where his services were retained until his retirement in 1584. There is a table (Fig. 90) at Hardwick directly inspired by his style, though known to have been constructed on the premises; it was possibly made by some of the foreign and English men working together in the employment of Bess of Hardwick, by that time Countess of Shrewsbury. It is of English walnut, but it is rash to presume that the Talbot hound-headed monsters supporting the table are carved by an English hand; the draw-top is also of walnut, inlaid with graceful arabesque and strap-work of holly and oak (a very English feature), with circles and irregular-shaped pieces of marble rather roughly

FIG. 89. *Small Walnut Table (French).* Property of COLONEL GEORGE KEMP.

FIG. 90. *Walnut Table with Draw-top.* Height, 2 feet 10 inches; length, 4 feet 10 inches; width, 2 feet 10 inches. Property of the DUKE OF DEVONSHIRE.

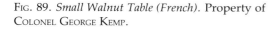

Fig. 91. *Oak and Walnut Cupboard*. Height, 3 feet 2 inches; length, 3 feet 7 inches; depth, 1 foot 10 inches. Property of the Duke of Devonshire.

Fig. 92. *Standing Buffet*. Height, 4 feet 2 inches; length, 3 feet 10 inches; depth, 2 feet. Property of Sir George Donaldson.

introduced; the open spaces between this strap-work are inlaid with the fruits grown in England at that time. The frame is carved with an alternate nulling and flat acanthus which centres on all four sides in a plaque, roughly carved with lions' masks and festoons of fruit. All this ornament was originally gilt, but no varnish has ever been applied; the frame and top is supported on four hound-headed, winged female monsters, who terminate in scaled tails; between them rise graceful balustered supports, two of which are missing. These monsters lie on a deep stand of plain walnut, painted on the sides to imitate plaques of marble; this again is supported on four tortoises, very English in their carving. The top and stand are by a distinctly different hand to the centre of the table. Fig. 91 is a cupboard of oak and walnut, also made at Hardwick about 1570, under the same circumstances. The top, which is supported by brackets at the sides, is of walnut, framed in a more recent moulding, and inlaid with a strap-work of coloured woods, now much faded. The front opens in two doors of architectural design, and above is a drawer inlaid with marqueterie, the marble plaques being imitated in stained ash; in the centre is a handle formed by a lion's mask; the panels on either side framing the cupboard are inlaid with an arabesque design in light woods, all much faded. The plinth on which the cupboard stands is original; the marqueterie of the top and front corresponds in its somewhat deep and rough workmanship with other marqueterie found at Hardwick. The same sense of importance in all this better class of furniture is to be found in the standing buffet, also of about 1570 (Fig. 92). This is of walnut and in two pieces. The front of the upper portion is composed of two panels opening as doors, inlaid with holly, in the same pointed arabesque design found on the top and sides of Fig. 86. These panels are framed in a flat, deeply carved with a Greek key pattern, and outside this a projecting guilloche worked in darker walnut; the uprights of the framework are carved with a delicate strap-work; the bottom rail is in projection and boldly carved; the sides are treated in a similar manner to the front. The general design bears an interesting resemblance to the simpler French work of the early years of Charles IX's reign, but it is less artificial and shows very distinctly the individuality of the new English taste. The lower portion or stand is some fifteen years later in date. Figures of women treated as caryatides support a frieze inlaid with floral arabesques in coloured woods; the shelf below is inlaid in a similar manner; the front carved with a bold nulling, rests on melon-shaped feet. The introduction of walnut into this better class of English oak furniture had towards the end of the sixteenth century found much favour, though the wood was evidently still scarce in this country;

indeed every novelty that taste could suggest was greedily adopted, and the nation seemed as eager for variety as the mind of its mistress. Harrison at the time wrote:

'For now the furniture of our house is grown in maner even to passing delicacie, and herein I do not speake of the nobilitie and gentrie onely, but even of the lowest sorte that have anything at all to take to. Certes in noblemens houses it is not rare to see abundance of arras, riche hangings of tapestrie, silver vessil, and so much other plate as may furnish sundrie cupbordes to the summe often times of a thousande pounde at the leaste, wherby the value of this and the reast of their stuffe doth grow to be inestimable. Likewise in the houses of knightes, gentlemen, merchauntmen, and some other wealthie citizens it is not geson to beholde generallye their great provision of tapistrie, Turkey worke, pewter, brasse, fine linen, and thereto costly cupboardes. But as herein all these sortes doe farre exceede their elders and pre-decessors, so in time past the costly furniture stayed there, whereas now it is descended yet lower, even unto the inferiour artificers and most fermers who have learned also to garnish their cupbords with plate, their beddes with tapistries and silke hanginges and their tables with fine naperie, whereby the wealth of our countrie doth infinitely appeare. Neyther do I speke this in reproach of any man, God is my judge, but to show that I rejoice rather to see how God hath blessed us with hys good giftes and to beholde howe that in a time wherein all thinges are growne to most excessive prieces we do yet find the meanes to obtayne and atchieve such furniture as here to fore hath been impossible.'

From these sentiments, written between the years 1577 and 1587, it is evident that the art of furnishing was occupying the serious attention of men's minds, and not only great improvements in design and execution were taking place, but that entirely new objects had been created, as, for instance, sideboards of double tier.

The first of these (Fig. 93) is of walnut, about the date 1585. The top is extremely thin, for at this time cornices to court cupboards and buffets became lighter in their proportions. The frieze is plain save for a simple geometrical inlay, and finely carved lions' masks at the corners; the bulbous supports that show the cup and cover origin very clearly are delicate in execution, and prove the great advantages derived from working in walnut. The shelves and bottom rail are inlaid with a squared pattern in a lighter wood; the back is left open, and the whole construction represents an innovation. The same motive, though different in execution, is apparent in Fig. 94, of Welsh make; this is of oak, and therefore of somewhat coarser touch, and though rich in effect, like all the oak furniture of Welsh origin, is lacking in finish. The cornice is very light, and neither the guilloche nor the lunette carving of the friezes show much originality, but the design of the supports is well considered. The open backs to these buffets were probably filled in with a rich piece of material as a background for the 'silver vessil' just mentioned. Another and later specimen is Fig. 95, also of oak, and about the date 1625. The original top is missing; the upper frieze that forms a drawer is decorated with an arabesque strap-work of a rather earlier design; the supports to this are slighter than the two previous examples, and the style of the carving is flat and small; the front of the lower shelves are inlaid with a rough checker of marqueterie. The back supports are carved in low relief with a laurelled design; the solid back is a modern addition, as are the bun feet on which the buffet stands; this form continued to be made until about 1660. The comparison of this with the other two specimens is instruc-tive, for although tradition of style is retained, the poverty of invention and execution is apparent, showing that by this time oak furniture had passed its apogee.

Fig. 96 is an interesting form of drawer-table, almost of trestle form, and of Welsh manufacture. The length of the bulbous legs, headed by a coat of arms, the scrolls and the bold simple nulling, point to the fashion of 1570; but as foreign design evidently filtered slowly into the Principality, types and fashion were irregular in their chronology, and did not always correspond in date with the contemporary work of the more enlightened English counties. The same type of long-shaped bulbous leg can be seen in the oak table (Fig.

FIG. 93. *Walnut Sideboard*. Height, 4 feet; length, 4 feet 1 inch; depth, 1 foot 7 inches. Property of E. A. BARRY, Esq.

FIG. 94. *Oak Sideboard*. Height, 4 feet; length, 4 feet 1 inch; depth, 1 foot 3½ inches. Property of LORD MOSTYN.

FIG. 95. *Oak Sideboard.* Height, 3 feet 7 inches; length, 4 feet; depth, 1 foot 6 inches. Property of MORGAN WILLIAMS, Esq.

97) of Gloucestershire make of about 1575. Here the frame is carved with a semi-classical frieze in very low relief, repeated on the legs. This close rich carving, found in the western counties, is very distinct in style from the more open ornament and strongly defined lines shown in the carving of the northern and eastern counties. The base of this table is much decayed, and the blocks supporting it are modern additions. Plate VII is a walnut standing buffet of about 1585. The top is thin, with a deep yet flat cornice of egg and tongue moulding above a frieze inlaid with a checker-work marqueterie of ebony, cedar and holly. The front is divided into three panels, two of which open as doors deeply recessed, and inlaid with the same woods in simple geometrical designs; these panels are set in deep mouldings between stiles corbelled out in acanthus carving. The lower portion forms a stand with the top rail carved in a flat guilloche and forming a drawer: the legs are of walnut and bulbous in form; they stand upon a lower shelf also faced with a checker

FIG. 96. *Oak Draw-table.* Length, 4 feet 9 inches; height, 2 feet 8 inches; width, 2 feet 9 inches. Property of LADY AUGUSTA MOSTYN.

FIG. 97. *Oak Table with Walnut Top.* Height, 2 feet 10 inches; length, 6 feet 9½ inches. Property of ARTHUR JAMES, Esq.

Fig. 98. *Oak Standing Buffet.* Height, 4 feet 4 inches; length, 3 feet 2 inches. Property of Ernest Crofts, Esq.

Fig. 99. *Oak Court Cupboard.* Height, 5 feet 2 inches; length, 5 feet; depth, 1 foot 8 inches. Property of Ernest Crofts, Esq.

of ebony and holly. The panels at the back and the internal structure of the piece are of oak; the colour of it is rich, and the condition is untouched.

The so-called court cupboard held a very important position in the furnishing of a house; the term court was used in opposition to the word livery. The wine, dry food and candles, used by the master and mistress and their family, were kept in the former; while the bread, cheese, butter, candles and odds and ends pertaining to the servants' livery, i.e. wages, were portioned out, in what were called livery cupboards, which were of much rougher construction. The court cupboard gradually became very ornamental, a favourite variety having the top portion triangular in form, with the roof forming a kind of canopy, supported on two uprights, somewhat bulbous in form during the latter part of Elizabeth's reign, but becoming lighter in construction as the seventeenth century progressed. The lower portion generally opened in two doors; occasionally the doors were omitted, when the uprights above would be repeated as legs below, forming a combination of standing buffet and court cupboard. This combination is found in Fig. 98, which is of oak; the upper structure is that of a court cupboard, while the lower portion, although not separate in construction, resembles the stand of a buffet. The cupboard is of triangular form, and the panels (the centre one forming a door) are inlaid in holly and bog-oak; the bulbous supports have lost all traces of cup and cover form. The centre drawer is lightly carved with rosaces and inlaid with a checker border in marqueterie; the little wooden handles are original; a lower shelf, with a broad bottom rail of shallow carving, completes the structure, which is undoubtedly of eastern county manufacture, for the ancestors of the present owner were living in Suffolk in 1590, which is the date of the piece. The court cupboard (Fig. 99) is from the same source, but made some twenty years later. The upper portion is triangular in form, the elaborate marqueterie of the panels being composed of a design of finches singing amidst conventional flowers; the bulbous and columnar-headed supports are plain, and the stopped flat channel moulding the open character of the carving show that the piece is not within the sixteenth century. The lower portion opens in a drawer and two cupboards, decorated with depressed arches supported by bulbous pilasters in high relief. The panels of the doors are inlaid with a charming design of birds and conventional flowers, and a small checker of marqueterie borders the rails and stiles.

The interest of Plate VIII (b) is apart from its style and workmanship, for it has already been shown that marqueterie had attained to an art far beyond what is represented in this example, though there is a certain direct and rich decoration in the rather coarse inlay of the different woods that is most effective. The chest is of oak, light in colour, and inlaid with two panels of marqueterie representing a building framed at the sides in narrow upright panels inlaid with small lantern-topped towers; above and below runs a frieze representing dormer windows; the whole is contained within a bead and reel inlaid border, repeated on the top and sides; the centre panel bears the initials I. C., with the date 1592. This same house in inlay work is found on many chests of this date, and represents the celebrated Palace of Nonesuch at Cheam, that Henry VIII built for himself towards the end of his life, from the designs of the Italian painter and architect, Totto del Nunziata, who lived over twenty years in this country. This remarkable building remained for upwards of a century the Aladdin's palace, that was considered one of the wonders of England. In 1555 the Earl of Arundel purchased the palace and park from the Crown, and completed the unfinished building, in memory of his former master, Henry VIII. Queen Elizabeth stayed there on several occasions and liked it so well, that she bought it in 1591 from the late Earl's son-in-law and heir, so that Nonesuch again became a royal residence; and we read that at the age of sixty-seven, the Queen, when there, 'was excellently disposed to hunting, for every second day she is on horseback, and continues the sport long'. There also the disgrace of Essex took place. Nonesuch remained in the possession of royalty until 1670, when Barbara Palmer was given the place and created Duchess of Cleveland and Baroness of Nonesuch; but this rapacious courtesan immediately proceeded to demolish the building for the value of the materials, till finally not a vestige of it remained.

Fig. 100 is from an original water-colour drawing of Nonesuch by Joris Hoefnagle, dated 1568. Fig. 102 is the reproduction, engraved by the younger Hoefnagle for Braun's *Cities*, published in 1582; and Fig. 101 is the engraving that probably inspired the furniture maker of the time. The Duke of Saxe-Weimar visited Nonesuch in 1613, and in his diary noticed the

FIG. 100. *Nonesuch Palace*. From the original Water-colour Drawing by HOEFNAGLE. Property of MRS ALFRED MORRISON.

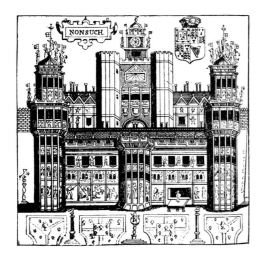

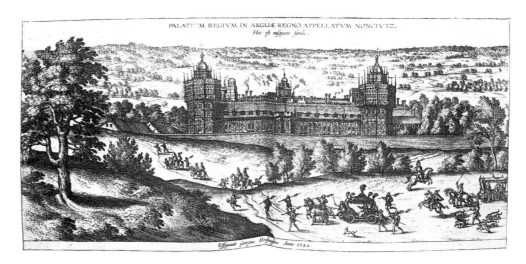

FIG. 101 (*above*). *Nonesuch.* (From Paul Hentzner's *Travels.*)

FIG. 102 (*right*). *Nonesuch.* (From Braun's *Cities.*)

exterior of the inner court, which was the part where Henry VIII resided:

'Beautifully and elegantly adorned with plaster work, representing the labours of Hercules and other histories; the other side, the Queen's lodgings, exhibited all kinds of heathen stories, with naked female figures.'

In the Survey of the Parliamentary Commissioners for 1650 we find:

'The gate-house leading to the outward court is a building very strange and gracefull, being three stories high, leaded overhead, battled and turretted in every of the four corners thereof, the highest of which stories contains a very large and spacious roome very pleasante and delectable for prospect.'

John Evelyn, in 1665-6 writes:

'I supp'd in Nonesuch House, whither the office of the Exchequer was transferr'd during the plague, and took an exact view of ye plaster statues and punchions of the outside walles of the court, which must needs have been the work of some celebrated Italian. I much admired how it had lasted so well and entire since the time of Henry VIII, expos'd as they are to the aire, and pitty it is, they are not taken out and preserved in some drie place; a gallerie would become them. There are some mezzo relievos as big as life. The storie is ye Heathen Gods, emblems, compartments, etc. The palace consists of two courts, of which the first is of stone, castle like, ye other of timber, a Gotic fabric, but these walls incomparably beautified. I observed that the appearing timber punchions, entrellices, etc., were all so covered with scales of slate, that it seemed carved in the wood and painted, ye slate fastened on the timber in pretty figures, that has, like a coate of armour, preserved it from rotting.'

Pepys in his diary also mentioned two visits to Nonesuch. 21 September 1665, he writes:

'To Nonesuch to the Exchequer by appointment . . . a great walke of an elme and a walnutt, set one after another in order, and all the house on the outside filled with figures of stories, and a good painting of Rubens or Holbein's doing; and one great thing is, that most of the house is covered, I mean the posts and quarters in the walls, with lead and gilded. I walked also into the ruined garden.'

Unfortunately there is no mention of the furniture inside this interesting building.

Fig. 103 is a large chest almost six feet in length, with this same interesting decoration as Plate VIII, and probably by the same hand. The front is divided into five panels, those narrow and upright being inlaid with the lantern-topped turrets of Nonesuch in light wood on a dark oak ground, the windows of the turrets being represented in the darker wood; these are bordered with a wide bead and spindle inlay, and framed in stiles of the finer checker-work marqueterie, found between 1580 and 1600. The two large panels are filled with a repeated representation of the central portions of the

FIG. 103. *Nonesuch Chest.* Property of SIR ASTON WEBB.

house set in elaborate borders of checker-work. Along the top, and treated as a frieze, run the dormer windows, which in Hoefnagle's drawing surround the tops of the towers. The colour of the oak forming the construction of the chest is light; the top and sides are decorated with borders of inlay checker-work, and possess the original handles. On opening the lid, the original tinned hinges can also be seen, and a small hanging box on each side, faced with marqueterie. In Fig. 104 a double portico entrance in projection is introduced, and in these a conventional design of flowering plants, probably emblematical of the celebrated gardens within the outer wall. At the side of these porticoes are introduced the Nonesuch turrets, and above are the ranges of dormer windows. The top and base of this chest are restorations, and although of the same date as the other specimens, it by no means represents the same state of preservation. Fig. 105 is another chest of this interesting make. In this instance the upper windows of the lantern towers are quatrefoiled, otherwise the same details are preserved.

A small chest of entirely different inspiration, though of about the same period, is Plate VIII (a), and is unusually rich in effect and execution. The top is in two panels set in a flat, with simple bold mouldings. The front is divided into panels, by three pilasters of terminal figures of satyrs, on plinths, decorated with bunches of fruit; these panels are contained within classical

FIG. 104. *Nonesuch Chest.* Property of A. L. RADFORD, Esq.

FIG. 105. *Nonesuch Chest.* Property of FRANCIS DARWIN, Esq.

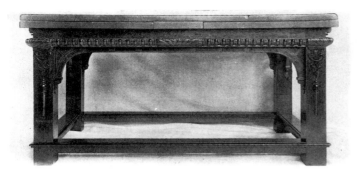

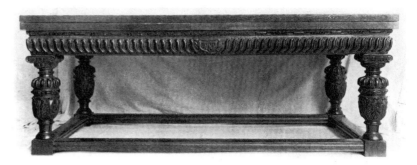

FIG. 106. *Oak Inlaid Table.* Length, 5 feet 3 inches; Height, 2 feet 7 inches. Property of SIR CHARLES LAWES-WITTEWRONGE, Bart.

FIG. 107. *Oak and Chestnut Draw-table.* Length, 7 feet 3 inches; width, 3 feet 8 inches; height, 3 feet 1 inch. Property of SIR CHARLES LAWES-WITTEWRONGE, Bart.

arches, and are carved in high relief with figures representing Faith, who bears the cup and cross (the latter emblem having lost the top), and Patience, who holds the lamb in her arms. Below the figures is a moulding in strong projection, and underneath are two long panels carved with the words Fides and Patienta. The sides are decorated with arches supported on vase-shaped pilasters, in the centre of which are the original iron handles. The carving of the figures, although coarser in finish than those found on corresponding and contemporary Flemish chests, are full of grace and spirit; the colour of the oak is very dark, and was no doubt stained at the time of manufacture. The design is a distinct departure from the usual decoration found in chests, but is in a style often met with in ecclesiastical work of the time.

This absolute diversity of taste is also shown in the two tables, Figs. 106 and 107. The example with marqueterie is German in inspiration; while the carved specimen is of purely home origin. The former is of unusual shape and but 5 feet 3 inches long; the frame is inlaid with a checkered diaper of pear and cherry woods, set in a bold walnut nulling, with corners ornamented with acanthus; the oak legs are square, veneered with panels of walnut bordered with checker-work; a raised pendant, a favourite ornament towards the end of the century, being applied on the upper face of these legs, which are connected by the spandrels and heading of a depressed arch. Fig. 107 is also a draw-table, the top of which is a restoration; the frame is chestnut, carved with a spiral nulling which centres on both sides in a coat of arms, bearing over one shield the motto 'Foy est tout', and over the other the date 1595; the ends bear a crest placed in similar positions. The foot-rail and legs are oak, the latter of bulbous form, yet refined with their bold capitals and carefully finished acanthus carving. This is the general type of table used throughout the end of the sixteenth century, it was continued with modifications until about 1660.

Fig. 108 is of the succeeding reign, about 1605. This table is of extremely neat workmanship and compact proportions; the frame is inlaid with a checker of marqueterie, but the shallow carving of the acanthus on the some-what clumsy bulbous legs shows signs of the commencement of a decadence

FIG. 108. *Oak Inlaid Draw-table.* VICTORIA AND ALBERT MUSEUM.

in the carved oak of this period. The beginning of a new order of taste was now about to make its appearance: the last traces of medievalism that were still faintly perceptible in artistic sentiment, even as late as the end of the sixteenth century, gradually ceased to be a natural form of expression, and what had hitherto been the occupation of cultivated intellects only, now became the stock-in-trade of the professional, and the hitherto noticeable self-effacement of the artist in every branch of his work rapidly became a thing of the past. A wave of eccentricity set in, and the royal Solomon, as James I was called, set the fashion for trunk-hosen, jerkins and doublets all preposterously stuffed and padded. This naturally affected the furniture, and the carved forms that had hitherto existed in bedsteads, chairs and benches gave place gradually to elaborate upholstery. Owing to neglect, havoc by moth, and the constant wear on delicate materials, there are but few genuine, untouched specimens of this upholstered furniture of the beginning of the seventeenth century in existence. At Knole there are a few chairs, couches and some beds of this period in their original condition. Of these, Fig. 109 is a chair of wide 'X' form, made in beechwood; on this throughout is glued a foundation covering of red cloth, over which the chair is upholstered in a beautiful crimson and silver damask, now faded to a pale brick colour; the back divided into panels, by crimson and silver fringe, is studded at the sides with large gilt nails and headed by egg-shaped finials; the arms are also padded and fringed; the legs centre with a rondel of the silk material stiffly lined, and pointed with a gilt boss, in place of the lion's mask or rose found on earlier forms of this type; the curves of the legs are also far shallower, and the crescents at the lower extremities smaller than in the chairs of the preceding reigns. Another chair of this type and period (Fig. 110), of rather smaller dimensions, stands in the same room. The back, which has lost its finials, is covered with plain aquamarine velvet, divided by broad bands of the same material, embroidered in a scroll-work of silver thread; down the centre and along the top run a fringe of silver and faded silk, once bright salmon colour. These combinations of colour must originally have been very beautiful, and the effect of these brilliant coverings makes up for the loss of carved form in the wood-work. In this instance the legs are painted in a white design of flowers and bands, on a dull vermilion ground: the original loose cushion is missing; it was probably converted to the present stuffed seat, which is not in the original style of its upholstery. A portrait of James I, seated in a chair of this description, hangs in one of the rooms of the house. Fig. 111 comprises two footstools of this period, of similar construction to the chairs, but they have been re-upholstered at a later date.

Furniture, similar to the tables last mentioned and these chairs, was probably used by James I and his Queen on the occasion of the banquet given on 24 August 1604, to Juan Fernandez de Velasco, Constable of Castile and Ambassador for Spain. The following account of this entertainment is translated from a contemporary Spanish pamphlet existing in the British Museum:

'The Audience Chamber was elegantly furnished, having a buffet of several stages, filled with various pieces of ancient and modern gilt plate of exquisite workmanship. A railing was placed on each side of the room in order to prevent the crowd from approaching too near the table. At the right hand upon entering was another buffet, containing rich vessels of gold, agate, and other precious stones. The table might be about five yards in length and more than one yard broad. The dishes were brought in by gentlemen and servants of the King, who were accompanied by the Lord Chamberlain, and before placing them on the table they made four or five obeisances. Their Majesties with Prince Henry entered after the Constable, and washed their hands in the same basin. The Price washed in another basin in which water was also taken to the Constable. Their Majesties took their seats on chairs of brocade with cushions; at the side of the Queen, a little apart, sate the Constable on a tabouret of brocade with a high cushion of the same; and on the side of the King the Prince was seated in a like manner. The principal noblemen of the kingdom were likewise at the table. There was plenty of instrumental music, and after the banquet, which was sumptuous and profuse, the King stood up and with his head uncovered

Fig. 109. *'X' Chair*. Extreme height, 4 feet 5 inches; width, 2 feet 7 inches. Property of Lord Sackville.

Fig. 110. *'X' Chair*. Height, 3 feet 9 inches; width, 2 feet 6 inches. Property of Lord Sackville.

Fig. 111. *Footstools*. Property of Lord Sackville.

drank to the health of the Constable and to the health of their Spanish Majesties. Immediately afterwards the Constable seeing that another opportunity might not be afforded him, rose and drank to the King, the health of the Queen, from the lid of a cup of agate, of extroadinary beauty and richness, set with diamonds and rubies, that he had brought with him, praying his Majesty would condescend to drink the toast from the cup; and the Constable directed that the cup should remain in his Majesty's buffet. After many other toasts of this character this divers beautiful cups, the cloth was removed, and every one immediately stood up; the table was removed from the dais to the lower floor, and their Majesties proceeded to wash their hands at it. A ball, bull- and bear-baiting and tumblers completed this entertainment, followed by a supper.'

The next entry in this interesting account is terse and suggestive:

'Monday, the 30th – The Constable awoke with a slight touch of lumbago.'

The luxury of feasting at this period was extreme, and we read that older courtiers of the preceding reign were shocked to see ladies and gentlemen of the present Court rolling about in a state of intoxication. Another writer of the time states:

'Among these luxurious livers was the Earle of Carlile, that brought in the variety of ante-suppers, not heard of in our forefathers' time, and for ought I have read, unpracticed by the most luxurious tyrants. The manner of which was to have the table covered at the first entrance of the ghests with dishes as high as a tall man could well reach, filled with the choycest and dearest viands sea or land could afford, and all this once seen, and having feasted the eyes of the invited, was in a manner throwne away and fresh set on to the same height, having only this advantage of the other that it was hot. I cannot forget one of the attendants of the King, that at a feaste, made by this monster in excesse, eate to his single share a whole pye, reckoned to my lord at £10, being composed of amber greece, magesteriall of perle, musk, etc., etc.'

The gaiety and intellectual refinement of Elizabeth's time sank into low frivolity in the next reign; the unsettled state that dimly heralded the approach of civil war was not conducive to serious condition; and the licensed immorality of the Court gave no encouragement to the throughful creation of beautiful things: the oak furniture, therefore, that demanded individual interest and originality of thought, was but repetitions of the forms and methods of the preceding centuries; at first good, but gradually growing less and less interesting, and finally dwindling into poverty of execution.

CHAPTER V

N the back of the oak chair (Fig. 112) of the beginning of the century, a pleasing sense of subdivision of proportion can be observed; the marqueterie of the panels is graceful in line and composed of the usual black and light coloured woods; the framing is also inlaid, which is unusual. The back is surmounted by the scrolled cresting, now rapidly becoming an important feature; the arms show a tendency to droop, and in this instance the supports, as well as the legs are fluted; the latter being further decorated at the top, with a flower in marqueterie. This is a north country chair and very different in motive to Fig. 113, which is of eastern county manufacture and rather earlier workman-ship, about 1590. It is one of a pair, and possesses the additional attraction of being made in walnut. The arms do not roll over in the usual manner, but are tenoned into knopped supports; the moulding of the seat-

FIG. 112. *Oak Inlaid Chair.* VICTORIA AND ALBERT MUSEUM.

FIG. 113. *Walnut Inlaid Chair.* Property of SIR GEORGE DONALDSON.

FIG. 114. *Oak Inlaid Chair.* Property of E. A. BARRY, Esq.

rail and the marqueterie are applied, and not incised. The back panel is geometrically treated with a bold checker inlay, framed in a richly carved moulding; the cresting is small and surmounts a broad inlaid top rail, supported by side brackets; these chairs with geometrical inlay continued to be reproduced in Norfolk, Suffolk and Essex, until the end of the seventeenth century, and many are to be found used as altar chairs in eastern county churches.

The handsome chair (Plate IX) belongs also to this early seventeenth-century group, and being represented in colour, gives a very good idea of the decorative effect of marqueterie. The introduction of inlay on the arms is rare, and only occurs at this period; the detail on the back panel much resembles that of Fig. 112. Fig. 114, in which the foot-rail and probably a cresting is missing, shows a carved diaper pattern on the arms, originally filled with marqueterie; and a raised panel, with a deeply inlaid network of fleur-de-lys in the usual two-coloured woods; on the top rail are inlaid the initials E. R., with the date 1603. Another chair of west country make, but without any marqueterie, is shown in Fig. 115. The cresting is a little more elaborate in design than is generally found at this time; the back panel is carved with a conventional flowering plant within an arch. The uprights, with their flat laurelling, and the carved oak seat-rail, are copied from an Elizabethan model.

FIG. 115. *Oak Chair.* Property of ARTHUR JAMES, Esq.

FIG. 116. *Oak Grandfather's Chair.* Property of the DUKE OF LEEDS.

It is difficult to assign an exact date to these chairs; but it should be observed that, up to the end of Elizabeth's reign, the top rail supporting the cresting is contained within the uprights, framing the back; and after this date it rests upon the uprights, and forms part of the cresting.

In the general shape of the chair there was evidently little variety, but occasionally one of the form of Fig. 116 is to be found. Being cumbersome in construction and taking up much space, they have, in company with the early roughly constructed settles, been destroyed, but must have been popular for a time, from the middle of the sixteenth century, as they are frequently represented in scenes of domestic life in tapestry and engravings. They are the prototype of the later grandfather chair, and were no doubt made for the use of old people as a protection against draughts. This example of about 1600, from Hornby Castle, is of oak, and stands 5 feet 8 inches high. It is staved, the construction tapering towards the base, and the joints are concealed by long fluted mouldings, while the arms, which are carved on the top and sides, scroll outwards. The roof of the chair is supported by a Jacobean cornice (originally continued round the front, and heading a carved arch and spandrels); the mouldings of the base correspond with those of the cornice. On the inside edges, traces of nailing are visible, showing that the chair was at one time lined; it would then, with the addition of cushions, have been an extremely warm and comfortable seat.

Indulgence in luxury at this period, consequent on a less dignified state of morals and manners, encouraged customs that in earlier and more austere times were considered undesirable; and society of the sixteenth century would have regarded with surprise the use of a piece of furniture on which the occupant reposed at full length in public. But the growth of day-beds, as they were called, did not become general till after the Restoration, developing at the end of the century into the form known as 'sopha', a term of Eastern origin. Fig. 117 represents a very early form of day-bed of about the date 1600, preserved in the long gallery at Hardwick. The structure is of oak, with two panelled ends that have an outward rake, the space between them at the top measuring 7 feet 3 inches. The oak is painted a deep chocolate red, and upon this runs a floral arabesque in white, red and green. In the centre of each of the upper panels are painted the arms of Bess of Hardwick, Countess of Shrewsbury, with those of Cavendish and Talbot, surmounted by a countess's coronet. On the face of the stiles framing these panels, baluster-shaped pendants are applied, and the top rail is supported by the little ears or brackets found on chairs of this period. The cushion, which is 6 feet 6 inches long, 3 feet wide, and 2 feet 3 inches from the ground, is covered with a deep rose damask of almost Gothic design, and is embroidered most elaborately on both sides in coloured silks and gold thread, the outside of the design being edged with a white cord. It is all much damaged, and has been repaired in many places with a silk damask of William III, of which the valance is now composed, but which originally would have matched the embroidered cushion. The head cushions, in a graduated set, are also missing.

FIG. 117. *Day-bed.* Property of the DUKE OF DEVONSHIRE.

F<small>IG</small>. 118. *State Bed*. Height, 12 feet; width, 7 feet 6 inches. Property of L<small>ORD</small> S<small>ACKVILLE</small>.

The reckless extravagance displayed at this time in the upholstery and embroidery of furniture and costume is unparalleled in our history. In a letter from John Chamberlaine to Mrs Alice Carton, written 4 February 1612, we read:

'About this day sevenight the Countess of Salisbury was brought a bed of a daughter, and lyes in very richly, for the hangings of her chamber being white satin, embroidered with silver and pearl, is valued at fourteen thousand pounds.'

This would be equivalent to at least £50,000 of our money.

An untouched example of a state bed and hangings of this description, and of about this same date, is shown in Fig. 118, and thoroughly typifies the profligacy of the period. The posts are slight and covered with deep coral taffetas, for the large carved posts were no longer in fashion for important beds, and were now quite plain, covered with material, and lost in the voluminous folds of the rich curtains that surrounded them. The valance to the tester is pure cloth of gold, of an early seventeenth-century design, edged at the top and bottom with a tasselled fringe of gold and silver: in each tassel is a coral tuft of silk, with a black centre. Ostrich plumes, springing from vases covered with cloth of gold, ornament the four corners. The inside of the tester and hangings are shown in Fig. 119. They are of deep coral taffetas silk, profusely embroidered with a bold floral design in gold and silks; the heading is embroidered in very high relief, with floral scrolls in gold and silver, surmounted by a royal crown. The pillows and quilt are of coral taffetas, now faded to a dull cream, and worked in the same manner. On lifting the fringe that trims the quilt it can be clearly seen that the metal it

FIG. 119. *Inside of State Bed*. Property of LORD SACKVILLE.

is composed of is alternately gold and silver; and under this heavy fringe, the silk that has been entirely protected from the light, keeps still its original burning coral colour. The curtains are of cloth of gold, lined with the embroidered taffetas, the lower valance being of the same. The feet of the posts, which are detachable, show traces of original gilding, and are in the form of lions couchant. It is impossible by description or illustration to convey any idea of the magnificence of this bed, and the impression it must have created when new. It was prepared for the reception of James I by Richard, third Earl of Dorset, at the cost of £8000; and if this King at all resembled the following description of him, written by his contemporary, Sir Anthony Weldon, the contrast between the bed and its royal occupant must have been startling:

'He was of middle stature, more corpulent through his cloathes then in his bodie, his cloathes ever being made large and easie, the doublets quilted for stiletto proof, his breeches in great pleits and full stuffed; his eyes large, ever rowling after any stranger that came in his prescence, insomuch as many for shame have left the roome, as being out of countenance; his beard very thin; his tongue too large for his mouth, which ever made him drink very uncomely as if eating his drinke, which came out into the cup on each side of his mouth; his skin was as soft as taffetas sarsnet, which felt so, because hee never washt his hands, onely rubbed his fingers ends slightly with the wet end of a napkin.'

Authentic portraits of this King are rare, as he had a great dislike to sitting for this purpose, and as his tastes were not directed towards any form of art, the demand for beautiful furniture languished at a Court where the pleasures of the monarch were confined to buffoonery with his favourites, eating and drinking, what he was pleased to call state-craft, and hunting. Although a singularly bad horseman, he was inordinately fond of the latter pastime; this is shown in a letter from Mr Joseph Meade to Sir Martin Stukville, dated 11 January 1622, and also refers to another bed in connection with the King:

The same day his Majestie rode by coache to Theobalds; after dinner, riding on horseback abroad, his horse stumbled and cast his Majestie into the new river where the ice brake; he fell in, soe that nothing but his boots were seen. Sir Richard Young was next, who alighted, went into the water and lifted him out; there came much water out of his mouth and body. His Majestie rid backe to Theobalds, went into a warm bedde, and as we heare is well, which God continue.'

Fig. 120. *Portion of Embroidered Cloth Bed-hangings*. Property of Lord Fitzhardinge.

Fig. 120 is a portion of some curtains belonging to a small bed of this same upholstered style and period at Berkeley Castle. The material is a heavy scarlet cloth, embroidered in yellow cord and silk, with a vine pattern, the grapes and leaves being of raised black velvet. The curtains, tester, valances, as well as the entire hangings of the wall of the room, are all of the same material and work. These upholstered beds at this period were often made to match the wall-hangings; but owing to their great cost, were few in number, and only used at Court or by the very wealthy, and carved oak bedsteads continued to be made till Charles II's reign.

In the Verney Letters there is a mention of a black mourning bed and hangings made for a widow in 1638, when the whole of the room was hung with black and the furniture covered with it. A list of thirteen 'pieces' is mentioned, 'blacke clothe hanginges three yardes deepe and foure and a halfe yardes longe', and two others 'three yardes deepe and three yardes long'.

Ordinary bedrooms still remained scantily furnished till about 1630, for it was not until then that the new forms, such as hanging cupboards, and chests with drawers, were introduced. A large amount of furniture was, however, constructed between 1600 and 1650 for ordinary households. The population of England had grown greatly during Elizabeth and James I's reigns, and we find continual reference to the vast amount of oak employed for building materials, joiner's work and furniture, although the greater part of the oak for wainscot panelling was not grown in this country, but imported from Denmark, with whom we then were in close alliance. Harrison wrote of that time:

'Altho' I must needs confess that there is good store of great wood or timber here

Fig. 121. *Oak Stool*.

FIG. 122. *Oak Stool*. Height, 15 inches; length, 15 inches. Property of MORGAN WILLIAMS, Esq.

FIG. 123. *Oak Stool.*

FIG. 124. *Oak Stool.*

FIG. 125. *Oak Stool.*

and there even now in some places of England, yet in our days it is far unlike to that plenty which our ancestors have seen heretofore when stately buildings were less in use. For albeit that there were then greater number of messuages and mansions almost in every place, yet were their frames so slight and slender that one mean dwelling house in our time is able to countervail very many of them, if you consider the present charge with the plenty of timber that we bestow upon them. In times past, men were contented to dwell in houses built of sallow-willow, plum-tree, hard-beam, and elm, so that the use of oak was in a manner dedicated wholly unto churches, religious houses, princes' palaces, noblemen's lodgings and navigation, but now all these are neglected, and nothing but oak any whit regarded. Of all oak growing in England, the park oak is the softest and far more spalt and brittle than the hedge oak. And of all in Essex, that growing in Barfield Park is the finest for furniture and joiner's craft, for often times have I seen of their works made of that oak as fine and fair as most of the wainscot that is brought hither out of Denmark, for our wainscot is not made in England. Nevertheless, in building, the hedge, as the park oak, go all one way, and never so much hath been spent in a hundred years before as in ten years of our own time.'

The possibility of obtaining oak at a lower price than formerly is shown by the words of another writer, a few years later:

'But the sale of crowne timber appeared of sadest consequence to the safety of the nation, in relation to the navy, the walles of the kingdome. English oake being then esteemed of as best for a sea fight, not being apt to cleave upon the receit of a shot, but rather boare: and of these millions were felled and sold at vile prizes, not only during the life of the Earle of Salisbury, but alle the raigne of King James.'

This enormous quantity of oak thrown upon the market, in conjunction with an increasing demand for furniture, produced results that can be compared to the output of a modern furniture establishment, where everything is made in dozens.

An article of furniture that found its way into every cottage and house was the joint-stool, of which many thousands must have been manufactured. By comparison of the following examples, it is easy to see that deterioration was taking place, as the supply and demand increase. Fig. 121 in a joint-stool of Elizabeth, about the year 1565; the frame, which is well carved in a guilloche, finishes on the lower side, in a widely divided nulling cornered with rough acanthus; the legs show the early and restrained bulbous form, the gadrooning being concave. Even the proportions of this small and comparatively unimportant piece are thoughtful, and a certain amount of grace is thereby attained. Fig. 122 is of extraordinary strong construction. The top framing, an inch thick, is sufficiently deep to form a box; this framing is carved on all four sides with the well-known Jacobean channelling. The hasp and lock do not show in the illustration, being on the further side; the legs are short, with a wide spread, but full of character; the date is about 1600. Fig. 123 is a stool twenty-five years later; this also is somewhat square in form and departs from the ordinary pattern of joint-stool. The top moulding is rather elaborate, and the legs still preserve a certain amount of character, as do those of the taller stool (Fig. 124), which is of about the same date, 1640, and altogether superior to the stool (Fig. 125) of Cromwell's time, which resembles the furniture of its period.

CHAPTER VI

I T is impossible in a work of this size, dealing with evolution, to represent a series of objects of entirely different form and purpose, and at the same time preserve their chronological sequence; it will therefore in many instances be necessary to revert back to certain kinds of furniture, in which evolution was only carried so far as uniformity in style permitted.

It has been shown that imitations of the lighter forms of imported foreign cabinets, such as Plates V and VI, were made here, but cabinets of entirely native origin at the beginning of the seventeenth century were still confined to varieties of the buffet and court cupboard. Plate X, of about 1605, represents a combination of these two types, and the comparative lightness of construction shows that it was intended for the parlour, a room that at this date was coming into general use for meals, rather than for the hall, which had hitherto been used for this purpose, and where the heavier type of court cupboards were placed. The upper portion, as in earlier specimens, is three-sided in plan, and composed of three panels, inlaid with elaborate marqueterie framed in carved arches of depressed form, the centre panel opening as a door. Above rises a carved and inlaid frieze, divided into two portions by carved corbels and headed by a dental cornice. This is supported at each end by a group of slender columns on plain plinths; the lower part of this buffet is headed by another inlaid frieze forming a drawer, and the face of the shelf beneath is carved with a flowering arabesque design. The legs are large in proportion and faced with bands of walnut, on which are applied pendants and heart-shaped bosses of the same wood, one of them forming a clutch in the centre of the drawer. The whole piece is rich in colour, of more elegant shape than is customary, and of eastern county manufacture.

Another variety of the more solid type of cupboard, a few years later in date, is shown in Fig. 126. It is of oak, five-sided, and without any

Fig. 126. *Oak Standing Cupboard*. Height, 4 feet 6 inches; length, 4 feet 10 inches; depth, 2 feet 1 inch. Property of Morgan Williams, Esq.

Fig. 127 *(left). Oak Court Cupboard.* Height, 5 feet 5 inches; length, 4 feet 7 inches; depth, 1 foot 9 inches. Property of Messrs Gill and Reigate.

Fig. 128 *(above). Oak Buffet.* Height, 3 feet 10 inches; length, 4 feet 1 inch; width, 1 foot 7 inches. Property of Sir Theodore Fry, Bart.

marqueterie. The top and lower panels of the front are richly carved in low relief with a design of subdivided circles, a Jacobean adaptation of a Gothic motive, the side panels being also carved, and framed in a flat roping of the same character; the long centre panels open in a drawer and two flaps, on which are carved initials; the extreme outside panels are plain. The rails and stiles throughout are bordered with a Jacobean reed moulding, and the bottom rail is cusped, finishing in each point with a cross. The lock and hinges, of Gothic form, are most effective, and are contemporary with the piece. Being an adaptation from more than one style, its date must necessarily be uncertain, but it is approximately about 1616. It is quite exceptional in form and construction, and its condition is untouched.

In early Jacobean court cupboards, the drawer surmounting the lower part is often omitted. Fig. 127, of about 1618, is a tall specimen in which the cornice is extremely shallow; but the bulbous uprights supporting it, as well as the frieze, are early in character and carving; this frieze is flat in execution, and the lower portion is entirely Jacobean in feeling. The upper and lower panels are filled with a geometrical inlay of black and light coloured woods; the feet have been cut at the bottom, the present balls being recent additions.

An elaborate and very beautiful court cupboard of 1640 is shown as the frontispiece, and although carved oak at this date was well past its zenith, the interest and care spent by client and craftsman in the conception and execution of this piece, shows that enthusiasm on the subject was not yet quite extinct. The cupboard is in three tiers; the upper, in the form of a canopy with a cornice of large dentals, has a thin top and two pendants, on which are inlaid the initials C. E. The panels are alternately carved with a pomegranate pattern, and inlaid with marqueterie in three coloured woods. The centre panels bear the inlaid date, 'Ye XXV DAYE OF JANUARIE 1640', and the Cavendish arms on a field or, three stags' heads couped and proper, with the Cavendish crest, a snake nowed. The two lower compartments are on the lines of an ordinary court cupboard. The interest centres on the frieze of the middle portion, on which, inlaid in light wood letters with black capitals, are the words 'VNTO VS A CHILDE IS BORNE'. This, no doubt, accounts for the unusual care and elaboration bestowed upon the whole piece. The vase-shaped uprights are much carved and of unusual pattern, but distinctly contemporary with the rest; the panels of this portion have the same alternate arrangement of marqueterie and carving, the pomegranate, the emblem of fertility, being introduced throughout the carving. The lower portion opens in two doors, between which runs the Cavendish scrolled bordure found on the Hardwick table (Fig. 81). The upper panels of the lower doors repeat the pomegranate design, those below being typical of late Charles I work, and the rails and stiles are inlaid with a most careful and elaborate checker. This exceptionally fine cupboard was no doubt made to commemorate a birth in the Cavendish family.

The combined buffet and court cupboard, such as Plate XI, continued to be made after the middle of the century. Fig. 128 is a dated specimen of the time of Cromwell. The bulbous supports to the cornice are narrow in their necking, and the middle rail is decorated with a shallow diaper. The piece bears the initials T. F., E. F., 1658. It is in perfect condition, and has remained in the owner's family since that date.

Fig. 129 is a later example of court cupboard of the reign of Charles II. The general structure is the same as that of earlier specimens, but the subdivision of these later cupboards generally consists of rows of four or more panels, making them greater in length than height. The top frieze, which bears the date 1672, rests on two turned supports, from which spring small brackets of S form; these supports do not finish in capitals, and their caps somewhat clumsily overlap the canopy. The doors and panels of the upper portion are lightly carved with the patterns that were by this time in their decadence, and the lower portion is divided into two long compartments, each opening in two doors, one of which is missing. The stopped reed mouldings that frame the panels are very indicative of the date. It is probably of northern manufacture, where carved oak furniture continued to be made till well into the eighteenth century.

Fig. 130 is another, still later, dated 1697, in which the frieze preserves characteristics of ornament which had now long since ceased to exist, except on contemporary later oak furniture. The supports to this have almost lost all trace of their original inspiration, and are turned in a series of meaningless rings. The nicking introduced on the outer stiles and upper rails was evidently suggested by the waved ebony mouldings that had been so much in fashion for twenty years on the foreign tortoise-shell cabinets. The whole front is divided into a series of panels, framed in bolection mouldings of pronounced Carolean type. These court cupboards were to be found in every gentlemen's and yeoman's house, varying in quality according to the owner's position, and they continued to be used in conjunction with oak chairs, tables and forms throughout the seventeenth century, and of plainer shape in country-houses into the eighteenth century. This later type, however, is so well known and so uninteresting that it is unnecessary to carry the evolution any further.

FIG. 129. *Oak Court Cupboard*. Property of SIR CUTHBERT QUILTER, Bart.

FIG. 130. *Oak Court Cupboard*. Height, 5 feet 10 inches; length, 6 feet 3 inches; depth, 1 foot 10 inches. Property of DR G. H. SAVAGE.

The crown timber of James I, felled in such quantities and sold at so low a price, cheapened the production of what had hitherto been expensive pieces of furniture, and added to the number of chests which at that date still fulfilled the office of holding clothes and linen, and frequently formed part of a marriage dowry; the use of a hanging cupboard forming part of the wainscot being confined to the garde-robes of the large houses. As no specimens of English domestic hanging clothes-cupboards are to be found much before the early part of the seventeenth century, it is safe to assume that the majority of clothes were laid down till about that time. The chests used for this purpose were sometimes divided into two compartments, the lower forming a drawer; and as the number of these increased, the piece was called a 'chest with drawers'. These chest fronts were usually decorated with a classical arcade, containing panels, which in the better specimens were inlaid, the general motive resembling the back of an Elizabethan bed. Inside is frequently found a little hanging box, about four to five inches in width, a survival from Gothic times, and was used by the women for trinkets and ribbons; tallow-candles were often put there as a preventative against moth. In one of the series of engravings of *L'Histoire de Civilisation* of about 1500, a young woman is to be seen in despair, standing by an empty chest; moth-eaten clothes are spread upon the floor, and she is holding a garment in her hands in which the ravages of moth are apparent, proving that a chest was not altogether a satisfactory receptacle for clothes. Many and varied are the stories connected with chests, but although interwoven in our folklore, these can generally be traced to foreign origin. The 'Contes Amoureux' of France and Italy of the sixteenth century refer to chests as a very usual place of concealment and popular with lovers. Plate XI is a good example of a chest with a lower drawer, about 1605. The panels on either side of the lock-plate are inlaid with floral arabesque, in self-coloured woods on a light ground; below this the front is divided into three arched compartments between uprights, carved with a design still showing signs of Elizabethan treatment. The arches are supported on squat pilasters, bulbous in outline, but flat in surface; within these are panels inlaid with flower-sprays on a light ground. A reeded plinth separates the front of the chest into two portions, the lower opening as a long drawer, carved with a delicate arabesque and chained patterned strap-work, framed in a lower plinth which is continued round the sides. It is all exceedingly rich in colour and in fine preservation. These chests, like other inlaid furniture, have in three hundred years mellowed to a beautiful combination of browns and yellows; but at the date of their make, when the green stained leaves and murrey coloured flowers of the inlay, shot lustre, and the light oak possessed the charm of cleanliness, they took their right place amidst the surroundings of new panelling and the many coloured cloaks and skirts of brilliant hue that moved amongst them. Now, it is as difficult to estimate what the different tone values of this inlaid furniture must have been, as it is to form any definite idea of the actual sound of the speech and language of those far-away times.

Fig. 131 shows what was once evidently a most brilliant chest of more than

FIG. 131. *Oak Chest*. Property of the HON CHARLOTTE MARIA, LADY NORTH, and R. EDEN DICKSON, Esq.

FIG. 132. *Oak Chest.*Height, 2 feet 7 inches; length, 5 feet 11 inches; depth, 2 feet.

ordinary finish and beauty. It is of a pattern found in the previous reign. The frieze, inlaid with floral sprays, is divided by plaques carved in low relief. The front is composed of three arched compartments, divided by carved and projecting acanthus corbels, enclosing carefully finished marqueterie panels; these stand upon a bottom rail, inlaid with a checker in light and black woods. The legs finish plain, and the keyhole plate is original. The piece is of eastern county work, about 1605.

It is interesting to compare this with the chest (Fig. 132) of Devonshire make, which is a few years earlier in date, and preserves the tradition of its style far more accurately; for the decadence of Renaissance design in oak furniture, in the west and north, was slower than in the home counties. A very distinct architectural effort is observable, but the lines of the detail are thin, and the efforts to avoid repetition in the design are over-emphasised, though the frieze carved in alternate cabochon and cartouche is simple and effective. The division of the front into four arched panels is uncommon; the inlaid scaling of walnut in conjunction with the ornamentation of the pilasters points to a date even before 1600. This chest was probably designed by one of the architects who at that time were erecting large houses in the western counties, for it corresponds in detail with much of the work found there.

Another good specimen of the beginning of the century is found in Fig. 133. This is admirable in workmanship and proportion, and the design of the semi-classical frieze ending in lion-headed bosses, as well as the panel forming a lower drawer, are unusually careful in execution. Between these are two long inlaid panels, the marqueterie design of which is unfortunately invisible in the illustration; the incised lozenge-shaped ornamentation on the lower panels of the sides prove that the date of the piece cannot be before 1605. Fig. 134 is a somewhat elaborate chest of about 1625. The construction of the front is curious, the top and bottom rail morticing half-way into the outer stiles; the top frieze is neatly and cleanly carved with a rosaced

FIG. 133. *Oak Chest.*Height, 2 feet; length, 3 feet; depth, 1 foot 6 inches. Property of SIR GEORGE DONALDSON.

FIG. 134. *Oak Chest.* Property of A. L. RADFORD, Esq.

Fig. 135. *Oak Chest.* Height, 2 feet 6 inches; length, 4 feet 5 inches.

Fig. 136. *Oak Chest.* Height, 3 feet 2 inches; length, 5 feet; depth, 2 feet. Property of Colonel the Hon Henry Mostyn.

guilloche. The two panels are carefully inlaid with the usual conventional flower-sprays, in two coloured woods, and contained in arches carved somewhat flatly, with a bold egg and tongue moulding, and spandrels that centre in a well-defined rose. The three upright stiles framing the arches are treated in a vine-branch pattern of early character on a matted ground; but the carving is thin throughout, showing decadence. The lid is a restoration. Fig. 135 is altogether more ordinary in execution of design, and was made about 1630, probably for a yeoman. This specimen was purchased from a well-to-do farmer in South Devon in 1875, and had been a possession of the family for generations. The decoration is composed of deep incised carving, the surface, with the exception of the flower-stalks on the stiles, being left flat. The chain pattern of quatrefoil and flower on a dotted ground forming the frieze is traditional of Elizabethan design, but the whole front is so barbaric in workmanship, and suggestive of a South Sea Islander's efforts in carving, that it can safely be assigned to the inspiration of a village carpenter. In the chest (Fig. 136) the lid is edged with a series of shallow dentals, and the front divided by a bold reeded moulding into uprights and horizontal panels, resembling in arrangement the base of a court cupboard. The two upper panels are carved in low relief, with a palmated chain pattern headed by a frieze of simple channel moulding. At the two corners 'Anno Domi' and '1625 W.N.' are lightly incised, and as a heading to the upper panels, the inscription, 'REMEMBER : THE : POOR : WHEN : THOV : OPPENES : THIS : AND : FORGET : NOT'. The four lower panels are decorated in lozenge with small incised circles; the channelling of the stiles and rails bear out the inscribed date; the added fret to the bottom rail is also characteristic of an ornament that began at this time.

The chest of this period, of which the foregoing are very representative specimens, was now to take a further step in evolution, and it is extraordinary that the inconvenience attendant on searching for an object buried at the bottom of a chest should have been endured for so many years. No doubt one reason was the great expense entailed by having more than one lock, for even as late as 1650 stock-locks on doors were considered so great a luxury, that when families moved from one of their houses to another, these locks were always taken with them.

Of these chests we give two varieties. In Fig. 137 the front is divided into three panels, two of which open as doors, framed in four pilasters, on which are applied terminal figures of men, with their hair and beards dressed in the manner of the time. Above these, and supported by bunches of fruit, are plain capitals inlaid with the initials J. S. repeated, and the date 1628. The door panels are inlaid with sprays of gillyflowers in vases of deal and black oak, while the marqueterie of the centre panel represents a water-gate with two swans inlaid in light wood. This is framed in a handsome nulling centred and cornered with acanthus, the same spiral nulling, waving in two

FIG. 137. *Oak Chest with Drawers.*Height, 3 feet 4 inches; length, 5 feet 3 inches; depth, 1 foot 9 inches. Property of ERNEST CROFTS, Esq.

directions, forming a central division. The lower portion, opening in two drawers, is coarsely carved with roses and a raised lozenge pattern; it is all in excellent preservation, and the irons to the drawers and cupboard doors are original. Fig. 138 is a later specimen from Berkeley Castle. In this instance the ordinary arcaded chest form is preserved. The carving is coarse throughout, and the redundancy of decoration is characteristic of Wales, where the chest was undoubtedly manufactured. This profusion of somewhat uninteresting detail with which the Welsh oak furniture of this period is covered is indicative of incapacity and want of originality. In this instance it may be noticed that not only are the sides carved in an exactly similar manner to the front, but also the feet and the plinth moulding, from which the carved bosses are missing. Its date is about 1640. Another interesting form of chest with drawers of about the same time is shown in Fig. 139. Here the top opens in one drawer, the front of which is inlaid with a ground of checker-work, a band of double S pattern running along the centre. The lower portion opens in two doors, concealing the drawers now missing; the panels are inlaid with a geometrical design, contained within two arches carved with the usual guilloche and roses in the spandrels; they are bordered all round with a triangular checker in black and yellow woods, and the rail at the bottom has the added fret found on oak furniture of this date.

FIG. 138. *Oak Chest with Drawers.* Height, 2 feet 10 inches; length, 5 feet; depth, 2 feet. Property of LORD FITZHARDINGE.

FIG. 139. *Oak Cupboard.* Height, 3 feet 1 inch; length, 3 feet 7 inches; depth, 2 feet 4 inches. Property of E. A. BARRY, Esq.

FIG. 140. *Oak Chest with Drawers*. Height, 3 feet 4 inches; length, 3 feet 3 inches. Property of S. E. Letts, Esq.

FIG. 141. *Oak Chest with Drawers*. Height, 4 feet 8 inches; length, 3 feet 10 inches. Property of S. E. Letts, Esq.

An interesting analogy can be drawn between the relief of the ornament on furniture and plate of this period, and that of the antique wood and metal-work, represented by the art of Byzantium. Forms once solid, round, and full of intention, became aimless, shallow and scattered, for the tradesmen of both these times sought only to cover the surfaces by ornament with the least possible trouble and thought, and so reverted to an archaic condition of technique entirely devoid of originality, wherein he was content to express himself by dots, circles and zigzag lines. This is exemplified in Fig. 139, and in other specimens of the next decade.

With such an oak chest as Fig. 140 a new style of decoration was introduced which lasted in fashion over thirty years. The well-considered proportions and details of this example suggest that it was probably designed by an architect. It is of about the date 1630. The top opens in a long drawer, in the centre of which a curved block of walnut forms a handle, repeated in plain corbels on the sides. The two doors, geometrically panelled, are framed in uprights decorated with applied pendants, bosses and strap-work of walnut, the centre of the panels being a plaque of ebony, inlaid with a design in bone and mother-of-pearl in the Moorish taste, a form of inlay that became extremely popular here, and no doubt was first inspired by caskets and furniture, that found their way to this country during the negotiations for the Spanish marriage. On opening the doors a series of drawers is disclosed, with their original knob handles. This specimen and the last are early examples of the complete chest with drawers. Fig. 141 is another, rather later in date. The top opens in a long drawer, the dividing uprights and the centre being inlaid in this same new manner. Below is another very deep drawer, panelled in strong projection, the bevels of which are of so-called zebra or snake-wood. The lower portion of this chest, opening in two doors over the usual arrangement of drawers, is decorated like the top. This chest is of oak, but in about 1680 it was, probably to match some other furniture, painted black and lacquered in what was then termed 'the Indian taste', so very fashionable for a time. The bone and pearl inlay is very cleverly imitated in the lacquer-work. The carving of the cornice, the brass ring handles, and the feet are of the date of the painting, but the irons on the inner doors are contemporary with the original chest.

N early Jacobean upholstered furniture, the design of the visible wood-work is seldom distinctive, and the materials with which it is covered, though of course principally of contemporary material, were often provided from hangings of an earlier time. It is therefore next to impossible to date such pieces within a decade. The furniture represented in contemporary pictures and engravings are reliable proofs that such forms were in existence at the time, but it does not follow that the artist always selected the fashion of the moment for his accessories. In a great number of Vandyke's portraits, a large piece of black and cloth of gold of the time of Henry VII is constantly introduced, proving this to be the case. But when embroidery is employed instead of a woven material, and the pattern corresponds exactly with the curves of the furniture, showing without doubt it was worked for the actual piece, it is no little assistance towards ascertaining a correct date. There is a record in the Verney Papers of one of Vandyke's sitters, Lady Sussex, giving much attention to materials for upholstery. She writes and spells as follows:

'My thinkes to you for my sattine, it cam very will, some of it i employ for the backes of chers, the rest i entende for cortines, when the chinese stofes come in, if you see any prity ons remember me i pray you for to or three peses. . . . I am very sorry i dide not consider of the figerde sattine when i was at Chelsey for truly though the prise be unreasonable i hade rather give it then by any of the figerde sattines that are to be hade hear, thorty shillings the yarde the axe, and the color lokes lyke dort to that i have . . . The carpet truly is a good on. . . . if i can have that and the other for forty ponde or a littell more i would by them, the woulde bee very fine for a bede but onlie if one may have a very good peniworth. For the carpets if the gronde bee very doll and the flowers or workes in them not of very plesent color i doubt the will bee to dole for to suet with my hanginges and chers. . . . Concerning the choice of a small carpet, If it will not sarve for a windo it will sarve for a fote carpet.'

These carpets referred to in the above letter were made in this country for nearly a hundred years; they were of so-called Turkey work, in imitation of Oriental carpets; the wool being threaded by hand, knotted and cut. There is a great tendency to pre-date much of the furniture made during the reign of Charles I, and assign it to James I or even to Elizabeth, but oak furniture continued to be made more or less on the old lines until many years after the Restoration.

It is probable that new forms of upholstered furniture were introduced from the French Court of Lousi XIII, the brother of Henrietta Maria, and copied by the rich families here. A couch inspired by French taste preserved at Knole (Fig. 142) is somewhat before the date of Henrietta Maria's marriage to Charles I. The construction is of beech, and is entirely covered with crimson velvet, or, as it was then termed, incarnadine or cramosie; this is divided by a gold galon into six upright panels, and further trimmed with a crimson and gold fringe, finished at the sides by large-headed gilt nails, and edged with a crimson and gold galon. The ends of the couch let down to any angle by means of a toothed rack, and have small fixed cushions; the arms are straight and square, covered with the velvet, and fringed; the front and sides are upholstered to match, but here the fringes are fixed on with small gilt-headed nails; the seat has been re-covered with modern velvet. It is instructive to find that no more comfortable form of couch has since been invented. Fig. 143 is a settee, somewhat similar in style, but the rounded sides are immovable. The legs and stretchers were originally gilt on a thick jesso preparation, some of which is visible, although the legs have at a more recent date been painted brown. The back, arms and sides are of crimson velvet, trimmed as in the last example; the loose cushion, which has been re-made, is of crimson damask, covered with a floral strap-work enclosing ovals, embroidered in silver, and worked in fine silks with allegorical figures. Fig. 144, of the same date, represents another novelty of construc-

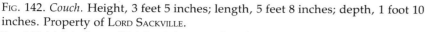

FIG. 142. *Couch.* Height, 3 feet 5 inches; length, 5 feet 8 inches; depth, 1 foot 10 inches. Property of LORD SACKVILLE.

FIG. 143 (*right*). *Settee.* Height, 3 feet 5 inches; length, 3 feet 8 inches. Property of LORD SACKVILLE.

FIG. 144. *Double Chair.* Height, 3 feet 5 inches; length, 3 feet 6 inches; depth, 1 foot 7 inches. Property of LORD SACKVILLE.

tion. It is an early form of the double chair, being 3 feet 6 inches long. The wood-work, again birch, originally gilt, is now painted brown. The back, seat and arms have lost their original covering, and have been re-upholstered at some time in crimson velvet and a richly tasselled fringe of the time of Charles II. These upholstered double seats became even more reduced in size later in the century, and were then termed 'courting chairs' and 'love seats'. Eventually, in the reigns of William and Anne, the backs of the seats became open and resembled two connected chair backs.

Stuffed stools or tabourets accompanied every suite of furniture, and were used according to their height by the younger or less important members of a household in precedence. One of these is shown in Fig. 144; it has been re-upholstered at the same time as the double seat. Another tabouret, also at Knole, of higher shape, is Fig. 145, which still possesses its original fringe and galon. The chair to match (Fig. 146) is of great interest, as although of a well-recognised shape, it is an early example of what was termed a farthingale chair. The farthingale had obscured the female form for nearly eighty years, and about 1612, when the proportions of this dress became outrageous, it was found that a chair without arms was better suited to this extreme style. In consequence of the growth of this eccentric fashion, an edict was issued by the King in 1613 forbidding ladies to come to the masque

FIG. 145. *Stool.* Property of LORD SACKVILLE.

FIG. 146. *Farthingale Chair*. Property of LORD SACKVILLE.

FIG. 147. *Arm-chair and Farthingale Chair. Left.* Height, 3 feet 6 inches; width, 2 feet 6 inches. *Right*. Height, 3 feet 3 inches; width, 1 foot 10 inches. Property of the DUKE OF DEVONSHIRE.

FIG. 148. *Upholstered Chair*. Height, 3 feet 4 inches; width, 2 feet 2 inches. Property of LORD SACKVILLE.

in 'these monstrous gowns', owing to the seat-room they occupied. Fig. 147 is an arm and farthingale chair from a large set at Hardwick, many of which are reproductions. Their framework of oak, thinly painted brown, resembles much of the Knole furniture. The velvet has in both these chairs been renewed, and some old embroidery in fine silks and gold thread reapplied. This embroidery is presumed to have been worked by Mary Stuart and her ladies during her long captivity when under the guardianship of the Earl of Shrewsbury and Bess of Hardwick. On the back of the arm-chair can be seen what is evidently intended to represent Queen Elizabeth and Leicester driving in state, the royal lion guardant forming part of the carriage. On the front of the seat can be seen the nowed snake of the house of Cavendish. The farthingale chair is very high in the seat and unusually low in the back.

Comfortable chairs made for the wealthy classes, who evidently wished for variety, quickly changed their detail at this time, and its is rare to find any one individial fashion lasting very long. There is a marked difference between the last chair with arms and Fig. 148, of about the date 1625. The frame of the latter is entirely and tightly covered with a purple velvet; the back (which has a slight rake), and the loose cushion to the seat, are embroidered on the velvet with a beautiful design in silver thread. The stretcher and all the edges of the chair are bordered by a narrow fringed silver galon, studded with small gilt nails; the tassels hanging from the cushion are of silver thread. It may be noticed here that the foot-rail in the

front of chairs is now being placed higher as a flat stretcher; this develops later into a twist, and later again into open carved work. In the low tabouret (Fig. 149) an exactly similar treatment has been pursued, but here the design on the velvet has been worked after it has been joined, and is in its original condition. Fig. 150 is a higher tabouret of 'X' form, much resembling a modern campstool. The legs and frame are of beechwood, and it is upholstered like the preceding specimens; all are trimmed round the feet with a silver-fringed galon. The velvet with which they are covered is still a beautiful colour, resembling the petals of the purple iris. The effect of the ladies in their butterfly coloured dresses seated on this furniture must have been charming in its fantasy.

Another and smaller chair of a set also at Knole is Fig. 151, and it is a few years later in date, about 1628. This entire set has been re-covered with late seventeenth-century cherry damask, but underneath this is visible in places the original covering, a damask of the same colour, but smaller in design; the straight fringe is contemporary with the chair. Furniture of this type, though rare in England, is found throughout the engravings of Abraham Bosse, which chiefly represent scenes of domestic life, proving that the design was introduced into this country about the time of Charles I's marriage; but such a strong dislike was entertained for this French marriage, and everything connected with that nation, that these new fashions found but little favour except at Court. The interests of this country were also beginning to be absorbed in those party quarrels, that were so soon to take serious form, and block the way to any fresh enterprise in art. In addition to this impending sense of insecurity, another catastrophe had taken place at the commencement of Charles's reign, which for the time paralysed everything. In the year of the coronation the plague destroyed 41,313 of the inhabitants of London – one-sixth of its population. The general depression caused by this event made the new ideas and gaieties introduced by the French followers of the Queen (who at one time numbered 440) extremely unacceptable to the English nation; but on their dismissial by the King, the opportunity of imbibing fresh influence ceased, as these courtiers not only took away with them their own possessions, but all the 'furniture and stuff' belonging to the Queen they could lay their hands on.

Individual taste was, however, largely developed in Charles I, who as a collector of beautiful objects was far in advance of his time, and but for the tasteless destruction and dispersion of his works of art, this royal collection would now be considered, as it was in those days, one of the finest in Europe. The inventory of furniture, hangings, pictures, plate and jewels, comprising the furnishing of nineteen palaces, took a year to complete, and the entire collection, so wantonly disposed of by Cromwell, three years to sell, the greater portion being purchased by foreigners. This accounts for the practical disappearance of all royal furniture before this date, and the reason why so little is left to represent the personality of our monarchs before the Restoration.

The introduction of human form in contemporary costume was not represented on English furniture after the reign of Charles I. In the walnut chair (Fig. 152) of about the year 1635, the supports to the arms are formed by ladies dressed in a costume of the time, and holding a rose. The dress is cut low, with lace falling on the shoulders; the arms are bare to the elbows; the hair is loose; the disappearance of the farthingale, and the introduction of panniers over a close skirt, clearly mark the change taking place in woman's dress since the beginning of the century. The arms, legs and stretchers of the chair are composed of an elegant twist which at this time commenced to be used. The upholstery is modern. The chair is foreign in inspiration, but entirely English in execution. A northern French chair is given in Fig. 153 to show how closely we copied their forms, though the double stretcher was hardly ever introduced on English examples. In both instances the women wear a single row of large pearls, the fashionable ornament of the time.

FIG. 149. *Stool.* Height, 10 inches; length, 1 foot 10 inches. Property of LORD SACKVILLE.

FIG. 150. *Stool.* Height, 1 foot 8 inches; length, 2 feet; depth, 1 foot 6 inches. Property of LORD SACKVILLE.

FIG. 151. *Chair.* Height, 3 feet 4 inches; width, 2 feet; depth, 1 foot 6 inches. Property of LORD SACKVILLE.

FIG. 152. *Walnut Chair.* VICTORIA AND ALBERT MUSEUM.

FIG. 153. *Northern French Walnut Chair.*

FIG. 154. *Walnut Chair*. Property of SIR
CUTHBERT QUILTER, Bart.

FIG. 155. *Oak Chair*. VICTORIA AND ALBERT
MUSEUM.

The twist in the legs of furniture beginning at this period was of slow growth, oak not adapting itself to this cutting. Fig. 154 is one of a set of chairs made in walnut with twisted legs, the arms being plain, covered with pigskin, like the back and seat. The low wide form is copied from the foreign type. Fig. 155 shows a later chair, less wide in the seat, more compact, and without arms; it is of oak, and the consequent angularity and coarseness of the twist is apparent. The original Turkey work covering is dated 1649 in the needlework on the back. This Turkey work was a favourite covering for furniture, and matched the carpets and curtains, but its destruction by moth has left but few examples.

Boxes, such as Plate XII, were much used in Elizabethan and Jacobean times for documents, daily accounts and other papers. When found of a rather later date and with a flat lid, they were termed Bible or lace boxes, and used for these purposes. The box (a) is of oak, and the top, of desk form, is inlaid with a parquet design of sycamore wood; the front is decorated with a little arabesque strap-work, and the sides are inlaid with the bead and spindle, or husk design so popular at this time. Another oak box (b), on the same plate, is some fifteen years later in date. This is in two compartments, the upper portion, opening as a lid, is decorated round the face and sides with a delicately carved cornice of classical design, supported at the corners with scrolled walnut corbels of acanthus. The lower portion, forming a drawer, is decorated in a similar manner; the front panels are inlaid with a floral design in coloured wood on a cedar ground; the lock-panel bears the letters S. G. G. The base is carved with a bold half-circle and tongue moulding, showing that this very highly finished piece of furniture was originally designed to be placed on a stand. Fig. 156 is of oak, also of desk form, of about the date 1610. The royal arms of James I are carved on the lid, and on the sides are incised the emblems of Great Britain. The lower portion is decorated with a bold nulling in high relief, finishing in a nicely moulded base. The lock-plates and hasp are original. Fig. 157 is another oak specimen of rougher make; in this instance the top is plain. The bottom opens as a drawer; the front and sides are carved with a double band of strap-work in low relief, the scrolling of which is ingeniously varied, and relieved here and there by the introduction of the classical honeysuckle.

Other small pieces of furniture were little hanging or livery cupboards. The daily distribution of liveries to the gentleman attendants and pages, as well as to the servants in a great house, was an important function. Fig. 158 is about the date 1635. The frame is inlaid with a charming checker of light and dark coloured woods; the door is carved with a well-known pattern of the time, and the row of balusters for the purpose of ventilation are of good design. These cupboards are generally divided by one or more shelves, the bread and small food being kept in the ventilated portion. Fig. 159 is a less elaborate example, a few years later in date, in which both compartments are ventilated by rows of straight balusters; the marqueterie that decorates the framing of the door is coarse, and surmounted by a flat and dental cornice.

FIG. 156. *Oak Box*. Property of E. A. BARRY, Esq.

FIG. 157. *Oak Box*. Property of H. A. TIPPING, Esq.

Fɪɢ. 158. *Oak Livery Cupboard.* Property of C. E. Kᴇᴍᴘᴇ, Esq.

Fɪɢ. 159. *Oak Livery Cupboard.* Height, 1 foot 6 inches; width, 1 foot 2 inches. Property of A. L. Rᴀᴅғᴏʀᴅ, Esq.

Fig. 160 is after the Restoration, and rough in construction, evidently intended for use in a farmhouse. These little cupboards are somewhat scarce, as owing to their open fronts they were considered useless and were broken up. They fulfilled the same purpose as the wheel pattern bread cupboard, found so plentifully throughout Brittany.

A distribution of livery in early times is described as follows in a Life of Wolsey, on the occasion of the Cardinal's visit to Charles V at Bruges:

'Also the Emperor's officers every night went through the town from house to house where as any Englishman lay or resorted, and there served liveries for all night, which was done after this manner. First, the Emperor's officers brought into the house a cast of fine manchet bread, two great silver pots, with wine and a pound of fine sugar, white lights and yellow, a bowl or goblet of silver to drink in, and every night a staff torch. This was the order of their liveries every night.'

This distribution would have been much the same in England, and would have been carried on in the great houses on similar lines till the Rebellion.

Fɪɢ. 160. *Oak Livery Cupboard.* Property of A. L. Rᴀᴅғᴏʀᴅ, Esq.

CHAPTER VIII

HE sharp spell of domestic misery and trouble that swept over England between the years 1643 and 1653 is happily unparalleled in our history; for during the civil wars of the fifteenth century the classes actively involved were divided into two large sections, both more or less accustomed to warfare. But at the time of the Rebellion the prosperity of the country had created a large and influential body of peaceable country gentlemen and merchant citizens, who found themselves forced to take part in the quarrel between the King and Parliament. As the struggle proceeded every form of trade was paralysed, every form of art neglected, its patrons being either actively engaged in the war, or taking refuge from the storm abroad. It is therefore not surprising to find that the furniture of this time is lacking in interest, showing advancement neither in construction nor decoration.

Society, as we understand the term, after the battle of Marston Moor, ceased to exist for the time being, and as the creation of better-class furniture has always been dependent upon entertainments and social gatherings, the dearth of this impetus accounts for a stagnation in its manufacture, and also for the somewhat dull and uninteresting appearance of the small quantity that was made, the public taste being entirely influenced by Cromwell and his followers, who had usurped the government. In addition to the absence of active taste, the desertion of the fine houses, and the wanton destruction of furniture and works of art by the troops of both parties quartered upon private individuals, greatly diminished the number of the more delicate pieces, and practically destroyed all the existing upholstered furniture. In some instances this destruction was wholesale. In a number of the *Mercurius Rusticus* of 1643, there is a graphic description of the besieging of Wardour Castle in that year by Sir Edward Hungerford, then chief commander of the rebels in Wiltshire. After a siege of three days, Lady Arundell, who was in sole charge, surrendered on the understanding that she and all others in the castle should have quarter, that all furniture and goods in the house should be safe from plunder, and that the ladies and servants should carry away all their wearing-apparel. The extract goes on to say:

"'Tis true they observed the first article and spared the lives of all the besieged; but for the other two, they observed them not in any part. As soon as they entered the castle, they first seized upon the several trunks and packs which they of the castle were making up, and left neither the ladies nor servants any other wearing clothes but what was on their backs. There was in the castle one extraordinary chimney-piece, valued at two thousand pounds; this they utterly defaced, and beat down all the carved works thereof with their pole-axes. There were likewise rare pictures; these in a wild fury they break and tear to pieces. In triumph they bring five cart loads of their richest hangings and other furniture towards Dorchester, and since that, contrary to their promise they plundered the whole castle, so little use was there of the inventory, unless to let the world know what Lord Arundell lost, and what the Rebels gained. This havoc they made within the castle. Without they burnt all the out-houses, they pulled up the pales of two parks, they burn three tenements and two lodges, they cut down all the trees about the house and grounds. Oaks and elms, such as but few places could boast of the like, these they sold for four-pence, sixpence, or twelve-pence a-piece, that were worth three, four, or five pounds apiece.'

And in the Verney Papers we read that, after four years' absence, Mary Verney revisits Claydon, and finds

'The house most lamentably furnished, all the linnen is quite worne out, the fire-irons and other odd things are so extreamly eaten with Rust thatt they cannot be evor of any use againe – the cloath of the musk colored stools is spoyled and the dining room chairs in Ragges – to-morrow I intend to goe and I shall leave ye house soe full of soldiers, thatt I feare they will make us very poore as beggers. I protest I know nott which way we shall live if the countrey may all wayes quarter soldiers.'

In many instances the furniture was used as firewood. Its commercial value at this time is shown in another letter from Sir John Leeke to Sir Edward Verney at an early period of the war:

'I protest I am most miserable, for though I have friends yet noe friend to lend me tenn pounds, no man will part with a penny of money, monies are not to be had for anything unless arms, swords, and muskets, which are gold and silver, plate and household stuff are not merchauntable.'

In spite of this lamentable state of affairs, by which society was shaken to its foundations, the unprotected state of women compelled even those who had lost their husbands in the war to a speedy re-marriage, and consequently the cradles and baby chairs that passed through this period have a particular interest attached to them.

Oak cradles much resemble each other, save in the variety of carving, and being of extremely strong construction, they did service for several generations of babies. Fig. 161 is an early specimen of this period with a deep chanelling, sunk on the top rail and side panels; the posts terminate in knobbed finials; the back is headed by a carved lunette, underneath which is the date 1620. The carved spandrels give a charm to the usually rather ugly angle in cradles, where the sides are tenoned to the uprights; the rockers are original, and show signs of much foot-wear. Fig. 162 is of the succeeding reign, and is of rougher workmanship; here the finials, six in number, are shaped as acorns. The upper panel bears the date and initials, 16 M. B. 35, in an escalloped border, the heading and corner panel are coarsely carved with masks, the design on the side panels is most unusual – suggesting Flemish influence. Fig. 163 was evidently made for the first of a family, as the words 'Unto us a child is born' are carved on the upper rail, which has the original yew pegs on which the bedding was slung; the head is surmounted by a hood, the side panels being carved in lozenge; the back bears the date 1664, with the initials B. M. D. The rockers are carved and show signs of foot-wear. These three cradles are of Yorkshire origin. Fig. 164 is also hooded, and the panels are inlaid with sprays of tulips in two-coloured woods; the uprights and rails are inlaid with a large checker; the edges have been repaired, and the rockers are restorations. A later and rougher type made for a child of humble origin, and bearing the date 1691, is given in Fig. 165; in this instance the two ends are left open, and the rockers finish at the top in a rude trefoil; the headings to the posts are turned in baluster fashion. These cradles were sometimes upholstered in material. There is a specimen at Badminton, made early in the seventeenth century, shaped in the manner of Fig. 164, covered close throughout in crimson velvet, and studded with gilt nails.

In early times congratulatory visits on the birth of a child were important functions in society, the 'lying-in chamber' being especially decorated for the occasion, and the cradle covered with an elaborately worked quilt. Engravings of the seventeenth century show the entertainment and refreshment of the guests proceeding in the room, with the mother and child in bed. A pincushion of an elaborate pattern, with 'God bless the babe' in pins, was a favourite form of gift on these occasions, and we read that in 1665, 'one of the ladies of the Verney family, though partially insane, takes pleasure in the adornment of her baby's "peencushion" '. In the same letter mention is made of a fine white mantle to lay over the head of the cradle, with a smaller one to match, to form a quilt. In the next year, that of the great fire, much difficulty was found by a member of the same family in obtaining a cradle in London, 'such things being very deare now, as all their stores are burnt'.

Other interesting pieces of furniture connected with children of the seventeenth century are their chairs. The first of these (Fig. 166) is of about the date 1635. The back is low, the panel and seat-rail lightly carved, and surrounded by a low scrolled cresting; the arms roll over at their extremities, which are pierced to hold a bar; the supports to these arms are early in type, finishing in straight legs; the foot-rest is missing. Fig. 167 is a taller chair, about fifteen years later; the height of the cresting, the applied half-baluster ornament now coming into fashion that rises above the arms, the plain panel with bolection moulding, and the simplicity of the arm supports and legs,

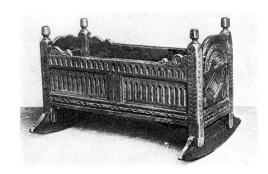

FIG. 161. *Oak Cradle.*

FIG. 162. *Oak Cradle.* Length, 3 feet 1 inch; height, 2 feet 1 inch; depth, 1 foot 4 inches. Property of SIR THEODORE FRY, Bart.

FIG 163. *Oak Cradle.*

FIG 164. *Oak Cradle.* Length, 3 feet 1 inch. Property of the EARL OF CARRINGTON.

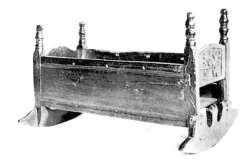

FIG. 165. *Oak Cradle.* Length, 2 feet 11 inches; height, 1 foot 3 inches.

FIG. 168. *Child's Oak Chair*. VICTORIA AND ALBERT MUSEUM.

FIGS. 166 and 167. *Children's Oak Chairs. Left.* Height, 3 feet 1 inch; height to seat, 2 feet; width of seat, 11 inches. *Right.* Height, 3 feet 11 inches; height to seat, 2 feet 5 inches; width of seat, 1 foot. Property of MORGAN WILLIAMS, Esq.

FIG. 169. *Child's Oak Chair*. Height, 3 feet 10 inches; width of seat, 1 foot 1 inch. Property of H. MARTIN GIBBS, Esq.

point to the date 1650. The holes in the arms for the bar, and those for the foot-rest, have been pegged up. Fig. 168 is some years after the Restoration, the knobbed legs and stretchers, the flat carving of the back, and the sunken seat panel corresponding with the other chairs of the time; the foot-rest is not original. Fig. 169 is an example in which the back panel and frame are inlaid with marqueterie. The legs in this instance are parallel, the foot-rest being supported by those in projection; the cresting and ears are large in proportion to the chair, and, in conjunction with the elaborately turned half-baluster applied ornaments, conform to a date approximating 1670.

Movable hanging cupboards or wardrobes were introduced as part of the furniture of a bedroom early in the seventeenth century. Previous to this time they would have formed part of the panelling or been of simple structure, opening in a single door and containing shelves, the elaborate linenfold cupboards seen in drawings being either for ecclesiastical or royal purposes. Plate XIII is a good example of a Welsh cupboard with shelves, and dated 1618. The front originally opened as one door. The panels are framed in a bolection moulding on the inner side, the outer and lower mouldings being plainly bevelled; the centre panel is further decorated with two grotesque profiles. The frieze-rail and two upper panels are carved in the style of 1615; the introduction of carving on the uprights and lower rail is characteristic of Welsh oak furniture.

Fig. 170 is a distinct hanging wardrobe, of about the date 1650. This opens in two doors, which extend rather more than half-way down the piece; the remaining portion is a fixture and opens in three narrow drawers framed in a late Jacobean moulding, with later handles. The doors are headed by two oblong panels of shallow scrolled carving, the remainder of the panels being deeply cut in lozenge, giving a particularly quiet and decorative effect; the rails and stiles are cleanly worked with a broad channel moulding. The doors have their original button handles of yew, and within are the original wooden pegs on which the clothes were hung. It is of great weight, being of oak throughout, and constructed in one piece. A smaller wardrobe of this same description, though later in date, is Fig. 171. Here the panels are consequently larger, being but two to each door, yet, after a lapse of twenty

FIG. 170. *Oak Hanging Wardrobe.* Height, 6 feet 8 inches; width, 5 feet 7 inches; depth, 1 foot 1 inch. Property of PERCY MACQUOID, Esq.

FIG. 171. *Oak Hanging Wardrobe.* Height, 5 feet 11 inches; length, 5 feet 3 inches; depth, 1 foot 8 inches. Property of H. MARTIN GIBBS, Esq.

FIG. 172. *Oak Hanging Wardrobe.* Height, 7 feet 5 inches; width, 5 feet 11 inches; depth, 1 foot 11 inches. Property of the HON CHARLOTTE MARIA LADY NORTH and R. EDEN DICKSON, Esq.

FIG. 173. *Oak Table.* Length, 7 feet 6 inches; height, 2 feet 7 inches; width, 2 feet 6 inches. Property of MORGAN WILLIAMS, Esq.

FIG. 174. *Oak Table.* Length, 12 feet; height, 2 feet 11 inches; width, 3 feet. Property of FRANK GREEN, Esq.

years, decorated with the same lozenge pattern; and this pattern is so frequently found upon this class of cupboard devoted to the use of woman, that one can only presume it bore an heraldic significance. The frieze is flatly carved with a sunflower pattern in lunette, and the rails of the doors are ornamented with a similar quality of work. In the western counties these wardrobes are frequently found with the carved friezes picked out in colours; two decorated in this manner in red and blue are in existence at Clevedon Court. Another of these interesting, though rather cumbersome, hanging cupboards is Fig. 172, of about the date 1670. Here the cornice is supported by corbels, with the frieze beneath decorated in two raised and deeply bevelled panels, forming a drawer, on which the centre ornament is hollowed out as a clutch handle. The front opens in two doors, panelled with Carolean arches framed between pilasters with fluted bases, the lower portion being fixed and decorated with the panels similar to those on chests with drawers of this time. A little waved border finishes the panels; the plinth has the same ornament in lozenge, and stands on ball feet, which are restorations.

The large oak joined tables of the preceding reigns continued to be made throughout the seventeenth century, and though certain modifications in structure and detail took place, and the drawer-top gradually disappeared, the original form lasted for considerably over a hundred years. In Fig. 173 the top is single, and the frame is without ornament, save for a deep channel moulding that also runs round the foot-rail. The legs are chamfered, a feature at this date which somewhat detracts from their dignity. Underneath this table six stools are fitted, and supported by a centre stretcher, and a groove sunk in the foot-rail to receive their edges. The stools are more elegant in form than usually found at this period, and together with the table are in an admirable state of preservation; they are of South Wales manufacture, of about the date 1640. Other tables of this character were fitted with forms as in Fig. 174. Here the frame is carved with a bold, straight nulling, centred with the initials W. G., and the date 1686. The legs, six in number, are of large bulbous form, finishing at the feet in plinths, and the foot-rail that receives the forms is deeply channelled on the outer side; the design of the legs was evidently taken from a far earlier specimen, as this large round bulbous form had at the date of this table long ceased to be made; the nulling throughout, however, is exactly contemporary with the table. Forms and stools were the recognised side seats, but the top and bottom of these tables were furnished with chairs. Sometimes the frames of the forms were carved to resemble the tables. Fig. 175 is a well-preserved and perfect specimen of an ornamental bench of about 1635.

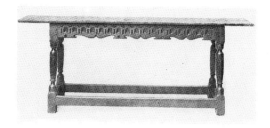

FIG. 175. *Oak Bench.* Property of ERNEST CROFTS, Esq.

It is unnecessary to illustrate all the later developments of these long oak tables, and two more only are given to show the disappearance of the bulbous leg and its evolution to baluster form, as in Fig. 176, which bears the late date of 1697, though the strap-work carving is of much earlier design; and Fig. 177 of the same date (accompanied by its form), in which the baluster is high-shouldered and connected to the frame by brackets. After this date the legs became straight, and continued so, well into the eighteenth century. This form of table was also much used in Jacobean times for altars. When made for this purpose, they invariably had the front and sides of the frame carved and the back left plain. The small long-shaped tables were merely reproductions of those of larger size; it is therefore unnecessary to illustrate them, but few were made, and it was not until the introduction of coffee, chocolate and tea, that the demand for small tables increased. Coffee, as a curiosity, was introduced here in 1615, but not as a drink until 1645, and became sufficiently popular in 1652 to justify a Greek opening a coffee-house in St Michael's Alley, Cornhill. Although a tea brewed of herbs was drunk in Elizabeth's time, and the word 'Tee-pot' occurs in the list of plate made at Hardwick in 1583, an early well-known reference to tea in England is the advertisement in the *Mercurius Politicus* of 1658:

'That excellent and by all physitians approved, China Drink, called by the Chineans Tcha, by other nations Tay, *alias* Tee, is sold at the Sultaness Head, a cophee-house in Sweeting's Rents, by the Royal Exchange, London.'

And the following appeared in the *Public Advertiser* for 16 June 1657:

'In Bishopsgate Street, in Queen's Head Alley, at a Frenchman's house, is an excellent West India drink called chocolate, to be sold, where you may have it ready at any time, and also unmade, at reasonable rates.'

The great increase in the quantity of small tables made after 1660 is no doubt due to the taste for these drinks, coming so rapidly into fashion, that in 1675 Chargles II attempted to suppress coffee-houses as public nuisances. The table (Fig. 178) is an early instance of a small flap table with folding-legs of about 1638. When the flap was not in use the table could be placed flush against the wall, and with but slight alteration the method of folding-leg has been continued to the present day. The frame is carved with a waved and

FIG. 176. *Oak Table.* Property of the DUKE OF DEVONSHIRE.

FIG. 177. *Oak Table.* Property of the DUKE OF DEVONSHIRE.

FIG. 178. *Oak Table*. Property of SEYMOUR LUCAS, Esq.

FIG. 179. *Oak Table*. Height, 2 feet 6 inches; width of top, 2 feet 10 inches. Property of T. VALENTINE GARLAND, Esq.

incised band, and has a single drawer; the legs are columnar in form and ringed; they support small arches with the usual spandrels. A deep and strong lower rail connects the plinths of the legs; at the back, moving on a pivot, are the extra legs to support the flap. The folding-flap, open, is shown in Fig. 179; this table closely resembles the last specimen, with the exception of the lower rail (which is missing at the sides); the rest of the table is quite plain, save for a few lightly carved lines; the top is original. Fig. 180 is a larger and later development, its ringed legs, six in number, pointing to a date about 1663. The back is given in order to explain the position of the folding-leg when not in use; the broad stretcher is unusual. Another form is shown in Fig. 181, date about 1648. It is triangular in shape, with an octagonal top, the legs of plain baluster form being divided into two tiers by a triangular shelf. These small tables are the first portable forms used for light refreshments. Seward, in his anecdotes of the great physician Sydenham, who lived in Charles I's and II's time, writes in connection with one of these small tables:

'Whilst suffering from gout, he was sitting near an open window, on the groundfloor of his house in St James's Square, respiring the cool breeze on a summer's evening and reflecting with a serene countenance, and great complacency, on the alleviation to human misery that his skill in his art had enabled him to give. While this divine man was enjoying one of these delicious reveries, a thief took away from a small table near to which he was sitting, a silver tankard filled with his favourite beverage, small-beer, in which a sprig of rosemary had been immersed, and ran off with it.'

A side-table with a cupboard in front, also about the date 1648, is given in Fig. 182; the panels are rudely carved, and the rails and stretchers inlaid with bands of coarse diagonal marqueterie. Such a piece of furniture might have been used in a bedroom as a washing-stand or dressing-table, and a good many are in existence. A rather more ornamental small table is Fig. 183, of about 1660. This is faced with two drawers, panelled with yew mouldings in the fashion of the time, and supported by plain and ogeed brackets; the legs break out into balls, a plain survival of a former taste. The knob handles to the drawers and the stretchers and feet are restorations.

The long seat, with an upright panelled back and arms, called a settle, is of very early origin, and was usually placed in the great halls of houses. In the early specimens the ends forming the arms were panelled, and the backs were very high. Being exceedingly cumbersome pieces of furniture, these were gradually superseded by a lighter form, with open arms and a lower back. French 'bancs', of the time of Francis I, are still in existence, with the panels beautifully carved in Renaissance design, while the lower portion is decorated with linenfold. It is probable that pieces of this description were also made here during the reigns of Henry VIII and Elizabeth, but they no

FIG. 180. *Oak Table*. Width, 5 feet; height, 2 feet 6 inches. Property of FRANK GREEN, Esq.

FIG. 181. *Oak Table*. Height, 2 feet 3 inches; width of frame, 2 feet. Property of C. E. KEMPE, Esq.

FIG. 182. *Oak Side Table.* Property of MORGAN WILLIAMS, Esq.

FIG. 183. *Oak Table.* Property of A. L. RADFORD, Esq.

longer exist. The seat in all early settles opened in box form; in the later specimens this is also general, though occasionally they are found with an open front composed of legs and foot-rail. The simplicity of Fig. 184 suggests Puritanical taste, and a date about 1645. The top rail is carved with a chain-cartouche pattern; the upper row of panels, three in number, are carved with a double loop, the surface of the panel being left plain to form the pattern. The arms are set unusually high, and the supports are of Cromwellian type; the seat forms a box, and the front is divided into two large plain panels framed in rails and a centre stile with a deep channel moulding. The handsome settle (Fig. 185) is dated 1647. The cresting, composed of somewhat meaningless scrolls, runs almost the entire length of the top rail, which terminates in two worked finials. The back is formed of five tall panels, carved with conventional flowers and swans on a grained ground in arched compartments; these are divided and framed by stiles inlaid with a neat checker-work of two coloured woods. At the bottom of the panels are the initials of the original owner, Alexander Lindsay, the date 1647, and the motto of the Lindsay family, 'ASTRA CASTRA, NUMEN LUMEN', 'The stars (our) citadels, God (our) light'. All the uprights and rails are inlaid with the same checker pattern. The seat opens as a box working on S hinges, and the hasp and the lock-plate are also original; the bottom is divided into three panels, with the large and rather flat carving on a grained surface, much used about this time. Alexander, second Baron Lindsay of Balcarres and first Earl of Balcarres, to whom this settle once belonged, became hereditary

FIG. 184. *Oak Settle.* Length, 5 feet 2 inches; height, 3 feet 5 inches. Property of SIR CHARLES LAWES-WITTEWRONGE, Bart.

FIG. 185. *Oak Settle.* Length, 6 feet 1 inch; height, 3 feet 9 inches; depth, 1 foot 7 inches. Property of C. E. KEMPE, Esq.

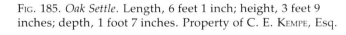

FIG. 186. *Oak Table Settle.*Length, 5 feet 10 inches; width of top, 2 feet 4 inches. Property of H. Martin Gibbs, Esq.

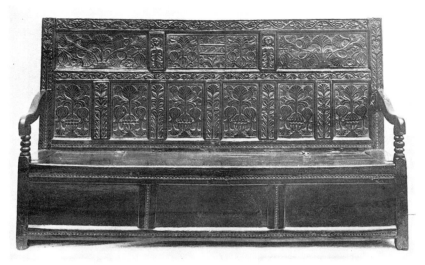

FIG. 187. *Oak Settle.* Length, 6 feet 7 inches; height, 4 feet 2 inches. Property of H. Martin Gibbs, Esq.

FIG. 188. *Oak Table Chair.* Property of F. W. Phillips, Esq.

Governor of Edinburgh Castle, Secretary of State, and High Commissioner to the General Assembly, and died in exile at Breda in 1659. The settle was discovered in a house in Canongate, Edinburgh, and the brilliancy of its appearance was evidently a protest by an adherent of the King's against the gloomy fashions of the Parliamentary party.

An uncomfortable and economical effort of Cromwellian inspiration was the table-settle, where the back, working on pins, could be pulled over to rest on the arms, and so form a table top. Fig. 186 is one of these, of about the date 1655; the carving on it is extremely rough; it stands on ten legs, connected by a foot-rail mounted on to a base, for further security; in this instance the base is a restoration. This make was also extended to chairs, as in Fig. 188. Here the top is round, and when let down forms a small table. The incised arched design follows out the lines of a chair of the time. Settles continued to be made throughout the eighteenth century; they gradually became plain in type, and chiefly in demand for inns, farmhouses and servants' quarters. A late specimen of the Jacobean type is given in Fig. 187. The decoration on the top rail is open and scanty; the knob finials are missing, though the holes for them are visible; the back is divided into three oblong and six upright panels, carved flatly in debased conventional ornament, the upper stiles being worked with barbaric representations of female terminal figures, and the panel between these bears the initials I. M. C., with the date 1720. The seat opens as a box, and the front is divided into three plain panels, with a toothed beading down the centre of the stiles and rails.

CHAPTER IX

ARLY forms of Cromwellian upholstered furniture were remarkable for severity and discomfort. This can be seen in the couch (Fig. 189), which has its original pigskin covering on the back and rails; that of the seat, hidden by a rug in the illustration, has been renewed; the rake of the sides, which are in one piece with the legs, must have entailed a considerable waste of wood. The chairs (Fig. 190) correspond in period and design to this couch; the leathers on the seats and backs of both are original, and on the taller specimen has been lightly tooled; the nailed banding to the seat-rail is missing on the smaller chair. The front legs and stretchers are knobbed, a pattern which found favour with the Puritans; this

FIG. 189. *Oak Couch*. Full length, 5 feet 11 inches; length of seat, 4 feet 6 inches; height, 2 feet 10 inches. Property of C. E. KEMPE, Esq.

FIG. 190. *Oak Chairs*.

FIG. 191. *Oak Chair*. Property of SIR GEORGE DONALDSON.

FIG. 192. *Oak Chair*. Height, 4 feet 2 inches. Property of the DUKE OF DEVONSHIRE.

FIG. 193. *Oak Chair*. Height, 4 feet. Property of the DUKE OF DEVONSHIRE.

FIG. 194. *Oak Chair*. Property of ERNEST CROFTS, Esq.

fashion began about the date of the King's execution, and continued into the reign of Charles II.

Towards the end of the Commonwealth, a desire for more cheerful-looking furniture arose, and this type of chair was then consequently covered with the stamped and coloured leathers imported from the Continent. In the Verney Papers there is a letter from a clergyman, written in 1658, with a reference to this taste:

'Rather than go to a much higher price for Hangings, etc., I would gladly bestow a matter of £8 in wainscot for my parlor, then I should like very well this painted leather for a suit of chairs and stools.'

This coloured stamped leather would have had but a short life when used for chair coverings, as neither the lacquered silver nor the paint could resist the friction of wear. The panelled-back arm-chair still continued to be made, and there are many dated specimens after the Restoration in existence. Fig. 191 is of about the date 1660; the panelled back is high, surmounted by a tall scrolled cresting, finishing at the sides in ears and centred by a bearded mask; the carving of the panel – a representation of the seed-pod and flower of the cocoa-tree – is thin in execution; the uprights framing it are decorated with a triple channel moulding, and finish below in very broad back legs; the arms, set low, are narrow, the supports finishing with legs turned in baluster fashion. The chairs from Hardwick (Figs. 192 and 193) show the development of the ringed baluster which came in at this time. In Fig. 192 a mask again centres the scrolls of the cresting, but the back is divided into two panels, the upper being dated 1662, and the lower carved with a pattern much found on ceilings of the time. Fig. 193 has the same subdivision of the back panel, but resembles early chairs in its compact form; the upper panel is carved with monsters in low relief, the lower with a fine strap-work; the arm supports and legs are ringed. Another chair, a few years later in date (Fig. 194), has the same high scrolled cresting, ringed arm supports, and broad back legs; the design, however, of the back panel in its flowing lines foreshadows the decoration of the coming reign.

Plate XIV shows a pair of double chairs or love-seats. They are made on the same lines as other Jacobean oak chairs; their date is about 1700, and the interest chiefly centres on their proportion, which is rare. A very distinct effort, inspired by Italian chairs of a rather earlier date, is to be found in the oak chairs of Yorkshire and Derbyshire origin, made between 1650 and 1675. These are the real progenitors of open back chairs, for those of Elizabeth's reign were of too intermittent and exceptional an occurrence to have created a fashion. In the early specimens of these, the back opens in an arcade and knobbed finials, supported on turned balusters standing on a centre rail. Fig. 195 has this rail carved in the style of about 1650, with the uprights of the

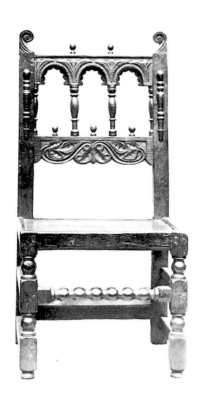

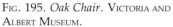

Fig. 195. *Oak Chair.* Victoria and Albert Museum.

Fig. 196. *Oak Chair.* Property of A. L. Radford, Esq.

Fig. 197. *Oak Chair.* Victoria and Albert Museum.

Fig. 198. *Oak Chair.* Height, 3 feet 6 inches. Property of Sir George Donaldson.

back ending in scrolled finials, which are all that remain of the previous Jacobean cresting and ears; below these are the applied split baluster ornament so much in favour at the time; the seat is sunk for a squab, and the legs are knobbed in the Cromwellian manner. In Fig. 196, a few years later in date, a similar treatment is followed without the arcading, and the broad and flat rails at the back are hooped and escalloped; the knobbed finials are here reversed as pendants. A still later form is Fig. 197, approximating in shape the tall walnut chairs of the end of Charles II's reign, with which it is contemporary. The lunette at the top, carved with a traditional rose, the incoming C scrolls to the centre rail, and the plain baluster stretcher, are transitional details that should be noticed; it is also interesting to compare with this the late panel-back chair (Fig. 198), dated 1691. In this last specimen there are traces of all the motives that once decorated panel-back chairs. The scrolled cresting, here abnormally hooped, the human mask, the arch with pilasters and flowering plant, the nicking that represents the upright laurelled pattern of the Renaissance – all show that the first-rate craftsman had discarded these patterns, and that in less efficient hands their intention had become without purpose.

An interesting form of court cupboard, with an extra canopy and shelf for the display of china, was much made in Wales, and known there as a cwpwedd tridarn. A specimen, dated 1662, exists at Gwydyr Castle, the decoration and lower portion corresponding with the ordinary court cupboard of the time. Fig. 199 is a tridarn dated 1695. The frieze of the canopy is plain, the lower moulding being perforated for a spoon rack; the supports to this are columnar and ringed, and high enough to allow a row of plates to be arranged on the back shelf, the smaller china, etc., being placed in front. In the inlaid cornice of the second tier there is a secret shelf, accessible only through the cupboards immediately underneath; the remainder of the piece is on the lines of the ordinary court cupboard. The decoration throughout is simple, and the carving on the lower doors represents the favourite dragon design, so frequently found on Welsh furniture.

Plate XV is another example of about 1700. Here, in the centre comparment, the balusters, which in early types supported the canopy, are replaced by pendants; the bottom doors are composed of single large panels,

FIG. 199. *Oak Court Cupboard (Tridarn)*. Height, 6 feet 3 inches; width, 4 feet 6 inches; depth, 2 feet. Property of HENRY GROGAN, Esq.

FIG. 200. *Oak Dresser*. Height, 2 feet 2 inches; width, 3 feet. Property of ERNEST CROFTS, Esq.

a change that came in at this time. It will be seen that this style of carving has now lost all interest of design, but the cross mouldings are very neatly run.

A distinct form of small dresser is shown in Fig. 200, in which there is a curious combination of decoration. The strap-work scrolls (which have lost their centre finial) of the top, the panels at the back, and the brackets supporting the shelves, are of a much earlier design than the construction of the lower portion or cupboard, which, with its inlaid emblems and various mouldings, is of about the date 1665. It is probably, like so many of these pieces that are composite in style, of country make.

Chests continued to be made during the Commonwealth, though not in such large quantities as before. Fig. 201 is an unusually elaborate chest for

FIG. 201. *Oak Inlaid Chest*. Length, 4 feet 6 inches; height, 3 feet. Property of ERNEST CROFTS, Esq.

FIG. 202. *Oak Chest*. Property of C. E. KEMPE, Esq.

this period, dated in marqueterie over the arches AD 1653, and is a very late representation of the early style, combining marqueterie, carving and terminal figures. It was very possibly inspired by Fig. 137, also in the possession of the same family. The front is divided into two panels, under broad depressed arches carved with palm branches, and headed by the mask of a savage; each panel is inlaid with the portico of a building, out of which a man armed with a sword and gun issues; on the outer stiles are male terminal figures, with hair and beard dressed in cavalier fashion, and the figure in the centre represents a female savage. The bottom opens in one long drawer, inlaid with marqueterie, in a design of the previous reign, but the marqueterie on the frieze beneath the lid is tending towards the scrolled lines that formed so important a decoration on furniture towards the end of the century; the feet and the corbels are carved. Although a very interesting chest in colour and general effect, it is easy to trace decadence in almost every line of its design; the joinery, however, shows that this craft was now making rapid strides. This good workmanship is shown again in Fig. 202, a Scotch chest from the same source as the settle (Fig. 185), and very likely by the same hand; the top and side panels are carved, a feature often found on late chests; the divided palm branch that decorates the uprights of the frame is an unsatisfactory novelty, but the design of the frieze on the upper rail is good; the lower rail is neatly inlaid above a well-run moulding. The interest centres on the inscription . THOMAS . IV . CHA . REX . II . SPENCER . signifying the date 1653 – the piece being Scotch – as in that country the adherents of Charles II considered his reign began on the day of his father's death.

These carved oak chests practically ceased to be made for the richer classes after this date, and, when replaced by lighter furniture, were probably sold or given away, in many instances to the servants attached to large houses on the occasion of their marriage, thus drifting into the cottages and farmhouses, where they were found constantly used as cornbins in Victorian times.

Another form of chest with drawers is shown in Fig. 203, where the top opens in a shallow box for clothes, the doors beneath opening on two drawers, and the bottom compartment being composed of one long drawer. The decoration throughout is a mixture of carving and applied work, the arcading on the doors resembling the backs of the north country chairs, as in Figs. 195 and 197. The date is approximately 1655.

There appears to have been an interval between the introduction of the pearl and bone inlaid chest with drawers, such as Figs. 140 and 141, and the later renewal of this fashion. Soon after 1650 a certain interest in furniture again arose, and these chests with drawers point to a revival of the taste that was then taking place. An interesting series of these is given in the following illustrations, though their chronological order is difficult to place, as only in one instance is the piece dated.

The earliest is Fig. 204, of about the date 1648. It resembles in construction

FIG. 203. *Oak Chest with Drawers*. Height, 3 feet 9 inches; length, 3 feet 7 inches; depth, 1 foot 8 inches. Property of S. CAMPBELL CORY, Esq.

FIG. 204. *Oak Chest with Drawers*. Property of MESSRS MORANT.

FIG. 205. *Oak Chest with Drawers.* Height, 3 feet 8 inches; width, 3 feet 8 inches; depth, 2 feet. Property of MESSRS J. MALLETT AND SON.

FIG. 206. *Oak Cupboard with Drawers.* Height, 3 feet 8 inches; width, 3 feet 8 inches; depth, 1 foot 9 inches. Property of PERCY MACQUOID, Esq.

the carved oak specimen (Fig. 139). Underneath the corbelled cornice and thin top is one long drawer, inlaid with a chess-board pattern of ivory and zebra-wood; the two doors beneath, opening on a series of drawers, are geometrically panelled and inlaid with ivory, centring in a highly bevelled octagon, the sides of which are faced with zebra-wood; this piece was originally mounted on a low stand. The next link in this series if Fig. 205, in which the octagon idea is elaborated, the mouldings of the panel carrying out the motive. The upper portion opens in one very deep drawer, panelled in two octagons, but divided by a deeply recessed representation of an arch and stairway, a decoration copied from Italian cabinets; the lower portion is separated from the upper by a narrow moulding which at a later date increases in width. The doors are treated like the drawers, with the addition of a fine zigzag line of ivory and an inlay of snake-wood; the split baluster ornament takes here a much more important place. This has been variously named split baluster, cannon or mace decoration, but in reality is only the Elizabethan and Jacobean applied walnut pendant, inverted and elaborated. The base moulding is of the knobbed Cromwellian pattern found on chairs; the sides are plainly panelled. Drop handles replace the original wood and ivory peg handles. Fig. 206 is of earlier design, and of about the same date as the last piece, from which it only differs in construction by the introduction of two top drawers; these are inlaid with bone and mother-of-pearl decoration; the subdivision of the panels is rectangular; the archway in the centre is here represented by a flat inlay of the pearl and bone, and on the uprights that frame the drawer inverted pendants of early form are applied. A further interest lies in the wood which forms the bevelled centre of the panels, as it is, with the applied pendants, corbels and bosses, of mahogany. This wood was not used for the construction of furniture till the end of the seventeenth century, and it has generally been accepted as a fact, that no introduction of it, even as ornament in decoration, is to be found before 1670, though this example is not later than the date 1655. The open door shows the usual arrangement of the drawers in these pieces; the centre rail and plinth are of bold character. In Fig. 207 the upper portion opens like a chest; the lid and corbels resemble the last specimen in their mouldings; the corners and centres of the panels are inlaid with bone and mother-of-pearl; the archway is very deeply recessed, and the circular mouldings within the octagons are spoked. The applied pendants have now become elongated, and are losing the trace of their origin. The lower portion opens in two drawers, and the

FIG. 207. *Chest with Drawers.* Height, 3 feet 6 inches; length, 4 feet 5 inches; depth, 1 foot 10 inches. Property of ARTHUR JAMES, Esq.

FIG. 208. *Oak Chest with Drawers.* Height, 4 feet 6 inches; width, 3 feet 9 inches; depth, 2 feet. Property of SIR CHARLES LAWES-WITTEWRONGE, Bart.

FIG. 209. *Chest with Drawers*. Property of MESSRS MORANT.

FIG. 210. *Chest with Drawers*. Height, 4 feet 8 inches; length, 4 feet 1 inch; depth, 2 feet 2 inches. Property of ARTHUR JAMES, Esq.

centre panel between them bears on an escutcheon the date 1661. This chest is upon its original stand, the type on which all these low-standing pieces of furniture were placed. The fashion for these chests must have been great, as many varieties of them are to be found following rapidly upon one another in date. Fig. 208 is a very carefully finished example, though the feet are restorations. The corbels of the frieze are in this instance flat, and inlaid with channels of snake-wood, studded, top and bottom, with small ebony bosses.

As the evolution of this motive continues, the decoration becomes more and more dotted and bossed, and ornaments are glued on in imitation of the solid work of a former time. In Fig. 209, of about 1675, the construction is still the same, but the upper portion is divided into six drawers, and stand on a plain and projecting moulding that forms a cornice to the lower portion; the bottom opens in two very narrow drawers over the doors. The split baluster ornament has here developed into small columns mounted on tall plinths; the fronts of the drawers and bevels of the panels are faced with snake-wood, the corners being ornamented with discs of ivory.

In Fig. 210 the front is so overlaid with strips and panels of rosewood and snake-wood, that but little of the original oak surface show. The inlaid arch with a checkered floor is still retained in the centre of the upper portion, but the sharp angles to the panel mouldings in the upper drawers, and the narrow panels which break on the angle of the central division, infer that the date is about 1680; the flat corbelled projection of the two friezes also point to this date. In these last two examples there is an attempt at architectural construction, which in some degree redeems the poverty of imagination, and in the pearl inlaid specimens there is a decided decorative effect; but in other oak furniture of this period, of which Fig. 211 is a characteristic example, the decoration is no better than that found on a birthday cake. The weakness of the applied process is apparent, for though evidently subjected to no undue hard usage, many of the glued-on bosses have dropped off.

Figs. 212, 213 and 214 represent the final development, where the lower cupboard doors are discarded, and the piece of furniture assumes the form known as the 'chest of drawers'.

The so-called snake-wood was imported from Demerara; it is known technically as *Poratinera Guianensis*. Zebra-wood is produced by the tree known now as *Omphalobium Lamberti*.

FIG. 211. *Oak Double Cupboard*. Height, 4 feet; width, 3 feet 8 inches; depth, 1 foot 7 inches.

FIG. 212. *Chest of Drawers*. Property of ARTHUR JAMES, Esq.

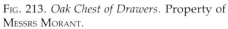

Fɪɢ. 213. *Oak Chest of Drawers.* Property of
Mᴇꜱꜱʀꜱ Mᴏʀᴀɴᴛ.

Fɪɢ. 214. *Oak Chest of Drawers.* Property of
A. L. Rᴀᴅꜰᴏʀᴅ, Esq.

There are many small articles of oak furniture which it has been found impossible, for what of space, to touch upon, and though in many instances finer isolated specimens could have been given in illustration, it has been thought better throughout this work to avoid what does not bear directly on the evolution of each period.

Of these periods, it has already been shown that so little English Gothic furniture is in existence, that we are forced to construct in imagination, from architecture, pictures and the more numerous specimens of foreign furniture, the many missing links. It must be remembered, in reviewing this period, that the foreign fashion in furniture practically controlled the taste here, and that an individual fashion was then more widespread than it is today.

By the end of the fifteenth century – the period selected for the beginning of this book – Gothic had already passed its zenith, and the later developments reproduced on English furniture were soon set aside by the vigorous and material feeling of the Elizabethan Renaissance, which laid the foundations of an individual style, the details of which lasted as long as the fashion for oak furniture continued. The simplicity and austerity of Puritan taste was not without charm, but this taste, being content with the abolition of ornament, without the development of any new or true proportion, came to a somewhat sudden termination; the last attempts in decoration to relieve the dreary monotony, being uneducated in form and artificial in method.

With the Restoration, the Age of Oak came to an end. The solidity and strange originality of beauty, which in so vivid and virile a manner pervaded the furniture and all art of the fifteenth and sixteenth centuries, gradually disappeared, giving way to more modern forms of thought, where in furniture the guiding principles consisted of constructional excellence, comfort and, above all, what was suitable to gaiety and the joy of living.

English oak furniture of Gothic, Elizabethan and Jacobean times represented the temperament of those for whom it was made, and in endurance and solidity was typical of the people who lived in those ages.

THE AGE OF WALNUT

CHAPTER I

O N 3 September 1659 the Lord Protector Oliver Cromwell died, and with him died the simple taste, that, owing to dearth of imagination, had gradually drifted into the commonplace. Had this taste continued, the evolution must have been devoid of artistic interest, and would have added no rung in the ladder of the beautiful, as the initial motives were not founded on true principles.

The Restoration of the Monarchy was accompanied by entirely new forms of thought, for not only were the tastes of the sovereign very strongly tinctured with those of France and Flanders, but the return here of a large number of adherents who had shared his exile in these countries, created a sudden change of fashion and manners in strong contrast to the existing conditons of social England. Owing to personal charm and easy familiarity of manner towards those who surrounded him, the new King was not only easy of access, but a very attractive model. The average English country home was, however, at first but little influenced by the licence of the Court, and the bulk of the people openly resented the immorality and luxury of Whitehall, but gradually this luxury left its mark upon a nation, which till this time had been content with simplicity, for the eccentric extravagances of the very rich in the preceding reigns were by no means representative of English taste. By 1673 this tendency towards extravagance must have been widespread, as John Evelyn wrote in that year, describing a visit to the Countess of Arlington, as follows:

'She carried us up into her new dressing-room at Goring House, where was a bed, two glasses, silver jars, and vases, cabinets, and other so rich furniture as I had seldom seen; to this excess of superfluity were we now arrived, and that not only at Court, but almost universally, even to wantonness and profusion.'

A few years later, Celia Fiennes writes in her diary about the household of an apothecary in Bury St Edmunds, that

'This house is the new mode of building; 4 roomes of a ffloore pretty sizeable and high, well furnished, a drawing roome and Chamber full of China and a damaske bed Embroydered: 2 other Roomes, Camlet and Mohaire beds; a pretty deale of plaite in his wives Chambers and parlours below, and a large shop.'

This description of a tradesman's domicile in a country town proves very clearly that, in twenty years, the desire of rich furnishing had spread to the middle classes.

Towards the end of the seventeenth century, the last details, and nobility of proportion in Elizabethan decoration and furniture, disappeared, giving way to the somewhat exaggerated mouldings and contrasted curves, prompted by the vagaries of the Italian artists Lorenzo Bernini and Francesco Borromini. The new forms found their way here through France and Flanders, and obtained a sure footing when modified to suit the quieter taste of this country. Although picturesque in the more elaborate and later developments, this style was only redeemed from frivolity by faultless execution. This change naturally was not effected in weeks or months, but represented a long and deliberate evolution.

The Protector, by the year 1657, to the disappointment of the majority of his followers, had assumed certain forms of state, pomp and ceremony; and consequently society, in a rather ponderous manner, had aroused itself during the last two or three years of his government. The inventory of his rooms at Hampton Court Palace proves that some of the finest state furniture had been reserved for his own use, the subjects of the tapestries retained in the bedroom being by no means in accordance with his austere views. Owing to this attempt at a court and semi-state, gayer furniture once more struggled into fashion, and the following list of possessions of the newly widowed Countess of Warwick – who was redecorating her house in honour of her approaching fourth nuptials with the Earl of Manchester – shows that in this respect the tide was in reality turning before the Restoration. In the withdrawing-room mention is made of

'Two complete suites, one of blew wrought velvet, fringed with blew, another in Crimson figured satten, with silk fringe and gilt nailes. Four crimson wrought window curtains lined with crimson wrought satten, and one greate crimson velvett Cabinett, each suite has chaires, stooles, and carpet to match. A crimson figured satten bed trimmed with imbroidered buttons and loopes, with carpet, chaires and stooles suteable, two little china carpets with colored silks and gold, one scarlet cloth bed lined with satten, a counterpane of satten trimmed with gold and silver fringe, and a rich gold and silver ffringe about the vallins.'

Another bed is upholstered in 'carnation quilted satten', and a fourth in 'grene cloathe with Isabella taffety and sheetes edged with purle'. Her widow's bed – which must have been more for show than use – is described as of 'fyne blacke imbroidery, with a sheete wrought with blacke silke, and blacke chairs, stooles and carpet to match'.

For some time previous to the Restoration walnut had been adopted as a light wood suitable to carry these silks and satins. A vast number of these trees had been planted during Elizabeth's reign, and their timber had by the middle of the seventeenth century attained maturity. The walnut was imported from Persia into Italy about the date of the Christian era, and was brought over here with the elm, yew and other trees during the Roman occupation, but the first distinct notice of its regular cultivation in this country is in 1562. Throughout Italy, France and Spain this wood was used freely for furniture during the sixteenth and seventeenth centuries, but, owing to its scarcity in England, was in Elizabethan and Jacobean times only introduced as a decoration in conjunction with oak. Occasionally, as has been shown, pieces were made almost entirely of walnut; this timber, however, was probably imported from abroad.

The new style that commenced in England about the middle of the seventeenth century was particularly suitable for the employment of walnut, as twists and curves, when on the cross-grain, were less liable to chip in this wood than in the more porous oak; and although the general construction and lining of cabinets and small furniture continued to be made

FIG. 215. *Walnut Turned Chair*. Height, 3 feet; width, 1 foot 6 inches.

FIG. 216. *Beech Turned Chair*. Property of the DUKE OF DEVONSHIRE.

FIG. 217. *Walnut Chair*. (a) Height, 3 feet 6 inches; width, 2 feet. (b) Height, 3 feet 2 inches; width, 1 foot 8 inches.

FIG. 218. *Walnut Stool and Bed-step.* Property of FRANK GREEN, Esq.

of oak, the outer surfaces were veneered with walnut, with applied mouldings worked in the same wood. In chairs, the lightness derived from walnut was at once appreciated; but our ancestors, by the end of the century, had discovered its liability to decay by worm, and welcomed the new substitute provided in mahogany.

Fig. 215 shows in its walnut rails, uprights and stretchers an interesting combination of twisted and knobbed turning, and is of a date just previous to the Restoration. The seat panel, sunk to hold the squab, is of oak, and the chair has its original varnish. Fig. 216 is another of these turned chairs, somewhat later in date, and made of beech; the back is composed of a series of carefully turned balusters, with uprights of a sturdy type; the stretchers are ringed, and rushing has replaced the original seat panel. Fig. 217 is from a set of chairs, turned throughout in a neat twist; the backs and seats are early examples of the new fashion of caning. This in (a) is original, large in the mesh, of about the date 1660; the framing to receive the caning is left plain, but in many instances the frames of these chairs will be found lightly incised with a diagonal pattern. It should be noticed that the rails of the back are now slightly curved, and that in (b) the arms are flat and bowed; the cresting found on previous arm-chairs is omitted, and round finials are the solitary attempt at decoration. Fig. 218 (a) is a stool or tabouret from a somewhat similar set, while (b) is a bed-step of the same description; the incised pattern on the seat-rail is clearly visible in these two last specimens. An alternative to caning in these plain turned chairs was the insertion of a number of flat uprights in the back; there are several examples of this description at Hardwick, and Fig. 219, from another collection, is an arm-chair treated in this manner. All these specimens are a distinct departure from anything that had been made before, for up to this time, except for the so-called Yorkshire and Derbyshire chairs, the backs to chairs were in almost every instance solid, either panelled or padded. These twisted chairs are mentioned by Mary Verney in a letter of 1664, as follows: 'For a drawing roome i should have 2 sqobs and 6 turned woden chairs of the haith of the longe seates. Be pleased also to by a tabel and stands of the same coler.' An answer to this is returned, 'That no tolerable chairs can be found under seven shillings a piece and the sqobs ten shillings.'

It is interesting to follow the evolution of this new form of chair, so far as it continues to be invested with its first motive. The stool (Fig. 220) is contemporary with Fig. 218, and of the same design, save for the introduction of a flat stretcher coarsely carved with roses and acanthus. This broad carved stretcher now for the first time made its appearance in chairs, stools, couches and day-beds, and lasted so long as the original type of these objects continued to be made. The decoration on these stretchers was repeated as a cresting on the chairs, and consisted of large and flat scrolls of acanthus centring in flowers or fruit, amidst which was often introduced a crown supported by cherubs, in allusion to the restoration of the Monarchy. The character of this ornament resembles that found on the silver-plate between 1665 and 1675, and, though picturesque and barbaric, was but a sudden and uneducated effort against the universal dulness of the Cromwellian period. Plate XVI (a) is an armchair of this description, and a good example of the type made in such large quantities during the first years of Charles II's reign; they were evidently often made in sets, with and without arms. In a mis-

FIG. 219. *Walnut Turned Chair.* Property of A. L. RADFORD, Esq.

FIG. 220. *Walnut Stool.* Property of FRANK GREEN, Esq.

Fig. 221. *Oak Chair*. Property of
Ernest Crofts, Esq.

Fig. 222. *Walnut Child's
Chair*. Height, 3 feet 7
inches; width of seat, 1
foot 3 inches. Property
of Sir Edmund and Lady
Elton.

Fig. 223. *Walnut Chair*. Property of Sir
Charles Lawes-Wittewronge, Bart.

Fig. 224. *Walnut Chair*. Height, 3
feet 8 inches. Property of Lord
Mostyn.

leading manner they are invariably catalogued as 'oak chairs' at sales,
though on examination not one in a hundred will be found to be of this
wood.

Fig. 221 is a Welsh variety of this kind made in oak, and the difference of
treatment is very apparent. Fig. 222 is a baby chair of Restoration make,
where cherubins form the centre decoration of heading the stretcher; parts of
the front legs are knobbed in order to receive the foot-rest, which is missing.
An altogether better class of design and workmanship is shown in Fig. 223,
where the carving is more delicate and artistic in treatment; the cherubs
support a vase of flowers, and it corresponds in decoration to the silver-plate
of 1679; the supports to the arms were so worm-eaten that they have been
restored by the present owner. In Plate XVI (b), of about the same date, the
element of the decorated C scroll is preponderant, and the carving is of
extremely fine quality; the arms have a bold roll over, and are well carved on
the upper surface; the supports to these and the legs are gracefully curved
and shouldered with beaded acanthus, and the front stretcher centres in a

Fig. 225. *Walnut Chair*.
Property of Frank Green,
Esq.

Fig. 226. *Walnut Chair*. Height, 3
feet 10 inches; width, 1 foot 9
inches. Property of the Earl of
Carrington.

Fig. 227. *Walnut Chair*. Property of
H. Martin Gibbs, Esq.

Fig. 228. *Walnut Chair*.
Property of Ernest Crofts,
Esq.

fleur-de-lys. The caning, which at this period became finer, is original on both seat and back. Figs. 224 and 225 are this Restoration type without arms, and of an altogether coarser quality. Fig. 224 is another well-known variety, in which the crown is introduced five times, the finials also repeating the same detail; the caning has been replaced by a panel seat, and the lower stretcher is missing. The scrolled leg, which later developed into the so-called cabriole form, was introduced into England as a fashion on these chairs, though the twisted leg was not finally discarded for many years. Fig. 226 is a chair from Gwydyr Castle; in this instance a broad central splat takes the place of the caning, and is carved in a manner strongly indicative of the French patterns that were being introduced from the Court of Louis XIV, though the rest of the work retains the original English freedom, in this case an eagle is introduced as a central ornament. Fig. 227 is a still later specimen of the finer type of these arm-chairs; the uprights of the back are balustered, and the scrolled legs are set in an oblique manner to receive the cross stretchers. Fig. 228, in which some necessary restorations have been made in oak, shows the Restoration pattern in its decadence, but the chair possesses interest as having been made during the three years' reign of James II, and evidently for use in his household, as the cresting bears the arms of England; the uprights of the back, which are still twisted, finish in human heads; the back is formed of a narrow panel of carving, framed in an open and feeble scrolling, amidst which are the inevitable cherubs, who have descended from the cresting, and bear shields with the letters I. R.; the front stretcher is thin in design, and the cherubs that bear the crown are peculiarly shapeless. Another point of interest is the introduction of the roughly carved animals couchant as feet to the front legs, a finish that will be seen also on the chairs in Fig. 241.

The revival of the day-bed, attendant on a more luxurious mode of living, is proved by the number of these in existence of post-Restoration date, and the extreme rarity of specimens before that time. Doubtless the soldiers, quartered in so many houses of importance during the war, had caused great destruction to all forms of couches that could have been utilised as beds, and the rough usage that ensured must soon have rendered them useless. The new day-beds repeated the motives of the Restoration chairs, and followed exactly the same evolution, the backs being adjustable by means of chains or chords. Fig. 229 is one of the early and simple type of about 1660; the back rest is roughly carved with large roses and acanthus, the sides of the frame are lightly incised, and the seat caned to receive a squab that would have been covered with silk, velvet or needlework; the legs and stretchers repeat the twist of the early chairs. In Fig. 230, a few years later in date, the stretcher and cresting are carved with cherubs and crown; the back is a fixture, and velvet replaces the original caning. Fig. 231 is a much later specimen, which, from the form of the hooped scroll of its stretchers and the

FIG. 229. *Walnut Day-bed.* Height, 1 foot 3 inches; width, 1 foot 9 inches; length, 5 feet 3 inches. Property of C. E. KEMPE, Esq.

FIG. 230. *Walnut Day-bed*. Length, 5 feet. Property of E. A. BARRY, Esq.

FIG. 231. *Walnut Day-bed*. Length, 5 feet; height, 3 feet 7 inches; width, 1 foot 8 inches. Property of C. E. KEMPE, Esq.

clubby curved legs, with their pear-shaped tops, is probably as late as the accession of William III; the very fine caning of the back, the broken pediment of the tall heading, with its wide ogeed mouldings, also pointing to this date. After this time day-beds ceased to be carved, and were upholstered.

These carved, high-backed, caned chairs and couches, with their brilliant silk cushions, must have been most becoming frames to those who used them. The revival of colour was the first protest against the greys, browns and drabs of the previous decade, and represents the early Carolean feeling of fashionable decoration which was presided over by Castlemaine and Gwyn. What followed later in the reign was more emphasised in style and more gorgeous in colour, being prompted by the influence of Louis XIV and the Frenchwoman Louise de Keroualle; the latter, while leading the fashion here, combined the offices of mistress to the English king and spy to the French king. These women of the Court had the greatest influence on matters relating to furnishing, and lavished enormous sums of money in decoration, thereby creating entirely new fashions. The male favourites of previous reigns, though they largely indulged in the building of beautiful houses, with the finest architectural decorations, took much more interest in their retinues, equipages, horses and personal adornments, than in novelties of furniture and luxurious comforts.

It is quite possible to form a correct picture of these people, even to minute

FIG. 232. *Oak Bird-cage*. Property of SIR GEORGE DONALDSON.

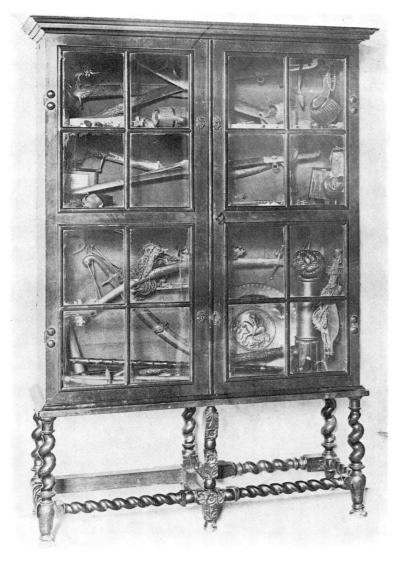

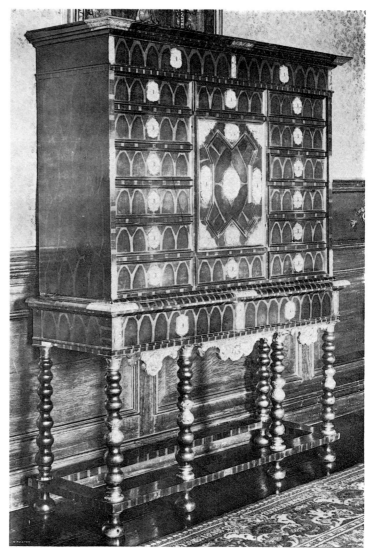

Fig. 233. *Oak China Cupboard*. Height, 6 feet 6 inches. Property of the Duke of Leeds.

Fig. 234. *Walnut and Laburnum Cabinet*. Height, 6 feet 7 inches; length, 4 feet 6 inches. Property of Robert W. J. Rushbrooke, Esq.

details, so perfect in condition are many of the things that have come down to us, so modern were their methods, and so near was their civilisation to our own. The oak bird-cage (Fig. 232), which is about the date 1670, is in construction like those of to-day; in such a cage Nell Gwyn might have kept her white sparrows, then so fashionable as pets. Fig. 233 is a china cupboard (now filled with military relics) of about the date 1675, but as modern in feeling as the bird-cage. Evelyn makes constant references in his diary to the then existing rage for collecting china and small curiosities, and from his description these collections evidently differed but little from those of to-day. We read also that one of the King's mistresses, the Duchess of Mazarin, was in the the habit of personally searching the ships that had freshly arrived from India for Oriental curiosities. In Fig. 233 the framing of the sides and doors are faced with walnut, and the mullions to the glass are a half-rounded moulding of the same wood; the butt-hinges are pinned on the outside of the doors with escalloped gilt bosses; the cornice and plinths are simple and well proportioned in projection; the old handle is missing, but the key-plates are original. The stand resembles early chairs of the time, in the arrangement of the twist and carving of the central leg, though the feet show a later development. One of the original back stretchers is missing.

One of a pair of most interesting cabinets, both from historical association and extreme rarity of design, is given in Fig. 234. The cornice is bold and in the strong projection of the time; below this the front opens in two long drawers, fourteen smaller drawers and a central cupboard. The whole is faced with laburnum wood, cut from long transverse sections of the tree, the lighter portion of the wood next the bark being retained as an ornament, instead of being trimmed away, as is usual in this sectional veneer. The drawers are bordered with finely run mouldings of walnut, and the door has centre panel mouldings in the same character; on each drawer is an elaborate repousse key-plate of English silver work, and on the centre of the door is a silver monogram composed of the letters H. M. R. – Henrietta · Maria · Regina. The frieze moulding and plinths are clamped at the corners, and also centre, with embossed acanthus. The stand is even more elaborate than the cabinet, and is composed of six legs of ball turning, with embossed silver caps, bases and central neckings of acanthus, supporting a frame which open in two drawers resembling the cabinet; flat pendants, covered with very fine embossed silver, with the Queen's monogram repeated in the centre, complete the structure. The outer mouldings and flat stretcher are alternately inlaid with the light and dark coloured parts of the wood, the colour of the darker part being a rich olive brown. These remarkable cabinets were once the property of Queen Henrietta Maria, and were given by her, with other things, to her former Master of the Horse and reputed lover, Henry Jermyn, afterwards Earl of St Albans, who left them to his nephew, and they have remained at Rushbrooke Hall since that time. Jermyn accompanied the Queen during her exile in France. It was he who broke the news of Charles I's death to her, and there appears every reason to suppose that she was secretly united to him after this event. On Henrietta Maria's return to this country in 1660 the Parliament made her a large grant, and Somerset House, bestowed upon her as a residence, was decorated and furnished by her with great taste. It is probable that these cabinets formed part of the furniture, during her residence there from 1660 to 1665, and on her leaving this country again she gave them to Jermyn. They correspond in style and workmanship to furniture of about this date, and apart from their remarkable interest in being associated with this turned-down page of history, are most beautiful examples of English silver and cabinet work in combination.

CHAPTER II

AK bedsteads continued to be made during the reign of Charles II, more or less on the old lines, only lighter in form; those remaining from Elizabethan and Jacobean times being still in general use, though the plague and fire account for the destruction of nearly all such specimens in London. State beds and very important beds continued to be made in the upholstered style already described.

Fig. 235, a bed at Knole, associated with the name of Lady Betty Germaine, is a small and simple example of this kind; its original construction is, however, earlier than the hangings. The embroidery of the valances and curtains, in leaves of bold design worked in bright-coloured crewels, has been reapplied on to linen, the original shape of the hangings being preserved; the quilted cream silk linings to the back and valances are in their original state; the quilt and lower valances are composed of old materials. The bed-step at the foot, which has its original caning, is about the date 1675. A portion of a very fine English Turkey-work carpet of about 1600 is also shown in the illustration. It bears the Curzon arms, and belongs to Mary Curzon, who inherited the carpet from her father and married the fourth Earl of Dorset in 1611. She was governess to the children of Charles I.

A very perfect bed, in untouched condition, is given in Plate XVII. This was made in the reign of Charles II for Sir Dudley North, and is still at

Fig. 235. *Upholstered Bed*. Height, 8 feet 6 inches; width, 4 feet 3 inches. Property of Lord Sackville.

FIG. 236. *Upholstered Bed*. Height, 11 feet; length, 7 feet. Property of ROBERT W. J. RUSHBROOKE, Esq.

Glemham Hall, where he lived, and in possession of a member of the same family. The cornice to the tester headed by ostrich plumes, and the four bold mouldings, are covered in crimson velvet of the finest quality, and embroidered on the lower member with a delicate arabesque of flowers in cream-coloured silks; from this hangs a valance of crimson velvet with a deep border of white, buff and silver guipure and embroidery, edged with a thick fringe of brown, cream and tawny tassels; the valance is panelled at the corners with a very highly raised embroidery, the edges being frogged and looped. The ceiling of the tester is of cream embroidered satin, the back being in alternate plain and draped panels of the same, and the early scrolling above the pillows is also covered with cream satin; the quilt matches in material and design. The posts are small and octagonal, and were originally covered with cream satin; the feet finish in removable bases of scrolled design, painted and carved with gilded cherubs. This bed is of about the date 1670, and was slept in by Charles II.

Fig. 236 is another of these state beds, preserved in Rushbrooke Hall, and some few years later in date. Here the cornice to the tester has lost the early simplicity, and is composed of a series of beautiful flat scrolls covered in deep crimson velvet, alternating with large acanthus leaves of embroidered white velvet; the pleated velvet valances are headed, divided and bordered, with rich fringes of white and canary coloured tassels, the curtains and lower valance being treated in the same way; the ceiling of the tester and the elaborate scrolled and acanthus heading above the pillows are covered with white satin embroidered in a beautiful design, and edged with the white and canary coloured tasselled fringe; the quilt is a brilliant canary colour embroidered with flowers. The feet terminate in open-work scrolls painted black and gold. The whole bed is most rich and yet refined in colour; it is rather smaller than the preceding specimen, and was also slept in by Charles II.

By this time the bedrooms of the nobility were universally furnished with a degree of luxury that up till now had been confined to the few who had been remarkable for lavish expenditure, and the introduction of gorgeously upholstered chairs, cabinets and other articles of furniture into the bedrooms became general amongst the rich. We read in an extract from a document of the time, that at Kimbolton, in 1675, Robert, third Earl of Manchester, slept beneath an Indian quilted counterpane within yellow damask curtains, while no less than three elbow-chairs of yellow damask had arms open to receive him, and stools of the same bright hue were ready to support his feet. My lady reposed 'in a room hung with six peeces of haire, called silk watered moehaire, the bed hung with moehaire curtaines garnisht with Irish stitch and ffringe and four Irish stitch slips, all lined with white watered tabby, with counterpanes suitable to the bed, kept down by four guilt lyons' clawes'. The document goes on to say that the remainder of the furniture might have found place in the sleeping-chamber of a Queen. In other rooms there was a profusion of all needful furniture, and the little waiting-room near the great hall was hung 'with sadcullor bayes and had one pair of tables, tablemen and boxes, one chess bord and men, and one bord to play at fox and gouse'.

The three elbow-chairs of yellow damask, mentioned in the above quotation, would have had the tall padded backs that were now coming into fashion, supplanting those with carved and caned backs. Plate XVIII is of this type and one of a set of six, made to match the Dudley North bed in Plate XVII, and formed part of the furniture of the state bedroom. The back and seat are upholstered in the identical crimson velvet, and tawny and brown tasselled fringe of the bed. The arms and their supports are scrolled, and the sides of the former are gilt and carved with an egg and tongue moulding, the plain surfaces being painted cream with a delicate pattern of coloured flowers like the rest of the bed; the front legs are of pronounced scroll form, cherub-headed, and finish in scrolled feet also painted and gilt; the stretcher is composed of recumbent angels with trumpets, surrounded by the usual ornamentation of the time. The effect of these chairs and bed, with tall gilt looking-glasses and black Japan cabinets against the tapestry hangings would be very representative of the best bedroom in a fine country-house at this period.

A plainer and later variety of these chairs is Fig. 237. Here the rake of the back is more emphasised, and the arms, front legs and stretcher are simple, with but little carving; the whole of the wood-work has been painted black and decorated with a delicate flower pattern in gold lacquer; its date is about 1680; it does not possess its original covering. Fig. 238 is a specimen that shows in embryo the side ears that became so popular on easy-chairs during the next century. The back is upholstered, but retains the early cresting, which is composed of two broad flat scrolls surmounted by a ducal crown, carved in a very large but masterly style; below this, on each side, spread the small ears, upholstered only on the inner side, and carved on the outer with a cherub and acanthus; the rake of the back is excessive, and the arms are unusually long; the seat-rail is carved in a waved moulding. Fig. 239 is one of a set of six chairs, made to match the bed (Fig. 236). They are covered with the same deep crimson velvet, and the arrangement of fringes corresponds to the valances of the bed; the date of both chairs and bed is between 1680 and 1685, and this is shown by the outward curve to the plain scrolls of the arms and the protuberance of the whorl, in which these and the feet finish. The arm supports and legs are of strong cabriole form, carved in plain mouldings, and show an interesting evolution from the perforated Chinese leg of this character found on the stands to the lac cabinets imported with so many other Oriental objects at this time.

An interesting ruin, still later in date, also from Rushbrooke, is given in Fig. 240. Here the outward curve in the arms is still more pronounced, and the supports and the legs are perpendicular; the double caps, the upper of

FIG. 237. *Walnut Chair.* Property of the Hon Charlotte Maria Lady North and R. Eden Dickson, Esq.

FIG. 238. *Walnut Arm-chair.* Property of S. Campbell Cory, Esq.

FIG. 239. *Walnut Chair.* Property of Robert W. J. Rushbrooke, Esq.

FIG. 240. *Walnut Chair.* Property of ROBERT W. J. RUSHBROOKE, Esq.

which are perforated, are strongly Chinese in feeling; the remains of the serpentine stretcher and the ball feet denote the change introduced with the accession of William III. This chair is covered in azure blue velvet, and thickly and gracefully trimmed with a richly tasselled fringe of the same colour.

Fig. 241 represents two chairs at Ham House, about the date 1673, described in an inventory of the time as 'sleeping chairs'. The backs, sides and seats are padded and covered with satin, which is the colour of a scarlet cherry, figured with gold. The backs have deep sides, and can be tilted to an angle by a steel ratchet; their tops are of engrailed form, and together with the sides and seat are trimmed with a gold fringe fixed on with gilt nails. The arms, which are straight and padded, are supported on a twist, continued in the legs below, finishing in feet formed as sea-horses. The front stretchers are decorated with infant bacchanals finely carved, the other stretchers being plain and bold in their curves; all the wood-work is gilt. Although a great deal of upholstered furniture of this time exists with its original covering, it is generally to be found composed of velvet, for the satins, being more delicate, have perished. The alcove in which these chairs stand is decorated in the taste of 1675, and the piece of tapestry bearing the Duke of Lauderdale's arms is of Mortlake manufacture. These actual chairs were used by the Duke of Lauderdale and Elizabeth Dysart, his second wife, when discussing the schemes of the Cabal. Burnet wrote at the time of Elizabeth Dysart, 'that she was wanting in no methods that could bring her money, which she lavished out in a most profuse vanity, and that she came

FIG. 241. *Alcove with Walnut Chairs – Gilt.* Height of chairs, 4 feet 5 inches; width, 2 feet 3 inches. Property of the EARL OF DYSART.

to have so much power over the Lord Lauderdale, that it lessened him much in the esteem of all the world'. On the death of his first wife, she married the Duke in 1671; these chairs are about that date, and formed part of the rich furniture that this remarkable woman accumulated round her. The floor of the room, of most elaborate parquet, is interwoven with her initials and those of the Duke, and the walls are covered with the same red and gold figured satin as the chairs, which, according to the inventory, were re-upholstered, on the occasion of Queen Catherine's visit to Ham House.

Fig. 242 is a chair, similar in type, of about the date 1685. The back and sides are in this case a fixture; it has the original covering of crimson velvet, now much worn, and is richly edged with a silk fringe of cherry and cream coloured tassels; the arm supports and front legs are short, and the scrolling is rich and effective. The knees are carved in low relief in the later style of Charles II, the front stretcher being a rich combination of small C scrolls, centring in a bunch of flowers.

Elaborate and handsome fringes are a very distinctive and characteristic mark in upholstery from the middle of the seventeenth century. Many of these patterns were of foreign importation, and the series on Figs. 243 and 244 are illustrations taken from old existing specimens. The earlier fringes of the sixteenth century were straight and simple, with important headings, sometimes elaborately netted. The first tassels introduced hung distinct, and were of twisted silk. In Fig. 243 *A*, the straight little fringe of about 1560 has a velvet and knotted edging; *B* is Elizabethan, and of the kind much used on important beds; it is composed of a series of flowers with raised and separate petals, and scrolls in needlework, applied on to a netted ground of silk and gold thread; such a fringe would to-day cost about £10 a yard to make. Those lettered *C, D, E* and *F* are of the beginning of the seventeenth century; in *G* and *H* the netted heading is made of more importance, and is Spanish in type, *I* is a French fringe of about 1630; *K* and *L* are of the middle of the same

Fig. 242. *Walnut Arm-chair*. Height, 4 feet 1 inch; width of seat, 2 feet 1 inch. Property of Lord Sackville.

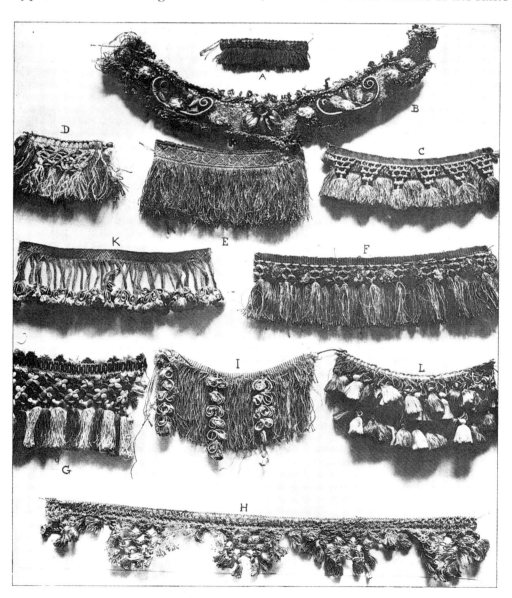

Fig. 243. *Sixteenth- and Seventeenth-century Fringes*. Property of Messrs Morant.

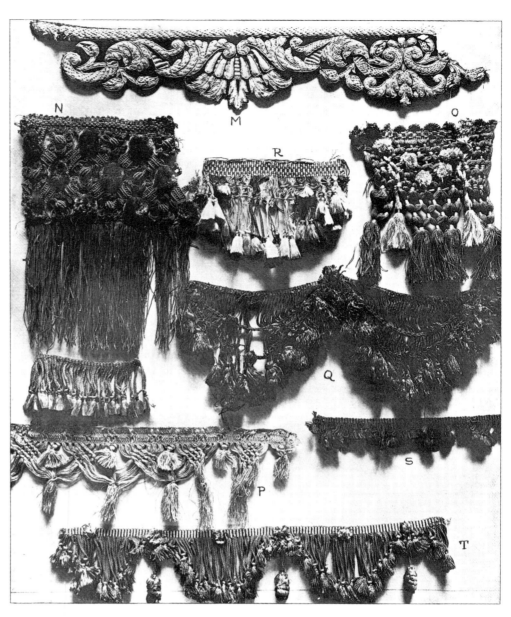

FIG. 244. *Seventeenth-century Fringes.*
Property of MESSRS MORANT.

century, and show the commencement of the floss silk tassels. On Fig. 244, *M* is an edging of a flowing design, worked in white silk and silver, on a ground of crimson velvet, whilst *N, O, P* have headings elaborately corded and netted, and embellished with small round tufts of floss silk; *Q, R, S* and *T* are frindges of the type found on the furniture of Charles II and until the end of the seventeenth century.

A large quantity of the silks, velvets, fringes, etc. employed both for furniture and dress, were made in this country. In 1638 a proclamation was issued, stating that if English men and women must buy silk, to buy it of home manufacture. The stuffs mentioned are gold and silver tissues, tuftafaties, plushes, velvets, damasks, wrought grograines, silk, mohair, figured satins, etc., and a prohibition was made against making goods of silk mixed with cotton. After a list, enumerating the ordinary and more brilliant colours, for which legitimate and permanent dyes could be used come 'Sadd colors, the following, liver color, De Roy, tawney, purple, French greene, ginger lyne, hare color, deere color, orange and graine color.' In 1681 letters of naturalisation were granted to French Huguenot refugee silk-weavers, and between the years 1670 and 1690, 80,000 people belonging to these textile industries landed in England, and as by 1689, 40,000 families were living by silk-weaving, we may very safely assume that a great part of the fabrics and fringes used in covering the furniture of this period was manufactured in England.

About 1668 mention is made by a foreign traveller here of the greater opportunities afforded in this country for conviviality by rounded dining-tables. He no doubt alluded to another and larger version of the flap-table of Jacobean times, introduced now with two flaps, and called a gate-table. Fig. 245, of walnut, is about the time of the great fire; it stands upon eight legs, fine both in turning and proportion. Fig. 246 is of oak, with the stretchers all

FIG. 245. *Walnut Table.* Height, 2 feet 6 inches; width, 3 feet 1 inch.

FIG. 246. *Oak Table.* Length, 5 feet 10 inches; height, 2 feet 6 inches. Property of DR CHARLES EASTWICK FIELD.

radiating to the centre, and with somewhat coarser twist, whilst in Fig. 247, of about the date 1675, the first subdivision of the table can be noticed, and with the addition of middle portion or portions, could be converted from a round to an oval table. Such a table is mentioned in the travels of Cosmo III, Duke of Tuscany, at a supper he gave in his lodgings to Charles II in 1669. An extract from the description of the ceremony is given, and it is interesting to note that stools were evidently still the usual form of seat for meals, in this country.

'The staircase was lighted by torches which were carried before and close to His Majesty, he was preceded by one of his Highnesses' gentlemen with a candle to the saloon appointed for the supper. From the ceiling was suspended a chandelier of rock cristal with lighted tapers. In the middle of the room the table was set out, being of oval figure, convenient both for seeing and conversing. At the upper end was placed on a carpet a splendid arm-chair, and in front of it by themselves, a knife and fork tastefully disposed for his Majesty, but he ordered the chair to be removed, and a stool without a back, according to the custom of the country, and in all respects similar to those of the rest of the company, to be put in its place. Other guests to the number of 17 were accommodated round the table, and the entertainment was most superb, the supper being served up in 80 magnificient dishes.'

Of the smaller tables, Fig. 248 is an early specimen of the gate-table variety, of about 1650; it has six legs, which are fretted out of flat material, the centre legs being mounted on to a broad base and stretcher.

FIG. 247. *Walnut Table.* Height, 2 feet 6 inches; width, 4 feet 4 inches. Property of SIR FRANCIS BURDETT, Bart.

FIG. 248. *Oak Table.* Height, 2 feet 2 inches; length of top, 3 feet 10 inches; width, 2 feet 2 inches. Property of T. CHARBONNIER, Esq.

FIG. 249. *Walnut Table*. Length, 2 feet 2 inches; height, 2 feet 5 inches; width, 2 feet.

FIG. 250. *Oak Table*. Property of C. E. KEMPE, Esq.

Of small square Carolean tables, Fig. 249 is also an early example, about the date 1665; the arrangement of the high stretcher and the long twist is unusual. The single twist table (Fig. 250) is of oak, about the date 1675; the flat serpentine stretcher was introduced at this time. Another small table of this period and character is Fig. 251. In this the legs, stretcher, top and sides are painted black, and lacquered with imitation Chinese drawing in the taste of the time. The purposes which called forth so many of these small tables at this period have already been explained.

A small side-table, with panelled front and sides, and a well-moulded capping, is shown in Fig. 252. The legs, seven in number, are original in their arrangement, and the serpentine curves of the flat stretcher give charming variety to the base. The introduction of the pendants show that the piece is of quite the end of Charles II's reign.

FIG. 251. *Lacquer Table*. Property of ROBERT W. J. RUSHBROOKE, Esq.

FIG. 252. *Walnut Side-table*. Height, 2 feet 10 inches; length, 5 feet 3 inches. Property of the REV J. O. STEVENS.

CHAPTER III

BOUT 1675, small tables, clocks and certain other forms of furniture began to be ornamented by marqueterie, and this revived style of decoration is a very distinctive mark in the change of taste. It differed from early marqueterie in the process of construction, the pattern, together with the background, being now laid down as a veneer, and for this reason the shapes of inlaid furniture of this period are frequently sacrificed in order to obtain suitable flat surfaces. It is impossible to state the exact date when this revival of marqueterie began. At first the design of acanthus-leaved arabesques and birds, inlaid in brown and buff coloured woods, was probably inspired by the Italian inlay of the time, whilst that representing flowers and birds in the altogether more realistic manner produced rather later, was of Dutch inspiration. These two styles amalgamated towards the end of the reign of William; then by degrees the flowers were left out of the design, and the marqueteries became an intricate series of very fine scrolls. The observance of this evolution will be found a certain way of dating these late seventeenth-century pieces.

Fig. 253 is the top of a table, having the usual twisted legs, of about the date 1675. The surface is divided by a broad band of walnut into the Jacobean arrangement of an oval centre and four triangular corners; and this subdivision, with the spaces filled with marqueterie, is found universally continued on table-tops and chests of drawers until the end of the century. In this instance the design is formed of foliated arabesque terminating in flowers, the pattern being of walnut on a ground of light wood; the triangular compartments have sprays of the same design issuing from cornucopia, a very favourite filling to the narrow corners of these panels. The birds represented on all this marqueterie are generally of the parrot tribe; occasionally other birds form the leading motive, with the scrolling starting from their wings or tail. Plate XIX is a chest of drawers decorated in this manner; the face of the drawers is inlaid with oval panels, an arrangement found on all these marqueterie chests of drawers; the birds represent eagles, dark on a light ground. The top of this chest, shown on the same plate, is inlaid with marqueterie of similar design; the coarseness of the laurel borders, with the conventional treatment of birds and flowers, point to a date before 1680; the decorated drop-handles, with their rose-shaped plates, are contemporary. The original stand to this piece is missing, and the feet are restorations.

In cutting these marqueterie patterns, the ground was not wasted, and Fig. 254 shows a chest of drawers of the same design, and probably by the

FIG. 253. *Top of Walnut Table Inlaid with Marqueterie.* Property of the VISCOUNTESS WOLSELEY.

FIG. 254. *Walnut Inlaid Chest of Drawers.* Height, 3 feet 2 inches; width, 3 feet 1 inch; depth, 1 foot 11 inches. Property of J. F. SNOOK, Esq.

FIG. 255. *Marqueterie Chest of Drawers.* Property of MESSRS J. MALLETT AND SON.

FIG. 256. *Walnut Inlaid Clock.* Property of the HON CHARLOTTE MARIA LADY NORTH and R. EDEN DICKSON, Esq.

FIG. 257. *Walnut Inlaid Clock.* Property of the GROCERS' COMPANY.

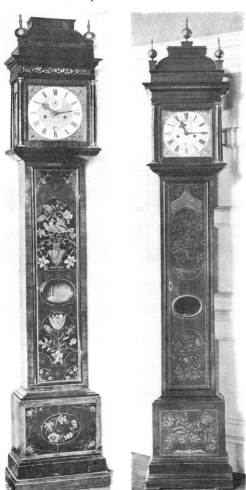

same hand, as Plate XIX, in which the dark wood cut away from the birds, becomes the ground, and vice versâ. Another example of this early scrolled marqueterie is Fig. 255, where an additional charm is given to the flowing lines of the inlay by the employment of other colours besides the brown, buff and black wood used in the preceding specimens, and an extremely rich effect is produced by the introduction of deep reds and greens amidst the quieter colours. The appreciation of colour in furniture was still further developed in the marqueterie which immediately followed. This consisted of sprays, groups of flowers and birds, in woods stained to resemble the colour of these objects, with leaves of green-stained bone or ivory; jessamine flowers, in bone and ivory, were also frequently introduced. The clock (Fig. 256) made by John Ebsworth about 1678 is an early example of Dutch influence; the flowers are somewhat formal and separate in their arrangement, and the panels containing them are set well apart, more space being devoted to the walnut ground-work than the inlay. The distribution of this floral marqueterie is a sure index of its date. Another clock (Fig. 257), made by Richard Ayres, presented to the Grocers' Company by Phineas Shower, Druggist, in 1683, shows a rather more realistic treatment of the flowers, but the spaces between the panels are still wide; the columns and the bandings are of ebony. This clock case bears the original brass plate engraved with the date of presentation to the Company, and this conclusively settles the period of its inlay.

The cases of these so-called Grandfather clocks originated in a desire to conceal the weights and pendulum of the so-called 'sheep's head and pluck' clocks that were fixed on the walls, and made during the first half of the seventeenth century. These clock cases quickly assumed the characteristics of movable and very decorative pieces of furniture. The early specimens were narrow in shape, and more graceful in proportion, than the elaborately decorated, and later forms.

The table-top (Fig. 258) is contemporary with the first of these two clocks, and the arrangement of the marqueterie is similar in character. The ground to the inlay is ebony, in which leaves are represented by brilliantly green-stained ivory, and the breasts of the birds and centres of the flowers are stained a deep red; the walnut ground between the panels is cut plain, and the banding of the ovals and corners is narrow; the distribution of design is open throughout, and the legs and stretcher resemble those of the following table. A further step of decoration in this interesting English marqueterie is shown in this table (Fig. 259), a little later in date, and of the last years of the

FIG. 258. *Top of Marqueterie Table.* Length, 2 feet 8 inches; width, 1 foot 11 inches. Property of PERCY MACQUOID, Esq.

FIG. 259. *Top of Marqueterie Table.* Property of SIR GEORGE DONALDSON.

reign of Charles II; the banding between the panels has become broader, in order to accommodate the so-called oyster shells of walnut of which the veneer is composed; these were taken from the boughs, sliced up into transverse sections, and were for many years a favourite feature on English walnut furniture. In this table it will be noticed that the flowers, which are inlaid on ebony, are more elaborate and less conventional, and that the jessamine flower in white ivory is introduced with green leaves of the same material; the other parts are of bleached walnut, and the legs (Fig. 260) form an open and early twist centring in a ball, and finish in a serpentine stretcher of the time. This original and intentional bleaching of walnut is also seen on the little chest of drawers and stand (Fig. 261); the top is almost identical with the last table, to which it corresponds in date, and the same design is repeated in oval panels on the face of the drawers, the ground being formed of oyster-pieces of walnut. The stand is formed of one long drawer on short twisted legs, and the stretcher is further ornamented by the addition of two heart-shaped panels of inlay. Fig. 262 is another of different design and coarser make. This marqueterie was generally laid down on deal, the drawers being of oak, and the half-rounded walnut mouldings being about a quarter of an inch thick.

It can be easily understood that these brilliant and remarkable tables and chests of drawers called forth a demand for cabinets of the same description,

FIG. 260. *Walnut Table Inlaid with Marqueterie.* Property of SIR GEORGE DONALDSON.

FIG. 261. *Walnut and Marqueterie Chest of Drawers.* Length, 3 feet 2 inches; height, 3 feet 5 inches; depth, 1 foot 10 inches. Property of MESSRS J. MALLETT AND SON.

FIG. 262. *Walnut and Marqueterie Chest of Drawers.* Property of MESSRS MORANT.

and Plate XX represents one of these on its original stand. The cornice surmounts an ovolo frieze, a universal feature on the cabinets at this time; it lies between two bands of waved inlay, and is faced with walnut oyster-pieces, framing two panels of flowers in coloured woods and green ivory; the doors beneath are edged with a sand-burnt laurelling (which after this date continued to be a favourite design and border in marqueterie), and the oval bands surrounding the centre are veneered with transverse sections of laburnum wood. It can be seen in the other panels that the cornucopia, from which the flowers start, are fringed with the same acanthus introduced in the centre, an indication of the amalgamation of the two styles of marqueterie, floral and acanthus. The inside of these doors are inlaid with macaws, perched on cherry boughs, in deep rich reds and browns, and bordered with narrow bands of sycamore framed in oyster-pieces, which are again edged with walnut veneer cut on the straight. The inner face of the cabinet opens in ten drawers decorated like the frieze, and a cupboard, which again opens on a further compartment filled with four drawers, enclosing still further a small secret drawer; the macaws are repeated on the sides of the cabinet. The stand is headed by two drawers, supported on five legs gracefully twisted, resting upon a curved stretcher, the square blocks that serve as feet being the only portion of the cabinet not in its original condition. In this piece, every advantage has been taken of the different colours and cuttings afforded by walnut, and its preservation is so perfect, that the colour and general appearance can have altered but little since it was made.

Judged by the standard of cultivated taste, isolated specimens of this Charles II furniture may at first sight seem somewhat gaudy, but elaborated notes in decoration have always been introduced as a setting, when clothes without pattern were in fashion; the employment of brilliant damasks and velvets upon the wall also demanded vivacity in the accompanying furniture, and this variety must have been well thought out as a background for the occupants of these rooms. The King himself almost invariably wore black when indoors, and nearly every portrait of this time represents the red-lipped and ringleted beauties of the Court dressed in brilliant-coloured satins. The flowered tabby dresses, which Pepys mentions as so becoming to his wife, were evidently somewhat of an exception, and perhaps only for out-of-door wear. This affectation of simplicity in dress was carried into the ruffles, which at this time were composed only of fine lawn; but simplicity was confined to such details, all else that surrounded these people was ornate; even the tall Charles II wall panels, that now seem so plain, were in those days earlier painted with landscapes, mythological subjects, or in imitation of coloured marbles. Celia Fiennes mentions in her diary that at Wilton

'There is a drawing roome and antiroome, ye wanscote is painted with ye whole History of ye Acadia romance made by Sir Philip Sidney.' Also, 'There are three or four dining roomes and drawing roomes of state with very good bed-chambers and well furnished; damaske and tissue.'

About Burghley she writes:

'My Ldy's Closet is ver ffine, the wanscote of the best Jappan, the cushions very rich work, there is a chamber My Lady used to Lye in, in the winter, a green velvet bed and the hangings are all Embroydery of her Mother's work very ffine.'

At Agnes Burton she mentions

'A very good little parlour with plain wainscote painted in veines like marble, dark and white streakes.'

Some rooms, however, continued to be wainscoted with different coloured woods, or carved with elaborate festoons of birds, fruit and flowers in the manner of Gibbon and his pupils, and when at Lord Orford's at Newmarket, this same enterprising young lady remarks, that

'The Hall is wanscoated with wall nut tree—the pannells and Rims round with mulberry tree, yt is a Lemon Coullour and ye mouldings beyond it round are of a sweete outlandish wood not much differing from Cedar but of a finer graine, the Chaires are all the same. The whole house if finely furnish'd with differing coulld Damaske and velvets, some ffigured and others plaine, at least 6 or 7 Richly made up after a new mode. In ye best drawing roome was a very Riche hanging, gold and silver and a little scarlet, mostly tissue and brocade of gold and silver and border of green damaske round it; ye window curtain ye same greene round it and doore curtains.'

'The sweet outlandish wood 'she refers to would probably have been yew,
    Of another part of this same house she writes:

'The roomes were all well wanscoated and hung, and there was ye finest Carved wood in fruitages, herbages, gumms, beasts, fowles, etc., very thinn and fine, all in white wood without paint or varnish; there was a great flower pott Gilt Each side of the Chimney in the dineing Roome for to sett trees in. There is very fine China and silver things and irons and jars and perfume potts of silver.'

Celia Fiennes took several tours on horseback through England in William and Mary's reign, and her impressions of the later forms of decoration and furniture of Charles's time are most interesting and reliable.

In addition to all these decorations on the wall, quantities of portriaits, fresh and bright in colour, were painted at this time, so that all these brilliant methods formed a varied background, which it is necessary to realise before attempting to criticise the taste of floral marqueterie.

In the cabinet (Fig. 263), which is about the date of the accession of William III, the jessamine forms a prominent detail in the design; the bandings and edgings of the green ivory leaves are foliated as in Plate XX. In the centre of the doors, acanthus in brown and yellow woods is introduced round a rather elaborate vase; the insides of the doors centre in lion masks. This cabinet originally stood upon a chest of drawers of similar workmanship, or a stand with twisted legs, which is now missing. The jessamine flower and green bone leaves are again very apparent in the chest of drawers (Fig. 265), of which the stand is also missing; but in Fig. 266 a quieter form of this same marqueterie is shown, where the jessamine flower is introduced, but in buff

Fig. 263. *Walnut and Marqueterie Cabinet.* Property of H. Martin Gibbs, Esq.

Fig. 264. *The same Cabinet, Open.* Property of H. Martin Gibbs, Esq.

wood, the other woods used being brown and blacks. The stand to this, which is probably a few years later than the chest, is a very early example of the cabriole leg. This quiet form of bird and floral inlay, with the foreign influence still visible, ran contemporaneously with the highly coloured varieties. The cabinet (Fig. 267) evidently formed part of the same suite of furniture as the last chest of drawers, and both were made about 1690; the marqueterie shows very clearly the union and predominance of acanthus over the varied flowers of the previous years; the form also marks an innovation in construction – that of a writing cabinet supported on a chest of drawers. The frieze, of ovolo shape, is inlaide with the usual two panels, and below this a large and heavy flap of oak veneered with walnut and marqueterie lets down, disclosing a series of eleven inlaid drawers, a cupboard and eight pigeon-holes; the design on the flap consists of one large and four small corner panels, so that when closed, as in Fig. 268, the design is carried out into the drawers beneath; the sides are also decorated with large inlaid panels. The internal structure is entirely of oak, and the handles and key-plates have the cherubim's heads, that were introduced about 1690. It is rare to find this exact form of furniture decorated with English floral marqueterie.

A lace box, given in Fig. 269, is of the same type and period. The inside is divided into compartments lined with pink silk, and the lid is fitted with a glass. Many of these boxes were made at this time, and they much resemble each other, except in the character of the veneer; they were usually made to

Fig. 265. *Walnut and Marqueterie Chest of Drawers.* Property of C. E. Kempe, Esq.

FIG. 266. *Walnut and Marqueterie Chest of Drawers.* Property of the DUKE OF BEAUFORT.

FIG. 267. *Walnut and Marqueterie Writing Cabinet.* Height, 4 feet 4 inches; width, 3 feet 6 inches; depth, 1 foot 6 inches. Property of the DUKE OF BEAUFORT.

FIG. 268. *Same Cabinet, Closed.* Property of the DUKE OF BEAUFORT.

FIG. 269. *Walnut and Marqueterie Lace Box.* 2 feet by 1 foot 6 inches. Property of Messrs J. Mallett and Son.

match the chests of drawers on which they were intended to stand.

Fig. 270 is a cabinet with doors and inner drawers of similar construction to Fig. 263, but possesses its original stand in the shape of a chest of drawers. The open distribution of the marqueterie infers a date of about 1687; the colour is subdued in tone, the leaves being composed of wood stained an olive green, and the artificial bleaching of the walnut bands gives great variety to the quiet shades of fawn employed in the veneer. Macaws, similar to those found on Plate XX, are introduced on the inside of the doors; the design of the marqueterie throughout is attractive, simple and not over-crowded in its long flowing lines. The bun-feet are contemporary with the piece. Fig. 271 is the upper portion with the doors open.

In the very elaborate cabinet faced with ebony (Fig. 272) it will be noticed the marqueterie design has become closer and more involved, and that the flowers form a border to the central panels of the doors on which butterflies are represented in addition to the usual birds; a broad edging was introduced from Holland about 1695. The design on the inside of the cabinet (Fig. 273) closely resembles those already given, and the leaves throughout are represented in the green ivory; the sides of the little central cupboard are also inlaid, and finish at the back in three drawers. This cabinet bears the strongest foreign influence, but the joinery, etc., are of English workmanship.

The question naturally arises, How far does this foreign influence go, and what are the distinguishing features between English and foreign marqueterie? Much of the English work has erroneously been ascribed to the latter manufacture, and it is a very usual way out of the difficulty to assign uncommon specimens that cannot easily be classed to foreign sources. A little deliberation will show that importation on a scale large enough to supply all that is supposed to have come from abroad at the date of manufacture would have been difficult and expensive, and impossible during times of war. A very large number of English cabinet-makers and artisans existed by the manufacture of high-class furniture, and these numbers were continually supplemented by talented French craftsmen, who sought the protection of this country against the religious intolerance of their own, and who, whilst working in conjunction with the Englishman, could not help asserting their own individual taste.

In foreign marqueterie a curved surface on the furniture is of frequent occurrence, and the general tone is that of a strong colour on a black or dark ground; or lightly stained flowers with the leaves of green-stained wood on a red-brown walnut ground; the inlay of light colour on a light sycamore ground was seldom attempted. In the drawing of the acanthus or endive

FIG. 270 *(left)*. *Walnut and Marqueterie Cabinet.* Height, 5 feet 9 inches; width, 3 feet 11 inches. Property of W. S. Curtis, Esq.

FIG. 271 *(below)*. *Top of same Cabinet, Open.* Property of W. S. Curtis, Esq.

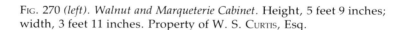

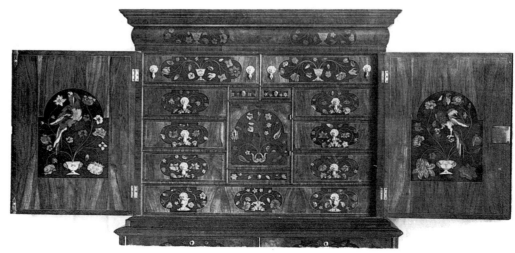

Fig. 272. *Ebony and Marqueterie Cabinet.* Height, 4 feet; length, 3 feet 1 inch. Property of the Earl of Dysart.

Fig. 273. *Same Cabinet, Open.* Property of the Earl of Dysart.

pattern, the points to the leaves are blunt, as opposed to sharper points found on English work, the sprays more complicated, and the 'shadowing' on these and the flowers is in Dutch, French and Italian marqueterie far more elaborate; the borders are also more often of black-stained wood, and the birds represented are in stronger action than in English specimens, and although in the latter, cherubs and sphinx forms are occasionally repre-sented, the introduction of figures, as on the specimen (Fig. 270), is rare. A great difference lies also in the dovetailing and joinery of the internal work-manship, and in the different cutting of the veneers.

IT has been already shown that the stool was a very useful and important piece of furniture in former reigns, and even as late as William III, the usual seat for meals. In Charles II's reign many elaborate and upholstered stools were introduced for the sitting-rooms; and some of these in their original condition are in existence. In the ante-rooms and passages of the palaces, these upholstered stools quickly took the place of the chests and coffers, hitherto used as seats, but in the drawing-rooms and presence-chamber of the Court itself, they served a different purpose, for their use there implied distinction; this custom had been gradually introduced from the Court of Versailles, where the right to use a 'tabouret' in the presence-chamber was permitted to no one of lower rank than a duchess, and was the greatest honour that could be bestowed upon a Frenchwoman by Louis XIV. Even in ordinary households, the use of a chair was by no means yet extended to the younger members of a family. Sometimes stools were made in sets of six or more; at Hampton Court Palace, and in some of the very large houses, these sets are to be found in their original condition.

FIG. 274. *Walnut Seat*. Property of SIR GEORGE DONALDSON.

Fig. 274 is a long seat of stool form made to match the tall cane-backed chairs of 1670 and originally cane-seated to carry a squab; in this instance the seat has been re-upholstered in needlework of the time; the C scrolling of the legs is so pronounced that the corners are placed angleways as in the chair (Fig. 227). The number of seats on occasions must still have been limited even at this date, and we can only presume were moved with the families to their different residences. Pepys gives an account of an important entertainment at the Duke of York's, on which occasion the furniture was evidently elsewhere. He writes on 4 March 1669:

'And so walked to Deptford, and there to the Treasurers house where the Duke of York is, and his Duchess, and there we find them at dinner in the great room, unhung; and there was with them my Lady Duchess of Monmouth, the Countess of Falmouth, Castlemayne, Henrietta Hide, and my Lady Peterborough. And after dinner Sir Jer. Smith and I were invited down to dinner with some of the maids of honor. Having dined and very merry etc. . . . and so we up; and there I did find the Duke of York and Duchess, with all the great ladies, sitting upon a carpet, on the ground, there being no chairs, playing at "I love my love with an A, because he is so and so, and I hate him with an A, because of this and that'; and some of them but particularly the Duchess herself, and my Lady Castlemayne were very witty.'

Pepys, however, in his Diary makes but little mention of furniture in detail, and in two instances only does he name a price for what he bought. On 1 July 1661, he writes:

'This morning I went up and down into the city to buy several things, as I have lately done for my house; among other things, a fair chest of drawers for my own chamber, and an Indian gown for myself, the first cost me 33s., and the other 34s.'

FIG. 275. *Walnut Seat*. Length, 4 feet 4 inches; depth, 1 foot 6 inches; height, 1 foot 10 inches. Property of the DUKE OF DEVONSHIRE.

In April 1666, he grumbles at having to pay 'near £40 for a set of chairs and couch'.

Fig. 275 is a stool from a set at Hardwick, of about the date 1678. The frame is plain save for isolated spaces of carving in low relief, and similar to that employed on the frames of portraits at this time; the squab is original and upholstered in crimson velvet now much worn. The legs, terminating in octagonal bun-feet, are more marked in their scroll than the illustration infers, but become straight towards the feet, a fashion that was now suggesting itself; the stretcher, bold and original, rises towards the centre, and in the coarse C scrolls the dolphin origin is clearly observable. Fig. 276 is one of a set of smaller stools of similar design but of more uncommon shape, being round; some traces of silver embroidery still remain on the original squab.

Fig. 277, long and short stools of elaborate workmanship and of about the date 1680, form part of another set also at Hardwick; the fronts of both are richly decorated with very elaborate carving, in which the flat scrolls are almost concealed by curled acanthus and representations of roses and other flowers strongly suggestive of Gibbon, or Gibbons, as he was afterwards called. The legs are also wreathed with flowers, the whole of the wood-work has been gilt in the eighteenth century, and the seats have been re-upholstered. Fig. 278 shows a long stool at Hampton Court Palace, of which

FIG. 276. *Walnut Stool*. Height, 1 foot, 10 inches. Property of the DUKE OF DEVONSHIRE.

FIG. 277. *Walnut Seat and Stool, Gilt*. Seat – length, 6 feet; height, 1 foot 6 inches; depth, 1 foot 10 inches. Stool – length, 2 feet 6 inches; height, 1 foot 6 inches.

FIG. 278. *Walnut Seat and Stool*. HAMPTON COURT PALACE.

FIG. 279. *Walnut Stool*. HAMPTON COURT PALACE.

FIG. 280. *Walnut Stool*. Property of the DUKE OF LEEDS.

FIG. 281. *Walnut Stool*. Property of the DUKE OF DEVONSHIRE.

FIG. 282. *Walnut Stool*. Property of FRANK GREEN, Esq.

FIG. 283. *Walnut Settee*. Length, 6 feet. Property of J. FRANCIS SNOOK, Esq.

there are several, forming part of the suite to the bed used by Queen Anne. The form of these stools is, however, earlier than this bed, and they were probably re-upholstered about the date of Anne's accession. The small carved stool in the same illustration is of the end of the reign of Charles II, and is covered with the same velvet; both these stools would have been trimmed with tasselled fringes, now replaced by gimp of much later date.

After 1680, it will be observed that the stretchers to stools are serpentine and often centre in a turned finial. Fig. 279 is a specimen of small size from Hampton Court Palace, with the original covering of cherry-coloured damask and tasselled fringe, looped at the corners and centres in the style of late Charles II. The legs have an inward scroll ending in perpendicular feet, and the stretcher rises up to a central finial. Fig. 280 is a few years later in date, about 1690, with the original covering of yellow and green velvet of English manufacture; the border of the frame is carved in low relief and gilt; the legs, square in form, are decorated in a similar manner, the ground-work being painted black. The introduction of black and gold paint on walnut furniture was adopted at this time, in order to harmonise with the cabinets and tables of lacquer-work that were now becoming fashionable. The majority of walnut furniture was, however, left in the natural colour of the wood, and Fig. 281 is a stool from Hardwick of about 1690, simple and beautiful in design, and in the taste which was by that time slowly growing more restrained and classical. The frame of this stool is cornered and centred with both acanthus; the caps to the square legs, which gradate rapidly towards the feet, are carved with the same effective nulling found upon the contemporary silver plate; the stretcher is delicate and centres in a tall finial; the covering to the seat is of red velvet, now almost perished, with a centre band of highly raised silver embroidery. Fig. 282 represents a stool made during the first years of William III's reign; in this instance there is no carving, but a great charm is conveyed by accuracy of proportion, and well-considered facets of the wood that reflect the light; it has been re-upholstered.

Walnut settees of late Cromwellian and early Restoration type are rare; they resemble the simple turned chairs of the period. Fig. 283 is a specimen of about 1658 made in walnut, the stretchers and front legs being turned in ball and ring fashion similar to the stand of the Henrietta Maria cabinet (Fig. 234). It has been re-upholstered. In its original state it would have been covered with either Turkey-work or leather.

The settees and chairs of the latter part of the seventeenth century were evidently constructed with a view of forming backgrounds to the prevailing fashions in costume; the strongest characteristics at this time being an extremely high-backed seat to suit the voluminous periwigs and tall head-dresses of the women. Fig. 284 resembles two tall upholstered chairs joined in one, on the principle of the smaller double chair or love-seat, the back being conspicuously higher than the sitter's head. The legs and stretchers, composed of simple scrolls, repeat the details of the chairs of 1675, with

FIG. 284. *Walnut Upholstered Settee.* Length, 4 feet 2 inches; height, 3 feet 9 inches. Property of LORD SACKVILLE.

which this settee is contemporary; the covering is a white, green and blue Genoa velvet of eighteenth-century design, but in recovering this interesting piece of furniture the cushion has been made much higher than in its original state. Another of these rare settees of double-chair shape is Fig. 285, of about the date 1685; this introduces upholstered wings and arms of outward and scrolled form; the front stretcher is composed of bold scrolls; parti-gilt; the legs are perpendicular, with peg-top shoulders; the damask, with which the seat is covered, is not contemporary with the piece, and the squab is missing; it was originally covered with a purple and white Genoa velvet, but the fringe and galon trimming are all that now remain of this upholstery.

Plate XXI is a double-backed settee of unusual form. The headings of the back resemble chairs of the date 1690; it is from a set at Hornby Castle. The wings of this settee finish on the outside in spiral whorls, and the arms roll over as in the example from Penshurst, finishing below in an outward and forward scroll; the wood-work is painted black, the carved ornament being gilt; it has the original covering of rich Genoa velvet of blue, black and brown on a cream ground, the divided squab being a usual adjunct at that time.

FIG. 285. *Walnut Upholstered Settee.* Property of LORD DE LISLE AND DUDLEY.

FIG. 286. *Walnut Upholstered Settee.* Property of the DUKE OF LEEDS.

FIG. 287. *Walnut Upholstered Settee*. Property of the DUKE OF LEEDS.

This very scarce piece of furniture is in its original condition, the two side cushions only are missing. Such cushions are shown in Fig. 286, a settee not quite so elaborate in form. The stretcher, which is missing, would have been of serpentine form, centring in a finial, and the design will be seen on a chair given later belonging to the same suite: all are covered with contemporary green and yellow velvet of English make, the edges being trimmed with a broad yellow braid in a picturesque and effective manner. After 1675 many innovations were introduced into the form of the couch, and eventually they were made long enough to lie down on, at full length, and so in time superseded the day-bed. Fig. 287 is a long settee or couch with five cushions, of about the date 1695; the back is headed by three crestings of decorated pediments, each centring in a ducal crown over an escutcheon bearing the cipher of the first Duke of Leeds, the date of the creation being 1694. The day-bed (Fig. 288) is of the same style and make. These two couches have been vaguely assigned to French manufacture, but the carpentry, carving, painting and gilding are distinctly English, and, moreover, in 1694, the approximate date of these two settees, we were at war with France. The only

FIG. 288. *Walnut Upholstered Day-bed*. Property of the DUKE OF LEEDS.

Fig. 289 *Walnut Upholstered Day-bed.* Length, 5 feet; height, 2 feet. Property of Lord de Lisle and Dudley.

part of doubtful origin is the velvet, and though unusually unobtrusive in pattern for foreign manufacture of that time, it is probably Italian. It will be interesting to compare the details in the stool from Hardwick (Fig. 281) with these two pieces from Hornby. The wood-work in both couch and day-bed is carved in a well-proportioned nulling gilt on a black ground; the arms, which finish in scrolls, being further ornamented with floral tracery; the legs taper, and are quadrangular, united at the base by a horizontal series of oval stretchers; the bun-feet supporting these have been cut to receive casters; in their original state they would have had the proportion of the legs on the Hardwick stool and chair (the latter to be given later), which are untouched. The long squabs are supported on a foundation of cords and sacking; they are entirely covered with the velvet, which is of superb quality, small and refined in design; the colours are crimson, green and cinnamon on a dark cream satin ground, and edged with an irregular and deeply tasselled fringe. These two couches represent remarkable examples of luxury in the upholstered furniture of this time.

Fig. 289 is another beautiful day-bed, but of earlier date, for the legs with their inward scroll and waved stretcher, prove a time towards the end of the reign of Charles II – about 1680. The back rolls over and is headed by a shell carved in walnut wood and covered in rose damask and velvet; the frame of the seat and back is sharply carved in floral tracery, thickly gilt; curved valances of rose damask, stained on wood, and finishing in tassels, are inserted between the legs; the squab, back and cushion are of rose damask covered with an appliqué of yellow, green and cream-coloured silk, and trimmed with a yellow galon with little green tufts. The legs and stretchers are thickly gilt, and the former resembles the type on the seat from Hardwick (Fig. 275). This day-bed has been described in the guide-books to Penshurst as of Tudor interest, but its charm is enhanced by the assignment of a proper date that enables one to realise its correct surroundings.

The surroundings of this time were of a nature that have never been repeated in this country, luxury and pleasure predominating over everything. The bedrooms and ante-chambers of Mazarin, Castlemaine and Portsmouth were amongst the sights of London; but although the often described silver bed of Neil Gwyn represented an unaccountable extravagance, her other immediate surroundings appear to have been in reason. This witty and talented actress really cared for Charles, and was the only favourite liked, or tolerated, by the nation. Castlemaine was a rapacious termagant, who, during one period of eight months, abstracted over forty thousand pounds from him. Louise de Keroualle, Duchess of Portsmouth, equally avaricious and acquisitive, under the guise of tender affection, sold

Charles to the French King, and was in consequence most hated of all the favourites, while the £60,000 a year that Charles II received from Louis XIV was very rapidly dissipated on the extravagant furnishing of the various apartments of these stars of the Court. Evelyn, in his Diary, 10 September 1675, states:

'I was casually showed the 'Duchess of Portsmouth's splendid apartment at Whitehall, luxuriously furnished, and with ten times the richness and glory beyond the Queens's, such massy pieces of plate, whole tables, and stands of incredible value.'

Eight years later he again calls attention to the profusion with which this woman furnished her rooms:

'Following his Majesty this morning through the Gallery, I went with the few who attended him, into the Duchess of Portsmouth's dressing-room within her bed-chamber, where she was in her morning loose garment, her maids combing her, newly out of bed, his Majesty and the gallants standing about her; but that which engaged my curiosity was the rich and splendid furniture of this woman's apart-ment, now twice or thrice pulled down and rebuilt to satisfy her prodigal and expensive pleasures. Here I saw the new fabric of French tapestry, for design, tenderness of work and incomparable imitation of the best paintings, far beyond anything I had ever beheld. Some pieces had Versailles, St. Germains, and other palaces of the French King, with hunting, figures and landscapes, exotic fowls, and all to the life rarely done. Then for Japan cabinets, skreens, pendule clocks, great vases of wrought plate, tables, stands, chimney-furniture, sconces, branches, braseras, etc., all of massy silver and out of number, besides some of her Majesty's best paintings.'

There are a few bills in existence referring to the household and furnishing expenses of Nell Gwyn during the years 1674, 1675 and 1676. These include charges for a bedstead with silver ornaments, great looking-glasses, dress furniture, and lavish clothes. The bedstead is described as covered with representations of the King's head, slaves, eagles, crowns and cupids, and Jacob Hall, the tight-rope dancer, all in silver embossed work. The account for this is dated 1674, and headed: 'Work done for ye righte HONble Madame Guinne, John Cooqus, silversmyth his bill.' The King's head weighed 197 oz, and the rest of the ornaments 2168 oz, and cost in those days £906, so that by the time the elaborate hangings and fringes were added, the bed would have represented a very vast sum of money.

The custom of using silver tables, mirrors and furniture decorated with applied work in silver was by no means confined to these ladies of the Court.

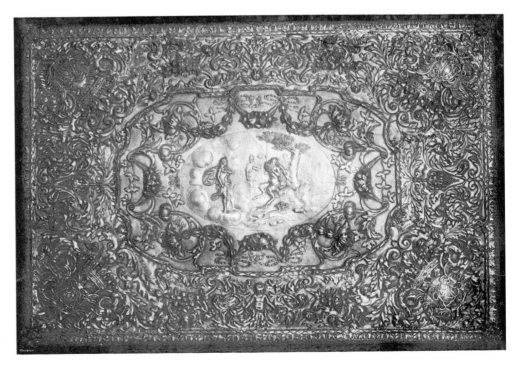

Fig. 290. *Top of Silver Table*. Property of Lord Sackville.

After her visit to Bradby, the Earl of Chesterfield's, Miss Celia Fiennes writes in an interesting manner in connection with one of these silver bedrooms, as follows:

'Ye drawing Roome had Company in it, ye Earle having just marry'd his Eldest daughter Lady Mary to one Mr. Cooke a Gentleman of a good Estate hard by, so there was Company to wishe her joy; but I was in severall bed Chambres, one had a Crimson damaske bed, ye other Crimson velvet set upon halfe paces: this best was ye bride Chamber wch used to be Call'd ye silver roome where ye stands, table, and fire utensills were all massy silver, but when plaite was in nomination to pay a tax, ye Earle of Chesterfield sold it all and ye plaite of ye house, so when ye table was spread I saw only spoones, salts and forks and ye side board plaite, noe plaites or dishes and but few salvers.'

The tax she alludes to was that of William III in 1696 and 1697, when plate was called in at five shillings and fourpence per ounce. Great quantities of Charles II silver furniture was no doubt melted on this appeal to the country, and the higher standard, represented by the hall-mark of Britannia, etc., was substituted for the lion passant and leopard's head, which had hitherto stood for the sterling value.

At Windsor there is a table and two guéridons covered with silver, embossed and chased, of which there are very good electrotypes in the Victoria and Albert Museum. The top of the table bears the royal crown and cipher of the King; the legs are of silver resembling the wooden turned twist of the time. It bears the London hall-mark of 1680.

The stands of guéridons were for lights, or the large silver and china potpourri jars, that were used so much in the decoration of the finely furnished rooms of the time. There is another of these silver tables at Knole,

FIG. 291. *Set of Silver Furniture.* Property of LORD SACKVILLE.

Fɪɢ. 292. *Set of Silver-mounted Fire-irons.*
Property of the Eᴀʀʟ ᴏꜰ Dʏꜱᴀʀᴛ.

of the date 1680, two guéridons to match, and a large mirror, all in embossed silver. Fig. 290 is the top of this table, in which the central oval design represents the musical contest between Apollo and Marsyas, and is set in a border composed of swags of garrya bloom and bunches of fruit; the table-top is further decorated with fine acanthus scrolls of chased and embossed work, starting from cherub's torsos, whilst at the four corners are the super-imposed cipher and coronet of the Earl of Dorset. The frame is embossed in a frieze of single acanthus leaves inverted, similar to what is found upon the porringers and cups of 1680, and finishes in a deep pendant with cherubs holding an Earl's coronet over the Dorset cipher. The legs scroll in the manner recently introduced in small tables of the time, and rest upon claw-and bun-feet. The guéridons at the side are of similar workmanship, and support two large perfume pots. The glass above is most elaborate in its work, repeating the design found upon the table; at each side are one branch sconces of silver. The table bears the London hall-mark of 1680.

The illustration (Fig. 291) of this set of silver furniture preserved at Knole gives a good idea of the extravagance of the time. The reflection in the mirror shows the bed prepared for James I and the dwarf on the tapestry behind the left-hand sconce is a portrait of Geoffrey Hudson, his Court dwarf.

Fig. 292 shows a set of fire-irons, bellows and brush, also decorated with silver in the manner of 1680. The handles, shovel and legs of the tongs are of iron, capped and clasped with silver knops, terminating in acanthus husks; on the bellows is the cipher of the Duke of Lauderdale, with ducal coronet and feather mantling. The little lion is one of a pair, that forms the rests to the fire-irons. The feet of the fire-pan (Fig. 293) are splayed, and teminate in broad flanges of acanthus. There are many sets of these beautiful silver grates and fire-irons in Ham House, all of about the same date.

Tables and cabinets, during the latter part of the seventeenth century, were often decorated with applied corners and centres of this embossed English silver-work, but in consequence of the thinness of the silver, the metal has loosened from its fastening, and so but few perfect specimens

Fɪɢ. 293. *Silver Fire-pan.* 1 foot 8 inches by 1 foot 4 inches. Property of the Eᴀʀʟ ᴏꜰ Dʏꜱᴀʀᴛ.

FIG. 294. *Ebony Table-top Mounted in Silver.* Length, 2 feet 7 inches; width, 1 foot 11 inches. Property of the EARL OF DYSART.

remain. A table-top, decorated with silver in this manner, is Fig. 294, made for Elizabeth Dysart about 1680, and whose cipher is applied on the open silver-work of the decoration. The frame (Fig. 295) is ogeed, and both this and the top are of ebony; they are supported by four graceful female terminal figures, finishing in lion claw-feet, connected by scroll-work interwoven by laurel garlands. The admirable carving of these figures, which are of walnut, suggests the work of Gibbon or one of his pupils. The stretcher is plain, and the blocks supporting the feet are additions. The ebony of the top is supposed to be earlier than the rest of the table.

Fig. 296 is a walnut table of similar form from the same collection and presumably a copy of the preceding specimen, made a few years later; the figures are deficient both in life and style; the walnut top is bordered with a herring-bone inlay of the same wood.

Another highly finished table of this kind, made of maple-wood, is shown in Fig. 297. The top is inlaid with a fine strap-work in silver lines. The half-round moulding of the edge is carved with the bold acanthus of 1680. The frame is plain and veneered with the knotted portions of maple, opening in a drawer, which has the original drop-handles. This frame is supported on small cushions that cap four finely carved female heads; the legs below these are of double C scrolled form; the stretcher is serpentine, with a central finial carved as a lamp and flame; the feet are flattened and scrolled; the whole of the carving is thickly gilt, the plain parts being left in the natural colour of the

FIG. 295. *Walnut Legs of same Table.* Height, 2 feet 5 inches. Property of the EARL OF DYSART.

FIG. 296. *Walnut Table.* Property of the EARL OF DYSART.

FIG. 297. *Maple-wood Table.* Length, 3 feet 10 inches; height, 2 feet 7 inches; width, 2 feet 6 inches. Property of the DUKE OF DEVONSHIRE.

FIG. 298. *Walnut Table.* Height, 2 feet 5 inches; length, 2 feet 5 inches; width, 2 feet 2 inches. Property of S. CAMPBELL CORY, Esq.

FIG. 299. *Lime-wood Table.* Length, 2 feet 9 inches; width, 1 foot 6 inches; Height, 2 feet 5 inches. Property of SEYMOUR LUCAS, Esq.

wood. The same idea is seen on the walnut table (Fig. 298), of about the same date. The heads of the scrolled legs are delicately carved in the pattern of chairs and stools of this time, and the stretcher and feet correspond; the top is edged with a waved border not often found on English furniture.

The individual touch of Grinling Gibbon is clearly seen on the table (Fig. 299), his mastery of movement being shown in the portrayal of the cherubims' active expression in combination with their beauty; the delicate irregularity of their pinions, the subtle and lifelike manner in which the wreaths of flowers are introduced, all denote the work of a very great artist. Few pieces of Gibbon's statuary and furniture remain, but his architectural decorations in wood-carving claim for this untutored genius the highest place in this craft.

Gibbon was practically discovered by Evelyn, who wrote of him on 18 January 1671 as follows:

'This day, I first acquainted his Majesty with that incomparable young man, Gibbon, whom I had lately met with in an obscure place by a mere accident, as I was walking near a poor solitary thatched house in a field in our parish near Sayes Court. I found him shut in; but looking in at the window I perceived him carving that large cartoon or crucifix of Tintoretto. I asked him if I might enter; he opened the door civilly to me, and I saw him about such a work as for the curiosity of handling drawing and studious exactness, I had never before seen in all my travels. I questioned him why he worked in such an obscure and lonesome place; he told me it was that he might apply himself to his profession without interruption, and wondered not a little how I had found him out. I asked if he was unwilling to be made known to some great man, for that I believed it might turn to his profit; he answered, he was yet but a beginner, and would not be sorry to sell off that piece; on demanding the price, he said £100. In good earnest, the very frame was worth the money, there being nothing in nature so tender and delicate as the flowers and festoons about it, and yet the work was very strong, etc.'

As a proof of Gibbon's obscure origin and want of education, the subjoined letter, written by him to Evelyn in 1682, is also given:

'Honred
'Sr I wold beg the faver wen you see Sr Joseff Williams again you wold be pleased to speack to him that hee wold get mee to Carve his Ladis sons hous my Lord Kildare for I onderstand it will be verry considerabell ar If you haen Acquantans wich my Lord to speack to him his sealf and I shall for Ev're be obliaged to You I wold speack to Sir Josef my sealf but I knouw it would do better from you.
'Sr youre Most umbell
'Sarvant
'G. GIBBON.'

FIG. 300. *Carved Lime-wood Mirror*. Property of RANDOLPH BERENS, Esq.   FIG. 301. *Gilt Mirror*. Property of the MARQUIS OF EXETER.

The English wood-carving of the eighteenth century owes its technical excellence of execution to the schools of Gibbon and Cibber, for until their time but little in the shape of realism in decoration had been attempted, and however widely Gibbon's followers drifted from his original methods and school of design, it was to the influence of these carvers in Charles II's and William's reigns that English wood-carving eventually rivalled that of foreign countries.

Fig. 300 is a frame to a mirror carved by Gibbon; the open tracery and delicate detail of the flowers and fruit are a good example of his early style.

The gilt frame of the mirror (Fig. 301) is of the school of Cibber, and of about the date 1680. The carving represents an elaborate and open-work acanthus scroll intermingled with flowers; the top heading is formed of two very finely carved figures of cherubs supporting an earl's coronet; the cherubs are repeated on the base, but here they lack the style of those on the heading. The plain half-round moulding that holds the glass is of black lacquer, with gold and coloured flowers.

What may be termed 'freaks' in the shape of mirrors occur frequently at this time. Some are bordered with panels of needlework representing biblical or historical subjects, some framed in borders of bead-work, others with the ornaments made of thin cardboard, papier-mâché and shells. Fig. 302 is one of the latter description of about 1688. The frame is of black and gold lacquer, the divisions of which are filled with representations of baskets of flowers; the top panel, crested with carved and gilt flowers, contain the frontage of a small house with figures at the windows. The details of this 'conceit', as it was called at the time, is composed of small rolls of stiff paper set edgeways and gilt, and the work representing flowers is most delicate and remarkable; at the bottom is a grotto composed of little shells. This piece is very representative of the childish taste indulged in occasionally by the ladies of fashion at that time. Other favourite forms of mirrors were those framed in a broad half-round of walnut in strong projection; these kind of frames were often inlaid with marqueterie; they were chiefly used in

FIG. 302. *Lacquer Mirror*. Property of MESSRS ISAACS.

FIG. 303. *Marqueterie Mirror*.

FIG. 304. *Ebony Mirror*. Property of MESSRS ISAACS.

bedrooms, and matched in design the chests of drawers and lace boxes over which they were hung.

Fig. 303 is a mirror evidently made by the same hand as the chest of drawers, Plate XIX, for the colour of the woods employed and the pattern of the marqueterie are the same. The frame to this class of mirror has frequently a flat heading of escalloped or hooded form, sometimes fretted; in this instance eagles under a crown are introduced as a cresting. Occasionally the green-stained ivory leaves and jessamine of the cabinets are also added.

Fig. 304 is an ebony mirror, and a specimen of English furniture that obtained some favour here after the Restoration. The originals of this ebony furniture were introduced by Catherine of Braganza; they included settees and chairs, and were a very favourite form of royal gift with Charles II. The source of this ebony furniture was Goa, and a certain amount was copied in this country from the Indo-Portuguese importations. The outlined carving of the flowers on this frame corresponds with that found on English plate of the time.

CHAPTER V

OOKING-GLASS of every description was much esteemed for the purposes of decoration and furnishing towards the end of Charles's reign, in the form of mirrors, and let into the wall as panels. In a contemporary description the dining-room at Chatsworth, the distribution of looking-glass reads almost early Victorian in its arrangment.

'At the end of the dineing roome is a large door all of Looking glasse in great pannells all diamond Cutt. This opposite to ye doores that runs into ye drawing roome and bed chamber and Closet so it shows ye roomes to Look all double. Ye Dutchess's Closet is wanscoted with ye hollow burnt japan, and at Each corner are peers of Looking glass. In all ye windows ye Squares of glass are so large and good they cost 10s. a pannell.'

These window-panes would have been bevelled, like those still in existence at Hampton Court Palace, which measure about 14 by 10 inches.

Elaborate bathrooms were at this time frequently introduced into the large houses. Mention is made in the same letter of a bathing-room at Chatsworth.

'Ye walls all with blew and white marble – the pavement mixed, one stone white, another black, another of ye Red Vaned marble. The bath is one Entire marble all white finely veined with blew and is made smooth, it was as deep as ones middle on the outside, and you went down steps into ye bath big enough for two people. At ye upper end are two Cocks to let in one hott, ye other Cold water to attemper it as persons please – the windows are all private glass.'

The windows of the gallery in Whitehall were all glazed with bevelled glass. This was 'the glorious gallery' that Evelyn alludes to, as furnished with such inexpressible luxury, and where he witnessed that last Sunday evening of Charles II, surrounded by his mistresses and dissolute courtiers. The next day the King had an apoplectic fit, and his death, which took place five days after, stemmed for a time the tide of profligacy; and the sense of extravagance and profusion, that had existed for thirty-six years, was replaced by the quieter Courts and influences of James II, and William III.

With this attempt at improvement in the morals of society, a certain element of picturesqueness disappeared, and the furniture soon became more sedate and practical. The caprices of a Court have always been to some extent responsible for the evolution of taste in furniture, and it will be noticed that change of a distinct kind in any of the applied arts can often be attributed to political associations. William III was Dutch on his father's side, and his preferences and manners were distinctly those of that nation; while the importations from Holland that he encouraged produced a more orderly and neater style of furniture, that eventually developed into simplicity and elegance.

The immediate surroundings of William's Court were gorgeous, for much existing in the previous reigns was retained; and although the new style of furniture tended towards simplicity, the decorations and materials employed were still sumptuous; the marqueterie introduced on furniture became quieter, more colourless, and the chairs less decorated, and more dependent upon graceful curves. It will be necessary in dealing with this large area, comprising so many different classes of furniture, to resume individual evolutions at the point where they were dropped, and introduce, in their proper place, pieces belonging to a former reign. In Miss Fiennes' description of some of the rooms at Windsor, written about 1698, it is evident that much of the furniture belonging to the Court of Charles II was still retained and valued for its interest and beauty.

'I went up staires into a Large dineing roome, Damaske Chaires and window Curtaines, wanscoated, and severall fine pictures. The Roofe of this was well painted also, but they are soe Lofty its enough to Breake ones neck to Looke on them. Thence into ye Drawing roome where is the large Branch of silver, silver table, and stands, and Glass frames and Chaire frames. Next is ye Queenes Chamber of state. Here's a silver table, and stands, and Glass fframe. Thence into ye King's dressing roome almost all Glass; ye windows of all ye roomes are Large sashes as big as a good Looking glass and are all diamond Cut round the Edges. Thence into the kings Constant bed chamber, being one of yr halfe bedsteads of Crimson and Green damaske, inside and outside the same hangings, and Chaires and window Curtaines the same; it was Lofty and full with food ffringe; here was tables, stands, Glass frames Gilt gold fine Carving etc. etc. Next this is the drawing roome of state, the Cannopy and throne and ye part behind is all green velvet Richly Embroyder'd with silver and Gold, of high embossed work, and some Curiously wrought Like needlework that you can scarce see ye Ground or stuff its wrought on, and the Crown of Crimson velvet Embroyder'd just over the Chaire or throne of state. The Cannopy was so rich and Curled up and in some places soe ffull it looked very Glorious, and was newly made to give audience of the Ffrench Embassadour to shew ye Grandeur and magnificence of the British Monarch – some of these ffoolerys are requisite sometymes to Create admiration and regard to keep up the state of a kingdom and nation.'

Windsor had always surpassed Whitehall in magnificence, and after the fire of 1698, when the latter palace, which had consisted of over a thousand furnished apartments, was, with the exception of the banqueting hall, utterly consumed, Windsor remained the royal residence for furniture and decoration, Hampton Court Palace being incomplete, and Kensington Palace being on a much smaller scale.

It is difficult to exhaust the many varieties of chair made during the latter part of Charles II's reign, in which scroll-form was the leading motive of the carving, the backs being cane-backed, splat-backed or upholstered, but invariably tall. The older type of upholstered arm-chair, as the development proceeded, was frequently covered in gorgeous patterned velvet. There are many such chairs at Knole, and Fig. 305 is one of about the date 1675. The legs, arm-supports and stretcher are formed of simple scrolls, but the arms are upholstered with the velvet, which is fine in design and of a beautiful blue; the tasselled fringe is of the same colour, and greatly enriches the rather simple form of the wood-work.

Fig. 306 is a most elaborate and ornamental chair, of about 1680. The cresting, frame, arm-supports and stretchers are composed of a series of highly decorated scrolls, the points of interest being emphasised by the introduction of lions' and cherubs' heads; the back is composed of four splats carved in a similar design, and the seat is caned to receive a squab; the legs, of contorted form, begin and finish in lions' heads; the whole of the carving is executed with great spirit, and although the detail is somewhat overlavish and redundant, the effect is imposing. The double cherubs' heads are suggestive of the favourite form of ornament so often introduced by Gibbon, but the touch of the carving is too heavy for that school. From the frequency with which the lion is introduced into the decoration, the chair was probably in some way connected with royalty, and the historical tradition in connection with it is as follows. Harraden, in his *Cantabrigia Depicta*, 1809, mentions the ancient gallery at St John's College, hung with portraits, and possessing a set of very curious chairs, said to have been presented to the Master's Lodge by Charles II, one of them being 'A large elbow-chair, curiously ornamented with cherubims, lions' heads, etc'. But Cooper, in his *Memorials of Cambridge*, says, 'A large, richly carved arm-chair, which is in one of the apartments, is supposed to have been made for the use of Charles II when he visited the College with his Queen in September 1681.' The ornate work of the scrolling and carving corresponds in date with this visit to the University, and it is probable that the King gave the chair, to be used by the Master of St John's, then Vice-Chancellor of the University, for had the chair been specially prepared for the King, the royal arms would certainly have been introduced.

Fig. 307 is an early and tall form of what is termed a ladder-back chair, the splats or bars being in this instance constructed of double scrolls, horizontally inserted into knobbed and collared uprights, carved with rough

Fig. 305. *Walnut Upholstered Chair*. Height, 4 feet 5 inches. Property of LORD SACKVILLE.

Fig. 306. *Walnut Chair*. Property of ST JOHN'S COLLEGE, CAMBRIDGE.

FIG. 307. *Walnut Chair.* Height, 4 feet 2 inches. Property of ROBERT W. J. RUSHBROOKE, Esq.

FIG. 308. *Wa'nut Chair.* Property of FRANK GREEN, Esq.

FIG. 309. *Walnut Chair.* Property of MESSRS MORANT.

acanthus. The cresting represents two cherubs supporting an effigy of King James II, and on the front stretcher that of his Queen, her hair down and breast uncovered, as at her coronation; which event this chair must have been intended to commemorate, as its date, 1685, coincides with that event; the finials also are formed as crowns. The frame to the seat is carved in an irregular form, and still possesses the original caning, which is circular. Although we know stools were constantly used as seats for meals, during the reigns of James and William, sets of tall chairs, without arms and with very narrow backs, were also made for the dining-rooms.

An interesting arm-chair, of about 1685, and one of a pair, is Fig. 308. In this instance the scrolled splats are perpendicular, and the uprights of the back being balustered, the arms are set at some distance from the front of the seat, as the rake of the chair is considerable; the legs have a very pronounced outward curve. This chair is painted black, a prevalent fashion at the end of Charles's reign. Fig. 309 is another variety of small chair of this time; the walnut frame is carved with coarse acanthus, and the form is interesting and unusual.

About this time a type was introduced from France, in which one open but connected splat formed the back, surmounted by a high cresting. The carving of this back and cresting was in many instances of very fine quality, and this shape was probably confined to the richer section of the community, as it is rare to find a genuine chair of this character indifferently carved. They were probably in a great many instances made by French workmen domiciled in this country, as they invariably lack the originality of indigenous work. Fig. 310 (a) is a well-carved specimen of about the year 1687; the uprights of plain baluster shape give great value to the elaborated back legs and stretcher; the carved patera at the tenons repeat the design of the early Restoration chairs, the legs are still of scroll form, but here end in lion claws, and the front stretcher repeats the form of the cresting. Fig. 310 (b) is another and later specimen, in which French inspiration is even more apparent; the stretcher is dropped on account of the baluster leg, and the

(b) FIG. 310. *Walnut Chairs.* (a) FIG. 311. *Pear-wood and Mahogany Chair.* Property of JAMES ORROCK, Esq.

uprights of the back are not so good in proportion as in the preceding specimen. Fig. 311 is of about 1690, the cupped leg and serpentine stretcher pointing to this date; the concave and semi-Gothic moulding of the uprights is very unusual; the open design of the back is due to the interesting fact that the splat being made of mahogany can bear a greater strain; the rest of the chair is pear-wood; the seat to this type of chair was invariably upholstered. The desire to give a lighter appearance to the backs of chairs was evidently increasing at this time, and the top rail, which had hitherto been tenoned within the uprights, now formed a capping, and increased in height, so that towards the end of the century finials disappeared altogether, and the top rail finished the uprights. In Fig. 312, of the date 1686, this increase of lightness is very apparent. Down the centre are two long strings of conventional decoration representing the catkins of the *Garrya eliptica*, framed on each side by a graceful border of open scroll-work, a hooped cresting heads the fluted uprights, and the perforated knees resemble those of earlier chairs; the knobbed union with the seat-rail generally occurs at this time.

Fig. 313 is a spray of the *Garrya eliptica*, the flower from which the swags, and pendants of so-called husks, were taken; in the late eighteenth century this ornament became a most prominent feature in decoration. Fig. 314 is another arm-chair of this new and light type, with a more elaborate cresting and carved back; the arms and legs scroll outwardly, but in their somewhat purposeless curves show the end of an evolution; the front stretcher still repeats the form of a cresting, though a certain amount of emptiness is apparent in the effort to obtain lightness of construction. These chairs suffered, inasmuch as they were built upon traditional form that had ceased to be invested with its original feeling. Fig. 315 is a chair, somewhat similar, without arms, and one of the narrow-backed variety made for the dining-

Fig. 312. *Walnut Chair.* Property of Frank Green, Esq.

Fig. 313. *Flower of the 'Garrya Eliptica'.*

table; in Fig. 316, for the same purpose, a year or two later in date, the finials are still preserved; the frame to the carving is escalloped, but the workmanship of the chair is very elementary, and suggest country origin. A chair, with a similar motive in the back, but of higher class of workmanship, is shown in Fig. 317. Here the cresting heads the uprights of the back, and three moulded bars take the place of caning; the cup-topped legs are in octagon, finishing in scroll-feet; the serpentine stretcher and these legs are of the date 1690; the seat is caned, but there are no traces that the back has ever been treated in this manner, and the three upright mouldings are original.

In the withdrawing-rooms of the rich, upholstered and padded chairs still continued to be in request, giving great opportunity for the display of gorgeous English and Genoa velvets, which were put on with an upholstery of less elaboration than in the last reign; and flat galon often took the place of the previous tasselled trimmings and fringes, this selection being guided by a quieter and more restrained taste. The furnishing and decoration of the new buildings at Hampton Court Palace gave opportunity for much that was new, and the descriptions of the energetic Celia Fiennes again give interesting details of the furniture in some of the new rooms in William and Mary's reign, when evidently chairs, etc., of a previous time were re-upholstered. Fig. 318 is one of these, for the wood-work is of about 1680, and the crimson and cream-coloured Genoa velvet is a rather later date. Fig. 319 is a narrow, tall-back arm-chair, the upholstery being framed in wood; the only attempt at carving is the cresting composed of a series of short C scrolls; the covering is not original.

Fig. 320 represents a walnut arm-chair from a fine set at Hardwick, of about the date 1690. The cresting preserves the strong Carolean irregularity of form found on scroll-back chairs, but the arm-supports and legs are in the

Fig. 314. *Walnut Chair.*

FIG. 315. *Walnut Chair.*
Property of FRANK E. BURTON, Esq.

FIG. 316. *Walnut Chair.*
Property of A. L. RADFORD, Esq.

FIG. 317. *Walnut Chair.* Height,
4 feet 4 inches. Property of the
HON CHARLOTTE MARIA LADY
NORTH and R. EDEN DICKSON,
Esq.

FIG. 318. *Walnut Upholstered
Chair.*
HAMPTON COURT PALACE.

newer style, resembling those of the day-bed and settee from Hornby (Figs.
287 and 288), which cannot be before 1697. The long garrya pendants that
edge the back are exceedingly original and fine in execution; the frame, arms
and seat-rail are carved with panels of alternate floral tracery and acanthus;
the back and seat have their original covering of crimson velvet, with a broad
band of highly raised silver embroidery, now almost perished. This is one of
the most remarkable chairs in England, both for beauty and originality, and
coming as it does at the end of an evolution, is surprising in its excellence. In

FIG. 319. *Walnut Upholstered
Chair.*
Property of the DUKE OF
BEAUFORT.

FIG. 320. *Walnut Upholstered Chair.* Height, 4
feet 9 inches; width, 2 feet 3 inches.
Property of the DUKE OF DEVONSHIRE.

FIG. 321. *Walnut Upholstered Chair.* Property of the
DUKE OF LEEDS.

Fig. 321 the strange outward scroll below the arms found on the settee (Plate XXI) has been reproduced in chair form, but although exceedingly quaint, cannot be pronounced beautiful, as the sides overweight the back; it is probably a kind of sleeping-chair, and the lower side scrolls could be used as a leg rest; the serpentine stretcher is missing, greatly detracting from the appearance of the lower portion. The covering is now a deep mulberry velvet, studded at the edges with nails, and put on probably some time during the eighteenth century; the eccentric form of the chair does not suggest an original covering of plain material; the cresting of the top, consisting of curved scrolls, is covered in the velvet. In Fig. 322 (a) the back has no visible wooden frame, and is entirely formed of padded upholstery, as in earlier Charles II chairs; the arms are very marked in their curve, and where they scroll over have a strong outward turn; the arm-supports and legs are capped, and the latter finish in scroll-feet; the wood-work of this chair, although of walnut, is painted black, and ringed with a bronze gold; the set is mentioned in an inventory of about 1700, at Hornby Castle, as being painted in these colours; the velvet with which they are covered is Utrecht quality but of English make; the design is extremely effective and evidently calculated for this width of chair; the broad scrolled galon on the seat carries out the other lines, and the upholstery of the end of the seventeenth century is most interesting, and proves that much thought was still given to the finishing of furniture. Fig. 322 (b) is an upholstered chair without arms, forming part of the suite to the stool and double settee, from Hornby, already illustrated; the wood-work is painted black and gold, and the lower rail of the back repeats the serpentine lines of the cresting; here the seat and back are framed in carved wood; these were originally covered in figured velvet to match the settee, but have been replaced by the present crimson damask. Fig. 323, from Hampton Court Palace, given to complete this series of late seventeenth-century chairs, was probably made about 1695, and re-covered during the next reign, when the bed and stools, to which this suite belongs, were evidently upholstered in the present rich tawny, cream and claret velvet that is still in sound condition. The scrolled arms of the tall-backed settees are repeated on this chair, and die in a cone-shaped roll that rests upon the front rail of the seat, a finish that was adopted on sofas and

(a)   Fig. 322. *Walnut Upholstered Chairs.* Property of the Duke of Leeds.   (b)

Fig. 323. *Walnut Upholstered Chair.* Hampton Court Palace.

tall-back easy-chairs for many years during the following century. The original galon trimming has been replaced by a modern gimp, and the velvet is an interesting instance of the so-called Genoa or Venetian velvet, made in England about 1702; the rather crude drawing of the design and peculiar flatness of the manufacture point to this period, when great attempts were made to restrict all importations of silks and velvets, though at the same time the retailers found it necessary to ascribe these products to foreign origin in order to obtain a ready sale. The number of Huguenot silk-weavers that took refuge in this country has already been given; their influence upon the silk trade left a permanent impresion, and during the reigns of William and Mary and Anne this manufacture made great progress. Although the English silk-weaver had learnt all his trade secrets from the French workman, he naturally resented the term 'French make' being applied to goods made in England under foreign influence. The Government, however, regarded these refugees as a profitable investment, and in 1709 granted £24,000 towards the support of artisans of all trades that arrived in this country during that year. Before the revocation of the Edict of Nantes, England had spent as much as £200,000 per annum on the importation of foreign silks; by the year 1698, the English silk and velvet manufacture had become so successful, that importation was totally forbidden for a time. In 1692 a company petitioned to be incorporated, showing that 'Having with great expense and industry attained the new invention of making, dressing, and lustrating of silks. That they have already caused to be made great quantities of the said silks at least equalling the manufacture of France, and being further resolved to promote the same to the good of the nation so as to thereby employ many thousands of poor people, and also to prevent the sending of vast sums of money to France for the said silks, they pray to be incorporated.'

Marqueterie furniture had much in common with these richly patterned fabrics, and continued to be greatly in demand. Plate XXII represents a table manufactured during the reign of James II, richly inlaid with the coloured marqueterie already described; the jessamine flower is sparingly introduced, and it is unusual to find the green ivory leaves in combination with so much acanthus and other conventional form. The broad feather-edged border of pear-wood, and the laurelled oval of the same wood, is tied with ribands in sycamore; the groundwork of the top frame and stretcher is veneered in ebony; the legs are cylindrical, solid and of the same wood, inlaid on the round in a most skilful manner with marqueterie; the difficulty of bending the green ivory is admirably overcome; the stretcher uniting these legs is inlaid with the same coloured flowers.

It has been customary to ascribe these elaborate and strongly coloured specimens to Dutch workmanship; but investigation proves that, compared with the English manufacture, Dutch marqueterie is always duller in colour and more disconnected in design. Italy supplied the real suggestion of

Fig. 324. *Walnut Inlaid Table-top.* Length, 3 feet 4 inches; width, 2 feet 8 inches. Property of S. Campbell Cory, Esq.

Fig. 325. *Same Inlaid Table.* Height, 2 feet 5 inches.

FIG. 326. *Walnut Inlaid Table-top.* Length, 3 feet; width, 1 foot 11 inches. Property of S. CAMPBELL CORY, Esq.

colour for our inlay in stained woods, whilst France, in exiling her workmen, introduced to us the patterns of Boulle, which was the later development of this highly decorated style. This table portrays a coming change in marqueterie, when the flowers disappear altogether, giving way to fine acanthus and minute scroll-work of seaweed form.

Between this and the table-top (Fig. 324), of about 1690, there is a gap that it is difficult to fill. Here the same treatment of acanthus foliage, with a still slighter introduction of the floral element, is apparent; the motive of the oval and four triangular panels is abandoned in favour of a field of elaborate design, which is so complete, that the hand of the domiciled foreign artist is strongly suggested, but the cutting of the marqueterie and the execution are entirely English; the ground is a dark walnut, the pattern being inlaid in sycamore or a rich yellow colour, and the influence of the brass and tortoise-shell designs of Boulle is secondary in feeling to the English arrangement and colours of the woods. The legs (Fig. 325), inlaid with the same fine marqueterie, are of double C form, a pattern that remained in fashion till the commencement of the seventeenth century. Fig. 326 is a little later in date. Here the marqueterie is contained within circular and trefoil form, and is of rather coarser cutting; conventional birds are introduced in the centre panel, and the acanthus begins to simulate fine seaweed design. The ground is walnut, cut on the straight, and a sand-burnt feather border of marqueterie surrounds the edge. The legs resemble those of the last specimen, being of double C scroll shape. Fig. 327 is another little walnut table inlaid with

FIG. 327. *Walnut Inlaid Table.* Property of C. E. KEMPE, Esq.

FIG. 328. *Walnut Game Table.* Property of FRANK GREEN, Esq.

FIG. 329. *Walnut and Holly Game Table-top.*
Formerly belonging to SAMUEL PEPYS.
Property of MISS COCKERELL.

panels of marqueterie of this type, but with the cupped and turned leg found on cabinets and chairs late in William's reign. Another interesting inlaid example is shown in Fig. 328. Here the top lifts out, and in the well are inlaid the points of a backgammon board, the top being treated in the same manner for chess or draughts; this table is heavy, and consequently supported on six legs, cleverly worked in an open twist; the stretcher uniting these is of the usual serpentine form and rest on bun-feet. There are parts of a similar table, once the property of Samuel Pepys, and still in possession of a member of the family; it has unfortunately been added to, and mounted on nineteenth-century legs. Fig. 329 shows this table-top (which is in the original condition) with some of the chess-men, of white and green ivory, no doubt those actually used by Pepys.

Another piece of furniture connected with this interesting person, and originally made for his private use, is one of the oak bookcases (Fig. 330) from the Pepysian Library at Magdalene College, Cambridge. There is a reference to them in his will as follows:

'6thly That the whole number and bulke of my books being soe ascertained one or more new presses be provided for the convenient containing them soe as to be neither too much crowded nor Stand too loose.'

These bookcases are twelve in number, and all are 7 feet 9 inches high and 4

FIG. 330. *Oak Bookcase.* Formerly belonging to SAMUEL PEPYS. Property of MAGDALENE COLLEGE, CAMBRIDGE.

feet 7 inches wide, united by narrow mirrors about 8 inches in width; the cornice of each is delicately carved with laurel branches, alternately upright and inverted, between a waved ribbon. The cupboards open in four doors, in which the lock-catches are hidden and intricate; the surbase moulding to the lower compartment is richly carved with acanthus. In this particular press the original cipher volumes of the celebrated Diary can be seen on the right-hand side of the cupboard on the third shelf.

It is probable that many of the decorated tables were used for cards and tea, the afternoon and evening amusements of ladies of fashion. The folding card-table, with its wells for counters and money, hand not yet been introduced, and cards were played on small marqueterie, oak or walnut tables, as in the previous reigns. Cards were much played during the Tudor and Jacobean times, and during the reign of James I the fashion had become so great that the audiences used to amuse themselves with cards at the play-house while waiting for the piece to begin. During the Commonwealth the practice declined, and cards were entitled the 'Devil's Books', but after the Restoration the passion recommenced. In the Verney Papers of 1685 there are letters passing between Sir Ralph Verney and his sister, Lady Gardiner, who is evidently addicted to gambling, and who asks him to lend her £100. He answers: 'I doe not wonder that play (which has ruined soe many Families and soe vast Estates) has reduced you to soe great Extremitys as almost to see the destruction of Youres.' He sends her the £100, but adds: 'You are noe way qualified for a Gamester but lie at the mercy of All who play with you.' However much they were reprimanded, women continued to play, the very fashionable game being Ombre, introduced by Catherine of Braganza. Basset, said to have been invented by a Venetian, who was exiled for his ingenuity, was brought to England by the French friends of Louise de Keroualle; but these small tables could not have been used for basset, as in this game the bank, in a large pile of gold, was spread upon the table, and the players were several in number. Faro, or Pharoah, is mentioned by Pepys. At one of these games Barbara Castlemaine, in 1667, won £15,000 in a night and lost £25,000 on a subsequent evening. Quadrille, though much played in William's and Anne's reigns at small tables, never took so strong a hold upon society as ombre, whilst Whist was a game played for many years in the servants' hall under the name of whisk or swobbers, until some gentlemen who met at the Crown Coffee-house studied its principles, and

Fig. 331. *Walnut Inlaid Writing-table*. Height, 3 feet 1 inch; width, 3 feet; flap, 1 foot 1 inch. Property of the HON CHARLOTTE MARIA LADY NORTH and R. EDEN DICKSON, Esq.

Fig. 332. *Walnut Inlaid Writing-table*. Property of FRANK E. BURTON, Esq.

established rules that were finally formulated by Hoyle in 1743. These small tables were all furnished with a drawer for the cards and counters. Specimens, with a panel of needlework inserted on the top, exist, worked with representations of playing-cards.

Other small articles of table form are writing-desks, such as Fig. 331. The top opens in a flap 13 inches in width, disclosing a series of drawers and pigeon-holes; this, when let down, is supported by the two centre legs that swing forward on pivots, forming brackets; for the sake of strength, an upper serpentine stretcher is also introduced, uniting the four outside legs at their shoulders; these are an early instance of the spindle-shaped leg, and are of yew, exceedingly rich in colour. The marqueterie, covering the inside and outside of the piece, is of arabesque pattern, walnut on a light ground, and bordered with the favourite feather-edging; yew pendants are introduced between the legs on the front and sides. Fig. 332 is another of these somewhat rare pieces. In this case the ground is walnut and the inlay sycamore; the construction of the upper portion exactly resembles the last example, and shows the working of the supports to the flap; the legs are of yew, and the stretcher is single, working on a wooden hinge. The plainness of this stretcher is relieved by an inlay of marqueterie on the top surface, which is not visible in the illustration.

There is much interesting furniture at Burghley, and at one time specimens of marqueterie must have been numerous, as parts of this enormous house were evidently redecorated and refurnished towards the end of Charles II's reign. Walpole refers to the decorations of the walls, painted by Verrio, and his words give a good idea of the general aspect of the place:

'The House itself, at least the new apartments may be said to be one entire picture. The staircase and ceilings of all the fine lodgings, the chapel, the hall, the late Earl's closet are all finely painted by Varrio; of whose work I need say no more than this, that the Earl kept him twelve years in his family, wholly employed him in painting those ceilings, staircase, etc., and allowed him a coach and horses, and equipage, a table and servants, and a very considerable pension.'

The decorative work of Verrio that still remains is by no means attractive, and the ceilings and walls at Hampton Court Palace, painted by him, prove that even the most ornate marqueterie and gorgeous upholstered furniture must have seemed tame and quiet beside the sprawling nudities and crude draperies so typical of this artist.

One of these elaborate pieces of furniture at Burghley is Plate XXIII, of about 1690; it stands over 7 feet in height, and represents one of the most important examples of English marqueterie in existence. The cornice is curously out of character, being composed of a plain frieze; the doors are inlaid with a fine design of flowers and scrolled acanthus in yellow and brown woods on a black ground; two sprays only of the white jessamine are introduced, and without any green leaves, an expiring effort of this fashion; and the long scrolled form of the endive-leaved acanthus is seen gradually overpowering the flowers. The border is of isolated panels of the same marqueterie on a ground of walnut oyster-pieces, the inside of these doors being also veneered in the same way; the lower portion is formed as a chest of drawers, but introduces the unusual feature of the design occupying the surface of three drawers; the handles, for this reason, are kept unobtrusive and of wood. The cross-bandings and mouldings of walnut are of beautiful workmanship; the feet are an early introduction of the flat bracket kind, that later became universal. Fig. 333 is another of these cupboards of the same date, in this case mounted on a stand; the acanthus scrolls are unusually interesting, and the floral portion of the design is entirely subservient to their curves. The groundwork to the marqueterie is composed of ebony; the inside, as in the former example, is an open cupboard originally filled with shelves; the plinth is inlaid with the same large and free marqueterie, and rests upon a stand composed of six well-turned yew legs, united by an undulating flat stretcher of the time.

A cabinet of rather later date, with much finer marqueterie, is seen in Fig.

THE AGE OF WALNUT

COLOUR PLATES

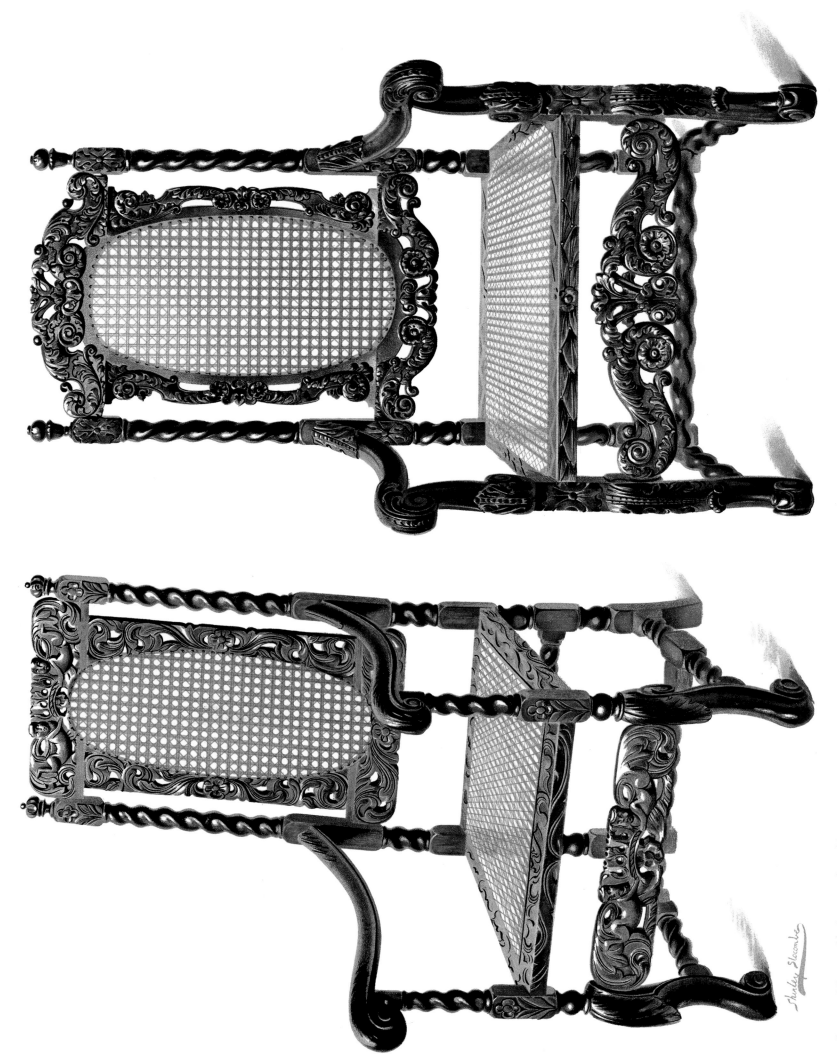

PLATE XVI. (a) *Chair.* Height of back, 3 feet 10 inches; height of seat, 1 foot 4½ inches; depth of seat, 1 foot 5 inches. Property of P. Macquoid, Esq.   (b) *Chair.* Height of back, 3 feet 10 inches; height of seat, 1 foot 5 inches; depth of seat, 1 foot 6 inches. Property of Arthur S. Cope, Esq.

PLATE XVII. *Upholstered Bed*. Height, 13 feet 10 inches; length, 7 feet; width, 6 feet 9 inches. Property of the Hon Charlotte Maria Lady North and R. Eden Dickson, Esq.

PLATE XVIII. *Upholstered Chair*. Height of back, 3 feet 11½ inches; height of seat, 1 foot 6 inches; depth of seat, 1 foot 7 inches; breadth of seat, 2 feet 2 inches. Property of the Hon Charlotte Maria Lady North and R. Eden Dickson, Esq.

PLATE XIX. *Chest of Drawers Inlaid with Marqueterie*. Length, 3 feet 3 inches; height, 3 feet 3 inches; depth, 2 feet.

PLATE XX. *Walnut Cabinet Inlaid with Marqueterie.* Height, 5 feet 7 inches; depth, 1 foot 8½ inches; breadth, 3 feet 7½ inches. Property of the Hon Charlotte Maria Lady North and R. Eden Dickson, Esq.

Shirley Slocombe

PLATE XXI. *Settee*. Height of back, 4 feet 8½ inches; height of seat, 1 foot 7 inches; length, 5 feet 8 inches. Property of the Duke of Leeds.

PLATE XXII. *Table Inlaid with Marqueterie*. Height, 2 feet 6 inches; length, 3 feet 6½ inches; width, 2 feet 3½ inches. Property of Lord Zouche of Haryngworth.

PLATE XXIII. *Cabinet-press Inlaid with Marqueterie.* Height, 7 feet 3 inches; length, 5 feet 4½ inches; depth, 1 foot 11 inches. Property of the Marquess of Exeter.

PLATE XXIV. *Chest of Drawers Inlaid with Marqueterie.* Height, 3 feet 10 inches; length, 3 feet 1 inch; depth, 2 feet.

PLATE XXV. *Lacquer Cabinet*. Height, 7 feet 1 inch; breadth, 3 feet 4 inches; depth, 1 foot 9 inches. Property of C. Assheton Smith, Esq.

PLATE XXVI. (a) *Clock Inlaid with Light Marqueterie*. Height, 7 feet 2 inches.
Property of Percy Macquoid, Esq.
(b) *Clock Inlaid with Dark Marqueterie*. Height, 7 feet 9 inches. Victoria and
Albert Museum.
(c) *Walnut Chair Inlaid with Marqueterie*. Height, 3 feet 3 inches; depth of seat,
1 foot 3 inches.
(d) *Mirror*. Height, 2 feet; breadth, 1 foot 5 inches.

PLATE XXVII. *Upholstered Bed*. Height, 19 feet 6 inches; depth, 8 feet 3 inches; length, 7 feet. Hampton Court Palace.

PLATE XXVIII. *Walnut Chair Covered with Needlework.* Height, 3 feet 2 inches; width, 2 feet 8 inches. Photographed direct from the object.

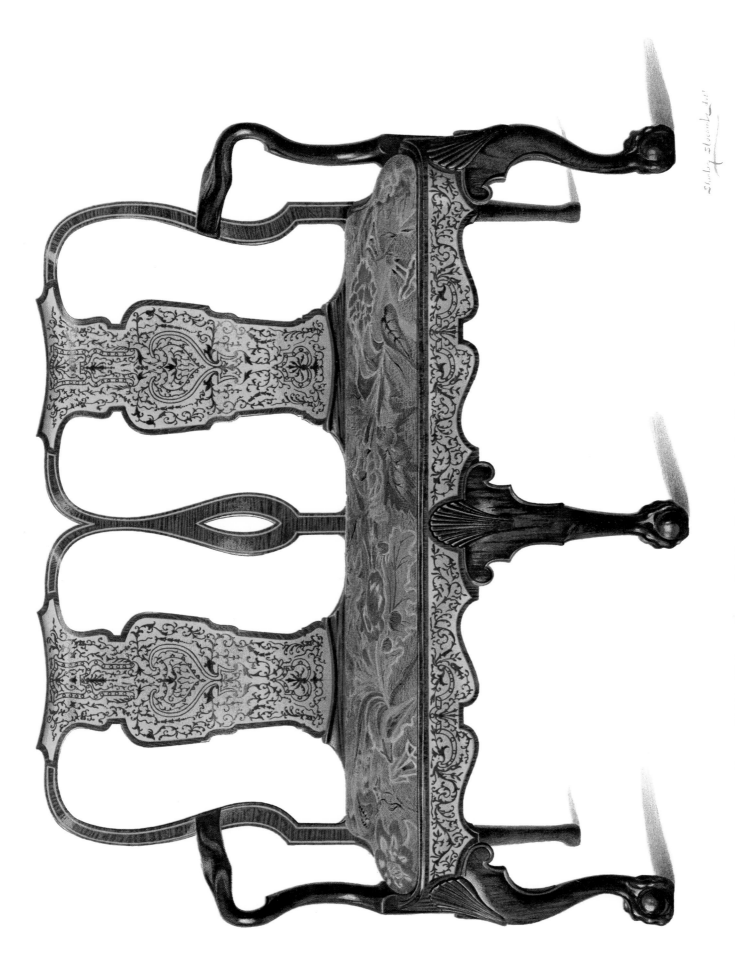

PLATE XXIX. *Walnut Settee Inlaid with Marqueterie. Property of Percy Macquoid, Esq.*

PLATE XXX. *Walnut Inlaid Writing-cabinet*. Height, 7 feet 2 inches; width, 4 feet; depth, 1 foot 10½ inches. Property of Alfred A. de Pass, Esq.

Fig. 333. *Walnut Inlaid Cupboard.* Property of Sir George Donaldson.

Fig. 334. *Walnut Inlaid Cabinet.* Height, 5 feet 4 inches; depth, 2 feet 8 inches; length, 3 feet 8 inches. Property of Messrs J. Mallett and Son.

334; the cornice and ovolo frieze are well defined, and the surface of the whole cabinet is covered with circular designs, filled with very fine marqueterie of the seaweed type, in light wood on a light walnut ground; these patches of brilliant yellow colour are surrounded by a darker inlay of laburnum. The cabinet opens on the usual series of small drawers, inlaid with the same fine marqueterie, that on the inside of the doors being somewhat coarser; the stretcher and the arrangement of the double C scroll legs to the stand are most unusual; marqueterie runs down the upper surface of these legs, which are made in short portions, joined together, and veneered only on the outer side. This style of leg is late for the date of the cabinet, which is about 1695, for it was not until the end of the century that this very fine marqueterie obtained favour.

Marqueterie furniture had now arrived at a style that is peculiarly distinctive to the end of William's reign, a style in which external form is very simple, but with a surface decoration so minute and elaborate, that from a little distance it is barely perceptible. From 1690 to 1695, public taste was very strongly influenced by that of Queen Mary, which was exceedingly refined and original. Defoe writes in his *Tour through Great Britain:*

'The Queen brought in the custom or humour as I may call it of furnishing houses with china ware which increased to a strange degree afterwards, piling their China upon the tops of cabinets, scrutores and every chymney Piece to the top of the ceilings, and even setting up shelves for their china ware, where they wanted such places, till it became a grivance in the Expence of it and even injurious to their Families and Estates.'

He also says, in describing the tastes of this Queen during the rebuilding and redecoration of Hampton Court Palace:

'Her Majesty had there a fine apartment, with a Sett of Lodgings for her private

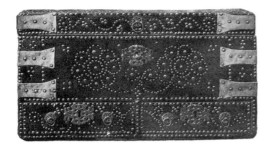

FIG. 335. *Leather-covered Travelling Chest.* Formerly belonging to WILLIAM III. Property of DUDLEY FALCKE, Esq.

FIG. 336. *Top of same.* Formerly belonging to WILLIAM III. Property of DUDLEY FALCKE, Esq.

Retreat only, but most exquisitely furnished; particularly a fine Chintze Bed, then a great curiosity – another of her own work while in Holland very magnificent, and here was also her Majesty's fine collection of Delft ware, which indeed was very large and fine, and was also a vast stock of fine China ware, the like whereof was not to be seen in England.'

At Windsor, he also notices in her room 'A bed hung with Atlass and Magglapatan Chintz'. Burnet was enthusiastic about the virtues and industry of Mary, and in reference to her needlwork wrote:

'In all those hours that were not given to better employment she wrought with her own hands; and sometimes with so constant a diligence, as if she had been to earn her bread by it. It was a new thing, and looked like a sight, to see a Queen work so many hours a day.'

The interest in needlework as a covering to furniture was widespread, owing to the Queen's example; for a great deal of the furniture in the royal apartments at Hampton Court Palace was covered with her handiwork, and was for many years one of the sights of the palace. William's mind, equally energetic, devoted itself more to the reconstruction of this building than to the furniture. His taciturn nature, inherited from his father, was no doubt augmented by his continual ill-health, and the remedies prescribed, which included garlic, crab's eyes and pounded hog's lice, were not calculated to increase his taste for art. Of the furniture personally connected with this King but little remains; there is a small marqueterie writing-table at Windsor, mounted in silver, and a bed at Hampton Court Palace, given later in illustration; the leather-covered travelling-box (Figs. 335 and 336), bearing his crown and initials in gilt nails, is therefore of interest.

Fig. 337 shows a writing-cabinet of the same shape and construction as that from Badminton (Fig. 267), but inlaid with the fine seaweed pattern of

FIG. 337. *Walnut Inlaid Writing-cabinet.* Height, 5 feet 7 inches; length, 3 feet 4 inches; depth, 1 foot 6 inches. Property of J. ANNAN BRYCE, Esq.

FIG. 338. *Walnut Inlaid Press.* Height, 5 feet 3 inches; length, 3 feet 3 inches; depth, 1 foot 7 inches. Property of S. H. S. LOFTHOUSE, Esq.

Fig. 339. *Walnut Inlaid Writing-cabinet*. Height, 6 feet 8 inches; length, 3 feet 1 inch; depth, 1 foot 9 inches. Property of J. Annan Bryce, Esq.

Fig. 340. *Walnut Inlaid Knee-hole Writing-table*. Height, 3 feet 4 inches. Property of Sir George Donaldson.

about 1698. It is veneered in plain walnut, with panels of dark marqueterie on a light ground, the sides being also decorated in this manner. Fig. 338 is a small press, surmounting a chest of drawers; the doors and face of the drawers are inlaid with seaweed marqueterie in oval-shaped panels, and the piece is of the compact and useful form characteristic of the close of the seventeenth century. Fig. 339 is a rarer shape to find inlaid with this marqueterie; it is a cupboard surmounting a chest of drawers, the top forming a writing-desk. The frame and heading have narrow panels of marqueterie in delicate arabesques which hold the original looking-glass panels; the desk opens in a flap inlaid in the same manner; it is of about the date 1700, it is in untouched condition, and con-sequently beautiful in colour.

The form known as the knee-hole writing-table (Fig. 340) was introduced about 1700. The top here is hinged in the centre, and folds back, the front opening as a flap, forming a writing-desk; within are a series of small drawers. The lower portion is divided into eight small drawers with a narrow recess, in which is a cupboard that opens on other small drawers, and is surmounted by a single drawer. The top, sides and front are veneered with walnut of fine figure, and inlaid throughout with oval panels of very delicate seaweed marqueterie, dark, on a light ground, and bordered with a sand-burnt edging. The stand is an early instance of the flat fretted leg, and is also inlaid; the handles, of button shape, are of turned walnut; the simple half-round mouldings are applied on a framing of deal. The remarkable finish of this piece, and the care with which the veneer is selected, rivals some of the French productions of the eighteenth century.

Plate XXIV represents the top and front of a chest of drawers of similar workmanship, and of about the same date; the handles of cherub form are in silver.

CHAPTER VI

CCASIONAL specimens of lacquer, such as cups, trays and small boxes, had, with other Eastern curios, found their way into this country in Tudor times. The invention originated in Japan in the third century BC, and red and gold lacquer is mentioned in Japanese writings of AD 380. This decorated lacquer was at first applied to drinking-vessels and other personal articles, as an impenetrable glazed protection to the surface, and eventually used decoratively to rooms, furniture and especially screens, and represented an important form of Japanese art. Indian cabinets, as they were called at that time, are to be found occasionally mentioned in inventories at the end of Elizabeth's reign, and during the first thirty years of the seventeenth century a few cabinets and screens were brought over to this country from Holland by wealthy travellers. The Portuguese and English carried on a trade intercourse with Japan in Elizabethan times, but were expelled in 1637. The Dutch trade with the Japanese began about 1600, under severe restrictions, and was continually being suspended, so that the majority of the imported lacquer must have come through trade with China and the East India Company. It is not possible to name the date when these imported examples first inspired the English and Dutch craftsman to attempt an imitation of Oriental lacquer in connection with furniture, but it is certain that by 1689 the art of japanning, as it was then called, was widespread, and taught as an extra accomplishment in girls' schools, for in a letter dated 1689, from Edmund Verney to his young daughter Molly, then at school at 'Great Chelsey', he wrote:

'I find you have a desire to learn to Jappan as you call it, and I approve of it; and so I shall of anything that is good and virtuous, therefore learn in God's name all good things and I will willingly be at the Charge so farr as I am able – tho, they come from Japan & from never so farr and Looke of an Indian Hue & odour for I admire all accomplishments that will render you considerable & lovely in the sight of God & man, & therefore I hope you performe your Part according to yr word & employ yr time well & so I pray blesse you. To learn this art costs a Guinea entrance & some 40/s more to buy materials to work upon.'

This japanning became a fashionable pursuit, and in the garrets and top galleries of old country-houses can still be seen worn-out boxes and tables, covered with specimens of this amateur decoration, that for a time developed into a craze.

In true Oriental lacquer, the ground is much smoother and more brilliant than in the imitations by England, France and Holland. The colour and lustre of the different golds are also far more metallic, the designs are drawn with the peculiar sharp touch of the Oriental artist, and the distribution of the detail is more connected. Frequently unmounted Oriental panels were imported and made up into furniture here, but the finished cabinets from the East, entirely of native origin, were the most highly prized. In the household accounts of Charles II there is an entry of £100, paid for 'two Jappan cabinets'; these would probably have been of what is termed cut lacquer, which consisted of hollowing out in the wood the objects in the design, leaving fine black raised outlines, and filling in the spaces with brilliant colours; no reproduction of this particular process was, however, attempted with any success in this country.

Fig. 341 is an English lacquer cabinet of bold and effective workmanship; the outside doors are decorated with water-birds, representations of a pagoda, and a group of flowers in high relief in reds and greens on a black and gold ground; the hinges, corner and lock-plates are brass, pierced and punched with a fine pattern; the doors open on a series of small drawers, lacquered in the same gold and effective manner. The inside of the doors (Fig. 342) represents a tree of blossom in very high relief, the reds and green of the lacquer employed being most brilliant; the drawing of the descending

FIG. 342. *The same Cabinet, Open.*

FIG. 341 (*left*). *Lacquer Cabinet on Gilt Pine-wood Stand.* Height, 5 feet 1 inch. Property of SIR SPENCER C. PONSONBY FANE.

duck, and also the tree, shows the work cannot be Oriental; on the other door are representations of a brace of pheasants; the work of the flowers, house and birds with which the small drawers are decorated prove but a crude acquaintance with Oriental drawing, and infer that the piece is an early attempt in English lacquer and perhaps of Suffolk origin, where the taste for this art first started. The stand is deal, carved in the full and florid style of 1670 to 1675; the ornament alternates in silver and gold. Fig. 343 is another cabinet of this description from Badminton. Here the water-birds with green necks and red backs are again repeated, and a tree in flower is introduced on the other door; at the bottom of each panel is a river with swans in flat painting; the brass hinges and corners correspond in design to those on the former cabinet, but the lock-plate is more elaborate. The decoration of the inside (Fig. 344; is somewhat diversified; a tree with brilliant red blossoms and green leaves and pheasants, are again introduced on the insides of the doors. The black lacquered stand is carved at the corners with the decoration of about 1680, and is supported by twisted columns; the stretcher takes the form of a shelf. In both these cabinets the relief of the lacquer is very high, and the colours far more brilliant than on Oriental specimens; they are very characteristic examples of this English craft. The demand for lacquer increased rapidly, and books were written on the

FIG. 343 (*left*). *Lacquer Cabinet and Stand.* Height, 5 feet 6 inches. Property of the DUKE OF BEAUFORT.

FIG. 344. *Same Lacquer Cabinet, Open.* Property of the DUKE OF BEAUFORT.

subject, containing numberless recipes for the instruction of both professionals and amateurs. In 1688 John Stalker of the Golden Ball, and George Parker of Oxford, published a work entitled *A Treatise of Japanning and Varnishing*, apparently for the use of amateurs, and the following extract shows how seriously lacquer must have occupied the public taste in those days:

'Since our Gentry have of late attained to the knowledge and distinction of true Japan – they are not so fond of colours but covet which is rightly imitated, rather than any work besides this never so finical and gaudy. The most excellent therefore in this Art copy out of the Indian as exactly as may be in respect of draught nature and likeness. Well then as Painting has made us an honourable prevision for our Bodies, so Japanning has taught us a method, no way inferior to it, for the splendour and preservation to our furniture and Houses. These buildings like our bodies continually tending to ruin and dissolution, are still in want of fresh supplys, and reparations, on the one hand they are assaulted with unexpected mischances, on the other with the injuries of time and weather; but the art of Japanning has made them almost impregnable against both. No damp air, no mouldring worm or corroding time can possibly deface it, and which is more wonderful, though its ingredients, the gums are in their own nature inflammable; yet this most vigorously resists the fire, and is itself found to be incombustible.'

The authors, after many remarks of this, proceed to give a long list of recipes for gilding and bronzing in every possible form, some of the directions being interesting and quaint. Of gold dust they say:

'To speak of the Brass dust commonly called amongst the Artists Gold dust, the best gold dust is that, which is finest and of the brightest and most Goldlike colour, which you may best discern by taking a littel in your finger and squeezing it along your finger with your thumb, if bad it will appear of a dull clayish colour and will never work lively or bright.'

The usual process was first to draw the view and objects, then model the

Fig. 345. *Lacquer Cabinet on Gilt Stand.* Height, 5 feet 8 inches. Property of Sir Spencer C. Ponsonby Fane.

Fig. 346. *Scarlet Lacquer Writing-cabinet.* Property of Lord de L'Isle and Dudley.

rocks and figures in composition and apply the gold size, and as the writer of the book says, 'When it is clammy and sticks somewhat to your fingers but not so as to bring off any, then it is high time with your leather to lay and rub on the gold dust, if it clings to your finger, but not so as to bring off any with it, then know it is not sufficiently drie.' After endless recipes for lacquering and gilding comes a series of Anglo-Oriental drawings, representing somewhat indifferently the objects introduced by the Chinese and Japanese into the decoration of their lacquer, but that the authors were under the impression that their illustrations were an improvement on the native drawings is evident from the following remark:

'In the Cutts or patterns at the end of the book, we have exactly imitated their Buildings, Towers and Steeples, Figures, Rocks and the like according to the Patterns which the best workmen amongst them have afforded us on their cabinets, screens, boxes, etc. Perhaps we have helpt them a little in their proportions, when they were lame or defective, and made them more pleasant yet altogether as antick.'

In Fig. 345 a more advanced style and higher finish is perceptible than in the last cabinet. The composition of design on the doors is more truly Oriental, but the detail shows very clearly this cannot be the case; the Chinese dresses of the male figures, with pigtails in combination with the unduly large feet, hairdressing and clothes of the female figures, prove that the artist was but little acquainted with native Chinese and Japanese customs. The colours employed in this lacquer are only black and gold, and the lock-plates and hinges are examples of the best English metal-work of about 1690. The stand is probably the work of a Frenchman domiciled in this country. It was evidently the fashion to place these cabinets on most elaborately carved gilt stands of this character, with sometimes a cornice to match, till nearly the end of the century. The lacquer decoration of this cabinet possesses both artistic merit and excellent imitative qualities.

In letters and diaries of about 1700 constant references to the fascination of japanning infer that the demand was supplied from well-recognised sources. Sir Ralph Thoresby in his diary mentions a visit to 'the ingenious Mr Lumley, an excellent artist in many respects, paints excellently, japans incomparably, and what I was most pleased with, works mezzo-tint plates'. This proves the art was not confined to Stalker, Parker and young ladies, but that competent artists made it a profession. The greater portion of lacquer furniture was black, with gold design, but occasionally the ground was an intense red, being composed of Spanish vermilion and Venice lacquer. A fine cabinet of this description is Fig. 346, preserved at Penshurst. It is made of oak throughout, the upper portion being surmounted by the bold hooded cornice that was adopted after 1700; the doors are decorated on both sides with large single figures of Chinamen, in gold and black lacquer, with silver faces; the inside is divided into pigeon-holes and compartments above a series of drawers decorated with the more ordinary designs furnished by Stalker and Parker in their book. It may be noticed that at this time the drop-handles of the previous century have given way to a ring-handle and plate, which is engraved, but not yet perforated. The ground of this piece is throughout of a most intense red, with a brilliant surface.

A marked preference for height in cabinets began at this time; the increasing loftiness of the rooms in conjunction with the tall deal wainscot panelling demanded a corresponding feeling in the furniture, and to conceal a certain sense of bareness in the corners of the rooms corner-cupboards were introduced; in these, the highly prized tea-services were kept, used on rare occasions, or when the mistress of the house had her weekly afternoons at home for tea and cards. By the beginning of the century these at-home days had become an institution in ordinary households; this is shown by a letter from Lady Wentworth to her son in 1705, when she writes:

'She and her husband came this afternoon to see me, and Bell and hers, and Peter and his boy, it being my veseting day, and I take the same freedom you gave me when you was hear in making a great show with your tea tables and dishis; but you left but one tea-pott, that is, the little blew and white one, etc.'

Fig. 347. *Lacquer Corner Cupboard*. Height, 7 feet 10 inches; width, 2 feet 7 inches. Property of Messrs J. Mallett and Son.

Fig. 348. *Lacquer Writing-cabinet*. Height, 7 feet 9 inches; length, 3 feet 2 inches; depth, 1 foot 11 inches. Property of Rev J. O. Stephens.

Fig. 347 is one of these corner-cupboards in black lacquer, of about 1700; the cornice consists of a broken pediment centring in a small vase; the doors, which are set in a wide framing decorated with sprays of flowers in gold lacquer, are closely covered with a design of figures, ships, birds and landscapes; a great deal of effect is produced by the contrast between the raised detail of the figures and the flat treatment of the landscape; the hinges are of early type.

Another cabinet of tall and elegant shape is shown in Fig. 348; the hooded cornice is formed as a broken pediment with a deep embrasure, the curves in conjunction with those of the looking-glass panels are exceedingly original and graceful; the introduction of a shell and vase as a centre, and the banded ornament on the cornice, are purely European – the rest of the decoration being Oriental in taste. A slide divides the two upper portions, the upper of which opens as a writing-desk surmounting a chest of drawers; all is decorated in very clear and bright lacquer with scenes of Chinese life and the usual landscape. The lock-plates are plain, with ring handles; the date of this cabinet is soon after the accession of Anne.

The passion for lacquer and Eastern objects took a very strong hold upon society, and was continually being stimulated by the sales of curios and Oriental objects held every month at the docks by the East India Company. In 1692 one Edward Hurd petitions the State and sets forth:

'That by his great industry and expense, he has attained and brought to perfection the art of lacquering after the manner of Japan to such a degree of curiosity and durableness as to equal any brought from India, and prays for letters patent for the sole use exercise and benefit of the said invention for 14 years.'

In some cases we read that even the wainscots of the rooms were lacquered, and after her first visit to Hampton Court, Celia Fiennes mentions the new fashion:

'I went to see Hampton Court. Ye old buildings and ye New part. Ye Queen took Great delight in it. Ye new was but just ye shell up and some of ye Roomes of State Ceiled but nothing ffinished. Beyond this came severall Roomes, and one was pretty Large, at ye four corners were little roomes like drawing roomes, one pannelled all with Jappan, another with Looking Glass, and two with fine work under glass.'

Sometimes this Japan wainscot was low, and the wall hung with the wall-papers that were now being imported from China representing flowers, trees and exotic birds; but that this importation was also quickly copied here, is shown by the Government grant to William Bayly in November 1691:

'For the sole use of his new invention of printing all sorts of papers of all sorts of figures, and colours with several engines made of brass, without paint or stain, which will be useful for hanging in rooms, and which has never been known before.'

This Oriental taste was at its height about 1710, continuing as a fashion for many years. The *Spectator* of 12 February 1712, contains a complaint signed 'Jack Anvil' against his wife, of whom he says:

'She next set herself to reform every Room of my House, having glazed all my chimney-pieces with Looking glass and planted every corner with such Heaps of China, that I am obliged to move about my own house with the greatest Caution & Circumspection for fear of hurting our brittle Furniture.'

A fine specimen of highly furnished lacquer is shown on Plate XXV. The upper portion opens in two doors on which are representations in gold and red on a black ground of Oriental figures on islands, covered with trees and rocks; these rocks are diapered with fine gold patterns in imitation of the best Japanese lacquer; the cornice is double-hooded in the style of 1700, and surmounted by three finials of vase-shaped form, beneath which an unusual arrangement of arched drawers takes the place of a frieze; the hinges and lock-plates are good examples of English metal-work. The lower portion is formed as a chest of drawers and decorated with the usual plants, birds and Chinese tea-parties; the feet are original.

Sometimes an attempt was made to introduce an Oriental feeling into the structure of the furniture; this is strongly marked in the lower portion of Fig. 349, a double chest of drawers. Here the surface is recessed into deep arch-headed channels; the ground throughout is painted in imitation of red tortoise-shell; the lacquer decoration, which has been retouched, is comparatively flat, and points to a date after the accession of Anne. The form of this piece is unusual, and its nationality is not very clearly defined. Another example of flat lacquer in black and gold is Fig. 350, a linen chest of about 1710; it is probably the work of a successful amateur, as the somewhat feeble drawing of the disconnected islands and rocks show very superficial skill in portraying Oriental feeling; the indifferent quality of the lacquer also points to the work of an unprofessional hand. The stand is simple and effective, the deep hollow over the short cabriole leg being most suitable to its low proportion.

It is rare to find English lacquer with the ground of a colour other than black, red or green, but occasionally a buff ground was introduced to imitate

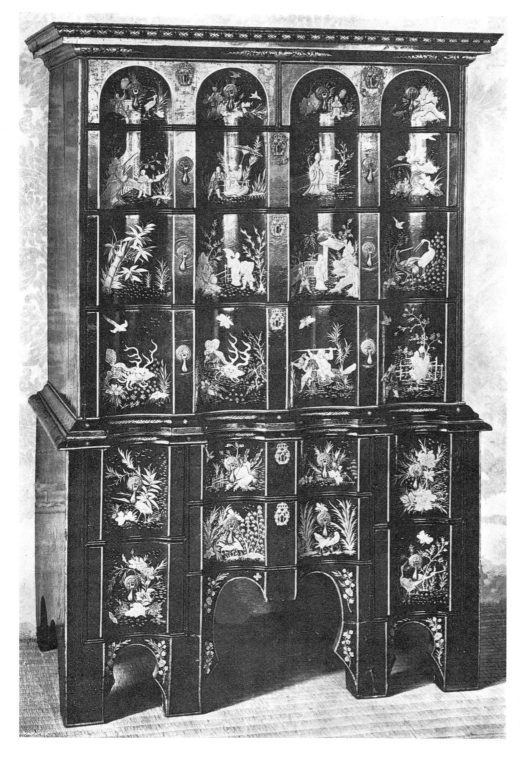

FIG. 349. *Lacquer Double Chest of Drawers*. Length, 5 feet 1 inch; width, 3 feet 4 inches; depth, 2 feet. Property of the VISCOUNTESS WOLSELEY.

FIG. 350. *Lacquer Linen Chest*. Length, 4 feet; height, with stand, 3 feet 8 inches; depth, 1 foot 11 inches. Property of the DUKE OF BEAUFORT.

the light sycamore ground of marqueterie. Fig. 351 is a clock-case of this rare lacquer. The design is small and in various colours, the pilasters at the sides being also lacquered. The maker's name is W. Webster, who was working about 1710, which is the date of the case; the top is hooded, a fashion that began on clock-cases about this time. Tall clocks of this period had by now lost the narrow and elegant shape of the former reigns, becoming broader throughout. Many tall clock-cases were made during Anne's reign in the ordinary flat black lacquer, and so many of these are still in existence, that it is unnecessary to give an example.

Marqueterie clock-cases followed the evolution of all other inlaid furniture; early specimens with coloured birds and flowers in panels have already been given in Figs. 256 and 257. In the next development, the entire surface was inlaid with flowers in brown and yellow woods, introducing the acanthus, which eventually developed into the fine seaweed pattern without floral decoration. Fig. 352 is of about the date 1690. In this clock-case it will be noticed that the heading is still square and the waist comparatively narrow; the surface of the case is covered with a floral marqueterie in brown and yellow woods springing from acanthus husks, the sides being also inlaid, a most rare feature in clock-cases. Fig. 353 is of the same character, rather later in date; in this instance the door to the hood is framed by two twisted columns in place of the ordinary straight shafts, the cupola to the hood being an early instance of this feature.

Plate XXVI (a) shows what is technically termed a yellow clock; the groundwork being of sycamore inlaid with light brown and black woods; the acanthus pattern of seaweed form combines with a strap-work which breaks up the monotony of the inlay. The maker, Bennett Mansell, was working in 1695, which is about the date of the clock. Fig. 354 is a still finer specimen of these rare yellow clocks, and where greater variety is effected by the introduction of small flowers and figures; the same treatment is continued round the framing of the door, and the cupola is also inlaid; the tall proportion and finish of this clock are remarkable. On Plate XXVI (b) it may be noticed that the design has become a pattern of finely cut arabesque marqueterie, dark on a light ground, spreading over the surface. The dial in this instance does not belong to the case, which is of about the date 1700. These clock-cases are a sure guide to the chronological arrangement of the different periods of marqueterie, inasmuch as the dials almost invariably have their maker's name, whose dates of entry into the Clockmakers' Company are registered in the Company's records. It must be borne in mind that occasionally these makers were working previous to their date of entry, and that in some

FIG. 351. *Lacquer Clock.* Height, 5 feet 8 inches; width at base, 1 foot 6 inches. Property of the REV J. O. STEPHENS.

FIG. 352. *Walnut Inlaid Clock.* Height, 7 feet 5 inches; width at base, 1 foot 4 inches. Property of D. F. WETHERFIELD, Esq.

FIG. 353. *Walnut Inlaid Clock.* Height, 7 feet 6 inches. Property of S. H. S. LOFTHOUSE, Esq.

FIG. 354. *Walnut Inlaid Clock.* Height, 7 feet 8 inches. Property of H. MARTIN GIBBS, Esq.

instances the dials have been changed; but in a case like the Grocers' clock (Fig. 257), where it is known that the dial has never been changed, and where the brass plate bearing the inscription is contemporary with the date of gift, the proof is incontestable.

Marqueterie and lacquer, although in great request from 1685 and onwards, was by no means representative of the ordinary class of furniture produced at that time. The demand for plain walnut furniture increased towards the end of the seventeenth century, and a large quantity was consequently made, attractive through simplicity of shape and quiet elegance of design. These objects were a fitting accompaniment to the many small houses of red brick that were now being erected in place of the more romantic-looking but less convenient stone houses of the first half of the century. No doubt the plainness of the furniture was in some measure due to the reduced finances of the nation, impoverished during the greater part of William's and Anne's reigns by wars that not only exhausted the resources of the people, but paralysed trade, the latter being so restricted for a period that the number of self-made merchants of former times who had so ostentatiously and lavishly spent money on furniture and decoration was now greatly reduced. Retrenchment and economy became a necessity among many of the county families, and consequently a certain mediocrity of imagination and general lethargy in art became universal, and with the exception of the few very wealthy landowners, the community was content with less luxurious surroundings. In the middle classes printed calicoes and cottons were substituted for silks, and wall-papers for tapestry and wainscot panelling. In the *Postman* of 12 December 1702, an advertisement is to be found stating that:

'At the Blue Paper Warehouse in Aldermanbury (and nowhere else) in London are sold the true sorts of figured Paper Hangings, some in pieces of twelve yards long, others after the manner of real tapistry, others in imitation of Irish stitch, flowered Damasks, Sprigs and Branches, others yard wide, in imitation of marble and other coloured wainscoats, others in yard wide Embossed work, and a curious sort of Flock work in imitation of Caffaws, and other hangings of curious figures and colours.'

Another advertisement in the next year mentions:

'Imitations of Marbles and other coloured Wainscoats, which are to be put in Panels and Mouldings made for that purpose, fit for the Hangings of Parlours, Dining Rooms and staircases; and others in yard wide Embossed work in imitation of gilded Leather.'

The older hangings were, however, still remarkable commodities in 1704, as an advertisement of this date in the same journal mentions:

'Three suites of Hangings, one of Forrest Tapistry, one of clouded Camlet, and one of blue Printed Linsey; the first two very good, scarce the worse for wearing, to be sold very reasonable.'

Wall-papers were used in the bedrooms of the larger houses and in the dining-rooms and parlours of the smaller houses, that were being built early in the century on the outskirts of London and other large towns, and in which, doubtless, so much of the smaller pieces of walnut furniture were used. Macky, in his *Journal through England* at this period, notes that:

'About two miles from Wainstead in my way to London, is a large village called Stratford, where there are about two hundred little country houses for the conveniency of the Citizens in Summer; where their Wives and Children generally keep, and their Husbands come down on Saturdays and return on Mondays.'

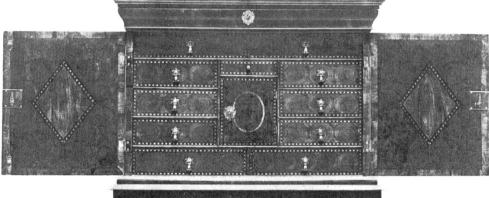

FIG. 355. *Walnut Cabinet*. Height, 5 feet 2 inches; width, 3 feet 4 inches; depth, 1 foot 6 inches. Property of MESSRS MORANT.

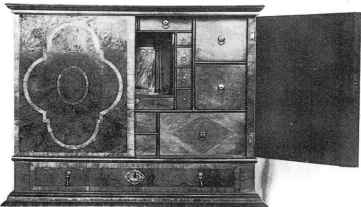

FIG. 357. *Outside – same* (FIG. 356).

FIG. 356 (*left*). *Walnut Cabinet*. Height, 4 feet 9 inches; width, 2 feet 10 inches; depth, 1 foot 6 inches. Property of MESSRS MORANT.

The quotation is interesting, as it proves the Saturday till Monday out of town was a fashion in existence two hundred years ago, and that the dangers of the road were braved for those week-end trips.

Fig. 355, a cabinet with a stand, is an early example of high-class simple walnut the doors are veneered in oyster-pieces of walnut, with a lighter border of the same wood; the drawers are faced in a similar manner, but edged with a chequer of holly and ebony; the ogeed line of the frieze is unusual, but resembles that on the frame of table (Fig. 295). The handles are

FIG. 358. *Walnut Chest of Drawers on Stand*. Height, 5 feet 2 inches; width, 3 feet; depth, 1 foot 7 inches. Property of HENRY HUXLEY, Esq.

FIG. 359. *Walnut Chest of Drawers on Stand*. Height, 6 feet; length, 3 feet 7 inches; depth, 2 feet. Property of the VISCOUNTESS WOLSELEY.

FIG. 360. *Walnut Writing-cabinet.* Height, 6 feet 9 inches; width, 1 foot 10 inches; depth, 1 foot 6 inches. Property of C. ASSHETON SMITH, Esq.

FIG. 361. *Walnut Writing-cabinet.* Property of the DUKE OF MARLBOROUGH.

of the star and drop pattern so prevalent at this time, and the legs of the stand are composed of a twist, and centre in a ball in the fashion of 1688, approximately the date of the cabinet. Fig. 356 is a few years later; it has no frieze, and the walnut veneer is cut on the straight, the outside of the doors (Fig. 357) being inlaid with oyster-pieces; the legs of the stand have a more open twist than the last specimen, and centre in an oval. These two pieces of furniture are very representative of the inexpensive type of cabinet used before 1700.

A favourite form of simple decorative furniture at this time was the chest of drawers mounted on a high stand such as Fig. 358. Here the frieze is divided into a flat and an ovolo member surmounting drawers, which are inlaid with a line of lighter wood; the stand, containing three drawers, is of oak and divided into arched compartments; the legs are of walnut, cupped and turned in the manner of 1690, and rest upon large bun-feet. Another of these chests of drawers and stand, veneered throughout in walnut, is Fig. 359, of about the date 1698. The top is hooded with a bold cornice moulding, which is somewhat out of proportion and disconnected with other parts of the piece, no use being made of the flat surfaces immediately below this cornice; the upper portion is divided into two parts, and no decoration is attempted save a cross-banding of walnut; the stand contains three drawers, and the arches of both this and the last cabinet are edged with a narrow fillet moulding, very typical of walnut furniture towards the end of the century, and the twisted legs are united by a slightly waved stretcher.

A writing-cabinet of rare shape is given in Fig. 360; the light hooded cornice is surmounted by three vase-shaped finials; the upper portion opens in two doors, bordered with a broad cross-banding of walnut, this edging being repeated on the writing-flap; the cupped legs in conjunction with the tall proportions of this piece give it great originality. Fig. 361 is an ordinary writing-cabinet of about 1700, preserved at Blenheim; the cupboard and cornice repeat the design of the preceding piece on somewhat heavier lines, the portion underneath the writing-flap being formed as a chest of drawers; the veneer is a mixture of oyster-pieces and plain walnut cut on the straight; the hinges overlap the doors and relieve the monotony of the plain uprights; the handle-plates on the two lower drawers are original, those perforated being of later make. Fig. 362 is a knee-hole writing-desk; it is veneered in plain walnut and supported on six legs, which taper towards the base and end in the usual feet, connected by a plain stretcher centring in a semicircle.

The double chest of drawers was a favourite piece of furniture in bedrooms from the beginning of the eighteenth century. Fig. 363 is an early example, surmounted by the curved and broken pediment with finials that began in William's reign, although the chamfered and channelled edges, the original open lock and handle-plates, distinctly point to about the date 1710. The centre of the semi-circular frieze is inlaid with a cross and square in dark wood on a shield of lighter ground; the face of the piece is veneered in burr walnut, each drawer being bordered with a cross-banding of the same wood.

Cupboards, with glazed and mullioned doors for the display of china, were much in use at this time, some hooded like the writing-cabinets, others with straight tops as on the bookcase. We read that Queen Mary had employed the services of Johnstone, who was the best cabinet-maker of that time, to make different varieties of these cupboards for her collection of china and Delft ware. Fig. 364 is of about the date 1690, and resembles the rather earlier specimen given in Fig. 233, but the difference is clearly marked in the solid construction of the lower portion resting upon ball-feet, in the place of the Carolean stand and stretcher; the frames to the doors are cross-banded in walnut, and the original crystal cut glass is contained in walnut mullions of a simple half-round moulding. Fig. 365 is a china cupboard of rather different construction, some twenty-five years later in date, with larger sized panels than in the preceding specimen, and bordered with a narrow gilt acanthus moulding. Many of these china cabinets were later converted into bookcases.

Much plain bedroom furniture, such as chests of drawers, dressing and other tables, was made towards the end of the century. Fig. 366 represents the type of dressing-table much in use about 1690; the arched and cusped finish to the lower portion of the frame is bordered with a narrow fillet; the long pendants carry out the graceful proportions of the cupped legs which are turned in yew, the serpentine stretcher being walnut. Fig. 367 is a larger dressing-table of the same type and date, somewhat sturdier in design, made throughout in walnut and bordered round the drawers with a herring-bone inlay of the same wood, a knee-hole space being left in the centre; the legs are six in number, united by an undulating stretcher. Fig. 368 shows one of the looking-glasses constructed to stand on these tables, a few years later in date; a flat heading is introduced in conjunction with the curves of a moulding peculiar to the end of the century; it has the original bevelled glass, but the ball-feet are restorations. Fig. 369 is another of these looking-glasses, made towards the end of Anne's reign; the mirror here is framed in a gilt and carved border of low relief, mounted on a double tier of small drawers. Occasionally these dressing-tables and mirrors are found of lacquer, to match other furniture.

Sometimes in tables the cup-shaped leg was elaborately balustered; this is the case in Fig. 370, a small oak table made towards the end of William's reign, for the occasional reproduction in oak of fashionable walnut forms in tables, chairs, chests of drawers and cabinets always continued, their rarity

FIG. 362. *Walnut Writing-desk.* Property of the HON CHARLOTTE MARIA LADY NORTH and R. EDEN DICKSON, Esq.

FIG. 363. *Walnut Double Chest of Drawers.* Height, 6 feet 4 inches; width, 3 feet 2 inches; depth, 1 foot 9 inches. Property of S. H. S. LOFTHOUSE, Esq.

FIG. 364. *Walnut China Cupboard.* Height, 6 feet 6 inches; width, 4 feet; depth, 1 foot 2 inches. Property of the HON CHARLOTTE MARIA LADY NORTH and R. EDEN DICKSON, Esq.

FIG. 365. *Walnut China Cabinet.* Height, 7 feet 10 inches; width, 5 feet 10 inches; depth, 1 foot 6 inches. Property of the VISCOUNTESS WOLSELEY.

FIG. 366. *Walnut and Yew Dressing-table.* Property of FRANK GREEN, Esq.

FIG 367. *Walnut Dressing-table.* Height, 2 feet 8 inches; length, 3 feet 4 inches. Property of C. E. KEMPE, Esq.

FIG. 368. *Walnut Looking-glass.* Property of the VISCOUNTESS WOLSELEY.

Fig. 369. *Walnut Looking-glass.* Property of the Rev J. O. Stephens.

Fig. 370. *Oak Table.* Height, 2 feet 4 inches; width, 2 feet 2 inches; depth, 1 foot 6 inches.

Fig. 371. *Walnut Side-table.* Property of the Hon Charlotte Maria Lady North and R. Eden Dickson, Esq.

being probably due to individual preference for this wood, or to country origin. Long oak dining-tables still continued to be made; a specimen, dated 1697, has already been given in Fig. 176 in 'The Age of Oak'. In the more modern and fashionable dining-rooms, oval and folding oak or walnut tables were often used; this can be proved by reference to prints of the time. Small walnut side-tables, with either marble or wooden tops, such as Fig. 371, came into fashion about 1700 in place of the somewhat cumbersome buffets and court cupboards, and the silver-plate originally displayed on these was now placed on the dining-tables. The so-called sideboard, as we now understand the term, was not developed until the middle of the century, and as neither knives nor spoons were changed, forks rare, and the food was placed in rotation on the table, no necessity for much side service existed until Georgian times. Another form of side-table is Fig. 372, which could be converted into a round shape by swinging legs on the movable back stretcher. It is of walnut throughout; the legs are of uncommon design, being of spindle form in octagon; they finish in feet that move on pivots approximating the construction of a castor, an invention that was certainly in use at this time, and can be seen on the walnut baby-trotter (Fig. 373), which is of about the date 1700. In this interesting piece, a portion of the upper ring opens to admit the child, and can be closed by a hook and eye; the lower portion is supported on six large wooden castors, working on movable pins.

Fig. 372. *Walnut Table.* Height, 2 feet 5 inches; width of top, 2 feet 7 inches by 2 feet 2 inches. Property of C. E. Kempe, Esq.

Fig. 373. *Walnut Baby-trotter.* Property of E. A. Barry, Esq.

CHAPTER VII

HE characteristics of important upholstered beds after the reign of Charles II were the elaborate mouldings and ornaments to the cornices and testers, the sometimes excessive height of structure, and the comparative absence of ornate tasselled fringes. The hangings up till this time had principally consisted of silk damasks, plain velvets embroidered in silks and gold thread, or of needlework tapestry. During the reigns of William and Anne, the hangings were sometimes composed of chintz, but mostly of figured velvets or damasks trimmed with galon. Embroidered bed-hangings, though exceptional, evidently still continued to be occasionally bought and sold, and were highly esteemed. In 1704 a bed is advertised in the *Postman* as 'a prize in a lottery by Her Majesty's permission', though it does not follow that the make of this bed is exactly contemporary with the notice.

'A Rich Bed, seven foot broad, eight foot long and about fourteen feet high in which no less than Two Thousand ounces of gold and silver, wrought in it containing four curtains embroidered on both sides alike on a white silk Tabby; Three Vallains with tassels, three Basses, two Bonegraces and four Cantoneers Embroidered on gold Tissue Cloth, cost £3000, put up at £1400.'

Basses were the ground valances; bonegraces (a French invention, from the word *bonnegrace* – a form of head-covering) were narrow fixed curtains that did not draw, closing the opening between the side-curtains and back of a bed, in order to protect the head from draughts. Cantonnières were narrow embroidered bands that hung from pendants, uniting the corners of the top valances outside the curtains, and performed the same office of protection and seclusion when the latter were drawn at the foot of the bed; it was therefore desirable to have height in a bed of this kind, not only on account of its appearance in the new lofty rooms, but also to avoid the asphyxiation of the occupant. These lofty rooms must have been extremely cold; the bedrooms up to Carolean times had been comparatively small and invariably low, but with the new style of building the size of the windows much increased, while the appliances for warming the rooms decreased, a small hearth-basket or tray, of what was then called sea-coal, being substituted for the roaring wood fires of earlier times.

The half-tester open bedstead, adopted from the shape called 'Duchesse' in France, received but little favour here, and consequently specimens of this style, which was alluded to by Celia Fiennes and other writers of that time as 'half tester beds in the new mode', or 'à la moderne', are almost impossible to find. Other simple forms, such as truckle and turn-up bedsteads, existed, used by the less important members of a household, but examples of these have also practically disappeared. In a letter of Isabella, Lady Wentworth, to her son, Lord Raby, dated 2 January 1711, there is an allusion to one of these turn-up bedsteads, and complaints about the temperature of the tall rooms of that time.

'My dearist and best of the children, Did I not tell you of the Queen's great loss? She had a dog shut up in a turn up bed and soe smothered. The Queen is better natured than I for sartainly I would have put away those that did it. . . . It is bitter cold in any roome but this, and this comfortable warme, but your lodgins ar excessif cold, the roomes soe large and soe high if the fyer be never soe great one syde freesis while the other burns.'

Oak bedsteads, even amongst people of quality, were still in use in Anne's reign, and in another letter written by Lady Wentworth in 1705, she mentions that:

'Our bedsteads being old and craysy, just as Betty stept into bed broak all to peesis; it cannot be mended I hope you will order Mr. Elleson to gett a new one.'

A few days later she writes to the same person:

'I have gott my bedstead mended, In my last I was afraid it could not be dun.'

Chintz had no doubt in many instances, by the beginning of the eighteenth century, replaced the ordinary hangings to oak bedsteads, and Swift, writing in 1712, and satirising the taste for things Oriental, mentions how a country squire from 'being a foul feeder grew dainty: how he longed for Mangos, Spices, and Indian Birds' Nests, etc., and could not sleep but in a Chintz Bed'.

The bed (Fig. 374), unfortunately somewhat mutilated, is connected with a very important event in English history – the birth of James Francis Edward Stuart – afterwards known as the Old Pretender, the youngest son of James II and his second wife, Mary Beatrice D'Este. The tester cornice, which has lost its top ornaments, shows the commencement of the scrolled and corbelled corners of carved wood, that in four or five years became so prominent a feature on these state beds. The material on the cornice is closely glued to the mouldings, and with the hangings and valances is of fine figured velvet, of English make, dark blue, green, crimson and salmon on a deep cream ground; the fringe is modern. The ceiling of the tester is untouched, and composed of canary-coloured satin, strained on simple architectural mouldings; the stain of the back has been renewed, and certain portions of the embroidery with which it was probably entirely covered, re-applied; the swags of flowers are of the highly raised original embroidery, in pale green and silver, the central and upright panel of ornament being still upon its original canary-satin ground; the ciphers on each side of this under small crowns are those of James II, whilst immediately over the centre

Fig. 374. *Upholstered Bed*. Height, 9 feet 8 inches; length, 6 feet 8 inches; width, 5 feet 9 inches. Property of Sir Algernon K. B. Osborn, Bart.

Fig. 375. *Upholstered Beds*. (A) Height, 16 feet; length, 8 feet; width, 6 feet 4 inches. (B) Height, 8 feet 6 inches; length, 7 feet; width, 4 feet 1 inch. Hampton Court Palace.

pillow, and surrounded by fragments of original embroidery, is a cipher containing the initials of the unfortunate Queen to whom the bed belonged. The scrolling of the pillow-heading, which has been re-covered, is strongly pronounced in the newest fashion of that time, and the padded quilt and quilted pillows have their original covering of cream satin. James Francis Edward, who for so long made pretensions to the British throne, was born in St James's Palace in this bed, on 10 June 1688. The interesting details of this event are described at length by Burnet, who leans strongly towards the supposition of a fraudulent birth; and the tradition of the introduction of a newly born child into the room through the medium of a warming-pan is in some measure due to his statements. This most interesting, though much restored, bed is now at Chicksands Priory; on the abdication of King James it became the perquisite of the Lord Chamberlain, by whom it was given to an ancestor of the present owner.

The next example in this series of beds is Fig. 375 (A), five or six years later in date, and used by William III, James's nephew and usurper of his throne; it is now placed in one of the small dining-rooms at Hampton Court Palace. The height of this magnificient bed is 16 feet, and the almost total disappearance of the curtains (their remnants being tied to the posts) adds to the loftiness of its appearance. The cornice consists of a series of fantastic scrolls supported by corbels at the centres and corners with large vase-shaped finials of elaborate form, from which the plumes have been removed; the ceiling of the tester is dome-shaped and matches the cornice in design; the double valances are bordered with a broad galon, and meet at the corners in scrolled projections, from which the cantonnières (now missing) hung; the pillow-heading is elaborately carved in scrolls and finials. The whole of the wood-work is covered in brilliant rose damask of English make, finished with a galon trimming, the curtains, valances and back being all to match; the bonegraces, whose uses have already been explained, are still left hanging; the feet are splayed, scrolled and covered with the damask. Some notion can be obtained of the arrangement of the bedding in those days by the inspection of these mattresses and quilts that are covered in their original cream satin, with green and red button-tufts; the long bolster is also covered with the same cream satin. By the side of this tall state bed made for so short a man, a small bed (B), used by George II, is shown, on which the inner leather covering to the feather mattresses can be seen, the satin having been removed.

A bed similar in construction and taste to that of Willian III's, but from which the vase-shaped finials have been removed, is Fig. 376, preserved at Hardwick. The cornice is carved in the same manner, but here pendants form the corners; the scrolls that held the cantonnières are also of carved wood, covered with rose-coloured damask with which the entire bed is upholstered, the trimming on the escalloped valances being bordered with a broad rose galon; the bonegraces, which can be seen where the back meets the sides, are decorated with one straight line of galon; the panel of silk immediately above the pillows is a restoration, and the quilt is comparatively modern. This bed is of about the date 1690, at which time the galon-scrolled trimming, centring in buttons, began to take the place of elaborate fringes on upholstered furniture.

The lavish expenditure that continued in the decoration of important beds shows that these still held the position of former times, and although it was no longer the fashion in England for men of high position to give audience in bed, ladies of quality still received in this manner, and royal beds were both in England and France guarded with especial precautions. In 1694 the Marquis de Dangeau mentions in his diary, that the Queen of England 'receives the Court whilst on her bed'. Here he refers to Mary Beatrice D'Este at St Germains. In the *État de France* of 1694, there are interesting directions for the protection of royal beds, and the appointment of ladies of the bed-chamber for the Queen, in place of the valets who had hitherto sat within the rails to guard the bed during the day, and these directions are stated to be founded on English Court ordinances of the time.

Plate XXVII shows another of these royal beds made for Queen Anne. The cornice is comparatively simple, surmounted by vase-shaped finials covered

FIG. 376. *Upholstered Bed*. Height, 13 feet; length, 7 feet; width, 6 feet. Property of the DUKE OF DEVONSHIRE.

in velvet, and the double valances are straight; the whole bed is upholstered in a richly patterned velvet of English make, and by tradition the product of Spitalfields looms; it is tawny, olive green and claret on a cream ground; the curtains are lined with cream satin, and the two mattresses, quilts and bolster still in existence are covered with the same material. No fringe or galon is used in the decoration of this bed, and its appearance therefore is somewhat bare.

Fig. 377 is a bed of about 1710, upholstered throughout in a beautiful figured velvet, olive green and rose on a cream ground; the cornice consists of simple mouldings which rise at the centres and form broken pediments enclosing ducal crowns; the valances are straight and trimmed with an early eighteenth-century fringe repeated on the curtains, all lined with sea-green satin; the ceiling of the tester is an elaborate design of carved scrolls covered with velvet and satin; the back has been re-covered, but possesses the original carved double escallop shells covered with velvet above a ducal crown worked in gold and silks; on either side are carved sprays of rush-leaved ornament covered in cream satin; at the corners of the cornice may be noticed the escallop shell again introduced, a favourite novelty in ornament at that time.

Fig. 378 is a bed, a little later in date, also preserved at Hardwick, and covered throughout in a patterned velvet of English make – green on a paler ground of the same colour; the cornice is here serpentine in outline and lighter in character than on the preceding beds. The top member is composed of a carved spiral nulling, centring and cornering in escallop shells

Fig. 377. *Upholstered Bed.* Height, 13 feet; length, 7 feet; width, 6 feet. Property of the DUKE OF DEVONSHIRE.

Fig. 378. *Upholstered Bed.* Height, 13 feet. Property of the DUKE OF DEVONSHIRE.

most skilfully covered with the velvet; the valances follow the lines of the cornice, and are trimmed with a fringe similar to that used on the last bed; the back is composed of the velvet without any ornamentation. The number of these magnificient beds of the same period existing at Hardwick proves that in a rich household this quality of bed was still predominant, for in addition to these given, there are many others; a large state bed also has been removed and another broken up to form a canopy in the long gallery.

It has been shown that, from about 1625 till 1700, the posts of important and fashionable beds were slender, octagonal or round in form, and covered with material; at the latter date this was discarded and the wood left bare, generally fluted on the upper portion, and finishing towards the end of Anne's reign in walnut legs of cabriole form.

Fig. 379 is a wooden bed of about 1710, with plain fluted posts, and it probably represents an isolated example of individual taste, perhaps copied from a French bed. The entire construction is of walnut, and the plain cornice is supported by a double frieze, carved and gilt with an early eighteenth-century design forming a valance-box to the curtains. The back is in four large panels, with gilt mouldings and applied pateræ of a sun and stars; the legs are of spindle form, and terminate in small bun-feet; the hangings, etc., are of later date. These fluted columns are again shown on the bed (Fig. 380) in which Queen Anne slept on the occasion of her visit to Brympton. The height is comparatively low, and the whole construction shows simplicity and elegance; the escalloped and nulled cornice upon which the damask is tightly strained foreshadows in its form and projecting corners some of the coming characteristics of the later eighteenth-century beds. The perforated and open vases are relics of the ostrich plumes which by this time ceased to be in request; this same form can be seen on the vase-shaped finials to the gate-posts of the entrance to the Orangery at

FIG. 379. *Walnut Bed*. Property of the HON CHARLOTTE MARIA LADY NORTH and R. EDEN DICKSON, Esq.

FIG. 380. *Upholstered Bed*. Height, 9 feet 6 inches; length, 6 feet. Property of SIR SPENCER C. PONSONBY FANE.

Kensington Palace. The valances are shaped, somewhat resembling in line those of the walnut bed (Fig. 379); they are trimmed with a simple fringe and pleated at the corners like the contemporary coat-tails; the carved pillow-heading, also covered in damask, is of bold scrolling; the legs are of cabriole form, carved on the knee and foot with the decoration of the time; the bed is entirely covered with red rose damask of English design and manufacture, the hangings of the room and window curtains being all to match.

CHAPTER VIII

T has been necessary to defer the definite introduction and description of the cabriole leg until now, although suggestions of its appearance in furniture have already been shown. So long as the backs of chairs remained comparatively rectangular, a distinctly curved leg was not considered necessary to carry out the design, but with the accession of William III a great change took place in chairs, and the fashion for a shorter back of hooped form with cabriole legs was introduced, presumably from Holland; this fashion ran contemporaneously with the tall and narrow cane-backed chairs, but being more convenient for meals and more comfortable to the sitter, eventually superseded the older type and formed the pattern for the later developments of the eighteenth-century chair.

The feet to these cabriole legs were first of scroll form as in tall-back caned chairs, then the scroll formed the fetlock-joint to a hoof-shaped foot, taken from the French *pied-de-biche,* but this soon lost its hoof form in a square and slightly spreading foot, and finally developed into the well-known club-foot of Anne and George I. The light curved form of this cabriole leg was accompanied by a similar treatment in the design of the back, a curve being introduced into its uprights, the splat assuming the shape known as fiddleback.

In Fig. 381, of about 1687, the cresting retains the feeling of the contemporary tall cane-backed chairs, the uprights are curved, and the splat is perforated and richly carved in the manner of Fig. 310, but suggesting the fiddle shape; the front of the seat droops in curved form and is united as in earlier chairs, by cappings to the cabriole legs; these are carved on the shoulders with floral pendants and finish in scrolls on slightly splayed feet; the front stretcher is recessed and of Carolean character; the back legs, as in

FIG. 381. *Walnut Chair.* Property of R. W. PARTRIDGE, Esq.

FIG. 382. *Walnut Chair.* HAMPTON COURT PALACE.

FIG. 383. *Walnut Chair.* Property of LORD FITZHARDINGE.

FIG. 384. *Walnut Chair*. Property of the EARL OF CARRINGTON.

nearly all early chairs of this type, are of scrolled form, finishing on square bases. This chair was probably originally covered in needlework. Fig. 382 is the next development of this new shape. Here the back is somewhat shorter and the cresting more simple than in the preceding specimens; the splat is more solid, but perforated in the centre with fine carving; the uprights are curved, but break at a sharp angle below the centre; the cabriole legs project in small curves on the inner side; a feature that continued for some years, and the feet are of hoof form; the rising stretcher is still Carolean. This chair is one of a set at Hampton Court Palace, and is covered with the original needlework tapestry made by Queen Mary and her ladies-in-waiting. Fig. 383 is one from a pair at Berkeley Castle, the treatment of the back being similar to that pursued in the last chair, except that the carving is rather more elaborate, the simple cabriole legs finish in hoofed feet, and the evolution of the scroll into the pastern of the hoof is clearly perceptible; the stretcher is flat, resembling that found on stools of about 1695, and the seat is covered with its original needlework. Genuine specimens of these hooped-backed chairs, with carved and perforated splats, are rare; they were made originally for the wealthy classes, being very expensive in manufacture, and by the time the demand for this shape became more general, much carving on the perforation of the spats was out of fashion. Fig. 384 is contemporary with these specimens, and the general outline is of similar shape; the cresting is far more elaborate and earlier in intention; the back is caned, and was probably originally gilt; the front rail of the seat droops, and is in the style of the back; the legs finish in scroll-feet. Another variety, with a tall cane-back, of about the date 1700, is Fig. 385; the cresting is simple but elegant in design, the uprights are straight, with a bold moulding that is continued in curved form on the lower rail of the back; the caning bears traces of the original gilding, and the legs terminate in the divided hoof form known as *pied-de-biche*; the back legs are scrolled, and finish in square plinths.

It may be noticed that up to this time the seat-rails to chairs were square-cornered, but soon after 1700 these corners became altered in character by the high cresting to the leg, the design of which was sometimes repeated in the middle of the front rail. In Fig. 386, of about the date 1709, the back is straight and upholstered; the legs show the curved cresting forming the corners of the seat, these finish in square club-feet, suggesting the hoof, in which the fetlock-joint is still perceptible; the edges and carved ornaments

FIG. 385. *Walnut Chair*. Height, 4 feet 3 inches. Property of S. CAMPBELL CORY, Esq.

FIG. 386. *Walnut and Gilt Upholstered Chair*. Property of the MARQUESS OF CHOLMONDELEY.

FIG. 387. *Walnut Chair, Gilt*. Property of the HON CHARLOTTE MARIA LADY NORTH and R. EDEN DICKSON, Esq.

Fig. 389. *Gilt Walnut Upholstered Stool.* Height, 1 foot 5 inches; length, 2 feet; width, 1 foot 3 inches. Property of the Hon Charlotte Maria Lady North and R. Eden Dickson, Esq.

Fig. 388 (*left*). *Gilt Walnut Upholstered Love-seat.* Height, 3 feet 6 inches; width, 3 feet 3 inches. Property of the Hon Charlotte Maria Lady North and R. Eden Dickson, Esq.

are gilt, the pendant on the front rail is broken. This example is one from a large set at Houghton in Norfolk, comprising chairs, stools and sofas; they are all covered in deep emerald-green velvet, trimmed with silver galon, and precede the building of the great house by about twenty years.

Fig. 387 is a chair from a suite of almost similar type from Glemham, but of more elaborate finish and decoration, the wood-work being entirely gilt and carved at the knees with bold cabochons surmounted by feathered trefoils; the feet are carved with acanthus. The seat and back of this chair are upholstered in rose damask of a later date, and in order to show the material with which this entire suite was originally covered, a stool (Fig. 388) and one of the double chairs or love-seats (Fig. 389) are also given. This material consists of a patterned cloth of gold, on a silver ground, through which run brilliant coral lines of satin; the trimming is a silver galon; when new it must have been most brilliant, and was evidently highly treasured by its first owner, Lord North, as we read in a contemporary letter, that he complains of the smoke from the chimneys of the Goldsmiths' Company injuring his new furniture to such an extent, that he was obliged to move it to his country-seat, Glemham, where it has since remained. In the love-seat, the arms curve outwardly and droop slightly; the upholstery of these specimens is in a remarkable state of preservation, the silver ground alone having tarnished in colour.

Fig. 390 is an interesting red lacquer chair, one of a set, of the first years of Anne. The width of the back increasing towards the top, the combination of the scarlet lacquer with the red and gold Cordova stamped leather, are most unusual; this leather is neatly strained with the original small gilt nails on a frame seat sunk in a rebate moulding, and the decorative effect is remarkable; the legs, of simple cabriole form, finish in round club-feet, the final evolution from the scroll and hoof.

Early hoop-back chairs (such as Fig. 381), in spite of the money evidently lavished upon them, were slow obtaining favour. The sentiment of the tall-back chair can still be traced in Fig. 391, one of a set, of about 1705. The cresting with the traditional vase and foliage has almost disappeared, but in the splat that divides the caning of the back, a cartouche of late marqueterie is introduced; the lines of the back are curved, and the lower edge of the seat-rail, and the long cabriole legs ending in club-feet, carry out the graceful lines of this back. The caning, which at this period became excessively fine, is

FIG. 390. *Red Lacquer and Leather Chair.* Height, 4 feet 7 inches. Property of the DUCHESS OF BEAUFORT.

FIG. 391. *Walnut Arm-chair.* Property of GUY LAKING, Esq.

FIG. 392. *Walnut Inlaid Chair.* Height, 3 feet 7 inches.

FIG. 393. *Walnut Inlaid Chair.* Height, 3 feet 7 inches. Property of S. CAMPBELL CORY, Esq.

original, and the stretchers still show a link with the chairs of the preceding century. The same sentiment of form is preserved in Fig. 392, which is without caning, and the shaped splat is treated plainly like the rest of the chair; the arms have an outward lateral curve instead of what has hitherto been vertical; the seat is loose, framed in a rebate moulding. A baby-chair on the same lines is shown in Fig. 393, but the reduced proportions make the back and legs somewhat clumsy. Fig. 394 is a chair with the splat enlivened by a panel of marqueterie again repeated on the seat-rail; stretchers, now about to disappear, resemble the preceding specimens, and fix the date as early in the century. In the beautiful chair, one of a set (Fig. 395), this departure is shown; the increasing width and strength of the shoulder of the cabriole leg at its union with the seat-rail was evidently called forth by this abolition, and the back legs became club-footed, and more in accordance with those of the front, and it may be taken as a general rule that, when back legs are found of this type and without a stretcher, the chair is after the date 1708. In this instance marqueterie decorates the splat, seat-rail, head of the hoop and knees of the legs; the front feet take the form of little shoes; the date of this chair is about 1708. Another chair of almost the same date is Fig. 396, with the same characteristics of shape, but decorated with the black and gold lacquer so much in vogue at this time. It is in an admirable state of preservation.

In assigning dates, it is only by the comparison of all small details that anything like a definite conclusion can be arrived at. It has been said before, that the general designs of a preceding taste may constantly overlap an innovation, and all the unobtrusive but practical parts of furniture should be equally taken into consideration; the stretchers, the height of the seat, the width of the hoop, and the form of the back legs of chairs are all details to be carefully observed. Vague references to the Stuart Period, or that of William and Mary, convey practically nothing in the arrangement of an evolution, and although a series of objects apparently resembling each other may seem dull, it is only by their close comparison that the differences in their dates can be arrived at.

FIG. 394. *Walnut Child's Chair*. Height, 2 feet 4 inches; width, 1 foot 1 inch. Property of ROBERT W. J. RUSHBROOKE, Esq.

FIG. 395. *Walnut Inlaid Chair*. Height, 3 feet 6 inches. Property of C. ASSHETON SMITH, Esq.

FIG. 396. *Black and Gold Lacquer Chair*. Property of the VISCOUNTESS WOLSELEY.

Writing-chairs, some of exceptional form, were made at the beginning of the seventeenth century. A favourite shape was Fig. 397; the back is curved, and formed of one solid piece of wood, inlaid with the initials in cipher of Lord Dudley North. The arms bow outwardly, and finish in scrolls on their curved supports; the seat is round; the legs present a strange combination of the spindle-shaped leg and the club-foot; the stretcher and back legs conform to a date very early in the century. Two more of these writing-chairs, of about 1710, are shown in Fig. 398, (a) with cabriole legs and club-feet, and (b) with the legs more quadrangular, and intersected below the shoulder by a triple moulding; the arms of this chair curve outwardly, and

FIG. 397. *Walnut Inlaid Writing-chair*.
Height, 2 feet 11 inches; width, 2 feet.
Property of the HON. CHARLOTTE MARIA LADY NORTH and R. EDEN DICKSON, Esq.

(a)

FIGS. 398 (a) and (b). *Walnut Writing-chairs*.
Property of the MARQUESS OF CHOLMONDELEY.

(b)

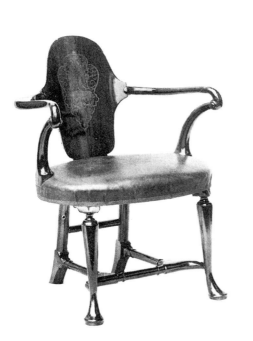

FIG. 399. *Walnut Inlaid Chair*. Property of MESSRS MORANT.

FIG. 400. *Mahogany Upholstered Chair*. Property of the EARL OF DYSART.

FIG. 401. *Walnut Upholstered Chair*. Height, 2 feet 3 inches; width, 1 foot 9 inches. Property of the HON CHARLOTTE MARIA LADY NORTH and R. EDEN DICKSON, Esq.

FIG. 402. *Walnut Chair*. Property of EDWIN A. ABBEY, Esq.

the padded back resembles in its lines the open hoop-back type. This specimen possesses great interest, as having belonged to Sir Robert Walpole, and being the writing-chair he constantly used.

Walnut chairs with upholstered backs, and cabriole legs without stretchers, also commenced to be in fashion at this time. Fig. 399 shows one of these. The knees of the legs are inlaid with marqueterie, and the club-feet are slightly splayed, whilst Fig. 400, from a suite of furniture at Ham House, comprising chairs, double chairs and sofas, is of mahogany, a wood, up to the first decade of the eighteenth century, used only as applied ornament, inlay or for the manufacture of quite small objects. The back and seat are covered with a figured velvet of English make and design, olive brown and red, on a cream ground; the mahogany legs are quite plain. Fig. 401 is another walnut upholstered chair in this new taste, one of a set, covered with Mortlake tapestry very finely woven, representing bunches of flowers in brilliant colours on a dull rose ground, and much resembling the needle-work of the time; the legs are somewhat slight, and there is a general appearance of bareness about the construction of the chair.

The manufacture of Mortlake tapestry began about 1620; at that date James I sent over to Flanders for tapestry weavers, and established a factory at Mortlake with a subsidy of £2000 per annum. So rapidly did this industry come into favour, that Charles I gave large orders, while both Rubens and Vandyke designed subjects and borders to be carried out in this manu-facture. The finest examples of Mortlake tapestry are the Acts of the Apostles, from the well-known cartoons of Raphael, and the History of Vulcan, now at the Garde Meuble in Paris. The celebrated pieces at Houghton, representing James I and his family, with small oval portraits of Charles I's children in the borders, were also made at Mortlake to the order of that king, and are given later as the background to a bed.

The sums lavished by Louis XIV and his minister Colbert upon Gobelins tapestry, revived in England an interest in the Mortlake manufacture which had languished during the Rebellion, and tapestry coverings of fine stitch for chairs, settees and cushions began to be made at this factory at the end of the seventeenth century.

The well-known claw- and ball-foot, adapted from the Oriental design of a dragon's claw holding a pearl, made its appearance in walnut furniture during the first years of the eighteenth century. In early specimens the legs are found connected by stretchers, proving that the fashion succeeded the hoof and early form of club-foot; this claw and ball type of foot, varied a little later by the introduction of a lion's paw, eventually became extremely fashionable. It must be remembered that a form of club-foot ran contemporaneously with both these patterns. Fig. 402 is one of an early set of these ball-and claw-footed chairs; the back is short and comparatively wide, but the legs are still united by stretchers, the back legs finishing on square bases, and represent a date early in Anne's reign. Although a somewhat plain specimen, it well represents the ordinary type of chair that was in favour for so many years, and in which sat the rather dull, plain-coated and be-periwigged people of this time. Plate XXVI (c) is another decorated example. The hooped back curves slightly forward, but is distinctly wider and flatter at the top than in earlier specimens; it is inlaid with two lines of holly, and the splat is filled with a marqueterie of fine arabesques, walnut on a holly ground. The corners to the seat are rounded, and the loose cushion, framed in a rebate moulding, is covered with original coarse needlework in a design of large flowers. The front rail of the seat is inlaid with a panel of marqueterie, and the cabriole legs, without stretchers, are wide and strong at their headings, and crested with a carved shell; the structure is veneered with a well-figured walnut, as in all important chairs of this kind, the legs being solid; the marqueterie, with the absence of stretcher, dates this chair about 1710. Fig. 403, a chair of very much the same shape, is decorated with black and gold lacquer and an enrichment of carved shells. In these early dragon-claw chairs it may be noticed that the energy thrown by the carver into the grip of the claw on the balls is excellent, whilst the later examples are often wanting in vitality. Shells and eagles' heads were favourite ornamental details during Anne's reign; it is rare to find them in combination, but in the chair (Fig. 404) the eagle's head ingeniously forms the scroll on either side of the shell; the splat is extremely broad, proving that the date is after 1710, but the grip of the claws lacks realism. A good type of chair, made about 1712, is Fig. 405, one of a set of particularly high finish, and furnished with a back stretcher. Towards the end of Anne's reign the splats commenced to lose their simplicity of outline, and fretted and carved openings, were introduced at the side, as in this specimen. Sometimes these are connected with the uprights, as in Fig. 406, which is practically the final

FIG. 403. *Black Lacquer Chair.* Property of FRANK GREEN, Esq.

FIG. 404. *Walnut Chair.* Property of the DUCHESS OF WELLINGTON.

FIG. 405. *Mahogany Chair.* Property of EDWIN A. ABBEY, Esq.

FIG. 406. *Walnut Chair.* Property of the DUCHESS OF WELLINGTON.

development of this walnut hooped-back type. Another point of interest in the transitional detail of the splat is the carved plinth, and the cresting, that slightly scrolls over at the top.

Having carried the development of hooped-backed chairs to this point, it will be interesting to trace the course of settees, day-beds and sofas that accompanied them. The term sopha, or sofa, was not applied to European furniture before 1685, and this Eastern word, adopted by us from the French, was evidently little in use even in France at the end of the seventeenth century, as St Simon, when annotating Dagneau's *Journal*, considers it necessary to explain the origin of the term in the following words:

'Le sopha est une manière d'estrade, couverte de tapis, au fond de la chambre d'audience du grand vizir, sur laquelle il est assis sur des carreaux.'

But a few years later another French writer, Madame d'Aulnoy, takes the term quite for granted when she writes in her *Barbe Bleue*:

'Elles monterent ensuite au garde-meuble, ou elles ne pouvent assez admirer le nombre et la beauté des tapisseries, des lits, des sophas, des cabinets.'

The term sofa, as we accept it, implies a long low couch somewhat like Fig. 287; but as this back is divided into chair form, it has been classed with the settees. In Fig. 407, remarkable for its high back, the lines of the scrolled

Fig. 407. *Walnut Upholstered Sofa.* Height, 4 feet 4 inches; length, 5 feet. Property of the Duke of Devonshire.

Fig. 408. *Walnut and Gilt Sofa.* Height, 3 feet 4 inches; length, 4 feet 6 inches.

arms are less sharp and pronounced than in later developments. The legs, connected by a simple stretcher, are of cabriole shape, finishing in cappings under the seat-rail, and in half scrolls at the feet; the central leg is an ingenious combination of those on the outside, and the result is an hour-glass form that is extremely original. It is of about the date 1705, and has been re-covered with a fine blue damask. In Fig. 408, the sofa form begins to be more clearly pronounced, the back is lower, the C scrolling of the arms is sharper, the stretcher is abolished, and the legs terminate in square club-feet, with traces of the fetlock-joint to the hoof still remaining: the carved portions possess their original gilding. This sofa forms one of a pair stated to have belonged to Nell Gwyn; they came from Lauderdale House, in which she lived for a short time, but she died in 1687, and the date of these sofas cannot be before 1700. They were both originally covered in needlework.

It is difficult to understand why comparatively so little of this partly gilt walnut furniture was made, as it is most beautiful in effect, and although age has now toned the gilding and the wood, even when new the combination must have been most decorative. Another of these pieces of furniture with this same combination of walnut and gold is Fig. 409, which much resembles the last example, although two or three years later in date, and here the

FIG. 409. *Walnut and Gilt Sofa.* Height, 3 feet 8 inches; length, 6 feet. Property of the MARQUESS OF CHOLMONDELEY.

interest is still further maintained by the original covering of deep emerald green velvet, trimmed with a gold galon; the arms differ in their lines from the preceding specimen, and curve outwardly; the pendants from the seat-rail are broken off.

The day-bed (Fig. 410), of about 1708, is of unusual breadth and length, the curves of the head-rest forming part of the motive of the cabriole legs; these are intersected with a triple moulding, and the familiar shell forms the cresting; the feet are of shoe form, and the connecting stretcher dates the piece as early in the century; the covering is modern. These specimens from Houghton, dating before 1722, are of great interest, as they must evidently have been moved from the older and smaller house into the new and magni-

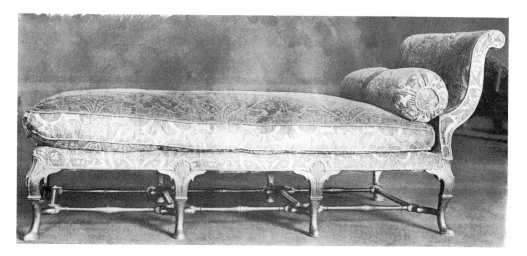

FIG. 410. *Walnut Upholstered Day-bed.* Length, 6 feet 8 inches; width, 3 feet 4 inches. Property of the MARQUESS OF CHOLMONDELEY.

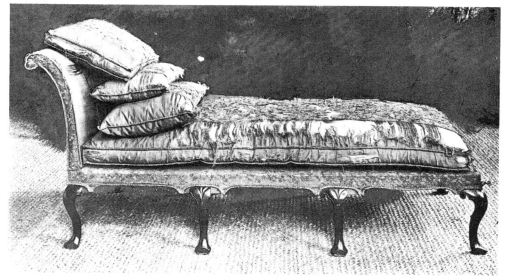

FIG. 411. *Walnut Upholstered Day-bed.* Length, 5 feet 6 inches; width, 2 feet 4 inches. Property of the DUKE OF DEVONSHIRE.

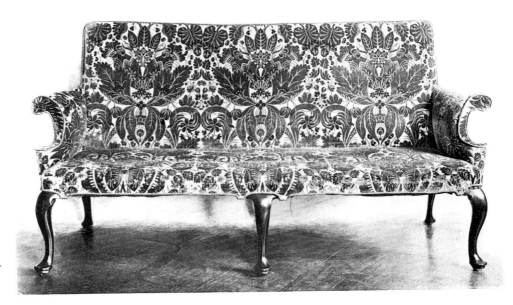

FIG. 412. *Mahogany Upholstered Sofa.* Height, 3 feet 4 inches; length, 6 feet 8 inches. Property of the EARL OF DYSART.

ficent building begun by the Prime Minister at that date. Fig. 411 is another day-bed a few years later. The seat-rail has by this time ceased to be carved as in earlier specimens, and is upholstered; the head-rest scrolls over, and the eight legs are of simple cabriole form without stretchers; the squab, frame and pillows are covered with a contemporary green damask, embroidered in silver, and ornamented down the centre with panels of elaborate raised needlework in silver thread; the whole is trimmed with a narrow green and silver braid, but no fringe is employed. These two day-beds are introduced to show that the shape continued to be in request, although rapidly being replaced by the sofa.

Fig. 412 is a mahogany sofa from Ham House, forming part of the suite already described, and of about the date 1715. The lines are long and narrow and the back is rather low; it is covered with the same English velvet as the rest of the suite, and well represents this early type of sofa without stretcher.

Tradition has assigned this entire set of mahogany furniture to the time of Charles II and to the use of the Cabal when they met at Ham House. It is always uncongenial to dispel the halo of romance that clings around old furniture and other objects, but period is inexorable, and tradition must give way at times to common-sense. At Holyrood, at any rate until quite recently, some Charles II furniture was misdated a hundred years, and assigned to the use of Mary Queen of Scots and Darnley, and these erroneous traditions have formed the basis of a system of incorrect dating in several works of reference on furniture. There is a set of well-known furniture, traditionally stated to have been used by Queen Elizabeth when on a visit to one of her ministers, and also preserved in an untouched condition since that date by descendants of the original owner, and so firmly did the present possessor believe in his family records, that although this set consists of exceedingly fine specimens of the full style of Chippendale, made in mahogany and covered with needlework of that period, he preferred to cling to historical tradition and assign them to Tudor times. There are many such traditional mistakes in many of the large houses.

A form of upholstered easy-chair with scrolled arms began to be very popular about 1700, but earlier specimens are rare. The legs and serpentine stretcher of Fig. 413 prove that this example is before that date; the C scrolling is repeated as a cresting to the back, and the early sweep to the arms is in bold curves; the chair is covered with needlework of the time in coarse stitch. Plate XXVIII is a very perfect example of another of these so-called grandfather chairs also covered with its original needlework of bold design in very fine stitch; the walnut cabriole legs ending in dragon's claw-feet approximate the chair to a date about 1710, the vigorous grasp of the claw also proving it is early in style; the form of the arms and legs of all these easy-chairs resemble those of the contemporary sofas. It is covered in needlework of very fine stitch, the ground being worked in rich green wools, and the large tulips, roses and carnations in brilliant silks. It is rare to find these chairs with their original covering for front and sides, like this example.

FIG. 413. *Walnut Upholstered Easy-chair.* Property of F. W. PHILLIPS, Esq.

Fig. 414. *Wool Needlework Carpet*. Length, 12 feet; width, 9 feet. Property of Percy Macquoid, Esq.

The fashion for needlework, stimulated by Queen Mary about 1690, continued all through the reigns of Anne and George I, consequently we find many of the sofas, easy-chairs and love-seats of these periods covered with this work. There is an elaborate bed quilt in existence at Madresfield Court, stated to have been worked by Anne whilst Princess, and Lady Marlborough. Carpets are also in existence, some of considerable size, made at this period and composed entirely of wool-work in fine stitch. Fig. 414 is a specimen of about 1690, with a blue ground-work covered with a yellow trellis, the centre and border being in a bold design of flowers and foliage in brilliant colours. This carpet measures 12 feet by 9 feet, and the amount of work entailed must have been enormous, as it weighs over 23 lbs, but the simple country life of those days gave ample opportunities to the ladies of the house for employment of this kind.

In Fig. 415, a love-seat of the beginning of the century, the legs are plain and connected by the ordinary stretcher of 1705, and the arms have a distinctive outward scroll; the design of the original needlework covering is conventional, in lines of blue and red with a buff-coloured pattern on a tawny ground, and the introduction of the large single carnation in the centre of the back and seat is effective. In Fig. 416, rather later in date, there is no stretcher, and marqueterie is introduced on the knees of the delicate cabriole legs; the design of the needlework is a series of scrolls of different colours on a dark ground. Needlework for the covering of such large pieces of furniture must have taken a considerable time to complete, and as it was generally designed to fit an especial piece, this accounts for the temporary undercovering of old silk which is so frequently to be found under the needlework on this class of furniture.

Fig. 417, of about 1710, has lost its original covering; the arms are not C scrolled; the legs are carved on the knees and square club-feet with shells and acanthus. Fig. 418 is one of a pair of small seats forming part of the mahogany suite already mentioned at Ham House; the legs here are shorter than in the preceding specimens, and the arms form complete sides.

About the middle of Anne's reign a new form of settee made its first

FIG. 415. *Walnut Upholstered Love-seat.* Height, 3 feet 5 inches; length, 3 feet. Property of C. ASSHETON SMITH, Esq.

FIG. 416. *Walnut Upholstered Love-seat.* Property of FRANK GREEN, Esq.

appearance; this in construction resembled two chair backs with their splats and usual ornamentation joined together by a top rail forming the hoops, and worked out of one piece of wood. So favoured and so fashionable did this seat become, that the motive was continued throughout the eighteenth century, and lasted nearly a hundred years. Plate XXIX represents an early specimen of these wooden chair-back settees; it is of walnut, the face covered with a highly figured veneer of the same wood; the splats are inlaid with walnut marqueterie on a holly ground; the arms are plain, with an outward curve and roll over at the elbow, and the legs are of ball and claw form, headed with carved shells; the waved seat-rail is also inlaid; the cushion seat is loose in a rebate moulding, and covered with needlework of large coloured flowers and leaves on a light olive-brown ground. The date of this piece is about 1710; it formed part of a set of two settees and eight chairs. In the fine settee (Fig. 419), a few years later in date, the splat is rather more

FIG. 417. *Walnut Upholstered Love-seat.* Height, 3 feet 4 inches; length, 3 feet 1 inch. Property of the MARQUESS OF CHOLMONDELEY.

FIG. 418. *Mahogany Upholstered Love-seat.* Height, 3 feet 5 inches; length, 3 feet 1 inch. Property of the EARL OF DYSART.

Fig. 419. *Walnut Settee.* Property of W. E. George, Esq.

elaborate in form, with carving on the scrolls, and is connected to the uprights by a horizontal extension, finishing in an elaborate heading centring in a shell; this shell is also introduced at the junction of the two backs, on the seat-rail, and as a cresting to the legs, which terminate in strongly defined claw and ball; the seat has the original needlework covering.

Another walnut settee of about 1718 is given in Fig. 420; here the hoops are carved with representations of eagle heads holding tassels; the splat and knees to the cabriole legs are also carved with acanthus and flowers in low relief; the arrangement of the four claws on the ball of the centre foot is unusual, and the gradation of the legs is not so pronounced as in the earlier examples. The chair with arms (Fig. 421) repeats the design of the last settee

Fig. 420. *Walnut Settee.* Height, 3 feet 4 inches; length, 4 feet. Property of Messrs J. Mallett and Sons.

FIG. 421. *Walnut Chair*. Height, 3 feet 4 inches. Property of MESSRS J. MALLETT AND SONS.

with very slight variation, and is given here to show how these chairs and settees were made to match.

Fig. 422, also about 1718, is perfectly plain, except for the eagle headings to the arms and claw-feet, and is veneered with a particularly fine figured walnut; the splats are not united to the cresting, but branch out to meet the sides. It should be observed that as this form of seat progresses, the chair back frequently becomes wider and more squat in form, and that the open elaboration of the splat is indicative of its late character. These settees must have been found convenient as giving plenty of room for the voluminous coats of the men, and enabling the women to show off their brocaded and preposterous hooped dresses. The plain skirts had gone out early in Anne's reign, giving way to those covered with frills and furbelows, with full sacque back and panniers. And as early as 1709 the *Spectator* mentions that 'the petticoats which began to heave and swell before you left us, are now blown up into a most enormous concave, and rise every day more and more'.

The arm supports of the arm-chairs that were made to match these settees curved backwards, and the seats were broad, to allow for the exaggerated fashions.

FIG. 422. *Walnut Settee*. Height, 3 feet 3 inches; length, 4 feet 6 inches; width of seat, 2 feet. Property of W. A. MEREDITH, Esq.

CHAPTER IX

THE cabriole leg, as it became popular, was also introduced on to different forms of tables, chests of drawers and stands to cabinets. The early and crude type is shown on the chest of drawers (Fig. 423) of a date about 1700, and is a late example of the low stand that had hitherto accompanied such pieces of furniture; the cornice and mouldings round the drawers, and the short clubby legs connected by the cusped and arched base-boarding, prove that its date must be early in the century, although the handle-plates are more perforated than is generally found at that time; the drawers are veneered with a facing of good figured walnut, and edged with a herring-bone inlay of the same wood. In Fig. 424, a chest of tall-boys shape, the cornice is admirable in its simplicity, and a so-called cock-bending is introduced as a finish round the drawers, which are veneered with tiger walnut and cornered with a narrow inlay of ivory and ebony. The lower portion of stand of this piece rests upon cabriole legs ending in claw and ball feet, headed by the favourite shell ornamentation, introduced as a pendant on the lower rail. Fig. 425 is a chest of drawers of this same period on a high stand, with slight cabriole legs ending in club-feet; it has no cornice, which is unusual on an example of this height; the walnut veneer is exceedingly dark, the drop-handles belong to the previous century.

The little table (Fig. 426), probably used as a dressing-table or wash-stand, somewhat resembles those already given with turned legs; this and Fig. 427 well represent the type of small table used in bedrooms during the first

FIG. 423. *Walnut Chest of Drawers*. Height, 4 feet 2 inches; length, 3 feet 5 inches; depth, 1 foot 10 inches. Property of W. A. MEREDITH, Esq.

FIG 425. *Walnut Chest of Drawers.* Property of the VISCOUNTESS WOLSELEY.

FIG. 424 (*left*). *Walnut Tall-boys Chest of Drawers.* Height, 6 feet; width, 2 feet 10 inches. Property of ARTHUR JAMES, Esq.

twenty years of the eighteenth century. An eccentric form of cabriole leg was introduced into tables about 1708 to 1715, which obtained but little favour, probably on account of its disagreeable appearance and inconvenient shape. Fig. 428 is a small plain example of this style; the top is of sycamore, and is moulded at the corners in a favourite manner of the time; the solid

FIG. 426. *Walnut Table.* Height, 2 feet 8 inches; width, 2 feet 6 inches.

FIG. 427. *Walnut Table.* Height, 2 feet 4 inches; width, 2 feet 6 inches.

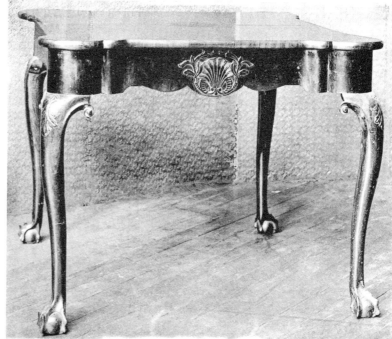

FIG. 428. *Walnut Table with Sycamore Top.* Height, 2 feet 7 inches; length, 2 feet 3 inches; width, 1 foot 6 inches. Property of T. CHARBONNIER, Esq.

FIG. 429. *Walnut Card-table.* Height, 2 feet 4 inches; width of top, 2 feet 8 inches.

walnut legs unite to the frame in the usual cabriole fashion, and break out into short but strong curves, descending perpendicularly in square and spindle form, breaking again at the junction of the fetlock-joint and square club-foot. This table no doubt fulfilled the office of a wash-stand, the top being of solid wood and not veneered. The card-table (Fig. 429) shows the adaptation of the cabriole leg to this popular item of furniture, of which many kinds were made soon after the beginning of the century. Their construction was various; sometimes the legs and sides folded in with the top, or swing legs supported the open flap; such tables invariably stood against the wall when not in use, and were not decorated on that side; they were also frequently made in pairs. The corners of these table-tops often

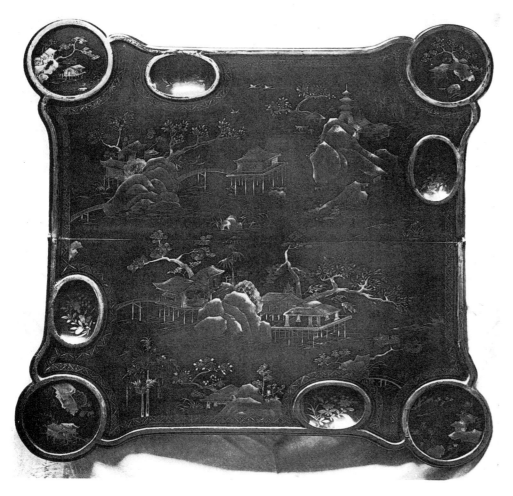

FIG. 430. *Top of Lacquer Card-table.* Property of C. ASSHETON SMITH, Esq.

FIG. 431. *Cabinet on Lacquer Stand.* Property of MESSRS MORANT.

finished in circles, slightly dished to hold candlesticks, and had sunken hollows for the counters and money. The shape of silver candlesticks underwent a complete change in about 1690, when the light-hammered variety, formed as a column with spreading base, began to give way to the more solid, shorter and cast manufacture with smaller base, and it is probable that this new fashion in candlesticks was prompted by their convenient use for the corners of these tables. Fig. 430 shows the top of a lacquer card-table of about 1712, showing these sinkings for candles and counters; the ground is black, and the decoration, consisting of landscape, houses and figures, is in red and gold lacquer. Another piece of English lacquer is Fig. 431, a cabinet mounted on a stand with elegant cabriole legs, the knees and feet of which are carved in the finest manner of 1712. Stretchers were by then no longer introduced on tables and stands, and the abolition of this feature is one of the most important structural differences between the late seventeenth-century chairs and tables and those of the succeeding century.

The gilt and partly gilt furniture, such as Figs. 388 and 408, seems likely to have been designed for a more gorgeous background than the simple tall wainscot panelling and wall-papers of the ordinary gentleman's house. Amongst the nobility and those connected with the Court, gilt furniture was evidently much on the increase towards the end of Anne's reign. The Palace of Blenheim, which was built at the nation's expense, between the years 1705 and 1720, from the designs of Sir John Vanbrugh, and which was the talk of all England, was furnished in the most lavish and extravagant manner by the Duchess of Marlborough, who was greatly answerable for this new departure in the gilded decoration of furniture. Lady Wentworth at the time writes as follows to her son in Flanders, proving the widespread interest taken in the building of this vast pile:

'My dearist and best of children

'I am much rejoysed at your fyne present, I wish you may often have such and better, till you ar as ritch as the Duke of Molberry whoe is billding the fynest hous at Woodstock that ever was seen, thear is threescore rooms of a flower, noe stairs only a little pair that goes to the uper roomes which are only for sarvents, and staitly wood, which he cuts out walks in, and fyne gardens that are fower myles about. It is beleeved furneture and al cannot cost les than three hundred thousand pd. why should you not be so fortunate as he?'

(This sum would be equivalent to about £1,000,000 at the present day.) In the Duke's letters during his campaigns we find that from time to time he sent home pictures and tapestries from abroad, and the following extract from one of his letters to the Duchess, shows that some difficulties were attached then to the importation of furniture even by so great a person:

'Tournay *April* 19 1710.

'I should be glad if you are in London, that you would give Mr. Maynwaring the trouble of speaking to some at the Custom House, I having sent by Captain Sanders one picture and some looking glasses. They are not of any value; but I find among other marks of declining favor, that I must meet with trouble at the Custom house. The best way will be to send nothing more from hence; for everything may be had in England perhaps a little dearer.'

The furnishing of the enormous palace was evidently entirely intrusted to the Duchess, who not only was a shrewd judge of a bargain, but took the greatest pains over the minutest details. In 1714 she wrote as follows to Mrs Jennens, the wife of her solicitor:

'Dear Mrs. Jennens

'I have looked upon this damask by daylight, the pattern is not so large as he stated; but hee has kept it so ill that it looks full as old as what I have, which is better than if it were a fine fresh Damask. But I think it is a good argument to him to sell it cheap, for tho' I like it very much for this use, I would not buy it for any other. But don't part with it, for I would have the whole piece on any terms that you can get it. I shall want a vast number of feather beds and Quilts I wish you would take this opertunity to know the Prices of all such things as will be wanted in that wild unmerciful Hous, for the man you go to is famous for low Prices. I would have some of the Feather beds, Swansdown, all good and sweet feathers, even for the servants. I am not in Hast for anything you are so good as to do for me.'

At times her instructions to Mrs Jennens are most involved, but show what an amount of pains the Duchess took in small details. The following extract from another letter is interesting in showing how much of the trimming of curtains, etc., was done at home:

'This narrow Fring is enough to put upon the Feet Base of the Bed and if the broad can bee made to do the two sides Bases, they are not seen at the same Time that the Feet is seen and if it is a little narrower I think it no great Matter. I say that because I fancy they may make it up of near half the Breadth it is now. Six Feet is wanted for the side Bases, and as much more as it will take up in putting on. It is to lye upon the Damask which require the less thicknesse. I shall want galloon of these sorts to lace the curtains and to turn the chairs and window curtains. May I ask what they will do it for an ounce. You will observe the fine colour of the Gold; tis being the best duble guilt which makes it last so long, and look so well for this has been made this eight years at least. . . . This is the Collour of the Damask of which this bed is made which I must match exactly because it will be so fine a Fourniture. I shall want of it two window Curtains, twelve Chairs and four Curtains for the Bed.'

The Duchess had at the date of this letter been for many years collecting vast quantities of stuffs for the furnishing of the palace, and that she had been in the habit of making use of everybody she could, is shown by the following letter, one of the many on this subject, written from Windsor Castle in the height of her power in 1708 to the Earl of Manchester in Venice:

'I have received the honor of your Lordships letter, You have had the goodness to give yourself more trouble in my small affairs than I thought it possible for a man to do, and are more particular and exact than ever I met with anybody in my life. I desire your Lordship will be pleased to give directions for to have made the quantities of damasks and velvets that I have put down in English measure – of the green damask 1300 yards; yellow damask 600 yards; crimson damask 600 yards; scarlet plain velvet 200 yards; plain blue velvet 200 yards; scarlet damask the same colour as the velvet 100 yards; scarlet satin 200 yards; blue satin same colour as the velvet 200 yards. Your Lordship says scarlet is the more difficult color, and seems to think they do not dye that so well as we do, for I think that you sent me was the most beautiful color I ever saw and I like it better for a bed than crimson being not so common. . . . The figured velvets of general colours are not much liked, though in the fashion, but I should like mightily scarlet figured velvet without any mixture of colours, and blue and green the same, and when your Lordship has the opportunity I should be glad to see a pattern of them.'

It is interesting to find that there are remnants of these foreign damasks still at Blenheim, but so late as 1720 it is certain that a large quantity of them was unemployed and that many of the rooms there must have been uncurtained, for on the occasion of some private theatricals at the palace in that

Fig. 432. *Gilt and Mahogany Bed.* Property of the Duke of Marlborough.

last year, these silks and velvets were evidently used as properties, for Lady Blaney in a contemporary letter writes:

'I played the high priest in an embroidered surplice that came from Holland. . . . I suppose we made a very grand appearance; there was a profusion of brocade rolls, etc., of what was to be the window curtains at Blenheim.'

The quantity of furniture required for this palace must have been very great, the library alone being 183 feet long and 32 feet wide; it was originally intended for a picture-gallery.

Fig. 432 is the only bed left at Blenheim contemporary with the building of the house; the dome and tester are in their original condition, the remainder of the bed having been cut down to almost half its height in order to fit the room into which it has been removed. It was originally in the State bed-chamber hung with blue damask interlaced with gold, and is probably the State bed referred to in the letter of the Duchess to Mrs Jennens, and for which she orders the gold lacing. The domed canopy is surmounted by a ducal crown, and the tester surrounding it is crested with a trellised cornice of shells and scrolls in the fashion of 1715, terminating at the four corners in plumed helmets. Beneath this runs a frieze carved with a delicate and floral acanthus scroll, gold on a cream ground; the ceiling of the tester is composed of architectural mouldings and ornaments elaborately carved and gilt; the foot-rail and sides are carved in guilloche decorated in cream and gold; the posts, which have been much reduced in height, are of mahogany, fluted and gilt. The original hangings of blue and gold are described in a guide-book of 1806; they were replaced by an upholstery of pink silk and Venetian rose point lace, recently again removed and transferred to a modern bed.

The console table (Fig. 433) formed part of a suite of gilt furniture made for one of the rooms at Blenheim and was very probably designed by Vanbrugh, as the same heaviness of touch and eccentricity of taste found in the general decoration of the house is noticeable in its proportions. The strange curved motive of the cabriole legs resembles that found on Fig. 428, in this instance finishing in scrolled and carved feet; the frieze is carved, with a classical banding centring in a shell, beneath which is a pendant edged with floral acanthus surrounding the cipher of John Churchill, Duke of Marlborough, surmounted by a ducal crown; the top is marble, and the legs are united by a straight stretcher of 'X' form to support the weight; the whole of the wood-work is thickly gilt on a gesso ground.

Fig. 434 is one of a pair of guéridons belonging to this suite; the shaft presents the broken and eccentric motive of the legs of the console table, and in its isolation outrages all laws of proportion and line; the top (Fig. 435) is of vase-shaped form, surrounded by leaves of acanthus; the upper surface is carved and worked in gilt gesso, with sprays of flowers and the Duke's cipher surrounded by four C scrolls. More examples of this type will be given later with other gilt furniture of this period.

The writing-cabinet (Plate XXX), of about 1710, possesses an interest of personal ownership apart from its construction, having been the property of Dean Swift. It is veneered with walnut and surmounted by a plain cornice, beneath which are two doors filled with crystal cut looking-glass and two drawers; these are framed in four pilasters of marqueterie in ebony and holly, the plinth being inlaid in a design of sphinxes and conventional ornament; the lower portion opens as a writing-flap (underneath which is a slide), and contains a series of pigeon-holes and small drawers in serpentine form, the divisions being inlaid; below this is a central cupboard and six drawers of concave frontage banded with lines of ebony and holly; the treatment of the well-proportioned stand and feet is particularly original. The plain handles are contemporary with the piece. Fig. 436 is a rather earlier specimen of the same type of cabinet. It is surmounted by a hooded and broken cornice and three vase-shaped finials; the upper portion in this instance opens in one door composed of crystal cut looking-glass contained within two pilasters) the lower portion is in the form of a writing bureau and chest of drawers; the handles and lock-plates are plain; the cock-beadings round the drawers are large and early in character.

FIG. 433. *Gilt Console Table*. Height, 2 feet 7 inches; length, 3 feet 8 inches; depth, 2 feet. Property of the DUKE OF MARLBOROUGH.

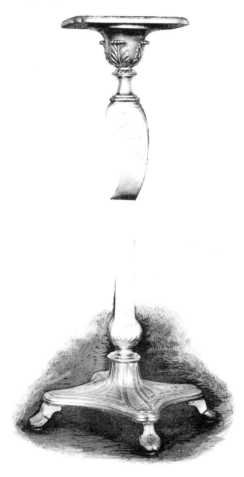

FIG. 434. *Gilt Guéridon*. height, 4 feet 8 inches. Property of the DUKE OF MARLBOROUGH.

FIG. 435. *Top of same.*

FIG. 436. *Walnut Writing-cabinet.* Property of MESSRS ISAACS.

FIG. 437. *Walnut Writing-cabinet.* Property of FRANK GREEN, Esq.

In the writing-cabinet (Fig. 437), of about 1715, the plain straight frieze in Plate XXX is repeated, and the top opens in two doors framed by fluted pilasters; the hooded form is suggested by a fine inlaid line of holly on the doors, which are bordered with a cross-banding of walnut. The figure and colour of the veneer are exceptionally fine. The lower portion comprises a series of small drawers and a writing-slide, underneath which is one long drawer; these are contained within two doors, cross-banded and veneered; the legs to the stand are of slight cabriole form.

But short mention has been made of the colour and character of walnut. Our ordinary English walnut differed from many of the varieties grown abroad, being lighter in colour and more open in the grain; it therefore seldom attained the bronze-like appearance found on the surface of foreign walnut furniture. Great numbers of walnut-trees must have existed here throughout the seventeenth century, having been planted at the end of Elizabeth's reign. The tree must be at least fifty years old before the dark centre of the wood is sufficiently large to cut from, the external and light-coloured portions next the bark being worthless. Walnut wood was occasionally used for high-class furniture and panelling as early as 1600, but the quantity of furniture made from this English wood during the second half of the seventeenth century was very great, the indigenous supply must have corresponded to the amount, and when mahogany sprang into fashion, a serious commercial loss must have been entailed by the importation of the latter wood. In estimating the bulk of walnut used between 1660 and 1720, it should be taken into account that the structure of all this furniture was oak or deal, and the surfaces only veneered in walnut; legs of chairs and tables were usually made of the solid wood.

Walnut furniture is much benefited by constant rubbing, and the occasional use of beeswax. Where the original varnish has chilled or discoloured, this should be removed (if possible by spirit and not by scraping), leaving the surface of the wood untouched, for in all restoration it is better to do too little than too much. Old varnish on marqueterie so frequently obscures the variety and colours of the different woods employed that its removal will in almost every case be found beneficial. As carving was naturally impossible on veneer, it was confined to those portions of the furniture that were of solid wood, decoration on the plain surfaces being obtained by the introduction of marqueterie or figure of the veneer.

The taste for this style of marqueterie lasted from about 1680 until 1710, when a sentiment of simplicity began to be effected, in which vivacity and colour gave way to a refined though somewhat joyless result, yet remarkable for practical excellence and handiwork.

After the death of Queen Mary the Court for a time lost all elements of brightness and polish, and Anne on her accession exercised no personal influence upon the arts of her day, her preferences being confined to domestic duties, dress and the free indulgence of a healthy appetite. Her somewhat lethargic temperament was typical of the people who surrounded her, at a time when all enterprise in Art, save in light satirical literature and music, was neglected for place-hunting, purposeless political party-feeling, cards and tea-parties; the interests of the nation being divided between the war with France and State lotteries.

The scientific porportions and well-considered mouldings of Sir Christopher Wren influenced the details of William and Anne furniture far more than the elaborated floral decorations of Gibbon. Sir John Vanbrugh, though considered by many at that time an 'Admirable Crichton', did little by his gigantic efforts in architecture to advance this art, and had practically no lasting effect on the furniture of this country.

The decline of walnut furniture was rapid and more decided than that of oak, but the character of its design and methods of construction continued to strongly influence the succeeding age of mahogany.

THE AGE OF MAHOGANY

CHAPTER I

THE first twenty-five years of the eighteenth century represent an almost stationary period in our artistic history; originality of design being practically quiescent for that time, with a dangerous tendency towards the destruction of what had previously existed. The advent of the line of Brunswick in 1714 brought about no immediate radical change in taste, for the fashions introduced at Court were those of an unimportant German Principality, a vulgar copy of Versailles. George I, on his sudden elevation to the English throne, did not attempt any serious encouragement of the English arts, his tastes remaining faithful to Herrenhausen, and his social sympathies with Kilmansegg and Schulenburg. The certain amount of opulent taste strongly marked by foreign preference that crept in amongst our more sober and national fashions was confined to the aristocracy and successful speculators, and very indicative of the occupation of the throne by a foreigner. Horace Walpole, writing of this time, said:

'We are now arrived at the period in which the arts were sunk to the lowest ebb in Britain. The new monarch was devoid of taste, and not likely at an advanced age to encourage the embellishment of a country to which he had little partiality.'

To this wave of spurious French taste, brought over from Herrenhausen, a more direct and purer influence was soon fortunately established by the new era of decoration that emanated from the Court of Philip, the Regent of France; for on the death of Louis XIV, the sombre state of French society burst into fresh life, being accompanied by great patronage for original capacity in all the industrial arts. This patronage came from a class that had not previously existed, for the rich speculator in stock had now become a member of society through the genius of the Scotsman, John Law; and the financial upheaval that took place in France under his auspices was accompanied here by the South Sea Scheme which, by 1720, had developed into a delirium, the attention of both nations being diverted from politics to the frenzy of speculation. For the benefit of those raised from comparative obscurity to sudden wealth, extravagant changes were originated, although some years elapsed before any real elegance and delicacy were established in the social surroundings of the English. The period of decoration known in France as 'Regence' inaugurated forms which there developed into the style termed Louis Quinze, and here formed a basis from which the so-called school of Chippendale sprang, for ever since the Restoration and the revocation of the Edict of Nantes, and in spite of the war and consequent protectionary legislation, French fashions and furniture had slowly gained ground in England.

Technical excellence in carving, originality of touch with traditional treatment, was for the first twenty years of the eighteenth century still influenced by Gibbon. In 1714 this artist was appointed Master Carver in wood to George I, with a salary of eighteenpence a day, and enjoyed this cautious acknowledgment of his genius for seven years until his death, which took place in August 1721. That the contemporary appreciation and influence of his work was even greater than it is to-day is shown in the criticism written by Horace Walpole:

'There is no instance of man before Gibbons who gave to wood the loose and airy lightness of flowers and chained together the various productions of the elements with a free disorder natural to each species.'

In the carving of this school, ornament interspersed with bands of flowers and fruit was an integral part of the structure of furniture, such as chairs and console-tables; the proportions were large and round, and the aim of the detail was realism. Soon after 1725 the ornament became flattened, introducing forms from the new French school, and took its place more on the

FIG. 438. *Oak Drawer*. Property of C. E. KEMPE, Esq.

surfaces of the furniture. At this time the plain panels of wardrobes and cabinets, enlivened in the three former reigns with marqueterie, were now enriched with mouldings and framed in carving and decorated borders, and furniture as a whole became lighter and smaller in character; for in every period of style elaboration of detail increases and its scale decreases as the evolution proceeds. Another cause leading to delicacy of treatment was the use of mahogany, which about 1720 began to supersede walnut. At first it was confined to the leaders of fashion, as the owners of the large houses contented themselves with their walnut furniture, gilt tables and lacquer-work, and continued to have these made. Consequently at this transitional period we find that English furniture was constructed simultaneously in oak, walnut and mahogany.

The heavy oak beds, chairs and tables of former times soon drifted from the large houses into important farmhouses, being there supplemented by unpretending and practical oak-panelled cupboards and dressers of local construction, more or less traditional in design but seldom in the new contemporary taste. Fig. 438 is a dresser of this type, of long shape and rough construction. The upper portion is divided into six drawers framed in bolection mouldings of the beginning of the century; a bold surbase moulding, stopped on the outside styles, separates the upper from the lower portion; below is a series of panels of large and small size, the latter forming the doors: the colour of the oak is light and almost modern in tone. Tall corner cupboards of oak, panelled in this manner, were also very usual pieces of furniture in small house-holds. Sometimes their doors are found inlaid with a star in black and yellow wood.

Great tracts of country at this time were still waste, uncultivated, and undrained, and the difficulties of locomotion preserved characteristics of local style, as every village of any size possessed a carpenter who repeated the models he had at hand. The counties of Suffolk and Norfolk were, however, by 1725, agriculturally far in advance of their time, and good representative pieces of mahogany were made there between 1725 and 1750. Farms let in these counties at the beginning of the century for £180 had in thirty years risen to a rental of £800, so that the better position of landlord and tenant was naturally accompanied by domestic comforts and the acquisition of novelties.

In the rich town and country houses a very gorgeous style of gilded furniture, still suggestive of foreign taste, became fashionable shortly before 1720. Certain characteristics of this type had existed during the reigns of Charles II and James II, but the development of gilt furniture that took place between the years 1714 and 1730, though lasting so comparatively short a time and confined to so limited a patronage, is a very distinct feature of the times. Reception-rooms were furnished with gilt console-tables, gilt sofas, chairs and card-tables. The console-tables, at first of bracket form with marble tops, were placed against the walls and between the windows, and often surmounted by tall looking-glasses. The designs of these console-tables were generally bold, florid and frequently exaggerated, carved in soft wood, and heavily gilt on a jesso ground. Sometimes portions of animals, human-headed, formed part of the bracket; in early specimens an eagle displayed often composed the support. On the knees of the cabriole legs were carved lion masks, shells or a contorted face. This human grotesque face, which varies little and originally borrowed from the designs of Beran

FIG. 439. *Gilt Fire-screen*. HAMPTON COURT PALACE.

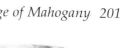

FIG. 440. *Gilt Guéridon.* Height, 4 feet 10 inches. HAMPTON COURT PALACE.

FIG. 441. *Gilt Guéridon.* Height, 4 feet 4 inches. Property of LORD DE LISLE AND DUDLEY.

FIG. 442. *Gilt Guéridon.* Height, 4 feet 8 inches. Property of the DUKE OF MARLBOROUGH.

FIG. 443. *Gilt Guéridon.* Height, 4 feet 9 inches. Property of the HON CHARLOTTE MARIA LADY NORTH and R. EDEN DICKSON, Esq.

and Boulle, was almost entirely confined to gilt furniture. Two early pieces of this gilt furniture in good taste are Figs. 439 and 440. The screen is of walnut and most delicately carved in strap-work clothed with fine arabesques, the ornamentation on the balusters recalling contemporary silver-plate. The treatment of the plinths forming the bases is bold and original, and the flattened C scrolls of the cresting and the work on the balusters prove this interesting piece to be about the date 1690. The centre of the screen is of the original red velvet trimmed with a broad silver galon. The guéridon or torchère (Fig. 440) is one of a pair, and resembles the screen in treatment; these were used for silver of china perfume jars or a branching candelabrum. In both these pieces the carving forms part of the structure: an impression of size combined with richness is thus obtained which is not seen in later work where the carving is confined to the surfaces.

Fig. 441, a guéridon, one of a pair at Penshurst, is of about the same date, though more simple in form; the vase shape supporting the top is in early guéridons concave in form, as in this instance, and those at Knole (Fig. 291, 'The Age of Walnut'), which bear the hall-mark of 1690, also show this characteristic. In the Penshurst example the lower portion of the baluster is square-sided and carved with husk design and strap-work of the period on a matted ground; this is surmounted by the flattened capping found on tables and chairs of the time; the decorated scrolls of the base are rich and rapid in their curves, but the claw-feet are probably additions to give stability, and the finish of the curve is somewhat marred by their introduction. Fig. 442, one of a pair, is solid in shape and of the beginning of the eighteenth century; the vase-shaped top is here bulbous in form and decorated with the plain acanthus that is found on so much of this gilt furniture, the proportions are unequal, and the introduction of the Ionic capital in the centre of the shaft arrests its grace. The scrolling of the feet, ending in whorls, is bold and simple. This pair of torchères was probably the property of the Duke of Marlborough before he moved into Blenheim, as they precede in style the other gilt furniture found there. In Fig. 443 the vase-shaped top is more spreading and is ornamented with a well-cut acanthus; the shaft is cylindrical and plain, save for some husk pendants in low relief; the scrolls of the base turn upwards and are surmounted by the grotesque head introduced so frequently about this time. Fig. 444, from Penshurst, is of the early part of George I's reign; the carvings and proportions of the baluster are large in

FIG. 444. *Gilt Guéridon.* Height, 4 feet 8 inches. Property of LORD DE LISLE AND DUDLEY.

character, but the acanthus on the legs, connected by swags of drapery, show the approach of a new epoch in decoration. The gilding on all these pieces is of the highest quality, beautiful in colour, and giving almost the appearance of hammered metal. The ground is dull throughout, the carved portions are alone burnished. These torchères must have greatly added to the stateliness of large reception-rooms, besides being an additional convenience for their lighting, as until the reign of Charles II, candelabra from the ceiling were small in size and few in number, the remainder of the light in those days being supplied by metal sconces on the walls. Towards the end of the seventeenth century, crystal, brass or wooden candelabra were made in large quantities, but even then the lighting could not have been good or well considered, and it is interesting to notice how few lights such a candelabrum as Fig. 445 (a) can hold in comparison to its size. This is one of a pair formerly at Kensington Palace and of about the date 1700. It is constructed entirely of wood and surmounted by the Royal crown; midway on the shaft is an ornament in the shape of a canopy with tassels, again repeated lower down, and from which spring ten exceedingly graceful and ingenious, widespreading arms, each supporting a candle cup. Few rooms could have contained more than three or four of these large objects, and the candles they held, even supplemented by those in the sconces, must have given a somewhat indifferent light in the large rooms of the time, and in great contrast to the blaze of candles that formed the lighting later in the century. The lighting at the coronation banquet of George II was evidently somewhat of a novelty, for in an interesting letter of Mrs Delany, wherein she describes the dresses, she appears much struck by the lighting of Westminster Hall:

'The room was finely illuminated, and though there were 1800 candles, besides what was on the tables, they were all lighted in less than three minutes by an invention of Mr. Heidegger's which succeeded to the admiration of all spectators; the branches that held the candles were all good gilt and in for the form of pyramids. I leave it to your lively imagination after this to have a notion of the splendour of the place so filled and so illuminated.'

The snuffing of all these candles must have been a very serious and difficult matter. It is difficult to realise that in the seventeenth century the

Fig. 445 (a). *Wood Candelabrum.*
Property of Sir Spencer C. Ponsonby Fane.

Fig. 445 (b). *Glass Chandelier.* Property of Frank Green, Esq.

furniture, silks and velvets, and the people who used them, could have been but little seen, though we gather that the ladies' complexions were calculated with a view of overcoming this difficulty. Want of light was comparatively unimportant to the business of the evening, which was chiefly connected with the card-tables, on which silver candlesticks were used. In Swift's sarcastic directions to a butler and footman we get an amusing glimpse into the manners and customs of servants and the trials connected with lighting by candles. The sconces alluded to would have been gilt mirrors bearing candle branches.

'Let your sockets be full of grease to the brim, with the old snuff at the top, and then stick on fresh candles. It is true, this may endanger their falling, but the candles will appear so much the longer and handsomer before company. When your candle is too big for the socket, melt it to a right size in the fire, and to hide the smoke, wrap in a paper half-way up. Sconces are great wasters of candles, therefore your business must be to press the candle with both your hands into the socket, so as to make it lean in such a manner that the grease may drop all upon the floor, if some lady's head-dress or gentleman's periwig be not ready to intercept it; you may likewise stick the candle so loose that it will fall upon the glass of the sconce and break into shatters: this will save yourself much labour, for the sconces spoiled cannot be used. Snuff the candles with your fingers and throw the snuff on the floor, then tread it out to prevent stinking: this method will very much save the snuffers from wearing out; you ought also to snuff them close to the tallow, which will make them run and so increase the perquisite of the cook's kitchen stuff, for she is the person you ought in prudence to be well with. And snuff the candles at supper as they stand on the table, which is much the surest way, because, if the burning snuff happens to get out of the snuffers, you have a chance that it may fall into a dish of soup, sack posset, rice milk, or the like, when it will be immediately extinguished with very little stink.'

Fig. 445 (b) is a graceful glass double-tiered chandelier, one of a pair made about the end of the seventeenth century. It consists of a series of globular and base-shaped forms, cut in diamond pattern, and two tiers of glass arms with candle cups. The simplicity of arrangement is effective, the design being suggested by the brass Dutch chandeliers of the time, though the wiring and fittings for electric light somewhat detract from the delicacy of its proportions. The manufacture of glass was an important industry in England at this period, and had in a great measure supplanted the foreign importation.

Throughout the first half of the eighteenth century the sideboard was still unknown, but the console-table, introduced here from France, formed a very prominent feature in the furniture of important rooms, and probably

Fig. 446. *Gilt Console-table.* Height, 2 feet 6 inches. Property of the Hon Charlotte Maria Lady North and R. Eden Dickson, Esq.

started the idea of mahogany side-tables with marble tops: a great many examples of consoles in soft wood gilt exist, which, doubtless, were used as sideboards.

Fig. 446 is an early specimen of about 1700, and one of a pair. The top is a thick slab of black and white marble resting on a frame carved with the spiral evolute termed 'wave pattern', in this instance singularly free and simple. It is supported by an eagle of remarkable strength and vitality; the grip of the claws upon the rock is tremendous in its strength and boldness, and the treatment of the plumage shows English carving of the time at its very best; the base is plain except for a simple rosette banding, and the wood is thickly and richly gilt; additional brackets at the side support the great weight of the top. A gilt mirror, which is architectural in construction and belongs to the console-table, is shown in Fig. 447; it is not by the same hand, and perhaps a year or two later in date. The broken pediment forming the cresting is admirable in proportion and possesses the original ornament to the centre plinth, but the carving of the acanthus sprays and the female bust at the base are lacking in vitality; the tassels of oak-leaves and acorns at the sides show a want of spontaneity, and are a feeble deviation from the garlands of Gibbon; the gilding is exceedingly beautiful, great variety being obtained by the burnished ornament lying on a sanded ground.

Fig. 448 is a tall mirror of about 1718, made to go over a console-table but not to form part of it; the same motive of the broken pediment, rather more ornate in character than the last specimen, is adopted, and the centre is a lamp with flames; the frieze is carved with a mask between acanthus sprays, the fascia on each side being decorated with swags of drapery; the framing of the sides is composed of oak-leaves, and the flat is decorated with shells and pateræ; there is no plinth, as the mirror is intended to hang on a wall, and the pendant is carved with the lion mask, now so rapidly becoming a fashion, and oak-leaves ending in eagle heads. The carving of this lower portion is full of character and superior to the rest of the frame.

Fig. 449 is a mirror of oval form of about 1728, with a richly carved and very interesting frame belonging to the school of Gibbon. It has characteristics of later design, especially in the mouldings surrounding the glass; the cresting is formed of a finely modelled head frame in five ostrich feathers and edged with broad foliated sprays; at the side are long cornucopiæ filled with fruit and flowers, realistic in treatment but wanting in the light touch of Gibbon; the base is clothed with large sprays of acanthus bordered with garlands of fruit and flowers. This mirror was probably designed for a room with florid surroundings and richly covered walls, as vevets, silks and Gobelin tapestry were still in great demand. We read that in Montagu House, Portman

FIG. 447. *Gilt Mirror*. Height, 6 feet 6 inches. Property of the HON CHARLOTTE MARIA LADY NORTH and R. EDEN DICKSON, Esq.

FIG. 448. *Gilt Mirror*. Height, 6 feet 6 inches. Property of LORD DE LISLE AND DUDLEY.

FIG. 449. *Gilt Mirror*. Property of W. H. LEVER, Esq.

FIG. 450. *Gilt Mirror*. Property of S. T. FISHER, Esq.

FIG. 451. *Gilt Console-table*. Height, 2 feet 6 inches; top, 2 feet 2 inches square. Property of the DUKE OF BEAUFORT.

FIG. 452. *Gilt Console-table*. Height, 2 feet 6 inches; length, 3 feet; depth, 1 foot 8 inches. Property of the DUKE OF BEAUFORT.

Square, in 1750, there was even a room hung with tapestry made of feathers. Mrs Montagu was the author of an essay on Shakespeare, and the chief of the blue-stockings of her day; she gave an annual feast to all the chimney-sweepers in London.

Fig. 450 is a good example of the ordinary type of small gilt mirror of this time.

Fig. 451 is another eagle console-table, one of a pair. Here the top is of wood carved with a strap-work in low relief of French design, clearly showing the influence of the Regence; the execution of both eagle and table suggest that the piece is of country workmanship. Fig. 452 is also one of a pair from Badminton, and the same rather elementary feeling is visible. The design is evidently an arrangement of details seen somewhere and but vaguely remembered by the carver; the drapery serves no purpose, and the

FIG. 453 (*left*). *Gilt Console-table*. Height, 2 feet 10 inches; length, 4 feet 9 inches; depth, 2 feet 2 inches. Property of the DUKE OF MARLBOROUGH.

FIG. 454. *Gilt Console-table*. Height, 2 feet 7 inches.

FIG. 455. *Gilt Console-table.* Height, 3 feet 6 inches; length, 7 feet 5 inches; depth, 3 feet 4 inches. Property of the MARQUESS OF CHOLMONDELEY.

useless acanthus growing out of the plinth show that the designer was not here quite in his element; the introduction of sphinxes with Egyptian head-dresses is interesting, being borrowed directly from the bracket supports of Renaissance furniture. These figures and animals are introduced on later consoles but without the plinth; scrolled or cabriole legs supporting the piece. Fig. 453 is from Blenheim; the design of the legs is suggestive of the taste of Sir John Vanbrugh, who in his efforts to obtain original effects appears merely to have succeeded in producing ugly and eccentric results. Horace Walpole said of this artist 'that he undertook vast designs and composed heaps of littleness; the style of no age, no country, appeared in his works; he broke through all rule and compensated for it by no imagination'.

The wave pattern running along the face of nearly all these console-tables remained a popular decoration for nearly thirty years, and the mahogany

FIG. 456. *Gilt Console-table.* Height, 2 feet 10 inches; length, 8 feet; depth, 2 feet 8 inches. Property of the MARQUESS OF CHOLMONDELEY.

FIG. 457. *Gilt Console-table*. Height, 2 feet 6 inches; length, 5 feet 1 inch; depth, 2 feet. Property of the MARQUESS OF CHOLMONDELEY.

side-tables, which ran contemporaneously with the later consoles, show instances of this same design.

About 1720 console-tables became more elegant, with legs of cabriole form. In Fig. 454 the top is of marble, and the front and sides of the frame are decorated with a bold egg and tongue moulding and the wave pattern; below this, an open work arabesque, composed of acanthus, fruit and flowers in the style of Gibbon, unite the legs, which are of unusual strength and grace. These are richly decorated on the shoulders with large escallops and husk pendants, and finish in lions' paws, a type of foot that for a short time superseded the dragon's claw; the gilding of this table is in excellent preservation. In the little console, Plate XXXI (b), the satyr face is introduced upon the legs, which, though hocked like a lion, terminate in claw- and ball-feet; the carving approximates that found on the mahogany furniture of 1725; the top is of fleur-de-pêche marble.

In 1722 Sir Robert Walpole commenced the building of Houghton Hall in Norfolk, and throughout this remarkable house are to be found many pieces of gilt furniture; the console-tables are especially interesting as they are contemporary with the building, many having been designed for the house by Kent and to suit the rather pronounced taste of the Prime Minister. Fig. 455 cannot be before the date 1726, as it bears on the pendant, underneath the framing, Sir Robert's crest encircled by the Garter. In 1725 Walpole persuaded the King to revive the Order of the Bath, described at the time 'as an artful bank of 36 ribands to supply a fund of favors'. Sir Robert was himself invested with this Order, but quitted it for the Garter in 1726, and for this he was commonly called 'Sir Bluestring' in the pasquinades of the time. In this console the top consists of a large slab of black and yellow marble resting on a carved frieze projecting in five corbels; it is supported on four scrolled legs of debased form, carved on the front with acanthus and guilloched ornament; the sides of these legs, as in all specimens of this class, are scaled. In the centre drops a pendant of acanthus arabesques containing Walpole's crest encircled with the Garter; on either side of the pendant are sphinx figures couchant on scrolls, surrounded by sprays of acanthus; garlands of oak-leaves connect the pendant with the legs. The execution of the figures is most careful, the heads being exceedingly beautiful, though the legs are very much out of proportion; the whole is carved in soft wood with the original gilding. On this table can be seen the famous bronze group by John of Bologna of his second composition of the 'Rape of the Sabines', which was presented to Walpole by Horace Mann, the King's Resident at Florence, and behind are the original crimson and cream hangings to the room, a patterned velvet of English make. Fig. 456 is one of a pair of smaller consoles, probably executed by the same hand; the beautiful modelling of the child backed by an escallop, the garlands of oak-leaves and acorns, is altogether better than the design. The rather hideous legs, and general confusion of line, of these last two tables, may be the unadulterated inspiration of Kent, but the animated beauty of the figures is probably due to

Fig. 458. *Gilt Console-table*. Height, 6 feet 8 inches. Property of the Earl of Radnor.

the skilled foreign craftsman who superintended so much of the furniture at Houghton. Fig. 457 is another table from the same house; the treatment here is more simple, and the design of the acanthus-scrolled front, centring in an elaborate shell, is graceful, but the caterpillar-like legs are bare in form, and the four bands of different ornament framing the marble top are quite meaningless in their relationship to one another. Fig. 458 is a very fine specimen from Longford Castle, where the same motive of the scrolled legs is more artistically treated. The sides of the thick marble top follow in their curves those of the frame; the front is slightly serpentine, and composed of garlands of flowers and fruit centring in a shell, the carving strongly showing the influence of Gibbon; the supports are eagle-headed, terminating in richly decorated scrolls, the wings ingeniously developing into acanthus sprays as they approach the central ornament, the crests of the birds breaking the line of the framing. A gilt table of more ordinary form, and a few years earlier than the last specimen, is shown in Fig. 459. The top is covered with a jesso strap-work of French origin in low relief and richly gilt, but the plain separated acanthus on the frame resembles that on the Blenheim guéridon (Fig. 442) and is distinctly British. The protruding

Fig. 459. *Gilt Table*. Height, 2 feet 5 inches; length, 3 feet 8 inches. Property of the Hon Charlotte Maria Lady North and R. Eden Dickson, Esq.

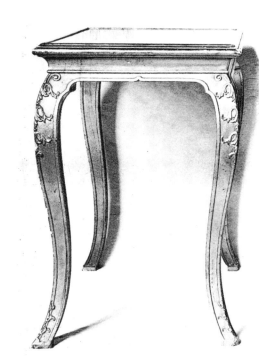

FIG. 460. *Gilt and Lacquer Table.* Height, 2 feet 5 inches; length, 2 feet 11 inches; depth, 1 foot 6 inches. Property of the EARL OF RADNOR.

surface of the front centring in a lion's mask, and the thin lines of ornament no longer forming part of the construction, mark this table as an interesting example of transition. Lions' paws are added to the ordinary square foot of the time, forming an artificial fetlock-joint. The gilding is in perfect preservation, and the ornament is burnished on an etched ground. Fig. 460 is a dressing-table, a combination of lacquer and gilding. The top is of black and gold lacquer, and the drawers, resembling in their arrangement the earlier walnut furniture, are also lacquered; the frame and legs are gilt and the latter end in hoof feet, a late example of this peculiarity; the legs are carved in very low relief with a meaningless quasi-French ornament. In the little gilt table (Fig. 461) the delicate relief seems to lend itself to the grace of the long, curved legs; the top (Fig. 462) is of glass, blackened at the back and with a gilt and cut cipher of Sir Robert Walpole and Katherine, his first wife, in an oval of C scrolls; the frame and square cabriole legs are somewhat Chinese in feeling but unusually elegant. It is of historical interest, being formerly the dressing-table of Sir Robert Walpole, and although before the date of the occupation of Houghton, was always used by him there.

This extraordinary house, designed by Ripley and begun in 1722, was not completed for ten years, and is closely connected with the subject of English furniture. Walpole had taken advantage of the public mania and bought largely in South Sea stock, selling out at the top of the market at £1000 per cent. profit; with the fortune thus acquired he built Houghton, and filled it with pictures and furniture, spending over £200,000 – an enormous sum in those days. It is not desirable here to describe the interior of Houghton at any length, but the internal fittings are known as the most elaborate effort in mahogany of any house of that time. The staircase is very finely carved in Cuban mahogany; on the first floor are over sixty doors of the same wood, nearly three inches thick, all having carved and gilt mouldings; the window-shutters of these rooms are to match, while one door and over-door in the saloon, a mass of carved mahogany, richly gilt in parts, is known alone to have cost £1000. This door leads to the hall, which in in stone, and a cube of forty feet; from the ceiling stone groups of cupids, considerably over life-size, hang by socles from their waists. One entire side of the dining-room is marble, with deep alcoves for two marble sideboards; in this room Walpole collected his friends, where they drank together till the greater number of them fell underneath the table. He had inherited this jovial disposition and love for the pleasures of the table from his father, who at convivial meetings had been accustomed to supply his son's glass with a double portion of wine

FIG. 461. *Gilt Table with Glass Top.* Height, 2 feet 6 inches; length, 3 feet. Property of the MARQUESS OF CHOLMONDELEY.

FIG. 462. *Top of same.*

FIG. 463. *Gilt Table.* Height, 2 feet 6 inches. Property of the DUKE OF DEVONSHIRE.

adding, 'Come, Robert, you shall drink twice while I drink once, for I will not permit the son in his sober senses to be witness to the intoxication of his father'. These hereditary instincts proved expensive, for in the *Craftsman* of 1730, there was a statement to the effect that the housekeeping bills at Houghton amounted to £1500 a week. These bills appear to have been for solid eating and drinking, which must have induced so material a taste that even the designs of Kent were thought beautiful. Kent was a popular pretender in art, who, not only content with advertising himself as architect, painter and ornamental gardener, aspired also to the merits of sculpture, and encumbered Westminster Abbey with some of his vulgar conceptions. Horace Walpole says of him:

'Kent was not only consulted for furniture, as frames of pictures, glasses, beds, tables, chairs, etc., but for plate, for a barge, for a cradle, and so impetuous was fashion, that two great ladies prevailed on him to make designs for their birthday gowns: the one he dressed in a petticoat decorated with columns of the five orders, and the other like a bronze, in a copper-coloured satin with ornaments of gold.'

More examples of furniture, in which the heavy hand of Kent can be

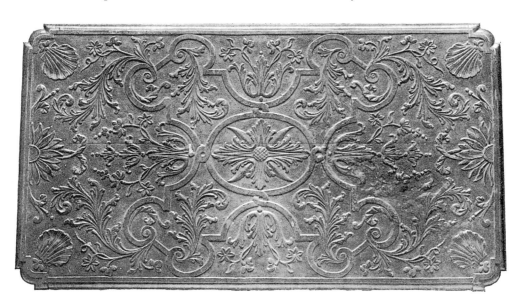

FIG. 464. *Top of Gilt Table.* Property of LADY NUNBURNHOLME.

traced, will be given later on. It is a relief to turn to the graceful gilt table (Fig. 463). The top is in carved and jesso strap-work, the intersection of the leg and frame moulding being unusual; the grotesque face is introduced on the shoulders, in this instance somewhat resembling a Red Indian with plumed head-gear, and is almost identical with the mask of this type introduced so much on sixteenth-century wood-work; the legs are slender and of cabriole form, finishing in scrolled feet clothed in acanthus; the date of this table is about 1720. Fig. 464 shows the decorated top of a similar table, the design of which is directly adapted from a French pattern. In some instances the ornamentation was entirely worked in jesso without any carving. It is a popular idea that all the good gilding was done by foreign workmen, but nothing definite is known to prove or disprove the incapacity of the English craftsman in this respect; but that furniture bought abroad was certainly gilt in this country is shown by a letter of Lady Mary Coke's in 1769:

'I've got my chairs from Paris, without being beholden to anybody; they have paid the duty, but I don't intend to have them covered with the damask, or have the frames gilt, till after I return from abroad.'

The following extracts from letters of the Countess of Pembroke to Mrs Clayton, afterwards Lady Sunden and Queen Charlotte's favourite, show that gilt tables were highly esteemed, the gift in question being a bribe:

'1728.
Dear Madam, – I intended to have seen Herbini's marble tables, but having by chance mentioned before my Lord that you wanted one, he has, without my knowledge, sent the best he had, which they call verde-antique, to your house, which he intreats your acceptance of as a small testimony of the sincere respect he has for you.'

In another letter to the same lady she says:

'I take the liberty to tell you that I have given my Lord's son all the drawings, prints, and books that are of great value, and the gilt sideboard.'

Sofas, chairs and stools were also made in this gilt style. Fig. 465 is a sofa, one of a pair of English type, of about 1712. The back is high and the arms terminate in C scrolls. It is covered in a deep sea-green contemporary damask of Spitalfields make, and bordered with the original nailing. The pendant and front of the legs are carved with fan-shaped ornaments and terminate in ball- and claw-feet; the wood-work is dull gilt, on a granulated ground, the ornaments alone being burnished; the back legs are of the early

Fig. 465. *Gilt Settee.* Length, 4 feet 6 inches; height, 3 feet 5 inches. Property of the Marquess of Cholmondeley.

FIG. 466. *Gilt Arm-chair*. Property of the
MARQUESS OF CHOLMONDELEY.

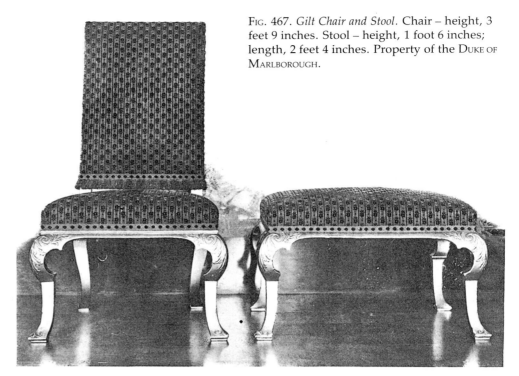

FIG. 467. *Gilt Chair and Stool*. Chair – height, 3
feet 9 inches. Stool – height, 1 foot 6 inches;
length, 2 feet 4 inches. Property of the DUKE OF
MARLBOROUGH.

FIG. 468. *Gilt Chair*. Height, 3 feet, 4 inches.
Property of the MARQUESS OF CHOLMONDELEY.

club-foot type. This granulated jesso on legs was generally discontinued about six inches from the ground in order to avoid scaling by wear. Fig. 466 is an arm-chair, one of a dozen belonging to the same suite, and is carved and gilt in a similar manner; the back is low, for this form now began to replace the tall and hooped-backed padded chair. The chair and stool (Fig. 467), covered in modern velvet, have broken cabriole legs and form part of a suite at Blenheim, of which the console-table has been given in 'The Age of Walnut' (Fig. 433). This shape is taken directly from Roman tables and stands of the first century AD; but in the antique the treatment is far more delicate, and the incurved point represents the hock of a deer, the foot finishing in a hoof. The same motive is preserved in the chair (Fig. 468), one of a dozen, in which the taste of the new Court is perceptible. The back is padded, of hooped form, carved with pendants of husks in low relief and surmounted with the shell that occurs on so much of the Houghton furniture; the legs have a double break, and the shoulders are treated in the same manner as the table from Hardwick (Fig. 463); the covering of crimson and cream Genoa velvet is original, and the whole chair is opulent in effect. Fig. 469 is a long couch matching these chairs, but the legs are too short to admit the broken curve; the undulated back is in three divisions: it is upholstered in Genoa velvet and has the original bolsters and cushions; the modern castors somewhat mar the appearance of the feet. At the back of the chair (Fig. 468) can be seen one of the mahogany and gilt doors of the room in which this furniture stands, and the velvet-clad walls must have formed a surprising accompaniment to the magnificent pictures that Walpole had collected, and to the brocaded satins and velvets worn by his guests. Although sumptuous and fine in colour the effect must have been rather unreal, and the desire to surprise rather too apparent, but is deeply interesting as representing a state-room of about 1730 in an untouched state. A finer taste in gilt furniture is seen in Plate XXXII, a chair of about 1728, one of a set of twelve. The cresting is high and of perforated design, reverting back to the period of 1690; the back is hooped with a fiddle-shaped splat, and plain but for a rectangular strap-work carved in very low relief, the open space and the seat being filled with fine gilt caning; the front rail is decorated with a small pendant, and the legs are carved with lions' masks and terminate in lions' paws. The height and delicacy of the construction evidently demanded some tie to the legs, four stretchers were therefore introduced, an unusual feature at this time; the gilding is original, and even upon the caning is extraordinarily fresh. Another interesting piece is the arm-chair on Plate XXXI(a), some two or three years later in date than the caned chair; the back is low, a shape that was becoming popular owing to the introduction of powder. To save the velvet and brocaded furniture, short silk flaps were

often attached to the backs of chairs and sofas, which could be brought over to the front in order to protect the tops from the grease and powder of the head-dresses of the time. The arms of this chair are serpentine, resembling those of earlier date, the supports are curved backwards, and like all arm-chairs belonging to this period, no longer form a continuation of the front legs, which are shouldered with the favourite Indian mask, here wearing earrings, and finish in small club-feet clothed in acanthus; the covering is the original needlework in 'the Indian Taste', as it was then called.

Needlework for carpets, as well as coverings to sofas and chairs, was still in great favour, and the fashion continued all through the eighteenth century. There are constant allusions to needlework in women's letters and diaries of this time. Mrs Delany, in 1740, writes to a friend:

Fig. 469. *Gilt Couch*. Length, 7 feet 4 inches; height, 3 feet 10 inches. Property of the MARQUESS OF CHOLMONDELEY.

Fig. 470. *Gilt and Painted Settee*. Length, 6 feet 2 inches; height, 3 feet 4 inches. Property of LORD FITZHARDINGE.

FIG. 471. *Gilt and Painted Chair.*
Property of LORD FITZHARDINGE.

'I have packed up a box of needlework for you, the great chair that was begun so long ago, with all the worsteds and silks that belong to it, which at your leisure I hope you will finish.'

In 1738 there is an entry in the diary of the Earl of Bristol for what was paid 'to lineing ye needlework carpet', and as late as 1774 the Hon Mrs Boscawen writes from Holkam, where she was staying:

'I think it is curious to see my Ly Leicester work at a tent stitch frame every night by one candle that she sets upon it and no spectacles, it is a carpet she works in shades, tent stitch.'

Fig. 470 is a long settee of about 1723, covered with the work of Elizabeth Drax, who married the fourth Earl of Berkeley in 1744; her initials, E. A. B., are introduced under the coat-of-arms. The existing set consists of one long and two small settees and four chairs, representing a most laborious and beautiful effort in needlework, but which certainly formed later coverings than the date of the furniture. In these coverings the Berekeley arms are introduced amidst sprays of brilliantly coloured flowers on a brown ground; this needlework is set in a delicate gilt egg and tongue moulding, the arms are simple and light, but the frame is more solid, and a band of the wave pattern surrounds the seat, which is supported by six curved and hocked

FIG. 472. *Gilt Arm-chair.* Height, 3 feet 8 inches; width, 2 feet 8 inches; height to top of seat, 1 foot 10 inches. Property of the MARQUESS OF CHOLMONDELEY.

FIG. 473. *Gilt Arm-chair.* Height, 3 feet 3 inches; width, 1 foot 10 inches. Property of the MARQUESS OF CHOLMONDELEY.

FIG 474. *Gilt Chair to Match.* Property of the MARQUESS OF CHOLMONDELEY.

legs shouldered with acanthus, and finishing in lions' paws. On most of these legs that suggest the anatomy of a lion, tufts of hair are introduced between the hock and pastern. The wood-work of this settee was originally entirely gilt, the introduction of the black being probably a Victorian addition. Fig. 471 is a chair belonging to the same suite, the hooped-back form is still preserved and covered with needlework similar to the settee; the proportions are somewhat lost in the photograph, and the added castors give an awkward appearance.

In the legs and frame of the tall-backed and winged arm-chair (Fig. 472), of about the date 1725, a definite movements towards the new style can be seen; the back wings, arms and seat resemble the usual grandfather chair of the period, and are covered in contemporary emerald green velvet trimmed with silver galon; the frame is in a curved projection carved in low relief, with two acanthus scrolls centring in a satyr's mark, the lion legs are distinctly hocked, and shouldered with lions' masks holding a ring and ribbon. This design marks the new taste found also on contemporary mahogany furniture. Fig. 473 is an arm-chair from the same set; the arms curve outwards, terminating in lions' heads, the uprights are ringed and scaled; the ordinary chair, one of twelve, is shown in Fig. 474, and coincides with the others. One of the stools can be seen under the console-table (Fig. 457). In the gilding of this furniture the ground is coarsely sanded, producing an extremely soft and unobtrusive effect.

The etiquette of the 'tabouret', even away from Court, was still preserved, which will account for the great number of stools to be found in large country-houses. In a letter of Mrs Pendarves to Mrs Anne Granville in 1727, describing the Lord Major's banquet after the coronation, she says:

'As soon as we had dined the Lady Mayoress got up and we followed her to a very pretty room with a good fire, at the upper end of which was placed two armed chairs, and two stools, for their Majesties and the Princesses.'

A little later we read in the diary of George Bubb Dodington:

'The Princess sent for me to attend her between 8 and 9 o'clock. I went to Leicester House expecting a small company and a little musick, but found nobody but her Royal Highness. She made me draw a stool and sit by the fireside. Soon after came in the Prince of Wales and Prince Edward and then Lady Augusta, all in undress, and took their stools and sate round the fire with us.'

Fig. 475 is an arm-chair, the upper portion of which is entirely different to any of the preceding specimens, and is comparatively modern in its notions of comfort; the back is low, and sufficiently raked to form one long curve with the arms; the seat probably originally possessed a loose cushion. The frame is carved in an ovolo moulding, supported on short scrolled legs, united at the front and sides by heavy garlands of oak-leaves; the chair is reminiscent of Kent, who may have supplied the design, as it bears very distinctly the heavy handiwork of that artist. It is of about the date 1730.

Fig. 475. *Gilt Arm-chair*. Property of the Viscount Enfield.

CHAPTER II

ETWEEN the years 1710 and 1715, mahogany (technically the wood of the *Swietenia mahogoni*, L.) began to be used in this country for the construction of furniture; up to this time it had only been introduced as a veneer or in a small portions for decoration, though such things as boxes, or quite small objects, were no doubt occasionally made previous to this date. The raised panels and split balusters applied to the cabinet of about 1660 (Fig. 216, 'The Age of Oak') are without doubt mahogany, but probably were made from a specimen of the wood brought from abroad as a curiosity. The chairs and settees at Ham House (Figs. 400 and 412, 'The Age of Walnut') are early examples of mahogany furniture whilst their coverings resemble in date those used on the bed that belonged to Queen Anne at Hampton Court; it is therefore reasonable to suppose that the date of the Ham House suite is before 1714. By the year 1720, mahogany was certainly being used for chairs, tables and settees, and rapidly adopted by those wishing to be fashionable, for at first it was no doubt more expensive than walnut. The figured walnut, reserved for the purposes of veneer, was too rare and too brittle to be used in solid construction when veneered walnut furniture was in fashion, and marqueterie had supplanted carving. Furniture makers quickly discovered properties of lightness in mahogany unknown in oak, and durability and strength deficient in walnut; the warmth of colour was also a novelty. In walnut furniture the mouldings and edgings had been kept plain; cross-banded in veneer, but with the new wood and in the new style as it developed, decorated framings, bandings and fillets were introduced, and panels of cabinets and wardrobes were carved. Our increasingly great trade and possessions in the West Indies encouraged the importation of mahogany, which after 1733 was shipped here in enormous quantities, as in that year Walpole removed the duty off imported timber.

The quality of mahogany varied greatly with the conditions of its growth; exposed situations and solid ground yielding the finest timber. The mahogany generally called 'Spanish', with 'clouded' grain, was especially prized, and obtained largely, though not exclusively, from San Domingo and Cuba. For many years only the finest and oldest trees lying near the coast were exported, which accounts for the rare excellence of all early mahogany; as these trees were used up, it became necessary to go further

FIG. 476. *Mahogany Bureau or Scrutoire.* Height, 3 feet 6 inches; length, 3 feet 6 inches; depth, 2 feet. Property of PERCY MACQUOID, Esq.

FIG. 477. *The same, Open.*

inland for this same quality of richly figured wood, transit increased the difficulty of shipment, and so Honduras mahogany began to be exported from the Bay of Campeachy. This variety is more open grained and occasionally much rippled in the figure, yielding logs sometimes over forty feet in length, but of inferior colour. The root of either variety, after attaining a certain size, is deeper in colour and the figure more marked than the wood of the trunk.

Although from 1715 to 1720 comparitively little mahogany furniture was made, it was all of high quality, proving that the wood must have been considered valuable, and used only by the best makers. Walnut was still employed, but as the shapes resembled those of mahogany, it is needless to give many examples of this period. Fig. 476 is an early plain and finely constructed mahogany bureau or escritoire of about 1720, resembling in its practical form those made contemporaneously in walnut. A diversion is, however, introduced by the tubbed front to the drawers, fairly simple of execution in solid wood, but not a desirable experiment in veneer; with this exception the piece shows no evolution in form from the lower portion of writing-cabinets of the previous twenty years. The top is kept narrow and the flap is very deep, the front is divided into four drawers, the tubbed and recessed surface entailing a sacrifice of three and a half inches of the wood; the moulding that frames the base, the pendants and brackets to the legs, are also similar to those found on Anne specimens. The interior (Fig. 477) shows a series of six drawers of serpentine front, surmounted by eight canopied pigeon-holes centring in a door, between two Corinthian columns; within these are two more drawers and many little secret drawers; the brasses on the front are contemporary and very picturesque in form; those on the top drawer are bent over to take the projecting curve. This piece possesses the polish of age attained by long and careful keeping, and is of beautiful colour.

Another escritoire or writing-table is Fig. 478, not only of great interest from its shape and early date, but from having been the writing-table of Sir Robert Walpole. The upper portion is perfectly plain, and the half-rounded mouldings between the drawers and that surrounding the top carry out this simplicity. The front and back exactly resemble each other, the centre drawers are concave, between others of convex form. The legs are quadrangular, set anglewise and carefully carved; they are united close to the ground by three X-shaped stretchers, moulded in a simple half-round; the handles to the drawers are of mahogany and the keyplates quite simple. The wood has faded to a cinnamon colour, never having been waxed or polished.

Fig. 479 shows Sir Robert Walpole's dining-table, and is also of this early period. The ends are semicircular and on the principle of a gate-table; it is 6

FIG. 479. *Mahogany Dining-table*. Width, 6 feet. Property of the MARQUESS OF CHOLMONDELEY.

feet wide, and when extended to full length by the introduction of intermediary pieces, is 16 feet 2 inches long. The legs are plain balusters, standing on oblong plinths over knobbed feet, and are thirty-two in number; it is of Cuban mahogany, the same quality used in the decorations and so much of the furniture at Houghton. To the left of the illustration can be seen one of the arched recesses containing one of the marble sideboards with which this side of the room is furnished. These recesses, faced with white marble, are framed between Corinthian columns. The sideboards, one of which is given in Fig. 480, are of violet, black, white and yellow marble; in the centre is a white escallop shell containing a silver tap, and beneath is a large grey granite cistern. The design of the sideboard conforms to the rest of the architectural surroundings of the room, and is both strong and simple in proportion. In this room the white marble mantelpiece is heavily carved with bunches of grapes, and the overmantel consists of a large panel representing a sacrifice to Bacchus; this structure reaches to the ceiling, which is covered with cupids and grapes in coloured mosaics. The overdoors are carved with a design of grapes in mahogany, partly gilt. The orgies that took

FIG. 480. *Marble Sideboard*. Length, 7 feet; height, 2 feet 9 inches. Property of the MARQUESS OF CHOLMONDELEY.

FIG. 481. *Mahogany Card-table.* Height, 2 feet 4 inches; top, 2 feet 6 inches square. Property of the MARQUESS OF CHOLMONDELEY.

FIG. 482. *Mahogany Card-table.* Height, 2 feet 4 inches; diameter, 2 feet 11 inches. Property of PERCY MACQUOID, Esq.

place in this room were the talk of all England at that time.

Fig. 481 is a card-table slightly earlier in date, and may even be the table on which the owner of Houghton, in spite of being one of England's most able Prime Ministers, gambled away the two magnificent marble staircases that originally formed the approaches to the back and front of the house, compelling all entrances in future to be made by the insignificant lower doors. The table possesses a double flap, so that it could be used for cards or chess, the legs are slender and almost straight; the circular corners of the lower flap are dished for the candlesticks and money. Fig. 482 is another of these combination tables, rather more ingenious in construction and circular when open; the front is fitted with shaped drawers, the runners and angles of which are calculated with great care and show the element of good cabinet work which was beginning to make its appearance at this time. The plain shell ornament that overlaps at the junction of the simple, almost straight cabriole legs, and the character of the mahogany, prove the table to be before 1720. The hinges and framing to the movable leg are of oak. It is evident that the early articles of furniture made in mahogany were rather plain in character, but the artist's table (Fig. 483) shows some tendency towards

FIG. 483. *Artist's Table.* Mahogany. Height, 2 feet 8 inches; length, 3 feet 2 inches; depth, 2 feet. Property of MESSRS HEWETSON AND MILNER.

FIG. 484. *Mahogany Dining-table.* Property of S. LETTS, Esq.

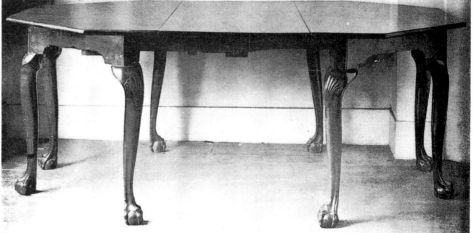

FIG. 485. *Oak Dining-table*. Height, 2 feet 6 inches; length, 4 feet 7 inches; width, 2 feet 9 inches. Property of FRANK GREEN, Esq.

FIG. 486. *Mahogany Wheel-chair*. Property of MESSRS J. MALLETT AND SON.

FIG. 487. *Walnut Wheel-chair*. Property of MESSRS J. MALLETT AND SON.

decoration. The top is edged with a simple half-round moulding between two fillets, and opens as a flap; underneath this is a series of compartments to hold colours, and a slab that can be raised to form a small easel; at the side are drawers for pencils and brushes. The frame is centred with an Egyptian mask, and lions' faces are introduced on the shoulders of the modelled legs, which finish in claw and ball feet; the brass handles are solid and simple, and carry out the character of the table, which is more interesting than beautiful; the easel, desk and small compartments for colours infer that it was used in the painting of miniatures or water-colours. Paint-boxes and tubes of colours were unknown during the eighteenth century; the colours were kept in powder or bladders and in the drawers of tables or cabinets, such as the highly finished little cabinet (Plate XXXIII), supposed to have been used by Sir Joshua Reynolds for this purpose. It is of walnut, and of about the date 1710; the cornice and ovolo frieze belonging to the end of the seventeenth century. The doors and inner doors are veneered with oyster-pieces of walnut, with cross-bandings of the same wood bleached; the comparative proportions of the lower and upper portions are unusual, and the stout cabriole legs are calculated to bear the weight of the cabinet; the handles and escutcheons are particularly good, but were probably added about 1745. This cabinet, apart from the interest of its ownership, represents a piece of furniture that has always been cared for and kept in beautiful condition, and evidently preferred by Sir Joshua for his personal use at a time when mahogany furniture was universal. The effect of light and air upon the exposed portions of the wood is very clearly seen in the illustration.

Fig. 484 is an interesting dining-table, octagonal in shape, of a date shortly before 1720, and which can be extended by means of a leaf to a size capable of seating ten persons. The legs are long and graceful, ornamented by simple shells, and terminate in dragon's claw and ball feet, on which it should be noticed that the tendons are prolonged and emphasised. The angle caused by the junction of the legs with the octagon frame is awkward, and these tables were consequently generally constructed with rectangular frames. Fig. 485 is a smaller oak dining-table of about the same date, constructed with a double flap. The legs are slender and headed with shells enclosed within a shield-shaped fillet, the feet are clubbed and ribbed; the arrangement of the centre legs is inconvenient for the sitter, a mistake in construction that occurs on many of these flap-tables.

Oriental taste is clearly perceptible in the mahogany chair (Fig. 486), made about 1720, a copy of the style of walnut chair made some twenty years before. The seat is circular and caned, the back semi-circular and composed of four balustered uprights, between which are three oval panels, perforated and carved in the 'Indian Taste', resting upon a waved rail of the same character; the seat is supported on six cabriole legs ending in lions' feet, united at the sides by scrolled stretchers and at the backs by knobbed stretchers, resembling in arrangement the spokes of a wheel, which no doubt suggested the name wheel-chair; in many instances the seat moves round on a centre pivot. Another name for this shape was 'Burgomaster's chair', inferring that the pattern came over here from Holland, where taste, owing to important trade with the East, was strongly tinctured with Chinese influence. Fig. 487 is the walnut prototype made about 1700, the true period of the shape, and closely resembles the former specimen, but the construction is not so light, nor is the carving of the back so delicate as in the mahogany chair; the acanthus on the legs is elementary yet the proportion of the whole is more pleasing.

After studying the evolution of form in chairs after 1720, it is very clear that the employment of mahogany suggested possibilities not to be found in oak or walnut, and although certain perforations of the splat took place early in the reign of James II, the great delicacy of treatment in this respect was reserved for later carvers in mahogany. This wood was first used at a plain period of fashion in furniture, but towards 1730 its decoration began and was hurried onwards in every conceivable variation by the various cabinet-makers, of whom Chippendale was perhaps the most consistent. Much mahogany furniture previous to Chippendale has erroneously been ascribed to him or his school, but it must be borne in mind that he was inspired and instructed by at least three waves of distinct taste that immediately preceded his own. The first of these periods was comparatively plain, of which the hooped-back chair (Fig. 488), of about 1718, is a fair example. The upper portion is divided into a flat strap of two loops headed by a shell; the vase shape, or so-called fiddle-back splat, is inserted beneath this, and the uprights of the back are pronounced in their angle; the scroll-over of the arms forms another sharp angle, and is of the fashion shortly before 1720; the seat-rail is decorated with a shell, carved in very low relief, and the legs are simple. In Fig. 489, the back is of plain Queen Anne type, but the legs and arms are more ornate than in the last chair; the arms turn outwards and end in lions' heads, a fashion introduced soon after 1720; the legs are decorated with a bold shell and pendant terminating in ball and claw feet. The settee (Fig. 490) is of the same date, being an early specimen of this form of seat made in mahogany; the double chair-back is perfectly plain, united in the centre by a shell; the broad splat is more for convenience than grace, and the arms turn outwards, finishing in lions' heads; the legs are distinct in character and more graceful than the rest of the piece.

A form of triple-back settee began to be made at this time, the greater strength and elasticity obtainable in mahogany enabling the chair-maker to construct the long, delicate rail that formed the top to the three hoops, and so extend the length of the piece of furniture. In the hooped-back chair (Fig. 491), rather later in date, the splat begins to show signs of subdivision, the arms turn outward and the legs are simple, but correspond admirably in

FIG. 488. *Mahogany Arm-chair.* Height, 3 feet 4 inches. Property of J. MALLETT, Esq.

FIG. 489. *Mahogany Arm-chair.* Height, 3 feet 3 inches. Property of W. H. LEVER, Esq.

FIG. 490. *Mahogany Settee.* Height, 3 feet 3 inches; length, 4 feet 6 inches. Property of W. H. LEVER, Esq.

FIG. 491. *Mahogany Arm-chair.* Property of J. MALLETT, Esq.

FIG. 492. *Mahogany Chair.* Property of HENRY HUXLEY, Esq.

FIG. 493. *Mahogany China Cupboard.* Height, 7 feet 7 inches; width, 4 feet 6 inches; depth, 1 foot 1 inch. Property of W. A. MEREDITH, Esq.

their curves to the rest of the chair, which, though plain, is lively and graceful in line; the seat is covered with needlework of the time. Fig. 492 is another early mahogany chair, one of a set, and probably of country make; the back is devoid of any beauty, and the perforation of the splat is elementary; the legs, however, possess a certain amount of charm, and are copies of the plain walnut type.

These plain examples may appear somewhat uninteresting and lacking in the grace of later work, but they constitute good types of the first period of mahogany; this and the two succeeding stages were more thoroughly representative of English feeling than the final distinct evolution, which was so strongly tinctured with French and quasi-Chinese design, and christened Chippendale after its chief promoter.

In the china or curiosity cupboard (Fig. 493), strong traces of the style of Queen Anne are still visible, though the waved bevel of the lower panels would have caused much difficulty in walnut veneer; the cornice is dentilled, a feature now introduced on cupboards and wardrobes; the doors are divided into twelve lights of serpentine shape, edged by mullions and transoms of elegant baluster form. The lower part open in two doors, with bevelled panels of the same serpentine design; these rest upon a simple plinth supported on short ogeed legs; the piece is of solid mahogany

throughout, the backing alone being of oak. The interest of this particular cabinet is considerable, as it has been in the possession of the same family ever since it was made; it was sent to America about the year 1723, and known to have been returned here about 1832. Much English mahogany furniture was sent to American during the eighteenth century, very beautiful specimens being still in existence there; these served as models to our colonists, and an independent school was evolved in that country and flourished, particularly at Newport, during the latter half of the century.

Fig. 494 is a chair of about 1725, which, though made in walnut, is representative of the second and more decorated period of mahogany. The plain splat and hooped back preserve the characteristics of earlier chairs, whilst the legs are ornamented with the favourite lion attributes. The designers at this time appear to have arrived at a decision how to treat the legs of chairs, but the back and divisions of the splats evidently still presented difficulties. Broad shoulders to cabriole legs, and shells with pendants, lingered in fashion for a long period, but after 1730 gradually disappeared. In the exceptionally fine settee (Fig. 495) made towards the end of George I's reign, full advantage is taken of the solid mahogany splats, and they are elaborately carved in the solid with a delicate tracery of distinctly foreign influence. A satyr's mask in full relief, placed low in order to avoid discom-

FIG. 494. *Walnut Chair.* Height, 3 feet 4 inches.

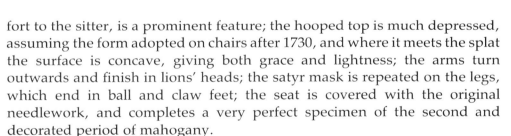

FIG. 495. *Mahogany Settee.* Length, 4 feet 6 inches; height, 3 feet 4 inches. Property of MESSRS J. MALLETT AND SON.

fort to the sitter, is a prominent feature; the hooped top is much depressed, assuming the form adopted on chairs after 1730, and where it meets the splat the surface is concave, giving both grace and lightness; the arms turn outwards and finish in lions' heads; the satyr mask is repeated on the legs, which end in ball and claw feet; the seat is covered with the original needlework, and completes a very perfect specimen of the second and decorated period of mahogany.

The constant changes in design occurring at this time in different parts of chairs, infer that taste was now in a very unsettled state, which renders the precise chronological arrangement of this transitional period most difficult. The chair (Fig. 496) shows the hoop-shaped back still in existence, but its uprights form a continuous line with the legs, and the stepped curve immediately above the seat, so marked a feature for the last twenty years, has disappeared. Occasionally, no doubt, individuals asserted their own taste, and insisted on certain details in their furniture being adapted on pieces of later fashion, and so created confusion of period; but such distinct points as the omission of the step in the uprights of chairs, or the division of their splats, clearly define a distinct and important change. The splat in this example is divided into three longitudinal openings, the rest of the chair presenting no new feature except the decoration of the seat-rail, which is carved with the wave pattern found on so many of th gilt console-tables of George I; the masks on the legs are those of lions holding a ring and

FIG. 496. *Mahogany Chair.* Height, 3 feet 3 inches. Property of W. H. LEVER, Esq.

FIG. 497. *Mahogany Stool*. Length, 1 foot 6 inches; height, 1 foot 5 inches. Property of W. H. LEVER, Esq.

FIG. 498. *Mahogany Stool*. Length, 1 foot 8 inches; height, 1 foot 5 inches. Property of W. H. LEVER, Esq.

pendant. This same wave pattern is found again on the serpentine seat-rail of the stool (Fig. 497), but the carving on the legs is more delicate and the curves more graceful than is generally the case on these stools, and the feet are ribbed in the manner of those of the table (Fig. 485), which infers a date soon after 1720. Another stool (Fig. 498) belonging to this same period is remarkable in representing a lion's front and hind legs; no masks are introduced on the latter, but the modelling of the hocks is very clearly shown. This particular treatment can be observed in the discoveries of furniture fabricated in Egypt and Assyria four thousand years ago.

In the two smaller stools (Fig. 499) lions' masks are repeated on all the legs; these pieces of furniture have been re-upholstered, and much of their proportion lost in the process. Our ancestors considered the coverings and trimmings of furniture as important as its manufacture, and in descriptions of individual pieces the coverings are more frequently mentioned than the carving. Every variety of covering was used at this time, and the materials employed represented a good deal of expenditure in both time and money. Chintz was used, and sometimes even linen elaborately embroidered, to protect the highly prized velvets, damasks and needlework. In 1757, Mrs Delany, one of the most celebrated needlewomen of the eighteenth century, wrote as follows to her friend Mrs Dewes:

'I am glad you are going to work covers to your chairs. I think you must alter your pattern, for they will have more wearing and washing than the bed or the curtains. I fear your cloth-work will not be firm enough. The border will be too broad for the chairs, something of the same kind of border to the bed with the mosaic pattern in the middle, and instead of cloth fill up part of it with stitches in thread, but don't you want your coverlid first?'

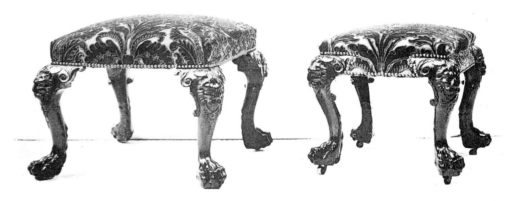

FIG. 499. *Small Mahogany Stools*. Height, 1 foot 4 inches.

Although cheap materials were manufactured in those days, they were seldom employed upon good furniture. Leather was largely used of all colours, even black. In the private accounts of John Hervey, Earl of Bristol, it is mentioned that he paid 'Tho. Phill, upholsterer, in full for ye Turkey leather chairs, £30, 2s. 6d.', and in 1726, 'Paid to John Sebthorpe for ten black leather chairs, £12, 3s., bought at Brigadier Munder's auction of goods'. Turkey leather was another name for morocco. It is interesting to see that so rich and important a peer as the Earl of Bristol not only bought furniture at auction, but also from personal acquaintances, as in 1702 there is an entry in his diary, 'Paid Colonel Parsons for ye black bureau, £6', and another in 1714, 'Paid Sir Harry Bond in full for a Japan cabinet, £35'. In all these prices it must be remembered that the value of money at that time was about three times greater than it is to-day.

Fig. 500 is a sofa of about 1725 to 1730; the back appears unusually high, as in the recent upholstering the loose squab has been omitted which would have completed the proper proportions of the piece. The arms are straight and padded and finish in lions' heads, the same design being repeated on the legs.

Up to this time mahogany had of necessity been used with caution, but the great amount imported by Walpole for the decoration of Houghton, and the removal of the tax on imported timber, no doubt suggested a more lavish use

FIG. 500. *Mahogany Sofa.* Length, 5 feet; height, 3 feet 8 inches. Property of W. H. LEVER, Esq.

of the wood. In the sofa (Plate XXXIV) a carved cresting is introduced, the arms are faced with mahogany, terminating in lions' heads; the front rail is elaborated with drooping pendants, the style of the carving being typical of the work done about 1730; the legs have the usual lions' masks and paws; the covering is a modern reproduction of a silk of the time. A suite, elaborately carved, of settees, chairs and stools of fantastic design, and also of about this same date, exist at Houghton. The settee (Fig. 501) is one of a pair; the cresting is high and solid, carved with graceful wreaths of acanthus on a scaled ground left in the natural colour of the wood; the arms are treated in a similar manner, and resemble in their downward scroll those of the end of the seventeenth century; the legs are surmounted with classical heads, and terminate in scrolled feet of the same date, and connecting these is a deep, openly carved design of acanthus scrolls centring in a large shell. The whole of the raised ornament is gilt, the plain surfaces being left in the mahogany; the seat and back are covered with a crimson and rose-coloured figured velvet of Spitalfields make, and the whole effect is very remarkable. Fig. 502 is one of the twelve arm-chairs that accompany these settees; the cresting is of the same character, and the uprights are carved with a ringed band

FIG. 501. *Mahogany and Gilt Settee.* Length, 4 feet; height, 4 feet 1 inch. Property of the MARQUESS OF CHOLMONDELEY.

FIG. 503. *Mahogany and Gilt Stool.* Length, 2 feet; breadth, 1 foot 10 inches; height, 1 foot 9 inches. Property of the MARQUESS OF CHOLMONDELEY.

FIG. 502 (*left*). *Mahogany and Gilt Arm-chair.* Height, 4 feet; width of seat, 2 feet. Property of the MARQUESS OF CHOLMONDELEY

FIG. 504. *Mahogany and Gilt Pedestals.* Height, 5 feet. Property of the MARQUESS OF CHOLMONDELEY.

terminating in husks, the scroll of the corners turning slightly outwards; the carved heads and shells are repeated on the legs, feet and pendant. Fig. 503 is one of the stools or tabourets, which are six in number, also belonging to this suite; this illustration is given in extra scale to show the details of the carving and gilding. The design of this set of furniture is extravagant, and suggests an elaborate effort of Kent in conjunction with the Italian carvers known to have been employed at Houghton at that time; the result carries on no evolution in mahogany furniture, for the details are composed of a medley of preceding styles, and the attempt at originality is quite abortive. Belonging to this same suite, but more beautiful, are the two high pedestals (Fig. 504) in the form of terms, carved and partly gilt; they are headed by the bust of a child bearing the capital of a column, composite in order; the terminals are scrolled in form, garlanded with fruit, and decorated from the feet upwards with one long acanthus leaf on a scaled round; the carving of the capitals and the children's heads is excellent, and the conjunction of the mahogany and gold in this instance most effective; the plinths are plain and square, with a rosette band. Fig. 505 is another pedestal, one of a pair; the carving is coarse and the design disconnected; it is interesting, however, as forming part of a suite of fine mahogany and gilt furniture at Longford Castle, that is contemporary with the specimens at Houghton, but altogether superior in style. This set of sofas, chairs and stools is very representative of the end of the second period in mahogany, about 1730. In the day-bed or couch (Fig. 506), which is of extreme length, the ends scroll over and are bordered like the frame in a fretted pattern, enclosed within fine bead and reel mouldings. The original green damask with which the couch and cushions are covered is strained underneath this gilt fretwork; it would therefore be impossible to re-upholster this furniture without removing the fretwork and the mouldings. The cushions are six in number and gradate in size, a fashion that had existed on day-beds since the sixteenth century; the frame is supported on eight legs, graceful for their height, carved with shells and acanthus, and finishing in lions' paws; these are connected by long scrolls of acanthus centring in shells. The carving, with the exception of the feet, is gilt, the remainder of the wood being left in the plain mahogany. Fig. 507 is a stool, five feet in length, and one of a pair; it is supported on six legs, and corresponds in design to the day-bed. The smaller stool (Fig. 573) is one of four. It is rare to find stools of this description with their original squabs as in these examples. The effect of the mahogany enriched with its old gilding, in conjunction with the greengage coloured damask, is very beautiful, but undoubtedly this quality of furniture was not often made, as its demand was confined only to the very rich. The arm-chair, one of a pair (Fig. 509), also from Longford Castle, in some way resembles the day-bed and stools, and was probably made about the same time. The previous hoop form to the backs of chairs had now given way to corners of square shape, a fashion that was adopted for many years; the carving of the top rail forms a cresting that finishes in inverted eagles' heads; the frame of the chair and the arm supports are a fretted banding of guilloche

FIG. 505. *Mahogany and Gilt Pedestal*. Height, 4 feet 6 inches. Property of the EARL OF RADNOR.

FIG. 506. *Mahogany and Gilt Day-bed*. Length, 7 feet; width, 2 feet 10 inches. Property of the EARL OF RADNOR.

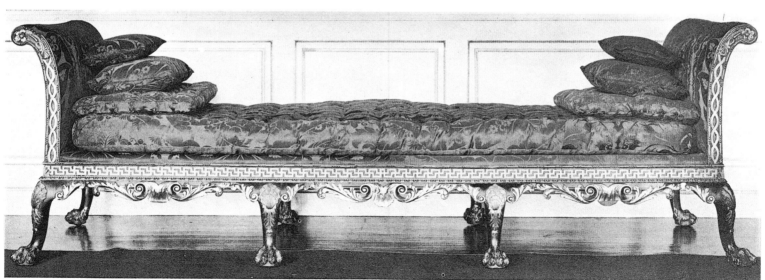

FIG. 507. *Mahogany and Gilt Long Double Stool.* Height, 1 foot 9 inches; length, 5 feet; width, 2 feet 4 inches. Property of the EARL OF RADNOR.

pattern gilt, through which the emerald green Italian velvet covering is visible; the arms are straight and upholstered, ending in lions' heads; the carving on the legs show a distinct departure from any previous decoration of this kind, being far more delicate and open in treatment; the cabriole form of the legs is still sturdy; the carved portions, with the exception of the lions' heads, are gilt.

Mahogany side-tables or sideboards with marble or wooden tops for dining-rooms were made contemporaneously with the gilt consoles already described, but probably not before 1720. Fig. 510 is an early table of this kind with its original mahogany top; the severe but admirable proportion of the frame and the slight legs are not calculated for a thick marble slab; the open character of the acanthus on the front, the isolation and peculiarity of feature on the lion's mask are typical of an early date. Fig. 511 is a sideboard of Irish origin with its old mahogany top. Here the treatment is more barbaric; the face and acanthus decoration show a less practised hand, but the legs at their junction with the frame are ingenious and original in treatment, producing a graceful and slender sense of line; the feet are curious in their conventionality, a series of balls representing the joints of the paws. Fig. 512 is another Irish sideboard, even more marked in character. The frame is plain, the lower portion being bordered with a carving of rough criss-cross divided with two well-carved escallop shells; a large barbaric lion's mask forms the centre, from which swags of oak leaves and acorns stretch to the rather delicate cabriole legs, which are shouldered with acanthus and terminate in many-jointed lions' paws. The top is original. No doubt the difficulty of transit of marble slabs encouraged the use of wooden tops to these Irish tables, which are most frequently found constructed in this manner. In these last two tables, which are between the years 1725 and 1730, the colour of the mahogany has attained a deep rich tone, and the surface resembles that of

FIG. 509 *(right). Mahogany and Gilt Arm-chair.* Height, 3 feet 8 inches. Property of the EARL OF RADNOR.

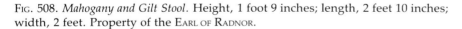

FIG. 508. *Mahogany and Gilt Stool.* Height, 1 foot 9 inches; length, 2 feet 10 inches; width, 2 feet. Property of the EARL OF RADNOR.

FIG. 510. *Mahogany Sideboard-table.* Length, 5 feet; height, 2 feet 7 inches.

FIG. 511. *Mahogany Sideboard-table.* Length, 5 feet; height, 2 feet 8 inches. Property of W. H. LEVER, Esq.

bronze. The furniture, decorations and silver plate of Irish workmanship of this time show great refinement of taste and perception of proportion; individual touch is especially noticeable in the plate, which is solid and of high quality, and the use of the little lion's mask on the cabriole leg ending in lions' paws, found so frequently on small jugs, sugar-basins and stands of the time, was practically confined to that country. The description in the following letter of Mrs Clayton's apartments, when resident with the Court, shows the standard of decoration at Dublin at that period. The letter is from Mrs Pendarves to a friend:

'DUBLIN, 1731.

. . . You must know, madam, yesterday being Wednesday, Mrs. Clayton opened her apartment and admitted all her acquaintance. I will describe to you how they are all disposed and furnished. First there is a very good hall well filled with servants, then a room of eighteen feet square, wainscoted with oak, the panels all carved and the doors and chimney finished with very fine high carving, the ceiling stucco, the window curtains and chairs yellow Genoa damask, portraits and landscapes very well done, round the room marble tables between the windows, and looking-glasses with gilt frames. The next room is twenty-eight feet long and twenty-two broad, and is as finely adorned as damask, pictures, and busts can make it, besides the floor being entirely covered the finest Persian carpet that ever was seen. The bed-chamber is large and handsome, all furnished with the same damask.'

In another letter written by this same lady a little later, she describes her own apartments in England as follows:

'Yesterday morning my upholsterer came and my new apartment will be very handsome. The drawing-room hung with tapestry, on each side of the door a Japan chest, the curtains and chairs crimson mohair, between the window large glasses with gilt frames and marble tables under them; the bed-chamber within hung with crimson damask; bed, chairs, and curtains the same.'

FIG. 512. *Mahogany Sideboard-table.* Length, 4 feet 11 inches; width, 2 feet 4 inches; height, 2 feet 8 inches. Property of J. ANNAN BRYCE, Esq.

FIG. 513. *Mahogany Sideboard-table.* Length, 5 feet 2 inches; height, 2 feet 9 inches. Property of W. H. LEVER, Esq.

FIG. 514. *Mahogany Sideboard-table*. Length, 4 feet 10 inches; width, 2 feet 2 inches; height, 3 feet. Property of the DUKE OF MARLBOROUGH.

It seems curious that mohair should have been used in the drawing-room and damask in the bedroom. In a description written about 1720, by Macky, of the Palace of Wanstead, built by Sir Richard Childe, the same characteristics of furnishing are mentioned:

'The apartment on the right fronting the area, called my Lord's apartment, consists of a parlour furnished with French prints, marble tables; an anti-chamber furnished with gold and blue brocade, velvet brocaded chairs and marble tables. A bed-chamber of crimson damask. The apartment on the right, called my Lady's, consists of a parlour finely adorned with China paper, the figures of men, women, birds and flowers the liveliest I ever saw come from that country; the anti-chamber is furnished with China silk, stained in colours, incomparably fine; the bed-chamber and dressing-room all also of China silk.'

By the middle of the century English wall-papers had arrived at great perfection in their manufacture, but were evidently expensive, as Lady Hertford states in a letter written to the Countess of Pomfret in 1741, that at a paper warehouse she was shown papers at twelve shillings and thirteen shillings a yard, also some at four shillings, but contented herself with one at elevenpence a yard.

In the table (Fig. 513), of about 1725 to 1730, the top is marble and the frame is plain but for a narrow bead and reel moulding; the legs are extremely bold; lion-headed, hocked and feathered like those of the chair (Fig. 471). In the centre is a deep pendant, but here unconnected with the legs; the numerous little scrolls of carving with which this pendant is embellished produces a somewhat restless effect, and the swag of drapery surrounding the female mask is not in scale with the rest of the table. The surface and colour of the wood in most of these sideboard-tables is

FIG. 515. *Mahogany Sideboard-table*. Length, 5 feet 2 inches; height, 2 feet 8 inches. Property of D. L. ISAACS, Esq.

remarkable; for the mahogany was of picked quality and probably in the first instance lightly covered with fiddle varnish or wax, which after a hundred and fifty years of rubbing has been cut down to the wood; at any rate, all gums or wax originally employed have disappeared, and only the bronze-like surface of the wood is left.

Fig. 514 is a specimen from Blenheim, one of a pair about the date 1730, with a mahogany top and projecting corners. The front and legs closely resemble in design some of the gilt tables already illustrated, but the heavy scrolling in the dark wood on this specimen overwhelms the lighter decoration to the front rail; it is unusual to find legs exactly of this type on mahogany furniture.

Plate XXXV is a sideboard-table about the date 1735, of fine design, made of light wood stained to resemble mahogany, and with a scagliola top; a cheaper imitation of the more expensive article made in mahogany and marble. The softer quality of the light wood lent itself to great freedom and richness in the carving, but this make of table is rare to find of such excellence, as the fine craftsman usually preferred to represent his work in more durable material. This staining of woods was very popular for a time, and the following extract on the subject in a letter to the *Annual Register* for 1764 is interesting:

'As I am very fond of mahogany furniture, I immediately (on reading a paper relating to a method of imitating it) entered on some experiments for that purpose.

'I took two pieces, one of elm and another of plane, both of which I stained well with aqua-fortis. I then took two drachms of powdered dragon's blood, one drachm of powdered alkanet root, and half a drachm of aloes, from all of which I extracted a tincture, with half a pint of spirits of wine; this tincture I laid over the wood with a sponge, and it gave it the colour of a piece of fine old mahogany. But may not wood be more uniformly and durably coloured while growing, since the bones of animals, as I myself have seen, are successfully coloured by feeding them on madder roots? The anhelent tubes by which trees suck their nourishment from the earth are analogous to the mouths of animals, and the circulating vessels of the former are much larger than in the bones of the latter.'

In Fig. 515, the perfection of execution and style in these tables is reached, and it is a good representation of the third period of mahogany from about 1730 to 1735, and that which most directly influenced Chippendale and his fellow-workers. The front consists of a carved frieze of finely scrolled acanthus, centring in a mask pendant, the lower rail of the frame being deeply and boldly gadrooned; the ornament on the legs resembles that on the day-bed at Longford (Fig. 506), but rings are introduced above the ball and claw feet. The top of this table was originally marble, but has been replaced by one of mahogany. As a substitute for marble tops to these tables, scagliola, an imitation of marble, was often used; these tops in many instances have cracked and been replaced by wood. Horace Walpole, in a letter of 1749, says, 'The scagliola tables have arrived.' This manufacture was invented in Italy as a cheaper substitute for marble at the end of the sixteenth century, and was introduced here for furniture and decoration about 1735. It was a composition of calcined gypsum, mixed with isinglass and Flanders glue; when in this state it was coloured to imitate the different varieties of marble, and laid on like cement; after hardening it was capable of very high polish. Another way of imitating costly marbles was by staining ordinary white marble according to the methods invented by Kircher and Mr Bird in the seventeenth century, and given at length in the *Philosophical Transactions* of the time. Kircher's method was to colour the marble

'By vitriol, bitumen, etc., forming a design of what you like upon paper, and laying the design between two pieces of polished marble; then closing all the interstices with wax, you bury them for a month or two in a damp place. On taking them up, you will find that the design you painted on paper has penetrated the marbles, and formed exactly the same design on them.'

Emanual da Costa, F.R.S., writing in 1759, says this method was recommended then, and in the same article he gives an interesting account of marbles stained by a Mr Robert Chambers about that time, and the tests to

Fig. 516. *Mahogany Card-table*. Height, 2 feet 3 inches; width, when open, 2 feet 6 inches. Property of Lord de Lisle and Dudley.

Fig. 517. *Top of same*. Property of Lord de Lisle and Dudley.

which they were subjected. He says:

'A piece of marble with several colours used on it, like a painter's pallet, being greatly saturated with aqua-fortis at different times for twenty hours, though the polish of the marble was quite effaced, yet there was not the least discharge of any of the colours, nor were they anywise dulled.'

He goes on to say that the results of the tests proved:

'That the colour permanently penetrated the marble without injuring it; it is therefore probable that Mr. Chambers' method of staining or colouring marbles is extremely good.'

Card-tables with the lion decoration were in fashion between 1720 and 1730, in both mahogany and walnut. Fig. 516 is a very highly finished specimen of about the latter date in mahogany from Penshurst; the legs are headed with lions' masks and long sprays of acanthus, they are hocked and covered with curious representations of little tufts of hair, and terminate in paws. The top (Fig. 517) is covered with an elaborate mythological scene in fine needlework of the time, and bordered round all the edges with a narrow silver galon; the corners of the table are dished for candles and receptacles for money and counters, the outer edges being carved. Fig. 518, a walnut specimen of about 1725, is also of the lion-headed pattern; the lower edge to the frame is serpentine. Card-playing, like all other forms of speculation, was much on the increase during the reign of George I, and this infatuation, which had hitherto been confined to the rich and those more or less connected with the Court, gradually permeated all classes of society. George II and his Queen set the example of card-playing every evening with very high stakes, and it is stated that no one was supposed to take a place at the royal card parties with a less sum than £200.

The Countess of Hartford, in a letter dated 1741, remarks that:

Fig. 518. *Walnut Card-table*. Height, 2 feet 4 inches; width, when open, 2 feet 6 inches.

'Assemblies are now so much in fashion that most persons fancy themselves under a necessity of inviting all their acquaintances three or four times to their houses, not in small parties, which would be supportable, but the boys and girls sit down as gravely at whist tables as fellows of colleges used to formerly; it is actually a ridiculous, though I think a mortifying sight, that play should become the business of the nation from the age of fifteen to fourscore.'

Dearth of intellectual amusement no doubt contributed to this love of gambling, which was carried to an even greater and more dangerous extent as the century advanced; the well-known picture by Hogarth of 'The Lady's last Stake', painted in 1759, being figurative of the evils that were attendant on this mania.

CHAPTER III

COMPARATIVELY little alteration took place in the decoration of important beds during the first thirty years of the eighteenth century, and that they were regarded as valuable items of household furniture is proved by the elaborate specimens that continued to be made, and the care that was taken in connection with their use. Even in the letting of a furnished house, the beds were evidently on occasions charged for as extras; the following letter from Sir Godfrey Kneller to Pope on this subject is interesting:

GREAT QUEEN STREET, 16*th June* 1719.

'SIR,

'I am in towne, and have louck'd for beds and bedsteads, which must cost ten pounds a year. When I promised to provide them you had maid no mention of the towne rates, which I am to pay, and will be £5 a year at least, and which would be £15 per annum with the beds; and that house did let for 45 a year when I bought it, so that all I have laid out being near 400 pound, would be done for nothing, of which you will consider and let me know your mind. The stables are fitted as you

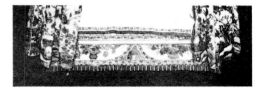

FIG. 519 (b). *Lower Portion of Bed.*

FIG. 519 (a). *Embroidered State-bed.*
Height, 14 feet; width, 6 feet; length, 7 feet.
Property of the MARQUESS OF CHOLMONDELEY.

Fɪɢ. 520 (a). *Velvet State-bed*. Height, 15 feet; length, 7 feet 6 inches; width, 6 feet 6 inches. Property of the Mᴀʀǫᴜᴇss ᴏғ Cʜᴏʟᴍᴏɴᴅᴇʟᴇʏ.

Fɪɢ. 520 (b). *Lower portion of Bed*.

Fɪɢ. 521. *Mahogany Bedpost*. Property of T. Cʜᴀʀʙᴏɴɴɪᴇʀ, Esq.

gentlemen ordered them to be, and all the painting will be done to-morrow or Thursday, with whenscoating in the quickest manner and best; and if you can stay till Saturday (the rooms shall be aired), and pray let me know your pleasure about the beds and bedsteads, for them I cannot provide. You may have 6, of which two are to have courtains for 10 pounds a year, etc.'

It is rare to find a bed of any period in an absolutely untouched condition, for not only was the upholstery liable to easy destruction, but the taste of successive owners often caused alterations. The two state-beds at Houghton are therefore of great interest, being now, exactly as they were originally made and in beautiful condition. The earlier is Fig. 519, which from its great height of fourteen feet necessitates division in the illustration. The tester, back, curtains, valances and quilt are composed of very fine Indian embroidery on a linen ground which is backstitched all over in fine thread; the cornice to the tester is of carved wood on which the embroidery is strained; at the four corners are carved escutcheons with the arms of Sir Robert Walpole in English needlework; the back is a tall scrolled design carved in wood and covered with the embroidered linen, and containing an elaborate representation of the arms, also in English needlework of the period. The basses are of the Indian work, the stitch of all being so fine that at a little distance the material might be mistaken for chintz. Horace Walpole, in his *Ædis Walpolianæ,* published in 1743, in describing the Embroidered Bedchamber, says:

'The Bed is of the finest Indian needlework; His Royal Highness Francis, Duke of Lorrain, afterwards Grand Duke of Tuscany, and since Emperor, lay in this bed when he came to visit Sir Robert at Houghton.'

This visit took place in 1733, a very few years later than the date of the bed.

The example Fig. 520 is the other state-bed preserved at Houghton, and a few years later in date. The tester consists of a series of simple mouldings, covered with green jaspé velvet, richly embroidered and fringed with gold; from this fall the curtains, each being six feet in width, of the same velvet, trimmed with gold embroidery and fringed with gold, and lined with cream-coloured silk; the ceiling of the tester is embroidered and fringed in the same elaborate manner. The back of the bed is of the green velvet, on which is a large escallop shell springing from a broken pediment, all carved in wood, and covered with velvet ornamented with gold; the quilt is composed of the same fabrics; the bed is mounted on a wooden plinth, covered to match the hangings. The ornaments and decorations of this state-bed are known to have been designed by Kent. To the right of the illustration can be seen a piece of the Gobelin tapestries with which the room is hung, representing the loves of Venus and Adonis, and to the left one of the mahogany doors alluded to before, with its richly carved and gilt frieze.

About 1715, bedposts once more began to be carved, and soon after that date were freely made in mahogany. Fig. 521 is one of a pair, formed of delicately fluted columns on vase-shaped bases ornamented with acanthus; the leg is headed with a design found on chairs early in George II's reign, an escutcheon centring in a cabochon ornament surrounded by acanthus; the

Fig. 522. *Mahogany Bed.* Height, 10 feet 6 inches; length, 6 feet 6 inches; width, 5 feet 6 inches. Property of Sɪʀ Fʀᴀɴᴄɪs Bᴜʀᴅᴇᴛᴛ, Bart.

Fig. 523. *Mahogany and Gilt Bed.* Height, 12 feet 6 inches; length, 7 feet; width, 7 feet. Property of the Dᴜᴋᴇ ᴏꜰ Mᴀʀʟʙᴏʀᴏᴜɢʜ.

foot is a lion's paw of fine execution. Posts and feet of this character can be seen again on the bed (Fig. 522), which is a simple specimen of about 1735. The cornice is boldly carved in a scroll-work of the mahogany, rising at the corners and centres into trefoil shape; there is no frieze, but the double valances are of unusual depth, the cantonnières being pronounced in form and finished on either side with tassels; the back is plainly plaited in the same material as the rest of the upholstery, which is a fine cherry-red mohair; the front curtains are missing, so the exceptionally good bedposts can be well seen; the ceiling of the tester is slightly dome-shaped, covered in the mohair, with corners and mouldings of mahogany. Fig. 523 is a more important bed, and perhaps a little later in date; the lines of the cornice, carved in mahogany and gilt, are of undulating form and of fantastic shape, the trefoil motives of the centres and corners resembling those of the former example; the valance follows the lines of the cornice, and is of rose-red damask trimmed with contemporary fringe. The damask of the upholstery is earlier in design than the bed, and probably formed part of the rolls of silk imported by the Duchess of Marlborough in 1720 for the furnishing of Blenheim. The silk at the back and part of the carved and gilt beading is missing; the posts are of mahogany, resembling Fig. 521 in their upper portion, but the plinths, partly concealed by the ill-arranged lower valance, are carved with a lattice-work tracery, a pattern beginning to find favour towards 1740. The constant references to important beds and bedchambers hung with red damask infer that this becoming colour was much in favour. In the more ordinary bedrooms, wall papers and embroidered linen hangings for the beds were used. Mrs Delany frequently mentions this work on linen in her letters, and in one dated 1743 to Mrs Dewes, her fellow-enthusiast in needlework, she says:

'Pray do not let my pretty chair interfere with your more important bed, which I hope you will finish as fast as you can; your hangings must be brown and white flowers, and ought to be the same pattern as your bed.'

This bed was the joint work of Mrs Delany and Mrs Dewes; the ground was nankeen, worked all over with patterns designed separately by Mrs Delany; the patterns were leaves united by bows of ribbon, cut out in white linen and sewn down with different varieties of knotting in white thread. She writes again in 1750:

'I have done up a little apartment, hung it with blue and white paper, and intend a bed of blue and white linen, all Irish manufacuture.'

These Georgian linen hangings have all nearly disappeared, or in some instances the work has been reapplied and so lost much of its interest. The previous custom of the mourning-bed, and how it was lent as occasion required to members of a family, has already been mentioned, and it continued even into the eighteenth century. Lady Bute, in 1726, witnessed one of these funeral receptions, held by the widow of her grandfather on the occasion of his death, which she described as follows:

'The apartments, the staircase, and all that could be seen of the house, were hung with black cloth; the Duchess, closely veiled with crape, sate upright in her state-bed under a high black canopy, and at the foot stood, ranged like a row of servants at morning prayers, the grandchildren of the deceased Duke. Profound silence reigned, the room had no light but from a single wax taper, and the condoling female visitors, who curtseyed in and out of it, and whose duty it was to tender in person their sympathy, approached the bed on tiptoe, and were clothed, if relations down to the hundredth cousin, in black glove mourning for the occasion.'

Fig. 524 represents the type of small domestic bed of the first half of the eighteenth century; in this instance the hangings are of white silk embroidered with an oriental design in colours; the back and tester being of satin with Chinese needlework, whilst the quilt and curtains are an English reproduction of the same design worked on silk. The tapestries on the walls

Fig. 524. *Upholstered Bed*. Height, 6 feet; length, 6 feet; width, 4 feet. Property of the MARQUESS OF CHOLMONDELEY.

are the celebrated series made at Mortlake representing James I and his family.

Plate XXXVI is a highly finished bed from Burghley, of about 1745. The cornice is of florid design and French in feeling, over which is strained crimson velvet. The skill required to so neatly cover the lines of the carving with material is great, for not a crease is visible, and the effect given is that the forms are carved out of red velvet. The valance is plain and follows the undulating and serpentine lines of the cornice; the cantonnière holders are formed of an acanthus spray terminating in tassels; the curtains and basses are also of red velvet trimmed with a tasselled fringe; the inner valances, ceilings, back and quilt are of turquoise-coloured silk, the carved and upright mouldings of the back being covered with a pale gold coloured silk. The posts are delicately carved with an upright laurelling, banded with a ribbon and terminate in square plinths, for at this time decorative feet to bedposts began to disappear; this bed shows the early commencement of true Chippendale style, and its lightness of design may be attributed to French influence. Fig. 525 is another bed also at Burghley. The cresting to the cornice is elaborately carved, forming curved and broken pediments at the sides and centres, on which is strained blue moiré silk; the cantonnière holders are of pagoda form, and the double valance is in serpentine curves and edged with the original fringe; the headings above the pillows repeat the design of the cornice, and the back is panelled and covered with cream silk closely pasted on to the carving, and so precise is the workmanship that no joins in the silk are apparent. The four original curtains, which would have been of the plain blue moiré, are missing, and are replaced at the head by

FIG. 525. *Mahogany Bed.* Height, 12 feet 6 inches; length, 6 feet 6 inches; width, 6 feet. Property of the MARQUESS OF EXETER.

blue and silver hangings of a silk of about 1765; the posts are well considered in their proportions, and finish in square plinths carved with a lion's mask and a string of garrya bloom. The height of beds during the reign of George II was considerably reduced, and did not again assume tall proportions.

The more florid and delicate taste in furniture that appeared in England after 1740 was chiefly due to the affectation of French manners and customs by the would-be leaders of fashion which encouraged the importation of foreign manufactures, but that a very strong feeling existed for the patronage of English silk manufactures as late as 1735 can be seen by the following extract from the *Monthly Intelligencer* of that year:

'March 1. Being her Majesty's Birthday, it was celebrated at Court with extraordinary magnificence. The Nobility, etc., were dressed in an exceeding rich and grand manner, the Ladies chiefly in stuffs of gold and silver, the gentlemen in cut and flowered velvet, and scarce any but of our own manufacture.'

Strong dissatisfaction against the foreign movement is seen by the many letters and essays published about that time. A correspondent in the *London Magazine* of November 1738 wrote:

'The ridiculous imitation of the French has now become the epidemical Distemper of this kingdom. The Travesty is universal; poor England produces nothing fit to eat or drink or wear; our cloaths, our Furniture, nay our food too, all is to come from France, and I am credibly informed that a Poulterer at Calais now actually supplies our polite tables with half their provisions. I don't mean to underrate the French, but like all true Mimicks we only ape their imperfections and awkwardly copy those parts which all reasonable Frenchmen themselves contemn in the originals. If this folly went no further than disguising both our meats and ourselves in the French Modes, I should bear it with more patience, but when even the materials for the folly are to be brought over from France too, it becomes a much more serious consideration. Our Trade and Manufactures are at stake, and what seems at first sight only very silly, is in truth a great national Evil and a piece of Civil Immorality.'

This mimicry of another nation at the expense of our own trade is again attacked in the same magazine a little later, as follows:

'The Increase in our Buildings, Furniture, wrought plate, and jewels is a proof of the Increase of our Luxury, but not of the Increase of our trade; for a man who is employed in Trade, knows better what to do with his money than to employ it in such vanities; the Increase in our luxury is chiefly among our Placemen, Stock-jobbers, and other Plunderers of their country, who like common gamesters and common prostitutes usually spend in extravagance what they have got by plunder.'

Even as late as 1786, letters and essays were still being written deploring the introduction of this foreign taste, as the following extracts from contributions to the *Lounger* of that year show:

'A well-educated British gentleman it may be truly said is of no country whatever, he unites in himself the characteristics of all different nations; he talks and dresses French, and sings Italian; he rivals the Spaniard in indolence, and the German in drinking, his house is Grecian, his offices Gothic, and his furniture Chinese.'

And again, describing a Frenchman staying in an English country-house:

'Comi fo, it seems means vastly fine in his language, though we country folks, if we durst own it, find the comi fo things often very ill tasted and now and then a little stinking. But we shall learn to like them monstrously by and by as Mons. de Sabot assures us. But my brother and my sister do all they can to wean him from his old customs. He fought hard for his pipe and spitbox, but my sister-in-law would not suffer the new window curtains and chair covers to be put up till he had given up both.'

The series of pictures of social life painted by Hogarth convey the manners, customs and surroundings of the early Georgian people more forcibly than any verbal description. Frivolous insincerity, uncleanliness of mind and body, with disregard of law and order, were their prevailing characteristics.

We see by the *Annual Register* for 1759 that this importation of foreign furniture and fabrics, on the other hand, in some instances stimulated the encouragement of home produce, as there is a note to the effect that:

'Six carpets made by Mr. Whitty of Axminster in Devonshire, and two others made by Mr. Jesser of Froome in Somersetshire, all on the principle of Turkey carpets, have been produced to the Society for the Encouragement of Arts, Manufactures, and Commerce, in consequence of the premiums proposed by the said Society for making such carpets, and proper judges being appointed to examine the same, gave it as their opinion that all the carpets produced were made in the manner of Turkey carpets, but much superior to them in beauty and goodness. The largest of the carpets produced is twenty-six feet six inches, by seventeen feet six inches.'

This Society in this same year offered a premium of £20 for:

'Making one quart at least, of the best, most transparent and colorless varnish,

FIG. 526. *Mahogany Coin-cabinet*. Property of SIDNEY LETTS, Esq.

equal in all respects to Martin's at Paris, commonly called copal varnish, the properties whereof are great hardness, a perfect transparency, without discoloring anything it is laid over, being capable of the finest polish, and not liable to crack. And for marbling the greatest quantity of paper, equal in goodness to the best marble paper imported, not less than one ream, £10.'

Many other rewards, amounting in all to some thousands of pounds, were offered in this year by this Society for different forms of pictorial and plastic arts, designs for fabrics and other native manufactures. Another interesting reference to an English carpet manufacture about this time is found in Lady Mary Coke's Journal in the year 1768.

'Went by the New Road to Moor Fields to the carpet Manufactory; they make several different kinds, and some remarkably fine; we saw one that was making for Lord Coventry, that he had agreed to give a hundred and forty guineas for; it is indeed excessively fine. There are other kinds like the persian and look quite as well. I believe I shall afford myself one of them for the room that I am furnishing.'

Mahogany cabinets made between 1720 and 1735 are very scarce; such as were made took the form of china or curiosity cupboards, but these were by no means general until after 1745. A coin or curiosity cabinet belonging to the second period of mahogany is given in Fig. 526. This is plain save for the introduction of a light leaf moulded cornice and plinth; it opens with two doors of dark Cuban wood, and within are a series of forty-two coin slides and two drawers. The stand is in great contrast to the plain top; the frame is deeply carved in a simple key pattern, and supported on highly decorated cabriole legs connected by a festoon of open-work flowers and leaves centring in a large lion's mask; the back legs are equally elaborate, and the carving is exceedingly bold and decided. The piece is known to have been in the possession of Horace Walpole at Strawberry Hill, and sold at the sale there. This famous house was bought in 1747 from a Mrs Chevenix, the proprietress of a celebrated toyshop, and Walpole immediately commenced making additions and decorating it in what he considered to be the Gothic style. Sir Christopher Wren, in his efforts to revive Gothic architecture, had not even grasped its first principles; Walpole's attempts in this direction, though trumpery in construction, first inspired in this country a revival of the domestic architecture of former times, and he was quickly followed by a host of imitative architects who adapted the characteristics of a previous period to their clients' requirements. In a letter dated 1753 from Horace Walpole to Sir Horace Mann, he thus describes Strawberry Hill and its decorations:

'Now you shall walk into the house; the bow-window leads into a little parlour hung with a stone-colored Gothic paper and Jackson's Venetian prints: from hence you come to the hall and staircase; imagine the walls covered with (I call it paper painted in perspective to represent) Gothic fretwork: the lightest Gothic balustrade to the staircase, adorned with antelopes, our supporters, bearing shields. The room on the ground-floor nearest you is a bed-chamber hung with yellow paper and prints framed in a new manner invented by Lord Cadogan, with black and white borders printed; over this is Mr. Chute's bed-chamber, hung with red in the same manner; in the tower beyond it is the charming closet where I am writing to you. It is hung with green paper and water-color pictures; out of this closet is the room where we always live, hung with a blue and white paper, adorned with festoons and a thousand plump chairs, couches, and luxurious settees covered with linen of the same pattern. Underneath this room is a cool little hall, where we generally dine, hung with paper to imitate Dutch tiles. We picque ourselves upon nothing but simplicity, and have no carvings, gildings, paintings, inlayings or tawdry businesses.'

The description conveys a strange mixture of ideas, but is a distinct and original departure in arrangement from the taste that surrounded Walpole. The elements of cheap building evidently began with the shoddy attempts in Gothic at Strawberry Hill, for the castellated parapet to the house, con-

FIG. 527. *Mahogany China Cabinet*. Height, 7 feet 6 inches; width, 5 feet 2 inches; depth, 7 feet 5 inches. Property of the DUKE OF MARLBOROUGH.

structed of lath and plaster, had to be renewed three times in thirty years. Pope's celebrated 'romantic grotto' at Twickenham, spoken of in such terms of contempt by Dr Johnson, is another instance of the puerile attempts in decoration by the fashionable amateur of this time. The walls of this grotto were covered with shells interspersed with pieces of looking-glass; there was a camera-obscura in one corner, and in another a passage opening to the river, paved with pebbles and shells. The furniture is described as being of the order called 'rustic', and was so highly valued by Pope that he bequeathed it in its entirety to his beloved female friend Martha Blount.

Fig. 527 is a stately china cabinet of about 1730, which stands 7 feet 6 inches high. The top is surmounted by a broken pediment with a small and plain plinth to hold a vase or bust, and is closely carved with acanthus and key pattern in low relief. The front is of architectural design, divided into three arched compartments, the spandrels and pilasters being left plain, and the carving confined to the headings, cappings, bases and borders; two fine scrolls and a carved cornice head the outer compartment; the rail of the stand is composed of a deep acanthus frieze supported on six well-proportioned legs that finish in scaling and lion paws; the hinges to the doors are in strong projection, adding greatly to the finish of the piece; the decoration is restrained throughout, and in scale accords with the careful proportions of the structure. It is an example filling an interesting link between the periods immediately before Chippendale. It was probably one of a pair made

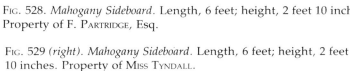

FIG. 528. *Mahogany Sideboard*. Length, 6 feet; height, 2 feet 10 inches. Property of F. PARTRIDGE, Esq.

FIG. 529 *(right)*. *Mahogany Sideboard*. Length, 6 feet; height, 2 feet 10 inches. Property of MISS TYNDALL.

originally to contain some of the important and celebrated china at Blenheim. This collection, at one time housed in a pavilion built for the purpose, was given to John Churchill, first Duke of Marlborough, on the understanding that a suitable arrangement should be made for its installation.

The same sentiment of decoration is noticeable in the sideboard (Fig. 528), which is a few years later in date; the frame supporting the marble top is carved with a large key pattern divided by square panels of acanthus, at some time cut through the centre; the legs are of terminal shape, headed with satyrs' masks, from which fall pendants of husks on a ribbed ground; the feet are square and foliated. Another sideboard of this type, of about 1745, is Fig. 529. The decoration of the frieze resembles in its character the preceding piece, and the legs are of the same terminal shape; the scrolled shoulders, are, however, headed with acanthus; the feeling throughout is classical, a feeling that was revived again later in the century, by the brothers Adam. This classical motive is also apparent in the writing-table (Fig. 530), made about 1740; the cornice mouldings at this date became more delicate in scale, and in this instance the capping consists of a fine leaf pattern, beneath which runs a frieze of the wave volute boldly treated. The front opens in doors on which are applied large foliated paterae enclosed in oval mouldings of French design; the panels are bevelled with a classical leaf moulding, the sides are also treated classically with a festoon of acorns, foliage and flowers, headed by a lion's mask holding a brass ring; the spandrels in the arch are carved with the cabochon and acanthus introduced about that time.

In Fig. 531, a chest of drawers with doors, is found the same admixture of classical and French tastes. The top is of marble, enclosed and edged with an open brass banding of diagonal pattern; the serpentine front opens in two

FIG. 530. *Mahogany Writing-table*. Property of VISCOUNT ENFIELD.

FIG. 531. *Mahogany Chest of Drawers*. Length, 4 feet 4 inches; height, 3 feet 2 inches. Property of MESSRS ISAACS.

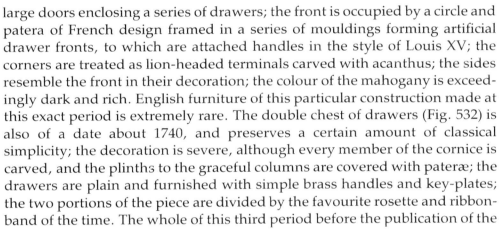

FIG. 532. *Double Chest of Drawers*. Height, 6 feet; width, 3 feet 6 inches; depth, 1 foot 8 inches. Property of MESSRS J. MALLETT AND SON.

large doors enclosing a series of drawers; the front is occupied by a circle and patera of French design framed in a series of mouldings forming artificial drawer fronts, to which are attached handles in the style of Louis XV; the corners are treated as lion-headed terminals carved with acanthus; the sides resemble the front in their decoration; the colour of the mahogany is exceedingly dark and rich. English furniture of this particular construction made at this exact period is extremely rare. The double chest of drawers (Fig. 532) is also of a date about 1740, and preserves a certain amount of classical simplicity; the decoration is severe, although every member of the cornice is carved, and the plinths to the graceful columns are covered with pateræ; the drawers are plain and furnished with simple brass handles and key-plates; the two portions of the piece are divided by the favourite rosette and ribbonband of the time. The whole of this third period before the publication of the

FIG. 533. *Deal Painted Overmantel*. Height, 6 feet; length, 5 feet 6 inches. Property of the EARL OF RADNOR.

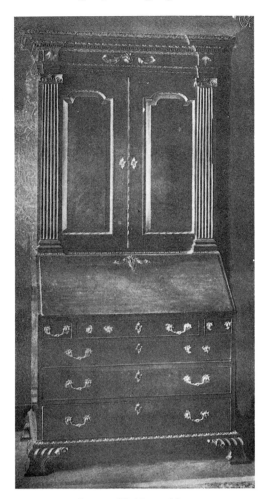

FIG. 534. *Mahogany Writing-cabinet.*
Height, 7 feet 9 inches; width, 3 feet 1 inch;
depth, 2 feet. Property of H. PERCY DEAN,
Esq.

FIG. 535. *Mahogany Book-case.* Height, 8 feet;
width, 6 feet 8 inches; depth, 1 foot 10
inches. Property of H. PERCY DEAN, Esq.

FIG. 536. *Detail of Mahogany Book-case.*
Property of H. PERCY DEAN, Esq.

Director by Chippendale shows signs of increasing ornamentation, and very frequently a tendency towards the French taste.

Another example, classical in feeling, of rather earlier date can be found in the overmantel at Longford Castle (Fig. 533). The broken pediment is most graceful in proportion, and the beautiful basket of flowers forming the centre is exceptionally delicate in its carving; it is of soft wood painted white, and was probably intended to contain a picture; it has been separated from its original mantelpiece. The writing-cabinet (Fig. 534) is a severe example of the classical taste, made very much on the lines of walnut scrutoires of the earlier period. The cornice and frieze are beautiful in their proportions and are of delicate workmanship; the doors, composed of raised panels, are framed in two pilasters; the lower portion is of bureau form, the escutcheon on the flap being of carved wood, which is of rare occurrence; the plinth is minutely carved, but the bracket feet are boldly gadrooned.

Plate XXXVII is a writing-cabinet similar in motive to the last example, but later in date, being about 1745. The pilasters framing the doors have ornate capitals, quite out of scale to their bases. The applied fretwork frieze is characteristic of this time; the graceful, undulating mouldings on the doors, with their decorated corners, redeem the otherwise empty and square proportions of the piece; the figure of the mahogany veneer is unusually fine, and of the variety termed 'clouded'. The lower portion opens as a writing-flap supported on the two small drawers; the handles are original.

Fig. 535 is a bookcase of exquisite workmanship made between 1740 and

1750, and undoubtedly by Thomas Chippendale. This remarkable piece of mahogany furniture consists of a centre piece with two wings; the former is in projection surmounted by a broken pediment, carved with an egg and tongue and small leaf moulding, a somewhat large plinth, delicately decorated with a slender wreath, filling the centre; the cornice, with its deep drip moulding, is supported and shouldered by two scroll brackets that terminate in eagles' heads holding pendants of husks and oak-leaves; these shoulders (Fig. 536) occupy the entire depth of the cabinet and pull open as secret drawers. The face of these scrolls is filled with superbly carved acanthus and husks on a matted ground in the Renaissance taste. The glass to the doors is framed in from the front by a rose and ribbon moulding, no putty being employed; the centre opens in an arch framed in egg and tongue, the spandrels and heading to this are plain, save for a laurel swag caught up by a central patera and ribbon bow; the pilasters supporting this arch and framing the door are faced with classic heads, backed by shells, from which fall laurel pendants. The lower portion is formed of three cupboards, the centre panel being decorated with a winged satyr's mask on a double shell, backed by laurel pendants. (This same design can be found on the key-board heading to the organ, Plate C. III, *Gentleman and Cabinet-maker's Director.*) The side-doors are plain; they open on a series of little compartments, and the doors are lined with narrow shelves and wire rails for small bottles. The plinth mouldings consist of a wide plain ogee framed between two carved borders; no keyholes are visible, as they are under the mouldings, and an absolute knowledge of the locks is necessary before any door can be opened; the colour of the piece is fine light chestnut, and the carving throughout is as sharp as chased metal; the inner construction and secrecy of the openings makes it probable that this cabinet was made for a doctor's use, and the upper compartment intended for books.

It is now necessary to again pick up the evolution of mahogany sofas and chairs, and the arm-chair (Fig. 537), one of a set at Ramsbury Manor, is a most interesting example of transition, for the hoop back and plain splat are retained whilst the front of the seat-rail is convex and carved with the decoration of 1730. The arm-supports are decorated at their bases, and the cabriole legs, although terminating in ball and claw feet, show a tendency to the lightness that was developing after the middle of the century.

The long settee (Fig. 538), one of a pair, matches this set, but the back, although of chair form, is upholstered; it has been re-covered with material of an earlier date.

The walnut love-seat, one of a pair, with the chair to match (Fig. 539), almost correspond in date to the last examples, proving that furniture of high quality was still made in this wood as late as 1735. The arms of the settee finish in small eagles' heads, but differ in shape to those of George I, while the curved supports forming their necks are indicative of the later date. The cabochon ornament, with its surrounding carving on the shoulders of the legs is rarely found on walnut, but much employed on mahogany chairs after 1738. This chair and settee, forming part of a set, were originally at Pewsey in Wiltshire, and it is probable that they, with the Ramsbury Manor

FIG. 537. *Mahogany Arm-chair.* Property of SIR FRANCIS BURDETT, Bart.

FIG. 538. *Mahogany Settee.* Length, 6 feet; height, 3 feet. Property of SIR FRANCIS BURDETT, Bart.

Fig. 539. *Walnut Chair and Settee.* Victoria and Albert Museum.

examples, were of Irish manufacture, which would account for certain anachronisms in the designs of both.

The upholstered arm-chair (Fig. 540) repeats the motives of the sofa (Plate XXXIV), and both evidently at one time formed part of a set. The back is low with a serpentine top; the arms, ending in lions' heads, are constructed for upholstery, and the supports have a rapid rake, the upper face of them being carved, a novel feature in the decoration of arm-chairs; the lower portion of the frame is convex and picks up the shoulder of the cabriole legs, and the carving is somewhat foreign in style. This sofa and chair are to all appearances by the same hand as the stained table (Plate XXXV), in all probablity by Giles Grendey of Clerkenwell.

There is a strong similarity of construction between this chair and Fig. 541, where the decorated frame is omitted; the arms in this instance finish in roses and the legs are hipped on to the frame; the feet end in scrolls in the French manner, the back legs are without carving. Fig. 542 is one of the plain chairs belonging to this set, and underneath it is the interesting label (Fig. 544) of Giles Grendey, who was evidently a cabinet-maker of French origin. These handsome, though heavy types, with upholstered backs made for the display of needlework or tapestry, were called at the time French chairs. In Fig. 543 the back is square in shape, the top rail ends in whorls, and the splat is divided into five simple perpendicular uprights, the arms terminate in dogs' heads, the legs are hipped on to a plain frame and finish in bold lion

Fig. 540. *Mahogany Upholstered Arm-chair.* Property of Messrs Isaacs.

Fig. 541. *Mahogany Arm-chair.* Height, 3 feet 2 inches; width, 2 feet 2 inches. Property of Messrs J. Mallett and Son.

Fig. 542. *Mahogany Chair.* Height, 3 feet; width, 2 feet. Property of Messrs J. Mallett and Son.

Fig. 544. *Label underneath Seat-rail.*

Fig. 543 (*left*). *Mahogany Arm-chair.* Height, 3 feet 2 inches. Property of Sidney Letts, Esq.

paws; the design of the carving coincides with the two preceding specimens. The width of these last chairs seems excessive, being two feet four inches, but the hoop had by this time assumed such outrageous proportions that chairs no doubt had to be constructed with a special view to its accommodation and display. In a letter to the *London Magazine,* dated January 1741, a correspondent makes the following remarks, which are interesting as showing an accurate picture of a fine lady of the time:

'As to the origin of the Hoop, whether it was an invention, as some say, of our Country women, or as others, that it was first imported from France, I will not venture to detirmine, and I have consulted the Records of Pantins and other Habit shops about Covent Garden without finding any satisfactory account. I am apt to imagine that it took its first rise only by enlarging the form of the antient fardingale, and was confined to a very moderate and decent circumference; but when Innovations of any kind are introduced, it is very difficult to know to what a degree they may be carried; this has been the fate of this very petticoat, which from its circumference originally took the name of a hoop, but which at present extending itself into a wide oblong form has nothing of the primitive Hoop but its mere name left. I have been in a moderate large room where there have been but two ladies, who had not space enough to move without lifting up their Petticoats higher than their Grandmothers would have thought decent: I believe every one has observed to what pains a Lady is put to reduce that wide extended Petticoat to the narrow limits

Fig. 545. *Mahogany Double Chair.* Length, 4 feet 4 inches.

FIG. 546. *Mahogany Chair*. Height, 3 feet; width, 1 foot 10 inches. Property of LORD ST OSWALD.

FIG. 547. *Mahogany Arm-chair*. Property of D. L. ISAACS, Esq.

of a Chair of Chariot: but let her manage her getting in or out ever so skilfully or modestly, yet she makes but a very odd grotesque Figure with her Petticoat standing up half-way the glasses, and her head just peeping out above them.'

The Countess of Hartford writes in one of her letters this same year:

'Few unmarried women appear abroad in robes or sacques; and as few married ones would be thought genteel in anything else. I own myself so awkward as to be yet unable to use myself to that dress, unless for visits of ceremony; since I do not feel at home in my own house without an apron; nor can endure a hoop, that would overturn all the chairs and stools in my closet.'

And even as late as 1772, Lady Mary Coke makes the following entry in her diary:

'I am very glad to dine by myself, for though the dress is very fine, a great hoop is a very troublesome affair at a great dinner.'

Madame de Bocage, in her description of London in 1750, seems to have been struck with the comparative scarcity of arm-chairs, for she says:

'There are scarce any arm chairs in their apartments, they are satisfied with common chairs. The women who use no paint and are always laced seem fond of these seats.'

Throughout the eighteenth century most arm-supports to chairs and sofas rake backwards, for the hoop died hard and lasted as a Court fashion well into the reign of George III. Fig. 545 is a double chair or settee, also of large proportion and much resembling the last specimen. In this instance the uprights of the splats are connected with small rosettes, the arms finish in lions' heads, and the outer legs are carved with masks; the centre leg is decorated in a different manner and shows a tendency towards French ornamentation; the pendants between the legs are rather solid in shape, and the carving on them is coarse. Fig. 546 is a chair without arms, evidently by the same maker as the settee to which it corresponds in every particular. It will be noticed that a slight beaded ornament is introduced in each instance on the shoe (that being the technical word for the projection which receives the base of the splat). Fig. 547 is an arm-chair of this same character, but possesses a more refined sense of lightness than hitherto met with in this square-headed type; the carving of the front rail and lions' heads suggest Irish workmanship, and the straight treatment of the arms is unusual for this period.

THE AGE OF MAHOGANY

COLOUR PLATES

PLATE XXXI. (a) *Gilt Chair Covered in Needlework.* Height, 3 feet 6 inches. Property of the Viscount Enfield.
(b) *Gilt Console-table.* Height, 2 feet 11 inches. Property of W. H. Lever, Esq.

PLATE XXXII. *Gilt Caned Chair*. Height, 4 feet 1 inch. Property of Clarence Wilson, Esq.

PLATE XXXIII. *Walnut Cabinet.* Height, 4 feet 2 inches; length, 2 feet 4 inches; depth, 1 foot 4 inches. Property of Edward Dent, Esq.

PLATE XXXIV. *Mahogany Sofa*. Length, 6 feet 4 inches; height, 3 feet 2 inches; depth, 3 feet. Property of Frank Partridge, Esq.

PLATE XXXV. *Stained Wood Table with Scagliola Top.* Length, 3 feet 9 inches; height, 2 feet 7 inches; depth, 2 feet. Property of C. J. Charles, Esq.

PLATE XXXVI. *Mahogany Bed*. Height, 12 feet 4 inches; length, 7 feet; breadth, 6 feet at the base of columns. Property of the Marquess of Exeter.

PLATE XXXVII. *Writing-cabinet*. Height, 7 feet 9½ inches; depth, 2 feet
2 inches; width, 5 feet. Property of H. Percy Dean, Esq.

PLATE XXXVIII. *Settee.* Length, 4 feet 2 inches; height, 3 feet 7 inches. Property of Miss Mills.

PLATE XXXIX. *Writing-chair*. Height of back, 35 inches; height of seat, 18½ inches; depth of seat, 19½ inches. Property of Thomas Wise, Esq.

PLATE XL. *Mahogany Commode.* Height, 29 inches; width, 49 inches; depth, 24 inches. Property of H. Percy Dean, Esq.

PLATE XLI. *Amboyna and Rosewood Cabinet*. Height, 8 feet 8½ inches; depth,
1 foot 8 inches; length, 6 feet 4 inches. Property of H. Percy Dean, Esq.

PLATE XLII. *Mahogany Writing-table.* Height, 2 feet 8 inches; length, 5 feet 2½ inches; depth, 2 feet 11½ inches. Property of H. Percy Dean, Esq.

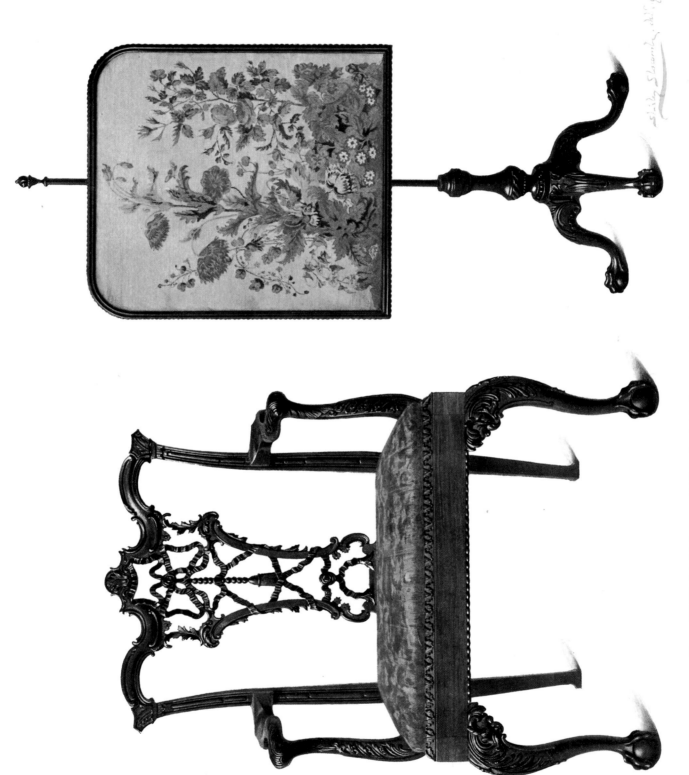

PLATE XLIII. (a) *Mahogany Ribbon-back Chair*. Height, 3 feet 4 inches; breadth, 1 foot 7 inches. Property of Lieut-Col G. B. Croft Lyons.
(b) *Mahogany Pole-screen*. Height, 5 feet. Property of H. Percy Dean, Esq.

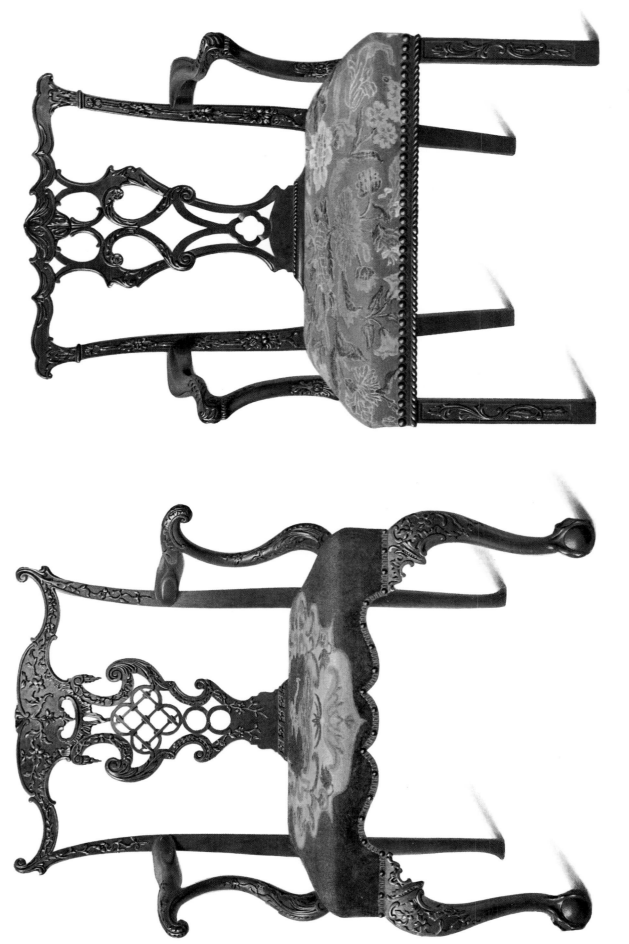

Shirley Slocombe del. 1907

PLATE XLIV. (a) *Mahogany Chair.* Height, 3 feet 2 inches; breadth, 2 feet 2 inches. Property of H. Percy Dean, Esq.
(b) *Mahogany Chair.* Height, 3 feet 1 inch; breadth, 2 feet 3 inches. Property of Percy Macquoid, Esq.

PLATE XLV. *Mahogany China Cabinet*. Height, 8 feet 9 inches; width, 5 feet 10 inches; depth, 1 foot 8 inches. Property of Messrs D. L. Isaacs.

CHAPTER IV

BOUT 1740 a change appeared in mahogany furniture, and elegance of line and form began to supplant the picturesque and more solid designs of the previous twenty years. The backs and legs of chairs were now treated more in sympathy with each other, the open work of the former being detailed into a series of curved flat strappings, developed by the hands of Chippendale and his contemporaries into ingenious variations of the same motive. Usually the design of this strapping was contained within the limits of a vase-shaped splat, but occasionally it is found spreading over the back as in the example, Fig. 548, which is one of a set made about 1735. The design filling this hooped back is very original, being an open convex strap-work in the form of a shell, supported by a flat double loop merging into the curves of the uprights; these latter still have the angle found on rather earlier chairs; the ball and claw legs shouldered with acanthus are of slight form. The pattern of this chair has been accepted as designed by Thomas Chippendale, and the delicate and accurate quality of the carving, in conjunction with the comparative lightness of construction, makes this supposition extremely probable. It has also been stated that this chair formed part of a large set made especially for Marie Antoinette by his firm, six of which are still in the Louvre, the remainder having come back to England in 1810. There is little doubt that this set of chairs was once in the possession of the unfortunate Queen, as the various traditions regarding them appear accurate, although they must have been completed by Chippendale at least fifteen years before she was born.

Fig. 549 is a chair-back settee of similar design made in walnut, and so fine in execution that it is probably the work of the same firm, and conclusively proves the early date of the chairs. It would be interesting if documentary evidence could be obtained proving the exact date of Thomas Chippendale's birth, as this would be a guide to the position he held at this time and so prove the influence of his earlier work upon his fellow-craftsmen.

It is quite possible that the chair (Fig. 550) is also a specimen of Chippendale's early work, as it possesses the sense of completeness rarely found in other contemporary furniture. The top of the back is hooped, but the uprights are straight, curling into rose-headed acanthus sprays. The flat strapping fills the back, taking the form of interlacing ovals; the arms scroll outwardly, and are lightly carved on the upper surfaces; the acanthus on the shoulders of the ball and claw legs is exceedingly careful in touch, inferring

FIG. 548. *Mahogany Chair*. Property of MESSRS J. MALLETT AND SON.

FIG. 550. *Mahogany Chair*. Property of D. L. ISAACS, Esq.

FIG. 549. *Walnut Settee*. Property of MESSRS J. MALLETT AND SON.

FIG. 551. *Mahogany Chair.* Property of
WEEDON GROSSMITH, Esq.

the work of a superior craftsman; the back legs are plain but perfect in their curves, and the frame is edged with an escalloped border. The whole chair is significant of an original effort in furniture, and conveys a most pleasing feeling of proportion. Fig. 551 is another interesting specimen of this same design, in all probability originating from the same firm. It is wider and lighter in character, and the ovals are more disconnected; the arms finish abruptly, and their supports are decorated. These three chairs and the settee represent an entirely new departure in the form of the back.

The carving on the sofa (Fig. 552) is open in character; the legs are rectangular, approximating the height of the back, and the legs, exceptionally good in curve, are hipped into the seat; the rail consists of a bold hollow moulding decorated with two pendants.

Arms are introduced of the earlier C scroll type, broad and pronounced in their curve, on the sofa at Penshurst (Fig. 553), of a date about 1735; it has the original silk covering – a design of birds, monsters, clouds and large flowers in various colours on a black background; the legs correspond in their curves to the C scroll of the arms and finish in very delicately carved lion paws. The

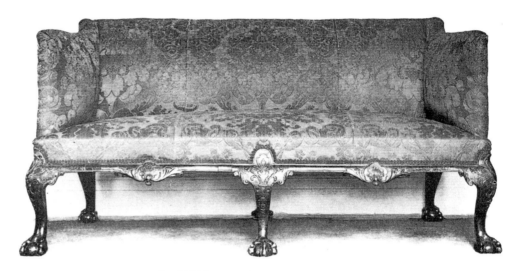

FIG. 552. *Mahogany Sofa.* Length, 5 feet; height, 3 feet 4 inches. Property of L. FLEISCHMANN, Esq.

FIG. 553. *Mahogany Sofa.* Length, 5 feet 6 inches; height, 3 feet 6 inches. Property of LORD DE LISLE AND DUDLEY.

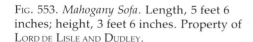

light, careful touch shown in the decoration resembles that found on furniture of a rather later date proved to have been the work of Thomas Chippendale.

But little is known of the career of this celebrated craftsman, and so much has recently been written on his work and influence that is is not necessary to attempt here to introduce his personality in connection with the furniture called after his name. It has been proved that he came to London before the year 1727 with his father, who was a carver, gilder and cabinet-maker; that he married his first wife in 1748, took a shop in 1749, moved to St Martin's Lane in 1753, and published his celebrated book, *The Gentleman and Cabinet-maker's Director,* in 1754. Facts also go to prove that he died at the age of about seventy. If the date of his birth was, say 1709, he would have been thirty-nine when he married and forty-four at the date of the *Director's* appearance. These dates are given merely to suggest that it was not till after the appearance of the *Director* that Chippendale's influence really affected English furniture.

Fig. 554 is an early form of the square-back chair, with a perforated splat so frequently and incorrectly associated with Chippendale's name; its date would be about 1740. The strap-work of this splat is varied in an uncommon manner by the introduction of a bold design of dolphins facing each other with open mouths; the carving of the top rail is simple, and well carries out the curved lines; the arms scroll outwards, finishing in flat eagles' heads, a decoration very popular with young collectors, and in consequence a large supply of chairs with these arms is always to be found. In this instance the carving is original, and also the needlework of the seat; the nulling along the seat-rail, introduced about this time, harmonises with the scaled decoration of the back. Fig. 555 is a chair certainly made after 1740; it is one of a set. A small piece of carved drapery with fringe and tassels forms the cresting, a very favourite ornamentation at this time that was sometimes accompanied by a decorative frilling, starting from the corners and finishing on the splat in two roses. The splat is perforated in a series of flat loopings, in which the upper present new features; the legs show the lightness and delicacy that was gradually being adopted, and are carved with cabochon decoration in place of the usual acanthus. The settee or double chair, one of a pair (Fig. 556), matches these chairs, and is also covered with the original needlework. The entire set was probably of country make.

Plate XXXVIII is another settee of about 1745, rather more elaborate, and with the same swag of drapery introduced below the top rail, the latter being carved with a complicated shell decoration again repeated as a cresting in the centre. The splats are broad and perforated with rather meaningless decoration, the arms being plain, reproducing those of an earlier period. The seat-rail is waved, to give an effect of lightness, and the ornamentation of the legs is similar in character to the top rail. Fig. 557 is an arm-chair, one of a pair, of about the same date, in which the drapery is more elaborated and entirely occupies the top rail; the tassels are prolonged into the strap-work, which is somewhat confused in design, and the arms terminate in eagles' heads, resembling in their treatment those on earlier chairs. The carving and execution again infer that the work is of country manufacture, probably of Suffolk origin. Ten plain chairs also exist, completing this set. Fig. 558 is of most extraordinary quality and elaborate workmanship; the back consists of a most ingenious combination of the Anne hoop forming a centre, with the square headings of later date on either side; the splats are very open and fanciful in character, and composed of sprays of oak-leaves and berries

FIG. 554. *Mahogany Arm-chair*. Property of MESSRS J. MALLETT AND SON.

FIG. 555. *Mahogany Chair*. Height, 3 feet. Property of W. H. LEVER, Esq.

FIG. 556. *Mahogany Settee*. Length, 4 feet 4 inches; height, 3 feet 2 inches. Property of W. H. LEVER, Esq.

FIG. 557. *Mahogany Chair.* Property of W. H. LEVER, Esq.

FIG. 558. *Mahogany Settee.* Length, 6 feet; height, 3 feet 2 inches. Property of H. PERCY DEAN, Esq.

intertwined with ribbons and framed C scrolls; the shoes forming the bases are unusually deep and solid. The arms are straight, terminating in animals' heads; the seat-frame is richly carved in perforated festoons, with escalloped edges, and centres in a grotesque mask pendant; the legs are particularly strong and solid at the shoulder, they are decorated throughout and finish in lions'-paw feet, the omission of centre legs demanding unusual strength of construction; the seat is covered with the original needlework, and the colour of the wood is a rich deep brown. The date of this remarkable settee would be shortly before 1750, and it is undoubtedly the work of Thomas Chippendale under strong French influence.

Plate XXXIX is an interesting writing-chair, resembling in motive those made in walnut early in the century. The back has a branching splat, carved in low relief, with disconnected floral sprays; the top rail is semicircular, finishing in scrolled ends starting from two flat rosettes; the uprights of the back are lyre-shaped, and the angle forming the base is the reverse of that found on walnut chairs; the arms turn rapidly outwards and finish in rosettes; the legs and shell-pendant have the characteristics of the chairs of 1730, which is probably the date of this example. The uncertain and flat

ornamentation, with the style of the feet, are indicative of Irish workmanship. In Fig. 559 can be seen the usual type of writing-chair of this period, in which two and sometimes three strap-work splats are introduced somewhat on the principle of the wheel-chair. In this example the front rail is serpentine and the centre decorated with a floral spray; the strap-work is of particularly good design, and the seat is covered with its original needlework. The legs do not present any new feature, excepting the claw, which in many instances towards the end of its existence began to be slighter, as in the present example. As Chippendale, in the first edition of the *Director*, does not once illustrate this form of foot, it seems safe to assume that he omitted it as old-fashioned and not in accordance with the more delicate and fanciful style he was desirous of introducing. Fig. 560 is a specimen lighter in construction; the semi-circular rail is here supported by three cylindrical uprights and two strap-work splats slightly raked outwards; the seat is set anglewise, often the case in these chairs. The small size of this particular example infers it was made for a woman's use. Fig. 561 is another form of writing-chair. The upholstered back and arms form one graceful curve, the latter terminate in dogs' heads supported by facings of a good ringed moulding that also surrounds the seat-frame. The front legs are in pure Chippendale style; the ornament on the shoulders in slight relief, and the rather delicate scrolled feet decorated with a cabochon, show the Louis XV feeling that was gradually influencing ornamentation. Fig. 562 is another upholstered writing-chair, and of rare shape. The arms are faced with carving of remarkable execution, each terminating in an eagle's head seizing an asp. The wave pattern introduced round the frame is divided by the

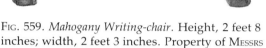

FIG. 559. *Mahogany Writing-chair.* Height, 2 feet 8 inches; width, 2 feet 3 inches. Property of MESSRS ISAACS.

FIG. 560. *Mahogany Writing-chair.* Height, 2 feet 6 inches; width, 1 foot 10 inches. Property of MESSRS J. MALLETT AND SON.

FIG. 561. *Mahogany Writing-chair.* Height, 2 feet 6 inches; width, 1 foot 10 inches. Property of D. L. ISAACS, Esq.

cresting surmounting the front legs, which are shouldered with eagles' heads and elaborate acanthus reaching down to the feathered claw. It would be difficult to find a chair of this class higher in technical excellence or capable of affording more practical comfort.

The easy-chair of 1740 still continued to be made on the lines of the earlier grandfather chair, high in the back, with wings at the sides, and very frequently covered with needlework. In Fig. 563 the principal characteristics of the Anne chairs are preserved, but the arm supports have no C scrolls and run straight with the seat. In this example their form is lost through recent bad upholstery; the loose squab is also missing. The legs are of ball and claw type of about 1745; the seat-rail is bordered with a gadrooned nulling of this time.

By the year 1745 mahogany furniture was employed in the bedrooms of the more recently decorated houses, though descriptions of rooms furnished in the new style are scarce. Bishop Richard Pococke, in his travels through England in 1754, describes some richly decorated rooms, and mentions mahogany furniture, though evidently the gilding, velvets and marbles chiefly attracted his attention.

'Beyond Salisbury, three miles we went to Langborough; it is esteemed as one of the best finished and furnished houses in England, and in the gallery are some very fine original paintings, marble tables and bronze groups, and the chimney boards throughout the house are made of Chinese pictures which show several of their customs. Our sleeping apartment is furnished with chintz and Indian paper. In one apartment the furniture is of mahogany, carved and gilt, and many fine Japan pieces of furniture.'

In writing of Eastbury, the house belonging to Mr Doddington, which cost £200,000, he describes the drawing-rooms as furnished with

'Consoles on which are the twelve Cæsars, the heads in bronze, the busts in a kind of agate, the walls and ceilings of stucco beautifully adorned with flowers and architectonick ornaments gilt. The best drawing-room is hung with flowered uncutt velvet of Genoa, and there are several very fine pictures in it; the next is a dressing-room hung with green satin, on each side of which large flower vases are painted in oyl colors. The room beyond it is the best chamber, all furnished with crimson velvet, and on each compartment a gilt eagle holds in his mouth a golden horn, the arms of the family, they are in bas-relief either of thick paper of pasteboard. There are several fine tables of green Silician marble and Oriental flowered alabaster.'

Of this same gentleman's house at Hammersmith, he says:

FIG. 562. *Mahogany Writing-chair.* Property of H. PERCY DEAN, Esq.

FIG. 563. *Mahogany Easy-chair.* Height, 4 feet; width, 2 feet 6 inches. Property of L. FLEISCHMANN, Esq.

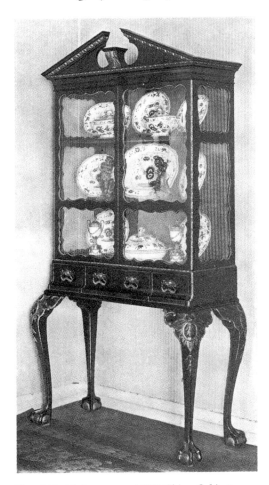

Fɪɢ. 564. *Mahogany and Gilt China Cabinet.* Height, 6 feet 9 inches; width, 3 feet 6 inches; depth, 1 foot 9 inches. Property of H. Oᴀᴛᴡᴀʏ, Esq.

'He has new model'd it in a very elegant taste, and 'tis finely furnished; but the gallery, which is the length of the house, is a very beautiful piece of architecture of the Ionic order; there is a Venetian window at each end, and two windows on each side of an arcade, supported by two fine pillars of Italian marble; in this arcade is a statue of Flora, and in a niche on each side a statue with bronze groups over them; on each side of the arcade and the Venetian windows are busts on terms, with bronze groups likewise over them. Between the windows are statues, as well as between the looking-glass opposite to the windows. At each end is a column with a vase on them of Oriental alabaster, and one of the pillars is of the same fineered, the other of some very fine marble. The pillars of the door at entrance are of lapis-lazuli fineered, which cost four shillings an ounce; the whole is paved with fine marbles in beautiful figures.'

This style of apartment clearly would not have been suitable for mahogany furniture, and held at the most a few sofas and chairs which would probably have been gilt Italian. The gilt mahogany furniture referred to by the Bishop was exceptional, and for this reason, no doubt, attracted his attention.

The very elegant china cupboard (Fig. 564) is one of a pair, and represents a specimen of this gilt mahogany furniture. The carving throughout, with the exception of the feet, is gilt, the pediment is lightly decorated with a string of carved moulding, and the framings to the doors are of escalloped and undulating form, edged with a carved roping; the transoms of the front and sides do not correspond in line, and the effect produced is charming and original. The base opens in three drawers, mounted with elaborate handles in the French taste; the legs are gracefully curved and decorated on the shoulders in the same manner. The date of this cabinet is about 1745, before the appearance of the *Director*, and is an early example of the china cabinet treated as an elegant piece of furniture.

Chests of drawers throughout the earlier part of this century presented no great novelties in form; the general proportions of the walnut and marqueterie types were maintained, but towards 1750 the fronts and sides were frequently serpentine in shape, and a separate stand to the rest of the piece was discarded in favour of a permanently fixed base. Fig. 565 is a chest of drawers of about 1740, dependent for decoration on elaborate handles and key-plates, and a stand which somewhat resembles in style the Longford settees (Fig. 497). The framing and cockbeading of the drawers are simple; a very strong French feeling is visible in the English brass-work, but the stand retains all the characteristics of native design. The piece is made of light-coloured rosewood, much valued at this time. In Fig. 566, of about 1750, the sides and front are serpentine, the corners being faced with pilasters, carved with decoration of a Louis XV character in high relief; these are headed by brackets of scrolled acanthus form. The cornice, base and intersections of the drawers are boldly carved in classical and rose and ribbon mouldings; the feet of bracket form are adapted from those found on Chinese bronzes, the

Fɪɢ. 565. *Rosewood Chest of Drawers.* Height, 3 feet 6 inches; length, 3 feet 6 inches. Property of H. Oᴀᴛᴡᴀʏ, Esq.

Fɪɢ. 566. *Mahogany Chest of Drawers.* Property of Vɪsᴄᴏᴜɴᴛ Eɴꜰɪᴇʟᴅ.

Fig. 567. *Rosewood Chest of Drawers*. Height, 3 feet 4 inches; length, 4 feet 4 inches; depth, 2 feet 4 inches. Property of John G. Griffiths, Esq.

Fig. 568. *Mahogany Chest of Drawers*. Length, 4 feet; height, 3 feet 4 inches. Property of L. Fleischmann, Esq.

brass handles and key-plates are of delicate and beautiful design in the French taste, and the mahogany with which the drawers and top are veneered is of the grain known as fiddle-back.

In Fig. 567 can be seen another fine specimen, made of rosewood. The front and sides serpentine in bold curves, the corners finishing in scrolls with whorled ends supported by richly carved pilasters. The chest is divided into three drawers constructed of deal, but faced with solid rosewood; the lower portion is in the form of a stand on ball and claw feet, united to the frame with broad shoulders, and decorated in the same style as the pilasters. The front and sides droop at the centre in pendants, and are carved from the solid, with very bold shelled scrolls, showing a largeness of touch rarely found at this period, when all carving was usually applied. The brass handles and key-plates are particularly beautiful, being in the same large character as the rest of the piece; they are admirable in their finish and interesting as repeating the design and exactly following the extreme curves of the front. The piece unfortunately has been cut at some time in order to convert the two lower drawers into a cupboard; the weight and hardness of the wood is remarkable.

It is comparatively rare to find carving round the edges of drawers on these chests, but in Fig. 568 a fine bead and reel moulding is introduced as a cockbeading. This piece is small, with a serpentine front of elegant proportions, and has a writing-slide between the top and second drawers. The inside cabinet work of these pieces of furniture is generally fine; the drawers

Fig. 569. *Mahogany Chest of Drawers*.
Length, 4 feet 2 inches; height, 2 feet 10 inches. Property of Messrs J. Mallett and Son.

Fig. 570. *Mahogany Chest of Drawers*. Height, 2 feet 10 inches; length, 4 feet 3 inches; depth, 2 feet. Property of the Duke of Beaufort.

Fig. 571. *Mahogany Chest of Drawers.* Property of Richard A. Canfield, Esq.

Fig. 572. *Mahogany Dressing Commode.* Length, 3 feet 6 inches; height, 2 feet 8 inches; depth, 1 foot 10 inches. Property of Lord St Oswald.

Fig. 573. *Mahogany Double Chest of Drawers.* Height, 6 feet; length, 4 feet. Property of L. Fleischmann, Esq.

are usually found of oak, mahogany fronted, in some special instances of cedar; but the carcase, as in earlier walnut chests of drawers, is almost always of deal, and of so well-selected and seasoned wood, that the drawers still travel perfectly on their runners. It is a wise precaution before buying a piece of antique mahogany furniture containing drawers, to carefully test their fit; these should never be too tight, for wood contracts with age and does not expand. Few elaborate mahogany chests of drawers were made at this period by inferior firms, and so the wood will almost always be found well chosen. Fig. 569 is a large specimen, also about 1750, the top and bottom carved with acanthus moulding, and the corners ornamented with wreathed and reeded pilasters terminating in scrolls; the feet are of unusual size, covered with a somewhat meaningless design in low relief; the handles and key-plates, of distinctly French taste, form an agreeable contrast to the plain face of the drawers; the mahogany is finely clouded and retains its original colour of warm cinnamon. In Fig. 571 the surface of the entire chest is perfectly plain, but the piece is mounted upon a gilt stand with legs of rococo ornamentation found on mirrors and sconces at the middle of the eighteenth century. The frieze of this stand is carved with a diagonal strap-work and cleverly connects the severity of the chest with the elaborate detailed feet. A chest of this kind was designed to carry some smaller form of cabinet or large china vases. In the present instance, this particular chest bears a glass case containing one of the shirts in which Charles I was executed, and which was given to his devoted adherent, the Marquis of Worcester, immediately after the King's death. It is shown later in Fig. 578. Fig. 571 represents a very elaborate chest of drawers shaped on the lines of a French commode of this period. It has a double serpentine front in three divisions, divided by pilasters carved with pendants of flowers in high relief. The nine drawers are edged with a roped cockbeading, and the brass handles are of English workmanship in the style of Louis XV, the corners bow outwards in bold shoulders of rococo design, and are supported on somewhat slender C scrolled legs connected by an elaborate base, the whole effect being distinctly florid, although the scale of decoration is imposing. Its date is about 1755, and it much resembles the design for a somewhat similar commode in the *Director.*

Occasionally the French taste was adopted without any attempt at our native style, and the many examples in illustrated furniture books of the time prove this. Such a piece as Plate XL is of this character. The long, low sweep of this commode is unusual, and the supports take the form of legs and not feet; the finish of the metal-work cannot compete with that of France, but the piece is full of life, and the proportions are simple and pleasing. Chippendale calls these chest of drawers 'commode tables', and gives an example in the third edition of his book; in the description of it he says, 'The ornaments, parts, are intended for brass-work, which I advise should be modelled in wax and then cast from these models.'

FIG. 574. *Mahogany Hanging Wardrobe.* Height, 7 feet; length, 4 feet. Property of L. FLEISCHMANN, Esq.

FIG. 575. *Mahogany Clothes-press.* Height, 6 feet 10 inches; length, 4 feet 2 inches. Property of L. FLEISCHMAN, Esq.

A smaller piece (such as Chippendale calls a dressing commode), far more restrained in taste, and purely English in style, made of dark Cuban wood, is Fig. 572. The front is divided into two cupboards, two small drawers and three larger, the latter being bow-fronted. It stands upon bowed legs exactly corresponding in form to those found supporting Chinese and Japanese bronzes; the only decorations to the piece are the beautiful handles and key-plates of English brass-work. Double chests of drawers (or tallboys) were still much used, and continued to be made until late in the eighteenth century, when the hanging wardrobe and press with sliding shelves superseded this somewhat inconvenient form of furniture. Fig. 573 is a neat and well-finished example, with the gradation between the upper and lower portions more marked than is usually found. The cornice and corners are enriched with delicate carving; the drawers are deep and the plinth is plain, supported on the broad and decorated Chinese legs peculiar to the middle of the century. These double chests of drawers were probably used for coats and dresses, as hanging cupboards of mahogany were rare, and even the sacque without its hoop would have gone into a comparatively small compass.

Fig. 574 is an early example of a mahogany hanging wardrobe. The cornice, with its Gothic upper members, is surmounted by a fretwork cresting of scrolled design, much resembling that found on the testers of contemporary beds; the doors, which open the whole height of the cupboard, are of fine clouded mahogany, panelled with mouldings of serpentine and oblong form; the legs resemble those found on chests of drawers.

During the first half of the eighteenth century, clothes cupboards forming

FIG. 576 (*right*). *Mahogany Clothes-press.* Height, 6 feet 8 inches; width, 4 feet 2 inches. Property of VISCOUNT ENFIELD.

FIG. 577 (*far right*). *Mahogany Clothes-press.* Height, 6 feet 10 inches; length, 4 feet 2 inches. Property of H. H. MULLINER, Esq.

part of the deal panelling of the rooms had taken the place of the rather cumbersome oaken wardrobes; no walnut hanging wardrobes appear to have been constructed, and so an hiatus must have arisen in this kind of furniture, until the use of mahogany for large articles became universal. The walnut cupboard with shelves, called at the time 'commode cloths-press', had been in much demand during the reign of Anne and George I, and this shape continued to be made in mahogany, of which Fig. 575 is a simple and well-proportioned specimen, about the date 1760. A rather earlier press, somewhat different in construction, is shown in Fig. 576; here the drawers in the lower portion are enclosed by two doors. The design and execution of this press is very fine in quality, and the decorated and serpentine mouldings forming the panels are in bold but admirable proportion to the piece. In Fig. 577 the same intention of construction is preserved, but here the lower portion takes the form of a chest of drawers; the cresting at the top is a Chinese railing with finials of the same style, whilst the large panels are framed in a delicate serpentine moulding with corners of French design; the handle plates are elaborate, finishing in little pagoda roofs; the feet are full of character, being octagonal in section.

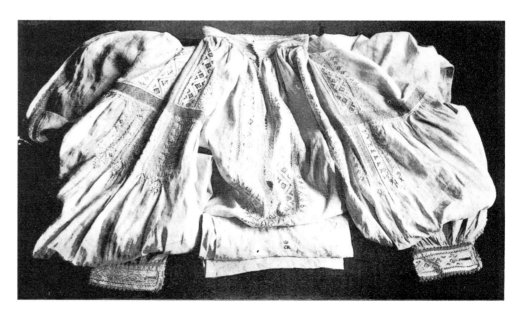

FIG. 578. *Shirt of King Charles I.* Property of the DUKE OF BEAUFORT.

CHAPTER V

E now arrive at the period of mahogany furniture that was the outcome of the books of designs published by Chippendale in 1754, by Matthias Darly, an architect and friend of Chippendale's in the same year, and by Sir William Chambers, who, on his return to England from his studies abroad, published a book on Chinese architecture and decoration in 1757. The designs in these books embrace three separate styles, known as the French, the Chinese and the Gothic. Our so-called French style differed from the corresponding period of Louis XV, chiefly in the absence of the finely chased and gilt metal fittings at the sides and corners; the gilding of the wood-work and the beautiful tapestry coverings; and its development here was principally confined to mirrors, sofas and chairs. The Chinese style was perhaps the most consistent of the three, as one apparent motive was preserved throughout; the principal characteristics were an open lattice-work, termed at the time a Chinese railing, pagoda roofs with bells as pendants, and in the mirrors and sconces, the introduction of mandarins, Chinese birds and little buildings among the decoration. The so-called Gothic was an attempt to introduce certain elements of that ancient taste, combined with later Georgian delicacy and lightness of construction; but the result was unconvincing and unsatisfactory. Occasionally these styles were interwoven, affording curious opportunities to the carver for eccentricity of design.

Chinese taste, which had to some extent died down, was strongly revived about 1750, and the great quantity of curios and porcelain imported from the East was found to demand a particular setting. Towards the end of George II's reign, the mania of collecting had widely spread, and the fashion increased for crowding the rooms and galleries of houses with china ornaments of every description. Over windows, doors and chimney-pieces and every other possible projection in a room, vases, basins, grotesque monsters and figures were displayed. Richardson described Sir Charles Grandison as having a fine arrangement of china in the state-rooms at Grandison Hall. In the earlier days of the mania Addison, writing in the *Lover and Reader*, said:

'There is no inclination in women that more surprises me than their passion for china. When a woman is visited with it, it generally takes possession of her for life. The common way of purchasing such articles, if I may believe my female informers, is by exchanging old suits of clothes for this brittle ware. For this reason my friend Tradewell, in the city, calls his great room that is nobly furnished out with china, his wife's wardrobe. In yonder corner, says he, are about twenty suits of clothes, and on that scrutoire, above, one hundred yards of furbelowed silk. You cannot imagine how many nightgowns, stays, and manteaus went to the raising of that pyramid, so that in reality this is but a dextrous way of picking the husband's pocket; who is often purchasing a great vase of china, when he fancies that he is buying a fine head or a silk gown for his wife.'

It was doubtless soon found advisable to secure the smaller and more valuable curios against theft and breakage by placing them in cabinets. These were at first of walnut or lacquer, with solid doors, although it has already been shown that attempts at glass-fronted cupboards were made towards the end of the seventeenth century. The lightness and strength of mahogany enabled the craftsman to easily construct a cabinet with glazed doors of decorative design, and so to well display its contents. In many instances these were used to contain books as well as china and curios, though no doubt in houses of importance where there was a library, books were confined to the shelves and cases of this room and not distributed about in cabinets.

Fig. 579 is a combination of writing-bureau and book-case, for here the framing to the doors is too wide and the glazed portion too small for the exhibition of china. The cornice is surmounted by an openwork pediment of

Fig. 579. *Mahogany Bureau and Book-case.* Height, 7 feet 4 inches; length, 3 feet 8 inches. Property of Messrs Morant.

FIG. 580. *Mahogany China Cupboard.*
Property of SIDNEY LETTS, Esq.

French design, for after the appearance of *The Gentleman and Cabinet-maker's Director,* a perforated pediment to cabinets took the place of the previous more solid and triangular structure; but the cornice is purely classical. Pendants of flowers carved in high relief are applied on the doors, which are supported on two drawers faced with a geometrical pattern of Chinese taste in the style known as card-cutting. The lower portion of this handsome and solid example consists of a cupboard and drawers, the top edged with a well-carved gadrooned border; the feet are double, and show signs of decadence in design, for the piece belongs to the end of a style, and is by no means original in motive. The date is about 1750.

Another specimen of this same date, formerly in the possession of Dante Gabriel Rossetti, is Fig. 580. This is distinctly a china cupboard. The glazed doors, bordered with a rosette and ribbon banding, are unusually large; the treatment of the stand, with its swags and festoons of delicately carved flowers and fruit in full relief, on straight Chinese legs, is original and beautiful. On the headings of these are escutcheons, bearing the arms of the Faulkner family, the original owners of the piece. Fig. 581 is probably a door to a recessed cupboard in a wall, to correspond with other wood-work of a room; the carving of the architrave is illustrative of the extreme delicacy of execution shown in the best work of this time. Fig. 582 is another book-case, on account of its great depth probably made to fit a particular recess. This exact design is given in the *Director,* plate lxxxix. The upper portion is in three compartments, of so-called Gothic, the style is not repeated in the lower portion, which is surmounted by a deep cornice beautifully splayed and carved in a lattice pattern. This lower portion opens in four doors, enclosing a series of small drawers with handsome brass handles. The plinth is very solid and plain, save for an acanthus heading.

It has been far too much the custom to attribute pieces of furniture corresponding in design to examples in Chippendale's book to that master of his firm. A very large number of subscribers to the work were cabinet-makers of the time, who purchased the book solely for practical purposes, in order to reproduce the designs, and these reproductions were at times so accurate that it is difficult to decide their origin without contemporary evidence. Peculiariity of touch in carving can in many instances be assigned to an individual firm, but perhaps undue importance has been given to the rather unimportant detail of tracing furniture to any one maker. Collectors of the Chippendale period are very apt to mentally cast doubts on the authenticity of a piece that does not exactly conform to the idiosyncrasies of the particular makers who have come under their notice, but it is unwise to be too freely prejudiced by unfamiliar details, or to accept even the want of surface abrasion as a proof of modern forgery. In some of this old mahogany furniture that has never been moved from its original position the surface is not always 'silky', and the colour is sometimes found like modern mahogany which has been wax-polished only. It has been possible, through the great kindness of the owners, to see specimens of Chippendale's furniture in their original positions. At Nostell Priory there is a library writing-table, so sharp and new-looking in all detail and colour, that without *primâ facie* evidence many well-informed enthusiasts might doubt its authenticity; but this

F ɪɢ. 581. *Mahogany Cupboard.* Height, 8 feet 7 inches; width, 3 feet 4 inches. Property of H. Pᴇʀᴄʏ Dᴇᴀɴ, Esq.

F ɪɢ. 582. *Mahogany Book-case.* Height, 7 feet 2 inches; length, 5 feet; depth, 2 feet 1 inch. Property of Mᴇssʀs Isᴀᴀᴄs.

Fig. 583. *Mahogany Bureau and China Cupboard.* Height, 8 feet; width, 4 feet 2 inches; depth, 1 foot 10 inches. Property of H. Percy Dean, Esq.

Fig. 584. *Mahogany Bureau and Book-case.* Height, 7 feet 6 inches; width, 3 feet 9 inches. Property of Messrs J. Mallett and Son.

particular table was made for the room in which it now stands, it is introduced with the side of the room as a background in a family group painted about that time, and Thomas Chippendale's bill, dated 1766, in which the item of the table occurs, has always been preseved in one of the drawers.

Cheaper reproductions began to be fashionable at this time for those who were not able to afford Chippendale's prices, and many were produced and made their appearance in the Strand shops and at auction. The interest taken in the sale of furniture and curios even attracted the attention of foreigners, and a Frenchman, Monsieur Grosley, who wrote a book on his tour to London in 1765, said:

'The finest shops are scattered up and down the courts and passages. The grand company which they draw together, the elegant arrangement and parade made by the shops, whether in stuffs exposed to sell, fine furniture, and things of taste, or the girls belonging to them, would be motive sufficient to determine those that walk, to make that their way in preference to any other. Even if they had not neatness and security to recommend them, the shops in the Strand, Fleet Street, Cheapside, etc., are the most striking objects that London can offer to the eye of a stranger. They are all enclosed with great glass doors, all adorned on the outside with pieces of ancient architecture, the more absurd, as they are likely to be spoilt by constant use; all brilliant and gay, as well on account of the things sold in them, as the exact order in which they are kept, so that they make a most splendid show, greatly superior to anything of the kind in Paris. The sad, gloomy air which smoke gives to buildings is one of the least injuries it does them; the inside of public buildings and of the houses is equally hurt by the most volatile, penetrating, and corrosive parts of the smoke. The furniture of houses, generally speaking, consists of large chairs, the seats of which are in part stuffed up very full and covered with morocco leather; and partly of mahogany tables. With regard to the walls, they are hung with cloth or printed paper, by those who are not satisfied with plain wainscot. As for the beds, they are made of stuffs more solid than brilliant, and which require to be frequently renewed if people prefer show to solidity. The humid and dark air which enwraps London requires the greatest cleanliness imaginable, and in this respect the inhabitants of that city seem to vie with the Hollanders. The plate, hearthstones, moveables, apartments, doors, stairs, the very street doors, their locks, and the large brass knockers, are every day washed, scoured, or rubbed. Even in the lodging-houses, the middle of the stairs is often covered with carpeting to prevent them from being soiled. All the apartments in the houses have mats or carpets; and the use of them has been adopted some years since by the French.'

No doubt, as Monsieur Grosley wrote, tables and chairs were the principal items of furniture in the rooms, but it is curious that he should have omitted to notice the book-cases and china cupboards, which were so largely on the increase at this time. Another show cupboard, with Gothic motive in the arrangement of glazing, is shown in Fig. 583. Here the pediment is a new departure, the C scrolls swooping upwards, being clothed on the outer edge with acanthus foliage, and perforated with Chinese fretwork; the hollow of the cornice is most delicately carved with an acanthus and flower divided by a waved line, an interesting adaptation of the lotus border, and a pattern seldom found on furniture. The lower portion of this piece is of bureau form, opening with a flap on a charming arcade of pigeon-holes, with perforated spandrels on either side of two classical pilasters, enclosing the usual looking-glass and secret drawers, but in this instance approached by a small flight of steps. Secret drawers, more or less in the same places, exist in almost all the scrutoires of the seventeenth and eighteenth centuries.

It appears certain that Chippendale and his followers adapted their work to the requirements of their clients' rooms and decoration, and therefore produced furniture of classical, French, Chinese and Gothic designs to suit different locations. The cabinet (Fig. 584) with looking-glass panels, of about the date 1755, but rather earlier in style, is severe in taste. In this instance the pediment is classical, but the fascia is perforated lattice-work, centring in the crown and feathers of the Prince of Wales. As the date of this cabinet is before 1760, it may possibly have been made for George III before he came to

FIG. 585. *Mahogany Book-case.* Height, 8 feet 4 inches; length, 4 feet 10 inches; depth, 1 foot 6 inches. Property of the DUKE OF BEAUFORT.

the throne. The framing to the doors is covered with a Chinese card-cut lattice-work, contained within two Corinthian columns; the lower portion of the piece is perfectly plain. This severe Chinese treatment is found again in the combined china cabinet and book-case (Fig. 585), belonging to the Duke of Beaufort, in which the wings are unglazed and covered with the original brass wire-netting for books, the glazed centre compartment being for china; the lattice-work frieze is perforated, but the lattice pilasters on either side of the centre opening are backed with looking-glass, and the same motive is carried out in the lower portion of the piece, producing a pleasing uniformity of design. At this period many instances occur of superfluity in ornament, but on careful examination, certain plain surfaces will always be found left to give proper value to the broken details of the carving. It is by the intellectual distribution of this activity and repose in decoration that the doubtful buyer should be guided, for simplicity is one of the many pitfalls to the forger, and a redundancy of ornament may often cover a multitude of sins. In the large and handsome cabinet or book-case in three compartments (Fig. 586), the scrolled and lattice pediment centres in a basket with flowers and two doves; the frieze to the cornice is perforated in a Chinese motive, the six doors are

Fig. 586. *Mahogany Book-case.* Length, 10 feet 3 inches; height, 10 feet. Property of E. H. Cuthbertson, Esq.

simple in treatment; the upper and lower portions of the piece are separated by a shelf, edged with a finely gadrooned moulding, and it is only the brass handles and key-plates to the doors that are ornate, and cleverly relieve what would otherwise be far too great an expanse of simplicity.

The unusually fine cabinet given in Plate XLI was probably made by the firm of Chippendale between 1750 and 1760, and is a masterpiece in construction, design and execution. The motive is Chinese, and the beauty of the undulating lines of the front is only equalled by the perfection of the veneer and the tasteful arrangement of the woods employed. The centre compartment rises in a dark rosewood roof of pagoda form, supporting an escutcheon and two candle-branches hung with ivory bells; the doors are veneered on the outside with fine amboyna wood, bordered in light rosewood, inlaid with a herring-boning of ebony and holly, the insides being veneered with plain panels of light rosewood; these doors open on a series of ninety-three drawers, faced with walnut, mahogany, amboyna, satin, laburnum, rose and other woods; in the centre is a recess, framed in two cluster columns set angle-ways, and backed by looking-glass; the wings are surmounted by a Chinese railing on a cornice composed of nine members; candle-holders, hung with ivory bells, forming pendants. The stand is of dark rosewood, decorated on the outer surfaces with a card-cut lattice-work in Chinese taste. There is a design for a cabinet of this description in the *Director*; the example given here was probably made for a wealthy botanical collector. Fig. 587 is a view of the same cabinet with open doors, to show the arrangement of the drawers.

Fig. 588 is a china cabinet with a perforated lattice pediment of purely Chinese feeling; the glazing to the doors, the frieze to the lower portion and the feet, corresponding in taste. Such a cabinet would have been used for either books or china. The following letter from Mrs Delany to Mrs Dewes, written in 1746, speaks of this Oriental taste:

'We got to Cornbury, where we were expected, and immediately conveyed into the apartment allotted for us, which is so neat and so elegant that I never saw

Fig. 587. *Inside of Cabinet*. Property of H. Percy Dean, Esq.

Fig. 588. *Mahogany China Cupboard*. Height, 8 feet; length, 4 feet 4 inches. Property of Lord de Lisle and Dudley.

anything equal to it. It consists of two large rooms and a bedchamber; the finest room is hung with flowered paper of grotesque pattern, the next room is hung with the finest Indian paper of flowers and all sorts of birds; the ceilings are all ornamented in the Indian taste; the frames of the glass and all the furnishing of the room are well suited; the bedchamber is also hung with Indian paper on a gold ground, and the bed is Indian work of silks and gold on white satin.'

Fig. 589 is a china cupboard of rare form and high finish, of about 1760. The pediment rises in the tall scrolls of this period, and is perforated in simple curved trellis; the hollow frieze is decorated with a series of the small pointed pendants that obtained such fashion on later cabinets, and the ornament on the framing of the doors is confined to carved pendants and borders of flowers. The divisions of the glazing are large; the lower portion forms a stand, headed by a well-carved moulding, the centre of the frame being decorated with a pendant formed of a shell between sprays of acanthus; the legs are of ball and claw shape, late in style. It may be well here to repeat that all carving on the flat surfaces of mahogany furniture of this period is applied; it is only upon the mouldings, the legs of chairs and tables, and the backs of chairs that decoration is cut out of the solid. A cabinet consisting entirely of drawers for papers, etc., is shown in Fig. 590. In this specimen both pediment and cornice are perforated and represent the only decoration. The small drawers are enclosed by doors, and each is numbered.

Fig. 591, although leaning towards a later taste, must be classified with the foregoing cabinets. In this case the glazed compartment is small, with drawers on either side; the cupboards open in cusped form; the lower portion of the piece is well in projection, taking the form of a chest with drawers standing on rather tall bowed feet; the handle-plates, which are original, point to a date about 1765, and are early examples of the solid plate, which fashion was revived about this time. The colour of the wood is exceedingly good. This form is classed by Chippendale as a 'dressing-chest and book-case'.

FIG. 589. *Mahogany China Cabinet*. Height, 8 feet 6 inches; length, 4 feet 9 inches. Property of VISCOUNT ENFIELD.

FIG. 590. *Mahogany Cabinet*. Property of L. FLEISCHMANN, Esq.

FIG. 592. *Mahogany and Gilt Writing-table*. Property of MESSRS J. MALLETT AND SON.

FIG. 591 (*left*). *Mahogany Cabinet*. Height, 5 feet 8 inches; length, 4 feet; depth, 1 foot 9 inches. Property of WEEDON GROSSMITH, Esq.

CHAPTER VI

IBRARY writing-tables have already been given in illustration, but after 1750 these were regarded as important pieces of furniture, and much care was bestowed on them. Their decoration was in accordance with the fashion, and their shape varied little. Fig. 592 is French in type and rather before 1750. It is remarkable for its simplicity, depending for charm upon proportion and undulation of line, even the top and bottom mouldings being uncarved. The only decorations are the gilt and carved borders of the long serpentine panels, the stringing and the well-curved feet. The top is covered with leather, no key-plates or handles are introduced; the mahogany is light in colour, having only been waxed. Furniture of this particular character is rare, and was probably the taste of one particular firm. The commode dressing-table (Fig. 593) is probably made by the same hand, the characteristics exactly resembling the last specimen. The same gilding round the lozenge-shaped panels, and the simplicity of the mouldings, would infer that these two pieces of furniture were made for one room. The legs are delicate, set in wide at the shoulder, and carved with cabochon and acanthus, terminating in scrolled feet. The whole effect is reminiscent of a French country-piece in oak of about the same time. Plate XLII shows a highly finished library-table, also about 1755, and is an undoubted instance of Chippendale's work. The design appears in

Fig. 593. *Mahogany and Gilt Commode.*
Property of H. H. Mulliner, Esq.

Fig. 594. *Back of Writing-table.* (Plate XLII)
Property of H. Percy Dean, Esq.

Fig. 595. *Mahogany Library-table*. Length, 6 feet 6 inches; width, 4 feet; height, 2 feet 7 inches. Property of Lord St Oswald.

Fig. 596. *End of Table shown in Fig. 595.*

plate lxxxv of the *Director*, and the workmanship is of the peculiar-finished character of that firm, though in this specimen the mouldings differ slightly from the design and are decorated. The frieze that surrounds the top is a fine card-cut lattice in Chinese taste; the eight panels, with their cluster columns, composing the lower portion of the piece, show almost every variety of Chippendale's design.

There is not space here to justify a further explanation of the plan and setting out of this carefully considered example. A reference to the above plate in the *Gentleman and Cabinet-maker's Director* may surprise a reader unacquainted with technical details of cabinet-making. On the back of this table – or rather the portion intended to stand out in the room (Fig. 594) – ornately carved panels are introduced, with carved Gothic octofoils, headed by garrya sprays. The carving on this remarkable piece is as sharp as metal-work, being equal in directness of execution to the bronze and marble of the Italian Renaissance. These fine tables, even at the time of their manufacture, were expensive; the wood was of the choicest, and none but the best crafts-men were employed. Fig. 595 is another specimen in the possession of Lord St Oswald, made by Chippendale for the library at Nostell Priory, and delivered there, June 1767. The bill for it lies always in one of the drawers, the detail referring to the table being as follows:

'To a large mahogany library table, of very fine wood, with doors on each side of the bottom part and drawers within on one side and partitions on the other, with terms to ditto carved and ornamented with Lions' heads and paws, with carved ovals in pannels of the doors, and the top covered with black leather, and the whole compleatly finished in the most elegant taste, £72, 10s.'

This was equivalent to quite £200 of our money at the present time, though the value of the table now is certainly over £2000. The design was probably by the brothers Adam, who, in conjunction with Chippendale, decorated the house and made much of the furniture. The piece is unique, as representing furniture in its original condition exactly as it left Chippendale's workshops, for not a panel has started, not a moulding has moved, and the carving is like wax-modelling by a skilful sculptor. The back and front of this table are treated alike; Fig. 596 shows one of the sides. This bill of Chippendale's is of great interest, and eight of the pages are given (Figs. 600 to 607). It is in sheets, foolscap size, sewn together, and includes a period from June 1766 to December 1770, and a sum of £1581, 8s. spent in upholstery. Other examples mentioned in this bill will be given later.

In the same room as the table there are some library steps (Fig. 597) of ingenious construction, which fold up into a box, carved in a severe Adam design. Another library book-table, of about 1765, is Fig. 598, from Badminton; the front and back are both partitioned for the reception of the large folios, so much the fashion at this time. The corners and centre compartment are flanked with finely designed terms, headed with lions' masks, each holding a loose brass ring; these are headed by a richly carved cornice, standing on a bold plinth. The colour, style and execution of this piece much

Fig. 597. *Mahogany Library Steps.* Property of Lord St Oswald.

FIG. 598. *Mahogany Book-table.* Length, 8 feet 4 inches; width, 4 feet; height, 2 feet 8 inches. Property of the DUKE OF BEAUFORT.

FIG. 599. *Tulip-wood Barometer Case.* Height, 4 feet; width, 1 foot 4 inches. Property of LORD ST OSWALD.

resembles the table by Chippendale at Nostell Priory, but it is useless to attempt to assign furniture to an individual maker, unless there are some very characteristic points of resemblance, or proved by document that it came from a particular workshop. It is impossible that Chippendale's firm could have made a tithe of the furniture assigned to them, though from 1750 to 1780 he was the fashionable cabinet-maker and upholsterer of his time, and there is but little doubt that he made all the best and most expensive furniture, and was employed by the richest classes both for their town and country houses. The bill at Nostell Priory includes various and quite ordinary forms of upholstery, in detail much resembling a modern account of the same kind. Among the items are forty-one picture-frames, that still hang in the house; they are very small in size, and simply carved. These frames in all amount to £98,10s. – nearly £200 of our money. There is a charge also of £34,10s. (£69) for a frame to a picture of Cleopatra, which is a large price for a picture-frame, but it must be remembered that the reputation of this firm had been founded in the reign of George I for looking-glasses and picture-frames. Again, on 20 October 1769, there is £25 charged for a barometer case, described 'as a very neat case for a Barometer with richly carved ornaments'. It is shown in Fig. 599, and is certainly of high finish, being inlaid with tulip wood and ebony, with a gilt cresting, gilt satyr terminals, and gilt base; but £50 would be considered a large price in the present day to give for a barometer case. In this interesting bill the cost of ordinary furniture compares favourably with that of modern manufacture, but directly a piece became at all enriched or of special design, Thomas Chippendale was not cheap.

In spite of the position gained by makers of furniture, and the popular interest which justified the publication of elaborate and expensive works on the subject, the demand for really fine specimens, even in 1750, was still very limited. The population of London consisted of 600,000 inhabitants, and but a very small percentage of these were patrons of art. The taste of the time, even in fashionable houses, showed a tendency to under furnish, rather than overcrowd a room according to modern ideas, although living-rooms probably had not quite that severe and empty appearance found in contemporary pictures and prints. An artist would naturally subordinate details to the importance of his figures, and at that time realism was by no means his aim. Hogarth's works were exceptions to the stereotyped and artificial productions of his age, and in 'The Marriage à la Mode' he goes further in detail than any of his contemporaries; but even the furniture he depicts is not of the finest quality, and he probably made sketches of important rooms for backgrounds, introducing furniture from his own surroundings, as the same chair and sofa is found constantly repeated in different pictures.

The rich people, for whom the finest furniture was created at this time,

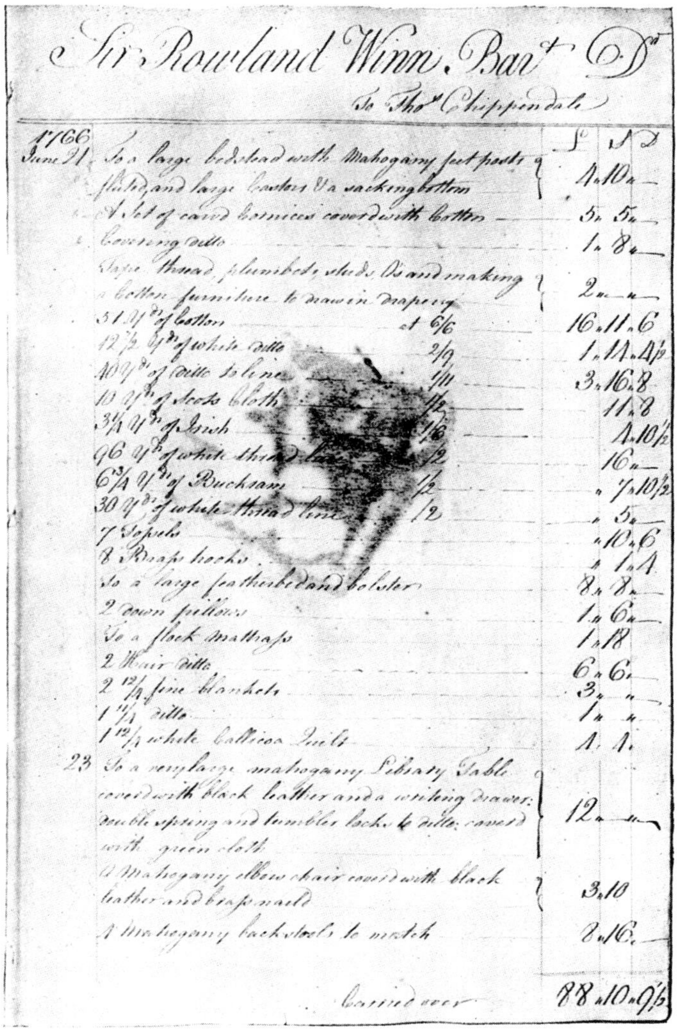

FIG. 600. *A Bill of Thomas Chippendale*. Property of LORD ST OSWALD.

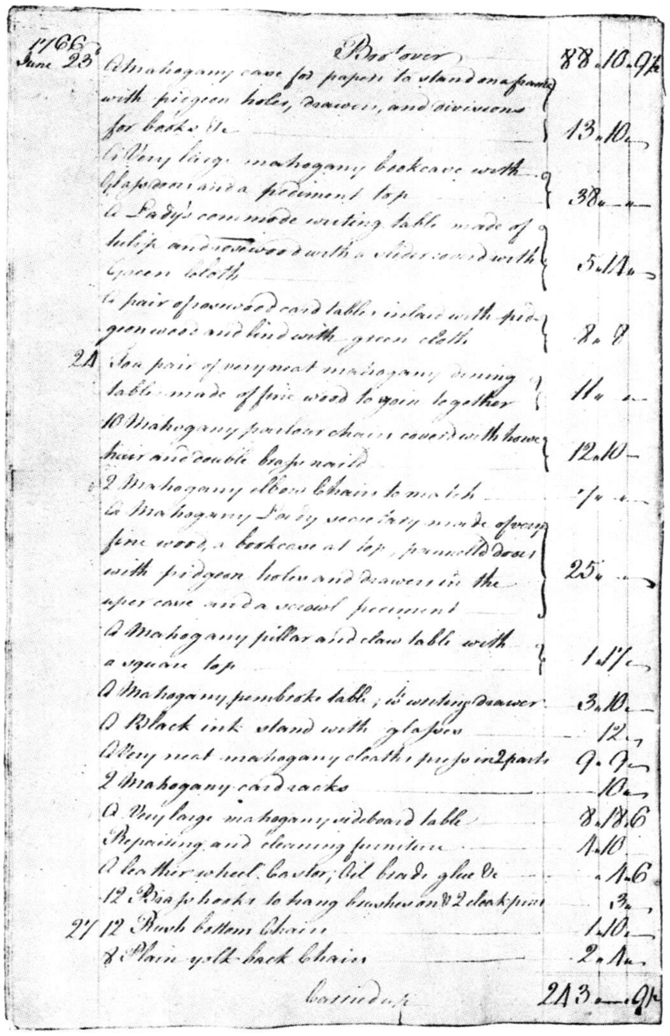

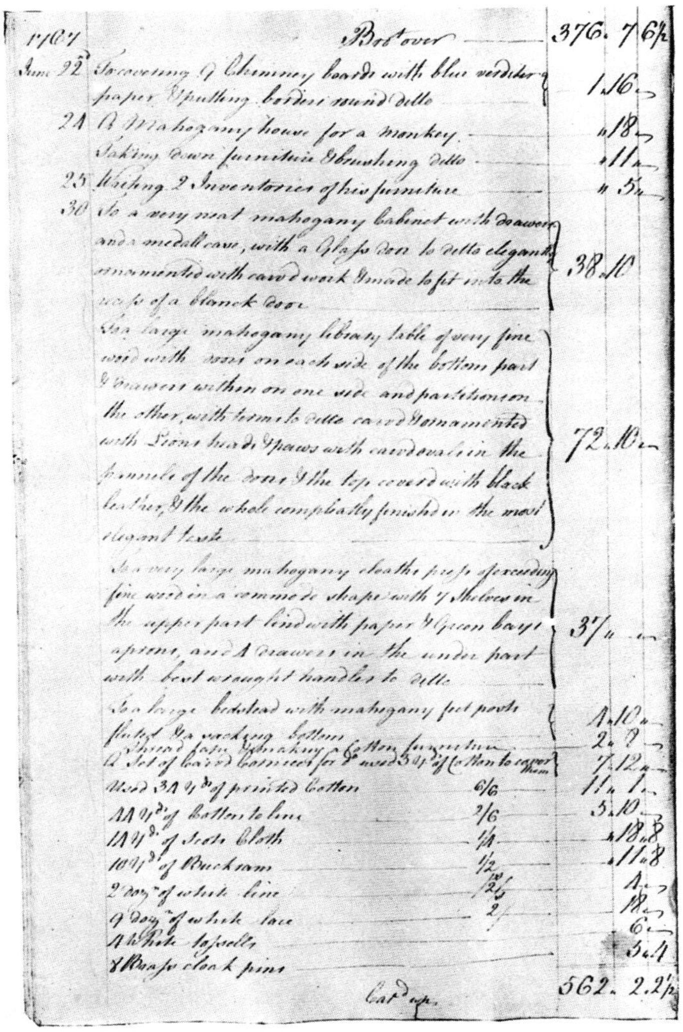

FIG. 601.

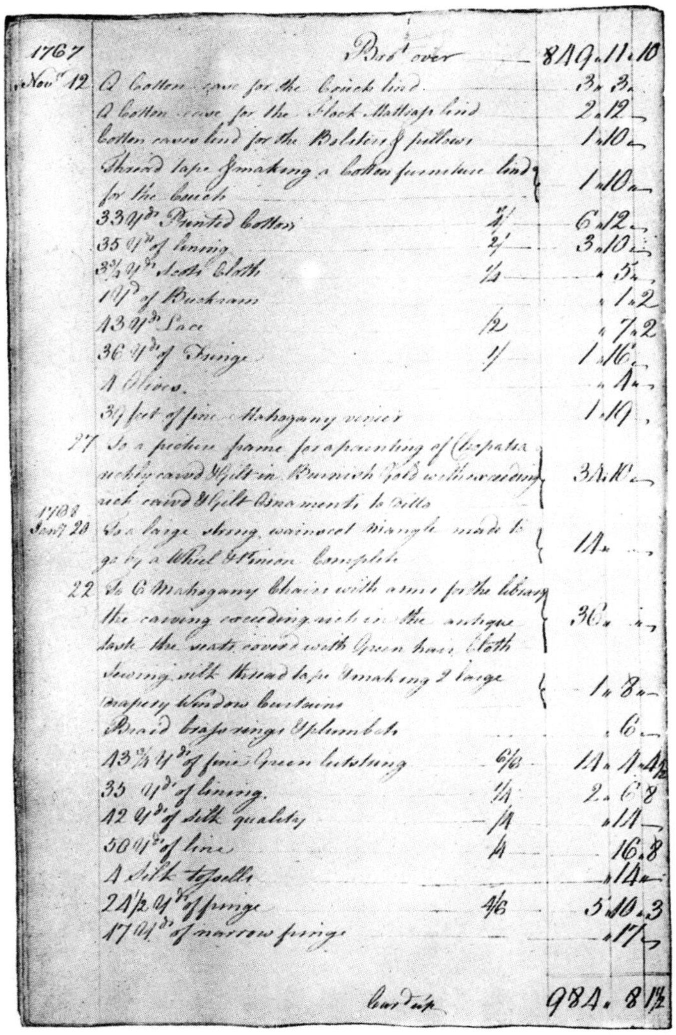

FIG. 602.

FIG. 603.

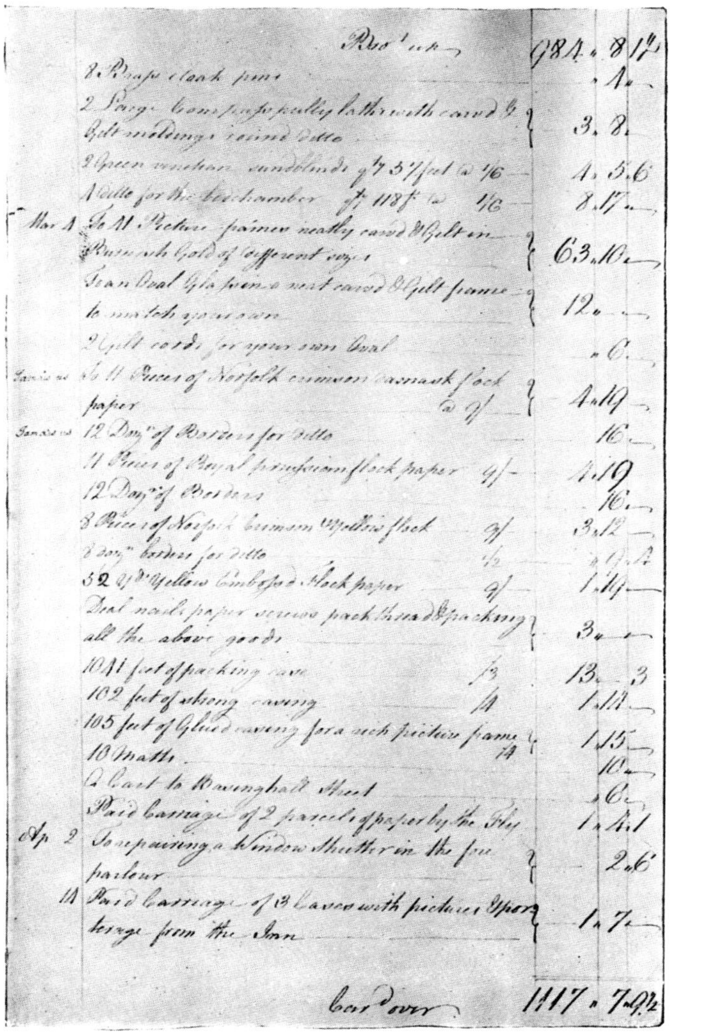

FIG. 604.

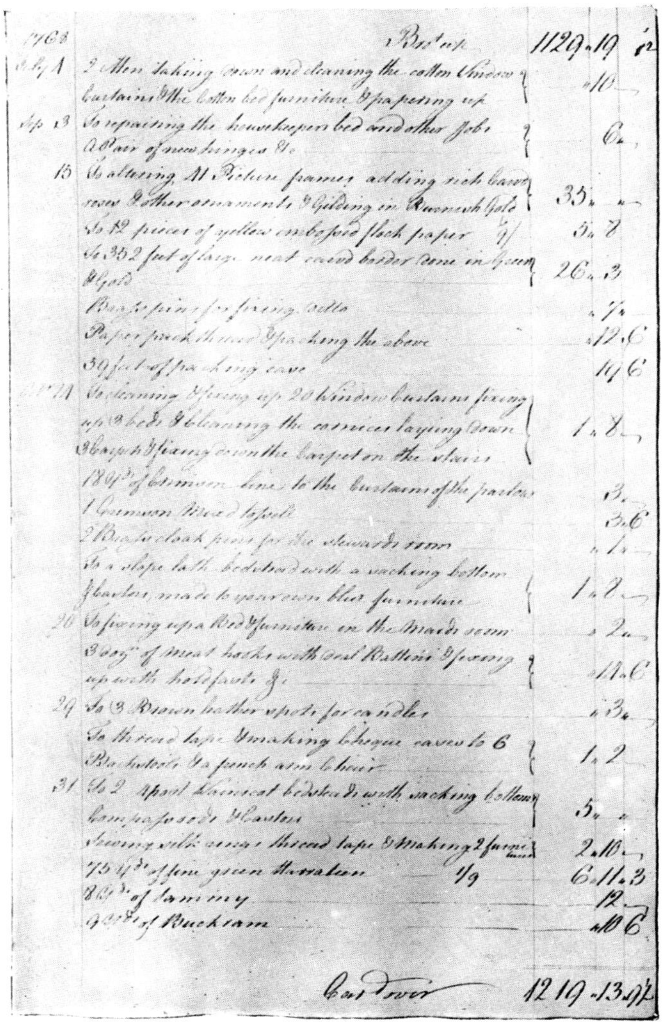

FIG. 605.

FIG. 606.

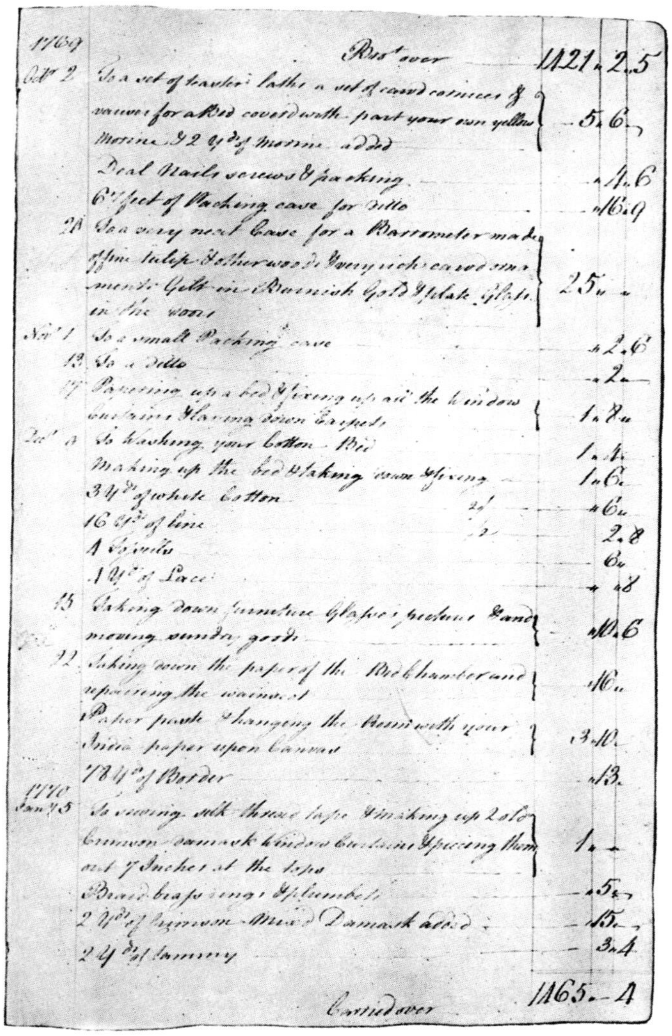

FIG. 607.

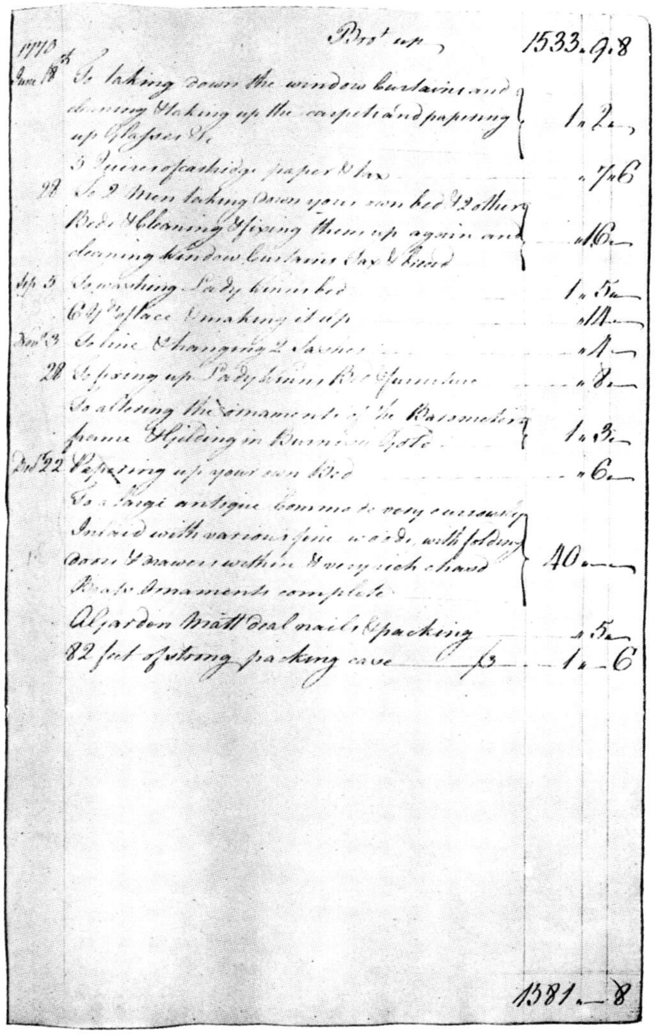

could not have made personal use of it. It was an age when the gentleman of fashion did little but amuse himself. He rose late, and after dining about three, spent the rest of the day in coffee-houses discussing scandals and the affairs of the nation, and his evenings in gambling, theatres or receptions at Vauxhall, etc. The ladies of fashion led much the same life, neglecting their children, their homes and virtue itself, for every possible form of frivolity. They must, however, have possessed refinement of taste, as even their saucepans and other kitchen utensils were beautiful, and are prized and collected to-day. This fashionable and extravagant set was supplemented, as has always been the case, by a rising and very powerful commonplace class, that rapidly became the backbone of the country. Monsieur Grosley, writing in 1765, gives a description of the daily life of this section of the community, and shows the other side of the picture:

'The manner in which the English bankers and merchants live, notwithstanding the care attending a commerce of such immense extent, is the same with that of the lawyers, physicians, and all the citizens in general. They rise a little of the latest and pass an hour at home drinking tea with their families; about ten they go to the coffee-houses, where they spend another hour, or meet people about business; at two they go to Change; on their return, they lounge a little longer at the coffee-house, and then dine about four; dinner concludes the day, and they give the remainder of it to their friends. In summer, the remainder of the day is passed either at some of the public walks, or in a country excursion, if they happen to have a villa near London. About ten at night they go home to bed, after taking a slight repast. In all seasons the London merchants generally retire to the country on Saturdays, and do not return till Monday at Change time.'

CHAPTER VII

CHAIRS of the school of Chippendale, made between 1750 and 1780, are very numerous, but it is only necessary to give a comparatively small number of examples, and these have been selected not so much for their quality, as to represent different and ingenious methods in treatment of the backs.

Fig. 608 is a chair of great interest, so unusual in proportion and design that is is difficult to place. The narrow back, the desultory but interesting character of the ornamentation of acorns and roses and the strange foliage on the shoulder of the legs would infer the same Irish origin as the writing-chair of rather earlier date, Plate XXXIX. The lively feeling of the curves, the scroll-back treatment of the top rail, with the low relief of the carving, all point to the school of Dublin. There is a curious want of practised design in the strap-work of the back of this chair, suggesting an amalgamation from more than one style. Its date is probably rather before 1750. Fig. 609, one of a set from Nostell Priory, is a so-called French chair of the time, also rather before the middle of the century. The back is upholstered in accordance with the shape in figured velvet, finished on the frame of the seat under open fretwork; the legs are hipped at the shoulders and carved in the French manner, but the feet finish in lion's paws. Fig. 610 is a well-known specimen of similar date; it preserves the old fashion hoop back, but the splat is elaborately decorated in Chippendale's style after 1750; the treatment of the seat-rail, and the carving of the legs ending in scrolled feet, are French in taste. The proportions of this chair are by no means equal to the richness of carving, which is over-elaborated for such narrow surfaces. In the chair (Fig. 611) the uprights of the back still suggest relics of the hoop shape. The corners finish in shells, and the splat is perforated in fan-shaped openings, the lower portion being plain, save for a trefoil headed opening and two wings of acanthus carved in low relief; the frame is of graceful and undulating form, carved with a shelled acanthus again repeated on the legs, which finish in vigorous ball and claw feet.

After the appearance of the *Director* in 1754, chairs became lighter in type, the legs varying between those of delicate cabriole form and the simple straight Chinese pattern; occasionally the treatment of the leg departs from both these principles. Fig. 612 shows a chair of the design known as 'ribbon back', a motive that Chippendale stated to be his best; in this instance the ribbon takes the form of a wheel supported by an elegant tracery of C scrolls

FIG. 608. *Mahogany Chair*. Height, 3 feet 3 inches; width, 2 feet. Property of PERCY HEATON, Esq.

FIG. 609. *Mahogany Upholstered Chair*. Height, 3 feet 2 inches; width, 2 feet. Property of LORD ST OSWALD.

FIG. 610. *Mahogany Chair*. Height, 3 feet 2 inches; width, 1 foot 10 inches. Property of R. W. PARTRIDGE, Esq.

FIG. 611. *Mahogany Chair*. Height, 3 feet 4 inches; width, 1 foot 10 inches. Property of LORD ST OSWALD.

FIG. 612. *Mahogany Chair.* Property of MESSRS J. MALLETT AND SON.

FIG. 613. *Mahogany Chair.* Property of H. H. MULLINER, Esq.

FIG. 614. *Mahogany Chair.* Height, 3 feet 2 inches; width, 2 feet. Property of MESSRS LAW, FOULSHAM, AND COLES.

and acanthus sprays; the uprights and top are comparatively simple but of beautiful undulation, and it is this subtlety of line that always stamps the chair of a good maker. The arms and their supports are thoroughly French, and the seat-frame, though shallow, is closely carved; the legs present a marked contrast to the usual type, being very delicate at the shoulders, and finish in dolphins. This beautiful set of chairs is now divided, the arm and plain chair (Fig. 613) belonging to different owners, who possess but single specimens. The design of the frame and legs of these chairs occurs in the *Director*, plate xxi. Fig. 614 is a more usual form of the ribbon-back, also with dolphin legs, and of beautiful proportion throughout.

Fig. 615 is a very perfect specimen of this ribbon-back pattern, so highly prized by collectors. The uprights of the back are strong, simply fluted, but of perfect proportion and graceful in undulation; the top rail is of fine serpentine curve, edged with C scrolls and centring in a shell; the splat is formed of two long C scrolls, united to the shoe and top rail by small curves in the same character, tied and interlaced with a delicate ribbon and tassel, forming the centres of the splat; the legs are delicate, and of ball and claw type most beautifully carved; the seat is covered with its original leather and nailing. It would be impossible to find a chair of more perfect workmanship and also adapted for practical use, strength, lightness and distinction of design; the ornament is combined in the structure, and is not merely, as in so many cases, an addition to the shape. Belonging to this set is a double chair settee ingeniously constructed for use as a bed. Fig. 616 shows the piece as a settee, the seat closed with a double fold. When extended as in Fig. 617, it is supported on two plain legs; the sacking and roping forming the bottom are original. The arms are of the French fashion and most beautiful in their curves. The colour of the mahogany in the wood of this whole set has lost all traces of the usual red and dark tones, having never been varnished or polished, and become the colour of a light-coloured cigar. It was quite a usual thing in country-houses at this time to make use of a settee bed in the sitting-rooms on an emergency. The fine execution of this entire set points to Chippendale as its author.

On Plate XLIII (a) is another of these ribbon-back chairs. It is one of the best type, much resembling those at Nostell Priory, and possesses the sense of strength that always accompanies a chair by a good maker. The uprights and top rail are fluted, the latter rising to a high cresting, and at their junction forming eared panels carved with a single leaf; the shoulders of the splat are high, and the ribbon that interlaces the two long scrolls of the splat is continued throughout its length, and ends in a small circle above the shoe; the arms are serpentine, finishing at the elbows in fluted whorls, and the supports are faced with foliage. The top of the seat-rail is carved with a fine leaf pattern, the lower side being delicately roped; although late in style, the

FIG. 615. *Mahogany Chair.* Height, 3 feet 3 inches; Property of LORD ST OSWALD.

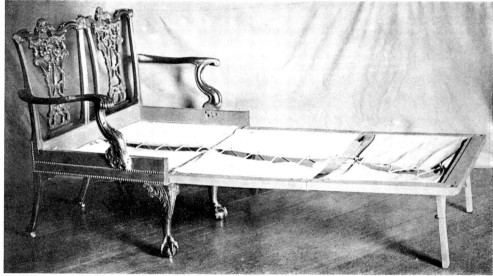

FIG. 616. *Mahogany Double Chair-bed.* Height, 3 feet 3 inches; width, 4 feet. Property of LORD ST OSWALD.

FIG. 617. *The same as Fig. 616, extended.*

FIG. 618. *Mahogany Chair.* Height, 6 feet 2 inches; width, 1 foot 10 inches. Property of the DUKE OF MARLBOROUGH.

ball and claw feet are well defined; the seat-covering is of late sixteenth-century Genoa velvet. The colour of this chair has suffered at the hands of the modern French polisher, who is answerable for the destruction of much surface quality on mahogany furniture. Five examples of these ribbon-back chairs have been given, as although the patterns are well known, genuine specimens are seldom seen, their great value being an incentive to modern reproduction. They vary very little in date, being perhaps most fashionable about 1755. Chippendale alludes to these chairs as follows:

'Three designs for Ribband Backs. Several sets have been made, which would have given entire satisfaction. If any of the small ornaments should be thought superfluous, they may be left out without spoiling the design. If the seats are covered with red Morocco, they will have a fine effect.'

It is evident that the difficulties attending the execution of some of these designs were severely criticised at the time, for in the rare third edition he wrote:

'Upon the whole, I have given no design but what may be executed by the hands of a skilful workman, though some of the Profession have been diligent enough to

FIGS. 619 and 620. *Mahogany Chairs.* Property of A. HALL, Esq.

represent them (especially those after the Gothick and Chinese manner) as so many specious Drawings impossible to be worked off by any Mechanic whatsoever. I will not scruple to attribute this to Malice, Ignorance, and Inability; and I am confident I can convince all Noblemen, Gentlemen, or others who will honor me with their commands, that every Design in the Book can be improved both as to Beauty and Enrichment, in the Execution of it, by Their Most Obedient Servant Thomas Chippendale. St. Martin's Lane. Feb. 27, 1762.'

Another representative type is the chair (Fig. 618) from Blenheim, one of a set of twelve. Here the uprights are deeply fluted, and terminate at the corners in scrolled acanthus with a fine backward twist, the tall C scrolls of the splat forming part of the top rail and giving great strength to the design; the centre is occupied by a foliated upright supported by a double loop resting on a plinth, rococo in style, that forms the bottom of the splat; the legs are well carved and are of ordinary slight ball and claw pattern. Chippendale gives this exact design in his third edition, 1762, plate ix. fig. 3, and writes on the subject:

'There are various designs of chairs for patterns. The front feet are mostly different from the larger choice. Care must be taken in drawing them at Large. The seats look best when stuffed over the Rails, and have a brass border neatly chased, but are most commonly done with Brass nails in one or two rows, and sometimes are done to imitate Fretwork. They are usually covered with the same stuff as the window curtains.'

FIG. 621. *Mahogany Chair.* Property of L FLEISCHMANN, Esq.

Figs. 619 and 620 are representative chairs of country make; the frames are rabbeted to receive the loose seats. Fig. 619 is the earlier of the two. Fig. 620 is rather more delicate in execution, the introduction of the fine bead and reel on the centre of the uprights being a rare feature. Fig. 621 represents an inexpensive chair of about 1760. The back is plain, depending for its ornament on simple, ingenious looping; the legs are straight and fluted, and the introduction of stretchers marks the reversion to a former construction. Stretchers are by no means necessary in a solid, well-made mahogany chair, so that it is difficult to account for their revival except in the hands of country or inexperienced makers. A large quantity of chairs, such as Fig. 622, were made for ordinary households. The specimen given is interesting inasmuch that it is constructed and veneered in walnut. A chair of great delicacy, also about 1760, is shown in Fig. 623. The ornamentation of the uprights and structure of the splats are in the Gothic taste. The combination of slightness and strength in these members is remarkable, showing a most careful choice of wood; the legs are entirely French in feeling, but in accordance with the extreme delicacy of the back, the seat has been re-upholstered with old needlework. Fig. 624 is a 'French chair', with upholstered seat and back; the

FIG. 622. *Walnut Chair.* Property of A. MEREDITH, Esq.

FIG. 623. *Mahogany Chair.* Height, 3 feet 2 inches; width, 2 feet. Property of PERCY MACQUOID, Esq.

FIG. 624. *Mahogany Chair.* Height, 3 feet; width, 2 feet 2 inches. Property of D. L. ISAACS, Esq.

FIG. 625. *Mahogany Chair.* Height, 3 feet 3 inches; width, 2 feet 2 inches. Property of the HON CHARLOTTE MARIA LADY NORTH and R. EDEN DICKSON, Esq.

design of the elbows resembles the last example; the legs have a fine cabriole curve, and are carved back and front in the same manner, the shoulders being decorated with a French motive that finishes in a delicately carved spray of flowers; the feet are finely scrolled. The date of this chair is not before 1760. The chair (Fig. 625) is one of eight chairs from Glemham Hall. Here the lines are even more French than the last example, and the arm supports are designed so as to pick up the mouldings of the back legs, the carving being very restrained in character. This pattern is represented exactly in the *Director* (1762), and foreshadows the period of simplicity shortly to be introduced by the brothers Adam and Hepplewhite, for Chippendale, however much he conformed to change in public taste, was never naturally severe, and his later adoption of simplicity, especially in chairs, was not natural to him. An additional attraction to these chairs are their coverings, for which a series of designs were drawn and worked by Lady Barbara North, daughter of the eighth Earl of Pembroke and wife of Dudley North. The original designs and separate drawings for each flower and bird still exist at Glemham. Fig. 626 is one of the outlines for the back of a

FIG. 626. *Design for Needlework.* Property of the HON CHARLOTTE MARIA LADY NORTH and R. EDEN DICKSON, Esq.

FIG. 627. *Water-colour Studies for Needlework.* Property of the HON CHARLOTTE MARIA LADY NORTH and R. EDEN DICKSON, Esq.

chair and Fig. 627 details of flowers and a bird. Fig. 628 is a chair of the same period, one of a set of four, with a sofa and two stools to match; the arm supports are unusual in their design, but the seat-rail and legs resemble the last example. The original needlework with which the chairs are covered is in a beautiful design of brilliantly coloured flowers on a cream ground. Fig. 629 is one of the pair of stools. The covering here is a modern copy of the old needlework.

The examples on Plate XLIV are good and interesting types of delicate decoration in low relief, but which has little reference to the lines of the chairs. Fig (a) is the earlier in period; the top rail is broad and flat, rising at the corners in two horned scrolls; this and the supporting uprights are carved with a fine tracery; the splat is vase-shaped, the centre being occupied by a slight quatrefoil, the delicate surface carving of flowers being repeated here; the arms and their supports are of the form anterior to 1750, but the slight ball and claw legs, ornamented with the same tender tracery, are of this date; the front rail is escalloped to produce an effect of lightness. The chair is covered with its original needlework. In Fig. (b), one of a set of two arm and eight single chairs, all having their original needlework, the lines of the back conform to the style of 1760, and the same distribution of fine floral ornament can again be seen, in this case travelling the entire length of the uprights; the arms are very representative of this date; the legs are of the straight shape given in the *Director* as an alternative to the earlier cabriole fashion; they are carved in panels of ornament, a rare feature; the seat rail is bordered by a narrow gadrooning. In both examples on this plate the space between the splat and the uprights is wide; in both the same scale of carving is preserved, and an effort of refined restraint is everywhere perceptible.

The last of this series is Fig. 630, made for the Chairman of the Corporation of the Poor, St Peter's Hospital, Bristol, which town was the first to establish, in 1696, a board of poor-law guardians. This chair is dated 1775, and is believed to have been made by Chippendale's firm for the Institution. On the top rail is carved a group in high relief of Charity, and beneath this the splat is composed of long foliated lines centring in a medallion bearing the badge of the Hospital and its date of foundation. The legs are of graceful French type, and show less signs of weakness than the rest of the chair; it is or purely domestic pattern, and is here illustrated to show the general decadence of the lines and decoration that once formed so high a school, for at the time this example was made, fresh influences were pervading English furniture, and new craftsmen were setting new fashions.

It is a curious fact that the majority of collections of old furniture begin with buying chairs, as collectors of silver generally commence with buying spoons. A great number of genuine single chairs have been furnished with arms in order to enhance their appearance and so add to their value, but the width of the seat is a sure guide to the original condition, for in arm-chairs this should always be greater than in single, about 24 to 22 inches. The colour of old mahogany in its original state is never red, and if any traces of this are apparent, the piece must be regarded with suspicion, as it has been coloured in order to disguise additions; a difference of colour between the splat and the uprights frequently occurs in old chairs, for good splats were often made of Cuban wood, which is hard, dark and capable of close carving, while the back, legs and uprights in the same chair are often found of Honduras wood, which is straighter in the grain and consequently capable of bearing a greater strain. The frames are found of oak, of mahogany and of beechwood faced with mahogany. In the last case sometimes an adventurous worm will have ventured to penetrate through to the mahogany; if this indication, with an old edge to the worm-hole is found, it is a certain proof that the frame has not been tampered with. By the following letter from a chairmaker to the *Annual Register* for 1764 can be seen the great care taken in the selection of wood, and also that certain recipes were then used for its preservation.

'Beechwood is very well known to be very much subject to breed the worm which presently destroys it; this worm is supposed, not without reason, to feed on the sap that remains in the wood after it is cut into scantlings, and wrought up – therefore I

FIG. 628. *Mahogany Chair*. Height, 3 feet 2 inches; width, 2 feet 2 inches. Property of W. JAMES, Esq.

FIG. 629. *Mahogany Stool*. Property of W. JAMES, Esq.

FIG. 630. *Mahogany Chair*. Height, 3 feet 10 inches; width, 2 feet 2 inches. Property of ST PETER'S HOSPITAL, BRISTOL.

FIG. 631. *Mahogany Sofa*. Length, 5 feet 2 inches; height, 3 feet 6 inches. Property of LORD ST OSWALD.

imagined the best way to preserve it was to take away the food that the worm fed on, by extracting in some manner the sap. I boil in a large copper which holds near two hogsheads, for two or three hours, all the beechwood I employ in smaller uses, which is no inconsiderable quantity in a year, being a chairmaker and turner by trade; and then before I dry it, I bestow another short boil on it about a quarter of an hour in some fresh water, the first being strongly impregnated with the sap, and acquiring a high colour and a bitter taste. This way of managing the wood takes out all the sap, it works pleasanter, is more beautiful when finished, and lasts without comparison longer. I have often thought that for many uses it would be a great improvement of this wood, if it was a third time to be boiled in some vegetable oil, or at least, if not boiled in it, managed in some manner that the pores of the wood should be filled with the fat juice; but as this is expensive, and I had no immediate occasion for such an improvement, I never made the trial, and it is too late in life for me to do it now.'

In genuine old chairs, the backs of even the most elaborate splats are found with irregular surfaces, the saw marks in the thickness of the fret are generally perceptible, and the ground of the carving is not so smooth in finish as the rest of the chair. These three details can be easily imitated, but not the worn and polished edge to each of these irregularities, for age alone can give this. Another suspicious characteristic is the yellow-brown colour found sometimes on the edges of the carving, which has been caused by being rubbed down with a bone or pumice-stone, to obtain the abrasion caused by age. However elaborate and finished the carving, if it appears motionless and without life, it is either a copy by an indifferent craftsman, or a modern reproduction, for the fine carvers varied their detail as they proceeded, considering the design rather than its execution. The surfaces of

FIG. 632. *Mahogany Sofa*. Property of D. L. ISSACS, Esq.

Fig. 633. *Gilt Sofa.* Height, 3 feet 6 inches; length, 6 feet. Property of the Marquess of Zetland.

chairs were not originally French polished and but rarely varnished; when old varnish is found, it is unwise to remove it; constant rubbing with a leather, or brushing with a stiff brush, will soon produce a surface that cannot be rivalled, and at no time should French polish be applied.

It was evidently considered desirable after 1750 to keep the backs of chairs as slight as possible, therefore examples in which thickness, clumsiness or crowding of the lines is apparent are not representative of the best specimens of that period. The firm grip of the claw upon the ball in a foot is characteristic of old work, and although towards the end of this fashion the claw became more slender and bird-like, there should always be intention of action and vigour in the grip of a genuine claw. Whole sets of old plain mahogany chairs have been recently recarved in Italy and France, as well as being entirely manufactured there; the carving of these will generally be found to be in low relief and rounded at the edges, and the colour of the wood a grey-brown, obtained by chemicals; an old chair, unless of Cuban wood throughout, is invariably lighter in weight than a modern forgery. Great skill is exercised in these manufactures, as the deceptions well repay the labour entailed.

Sofas became less severe in shape after 1750, the fluted motives of the legs being repeated on the rest of the piece. The old shape (Fig. 631) belonging to the set of chairs at Nostell Priory (Fig. 609) is before that date, the old-fashioned C scroll to the arms being much reduced; the trellis to the seat-frame and treatment of the legs exactly resembles the chairs. Fig. 632 re-presents a sofa of pure Chippendale shape, about the date 1753. The back consists of one long, sweeping curve edged with carving; the arms pick up the line of the back and terminate in ribbed scrolls with narrow gadrooned edges; the seat-rail is of graceful and undulating form, bordered with the same gadrooning, which is continued down each side of the legs; these are eight in number, rising in their centres to a bold, convex rib, which finishes

Fig. 634. *Gilt Sofa.* Height, 3 feet 4 inches; length, 7 feet. Property of the Marquess of Zetland.

FIG. 635. *Gilt Arm-chair*. Height, 3 feet 4 inches; width, 2 feet 4 inches. Property of the MARQUESS OF ZETLAND.

on the seat-rail in a delicately carved shell and foliated sprays; the feet are of scrolled form, carved with cabochons and acanthus leaves. The whole treatment is very simple, yet exceedingly rich in effect; the covering is modern, but correct in design to the period of the sofa.

Fig. 633 is another sofa, one of a pair, more ornate in form and much like some examples given in the *Director*. The lines are French in feeling, but of English workmanship; the back is serpentine, rising to a cresting which centres in a shell between two foliated scrolls; the corners are beautiful in their curves, depending for their decoration on simple mouldings and a dolphin-shaped shoulder; the legs are eight in number, short but graceful, and carved with the same simple mouldings, which continue in serpentine curves, and form the frame which centres in a shell surrounded with husked ornamentation. Fig. 634 is another specimen, one of a pair, rather more severe in treatment; the back, like the last example, rises to a cresting, but in this instance the shell is perforated and the ornament at the corners curves upwards; the arms rise slightly and scroll over; these and the frame are decorated with a delicate design of floral sprays, sphinxes and griffins; the ornamentation is exceedingly refined and of classical taste, resembling the forms employed on the earlier work of Robert Adam; the legs are comparatively straight, and end in lions' paws. The decoration of this sofa is exceptional, and is repeated on the fine arm-chair (Fig. 635), which is one of a set belonging to the suite.[1] In these three last specimens, the woodwork is entirely covered with English gilding, and it was proved, on stripping them recently for the purposes of re-covering, that they were of English workmanship throughout.

[1]Since writing the above, I have found at the Soane Museum the original designs, signed by Robert Adam, for Figs. 634 and 635, and made by him in 1764 for Sir Lawrence Dundas, Bart., Lord Zetland's ancestor.   P.M.

CHAPTER VIII

ABLES, like all other furniture, increased in variety towards the middle of the eighteenth century, and mahogany dining-tables were common by that time; these were mostly made with simple legs and sometimes with ball and claw feet; they show no great originality, and not being convenient for modern requirements, have been much broken up to imitate and repair old furniture. The more modern mahogany dining-table with sliding extensions being a far more practical construction, those of the eighteenth century have almost all disappeared.

Fig. 636 is a dining-table of about the date 1750, in which the legs swing out as brackets to support the extra leaves; it is of rare size and elegance, and the treatment of the long cabriole legs, twelve in number, is very clever, for although the ornament is by no means elaborate or continuous, an effect is given of the leg being entirely decorated, and the plain, empty feeling that generally accompanies a long cabriole leg is here overcome. At this time in many houses two oval or round tables were used, and the majority of these were plain, save for a little ornament on the shoulder and foot of the leg.

Sideboard-tables at this time grew somewhat lighter in construction, and the detail of their ornament was reduced in scale. The sideboard (Fig. 637), one of a pair from Nostell Priory, in anterior to the publication of the *Director*, and contemporary with the settee (Fig. 631). The top is a marble slab sup-

FIG. 636. *Mahogany Dining-table*. Property of H. Percy Dean, Esq.

FIG. 637. *Painted Wood Sideboard-table*. Length, 6 feet; height, 3 feet. Property of Lord St Oswald.

FIG. 638. *Drawing-room at Nostell Priory.*
Property of LORD ST OSWALD.

ported by a frieze carved in a waved volute, so favourite a pattern on these pieces of furniture. The centre is occupied by a goat's head on a shield, connected to the legs by long serpentine scrolls and vine wreaths, repeating the Bacchanalian motive of the frieze of the room in which these tables stand; the legs resemble the pilasters to the overmantel, and form a triple cluster; the vine sprays are interwoven amongst them, producing a most charming effect. These beautiful side-tables are carved in white wood, and though originally gilt, are now painted oak colour; they were evidently made for the

FIG. 639. *Mahogany Sideboard-table.* Length, 5 feet; depth, 2 feet 6 inches; height, 2 feet 8 inches. Property of J. OATWAY, Esq.

room (Fig. 638) in which they have always been. The ceiling of this room is an excellent specimen of plaster-work just before 1750, but the painted panels on either side of the mantelpiece are a few years later in date, and emanated from the hands of the brothers Adam, who reconstructed and decorated other parts of the house. Two octagonal dining- or breakfast-tables can be seen on each side of the fireplace; they are quite plain, but of the period of the room at the time of its decoration. The grate, fender and fire-irons are also all original to this time.

This idea of terminal legs connected with garlands is found represented in the first edition of the *Director*, plate lxi, of which Fig. 639 is an exact repro-duction, with the addition of a gadrooned top and acanthus on the feet. This piece is of mahogany, and probably a few years later than the preceding example (Fig. 637); the wave-patterned frieze is intersected with lion masks, and an entablature decorated with a swag of flowers occupies the centre; the carving throughout is delicate and of the highest finish. Fig. 640 is a sideboard-table of about the date 1750; the top is plain, and the frieze decorated with a large open trellis, bordered with half-leaves of acanthus alternating in their arrangement, the centre being in the form of a shelled pendant; the legs are slight, carved with the usual shoulder decoration, and terminating in ball and claw feet. Fig. 641 is a slighter specimen than the last example; the gadrooning of the edge is broad and fine; there is no frieze, its place being occupied by a row of dentals; the careful consideration of this table will show why in so many instances the slender terminal leg was doubled or even trebled at the corners, for when single, it comes at an awkward angle and produces an appearance of weakness. Even well as this table is carried out, it is lacking in the proportions generally found in good mahogany furniture of this time. Fig. 642 is what Chippendale names a 'Gothic sideboard-table'. This fine piece is topped with a marble slab, and the carving of the frieze is in extremely low relief, in design a mixture of the

FIG. 640. *Mahogany Sideboard-table.* Property of MESSRS J. MALLETT AND SON.

FIG. 641. *Mahogany Sideboard-table.* Length, 6 feet 6 inches; height, 2 feet 9 inches. Property of MESSRS J. MALLETT AND SON.

FIG. 642. *Mahogany Sideboard-table.* Length, 6 feet 6 inches; height, 2 feet 8 inches. Property of MESSRS J. MALLETT AND SON.

FIG. 643. *Mahogany Sideboard Pedestal.* Property of H. PERCY DEAN, Esq.

French and Gothic tastes; the centre ornament is composed of delicate foliated scroll-work; the legs are large and square, of Gothic open work, enclosing Dorice columns resting upon plinths of architectural construction. The design for this table without the columns is given in plate lx of the *Director*; these were, no doubt, an afterthought, as the perforation of the legs might have looked empty without this addition. The colour of this fine table is a warm cinnamon, and the wood has never been polished or varnished. It has been shown that until the middle of the eighteenth century the sideboard with drawers and cupboards was not invented, and so separate pedestals corresponding in design to the side-tables were sometimes placed on each side, and these contained drawers for the wine and table accessories. Fig. 643 is a handsome specimen of one of these pedestals, carved with gadrooning and the waved volute; the handles are almost triangular and well suited to the character of the piece. Sometimes the lower compartment was lined with metal and fitted with a grating, underneath which a red-hot iron was placed to keep the plate warm. Fig. 644 is a plain specimen showing this arrangement; the woodwork is much burnt at the bottom, and this primitive mode of heating plates was probably one of the many causes of fire in country-houses during the eighteenth century.

One of a pair of very interesting sideboard-tables is shown in Fig. 645. The top and frieze are perfectly plain, from which dropps a deep border of valance form, beautifully filled with long acanthus sprays in low relief, centring in a shell on a ground criss-crossed with fine lines; the legs, of exceedingly graceful form, carry out the convex shape at the shoulders, terminating in scrolls on small escalloped feet. These tables have not been varnished or French polished, and are of a light brown colour. Fig. 646 is almost similar to the last specimen and evidently by the same hand; here the centre shell is inverted and convex, and the shells on the corners of the frame are very prominent. There is no evidence of carving of this character by Chippendale or his school, and the free and open treatment of the flatness and largeness of design give an appearance of Irish origin. The wine-cooler from Badminton (Fig. 647) possesses exactly the same character, and much resembles Irish silver salt-cellars of this period; the introduction of the lions' masks at the junction of the legs and frame perhaps point to a rather earlier date than the last two tables, and the design of the deep border is different, but the character of all three pieces is virtually the same. Fig. 648 is a table made in octagon, fitted with chairs; it was no doubt the furniture for one of the many grottos, pavilions or summer-houses so fashionable in the eighteenth century, when people in the country dined, supped, played, sang and danced out of doors. The table is simple in construction on four spider legs, and the chair seats, more ingenious than comfortable, radiate to the centre of the table, their backs being of the style known as 'Rustic Chinese', and resembling in their perforation the trunks and limbs of trees. The table is capable of holding eight people, and when the chairs are packed round it, their top rails all touching, form a cleverly thought out open border.

An excessive spirit of gambling accounts for the large number of variously shaped card-tables made between 1740 and 1780. Walpole states that the young men of fashion in 1765 were in the habit of losing five, ten and fifteen thousand pounds in an evening at Almack's. 'Lord Stavordale', he says, 'not then one-and-twenty, lost eleven thousand pounds there last Tuesday, but recovered it by one great hand at hazard, when he swore a great oath, saying, "Now, if I had been playing deep, I might have won a million"'. It was considered no disgrace for titled ladies towards the end of the century to keep public tables for gambling; one kept by the Hon Mrs Hobart, afterwards Countess of Berkshire, being much frequented by the Prince of

FIG. 644. *Mahogany Sideboard Pedestal.* Property of MISS TYNDALL.

FIG. 645. *Mahogany Sideboard-table.* Length, 4 feet; height, 2 feet 8 inches; depth, 2 feet 3 inches. Property of H. H. MULLINER, Esq.

FIG. 646. *Mahogany Sideboard-table.* Length, 5 feet; height, 2 feet 8 inches; depth, 2 feet 6 inches. Property of MESSRS MORANT.

FIG. 647. *Mahogany Wine-cooler*. Property of the DUKE OF BEAUFORT.

Wales. Lady Mary Coke in 1768, according to her journal, hardly spends a day without playing cards, often losing £40 at 'Lu'. She also mentions Tresdille as a favourite game. Cribbage, Quadrille, Pope Joan and Whist, however, maintained their positions as the most popular games. She also alludes to the 'Low tables', so called from the low standard of stakes indulged in at the unfashionable season of the year, and which, she adds, 'brings out odds and ends that nobody thinks of inviting when better are to be had'. The magazines and papers of the day contain numerous notices of the passion to which gambling of all kinds was carried on amongst the young aristocracy, no medium apparently being considered too trivial, even to betting on which of two raindrops coursing down a window should reach the bottom first, or who would pull the longest straw out of a rick. The *Oxford Magazine* for October 1779 mentions that

'A few days since, some sprigs of our hopeful nobility who were dining together at a tavern at the west end of the town took the following conceit into their heads. After dinner, one of them observing a large maggot come from a filbert, immediately offered five guineas for it, which were accepted. He then proposed to run it against any other two maggots that could be produced at table. Matches were accordingly

FIG. 648. *Mahogany Table and Chairs*. Height, 2 feet 8 inches; width, 4 feet 8 inches. Property of H. H. MULLINER, Esq.

FIG. 649. *Walnut Card-table.* Property of H. PERCY DEAN, Esq.

FIG. 650. *Mahogany Card-table.* Property of W. E. GEORGE, Esq.

made, and these poor insects were the means of five hundred pounds being won and lost in a few minutes.'

Fig. 649 is a card-table of about 1745, but of the shape so much in favour earlier in the century. It is of walnut, but the decorative treatment in the carving is rarely met with in this wood; the legs are especially fine in their sweep, and the claws of the feet are deeply scaled. By the year 1750 the bases of silver candlesticks had become squarer in shape, so that circular corners were no more needed on card-tables to contain the octagonal and round bases of the earlier candlesticks. Fig. 650 is a good example, with square projecting corners; the edges are carved with a rose-and-ribbon band, and the plain fascia beneath is framed in a very open gadrooning, from which start legs of graceful form carved on the shoulders with a concavity in place of a cabochon, and finish in ball and claw feet. The style of this table is large and well carried out; it belongs to the type before 1750, while Fig. 651 belongs to the second half of the century. Here the front and sides are slightly serpentine, and the top is double-flapped for cards and tea; the

FIG. 651. *Mahogany Card-table.* Height, 2 feet 6 inches; length, 2 feet 8 inches. Property of H. PERCY DEAN, Esq.

FIG. 652. *Mahogany Card-table.* Height, 2 feet 6 inches; length, 2 feet 7 inches. Property of the DUKE OF BEAUFORT.

FIG. 653. *Mahogany Table*. Length, 2 feet 6 inches; height, 2 feet 4 inches. Property of L. FLEISCHMANN, Esq.

FIG. 654 (*right*). *Mahogany Table*. Length, 3 feet 2 inches; height, 2 feet 6 inches. Property of MESSRS J. MALLETT AND SON.

corners are squared, and the front is delicately treated with a central ornament in strap-work on a criss-cross ground; it is curious that the legs should be more highly decorated than the rest of the piece, but in this instance the balance of ornament is maintained. Fig. 652 is a table of later date, about 1765, with a triple-flapped top, one of which is marked out as a chess-board; the frame is decorated with a Chinese Gothic fret containing well-carved escutcheons; the legs show the first type of the taper square form coming into fashion.

Small mahogany tables were made of all sorts and sizes. A simple table of oblong form is shown in Fig. 653. This may have served as a dressing-table, and was evidently made to stand against a wall, as the square projections for candles at the corners only occur in the front; the legs are straight, edged on the outside by a narrow beading which also surrounds the drawers. A favourite and fanciful pattern is shown in Fig. 654, which is a mixture of

FIG. 655. *Mahogany Table*. Height, 2 feet 6 inches; length, 3 feet 2 inches. Property of H. PERCY DEAN, Esq.

FIG. 656. *Mahogany Table*. Length, 3 feet 6 inches; height, 2 feet 6 inches; width, 2 feet 2 inches. Property of H. PERCY DEAN, Esq.

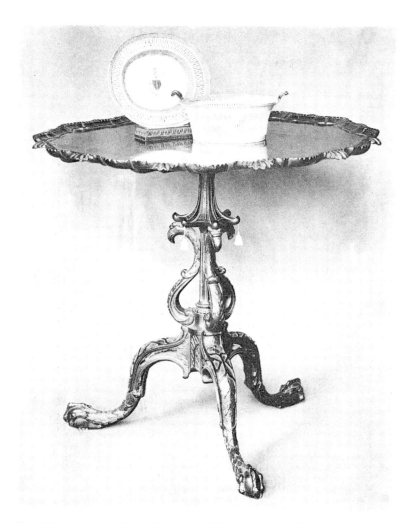 

FIG. 657. *Mahogany Table*. Property of H. PERCY DEAN, Esq.   FIG. 658. *Top of Table Fig. 657*

Gothic and Chinese design; the legs are composed of a cluster of four columns standing on square plinths, while the frame is perforated in a series of cusped and arched openings united by a round rail; little fretted brackets of Chinese design connect this with the legs; the top is of serpentine form, bordered by a rosette-and-ribbon band, and a cross-stretcher of saltire shape completes the lower portion. This was the lightest kind of table for its size that had up to this time been constructed in English furniture, and was a type much patronised by admirers of the so-called Gothic taste. These tables are comparatively easy to copy, and have been much imitated. Standing upon this example is a highly finished model of what Chippendale calls a 'cloths-press commode', probably made to contain trinkets, as it is too large for dolls'-house furniture, though many such toys were at this time made by the best workmen. Figs. 655 and 656 also represent highly furnished specimens of this light kind of table. In both instances Chinese railings surround the tops to protect the ornaments placed upon them, a very necessary precaution with the full skirts of the men's coats and women's dresses. Fig. 655 is of Chinese design throughout, with square fluted legs and a rising cross-stretcher of fretwork; the brackers connecting the legs with the frame are most elegant and simple in motive. Fig. 656, altogether more elaborate, is eight-sided and of serpentine form, the fretwork railing centring in four place in perforated arabesques. On the lower portion of the frame the Chinese motive is replaced by an escalloped leaf ornament; the legs, eight in number, are of the taper form introduced by the brothers Adam, and now beginning to be fashionable, but having here a Chinese treatment in their perforated feet, which are connected with four stays of the same character. The colour of this beautiful little table is a cinnamon brown, and its date is about 1765. It is reasonable to suppose from the introduction of these small tables placed about the rooms that by this date furnishing had assumed a delicacy hitherto unknown. Dress, too, at this time was becoming less exaggerated, giving way to a neater and less eccentric style; and though the hoop was worn at Court till 1780, it was much reduced from its original proportions.

A great many small round tripod tables were made after the middle of the

FIG. 659. *Mahogany Table.* Property of L. FLEISCHMANN, Esq.

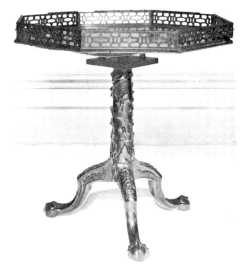

FIG. 660. *Mahogany Table.* Property of F. PARTRIDGE, Esq.

FIG. 661. *Mahogany Table.* Property of W. H. LEVER, Esq.

FIG. 662. *Mahogany Kettle-stand.* Property of ROBERT EASTWOOD, Esq.

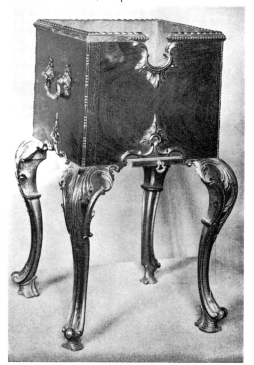

FIG. 663. *Mahogany Kettle-stand.* Height, 2 feet 2 inches. Property of H. PERCY DEAN, Esq.

century; these were for tea or needlework, and when surrounded by a gallery, used for china. The custom of having several such tables in a room at this period is evident from the following extract in Miss Hamilton's diary, written about this time, when she was staying with Mrs Delany at Bulstrode:

'At seven, Mr Keyes, the groom of the chamber, told us tea was ready. We had each our little table, our candles and work, conversed upon ye news of ye day, fashions, dress, etc.'

Fig. 657 is an unusually elaborate specimen of one of these tables. In this instance the central support opens out into finely carved scrolls terminating in birds' heads, and surrounded with a pagoda finial hung with ivory bells; the legs are feathered and terminate in claw feet. The top (Fig. 658), which is of rosewood, has a shell-and-ribbon edge. Fig. 659 is a simpler type, but a very practical and steady shape of tripod table; the top is of undulating and escalloped form, with a raised ribbon edge, and is supported on five short columns resting on a small platform. A far more elaborate china table is shown in Fig. 660, in which the central support is carved with the scattered and purposeless design, so representative of Irish origin. At the junction of the legs and shaft a Gothic cusped trefoil is introduced, quite irrespective of anything in the surrounding decoration, and the claw to the foot shows late characteristics. Fig. 661 is a very good table of this kind, in which the open edging is treated in basket form of scrolled acanthus and strap-work; the outer edge undulates in serpentine curves, and is bordered with a neatly carved leaf pattern; the stem and shoulders of the tripod are covered with carving. The ball and claw feet of these last two tables show great decadence, the foot of the dragon has descended to the lizard, and the pterodactyl prototype has sunk to the little reptile that crawls about ruins. These tripod tables may seem somewhat small for tea, but it must be remembered how small the teapots and cups were in those days, and the kettle, with its silver stand, was accommodated on a separate piece of furniture. Fig. 662 is one of these kettle or urn stands, surrounded by a trellised gallery, beneath which is a small slide to hold the teapot whilst being refilled; the legs are tall, decorated on the shoulder and foot with the same design. A kettle-stand of more elaborate workmanship is given in Fig. 663. It consists of a box without a top, resting on four cabriole legs of beautiful design; it has an opening for the spout of the kettle and a slide beneath; from its large size, this piece was most likely used in connection with hot drinks, such as punch, bishop, negus and other such beverages conducive to the gout of Georgian times. The inside lining is of metal. Fig. 664 represents another form of kettle-stand or table, of which a great quanitity were made in many different varieties; these were also much used to hold large bowls of flowers. Many of these small tables have tops of rosewood, a wood much employed in Chippendale furniture as an adjunct to mahogany, and later as an inlay. The finest

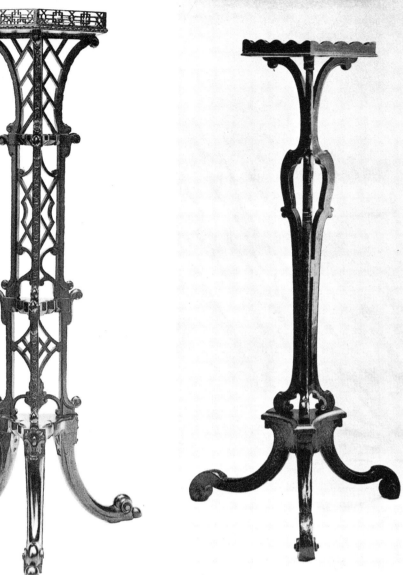

FIG. 664. *Mahogany Stand.* Height, 3 feet 8 inches. Property of D. L. ISAACS, Esq.

FIG. 665 (*right*). *Mahogany Candle-stand.* Height, 5 feet. Property of the EARL OF RADNOR.

FIG. 666 (*far right*). *Lacquered Candle-stand.* Height, 4 feet 10 inches. Property of the DUKE OF BEAUFORT.

rosewood comes from Rio de Janeiro and Bahia, and is mostly the wood of the tree *Dalbergia nigra*, a leguminous tree of great size; the heartwood attains large dimensions, but as it begins to decay before the tree arrives at maturity, is very often faulty and hollow in the centre; for this reason squared logs or planks are not imported, it being cut in half round flitches 10 to 20 feet in length and 5 to 12 inches in thickness, and owing to this irregular form is sold by weight, its value varying according to the richness of colour. The splinters of this wood are extremely poisonous, and great care has therefore to be exercised in its working.

Fig. 665 is what Chippendale designates as a candle-stand, and is a representative piece of Chinese lattice-work. These candle-stands were made to match every style of furniture of this period, and the lights placed upon them were usually silver candelabra. Fig. 666 is a specimen of rather earlier date; in this instance the surfaces are uncarved and decorated with black and gold lacquer, and the scrolling of the shaft and the tripod-stand are Chinese in feeling. Amongst this kind of furniture can be included such an example as Fig. 667, what is termed now a dumb-waiter; it exactly resembles the small round tables, but is in three tiers. Fig. 668 is an elaborately decorated washhand-stand, of the type generally in use about the year 1750. The circle to contain the basin is delicately carved and edged with a gadrooned border; this is supported on slight and ribbed columns; the plinths frame a compartment divided into two drawers, upon which is a round soap-box. The lower portion consists of a carved tripod to hold the water jug or bottle when the basin was in use. From this tripod rise four C scroll supports, beautifully carved in the French taste, which carry the upper portion of the piece. The bottle for the water was usually of globular form, and like the basin, of oriental porcelain; and as cleanliness was not customary at this time, these bottles are invariably found of very small dimensions. More simple tripod

FIG. 667. *Mahogany Waiter.* Property of D. L. ISAACS, Esq.

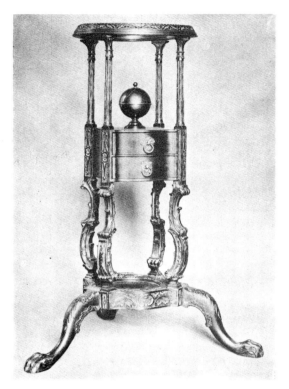

Fig. 668. *Mahogany Wash-stand*. Height, 2 feet 8 inches; width at top, 1 foot. Property of T. Oatway, Esq.

Fig. 669. *Walnut Fire-screen*. Height, 4 feet; width, 2 feet 3 inches. Property of the Earl of Carrington.

Fig. 670. *Mahogany Fire-screen*. Property of H. Percy Dean, Esq.

Fig. 671. *Mahogany Pole-screen*. Height, 4 feet 4 inches; width, 2 feet. Property of the Earl of Carrington.

wash-stands of this character still exist in great numbers; they are sometimes found with pewter fittings.

The writers in the eighteenth century allude very plainly to the want of personal cleanliness, even in the highest classes. Probably at no period of our civilised society were women so beplastered with paint and powder; it was therefore impossible that much use could have been made of water. In Georgian times several deaths amongst fashionable ladies were recorded as having occurred from the abuse of paint, among them Lady Fortrose, Lord Harrington's daughter.

Other small and popular articles of furniture were fire-screens, affording the opportunity of an additional piece of colour in a room, and the framing of specimens of the best needlework. In the earlier form of these screens, the panel was contained within two uprights, with a decorated cresting and bottom rail. Fig. 669 is an early specimen in walnut of the beginning of the eighteenth century; the needlework depicts the Judgment of Solomon, and the series of heads that line the steps are not those of spectators but representations of the golden lions that formed the approach to the throne. Fig. 670 is another example of the middle of the century, made in mahogany; the cresting is carved in the best manner of this period, the work on the uprights and feet being of the same character. The needlework here is not of fine quality, and earlier in style than the frame. Fig. 671 is the later form of screen in which the panel works up and down a pole. The subject of the needlework is very involved and of much earlier date than the woodwork of the screen, which is finely carved in the style of about 1755. Fig. 672 is an example of simpler and rather later kind; it is very well proportioned, and the needlework is contemporary with the screen. In Plate XLIII (b) the carving is of elaborate workmanship, and the whole construction of unusually large dimensions.

Mahogany furniture in lighter Chinese style was made simultaneously with the other types already mentioned; the slight lattice-work decoration so much introduced on it, though not practical in its strength, formed a charming accompaniment to other forms of Oriental arrangement. This furniture was made from designs by Chambers, Darly, Ince and Mayhew, Lock, Mainwaring and many others as well as Chippendale, and Mr Clouston's work on Furniture Makers of the eighteenth century gives detailed and interesting information on the merits and styles of these different firms.

Plate XLV is a china cabinet in simple Chinese taste; the centre compartment rises in a roof of pagoda form, and the whole piece is dependent on its proportions, and is practically without decoration. Fig. 673 is another of these cabinets; the roof is here supported on an open-work frieze of Chinese railing, and the padoga motive is repeated again in the highly decorated woodwork of the glazing; the inside angles of the legs are strengthened with columns, an unusual feature.

A lady's writing-table, with a superstructure of lattice-work shelves and six plain drawers, is shown in Fig. 674; the writing-slide is carried on two movable legs decorated with Gothic strapping; the fronts of the shelves are edged with light galleries; its date is about 1760. Fig. 675 is a piece of rare form, composed of lattice-work, containing two drawers, beneath which are deep shelves for the display of china; the fronts of these drawers are plain, but the corresponding panels at the sides and the pilasters are decorated with swags and pendants of flowers carved in high relief; it is very exceptional to find this raised and bold treatment of flowers in conjunction with Chinese fretwork. Fig. 676 shows a lady's work-table, the top opening as a box, with a lid decorated on the inside with two panels of fretwork and enclosing a series of small compartments; the sides are ornamented with a chained looping of applied fretting, and beneath this is a shelf surrounded

FIG. 672. *Mahogany Pole-screen*.
Property of PERCIVAL GRIFFITHS, Esq.

FIG. 673. *Mahogany China Cabinet*. Height, 7 feet 3 inches; length, 4 feet. Property of SIR BASIL MONTGOMERY, Bart.

FIG. 674. *Mahogany Writing-table.* Height, 2 feet 7 inches; length, 3 feet; depth, 1 foot 9 inches. Property of LORD ST OSWALD.

FIG. 675. *Mahogany China Case.* Height, 3 feet. Property of the EARL OF RADNOR.

on three sides by a Chinese railing; the legs are carved in low relief and are in admirable proportion to the rest of the table. Hanging china cupboards of this same character were made both in mahogany and soft woods; Fig. 677 is one of the latter painted white. The glazing of the doors is diamond-paned, and these are headed by a simple cornice, finishing in four vase-shaped finials; the pagoda-like erection surmounted by a peacock that forms the top is a bizarre mixture of French and Chinese motives. Placed in correct

FIG. 676. *Mahogany Work-table.* Height, 2 feet 6 inches; length, 2 feet. Property of the DUKE OF BEAUFORT.

FIG. 677. *Hanging China Cupboard.* Property of MISS TYNDALL.

FIG. 678. *Mahogany China Hanging Shelves*. Property of LORD ST OSWALD.

surroundings, such a piece of furniture would have had great decorative value.

A pair of mahogany hanging shelves for china in the same taste, but more restrained in feeling, are those belonging to Lord St Oswald (Fig. 678), and probably supplied by Chippendale in 1766 with other furniture for Nostell Priory. The centre compartment is headed by a pagoda-shaped roof rising to a finial, terminating in a baron's coronet; the lattice-work of the sides is somewhat stouter than is generally found, but the fretwork border of the top and bottom is delicate; the colour of this charming example is a warm light brown, and the wood is unpolished. There are many designs of this character in the *Director*, as ornamental shelves filled with china were a favourite form of decoration. Bishop Pococke, in his Tour in 1754, alludes to

FIG. 679. *Mahogany China Case*. Property of H. H. MULLINER, Esq.

'A Tower built by the Duke of Cumberland near Windsor, with a beautiful hexagon room, in which there are in the sides three doors and three windows, two of em lead to the round closets, in one are little shelves hung up for books for the Duke's use, in the other on such shelves is china for tea and coffee, the hexagon is most beautiful, the sides are adorned with festoons and flowers and fruits hanging down from them on each side of the doors and windows in stucco, and painted in their natural colours.'

The above quotation shows that the china was used direct from the shelves, and also that the pendants and swags of flowers and fruit so general at this time were sometimes painted realistically.

Fig. 679 is a china cabinet in this same fretwork style, the gallery forming the cresting being of most original design, and a cornice of pagoda shape is cleverly introduced; the framework of the stand is plain save for two small panels of card-cut lattice, and the three handles to the drawers are of fine brass-work and Chinese in sentiment; the two-sided legs are also open, the returns to the back legs being left solid. Chippendale calls such pieces 'China Cases'. Nothing more suitable for china has ever been designed than this fretwork furniture, the lightness of construction forming a background that never overweights the fragile ornaments it is designed to contain. This same fretwork treatment was also applied to sofas and chairs, but with a less

FIG. 680. *Mahogany Arm-chair*. Height, 3 feet 2 inches. Property of J. H. LEVER, Esq.

FIG. 681. *Mahogany Arm-chair*. Height, 3 feet. Property of H. H. MULLINER, Esq.

FIG. 682. *Mahogany Arm-chair*. Height, 3 feet. Property of the DUKE OF BEAUFORT.

FIG. 683. *Mahogany Stool*. Height, 1 foot 6 inches; length, 1 foot 8 inches. Property of S. CAMPBELL CORY, Esq.

satisfactory result, as it gave a sense of brittleness and insecurity, and the seats always appear to sacrifice comfort to ingenuity and eccentricity; it is therefore probable that this fashion in chairs was not of long duration. Fig. 680 is a highly finished chair of this type; it is purely Chinese in feeling except for the introduction of small pieces of French ornament on the cresting and where the uprights meet the seat. As it would obviously be most difficult to repeat the fretwork on the back legs and uprights, the unsuitability of this open-work design for seats is at once apparent. In arm-chairs of this character, panels of fretwork filled the spaces under the arms, and these were generally set at a slightly obtuse angle. Fig. 681 is a more solid specimen with a wooden seat, and with solid front legs with card-cut fretting and stretchers; the character of this chair lacks the grace of Chippendale's suggestions for Chinese furniture, and is probably from a design by Darly or Mainwaring. Fig. 682 is one of a set and particularly pleasing in shape; it corresponds in design to the table (Fig. 676); the seat is caned, and the colour of the mahogany is very pale and of the quality known as fiddleback.

Settees and stools were also made of this character to match the chairs. Fig. 683 is a stool in which the legs are solid, faced with card-cutting, but the

FIG. 684. *Mahogany Arm-chair*. Height, 3 feet 2 inches. Property of MISS TYNDALL.

FIG. 685. *Mahogany Arm-chair*. Height, 3 feet. Property of LORD DE LISLE AND DUDLEY.

FIG. 686. *Mahogany Arm-chair*. Height, 3 feet 1 inch. Property of WEEDON GROSSMITH, Esq.

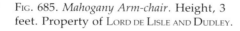

stretchers are perforated, and the brackets connecting the gadrooned frame with the legs are unusually simple. It is instructive to notice the more casual introduction of this lattice-work in combination with other styles, as in the chairs (Figs. 684 and 685). In the former the Chinese motive is introduced into the splat and uprights, the legs of the chair being of late ball and claw form, and the arms upholstered in leather. In Fig. 685, one of a set at Penshurst, the lattice-work forming the splat is surmounted by an earl's coronet and supported by a solid piece, pierced with an opening; the form of the uprights at their junction with the seat, the carving on the legs, and the serpentine and cornered front, suggest Irish workmanship of about 1768. The eccentricities in both these chairs are probably due to country manufacture. With these fretwork chairs may be classed the late examples of Gothic design. In Fig. 686 the splat is perforated with Gothic tracery, while the rest of the chair is plain save for the introduction of some foliated ornament in the French taste. The splat in Fig. 687 is of Gothic perforation, edged with a fine C scrolling, and the stretchers repeat this motive; the legs are treated as terms and finish in splayed feet; the carving and execution is good throughout. The design is better seen in the three-backed settee (Fig. 688), which must have at one time formed part of the set; this still possesses its original needlework.

A very interesting chair (Fig. 691), with a curious mixture of styles, is given at the end of the chapter to show what unexpected complications of design could be united in a fine piece of this kind. The hooped back and its decoration is of the time of Anne, the arms and their supports are about 1725, while the legs are about 1730, which is probably the date of the chair; it is of the finest quality throughout, and covered with its original needlework.

Beds of both Gothic and Chinese designs were also made between 1750 and 1765. Fig. 689 is a specimen with an elaborate Gothic cresting consisting of a series of arches filled with the same tracery; at the corners and centres are scrolled finials of acanthus, and cluster-columns form the posts. The hangings are entirely modern and incorrect in form. It should be noticed that the headings of beds at this time are somewhat reduced in scale and no longer assume the proportions of those made earlier in the century, for although in Fig. 690 the carving and design of the cresting is most intricate, the detail of the ornament is small, and the open-work tabs here introduced often formed an elaborate feature in beds later than this example; the posts are of fine workmanship, the frame and lions'-paw feet being carved in a rich manner; the pillow-heading rises in two long S scrolls enclosing a finer tracery. The date is about 1755.

It has been shown that towards the end of the seventeenth century decoration on furniture was principally represented by marqueterie or different processes of veneer, for the elaborate carving in soft woods, either gilt or painted, was chiefly used for console-tables, mirrors and beds. The early mahogany furniture of 1715 was solid and simple, and consisted principally of chairs, stools and settees, the decoration on these being generally confined to a shell on the shoulders of the leg, with some slight

FIG. 687. *Mahogany Arm-chair.* Height, 3 feet 4 inches. Property of MESSRS J. MALLETT AND SON.

FIG. 688. *Mahogany Settee.* Length, 5 feet 9 inches; height, 3 feet 4 inches. Property of MESSRS J. MALLETT AND SON.

FIG. 689. *Mahogany Bed.* Height, 8 feet 6 inches. Property of MESSRS ISAACS.

FIG. 690. *Mahogany Bed.* Height, 8 feet 8 inches. Property of FRANK PARTRIDGE, Esq.

ornamentation above the splat. The true spirit of the age of mahogany did not commence till about 1725 and terminated about 1770, when inlaying once more came into fashion. The carving of this 'Age of Mahogany' can be briefly divided into three periods. Beginning with an almost barbaric boldness, it culminated into a redundancy of fantastic and finely carved ornament, and finished finally in an altogether severer taste. After the gradual disappearance of the C scroll and cabriole leg, the influence of seventeenth-century design and the technique of Grinling Gibbon was exchanged for an adaptation of classical and Italian styles, of which Robert Adam and Pergolesi were the founders, Hepplewhite, Sheraton and Shearer being more or less their disciples. It is proved by the Nostell Priory library-table that the severer designs introduced by Robert Adam were in existence in 1766 and made use of by Chippendale when working in conjunction with him, but it is impossible to define the exact period when the gay and fanciful curves of Chippendale gave way to the more restrained and classical taste, or how far the florid style overlapped this latter fashion, with which it had little in common except the materials employed. It should be clearly understood that this volume is only intended to explain the historical evolution of artistic form in furniture by assigning dates according to the development of certain definite details, and not by theoretical attributions to individual designers and makers. It is always unwise to attempt to trace alterations in style merely by a date affixed to an illustration in one of the many books published between 1730 and 1765, for not only was plagiarism in design frequent, but the furniture had constantly been made some years before the publication of the book. Dates, in most instances, can only be fixed, and then only approximately, by careful observation in the steady evolution of individual characteristics and motives.

The admirable qualities of mahogany quickly developed the talents and enthusiasm of the English carver, and in the execution of ornament in this wood he stands unrivalled, for the beautiful mahogany furniture made in France by Reisener, Jacob, etc., had always plain surfaces and was largely dependent on its metal fittings.

Our fine mahogany furniture of the eighteenth century is essentially connected with the English, for little or none of its construction was borrowed from abroad, and it holds a unique and unassailable position in the history of European furniture.

FIG. 691. *Mahogany Arm-chair.* Height, 3 feet 3 inches. Property of T. BASSETT, Esq.

THE AGE OF SATINWOOD

CHAPTER I

T has been shown in 'The Age of Walnut' that the appreciation of lacquer furniture developed in this country soon after the Restoration, and that a great deal was made here during the reigns of William and Anne. This taste continued during the first half of the eighteenth century, and although large importations were made from Holland during the earlier period, it is improbable that Dutch lacquer was much in favour after 1725, as many books written on the subject by English authors show that this craft was firmly established here by that date. Chippendale states that many of his designs are suitable for lacquer decoration, but gives no details or directions for its use. The strong interest in Chinese art that arose about 1750, shown in mahogany furniture, wall-papers and gilt mirrors, strengthened the demand for lacquer furniture; the same designs and processes were employed as before, but the shapes generally conformed to those of contemporary mahogany. The ornament grew smaller in detail, and no longer boldly raised as in the earlier work; the employment of different colours in the patterns was generally omitted, the selection being confined to gold upon a black, red, bistre or green ground; of these black was by far the most favoured, red was rarely employed on account of its violent and distinct colour, and green considered undesirable on account of the great difficulty in preserving a brilliant and permanent hue.

Bedrooms were furnished throughout with lacquer, wall-papers, mirrors and chintzes in Chinese taste. The bedroom at Badminton, given a little later, is a good example of this fashion that appealed so strongly to the delicate and frivolous taste of the wealthier classes; a taste that had been influenced by pseudo-Chinese-French work, and the furniture of Simon Martin, who discovered his celebrated varnish about 1730, and whose decorations on furniture were at that time often oriental. The publication in England of various books on the subject, and reprints from those published earlier in the century, had no doubt helped to keep up the interest taken in lacquer. The following extracts are taken from a small work entitled *The Arts Masterpiece, or A Companion for the Ingenious of Either Sex*, 1700:

'THE CURIOUS ART AND MYSTERY OF JAPPANING. – To be proficient in this Art several matters are required, and these you must consider as suitable, not only in property but goodness, that your cost and labour may not prove in vain.'

After this rather vague statement, the author gives recipes for different varnishes, but the methods of producing the various coloured lacquers are founded more or less upon the first edition of Stalker and Parker, 1681, mentioned in 'The Age of Walnut'. The most important of these recipes is seedlac varnish, the substance, with which colour was mixed, to form a lacquer ground.

'SEEDLAC VARNISH, HOW TO MAKE IT. – Your Groundwork is good rectified Spirits – of which you may take a Gallon, put it into as wide a necked Bottle as you can get, that the Gums may the better come out. Then of the best seedlac add a pound and a half, let it macerate twenty-four hours, or till the Gums are well dissolved, with often shaking to keep them from clogging together. Then with Flanel strainers strain it into a Tin Tunnel placed in the mouth of the empty Bottle. Then let the Varnish settle and pour it off into other Bottles till it rises thick and no longer thin. Then strain the thick part and settle that again and keep the fine Varnish for your use, and this does as well without the danger of attempting to boil it which endangers firing the house and the Party's life.'

A recipe for red lacquer, a few pages further on, showing the gradual care taken in producing a fine ground, may be interesting to those who wish to restore or relacquer old furniture according to the original method:

'RED JAPAN, AND HOW TO MAKE IT. — The Reds are properly three, viz. The Common Red, the Deep Dark Red, and the light pale Red. In the first Vermillion is proper mixed with the thickest of seedlac. Warm the work and mix your Vermillion with the Varnish in a Medium, carry it over four times, permitting it to dry as the former; and if your Reds be in a good body and full, Rush it smooth then with ordinary Seedlac Varnish, wash eight times and after 12 hours Rush it again; and then for a curious outward covering give it eight or ten washes with Seedlac Varnish, and after five days polish it with water, Lampblack, and Tripoly.'

Regarding this Tripoly there are the following directions:

'It ought to be made into subtil powder and sifted, it is to polish your work after it is Varnished, and may be had at the Ironmongers in Foster Lane.'

Another book of the same date is *Poly Graphice, or The Arts of Drawing, Engraving, Etching, Limning, Painting, Vernishing, Japanning, and Gilding*, by William Salmon, M.D., MDCCI. At the end of the recipes is this sensible advice:

'These things have we given you for Example sake and thought good to make the Exempla in that of flowers a being that in which the greatest Nicety and Difficulty

FIG. 692. *Black Lacquer Cabinet.* Property of VISCOUNT ENFIELD.

Fig. 693. *The same, Open.*

lyes, it not being so easily performed as other things; and yet in this very thing the Licentia Picturalis is very large, the Artist being left chiefly to his fancy, only with this caution that everywhere he uses variety.'

It was upon these black, blue, red and yellow lacquer grounds that the time and care was bestowed. When they were polished and hard, oriental designs in gold, bronze, silver and colour were painted upon the finished surface. The art of lacquering in 1740 was still regarded as a polite occupation, for in the descriptive catalogue of the contents of Strawberry Hill, written by Sir Horace Walpole, he mentions a cabinet japanned by Lady Walpole, and also alludes to this fashion, in a letter to Sir Horace Maun, dated August 1743, 'My table I like, though he has stuck in among the ornaments two vile china jars that look like the modern jappaning by ladies.'

In the preface to the extracts from the mss. of the great Mr Boyle, published 1735, entitled *A New and Curious Method of Jappaning upon Wood,* the following remarks show that this amateur lacquering was resented by the professional craftsman:

'If any person should find a difficulty in the Performance of any article, I shall be ready to put them to rights for a reasonable satisfaction. I must confess I owe my knowledge of several valuable Receipts to some Manuscripts of the Great Mr. Boyle which have never been printed, and have fallen into my hands by means of the same noble Lord his relation whom I before mentioned in my Art of Drawing. I have been upbraided by some workmen in Curiosities for publishing Receipts of value to instruct the Gentry in the manner of Drawing and Painting and in Arts of the like kind, for they say it is a Damage to the workmen who get their livelihood by such things. I have a short Answer to this Argument, namely that there are none of the Receipts which I publish, but which are either my own invention or I have bought at a good Price, or else have been presented with by People of Fashion with their Desire to have them made publick; and these are such as would never come to the knowledge of the Workmen if I was not to communicate them in this manner. So that I can say from my own certain knowledge that many of them are obliged to me, and instead of complaining ought to thank me.'

In spite of this protest, the recipes that follow are practically repetitions of Stalker and Parker and other early authors on the subject, showing that the new enthusiasm in the art of lacquering had produced no discoveries. Many of these recipes of the great Mr Boyle leave much to be desired; the following is somewhat vague:

'Take any colour you have a mind to and grind it well with water with a stone and Muller, then let it dry and grind it in a Mortar and lift it if there is occasion, then instead of oil mix it with White Varnish, and painted it with what you think proper.'

In 1754 Edwards and Darly published a book of designs for use upon lacquered furniture that gave that art a more substantial help, and five years later a series of drawings for the same purpose was produced by Decker, a plagiarism on the former work, but with the following title: *Chinese Archi-*

tecture, Civil and Ornamental, being a Large Collection of the designs of Plans and Elevations from the Imperial Retreat to the smallest ornamental Building in China, from real designs drawn in China adapted to this climate.

Soon after 1760, it appears that lacquer became less popular, for in the *Handmaid to the Arts*, by Robert Dossie, published 1764, he alludes to a decline in the fashion for this furniture:

'By Japanning is to be here understood the Art of covering bodies by grounds of opake colours in varnish, which may be either afterwards decorated by paintings or gilding or left in a plain state. This is not at present practised so frequently on chairs, tables, and other furniture of houses, except tea-waiters, as formerly, but the introduction of it for ornamenting coaches, snuff-boxes, and skreens in which there is a rivalship betwixt ourselves and the French, renders the cultivation and propagation of this Art of great importance to commerce.'

The above extracts show the great interest taken in this lacquer manufacture; further reference to the above-quoted works will give much that is interesting and instructive.

It may be useful to mention some of the characteristics that distinguish English, Dutch and Oriental lacquer. The ground of the Chinese and Japanese manufacture is invariably smoother, and the enamel more brilliant than that of European origin; the execution of the landscapes, figures and other details is sharper and more rapid, and the work is but little in relief; the faces are more truly oriental and drawn with a finer line, and the gold throughout is brilliant. The hinges, corner-pieces, lock-plates and handles, if oriental, are more flimsy and less deeply incised than those of European make, and the doors and drawers are not of oak, unless the cabinet had been sent to the East for decoration, after being manufactured here. Lacquered panels for doors and drawer fronts, ready to be made up into cabinets in Europe, were also imported from China and Japan; the difference between the painting of the framework and the panels in these cases is clearly discernible. The distinction between the Dutch and English lacquer is more difficult to follow, but the structure is here a very certain guide, for in foreign pieces the internal joinery is coarse and the dovetailing large. The figures

Fig. 694. *Top of Lacquer Table.* Width, 4 feet.
Property of Mrs Assheton Smith.

FIG. 696. *Black Lacquer Table.* Height, 2 feet 8 inches; length, 3 feet. Property of the EARL OF JERSEY.

FIG. 695 (*left*). *Red Lacquer Cabinet.* Height, 5 feet 9 inches; width, 3 feet.

and birds of the ornamentation are also rather better drawn, and the relief is not quite so high as in English specimens. After 1725 the Dutch importations of lacquer into this country considerably diminished, and by the middle of the century the patronage of this industry was almost entirely confined to objects of home production and those of Eastern origin.

In the cabinet (Fig. 692), of about the date 1714, the raised ornament of the previous thirty years is still maintained, although somewhat lower in relief. The doors are mounted in the usual manner with elaborate brass fittings, the lock-plates are still cock-headed, a traditional pattern dating from the sixteenth century, and the large lacquered birds have become smaller in treatment, and lack the additional colouring to their plumage. The inside of the cabinet (Fig. 693) consists of the usual series of drawers, lacquered with Chinese scenery and figures of very careful execution, in distinct English drawing. A good many small tables for cards and tea were made in both red and black lacquer, but it is rare to find a table as large as Fig. 694, which is twelve-sided, and of about the date 1725. The edges are dished and rounded, the top is decorated with a bold design of cocks and hens, amidst flowering plants radiating to the centre; the lacquer is in high relief, most careful in execution, and its colour is black and gold; this top is supported on a central shaft, finishing in three curved legs, which are ornamented with pendants of peg-top form.

Another cabinet of very high quality, and of about 1745, is shown in Fig. 695. This, with its original stand, is 'the light pale red' lacquer described in the *Arts Masterpiece*. The decoration, which is delicate, consists of birds and plants in almost flat relief. The red stand is in true oriental character, being a deliberate copy of a Chinese rosewood table, and is most carefully decorated with gold and silver. A pair of tables very similar to this stand exist at Osterley; Fig. 696 represents one of these. The top is surrounded by a fretwork gallery as a protection to china, the colour of the lacquer being black and gold; in both stand and table it can be noticed that a Chinese treatment of the ball and claw foot has been adopted. Another specimen of red lacquer,

FIG. 697. *Black Lacquer Cabinet and Stand.*
Height, 7 feet; length, 4 feet 1½ inches;
depth, 1 foot 10 inches. Property of MESSRS
MORANT.

FIG. 698. *The same, Open.*

Fig. 699. *Gilt Mirror on Chinese Wall-paper.*
Height, 6 feet 6 inches; width, 6 feet.
Property of the Duke of Beaufort.

of about 1740, is shown in Plate XLVI, a corner cupboard in two compartments, united by a centre drawer. The red ground in this instance does not
possess the coral-hued delicacy of the lighter variety, and is termed in the
recipes of the time 'The Common Red'. The upper panels represent Chinese
family scenes in brown, black and gold lacquer; both the top and bottom
panels are bordered with a scrolled Georgian decoration, and the cupboard
is headed with a curved pediment of traditional shape. In the cabinet of
about 1755 (Fig. 697), a marked difference to the preceding specimens can be
observed, for a frieze and cornice are added which conform to the pattern of
contemporary mahogany furniture; the decoration is small in character, with
but little trace of real Chinese feeling; the metal-work handles and lock-
plates resemble those found on chests of drawers of the time, and the
construction of cabinet doors over a double tier of drawers is a novelty. The
stand, though original, is on very simple lines, and a useful pattern for
reproduction. Fig. 698 shows the inside, the centre being treated as a
classical portico, enclosing two gates fretted in the Chinese taste, with a
looking-glass background; the colour of the piece is black, a very little red
being introduced here and there amidst the gold ornamentation.

The decoration of bedrooms in this style has been so often alluded to, that
it will be interesting to give the complete furniture of one of these rooms as it
still exists at Badminton. The walls are hung with a paper made in China, on
which bamboos are depicted the full height of the room; these are
interspersed with camelias, jonquils and other flowers, amidst which fly
pheasants and other birds all in brilliant colours; on the walls hang gilt
looking-glasses of delicate design and fine execution in the Chinese
Chippendale taste. The most elaborate of these is shown in Fig. 699. The
outside lines are of fantastic shape, enclosing glass compartments divided
by carved framings; in the centre is a projecting canopy approached by a

FIG. 700. *Black Lacquer Bed*. Property of the DUKE OF BEAUFORT.

double flight of steps and a rococo balustrade; the canopy is supported by six slender columns of eccentric but graceful design, and above it sits a grotesque Chinese figure wearing a pagoda-shaped hat; a pagoda roof hung with two bells completes this elaborate structure. The whole of the carving is most deicate and graceful and possesses its original gilding.

Fig. 700 represents the bed. The canopy, which is of wood, decorated in black and gold lacquer, rises rapidly in pagoda form, terminating at its apex in a Chinese railing surmounted by a fantastic ornament; at the four corners, finials scrolling upwards in pure Chinese taste, support gilded dragons, carved with great spirit and character; the tester is tile-edged in the manner of all pagoda roofs, and the cornice is of the icicle pattern so frequently seen on mirrors of later Chippendale work; the back is a bold open lattice contained in a lacquered framing, originally no doubt backed by chintz. The posts are simple, in order to display their lacquered decoration. The original curtains and valances are missing, but were probably of fine oriental chintz. To the right and left of this lacquer bed are mirrors, and Fig. 701 is one of these. The dressing-table (Fig. 702) is of knee-hole shape, the opening having four drawers behind cupboard doors; the front, sides and top are closely decorated with a lacquer-work of rocks and trees, no figures, birds or animals being introduced into the design. On this dressing-table once stood a silver toilet service, decorated in Chinese taste; it bears a hall-mark of 1685, and may have belonged to an earlier room in this style, for there are seventeenth-century Chinese papers and lacquer furniture in the adjoining apartments. Three pieces of this toilet service are shown in Fig. 703.

The chairs (Fig. 704) that accompany the bed are of Chinese lattice-work of

FIG. 702. *Black Lacquer Dressing-table*. Height, 2 feet 9 inches; length, 4 feet 2 inches; depth, 2 feet 6 inches. Property of the DUKE OF BEAUFORT.

FIG. 701. *Gilt Mirror on Chinese Wall-paper*. Height, 10 feet; width, 4 feet 4 inches. Property of the DUKE OF BEAUFORT.

FIG. 703. *Part of Silver Toilet-service*. Property of W. JAMES, Esq.

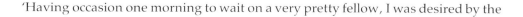

simple geometrical design, and lacquered in black and gold; the cresting is of pagoda outline, and the return sides to all the lattice-work are painted red, an addition which gives great relief to this furniture. In th example (Fig. 705), of about 1758, a pagoda motive pervades the entire back, even the corners of the uprights are carved in this manner, and the entire surface is lacquered in black and gold; the eagle headings to the latter are seldom found on a chair of so late a date.

The four little china cases in black and gold lacquer, one of which is given in Fig. 706, are also from Badminton. A pagoda roof hung with four bells is supported on two delicate twisted columns, and with a lattice-work balustrade forms the top compartment; the sides of the centre division are solid, but applied with a Chinese fret, whilst those of the lower compartment are of open work. These china cases formed part of the same set as the commode chest of drawers (Fig. 707), another rare and highly finished piece of lacquer. Here the top is of undulating shape, backed by a gallery of Chinese railing; the front is divided into three compartments of drawers lacquered with landscapes, buildings and figures, the side drawers being enclosed behind lattice-work doors, which give great variety to the surface; the handles are of the goffered type found upon mahogany furniture of about 1760. On the straight legs of the stand a herring-boning of lacquer is introduced that can also be noticed on the legs of the china case (Fig. 708). The returns of the lattice-work in these pieces are painted red, and correspond to the chairs of this interesting set. That Chinese taste in the decoration of bedrooms was not confined to important houses is shown by a description in the *Connoisseur* of 25 April 1755, of a fashionable 'spark's' apartments:

'Having occasion one morning to wait on a very pretty fellow, I was desired by the

FIG. 704. *Black Lacquer Chair*. Property of the DUKE OF BEAUFORT.

FIG. 705. *Black Lacquer Chair*. Property of Messrs J. Mallett and Son.

FIG. 706. *Black Lacquer China Case*. Height, 4 feet 2 inches; width, 1 foot 8 inches; depth, 10 inches. Property of the Duke of Beaufort.

FIG. 707. *Black Lacquer Commode Chest of Drawers*. Height, 2 feet 10 inches; length, 4 feet 8 inches. Property of the Duke of Beaufort.

valet de chambre to walk into the dressing-room, as his master was not stirring. I was accordingly shown into a neat little chamber hung round with Indian paper and adorned with several little images of pagods and bramins, and vessels of Chelsea China, in which were set various coloured sprigs of artificial flowers. But the toilette most excited my admiration; where I found everything was intended to be agreeable to the Chinese taste. A looking-glass, enclosed in a whimsical frame of Chinese paling, stood upon a japan table over which was spread a coverlid of the finest chintz.'

Another example of lacquered bedroom furniture can be seen in the clothes chest from Blenheim (Fig. 708), of about the same date. The gold lacquer, representing islands covered with trees, rocks and buildings, is almost flat in relief but extremely careful, the black ground being particularly brilliant and smooth. The design very clearly shows the disconnected attempt at irregular composition generally apparent in the late English adaptations of oriental drawing; each detail is so isolated that the charming irregularity of balance found on earlier specimens is lost. The spindle-shaped ornaments introduced on the border are of no definite style, and infer that lacquer was losing its true oriental character.

Many tables, screens and chairs of this flat lacquer were made. Fig. 709 is a chair of a set from Houghton, in which the old hoop shape of the panelled back is preserved, although the legs conform to the straight type of 1760. Another instance of highly furnished flat lacquer is shown in Fig. 710, forming part of a set of three china cabinets, probably made by Ince and Mayhew, as the design occurs in their book published 1768. The construction is of mahogany, lacquered in black and gold; the gallery and cresting is a fine Chinese railing gilt, centring in a fretwork pagoda surmounting an arch of Gothic tracery; below this is a china case opening in two glazed doors, the framing decorated with small and finely painted panels of flat lacquer. The divisions to the glazing are gilt, and the base of the cabinet and the top of the stand open in drawers faced with a gilt card-cutting on a black ground, framed in fine lacquer-work borders; the legs, straight and slight, are covered with a small design of trees, rocks and plants, and present a highly finished and delicate appearance. Fig. 711 is the corner cupboard that completes this set; the design on the framing is scattered and disconnected as in all cases of this late lacquer, but the composition of the picture on the lower cupboard is rather better than generally found at this time, and the dainty execution of the three pieces in a great measure atones for the want of picturesque originality found in the earlier lacquer.

The State bedrooms at Nostell Priory are other fine examples of Chinese decoration and exceedingly interesting. Their date is a few years later than the room at Badminton already described. The walls are hung with a Chinese paper of rose-coloured and white peonies, chrysanthemums, irises

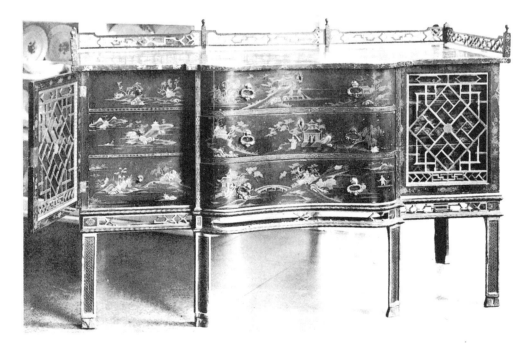

FIG. 708. *Black Lacquer Clothes-chest*. Height, 3 feet 2 inches; length, 4 feet 6 inches. Property of the DUKE OF MARLBOROUGH.

FIG. 709. *Black Lacquer Chair*. Height, 3 feet 9 inches. Property of the MARQUESS OF CHOLMONDELEY.

and tropical birds on a pale-green ground. The furniture to this room is of pea-green lacquer decorated with gold and silver designs. Lacquered furniture made under the direction of the brothers Adam is extremely rare, but there is little doubt that these specimens were made when this celebrated firm was remodelling the decorations of the house. In the commode, Fig. 712, the decoration is a strange mixture of Adam and oriental design; the front opens in three doors enclosing a series of drawers; the ground-work throughout is of a delicate green, lacquered in gold, silver and a little red, with British inspirations of Chinese life and landscapes; the carved Adam garrya pendant at the four corners, the ovals of the side-doors and fluted taper legs have nothing oriental in their character, but the proportions and colours are so cleverly blended, that this divergence of style does not seem amiss. In Fig. 713 the pattern of the beautiful wall-paper can be seen behind a wardrobe commode of about the same date as the last example, although of rather different style. The front, formed of two serpentine doors, opens on a series of sliding shelves, and is lacquered with the design of a tea-garden in gold and silver on a pea-green ground, in higher relief than is usual at this period; the lower portion opens in two drawers decorated to match the doors, and the sides are lacquered with designs of conventional Chinese birds and animals; the simple cornice and channelled frieze, with the introduction of garrya pendants at the corners, suggest a date about 1770. Fig. 714 shows the mantelpiece and mirror in this interesting room; they are of pure Adam style, and correspond in date to the furniture. Fig. 715 is a quaint wall lantern of brass, of about the date 1770, probably made in connection with these rooms. The top is of pagoda shape and surmounts the glass arranged to contain a lamp, now replaced by a modern electric fitting; the base is formed of a Chinese fretwork finishing in bells and pendants.

The very beautiful lacquer commode designed by Adam for Osterley is illustrated in Fig. 716; here the treatment is far more elaborate and severe than in the preceding specimens. The serpentine and hexagonal front is divided by six pilasters, decorated with pendants and headed by rams' heads and garrya swags, finely modelled in gilt brass. The top is banded with a guilloch moulding of the same material; the front opening in one long door is ornamented with fine black and gold lacquer of Chinese warriors in a landscape, the top drawer and sides being decorated with smaller designs. The feet are vase-shaped and fluted, standing upon the tapered block introduced by Adam on furniture. The effect of the whole piece is exceedingly rich, and its finish is remarkable.

Osterley, originally a Tudor house, was rebuilt by Francis Child about 1760 from designs by Robert Adam, who also designed most of the furniture. Horace Walpole, on visiting Osterley in 1773, says in one of his letters:

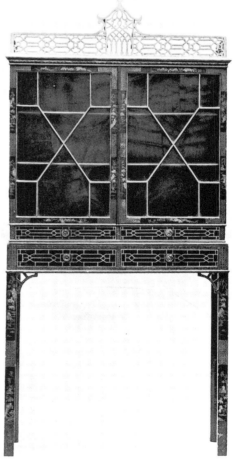

FIG. 710. *Black Lacquer China Case*. Property of MRS ASSHETON SMITH.

FIG. 712. *Green Lacquer Commode.* Height, 3 feet; length, 4 feet 8 inches; depth, 2 feet. Property of LORD ST OSWALD.

FIG. 711. *Black Lacquer Corner China Case.* Property of MRS ASSHETON SMITH.

FIG. 713. *Green Lacquer Commode.* Height, 5 feet; width, 4 feet. Property of LORD ST OSWALD.

FIG. 715. *Brass Wall-lantern*. Property of LORD ST OSWALD.

FIG. 714. *Gilt White and Green Overmantel and Mirror on Chinese Wall-paper*. Mantelpiece, height, 5 feet 6 inches; width, 6 feet 2 inches. Mirror, extreme height, 4 feet; width, 5 feet. Property at NOSTELL PRIORY.

'On Friday we went to see – oh the palace of palaces – and yet a palace sans crown, sans coronet; but such expense! such taste! such profusion! There is a hall, library, breakfast-room, eating-room, all *chefs d'œuvres* of Adam; a gallery one hundred and thirty feet long, and a drawing-room worthy of Eve before the fall. Mrs. Child's dressing-room is full of pictures, gold filigree, China and Japan. So is all the house; the chairs are taken from antique lyres and make a charming harmony.'

The top of a table (Fig. 717) is an interesting, late example of lacquer, being of about the date 1775, and of a light buff colour; the decoration is in brown and black, etched with a little gold; the drawing is extremely feeble in execution and shows the decadence of this art, which, almost abandoned towards the close of the eighteenth century, reappeared at intervals during the early part of the nineteenth in the form of work-tables, whatnots and tea-trays.

On the walls of small rooms, in place of real Chinese paper, a so-called Paper Mosaic work was sometimes employed, and made by ladies of fashion. This consisted of paper plants, butterflies and birds cut out and pasted on to a coloured foundation. Lady Mary Coke, in her diary, 1772, writes:

'I called on the Duchess of Norfolk, who I found sorting butterflies cut out of indien paper for a room she is going to furnish.'

Another favourite form of decoration for small rooms was the ornamenting of ceilings and cornices, lustres and candlesticks, with shells.

FIG. 716. *Lacquer Commode.* Height, 3 feet; length, 5 feet. Property of the EARL OF JERSEY.

'Mrs. Delany excelled in shell work and attained to such perfection in it, that she executed cornices of the most beautiful designs, formed of shells, which when painted or coloured over appeared like the finest carving, but for smaller objects like the lustre, etc., they were left in their natural colour, which, arranged by her, had the most beautiful effect, and united the brilliancy of enamel with the inimitable tracery and harmony of nature.'

These curious attempts by amateurs must have been more peculiar than beautiful, but were no doubt only called into a brief existence through the various eccentricities of the many Chinese crazes which have left a lasting mark on our furniture by introducing Chinese-Chippendale and English lacquer.

FIG. 717. *Lacquer Top of Commode.*

CHAPTER II

EFORE leaving the subject of what is commonly known as Chippendale furniture, it is necessary to give a few examples of this style, such as clocks, mirrors and commodes inlaid with various coloured woods that were contemporary with the early designs of Adam and his followers.

In Chippendale's bill, dated 1770, for the furniture supplied to Nostell Priory is an entry for the commode (Fig. 718). Although these English commodes of cabriole form are rare, the internal construction, the character of the inlay, and the inferior quality of the metal-work is unmistakable and conclusive of their origin. In the Nostell commode the undulating form compares favourably with good French work of the time; the front and sides are inlaid with graceful garlands of flowers in coloured woods upon a ground of stained sycamore, commonly called Hairwood or Harewood, and beneath these are inlaid classical vases supporting a broken column in the style of Adam, the whole being surrounded by a dark rosewood border of late Louis XV design. The inlaid top is edged with a brass guilloch moulding, brass fittings also decorating the shoulders, feet and lower edge of the doors. The inside is veneered with Hungarian ash stained grey, much resembling watered silk of that colour, then so fashionable; the handles are English in type, and of the kind employed on ordinary mahogany furniture.

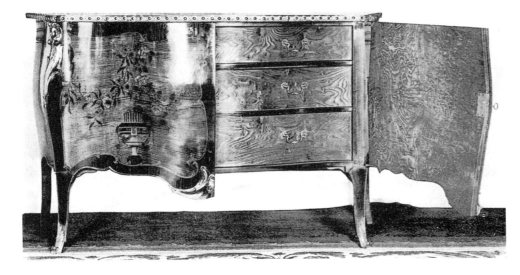

FIG. 718. *Inlaid Commode*. Height, 3 feet; length, 5 feet 2 inches. Property of LORD ST OSWALD.

FIG. 719. *Inlaid Commode*. Height, 2 feet 10 inches; length, 4 feet 2 inches. Property of the MARQUESS OF SALISBURY.

FIG. 720. *Inlaid Commode.* Property of the DUKE OF DEVONSHIRE.

FIG. 721. *Inlaid Commode.* Property of W. H. LEVER, Esq.

Fig. 719, from Hatfield House, is another brilliant example of these interesting commodes, evidently made by Chippendale, for the metal fittings to the top, shoulders, base and feet are cast from the same moulds as those of the last specimen. The front and sides are veneered, with panels of mahogany inlaid with coloured garlands and baskets of flowers, surrounded with broad borders of tulip-wood and small triangular panels of holly knots; where the doors meet, a trophy of Cupid's bow, quiver and torch is introduced, a detail much used by Adam; the legs are rather shorter than those of the preceding commode, but the same brass feet have been adapted to their use.

It can be noticed that the inlay and metal-work of these two commodes, although graceful and full of character, is rather coarser than that found upon good contemporary French work. A third example is given on Plate XLVII. Here the whole ground is a veneer of yew, inlaid with a serpentine

FIG. 722. *Gilt Mirror.* Width, 5 feet 6 inches. Property of MESSRS J. MALLETT AND SON.

FIG. 723. *Gilt Mirror.* Height, 5 feet 3 inches; width, 2 feet 7 inches. Property of CHARLES TUDWAY, Esq.

scrolled design of light wood, enclosing a bouquet of flowers; the top, base and shoulders are edged with a metal ornamentation of similar character to that used on the preceding commodes.

From the resemblance of Fig. 719 to Fig. 718 it is certain that inlaid commodes of foreign taste were introduced and made here by Chippendale, and that the development of this article of furniture, which later became so fashionable, was probably due to his introduction. The next step in their evolution is shown in Fig. 720, from Hardwick. Here the serpentine front is maintained, but the base is straight and rests upon ordinary bracket feet; the brass fittings are omitted, and the motive of the inlay is more or less in the style of Adam. The frieze is decorated with a large chain pattern of mahogany inlaid on satinwood, and opens as a drawer; beneath this are cupboard doors (enclosing drawers), inlaid with branches and swags of garrya in brilliant green on a satinwood ground, surrounded by a broad border of mahogany; a narrow feathering of brown and yellow inlay finishes the base.

The bellied front and cabriole legs of the earlier specimens is preserved in Fig. 721, but the front opens in three drawers, which are decorated with a coarse inlay of mahogany and satinwood on a sycamore ground. The central panel, representing a classical urn surrounded by sprays of flowers, is significant of the date which in both pieces is from 1770 to 1775.

A very great number of mirrors of the school of Chippendale still exist. These are of open and often fantastic ornament carved in soft wood and gilt. This style replaced the solid and unperforated frame surmounted by a pediment that was in fashion during the first half of the century. Fig. 722 represents the French rococo type of about 1750. It is divided into three compartments, the centre rising in a series of C scrolls, upon which is perched a crow with a bunch of grapes; the fox, out of all proportion to the bird, looks upwards from the lower portion of the frame. The carving is full of spirit, and the interlacement of the C scrolling ingenious. Fig. 723 is a more ordinary mirror of about the same date, with the pagoda motive as a cresting, the bells being repeated on the scrolled finials of the corners.

FIG. 724. *Gilt Mirror*. Height, 7 feet 6 inches; width, 4 feet. Property of CHARLES TUDWAY, Esq.

FIG. 725. *Gilt Mirror*. Property of SIR FRANCIS BURDETT, Bart.

FIG. 726. *Gilt Mirror*. Property of WEEDON GROSSMITH, Esq.

Although coarse in execution, this mirror is extremely effective, possessing great originality of line.

Another mirror of about 1758 is Fig. 724. Here the scrolled tracery is extremely light and graceful, becoming heavier in its proportions towards the top, and finishing in a bold trefoil of acanthus.

The mirror (Fig. 725) is of great interest, combining the florid C scrolls of Chippendale with the classical reticence of Adam; the oval, the honeysuckle finial, the vase, swags and pateræ being of this late style. It is therefore a very representative transitional piece of about the date 1763. In the background can be seen a good specimen of a Chinese paper, the marble mantelpiece beneath being of Adam design. A later mirror and its mantelpiece from the house, which this master is said to have built for himself in Bedford Square, is shown in Fig. 726. Here the structure is architectural, the detail delicate but severe, and in the full style of about 1770; a classical urn and two sphinxes form the cresting of this mirror, and in it can be seen reflected the ceiling of the room. The mantelpiece is of white marble, and probably executed by an Italian workman.

Tall clock-cases continued to be made in walnut and oak until 1725, the

FIG. 727. *Painted and Lacquered Clock.* Height, 7 feet. Property of PERCIVAL GRIFFITHS, Esq.

FIG. 728. *Mahogany Clock.* Property of the HON LADY CHARLOTTE MARIA NORTH and R. EDEN DICKSON, Esq.

FIG. 729. *Mahogany Clock.* Height, 8 feet 8 inches; width, 2 feet 2 inches. Property of H. PERCY DEAN, Esq.

FIG. 730. *Mahogany Clock.* Height, 8 feet 2 inches. Property of LADY RUSSELL.

latter being often decorated in lacquer or painted with pastoral designs. Fig. 727 represents a clock-case lacquered and painted with Watteau subjects in colour on a dark green ground, the drawing of the figures being unusually good for this class of work. Watteau was resident in this country in 1720, and no doubt this kind of decoration was inspired by his work. It is interesting to notice that the centre band of lacquer across the door of the clock repeats the design of the brass-work on the dial.

A large and finely proportioned clock in mahogany, a few years later than the last example, is shown in Fig. 728. The case is without decoration save for the introduction of some reeded panel mouldings and the usual fluted columns to the hood and sides; these are again repeated on the base, possibly with the idea of reducing its width. The mechanism is most elaborate and complete, being a fine example of eighteenth-century clockmaking.

Fig. 729 represents a finely carved specimen in mahogany of about 1745. The heading consists of a scrolled pediment centring in a vase-shaped lamp, supported on open fretwork pilasters; the body is plain but enclosed between three-quarter columns perforated in the Chinese manner; the bricking at the corners of the base is characteristic of Chippendale's cases, but does not harmonise with the rest of the ornament. Fig. 730 is a clock of rather later date. The mouldings of the heading are elaborate, and the double hollow to the door, surmounted by a carved lunette, is a rare feature. It can be noticed that the bases of these tall clocks increase in height towards the middle of the century.

Fig. 731 is a gracefully proportioned clock of about 1765, with a hood of pagoda shape, supported on extremely slender Corinthian columns. The body is panelled with plain mouldings cornered with pateræ of the period.

Cartel and Bracket clocks, during the reigns of George I and II, had to a great measure taken the place of grandfather clocks in rooms, and this change in fashion may account for the small number of highly finished tall

FIG. 731. *Mahogany Clock.* Property of W. JAMES, Esq.

FIG. 732. *Mahogany Cartel Clock*. Height, 1 foot 4 inches.

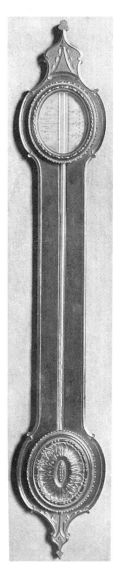

FIG. 733. *Mahogany Barometer*. Property of ALFRED DAVIS, Esq.

clocks that appear to have been between 1720 and 1750. Fig. 732 is a Bracket clock in mahogany of about 1750, made by Chippendale and illustrated in the first edition of the *Director*. The ingenious and elaborate top is of dome shape, supported at the corners by plain columns resting upon double feet, clothed and scrolled with acanthus. The carving is of fine execution, and the wood is of a rich dark brown.

A barometer-case (Fig. 733) shows the influence of Adam in the originality of its shape, which is both ingenious and practical; the date of this is about 1765, and is a good example of careful and minute carving.

Robert Adam, whilst studying architecture in Italy, based his style on that of his friend Piranesi, the Roman architect. The latter published a book of designs on decoration and furniture in the classical taste, dedicating it to Adam. In comparing the designs of Piranesi and Adam it is at once apparent how the former originated and the latter improved and adapted this Italian style to English requirements. There are pages of Piranesi's drawings that Adam reproduced fearlessly as his own, enlarging and simplifying the details of the originals; originals that had in their turn been taken from Estruscan, Greek and late Roman motives, for the art of decoration is but intelligent plagiarism. Full of his new discoveries, Adam returned to England in 1758, was appointed architect to the King in 1762, and introduced a style in architecture, decoration and furniture that influenced taste for nearly fifty years; the motives of late Chippendale, Hepplewhite, Sheraton, Shearer and even Empire being the outcome of his teaching and style.

In his first designs for furniture Adam combined the foliated C scroll with the classical detail so generally associated with his name, but soon commenced to influence the manufacture of furniture of simple and restrained taste, without inlay and with but little carving. The small escritoire with drawers (Plate XLVIII) is a good example of this quiet style. The upper portion opens as a writing-flap, and is headed with delicately carved festoons of garrya. This is divided by a carved moulding from the lower portion, which opens in seven drawers, cockbeaded and lined with ebony; long pendants to match the festoons decorate the corners of the serpentine front, which is most successful in its grace and proportions.

Another of these escritoires, a few years later in date, is Fig. 734, interesting for its double gallery of carved fretwork; the top compartment forms a writing-desk, and is decorated with light carving to match the top. The drawers are perfectly plain, fitted with brass handles of about 1770. The legs are of short taper form.

At the beginning of George the Third's reign, ordinary tall mahogany writing-cabinets were still in the form of a chest of drawers, surmounted by a glazed cupboard for books or china, and corresponded in shape to those of 1750, with the exception of the oblique writing-flap, which after this date was shaped like an ordinary drawer front, and let down by the means of two curved metal runners. A great many of these cabinets were made without any carving, except on the cornice and the framings to the glass, but it is not until after 1775 that they are found veneered with the satinwood that then became so fashionable. The low writing-bureau of earlier Georgian shape was also made in plain mahogany, and occasionally veneered with such woods as amboyna, maple and pollarded oak, but very seldom with satinwood. In the case of maple and oak, woods full of knots and veinings, an ebony stain was rubbed into the figure. This, when scraped, left a mottled yellow and black surface, somewhat resembling marble, that so disguises the character of the wood that many are puzzled by its appearance. Fig. 735 is one of these bureaux, of the shape so often made in mahogany, but here veneered with this artificially treated wood.

Chests of drawers are sometimes met with treated in this manner, and a barometer in the Guardroom of Hampton Court Palace is veneered with this stained wood. The most important form of furniture used for writing was still a table of pedestal shape. These were of mahogany, plain, except for the slight panel mouldings that were cornered with small round or oval paterae of Adam design; but as the taste for inlay succeeded that of carving, these tables, like all other furniture, were sometimes carried to an elaborate degree of finish in that respect. Fig. 736 is an early example of 1768, designed by

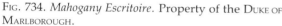

FIG. 734. *Mahogany Escritoire*. Property of the DUKE OF MARLBOROUGH.

FIG. 735. *Pollarded Oak Writing-bureau*. Height, 3 feet 2 inches; length, 2 feet 4 inches; depth, 1 foot 6 inches. Property of S. CAMPBELL CORY, Esq.

Adam, with a corresponding set of chairs and tables for the saloon at Osterley.

The top, covered with leather, and surrounded with a granulated banding of brass, is supported by tapering pilasters of rosewood, inlaid towards their bases with an acanthus leaf, and headed by open-work trusses of gilt brass, these frame drawers, and pedestal cupboards, veneered with sycamore, and inlaid with an open and classical design in delicately coloured woods; the pateræ at the corners of the panels are also of gilt brass.

On early specimens of this inlaid furniture the scale of the inlay is large, and the details are well defined: as the fashion proceeded, the ornament became smaller, more intricate, and the design more closely connected in its lines. Classical heads, full-length figures, broken columns and vases, were at first inlaid as centres to the surrounding marqueterie, which took the form of simple laurel wreaths, or a series of plain bandings in differently coloured woods; these very shortly developed at the hands of Adam, who was responsible for their first introduction into honeysuckled arabesques or foliated scrolls, springing from vases of fanned pateræ; borders of inlay surrounding these centres were copied from classical friezes; Etruscan vases, and Roman mosaics, rose, sycamore (hairwood) and satinwood forming the usual background. When first stained, these inlays were so

FIG. 736. *Inlaid Writing-table with Metal Mountings*. Height, 2 feet 6 inches; length, 6 feet; depth, 3 feet 2 inches. Property of the EARL OF JERSEY.

Fig. 737. *Inlaid Rosewood Writing-table with Metal Mountings.* Height, 2 feet 9 inches; length, 6 feet 10 inches; depth, 4 feet. Property of the EARL OF HAREWOOD.

Fig. 738. *Detail of Door of Inlaid Writing-table.* Property of the EARL OF HAREWOOD.

brilliant, that to an eye accustomed to their present faded condition, the original colour would almost seem crude.

It is somewhat surprising to find that Chippendale had in his old age adapted his taste to the new fashion, and that his firm carried out the inlaid furniture at Osterley and Harewood. Both houses owe their magnificent specimens to the happy combination of Robert Adam and Thomas Chippendale.

Fig. 739. *End of Writing-table*. Property of the Earl of Harewood.

The library table (Fig. 737), in many ways resembling the last example, represents this combination at its best. The top, 6 feet 10 inches in length, is covered with crimson morocco, to which age has given a fine deep tone; this edged with a bold acanthus moulding in brass, and supported by a frieze inlaid with rose and green stained pearwood, the design shaded in great finish; the taper pilasters which decorate the front, back and corners are headed by metal rams' heads from which hang garrya swags of the same cast and chased work. The doors (Fig. 738) are inlaid with beautifully drawn vases and foliated ornaments of classical taste in holly and other stained woods, on a light rosewood ground, framed in bands of satin and tulip-wood, and cornered with metal pateræ. The ends, one of which is given in Fig. 739, are of similar finish. The whole scheme of this inlay and metal work is extremely beautiful and broad in effect, and though composed of so many various woods, the general tone of the table is now of a delicate fawn colour, forming a perfect harmony with the rich gold of the mountings; it is unlikely that any English inlaid furniture of higher quality was ever made.

Library furniture was evidently considered of great importance in well-appointed houses of this time. Mrs Delany, whilst visiting Lord Bute in 1774, wrote to Bernard Granville as follows:

'You then go into the library, three or five rooms, one very large, one well pro-portioned in the middle, each end divided by pillars in which recesses are chimneys, and a large square room at each end, which, when the doors are thrown open, make it appear like one large room or gallery. I never saw so magnificent or so pleasant a library, extreamly well lighted, and nobly furnished with everything that can improve and entertain men of learning and virtue.'

A plain but very necessary piece of library furniture, folding up into the compass of a small table, is shown in Fig. 740; these steps are of mahogany, and though somewhat frail in appearance, make a perfectly reliable library ladder. Other forms of escritoires were adopted in the drawing-rooms and ladies' parlours. One of these, called in 1770 an upright writing-commode, is shown in Fig. 741. The shape, almost a reversion to the walnut scrutoires of William and Anne, though common in France and Holland during the latter part of the eighteenth century, was not popular in England after 1720. This example forms part of a set of inlaid satinwood furniture made for Hare-wood by Chippendale and designed by Adam, in 1773, and is fine colour and execution; the introduction of the black oval panels on the writing-flap and cupboard door, inlaid with a recumbent figure and classical urn, are very effective, and the brilliant green of the surrounding inlay forms a beautiful contrast to the golden satinwood ground. The shading and model-ling to the ornaments and figures on all this inlaid furniture was produced by

Fig. 740. *Mahogany Library Steps*. Property of Percival Griffiths, Esq.

FIG. 741. *Satinwood and Inlaid Commode.*
Height, 4 feet 6 inches; length, 2 feet 9
inches. Property of the EARL OF HAREWOOD.

FIG. 742. *Satinwood Inlaid Dressing Commode.*
Height, 3 feet 2 inches; length, 7 feet 2
inches. Property of the EARL OF HAREWOOD.

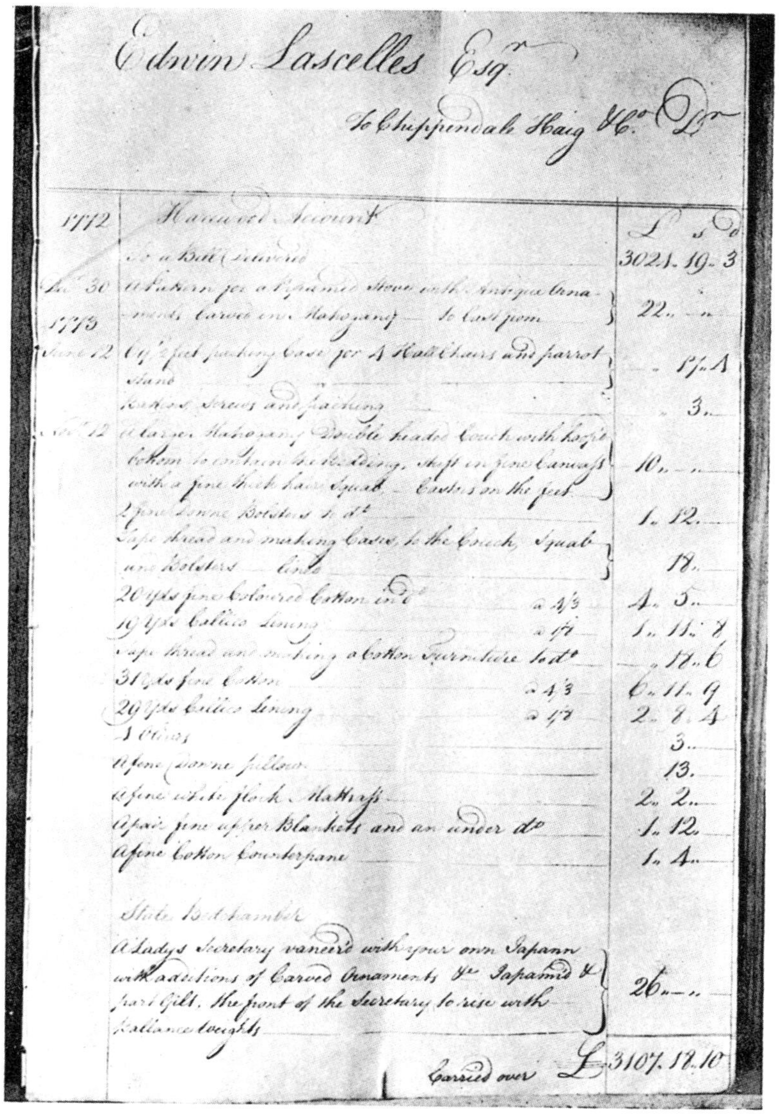

Fig. 743. *A Bill of Chippendale, Haig & Co.* Property of the EARL OF HAREWOOD.

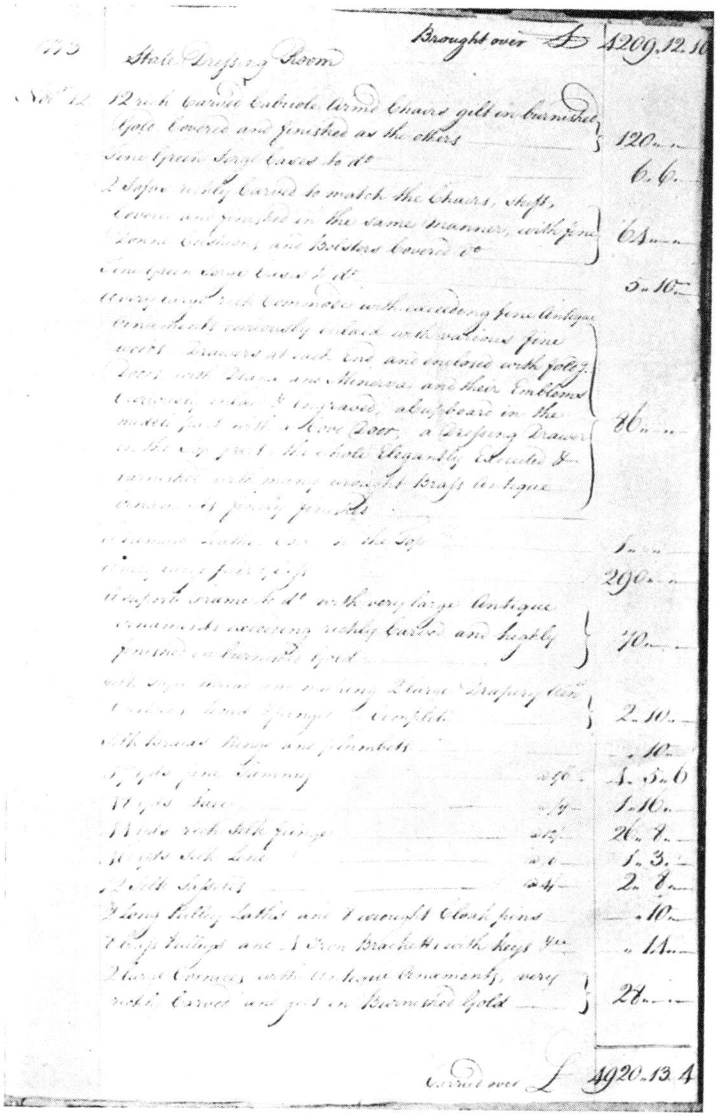

Fig. 744.

burning the surface of a light wood, such as pear, holly or poplar, with hot sand – the gradation of tone being regulated by the depth of the deposit.

Perfection of design, skill and finish can be seen in the dressing-table commode, Fig. 742; the veneered ground is of the finest satinwood, inlaid with an open design of swags and wreaths of once brilliant green garrya husks, now faded to a light olive; the wreaths frame seated figures of Minerva and Diana, inlaid in coloured woods and ivory on a black ground; carved satinwood beadings run down the face of the pilasters, which are headed with gilt metal leaves, and terminate in round taper legs on which the metal leaves are repeated. The concave lunette forming the kneehole is a masterpiece of cabinet-making, being composed of narrow mahogany staves shaped barrel-wise; on this curved surface the veneer and inlay has not moved since the piece was made, and the lustre in the satinwood produce reflections similar to those seen on a golden or brass basin. This superb satinwood commode was also designed by Adam for Harewood, and made by Chippendale and Haig in 1773.

Some pages from a bill of this firm to Edwin Lascelles, Esqre, Lord Harewood's ancestor, are given in Figs 743, 744 and 745, and amongst the items mentioned is this piece of furniture:

'*Nov.* 12, 1773. – A vy large rich Commode with exceeding fine antique Ornaments, curiously inlaid with various fine woods. Drawers at each End and enclosed with foldg Doors, with Diana and Minerva and their Emblems Curiously inlaid and Engraved a cupboard in the middle part with a Cove Door, a Dressing Drawer in the Top part, the whole Elegantly Executed and varnished, with many wrought Brass Antique ornaments finely finished, £86.'

To preserve the top a damask leather cover was also supplied at £1.

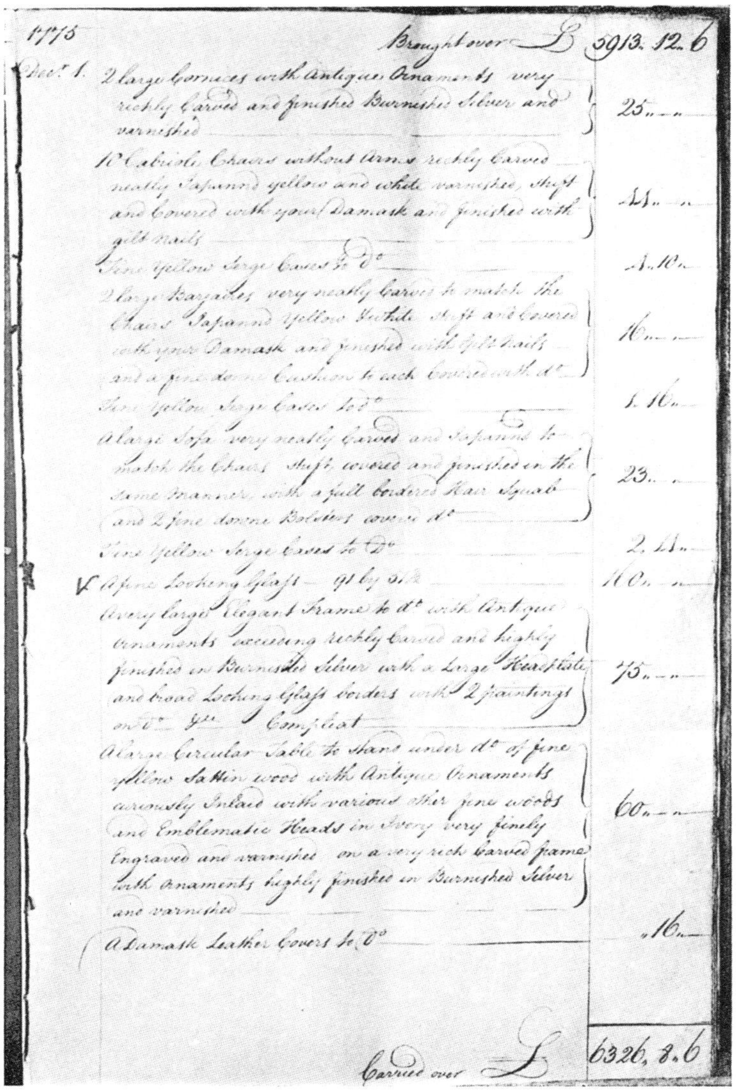

Fig. 745.

Fig. 746. *Satinwood Writing-cabinet*. Property of L. Fleischmann, Esq.

Descriptions of furniture supplied by Chippendale in his bills leave nothing to be desired; he is quite aware of its excellence, and never loses an opportunity of enlarging on its merits. It may here be interesting to call attention to the next item on this account:

'A very large pier Glass, £290.'

This would represent about £800 of our current money, and shows the great cost of very large sheets of glass in those days, for this sum does not include the frame, described as

'A superb Frame to ditto, with very large antique ornaments exceeding richly Carved and highly finished in burnished Gold,'

and charged separately at £70. Although these bills prove that Chippendale was veneering with satinwood very soon after its introduction in 1765, when it was ordinarily used as an inlay, it is more than surprising to find these elaborate effects of inlaid satinwood furniture, which are generally attributed to Sheraton, brought to such perfection twenty years before his arrival in London. Sheraton, in his *Cabinet Dictionary* of 1803, alludes to the use of this wood for the past twenty years, but does not recognise the achievements of earlier masters in this style. It is therefore probable that Chippendale and his firm led the taste in satinwood as they had already dictated the fashions in mahogany, and that much of the originality in inlaid furniture, attributed to other makers, is due to Chippendale and his connection with Adam.

Satinwood is cut from the tree *Chloroxylon swietenia*. The best comes from Central and South India, is short and broad in the figure, and with age attains a brilliant warm yellow. It is extremely hard, and gives out a curious aromatic scent when scraped. East India satinwood was generally used upon all the finest furniture; that cut in the West Indies is paler, although more distinct and horizontal in figure, but possesses neither the same lustre nor value as the former wood. Tulip-wood was much used in conjunction with satinwood, and generally formed the bandings and borders to inlaid furniture. It was applied on the cross, and when new, is distinctly pink in colour.

Zebra-wood, cut from the *Connarus guianensis*, comes from British Guiana, and is also much used for borders and bandings; it is a light yellow brown wood with dark vertical lines which almost give the appearance of a zebra stripe. Kingwood is a darker and redder wood of the same character, a species of Dalbergia, and marked with fine lines of a darker colour.

The green-stained wood, so much in favour as an inlay for garrya husks and leaves during the last thirty years of the eighteenth century, was beech or pear stained to a brilliant colour by an oxide of copper. This has now faded to pale olive tones, but the original brilliance of colour can be discovered by scraping the surface with a knife.

Harewood, or hairwood, is the same cutting of sycamore as that used in the manufacture of violins, and consequently termed fiddleback. This was stained an ashen grey, which, with age, became somewhat golden in colour.

Amboyna, a species of Pterocarpus, is a wood full of eyes and knots, much resembling bird's-eye maple, but of smaller and closer figure; the colour is a reddish brown, and furniture veneered with this wood was highly prized. In conjunction with these, walnut, yew, holly, pear, laburnum, cherry, ebony, rose and other woods were used for the different inlays that were considered so important in this late Georgian school of furniture.

A good example of plain East India satinwood is shown in the lady's writing-cabinet (Fig. 746) mounted upon taper legs. This is entirely de-

Fig. 747. *Rosewood Inlaid Sideboard-table and Wine-cooler with Metal Mounts*. Height, 2 feet 9 inches; length, 6 feet 6 inches. Property of the Earl of Harewood.

Fig. 748. *Detail of Wine-cooler*. Height, 2 feet 3 inches; length, 2 feet 6 inches. Property of the Earl of Harewood.

Fig. 749. *Rosewood Inlaid Sideboard Pedestal and Urn with Metal Mountings.* Height (in all), 6 feet. Pedestal, 1 foot 6 inches square. Property of the EARL OF HAREWOOD.

Fig. 750 (*above right*). *Detail of Sideboard Pedestal.* Height, 2 feet 11 inches; 1 foot 6 inches square. Property of the EARL OF HAREWOOD.

pendent for its decorative charm on the lustre of the veneer and perfect simplicity of its shape. It is interesting as an early and quiet example of the delicate and somewhat effeminate furniture that prevailed towards the end of the century, a period producing much that was graceful and charming, but at times trivial, and tinctured with a sentimental prettiness which formerly had been unknown.

It is unwise to assign an individual maker to such a piece, but it is probable that Seddon was making a great deal of fashionable furniture as early as 1770. Some writers have placed the work of this firm at a later date, but the following passage from the *Annual Register* for 1768 proves their mistake:

'A dreadful fire burnt down London House, formerly the residence of the Bishops of London, in Aldersgate Street, now occupied by Mr. Seddon, one of the most eminent cabinet-makers in London. The damage is computed at £20,000.'

This sum represents about £60,000 of our current money, large and valuable stock-in-trade for a maker to hold whose furniture is not even called after his name, and who must have been contemporary with Chippendale. In spite of the many similar and important firms of cabinet-makers turning out quantities of work in London about 1770, the furnishing of small country-houses was still scanty, and it can be seen from the following details of domestic country life that luxuries in middle-class life had increased there but little since the time of Anne. Gardiner, in *Music and Friends*, states that but 'few houses in the country possessed harpsichords and spinets, and that so late as 1782 no more than three such instruments existed in the town and neighbourhood of Leicester'. In Cowper's correspondence he mentions that a table, a looking-glass and a few chairs constituted the furniture of an ordinary country parlour, that easy-chairs were still very, very far from common, and that clocks in such a household were limited to one eight-day that stood in a corner of the principal sitting-room, or very often a cuckoo clock that hung upon the wall.

On the mantelpiece of such rooms stood two brass candlesticks, with a pair of snuffers on a tray side by side with a tinder and flint. Box-beds in some of the rooms were still largely used, the air being carefully excluded from their occupants during the night by means of sliding doors. Roasting-jacks were a luxury, and such cooking was done by spits, the wheels being turned by a servant or by a dog trained for the purpose.

W. Sydney, in *England and the English in the Eighteenth Century*, states that even towards the end of the century cooks were often to be seen running about the city of Wells eagerly inquiring for their dogs that had forsaken the spits. Wooden platters and trenchers were used in most households by the young people and servants. Large joints of meat were favourite dishes amongst all classes. Geese, ducks and poultry of all kinds and ham were considered luxuries. About 1780 the customary dinner-hour in good country families was two o'clock; wine was never placed upon the table during dinner, as beer was the general drink. Cock-fighting formed a very general subject for conversation after dinner amongst country gentlemen, and the birds being sent for and placed upon the dinner-table, a cock-fight would ensue.

The furniture of dining-rooms, even in large town and country houses, all through the eighteenth and greater part of the nineteenth centuries, were confined to a table, chairs and sideboard-table. These sideboard-tables, after 1750, were sometimes flanked on either side by separate pedestal cup-boards. A little later the pedestals were united to the table, forming one piece of furniture, called a pedestal sideboard, which in turn gave way to the well-

FIG. 751. *Mahogany Sideboard Pedestal and Urn.* Property of the MARQUESS OF EXETER.

FIG. 752. *Mahogany Inlaid Sideboard-table with Urns and Pedestals.* Property of the DUKE OF DEVONSHIRE.

FIG. 753. *Painted Deal Pedestal Sideboard.*
Height, 2 feet 9 inches; length, 6 feet 6
inches. Property of the EARL OF HAREWOOD.

known form flanked on either side by drawers or cupboards, and standing upon taper legs.

In the two first varieties the pedestals were often surmounted by vases of classical form, carved or inlaid to match the table; these were lined with lead; Hepplewhite in his *Guide*, published some years later says: 'These vases may be used to hold water for the use of the butler, or iced water for drinking, which is enclosed in an inner partition, the ice surrounding it. Pedestals are much used in spacious dining-rooms: one pedestal serves as a plate warmer, being provided with racks and a stand for heater; the other pedestal is used for other purposes.' The vases were sometimes divided into compartments to hold knives, forks and spoons, which, being very limited in number, were often washed in the room.

The sideboard-tables and pedestals of Adam were at first comparatively plain and severe. Occasionally very elaborate specimens were made for exceptional clients, such as the beautiful sideboard, pedestals, vases and wine-cooler, designed by Adam and carried out by Chippendale for the dining-room at Harewood in 1770. The top of this sideboard (Fig. 747) is of light rosewood edged with brass and inlaid with a broad rectangular banding of tulip-wood surrounding an oval of fanned ornament; on the rosewood frame beneath this is applied, on rosewood, a frieze of floriated and open scroll-work of brass in high relief; the legs, of rosewood veneered on the cross, are headed with pateræ and bold garrya swags also cast and chased in brass. The feet are top-shaped and finished in brass.

Underneath the table stands an oval wine-cooler; its detail is shown in Fig. 748. This also is of rosewood, enriched with bandings, festoons and satyrs' masks, all of gilt brass; on either side of the table are pedestals, surmounted by vases of solid rosewood mounted with metal in a similar manner. Fig. 749 represents one of these, and in Fig. 750 detail of the pedestal is given, in order that the exact arrangement of the inlay and surprising excellence of the brass-work can be appreciated. The modelling of these mountings is so large and full of spirit, that it even surpasses in style the work of the contemporary Frenchman, Gouthière. The furniture just mentioned has hitherto been

FIG. 754. *Inlaid Pedestal Sideboard.* Height, 2 feet 8 inches; length, 7 feet. Property of A. HALL, Esq.

FIG. 755. *Mahogany Inlaid Pedestal Sideboard.*
Property of MESSRS J. MALLETT AND SON.

described as of mahogany, but the rosewood is so faded, that the mistake is almost excusable. There is no means of ascertaining the original cost of such work, for the bills of Chippendale, 1773, preserved at Harewood, do not mention this furniture, but there is a balance of three thousand pounds brought forward from a former account, that probably included these items.

The sideboard pedestal (Fig. 751), one of a pair from Burghley, is about six years earlier in date than the preceding examples, and represents Adam at his best as a designer for carving. They correspond in style and execution to the library table at Nostell, and were probably made by Chippendale at the same time. The vase, of most remarkable finish, is in direct imitation of a Roman cinerary urn, but the handles are composed of the foliated C scrolls of 1755. The carving of the rams' heads and central trophy on the pedestal is superb, the hard Cuban mahogany giving a fine quality to the work. The sideboard-table that originally accompanied these magnificent pedestals is unfortunately now missing, but the small hole at the base of the vases shows that a tap was inserted here to drain off the ice-water, and therefore proves that they formed the accompaniment to a large sideboard.

It is unnecessary to give plain examples of these tables and separate pedestals, for they but repeat the structure and arrangement of the ornamented varieties; they are always of mahogany, and decorated with but little carving.

Fig. 752, from Hardwick, explains the next evolution in sideboards, for in this instance the leg and corner of a long sideboard-table has been actually cut away to admit the pedestals. These and the table are of plain mahogany, inlaid with the same wood of a lighter colour. The vases are ornamented with a plain inlay and fluting, and retain their taps for drawing off the water.

A pedestal sideboard of ordinary Adam type (Fig. 753) possesses interest – being made of deal; it was probably made for the steward's room, where it

FIG. 756. *Mahogany Sideboard.* Height, 3 feet; length, 5 feet 6 inches. Property of MESSRS J. MALLETT AND SON.

FIG. 757. *Mahogany Wine-cooler*. Property of R. EDEN DICKSON, Esq.

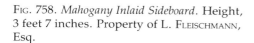

FIG. 758. *Mahogany Inlaid Sideboard*. Height, 3 feet 7 inches. Property of L. FLEISCHMANN, Esq.

now stands. The heading and the oak top are a later addition. Pedestal sideboards, inlaid with isolated full-length figures in arched panels, are generally the work of George Hepplewhite, who died in London in 1786, and obtained much celebrity as a designer of cabinets, settees and chairs; his work, though at times original, is hard and plain, lacking the delicate refinement of Adam, Chippendale and Sheraton. Fig. 754 is an unusually ornate and elaborate specimen by this maker. The table-front is concave, opening in one long drawer inlaid with delicate swags of garrya, but the beauty of the piece consists in the well drawn, stained, and inlaid figures on the pedestal doors. The draperies to these are in deep reds and greens, the faces and limbs being admirably modelled by burning on a light wood. The figures are set in arched panels of sycamore, surrounded by tulip-wood on a ground of mahogany; at the back is a low gallery of brass, which gives great finish to the top, and behind this is a plain brass curtain rail, often introduced at this time. In Fig. 755, of about the same date, 1780, the front is serpentine, and the pedestals divided into three drawers; the carved garrya pendants decorating the corners have lost the fat, round character found in earlier work, and have almost degenerated into a string of tassels. The introduction of the marqueterie shell into the channelled frieze, the spandrels of the arched opening and the inner shelf, infer that the sideboard is late for one of pedestal shape, as this style went somewhat out of fashion towards the end of the century, and was not revived until about 1800.

In the well-known type of sideboard generally associated with the last quarter of the eighteenth century, the pedestals were curtailed and took the form of drawers, or cupboard doors enclosing drawers, supported by taper legs. The earliest specimens are of Adam design, with fluted legs, generally headed by an oval patera; the frame and drawer in some instances being decorated with applied swags of fine carving. Fig. 756 is simple, but of good proportion; the drawers uniting the well-fluted legs are not sufficiently deep to contain bottles; a wine-cooler, or oval box for wine, such as Fig. 757, would also have accompanied the early sideboards of this shape, and filled the rather vacant space beneath the table, for a certain empty coldness and severity pervades the whole piece, representative of the feeling that is to be found in tables of this new school.

The brass handles used on furniture after 1770 often repeated the rounds and ovals of the inlay of the carving of the pateræ. An interesting sideboard in two tiers, of Hepplewhite design, is shown in Fig. 758. The front of both these tiers is serpentine, the ornament being limited to fine lines of light wood on a mahogany ground; the feet repeat the motive found upon

FIG. 759. *Satinwood Sideboard.* Height, 3 feet; length, 5 feet. Property of MESSRS GILL AND REIGATE.

Chippendale china tables of lattice-work design.

Another and rather later specimen of this maker (Fig. 759) repeats the serpentine front, but the entire surface is veneered with satinwood, the plain legs being relieved with long, sunk panels; it is unusual to find sideboards entirely of satinwood before the time of Sheraton. In this example, the wood, although East Indian, is pale in colour, the bandings and flutings being of tulip-wood. George Hepplewhite, who established the business of Hepplewhite and Co., died in 1786, his book of designs for furniture, *The Cabinet-maker and Upholsterer's Guide,* being published in 1788; his position as a cabinet-maker was therefore well established by the year 1775, and from the great quantity of furniture produced by his firm and his followers, it is probable that the name of Hepplewhite carried almost as great a weight with the public as that of Chippendale, although the productions of the former were never so ambitious, nor did they attain the variety and great perfection shown in the work of the latter master. It is only when we see Chippendale, at the age of sixty, departing from his original style, and adapting his work to the new fashions, that his versatility is realised.

The carving of Hepplewhite is delicate and his inlay careful, but both are lacking in life and spontaneity; the finish is admirable and the construction of his furniture scientific in its lightness and durability, but the results are seldom unexpected.

In Plate XLIX the decoration takes the form of plain inlaid and finely figured satinwood panels, the front is elliptical and beneath the centre drawer, the arch and its spandrels open as a lower drawer, this addition being found in sideboards after 1780. The brass rail at the back centres in two candle branches of careful execution, which with the original extinguisher are intact. The general simplicity of design and delicate proportions of this piece, combined with its careful internal construction, suggest the work of Thomas Shearer, a contemporary of Hepplewhite, and responsible for most of the designs in *The Cabinet-maker's London Book of Prices and Designs of Cabinet-work,* 1788.

Sometimes these sideboards were made with rounded backs, to fit the curved recesses so much favoured by Adam and his followers in the

FIG. 760. *Mahogany and Satinwood Sideboard.* Length, 16 feet. Property of S. WARING, Esq.

FIG. 761. *Inlaid Mahogany Sideboard.* Property of W. H. LEVER, Esq.

decoration of rooms, or where the recess was square the piece often filled the entire width. Fig. 760 is probably one of these very long sideboards, its length being no less than sixteen feet. It is of the same character as Plate XLIX, but in this case the cupboard fronts are veneered with clouded mahogany on a satinwood ground, the spandrels to the three arches being also of the latter wood. The legs show the extremely taper proportions introduced after 1780.

The semi-circular shape of Fig. 761, its general lightness of proportion, and the tasteful arrangement of its decoration, is generally attributed to Sheraton, but as this designer and cabinet-maker did not come to London until about 1790, it is difficult to imagine this sideboard is of quite so late a date. The ground is of finely chosen mahogany, the borders, frame and legs being inlaid with buff and light brown woods. The spandrels to the arch are wide and inlaid with large fans. Underneath this is a movable shelf which can be placed in position when required. The waved framing to the lower drawers, and the small ovals inlaid with flowers that head the legs, show that the piece is certainly after 1785. Hepplewhite describing these sideboards, states: 'That the drawer on the left hand should have two divisions, the hinder one lined with green cloth, to hold plate, etc., under a cover; the front one is lined with lead for the convenience of holding water to wash glasses, etc.; there must be a valve cock or plug at the bottom, to let off the dirty water, and also in the other drawer to change the water necessary to keep the wine cool. The long drawer in the middle is adapted for table-linen.'

These graceful sideboards continued to be made until about 1805, developing a still lighter construction, with rounded taper legs and elaborate inlay. They were replaced by an altogether heavier type, and finally reverted back to the pedestal sideboard of massive mahogany.

CHAPTER III

IDE-TABLES for the dining-room accompanied the sideboards, both being used for the display of plate and other necessities of the meal. The various dishes of food were placed upon the table and helped by those nearest to them, a custom that prevailed until after the middle of the nineteenth century. The design of Fig. 762 is rich though simple, every portion of the serpentine front is decorated in the early style of the new fashion, the urn with its well-defined garlands that forms the centre panel is effectively carved, and the frieze of serrated palm leaves gives a great sense of richness and repose; the flutings to the taper legs are without stops, details probably omitted to carry out the narrow perpendicular effect of the leaves above; the top is plain, and made in one thick piece of Cuban mahogany. Fig. 763 is of the same character, but still more severe, and so good in its proportions and execution, as to suggest the combined work of Adam and Chippendale; here also the entire surface is carved on classical lines, the mouldings and honeysuckle pateræ heading the legs being of the highest finish. In this instance the flutings on the legs are stopped, the space being outlined with a leaf pattern; the feet are bold and square, and give a good classical finish to the legs. The channelled frieze to this table has at some time been cut to form drawers, a circumstance much detracting from its beauty, and a piece of vandalism of by no means uncommon occurrence. The date of both of these examples is about 1765.

In Fig. 764, the style is transitional, the taste of the sprays and ribbon preceding in period the innovations of Adam, represented by the legs and

FIG. 762. *Mahogany Side-table*. Property of A. HALL, Esq.

FIG. 763. *Mahogany Side-table*. Height, 2 feet 8 inches; length, 5 feet. Property of D. L. ISAACS, Esq.

FIG. 764. *Mahogany Side-table*. Height, 2 feet 8 inches; length, 5 feet. Property of L. FLEISCHMANN, Esq.

their pateræ. The carving is free and vigorous, its open character and the introduction of the shamrock leaf clearly point to Irish origin, the insertion and treatment of the quatrefoil at the spring of legs is also indicative of that nationality; the colour of this handsome side-table is a deep brown, the surface possessing a bronze-like quality rarely found after 1760, for the darker and harder Cuban wood was being gradually superseded by that of Honduras, the latter being more suitable to receive inlay, and capable of a larger cutting.

Fig. 765, of the school of Hepplewhite, shows the extreme simplicity preserved at times in these large side-tables. The construction of this specimen shows great solidity, and is entirely dependent for its charm on correctness of proportion, the little ornament introduced being of a simple and uninteresting nature; the feet are especially graceful, and the wood throughout is of picked quality. An entirely different sentiment is conveyed by the table, Fig. 766, one of a pair from Nostell, designed by Adam and carried out by Chippendale in 1768. These were made for the hall where they now stand, and are of soft wood, and were doubtless originally gilt; at present they are painted a light brown. The fleur-de-pêche marble top is framed in a purely classical frieze supported by four terminal figures connected with boldly carved festoons of garrya husks. The modelling of the torsos and the careful detail of the faces is remarkable. The stretchers connecting the vase-shaped feet are quite straight and simple, and the centre patera bears the Wynne crest; the large open treatment and absence of metal-work is indicative of Adam's early style. In the gilt console-table (Fig. 767), also from Nostell, and evidently made at the same time, a somewhat similar motive is preserved, but in this case, medallions take the place of the daisy pateræ and torsos. As a heading to the honeysuckle pendants decora-

FIG. 765. *Mahogany Side-table*. Height, 2 feet 11 inches; length, 6 feet 8 inches.

FIG. 766. *Gilt Side-table*. Height, 3 feet 2 inches; length, 5 feet 2 inches; breadth, 2 feet 6 inches. Property of LORD ST OSWALD.

ting the legs, classical ox skulls with drapery are introduced. The origin of this detail in classical ornament is another instance of Art adapting an accidental arrangement to a permanent purpose; the skulls of animals used in sacrifice, together with their garlands and other emblems of ceremony, were frequently hung upon the walls of classical temples; these being reproduced in marble by Greek and Roman artists, became accepted details of decoration, were revived by the renaissance sculptor, and later again by Adam and the eighteenth-century Italian school.

The top of this table is of white marble inlaid with a classical design composed of coloured cement. This stone intarsia or marqueterie was brought to great perfection by an Italian named Bossi, one of the many clever craftsmen of that nationality, working in England under the auspices of Adam.

Bossi's ingredients and process were a secret, much of his work being carried out under lock and key in the actual houses of the Irish aristocracy, who formed his principal clientele. The mantelpieces and table-tops decorated in this manner were incised with a design, and filled in with a composition that hardened to the consistency of the surrounding marble, beautiful coloured effects being produced in this way.

There is a tradition that a certain nobleman, in whose house Bossi was working, took some friends to see the process without the knowledge of the artist, who consequently became so enraged that he threw up the work and returned to Italy, carrying with him the secret of his invention. Fig. 768 represents one of these table-tops, similar to that on the Nostell specimen, but a few years later in date, and without doubt from the secret workshops of Signor Bossi. The marble is Parian, without stain or flaw; the beautifully drawn and inlaid border of convolvulus is in a coloured composition of the

FIG. 767. *Gilt Console-table*. Height, 3 feet 1 inch; length, 4 feet 10 inches. Property of LORD ST OSWALD.

FIG. 768. *Marble Table-top Inlaid with Coloured Cements*. Property of W. H. LEVER, Esq.

Fig. 769. *Gilt Side-table with Inlaid Top.* Height, 2 feet 10 inches; length, 5 feet 9 inches; width, 2 feet 6 inches. Property of the EARL OF HAREWOOD.

most delicate blues, pale lilacs and greens; the accuracy of the work is remarkable, but as a process the results are rather hard.

The side-table (Fig. 769), one of a pair, was evidently made and supplied by Chippendale to Harewood at the same time as the dining-room furniture, but certainly never formed part of it, for the tops (Fig. 770) are of the most beautiful and elaborate inlay, and therefore not suited to the wear of hot plates and dishes; moreover, having always been excluded from the light, and protected by a covering, the stained woods have retained their original colour. The blues, greens, purples and deep amber gold of the delicately drawn inlay possess the lustre and colour of a peacock's back, the ground-work being of dark rosewood; the edging is a broad band of tulip-wood, which still retains an exquisite rose colour, the hoop and pheon pattern of the border and the central oval being of satinwood, the latter banded with green. The legs, festoons and frieze of these brilliant tables are carved in soft wood and entirely gilt in two shades. The inlaid design of the tops is in accordance with the plaster work wall-panels of this room (Fig. 771). Adam learnt the recipe for making composition ornaments in Italy, and carefully preserved its secret. The material is extremely hard, and has well stood the test of time, but is a totally different composition to that of modern carton-pierre. Amongst other items of great interest connected with the decorations of Adam at Harewood is the carpet for this room, which repeats the design of the ceiling, and the mahogany doors (Fig. 772), with their carved archi-traves, over a hundred in number, throughout the house.

Fig. 773 is a piece from Burghley, of unusual shape, and in the Hepplewhite style of about 1775. It forms a side-table, the front being divided into three tiers of drawers inlaid in the rather disconnected manner of this maker's early work; the legs and taper feet are most tasteful and delicate in their gradation, but the inverted lunettes, of fan inlay, are by no means necessary or successful.

Large tables to stand out in the drawing-rooms, even in Chippendale's best period, were not often made, and after 1765 they are extremely rare. Plate L, of about 1770, is so fine in its large character that it was probably carried out from a drawing by Adam; the top is of fleur-de-pêche marble, the frame and legs being gilt; the decoration of the former consists of a finely carved leaf moulding which runs all round the frame, from which hang festoons of very elaborately carved garrya husks; the petals are doubled and crimped, and resemble in their execution those introduced in Charles II and William III stonework; the legs are nearly plain, but curve outwards, and end in goats' feet. The table is exactly the same on all four of its sides, showing that it was not intended to be placed against a wall.

Smaller tables of what is called Pembroke shape were a great feature in late eighteenth-century furniture; these took the place of the china and round tables of the previous twenty years. At first the inlay introduced was com-paratively simple, but shortly became more elaborate, being occasionally distributed over the surface of the top. A few characteristic examples are selected from the large number of these still in existence.

Fig. 770. *Top of Side-table (Fig. 769).*

Fig. 774 of about 1768, still preserves the straight legs of Chippendale, which are united by a tray hollowed out for the convenience of a writer; the emblems inlaid on the oval satinwood panel of the top (Fig. 775), inferring that it is a lady's writing-table, represent an inkpot, pen, paper, eraser, a seal and wafers; the satinwood panels are surrounded with a well-figured veneer of sycamore, this being again edged with a banding of mahogany; the florid brass handle on the drawer is contemporary with the transitional date of the piece.

Fig. 776, a few years later in date, is oval when the flaps are extended, and show the combination of carving and inlay. The festoons at the end are still large in character, but the border at the top shows a tendency towards finer detail. This table is of mahogany, inlaid with rosewood and satinwood. The excellence of its finish, especially in such parts as the rule-jointing of the flaps, infers the work of some good maker, and suggests Hepplewhite. A rather disconnected effect is produced in the table (Fig. 777) by the legs being of carved and unpolished satinwood, whilst the top is composed of a series of bands in mahogany, satinwood and green-stained wood. The difference of tone, however, is more apparent in the illustration than on the table itself, which is original and brilliant in colour. It is difficult to assign a particular maker to the elegant little tambour writing-table (Fig. 778), but its date is

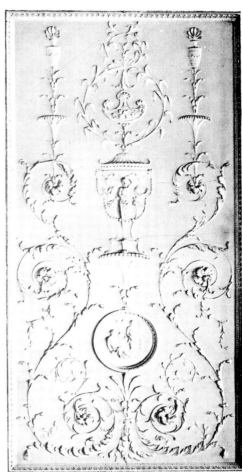

FIG. 771. *Plaster Panel.* MUSIC ROOM, HAREWOOD HOUSE.

FIG. 772. *Mahogany Door.* HAREWOOD HOUSE.

FIG. 773. *Mahogany Side-table.* Height, 2 feet 8 inches; length, 4 feet 6 inches. Property of the MARQUESS OF EXETER.

FIG. 774. *Harewood Inlaid Pembroke Writing-table.* Property of the MARQUESS OF SALISBURY.

about 1780. The inlay resembles the design of Hepplewhite, but the general proportion pervading the whole does not suggest that maker; the drawer front is fiddleback mahogany, the rest of the piece being of the same wood inlaid with panels of satinwood.

For the same reasons it is unlikely to imagine that Hepplewhite is the author of the Pembroke table (Fig. 779), although the character of its inlay is certainly antecedent to the advent of Sheraton (1790), to whom such tables are generally assigned. But whoever the maker may have been, the cabinet-work is remarkable, for one of the inlaid panels on the top rises as a secret box when a spring is touched at the side, the joint in the veneer enclosing the panel being quite imperceptible; under the other panel runs a drawer. The hairwood veneer forming the ground is beautifully rippled, the other woods employed being amboyna, ebony and holly.

A small satinwood folding-table of high finish is shown on Plate LI.

It is of unusual construction, the top swinging round on a pivot and opening in four triangular leaves, the corners of the frame forming their supports. This top is inlaid with four fanned lunettes of green-stained wood enclosed with lines of garrya husks, and the sides with minute circles of tulip-wood; the frame is perforated and elaborately inlaid, supported on legs

FIG. 775. *Top of Writing-table (Fig. 776).*

FIG. 776. *Inlaid Mahogany Pembroke Table*. Height, 2 feet 5 inches; length, 3 feet. Property of H. FRANKLIN, Esq.

FIG. 777. *Satinwood and Inlaid Pembroke Table*. Property of LADY PEARSON.

treated in the same manner with reeded channels of green wood. The inner surface, when open, presents a brilliant appearance, for never having been exposed to the light, the colours of the stained woods are in their original condition. This design centres in a lotus with golden anthers and petals of turquoise, olive green and pale mulberry, and is surrounded by the usual Adam pateræ, ribbon borders and wreaths of similar colours; the flaps, centring in urns, are in red, green, yellow and various tinted woods. The work forms a wonderful example of wood-staining, and even in so small a piece shows the delicate sense of colour possessed by Robert Adam.

FIG. 778. *Mahogany Inlaid Tambour-table*. Height, 3 feet 1 inch; length, 2 feet 7 inches. Property of the MARQUESS OF SALISBURY.

FIG. 779. *Harewood Inlaid Pembroke Table*. Property of COLONEL FEARON TIPPING.

CHAPTER IV

HAIRS after 1770 approach their final development, lightness, simplicity of line, with comparative absence of carving, being their chief characteristics, for although the latter feature died hard, slightness of construction and a very restrained taste in ornament was not conducive to opportunity in this respect, and after inlay had taken the place of carving, painting for a few years usurped the place of both. A comparison between a chair of Elizabethan times and one of Hepplewhite, the last of the great designers, gives a better idea of the change in manners and customs that had taken place during that interval of three hundred years, than any other furniture that has come down to us. The intermediate evolutions, though gradual, can be attributed to definite causes. The panel-backed chair of oak, with its cumbrous and barbaric severity, was constructed to resist the rough usage it constantly received, and was made of sufficient durability in texture and strength to receive a man heavily armed. To these succeeded the tall-backed chairs of the age of walnut, carved with a perforated cresting that formed a frame to the periwig of the sitter, and with free picturesque lines. Then came the plain walnut in an age when all things were plain, the back curtailed to avoid the grease and powdered heads of their owners, and as the gaiety and the lightness of French fashions were introduced, this heaviness gave way before the genius of Chippendale, and chairs corresponded in their fanciful forms with the frivolous appearance and artificial life of those who used them. In the designs of Adam and Hepplewhite the personal appearance of the occupant was not considered, the chair being constructed with simple outlines that combined lightness with comfort. At first the backs were at times hoop-shaped, but these rapidly gave way to those of rectangular shape, and the serpentine line of Chippendale was soon discarded.

The next innovation by Adam was a padded oval back, retaining the comfort but reducing the size of the so-called French chair of Chippendale. The ovals of these backs were also made in an open-work design of wood, and this form was still further varied by the heart of shield-shaped back introduced by Hepplewhite about 1770. In the legs of chairs of the new style, a tapered straight shape was adopted in place of the cabriole leg, the ball and claw and the scrolled foot being entirely abandoned in favour of a tapered and plinth-shaped block. These legs were plainly fluted or faced with a craved pendant of garrya husks. Cylindrical tapered or fluted legs were also introduced, intersected with rings and knobs of carved ornament, but as the evolution proceeded, its whole tendency became one of lighter construction, until the foot as a distinct finish finally disappeared. The seat also became smaller and slighter, for the cloth and silk of coats and dresses were of far thinner quality, cut with fewer folds, and so capable of being compressed into a smaller space; another reason for reduction in the general size of chairs was the great increase in their quantity, for during the last quarter of the eighteenth century more chairs were manufactured and used in the ordinary household than during the whole of the previous fifty years, so that the space occupied by them in an ordinary room became a matter for consideration.

Although it is naturally impossible to give the many varieties of chairs made during the last thirty years of the eighteenth century, it is advisable, even at the expense of being tedious, to attempt a representative selection. The first series of examples are known to have been actually designed by Adam, and according to documentary evidence carried out by Chippendale.

In Fig. 780 can still be seen traces of the earlier style. It is a chair from the dining-room set at Harewood, and was made by Chippendale for the house about 1768. The top rail is straight for the first time in the eighteenth century; the carving on this is channelled, and caps the uprights with pateræ on plain squares. The splat and cresting is florid, and in the style of the previous ten years, so the chair can be termed transitional; the taper legs, with their strong square feet, show the hand of a master in design, and the reticence of

Fig. 780. *Mahogany Chair*. Height, 3 feet. Property of the Earl of Harewood.

Fig. 781. *Painted Beechwood Chair*. Property of Lord St Oswald.

THE AGE OF SATINWOOD

COLOUR PLATES

Shirley Slocombe delᵗ 1907

PLATE XLVI. *Red Lacquer Cabinet.* Height, 7 feet 6½ inches; width, 3 feet
7 inches; depth, 1 foot 6½ inches. Property of H. Percy Dean, Esq.

PLATE XLVII. *Inlaid Commode.* Height, 2 feet 11 inches; width, 5 feet 2 inches; depth, 2 feet. Property of Lady Russell.

PLATE XLVIII. *Mahogany Escritoire.* Height, 3 feet 2 inches; depth, 1 foot 2 inches; width, 2 feet 3 inches. Property of Messrs Morant.

PLATE XLIX. *Satinwood and Mahogany Sideboard.* Height (to top of brass-work),
5 feet 7 inches; length, 6 feet 11 inches; depth, 2 feet 7 inches. Property of
Percy Macquoid, Esq.

PLATE L. *Gilt Table with Marble Top.* Height, 3 feet 1½ inches; length, 6 feet; depth, 3 feet 1 inch. Property of W. Ingham Whitaker, Esq.

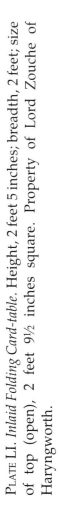

PLATE LI. *Inlaid Folding Card-table.* Height, 2 feet 5 inches; breadth, 2 feet; size of top (open), 2 feet 9½ inches square. Property of Lord Zouche of Haryngworth.

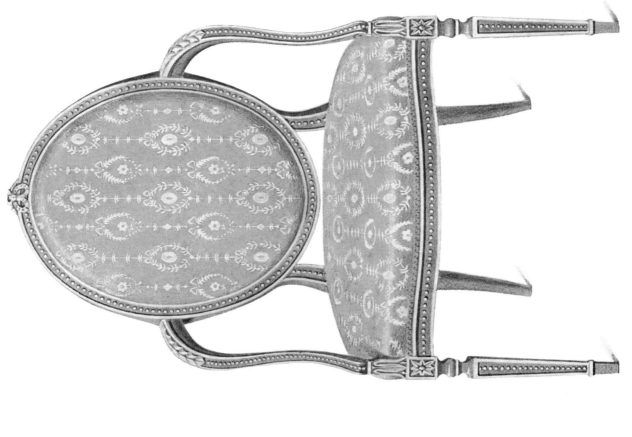

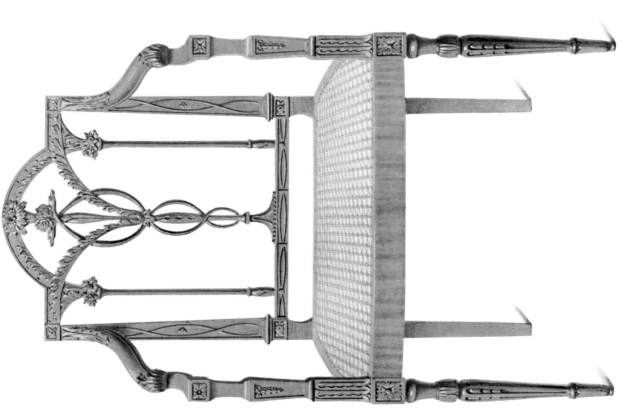

Shirley Slocombe. del.t 1908

PLATE LII. *Painted Chair.* Height of back, 3 feet 1 inch; height of seat, 1 foot 4½ inches; width of seat, 1 foot 11½ inches. Property of the Hon Mrs Whitaker.

Satinwood Chair. Height of back, 3 feet 1 inch; height of seat, 1 foot 6¼ inches; width of seat, 2 feet ½ inch. Property of Miss Scholfield.

Shirley Slocombe. del.ᵗ 1908

PLATE LIII. (a) *Inlaid Mahogany Pole-screen.* Height, 4 feet 11 inches. Property of Alfred Littleton, Esq.
(b) *Amboyna-wood Writing-cabinet.* Height, 4 feet 9 inches; depth, 1 foot 5½ inches; breadth, 2 feet 5 inches. Property of Alan Mackinnon, Esq.

PLATE LIV. *Mahogany and Satinwood Clothes-press.* Height, 6 feet 6 inches; breadth, 4 feet 1½ inches; depth, 2 feet. Property of Percy Macquoid, Esq.

Shirley Slocombe. delt. 1908.

PLATE LV. *Satinwood Commode.* Height, 2 feet 11½ inches; length, 5 feet 6 inches; depth, 1 foot 10 inches. Property of Alfred Littleton, Esq.

Shirley Slocombe. delt. 1907

PLATE LVI. *Painted Sideboard-commode.* Height, 2 feet 8 inches; length, 6 feet 4 inches; depth in centre, 2 feet. Property of Frank Partridge, Esq.

PLATE LVII. *Painted Satinwood Writing-cabinet.* Height, 7 feet 11 inches; depth, 1 foot 10 inches; width, 3 feet 6 inches. Property of Messrs D. L. Isaacs.

PLATE LVIII. (a) *Inlaid Satinwood Tea-caddy*. Height, 5¼ inches; length, 12 inches; depth, 5¾ inches. Property of Percy Macquoid, Esq.

(b) *Circular Knife-case*. Height, 2 feet 4½ inches. Property of Basil Dighton, Esq.

(c) *Painted Satinwood Chair*. Height of back, 3 feet 1 inch; height of seat, 1 foot 3 inches. Property of Basil Dighton, Esq.

(d) *Painted Chair*. Height of back, 2 feet 7½ inches; height of seat, 1 foot 3 inches.

PLATE LIX. (a) *Painted Satinwood Work-table*. Height, 2 feet 9½ inches; depth, 1 foot 8¾ inches; width, 2 feet 1 inch. Property of E. Marshall-Hall, Esq.
(b) *Painted Satinwood Dressing-table*. Height, 2 feet 10½ inches. Property of E. Marshall-Hall, Esq.

PLATE LX. *Painted Commode.* Height, 3 feet 6 inches; width, 3 feet 7 inches; depth, 1 foot 7½ inches. Property of W. H. Lever, Esq.

their ornament the incoming taste. The mahogany is light in colour, never having been varnished.

Another chair, but in this instance of the severest style, is Fig. 781, one of a set from the hall at Nostell Priory, and mentioned in Chippendale's invoice of 1766, which deals with much of the early furniture supplied by him to this house. The design speaks for itself, but the introduction of an oval for hall chairs is found before this date. The carving of the seat-rail and proportions of the legs and arms are especially good and careful.

The curious construction seen in Fig. 782 is of about the same date; the waved top rail, supported by a circle filled in with a fretwork and carved star resting on elongated C scrolls, being uncommon. The stretchers connecting the legs are contemporary, the whole set being finished in this manner, but the chairs are so light in construction for their period that this extra precaution may have been deemed advisable. The seats are covered in the original black horse-hair so largely used at this time.

Stretchers had been practically abandoned by the year 1720, but were revived with the straight-legged chair of Chippendale, and occasionally are found on examples of the Hepplewhite school, but apparently at all times they formed a feature in the construction of common chairs. By the middle of the eighteenth century cheap ordinary chairs were in greater demand, and largely took the place of the oak joint-stools and benches used in coffee-houses, farmhouses, inns, and especially in the numerous tea-gardens on the outskirts of the metropolis and other large towns. So great were the numbers of visitors to these places that attention was called to their increase in one of the contemporary weekly journals, where a calculation was made that on Sundays alone 200,000 people visited the tea-gardens situated on the northern side of London, and as half-a-crown per head was probably the least sum expended by them, it can be no exaggeration to state that £20,000 on a fine Sunday was taken at these places of amusement. Many cheap chairs must therefore have been required at such places of entertainment, and Figs. 783 and 784 represent the better class of common chairs made between 1760 and the end of the century for general country use. The backs and arms of these are made of hoops of yew, held together by a number of slender uprights and a perforated splat of the same tough and pliant wood; the seats were invariably of elm, as yew cut into a superficies of any size is liable to split; the legs and stretchers were generally of yew. In addition to these, ladder-back chairs of beech and oak were made all through the second half of the eighteenth century. In large houses plain walnut chairs of

Fig. 782. *Mahogany Arm-chair.* Property of the DUKE OF DEVONSHIRE.

Fig. 783. *Yew Arm-chair.* Height, 3 feet 6 inches.

Fig. 784. *Yew Chair.* Height, 3 feet 2 inches.

Fig. 785. *Oak Dresser*. Length, 6 feet; height, 7 feet. Property of Percy Macquoid, Esq.

George I and Anne descended to the servants' quarters, and can be found there to this day.

Other furniture in the living-room of a farmhouse or country inn consisted of a long oak table, often of Jacobean origin, perhaps discarded from a more important house, and a contemporary oak table with straight cylindrical legs united by stretchers. These were supplemented by a dresser of oak, either with or without a superstructure of shelves and cupboards, upon which earthenware plates and dishes were arranged, for by the date 1770 such commodities were commercially within the reach of modest householders.

Fig. 785 represents an oak dresser, the last evolution of the credence and court cupboard of earlier times, and made for the display of the pewter and crockery in daily use. The lower or side-table portion opens in three drawers, bordered with a cross-banding of mahogany outlined in a lighter wood; the legs are of clumsy cabriole shape, the lower rail uniting them being sawn to a waved outline; the upper portion is divided into shelves and two cupboards, the latter inlaid with a marqueterie shell. These dressers existed in great variety and were of common occurence throughout the country; the colour of the oak is invariably light, as time has not yet toned it to a deeper brown. A corner cupboard and tall clock, made in the same style, often completed the furnishing of such rooms.

The chairs designed by Adam for Osterley, and made by Chippendale, are deeply interesting, not only from their character, but because they establish a date that is beyond question, for Horace Walpole, in a letter dated 1773, quoted on page 315, alludes to their existence at Osterley, and remarks upon the singularity of their shape.

In Fig. 786, one of a set of twelve, the back-rail is trebly hooped and the uprights are perfectly plain, the splat being in the shape of a classical lyre, beautiful in its proportion and construction; the cords, of extreme delicacy, are also of mahogany. In these finely carved splats, the thickness is composed of layers of mahogany in three plies, which give strength and play to the back. The rest of the decoration on the chair is composed of flutings,

FIG. 786. *Mahogany Arm-chair*. Height, 3 feet 1 inch; width of seat, 2 feet; depth, 1 foot 4 inches. Property of the EARL OF JERSEY.

FIG. 787. *Mahogany Arm-chair*. Height, 3 feet. Property of the EARL OF JERSEY.

FIG. 788. *Inlaid Mahogany Arm-chair*. Height, 3 feet 1 inch. Property of the EARL OF JERSEY.

the front legs being headed by the inevitable pateræ, without which no furniture of this period seemed complete.

The hooped uprights of Fig. 787 are fluted and centre in a shell; a vertical lyre supported on two S scrolls, enclosing a finely carved patera, forming the splat; the arms, legs and seat-rail resemble the last specimen.

The beautiful inlaid chair (Fig. 788) is one of a set matching the writing-table (Fig. 736) from Osterley. The lyre-shaped splat is in this instance inlaid with tulip-wood and holly, and surmounted by a cameo of carved boxwood in place of a patera; the uprights, hooped rail and arms being inlaid with pendants of garrya husks in brilliant green wood; the seat-rail is treated in the same manner, with a waved volute of holly-wood on a rosewood ground; the legs are veneered with similar woods and headed by festoons of gilt metal-work.

Another of these chairs, designed by the same hand, is Fig. 789. Here the lyre occupies the entire splat, its base forming the shoe; the ornament is extremely simple and in the early style of Adam; the serpentine top rail, very rare to find in these chairs, shows a relapse towards a Chippendale shape,

FIG. 789. *Mahogany Arm-chair*. Height, 3 feet 1 inch. Property of LORD ST OSWALD.

FIG. 790. *Inlaid Mahogany Arm-chair*. Height, 3 feet. Property of the EARL OF JERSEY.

FIG. 791. *Painted Arm-chair*. Height, 3 feet. Property of the EARL OF JERSEY.

FIG. 792. *Painted Arm-chair*. Height, 3 feet 1 inch. Property of MESSRS ISAACS.

FIG. 793. *Painted Arm-chair*. Height, 3 feet. Property of the MARQUESS OF CHOLMONDELEY.

FIG. 794. *Gilt Arm-chair Covered in Tapestry*. Height, 3 feet 2 inches. Property of the EARL OF HAREWOOD.

but the carving of the seat-rail and legs is in the most accurate manner of the new classical school. All four legs at this period are often treated cylindrically, and depart from the original square and taper form, thereby offering fresh opportunities to the carver. Such chairs are generally found with arms, sets being made in this manner. The next two chairs, although designed by Adam for Osterley, are quite distinct in motive from the preceding specimens, for the uprights and the top rail are straight, and all carving is dispensed with. In Fig. 790, the surface, with the exception of the plain cylindrical legs, is inlaid with a classical design in bright green wood on a ground of mahogany banded with satinwood; the splat is straight in outline and inlaid with a palmated design. The excellence of this inlay is shown by its condition on the rounded surface of the elbows. The other chair (Fig. 791), one of a set for a room decorated in the Etruscan taste, has the splat shaped like a classical vase, and painting here takes the place of inlay.

In many of the preceding specimens the seat coverings are of the original horse-hair or leather, and it may be presumed that chairs about 1770 were largely covered in these materials, for the occupation of working covers for furniture had been superseded by the introduction of tapestry for this purpose from France, and a great deal of silk was also used for drawing-room sofas and chairs. It is certain that Adam made constant use of silk, and took the trouble to select or design suitable pieces for his furniture, as little cuttings of the materials chosen by him for its upholstery are in many cases still attached to his original drawings. But whatever the cause may have been, there was a temporary decline in the fashion for needlework coverings after the date 1770.

Occasionally a coarser woolwork, with a trellis pattern enclosing a flower, is found on 'grandfather' chairs and others of the above date. The interesting example (Fig. 792), one of a set painted green and white, is covered with this trellis needlework. The back is transitional in design, being a dislocated version of the honeysuckle pattern and centres in an escutcheon; the legs belong to the taste of the previous ten years. Fig. 793, although far more correct in style and some years later in date, has not quite the same picturesque appearance, but the seat covering is of the same work and design, and the chair is decorated in white and gold. This coarse woolwork not being of the same consistency and durability as the earlier and smaller stitch, is consequently seldom found in good condition, and the want of careful execution shows that this industry was no longer fashionable.

In France the adoption of tapestry in upholstering chairs and sofas as well as the later invention called 'parfilage', no doubt put an end for a time to needlework coverings. This 'parfilage' was called in England drizzling, and obtained much favour here. In the *Life of Caroline Bauer* we read that it was invented at the Court of Versailles, during the reign of Louis XVI, and was in vogue there for ten years. In pursuing this amusement, the most fashionable ladies of the Court felt no compunction in asking gentlemen of their acquaintance for cast-off gold and silver epaulettes, hilt bands, galloons and tassels, with which all dresses at that time were overloaded. They took these with them to every entertainment, and there picked out the gold and silver threads, and finally sold them. If a lover wished to please his mistress, he did not give her flowers, perfumes, finery and jewelled trinkets, but presented her with dozens of gold tassels and other objects spun over with gold thread. These gold-thread pickers were called 'parfileuses' from the word *parfiler*. A 'parfileuse' would take with her into 'company', and even to Court, a huge picking-bag for all the galloons and tassels received from gentlemen, and she was proudest who took home with her the best-filled bag. A beautiful and bold parfileuse would make over one hundred louis d'or a year by this extortion. At the New Year the customary presents given by gentlemen to ladies consisted of parfilage, and when betting with them they no longer staked so many louis d'or but so many tassels for picking. On one occasion the Countess de Genlis took from the Duc de Coigny four-and-twenty gold tassels, each worth twenty francs, because she had won a wager that she would walk up the steps of an aqueduct. In the evening she distributed these tassels amongst the ladies present because she hated the nuisance of parfilage. Mme de Genlis, by her sarcasms on drizzling in *Adèle and Theodore*, put an effective stop to this disgraceful fashion, and ladies were no more seen in society demanding gold lace from gentlemen, and Mme Bauer goes on to say, 'took once again to embroidery and the divers kinds of needlework which had once agreeably whiled away the time of our mothers and grandmothers'.

Although parfilage had gone out of fashion in France as early as 1782, it continued to exist in England under the name of drizzling for a generation after. The tortoise-shell and other small cylindrical boxes to which we are sometimes puzzled to assign a use were probably the cases to contain the tools necessary for this pursuit.

The French tapestry-coverings that took the place of needlework were much used in this country for chairs and sofas of Adam design. There is a

FIG. 795. *Gilt Sofa Covered with Rose du Barri Tapestry.* Length, 6 feet 6 inches; height, 3 feet 3 inches. Property of the EARL OF HAREWOOD.

FIG. 796. *Bergère Chair Covered in Rose du Barri Tapestry.* Height, 3 feet 2 inches. Property of the EARL OF HAREWOOD.

room at Osterley hung with Rose du Barri tapestry, the furniture being covered with the same. At Harewood are two sets of sofas and chairs similarly upholstered. All this tapestry is in perfect conditon, the ground being of a full rose colour, brilliant, as at the time of manufacture. These chairs, invariably oval-backed, with cylindrical carved legs, took the place of the so-called French chair of Chippendale, their shape being adapted by Adam from the Louis XVI taste.

Fig. 794 is from a large set made in this manner. The general treatment is in the contemporary French style, but the scale of detail is larger than that generally found in Louis XVI furniture of this quality, whilst the design of the legs and seat-rail are very clearly English. The cresting is somewhat confused and purposeless, but the strings of roses starting from the lion's masks and edging the shoulders of the oval are beautiful; the legs in their carving represent the metal-work of the palm-leaved character so often found on the rosewood and inlaid furniture already described. The wood-work of this chair is gilt so richly that it resembles solid metal. The tapestry is Aubuisson, representing vases of flowers on buff panels, surrounded by a ground of intense Rose du Barri. Matching these chairs are two sofas (Fig. 795), covered in the same manner, and some chairs of the shape called bergère (Fig. 796), which differ from the sofas in their ornament. Both sets are gilt, and the effect of this gold and tapestry in its original condition is rare and remarkable.

In Fig. 797, a tapestry-covered chair of about 1780 from another set at Harewood, the back is more shield-shaped than oval, and the arm-supports repeat the form of the legs, giving a somewhat disjointed effect. The carving does not call for any particular comment, except at the junction of the legs and seat-rail, where the ordinary square block is discarded in favour of foliated scrolls terminating in small quatrefoils, a florid detail that is somewhat out of place. These chairs are painted white, the ornament being gilt. The tapestry is a deep full rose, upon which are bouquets and garlands of flowers in brilliant colours on a cream-coloured panel.

The design of the grateful chair (Fig. 798) exists at the Soane Museum. It is from a set at Osterley and earlier in date than the last specimen. The oval of the back is concave and connected to the seat by two sphinxes of fine execution; the legs are slight, the feet being small and unobtrusive; the ornament throughout is in the full style of Adam, sphinxes being a very characteristic detail of his work at this period. The original covering was probably of cut velvet or silk, now replaced by a modern fabric.

Fig. 799 is very similar, and from a set at Nostell Priory designed by Adam

FIG. 797. *White and Gold Arm-chair Covered in Rose du Barri Tapestry.* Height, 3 feet 1 inch. Property of the EARL OF HAREWOOD.

FIG. 798. *Gilt Arm-chair.* Height, 3 feet 1 inch. Property of the EARL OF JERSEY.

FIG. 799. *White and Gold Arm-chair.* Height, 3 feet. Property of LORD ST OSWALD.

on purely French lines for that house. The decoration is in white and gold and of simple character, and represents the ordinary upholstered drawing-room chair of this time. The original covering has been replaced by a modern silk. It is very evident that by the date 1780 painted chairs were popular in taste, and that many makers adopted the coloured decoration on furniture introduced by Adam. A graceful arm-chair of about this time is shown on Plate LII. The low sweep of the arms introduces a fresh motive that carries out the light construction, and the introduction of colour emphasises the delicate lines that would be lost in plain mahogany. For this reason the fanciful satinwood chair on the same plate benefits from the light and golden colour of the wood, and its small proportions gain in value from the assertive properties of the material. Its date is between 1758 and 1790, and as Robert Adam did not die until 1792, it is probable that the rather unusual design of this specimen can be assigned to his work.

Although the coverings on some of the preceding examples are without doubt French, there was a manufactory of tapestry at Fulham as late as 1755, and at other places in London at a still later date. Muntz, in his *History of Tapestry from the earliest Times until the present Day*, states that Peter Parisot, a naturalised Frenchman, had an establishment at Paddington for the manufacture of this fabric, which he afterwards removed to Fulham, and adds:

Fig. 800. *Mahogany Arm-chair*. Height, 3 feet 6 inches; width of seat, 2 feet 6 inches. Property of the Earl of Jersey.

'The manufacture of Parisot consisted of tapestry-weaving after the manner of the Gobelins, and carpet-weaving in the style of Chaillet, besides dye-works. Connected with the manufactory there was a school of practical art, for a great number of artists of both sexes and for such young people as might be sent to learn the arts of drawing, weaving, dyeing, and other branches of the work. Parisot states that he employed a hundred workmen, but the success of the manufactory was short-lived, although it was under the powerful patronage of the Duke of Cumberland, and countenanced by other members of the Royal family. Doddington, Baron of Melcombe Regis, writes in his diary that he went to see the manufacture of tapestry from France, set up at Fulham by the Duke: "The work, both of the Gobelins and of Chaillot, called Gavonnerie, was very fine but very dear." Parisot published a pamphlet describing the manufactory in glowing terms, but the catalogue announcing the sale of all the stock, etc., in 1755, is sufficient comment.'

This catalogue gives valuable information of the kind of tapestries woven in the Fulham manufactory:

'A catalogue of the entire works of the Fulham Manufactory, consisting of beautiful tapestry hangings, large and small carpets, screens, backs, and seats for chairs, etc. All finished in the highest perfection after the manner of the Royal Manufactories at Chaillot and the Gobelins at Paris. Several of the pieces are made by English apprentices instructed in the new establishment brought into the kingdom under the patronage of His Royal Highness the Duke of Cumberland.'

The sale took place on 30 April 1755, and the following is an abridgment of the list of articles:

'A great many of these items include coverings for the backs of chairs such as –
'8 seats for stools after the manner of Chaillot.
'A pattern for a screen or French chair after the manner of Chaillot.
'A seat for a French chair, with poppies in a yellow ground, and 6 backs for chairs – Gobelin.
'4 patterns for large French chairs, with a parrot eating fruit – Gobelin.
'11 large chair seats, with curious baskets of flowers – Gobelin's work,' etc., etc.

In addition to the Fulham manufactory, London was the scene of many other small tapestry-weaving establishments during the middle of the eighteenth century. There is a set of tapestries belonging to the Duke of Northumberland, woven in Soho in 1759 from designs by Francesco Zuccharelli. Hutton Garden was also the scene of another workshop.

These English tapestry backs and seats were sometimes used upon such chairs as Fig. 800, and the earlier 'French chairs' of Chippendale. In this

Fig. 801. *Mahogany Arm-chair*. Height, 3 feet. Property of Viscount Enfield.

FIG. 802. *Mahogany Sofa.* Length, 7 feet; height, 3 feet 3 inches. Property of the EARL OF HAREWOOD.

example, made for Osterley about 1770, the distribution of the decoration is reticent, with the sense of solid construction that marks all Adam-Chippendale furniture. The carved laurelled bands that frame the seat-rails relieve the sense of severity that would otherwise be apparent, and the classical plinths forming the feet are doubtless the most pleasing and practical finish ever introduced on these legs. The ordinary covering to such chairs would have been in horse-hair or leather. Another form of arm-chair, with a concave back of open trellis, is shown in Fig. 801; here the upper portion is French and serpentine in line, whilst the legs are of the bold, vertical Adam type. Great comfort and strength is obtained by this combination, although the mixture of styles is not quite successful.

The mahogany sofas that accompanied the Adam chairs were extremely severe, for those with serpentine and flowing lines, which have been already described, were always of soft wood gilt or painted in white and colour, or white and gold, and resembled Fig. 795 more or less in their lines.

Fig. 802, of mahogany, from Harewood, is in the severe style, and about the date 1775; the carving is minute and delicate, and the covering is of leather. Horse-hair, black or coloured, was also much used for these sofas, and was not only confined to comparatively plain specimens, for Hepplewhite in his *Cabinet-maker's and Upholsterer's Guide* (1788) suggests it as a covering for some of his most elaborately designed chairs, and says, 'Mahogany chairs should have seats of horse-hair, plain striped, chequered, etc., at pleasure.' This material, however, on a sofa is extremely uncomfortable, but comfort at this time in furniture was often sacrificed to simplicity. A long settee without a back, resembling the Georgian day-bed, was also a very favourite form of couch. Fig. 803 represents one of a pair of these, carved in soft wood, painted white, and standing in the Hall at Osterley. The corners

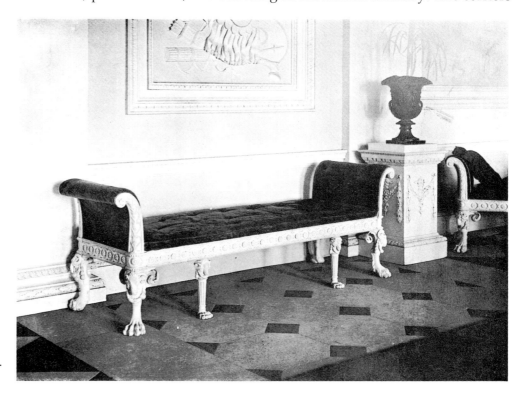

FIG. 803. *White-painted Settee.* Length, 7 feet. Property of the EARL OF JERSEY.

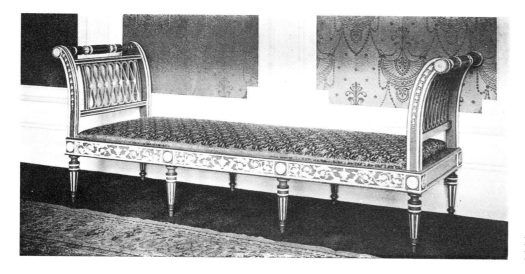

FIG. 804. *Painted Settee*. Length, 6 feet. Property of the HON MRS WHITAKER.

finish in four massive rams'-headed legs, which terminate in lions' paws, the seat-rail being supported by smaller legs of cylindrical shape, with heads and feet of the same character; the ends scroll over, and are upholstered like the seat. Another of elegant construction and a little later in date is shown in Fig. 804; the ends are of open work, and the seat-rail carved with an exceedingly graceful design in classical taste. The effect of the delicate carving is much enhanced by being painted white on a grey-green ground, and very lightly gilt in certain portions. This green ground, with its white detail, in great favour on this class of furniture, was doubtless suggested by the jasper ware of these colours introduced by Wedgwood in 1773, for which Flaxman and other artists furnished the models. The carving of both these examples is exceptionally fine, and leaves nothing to be desired. This same shape was adopted for small window-seats; there are several at Harewood, such as Fig. 805, in the windows of the long gallery; another (Fig. 806) is from Houghton.

This magnificent room, 80 feet by 24 feet, represents Adam at his best. The elaborate ceiling, the furniture, the frames to the Romneys, Reynolds, Gainsboroughs and Hoppners, with which the walls are covered, were all designed by him, for Robert Adam was indefatigable in the care and pains he bestowed upon his subject. The windows, five in number, are headed with elaborate gilt cornices and deeply draped valances of wood (Fig. 807), carved with great skill to resemble drapery. They are described in a guide-book, *The Tourist's Companion*, written by John Jewell of Harewood in 1817, as 'some rich mock curtains hanging in festoons and apparently ready to let down at pleasure, formed of wood carved and painted under the directions of Mr. Chippendale in so masterly a manner as to deceive every beholder'. The painting is deep blue, and their resemblance to dull silk is extraordinary. From these hang ordinary curtains of the same colour, completing the deception. Between these five windows are four pier-glasses, 9 feet by 7 feet 6 inches (Fig. 808), surmounting gilt pier – or console-tables covered with china of great value, the pieces here represented being of celadon ware with

FIG. 805. *Painted Window-seat*. Length, 4 feet. Property of the EARL OF HAREWOOD.

FIG. 806. *Window-seat*. Length, 2 feet 4 inches. Property of the MARQUESS OF CHOLMONDELEY.

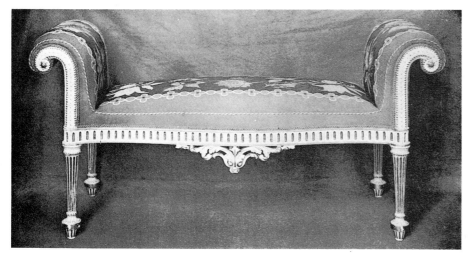

FIG. 807. *Wooden Valance Carved to Resemble Tapestry.* Property of the EARL OF HAREWOOD.

Louis Quinze mountings. The glasses are headed by oval paintings in the manner of Angelica Kaufmann, encircled with a garland of roses supported at either end by Cupids. In the glass can be seen reflected the frieze of the opposite wall and one of the Adam-Chippendale picture-frames – slabs of white marble form the tops of the tables, which rest upon eight rams'-headed and garlanded capitals, finishing in lions' paws. Altogether a most exquisite arrangement in decoration. Such pier-glasses cost in those days large sums of money; the comparative value of them and their frames can be seen by referring to extracts from the Harewood accounts (Fig. 744). In a rare little work, *The Plate Glass Book, by a Glass House Clerk,* 1771, are tables of these prices. The sizes mentioned in this book do not run beyond 60 inches by 42½ inches, and are priced at £81, 17s., plus a duty of 50 per cent., so the charge of £290, equal to £800 of our current money, for a sheet of plate-glass 11 feet high is easily accounted for.

The author naïvely apologises for the prices in the following manner:

'THE EXCEEDING BRITTLENESS of Glass, as well as the many unavoidable HAZARDS and ACCIDENTS it is always liable to (*in the working, Silvering, Framing, Packing, Ec.*), is so very considerable an affair, that it is (BUT REASONABLE) to allow the workmen on those Accounts a Profit from (251 *to* 301 *per cent.*), that is, 5s. or 6s. in the Pounds. But in things that are (*very curious*) this allowance is by no means sufficient.'

The directions for using the tables are involved:

'*When you cannot find* the sum *in the* TABLE *that you want* the Discount upon, *you must find the* next LESS sum, *and take* the Discounts upon THAT *instead of* IT.'

The author further states that:

'The *Chemists* hold that there is no BODY but may be *vitrified*, that is, converted into

FIG. 808. *Gilt Pier-glass and Console-table.*
TABLE – Height, 3 feet; length, 7 feet 6
inches. GLASS – Height, 9 feet; width, 7 feet
6 inches. Property of the EARL OF HAREWOOD.

Glass. By intense Heat, even Gold itself gives way to the Suns Rays collected in a
burning glass and becomes Glass. And it was a merry Saying of a very great Artist in
the Business of *Glass* that their Profession would be the last in the World; for that
when God should consume the Universe with Fire, all things there in would be
turned to *Glass*.'

Looking-glasses of every description formed an important item in Adam
decoration, differing entirely from those of the previous twenty years, in the
size of the glass surface and the symmetrical distribution of the ornament.
Fig. 809 shows an oval mirror of large size, in which the frame in contained
between two female figures holding garlands in their hands, and headed by
small medallions painted by Angelica Kaufmann. As a cresting to this graceful motive, a tazza-shaped vase of considerable height, surmounted by
another and larger medallion, also by the same artist, finishes the design.
The base is in the form of a flat bracket, decorated with rams' heads, from
which fall festoons of flowers – brackets of this character were frequently
made at this time as candle-brackets, and for china, glass or silver candelabra. The candle-stands or torchères, so numerous during the previous
thirty years, declined in number, and in the hands of Adam took the shape
of tripods; sometimes these were of elaborate design and beautiful work-

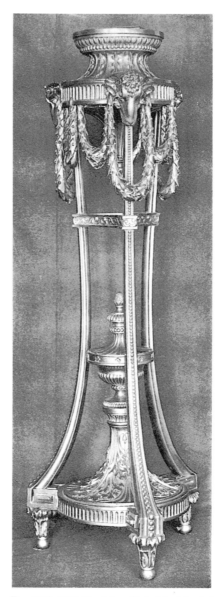

FIG. 809. *Gilt Mirror.* Property of the EARL OF HAREWOOD.

FIG. 810. *Gilt Torchère.* Height, 4 feet 6 inches. Property of the EARL OF JERSEY.

FIG. 811. *Gilt and Painted Torchère.* Height, 5 feet 8 inches. Property of the EARL OF JERSEY.

manship, gilt and inlaid with Wedgwood plaques or paintings.

Fig. 810, one from a set of four of about 1770, is of beautiful construction; the rams' heads, with their laurel festoons, are of great finish, and the base rising in the form of a lamp is a masterpiece of design. The supports to these tripods are invariably simple, and imitate classical bronzes of this kind.

Fig. 811 is of rather later character, the general motive of the design being sacrificed to finish and detail. The spaces between the tripod legs are filled with long tabs decorated in white and gold, enclosing paintings of classical figures in the manner of Cipriani; the lower portion being occupied by minutely carved and gilt open-work panels; the tripod finishes in lions' paws, which again rest upon another base composed of three sphinxes; it could be used either as a stand for a candelabrum, for the pastile or incense burner that surmounts it, or for flowers. Its design and decoration is interesting, for although made for Osterley before 1780, it foreshadows the style known as Empire, proving that the source of this fashion was by no means French, but that a simultaneous adoption of the New Italian style took place in France and England – one called after Adam, the other after Louis XVI – Empire being but the evolution of these tastes with many of the original motives retained. Fig. 812 is another specimen designed by Adam at Harewood.

Fig. 813 is one of a pair, a plain tripod of mahogany, admirably proportioned and still retaining its metal candelabrum. The arrangement of the candle-branches carried out the simplicity of the stand, for symmetrical composition in all objects had replaced the irregular and picturesque lines of the Chippendale period. The base of pole-screens were usually of tripod form, and in some instances solid. Plate LIII (a) represents one of these in mahogany, inlaid with shells and sprigs of oak with acorns. The screen is of white satin, delicately embroidered in flowers, in the long stitch of about 1785. Ornamental pedestals to hold vases or busts, placed upon the staircases or in the halls of Adam houses, were generallly of soft wood carved and painted to resemble marble. Fig. 814 is an early example of about 1768, columnar in character; the necking is carved with the ox skull and drapery motive already described, and the flutings of the shaft centre in a large and carefully carved oval patera; the dark portion is painted to resemble porphyry, the rest as white marble. On it stands a finely carved urn in black basalt of classical shape. The pedestal (Fig. 815) is a few years later in date, and is one of a pair standing on the staircase at Harewood. The flat surface and framings are painted as black and coloured marbles, and the ornament to resemble bronze. On one of these staircases is suspended the large wooden lantern (Fig. 816), carved in a most beautiful design of cherubs as terminal supports to the cupola, their outstretched wings rising and meeting in accordance with this shape. The carving is attributed to the personal work of Thomas Chippendale, who must have been over sixty in 1770 when the lantern was made, as he died in 1779.

Arrangements for lighting house and rooms had considerably improved by the year 1770. Glass chandeliers with innumerable pendants and drops were generally to be found in every well-furnished drawing-room. In addition to these, glass candelabra of graceful line, with ormula bases, sometimes inlaid with a Wedgwood plaque, as in Fig. 817, were used in great numbers. Hanging lamps and lamps upon column-stands were in the libraries and on side-tables in the dining-rooms, the dining-table being lit by silver candelabra and candle-sticks, for these had largely increased in number both with the rich and middle classes, and were placed about the rooms for reading or needlework, but the lighting of rooms in an ordinary household must still have been very inefficient.

Samuel Johnson was in the habit of taking the candle from the stick and holding it in his hands as he read. Boswell refers to his habits with candles as follows:

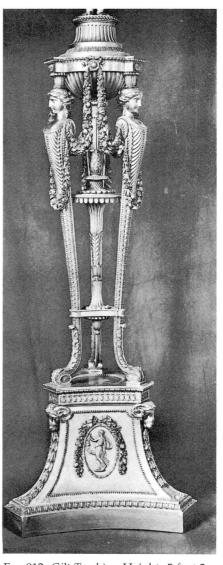

FIG. 812. *Gilt Torchère.* Height, 5 feet 2 inches. Property of the EARL OF HAREWOOD.

FIG. 813. *Mahogany Torchère.* Height, 4 feet 10 inches. Property of W. H. LEVER, Esq.

FIG. 814. *Basalt Urn and Painted Wood Pedestal.* Property of LORD ST OSWALD.

FIG. 815. *Painted Wood Pedestal.* Property of the EARL OF HAREWOOD.

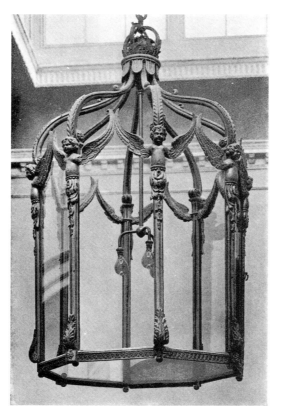

FIG. 816. *Carved Wood Lantern.* Height, 3 feet 4 inches. Property of the EARL OF HAREWOOD.

FIG. 817. *Glass Candelabrum with Wedgwood Base.* Height, 2 feet 6 inches. Property of PERCY MACQUOID, Esq.

'The truth is, that his irregular hours and uncouth habits, such as turning the candles with their heads downwards when they did not burn bright enough, and letting the wax drop upon the carpet, could not be but disagreeable to a lady.'

Stands were also made as tripods to support the large china vases and cisterns that decorated the halls and drawing-rooms. Fig. 818 is a representative specimen from Nostell of this type, corresponding in motive to most of the furniture designed by Adam about 1770; the laurel swag, however, is disproportionate to the piece of china, and is by no means helped out by the excessive size of the lions' paw-feet necessary to carry its weight. Another piece of furniture of similar construction is the drawing-room side-table, one of a pair (Fig. 819); here the hoof feet are in the right proportion to the goats' heads. The somewhat hazardous construction is not endangered by the weight of the top, as in this instance it is of wood beautifully veneered and inlaid in brilliant colours. The gilding of all this furniture is remarkable for its brilliance and depth of colour.

In considering this series of examples made from designs by Robert Adam, it must be remembered that the drastic change introduced by this artist is an isolated innovation in the history of our furnitue, for the individuality of one man was thrust upon his contemporaries with but little or no reference to any preceding style, apart from that of classical times; his furniture was a necessary accompaniment to his architecture and decoration. The energy of his nature and enthusiasm for his subject created a fresh series of decorative objects, original in motive, and entirely suitable to their surroundings. It was fortunate that these ideas were materialised in the best possible manner at the hands of Chippendale, who, although nearly sixty years old by the date 1765, was quickly appreciative of the new change in taste, and introduced, in collaboration with Adam, the beautiful satinwood inlaid furniture invariably attributed to the hand of Sheraton, but which documentary evidence given in this book very distinctly proves was due to the combined efforts of these two remarkable men. It is doubtful whether Chippendale's most elaborate carving ever entailed the same expenditure of time and care as the selection of rare woods, brass mountings and perfect workmanship found in the examples at Osterley and Harewood, and though it may be urged that such pieces are not really representative of their period, in tracing the development of any style, it is necessary to emphasise

FIG. 818. *Gilt Tripod Stand.* Height, 1 foot 10 inches; diameter, 1 foot 6 inches. Property of LORD ST OSWALD.

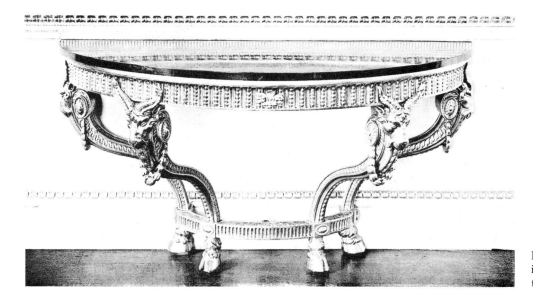

FIG. 819. *Gilt Console-table*. Length, 5 feet 2 inches; height, 2 feet 9 inches. Property of the EARL OF HAREWOOD.

the most ambitious of its examples, as more is to be learnt in observing these than by dwelling upon ordinary and commercial repetitions of the same ideas.

Beds after 1765 conformed to the new taste in their decoration, though they still resembled in structure those of the previous thirty years. The mahogany posts were simple in their flutings, the carving being confined to the bases and capitals, and consisted of an upright and palmated leaf pattern, or wheat-ears in low relief, the feet generally remaining plain and

FIG. 820. *Mahogany and Gilt Bed*. Height, 10 feet. Property of the EARL OF HAREWOOD.

FIG. 821. *Inlaid Satinwood and Gilt Bed.* Height to top of Dome, 16 feet; length, 8 feet; width, 7 feet. Property of the EARL OF JERSEY.

covered by the lower valance, the upper valance being festooned in folds of drapery. These in rich households were of damask, and in exceptional instances embroidered, but occasionally plain silk was used for both curtains and valances. Mrs Delany, who was still regarded as the authority on bed furniture, when staying with Lord Bute in 1774, writes as follows:

'The only objection to ye house is 42 stone steps, which you must ascend whenever you go up to ye loding appartments; one of these appartments is Lord and Lady Butes, and 4 for strangers. Up another flight of stairs leads to the attick, where there are as many appartments as compleat but not as lofty. The furniture well suited to all, the beds damask and rich sattin, green, blue, and crimson; mine was white sattin. The rooms hung with plain paper suited to ye colour of ye beds, except mine, which was pea green, and so is the whole appartment below stairs. The curtains, chairs, and sophas are all plain sattin. Every room filled with pictures, many capital ones; and a handsome screen hangs by each fire side with ye plan of ye room, and with the names and hands by whom the pictures were painted. The Chimney pieces in good taste; no extravagance of fancy; indeed throughout the house that is avoided. Fine frames to the pictures, but very little gilding besides, and the cielings elegant and not loaded with ornament, a great variety of fine vase, foreign and English, and marble tables.

A bed of early Adam taste from Harewood, and probably contemporary with the completion of the house in 1772, is Fig. 820. The ornament on the

FIG. 822. *Robert Adam's Design for Bed (Fig. 821).*

cornice still preserves the earlier feeling of gilt and foliated scrolls, but in this instance centring in a honeysuckle finial, and backed at the front of the tester by a shallow lunette covered in the same damask as the hangings. The corners finish in the traditional vase-shaped finials, here of classical form, and the mahogany cornice is carved in the dentals or tabs, which invariably formed the ornament to this portion of the bed. The red damask valance is draped, fringed, tasselled and lined with cream-coloured silk, and these tassels, with the folds of the silk, head the posts where the cantonnières of an earlier period formed a prominent feature. The damask of the back is panelled with flutings of the cream silk. The above forms a very good and simple example for those wishing to upholster a bed in the Adam or Hepplewhite taste.

State-beds, such as the magnificent specimen (Fig. 821) designed by Robert Adam for Osterley, were still made for great establishments, but by the year 1770 it was no longer a general custom to furnish a newly built house in the country with a state-bed. These very important and expensive

FIG. 823. *Embroidered Bed at Hampton Court.*

items of furniture were therefore after this date made only in exceptional instances and for the use of royalty.

The structure of this bed, probably made by Chippendale for Robert Child, Lord Jersey's ancestor, is most elaborate. Four columns of satinwood, inlaid with upright green laurelling and finishing in bases and capitals of chased metal, support a canopy that rises in a lofty dome; the cupola is covered in pale green silk, embroidered with a band of honeysuckle design, and at its spring is surrounded by a ring of carved and gilt plume finials surmounting a frieze of honeysuckled tabs, from which hang festoons of flowers most delicately carved and gilt. The cornice, projecting at the four corners into square cantonnières, is treated as that of a classical temple, and crested with the antefixes found on the roofs of such buildings; four winged sphinxes at the corners complete the structure, the whole of the wood-work being most admirably carved and gilt. The valance is of pale green velvet embroidered in coloured silks and edged with a fringe of tassels, and below this is a second draped valance of embroidered velvet; the curtains are of plain pale green silk, and the cream quilt is embroidered with colours in an Adam pattern. The bed stands upon a most interesting carpet, evidently designed by the same hand to match the bed with its elaborate upholstery. Fig. 822 is a reproduction of the original drawing by Adam existing in the Soane Museum, showing the great care and interest taken by him in its

Fig. 824. *Satinwood Painted Bed.* Property of
Mrs Assheton Smith.

production. In carrying out this design the double columns were omitted,
and the carved group of figures and their plinth, forming the bedhead,
evidently underwent alteration, but otherwise all details in the drawing
were adhered to. In these days great architects do not design upholstery, but
the innumerable designs for curtains, valances and their headings, made by
Adam and existing at the Soane Museum, show that keen attention was paid
to this important detail in the last half of the eighteenth century, and that the
architect of those times thought nothing beneath his notice that added to the
finish of his rooms. A royal bed, a few years earlier in date than the
preceding example, is shown in Fig. 823, probably designed by Adam for
Queen Caroline, wife of George III.

The cornice in his most severe style is hipped at the corners with the
akroter, which served in Greek buildings as an ornamental finish to the
corners of the roof; for although the Middle Ages and the Renaissance make
no use of the antefixe and akroter, it was adopted as decoration in modern
times. The valances are cornered in the old-fashioned cantonnières, and,
with the curtains, are of pale lilac silk, embroidered in flowers, brilliant in
colour and of tasteful execution; the back is of cream-coloured silk, worked
in a graceful composition of flower wreaths centring in a vase filled with
roses, anemones and lilac. The embroidery is of high finish, and a pictorial
realism is attempted both in colour and form that was unknown in needlework until this date, resembling in effect the contemporary silk tapestries
manufactured in France and signed Neilson.

Fig. 824 is a very interesting bed, for it is signed W. Coombes, and dated
1789, being another instance of a comparatively unknown maker turning out
first-rate fashionable satinwood furniture in the full style of Sheraton quite a
year before the latter arrived in London!

The bed is of satinwood, carefully painted with classical motives, the
decoration of the tabs being exceedingly happy in the variety and arrange-

Fig. 825. *Mahogany Clothes-press.* Length, 4 feet; height, 6 feet 6 inches. Property of the Earl of Harewood.

ment of their colour; the cornice, curved as a shallow lunette, centres on three sides in a classical urn and a coat of arms, from which hang festoons of laurel also painted in natural colours in the satinwood.

Plate LIII(b) is a small tambour writing-cabinet veneered with amboyna-wood; of delicate proportions and high finish, and very typical of the graceful little pieces of furniture so much in demand for boudoirs and ladies' dressing-rooms during the last quarter of the eighteenth century.

Other articles of bedroom furniture remained almost similar in shape to those of the previous twenty years, but small pieces such as shaving-tables, shut-up dressing-tables and medicine cupboards were introduced. The wardrobes were enlarged into three or four compartments, consisting of a press and chest of drawers, flanked on each side by hanging cupboards. The perforated cresting found in earlier specimens was replaced by a plain cornice, and the panels became more decorated; plain light carving, inlay or varied veneer taking the place of simple mahogany.

The clothes-press, with sliding shelves and a chest of drawers beneath, was still the favourite and fashionable receptacle for the coats and flowered waistcoats of George III's reign; for brocaded silk and cut velvet were worn with powder by gentlemen at Court and 'in company' as late as 1800. The tax upon powder was levied in 1796, and the first years of its introduction brought in £200,000 towards the revenue of the State, proving that this fashion still remained popular; and the many small pieces of furniture made for bedrooms or dressing- and powdering-closets were fitted with the

FIG. 826. *Mahogany Wardrobe.* Height, 7 feet; length, 7 feet 4 inches. Property of LADY PEARSON.

necessary compartments for the powders and cosmetics so much in vogue.

Fig. 825 is a clothes-press at Harewood in the style of Adam Brothers, and dates from the first occupation of the house in 1771. The large plain and arched panels of the upper portion are headed by carved spandrels of honeysuckle design and bordered by a sunken leaf moulding cornered at the lower extremities with carved pateræ; the drawers are long, for the width of the piece is unusual; the feet consist of plainly fluted plinths; the brackets connecting these with the frame do not improve the construction, and probably did not form part of the original design.

In Fig. 826, a few years later in date, the doors are carved in a light classical design of ovals, with scrolled branches and pendants of garrya with drapery, the ornament on the drawer fronts being confined to festoons interlaced with cords and tassles. The construction consists of a clothes-press flanked by slightly recessed hanging cupboards, embodying in its form the modern wardrobe; the carving is in the somewhat flat and lifeless style of Hepplewhite, but it is unwise to assign furniture of this type to an individual maker unless certain characteristics are prominently marked. The existence in 1760 of Seddon as an important upholsterer has already been referred to. Robert Gillow started work as a joiner and cabinet-maker at Lancaster early in the eighteenth century, and had established his reputation in Oxford Street at the date of his death in 1772: and so it is possible that much of the inlaid and satinwood furniture generally attributed to Hepplewhite, Shearer and Sheraton may be the work of the Gillows, whose firm is still in existence at the present time, and so the difficulty of attribution of pieces of this description, unless supported by documentary evidence, becomes great in a period when so many excellent firms, of whom we know so little, existed contemporaneously. In the beautifully veneered clothes-press on Plate LIV, a shallow satinwood cornice is inlaid with small dentals in ebony and boxwood; the doors, enclosing sliding shelves, are of a light-coloured and much rippled fiddlebacked mahogany bordered with zebra-wood and centring in large ovals of satinwood, the latter being surrounded by slight panel mouldings of box and ebony. This press, of about the date 1785, is selected to illustrate the veneered and inlaid type; the plainer examples were

FIG. 827. *Satinwood Wardrobe.* Height, 7 feet 4 inches; length, 7 feet 4 inches. Property of W. JAMES, Esq.

similar in shape, but of mahogany throughout, sometimes with fine lines or bandings of inlay. It is also represented in colour to show the peculiar character of the wood forming the ground-work of the veneer. This wood – miscalled by cabinet-makers snake-wood, sequoia and other names – is probably a light-coloured variety of mahogany, possessing the ripple and lustre of satinwood, but more open in the grain. In the Museum of Economic Botany, Kew Gardens, are slabs of 'black-wood' (*Acacia melanoxylon*) from Tasmania, exactly resembling this veneer in grain, colour and figure, but it is impossible that any wood was exported from this island until after the landing of Captain Cook in 1777; it is certain that this particular wood was used for furniture soon after this date, but on rare occasions, and although used more freely some ten years later by Sheraton, is, and has always been, of mysterious origin and highly prized. Snake-wood is cut from the poison-bearing tree *Strychnos nux vomica*; it is brownish-grey, hard and close-grained, and with its mackerel-striped figure presents a totally different appearance to the copper-coloured, richly rippled veneer found on Plate LIV.

Another fine wardrobe and clothes-press commode is Fig. 827, the lines of the hanging cupboards in this case being concave, whilst the centre portion is convex, the whole forming a serpentine front. The panels are veneered in East India satinwood of fine lustre, bordered with the same cut on the cross and edged with tulip-wood. The veneer on the drawer fronts is of partridge-wing satinwood and of a fine rich gold throughout. In the press (Fig. 828), probably the work of Hepplewhite's firm, the pediment is of simple classical form, the centre being inlaid with the initial G and fan ornaments. The frieze is of sycamore intersected by upright shells, a pattern that became very common after 1780; the door panels are inlaid with tall shields of a light-coloured mahogany on a darker ground; these again centre in smaller inlaid shields of satinwood of the same shape, from which radiate very fine lines in

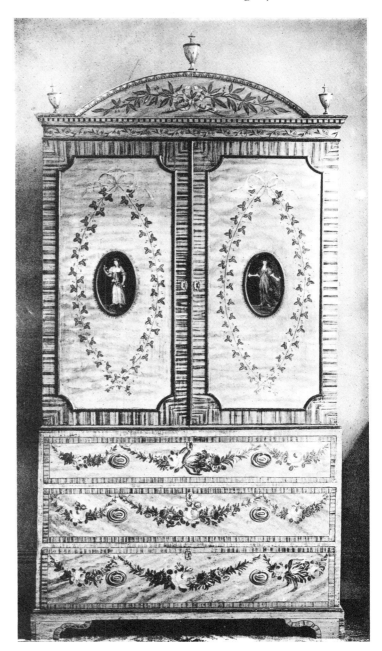

Fig. 828. *Inlaid Mahogany Clothes-press.* Height, 7 feet 3 inches; length, 3 feet 8 inches. Property of J. C. H. Kindermann, Esq.

Fig. 829. *Painted Clothes-press.* Height, 7 feet; width, 3 feet 6 inches. Property of the Rev J. O. Stephens.

holly resembling the leaders of a spider's web. Other fine lines and panel-mouldings complete the very decorative design of these doors; the remainder of the piece is comparatively plain.

Fig. 829 is interesting, for it is made of deal, and painting here takes the place of the inlays and veneers found on the better-class presses and commodes. The imitation of the various woods is somewhat coarse, but the swags of flowers are painted with grace and skill. The lunette cornice and painted decoration infer a date about 1790. Fig. 830 is in the style of Sheraton, who arrived in London about this time. The feeling of his furniture is rather taller, and the scale smaller, than that of the previous twenty years, and even greater finish is attempted. On this piece a pediment is almost discarded, the veneer is of satinwood, banded with fiddleback mahogany, the top opens in three cupboards, faced with looking-glass, the lower portion being shaped as a chest of drawers, and the top drawer opens as a writing-commode. The finish is extraordinary, and the satinwood is a very deep golden colour.

High chests of drawers were sometimes surmounted by two small cupboards, which were used for the medicines, cordials, different waters and washes favoured chiefly by ladies. That mysterious complaint, the 'vapours', so fashionable during the whole of the eighteenth century, with other like indispositions, called for many varieties of powders and cordials. The recipes for these elaborate concoctions were included in the cookery books of the time and were frequently manufactured at home; the medicine cupboard in consequence became furniture of importance. Fig. 831 repre-

FIG. 830. *Book-case and Writing Chest of Drawers*. Property of E. MARSHALL HALL, Esq.

FIG. 831. *Satinwood Chest of Drawers with Cupboard*. Height, 5 feet; length, 2 feet 11 inches; width, 1 foot 6 inches. Property of W. JAMES, Esq.

sents a very highly finished example in combination with a chest of drawers, the doors are headed with delicate festoons of garrya over ovals of amorini inlaid in holly on a rosewood ground; these and the drawer fronts are veneered with fine partridge-wing satinwood, banded with tulip- and lines of holly-wood; the legs much resemble those found on Dutch furniture of about 1785. The satinwood candlesticks correspond in period, and the vase is one of a pair beautifully inlaid with sycamore and burnt holly-wood, originally no doubt made for a small sideboard. Another and plainer example of these medicine cupboards, again mounted on a chest of drawers, is shown in Fig. 832; here the veneer is of mahogany throughout, the relief introduced being the usual banding of tulip-wood with fine lines of holly. The handles of mahogany, enclosed in brass settings, point to a date after 1790.

The small bedroom commode (Fig. 833), one of a pair from Harewood, is one ten years earlier in date than the two preceding pieces, and belongs to the earlier period of Shearer; the lines are exceedingly simple and attractive, and all ornament is confined to a centre banding of garrya husks and fluted headings to the legs.

Fig. 834 is a very much later example and of Sheraton make. The top and lower shelf are of green marble, the tambour front being of alternate satin-

FIG. 833. *Mahogany Commode.* Height, 2 feet 10 inches; length, 2 feet 6 inches. Property of the EARL OF HAREWOOD.

FIG. 832 (*left*). *Mahogany Chest of Drawers with Cupboard.* Height, 5 feet 6 inches; length, 3 feet 6 inches. Property of T. BASSETT, Esq.

wood and mahogany strips, and the delicate cylindrical satinwood legs are very distinctive of the small and elegant furniture made during the last fifteen years of the century.

Sets of satinwood furniture for bedrooms were made during the last quarter of the eighteenth century, but the veneer was still very expensive. Chests of drawers and wardrobes with their original veneer of satinwood are consequently by no means common, and much that passes muster as the work of this time is of old mahogany construction, veneered some thirty of forty years ago. The inlay introduced by Chippendale, Hepplewhite, Shearer, Sheraton and Gillow on bedroom furniture is open and reticent in its distribution, and a certain simplicity invariably pervades the whole design. Great caution should be therefore exercised in the purchase of elaborately inlaid or even plain satinwood furniture, for it costs but little in these times to cut marqueterie in packed slices with a machine-saw, face old mahogany chests of drawers, wardrobes and tables with satinwood, and inlay them with good designs. Fig. 835 is a good and genuine example of a commode chest of drawers of unusual shape. The three drawers forming a frieze are veneered with sycamore, inlaid with pateræ and swags of green-stained garrya. The sides, which open as cupboards, and small front drawers are inlaid with vases, arabesques and honeysuckle pattern, in coloured woods, the other drawers being in plain satinwood, the tulip-wood banding that surrounds these is unusually broad, and the satinwood feet are an adaptation of earlier Adam design. The colour of the whole piece is exceedingly delicate, and the character of its ornament points to the work of Hepplewhite.

A plainer specimen, but veneered with beautifully figured wood, is shown in Fig. 836. The corners are bevelled and finish in simple stops; the

FIG. 834. *Satinwood and Marble Tambour Commode.* Height, 2 feet 10 inches. Property of E. MARSHALL HALL, Esq.

FIG. 835. *Inlaid Satinwood Chest of Drawers.*
Height, 2 feet 9 inches; width, 5 feet.
Property of W. JAMES, Esq.

handles are of the octagon shape adopted about 1785, the balls to the feet being additions. The top forms a dressing-drawer, divided into numerous partitions for the paint, cosmetics and powders that formed so important an addition to Georgian beauty, immortalised by Gainsborough, Reynolds, Romney, Morland and others. Unfortunately these artists seldom introduce furniture into their pictures. The three ladies Waldegrave, by Sir Joshua, are grouped round a small satinwood table, but as a rule draperies hide the furniture occupied by his sitters. A realistic treatment of interiors was seldom represented in pictures of this time, so that these celebrated artists are of little use to us in verifying the furniture of this period.

Fig. 837 is a chest of drawers in the manner of Sheraton, for the drawers are narrow, with the lightness and grace of line peculiar to this designer; the use of the broad band of sycamore, with which the top and sides are veneered, is also a very favourite feature in his work; the drawer fronts are of satinwood bordered with rosewood and inlaid with a very fine chequer in box and ebony. The quick serpentine curve of the front, ending in small corners, was a fashion adopted after 1790, for lightness and elegance of line became more distinctly marked as the century approached its end.

Fig. 838 is another inlaid piece of beautiful finish probably for use in a fashionably furnished bedroom of 1780. It is in the form of a chest of drawers, surmounted by two small cupboards for medicines, etc. The doors

FIG. 836. *Satinwood Chest of Drawers.* Height, 2 feet 8 inches; length, 3 feet 6 inches. Property of W. JAMES, Esq.

FIG. 837. *Satinwood Inlaid Chest of Drawers.* Height, 2 feet 8 inches; length, 3 feet 8 inches. Property of E. MARSHALL HALL, Esq.

FIG. 838. *Inlaid Satinwood Drawers with Cupboard.* Height, 5 feet; length, 3 feet; depth, 1 foot 6 inches. Property of the HON MRS WHITTAKER.

are veneered with satinwood bordered with kingwood on the cross, the centre of the panels being occupied by ovals inlaid with classical figures in holly, surmounted by a key pattern border of ebony and holly. The top of this beautiful little cabinet is veneered in yew with an inlaid panel of other woods, and mounted in a bold framing of gadrooned brass; the sides are also inlaid with classical objects, the owl of Athene in an ivy tree, and an Etruscan base. The drawer-fronts are decorated with inlaid sprays of flowers, entwined round a Cupid's bow and arrow, and the key-patterned base is capped with a rather bold brass moulding. The wood throughout is most carefully selected, and the effect of colour is extremely rich and harmonious.

Another interesting variety of dressing-room furniture is shown in Fig. 839, a shaving-table commode of about 1775. The top, which opens in two portions, discloses a series of partitions for powders and soap, etc.; at the back is a shield-shaped glass, supported on arms which let up and down, and can be entirely concealed when the top is shut. The cupboard doors are inlaid with fan-shaped paterae, the handles and key-plates being rather earlier in style than the rest of the work. Other objects for bedrooms, such as cheval glasses, originally called Psyche, from an allusion to an incident in the

FIG. 839. *Shaving-table Commode.* Height, 2 feet 8 inches; width, 1 foot 7 inches; depth, 1 foot 6 inches. Property of MISS TYNDALL.

FIG. 840. *Satinwood Cheval Glass.* Height, 5 feet; width, 2 feet 2 inches. Property of W. JAMES, Esq.

FIG. 841. *Inlaid Satinwood Box.* Length, 1 foot; height, 7 inches; depth, 9 inches.

fable, were introduced towards the end of the eighteenth century from France. Fig. 840 is made practical by the ingenuity of its construction, as it runs up and down upon a chained strapping contained within the supports. The side-brackets and candle-holders may be of later origin, but such appliances are frequently found at this date. The inlaid box (Fig. 841), of about 1775, veneered with satinwood and inlaid with a vase and rough festoons in green-stained wood, was perhaps made for a jewel case; the tambour top is very unusual, and the strong handles infer that it is early in period.

The fashionable drawing-room from 1775 until the end of the century may be described as elegant and empty. The lacquer and tortoise-shell cabinets, or those inlaid with coloured marbles and stones and other highly prized importations of this description, had given place to more formal-looking commodes, veneered and inlaid with rare woods. The word commode is of French origin, dating from about 1700, and was evidently regarded as somewhat of a novelty even eighteen years later, for the Duchesse d'Orleans, writing in March 1718, says, 'The present the Duchesse de Berry has made to my daughter is very charming, she has given her a commode; a commode is a deep table with large drawers and beautiful ornaments.' The original invention no doubt answered to our chest or drawers, and was termed a commode, as it dispensed with the inconvenience of the chest or coffer, for until the end of the seventeenth century clothes and linen were kept in chests, and when some article was required that lay at the bottom the entire contents had to be turned over. The earlier decorative examples were made in the fashion of Boulle, inlaid with metal on tortoise-shell; this was soon discarded in favour of inlaid woods, and the commode soon became the most ornamental and highly prized piece of furniture in French rooms. It has been shown in Figs. 718 and 719, that Chippendale in 1767 was copying the shape, inlaying it with coloured garlands of flowers on satin and other rare woods, and ornamenting the tops, corners and bases with metal mountings. A little later, in conjunction with Adam, he introduced a more severe style inlaid with classical figures and ornament, and even more elaborately furnished with metal mountings, but it is rare to find at any time

FIG. 842. *Mahogany Commode*. Height, 2 feet 9 inches; depth, 1 foot 7 inches; length, 4 feet 8 inches. Property of MISS SCHOLFIELD.

mahogany commodes, for this shape was not considered suitable for the dining-room or library, and in mahogany was too heavy in colour for the drawing-room. Very occasionally such pieces were made for plate and wine, either to supplement a sideboard or to take its place in a small room.

Fig. 842 is in the early and rather sad style of Hepplewhite. The design of the doors is very simple, and the front is slightly serpentined, the drawers within being of oak banded with rosewood. Eventually commodes were often made in pairs, and they generally occupied the wall space opposite the windows, that between the windows being still filled with console-tables with their over-glasses. The ground of inlaid commodes was generally of satinwood or sycamore, sometimes painted, but rarely found of mahogany. The lacquered commode designed by Adam for Osterley, already given in Fig. 716, is certainly not after 1770; but the commode (Fig. 843) from Harewood may be a few years later in date, for the carved wood is gilt to imitate the metal mountings, and the lacquer design is poor and disconnected. The green ground is not very brilliant, but the inside, filled with various drawers, is a fine scarlet, an interesting example of what must have been a cheap piece of furniture probably designed by Adam for some unimportant room in the house.

The beautiful commode (Fig. 844) was designed by Adam and made by Chippendale for Harewood at the same time as Figs. 741 and 742, and is included with them in the bill of Chippendale and Haig, dated 1772, in Lord Harewood's possession. It is severe in form, but exquisite in detail and execution; the satinwood is of the finest quality, and the drawing of the designs and the ivory inlaid figures of the centre panel most accurate and

FIG. 843. *Green Lacquer Commode*. Height, 2 feet 8 inches; length, 4 feet 2 inches. Property of the EARL OF HAREWOOD.

FIG. 844. *Inlaid Satinwood Commode*. Height, 2 feet 8 inches; length, 4 feet. Property of the EARL OF HAREWOOD.

Fig. 845. *Painted and Inlaid Sycamore Commode.* Height, 2 feet 9 inches; length, 4 feet 6 inches. Property of the Earl of Jersey.

careful. There are no metal embellishments to the corners, legs or frieze, and it represents the best taste of Adam and Chippendale in this kind of furniture. It was to commodes such as these that the skill and attention of these two great men were directed, and though the result may be deficient in picturesque interest, in perfect execution they are unexampled in the history of English furniture. In the reproduction of Fig. 845, a fine commode also by Adam made for Osterley, the detail is unfortunately indistinct owing to its fixed position between two windows. The shape is semi-circular, and the ground is veneered with sycamore; the cornice and pilasters are of rosewood, banded and covered with elaborate metal ornaments; on the side panels are dancing figures, inlaid and etched on a rosewood ground; the centre panel, bordered in octagon, contains a painting by Angelica Kauffmann; the base finishes in a curious imbricated border of metal-work. It would be interesting to know the original cost of this very ornate commode, but when Mr Child paid the bills for the house and furniture, he threw them into the fire, so unfortunately no record remains.

It is evident that important cabinet-makers after 1700 concentrated their strongest efforts on the commode, that it was the most fashionable piece of furniture, and that a certain amount of competition existed in the production and patronage of this article. The specimens under the influence of Adam were more or less flat-fronted; the ornament was inlaid and no painting was introduced, but in every period imitation has succeeded reality, so marqueterie followed carving, and painting marqueterie. To constantly introduce variety into apparently the same limited shape must have been difficult, and it is remarkable what ingenuity was called forth in the process. The

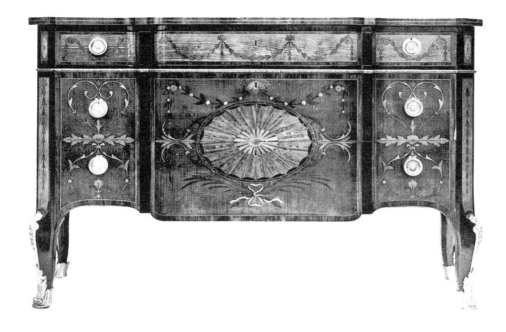

FIG. 846. *Inlaid Sycamore Commode.* Height, 2 feet 8 inches; length, 4 feet 2 inches. Property of W. H. LEVER, Esq.

commode (Fig. 846) is exceedingly simple and good. The lines of the inlay are well considered, and the colour of the sycamore of hairwood veneer is quiet and attractive. The ornament is open, and yet fills the spaces admirably; the legs are very slightly cabrioled, and mounted with metal, showing that the date is not later than 1770.

Fig. 847 is of about the same date, and probably by Hepplewhite, for it presents certain strong characteristics of his work, such as the honeysuckle frieze being drawn out and the spaces round the amorini miscalculated; the latter are of holly on a ground of snake-wood; the inlaid top is surrounded by a banding of metal-work, repeated in finer fillets beneath; the brass legs and feet are deliberate copies from Adam. Another of those straight-fronted commodes, of about 1778, mounted on tall sideboard legs, is shown in Fig. 848. The coved top, inlaid in two series of flutings and one of laurel wreaths, is rare, and gives great distinction to the upper portion; this alternation is again repeated in the inlay of the frieze. The design on the panels of the four doors is extremely simple, and in accordance with the framings and legs; the whole is in such admirable proportion that it suggests the satinwood work of Chippendale's firm, which still held the most important position amongst cabinet-makers and doubtless provided much of the better-class satinwood furniture attributed to other makers.

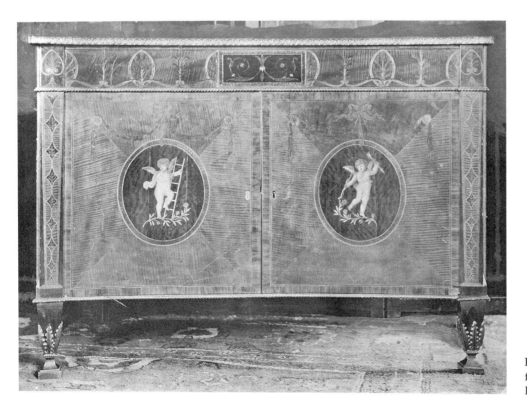

FIG. 847. *Inlaid Sycamore Commode.* Height, 2 feet 8 inches; length, 4 feet. Property of the EARL OF RADNOR.

Fig. 848. *Inlaid Satinwood Commode*. Length, 5 feet; height, 3 feet 6 inches. Property of R. H. Benson, Esq.

Fig. 849 is a still later design, probably adapted from Hepplewhite, for it has many of his faults without his excellent execution. The colour of the satinwood is fine, although its figure is not remarkable; it by no means follows that flashy satinwood is any sign of antiquity – such veneer being often found on doubtful pieces; a clear deep yellow is indicative of old wood, the orange colour so frequently seen being produced in the polish. The frieze of this commode is of high finish, and is very superior to the square inlaid panels of the sides, the drawing of the figures being very elementary; the shape is semi-circular and mounted upon a taper leg, that is a long and slender reproduction of an earlier style. A very good specimen of the ordinary better-class commode is shown on Plate LV; it is semi-circular, and dependent for decoration on inlaid work and the colour of the satinwood, for it is without painting or metal mountings.

Fig. 850 is another specimen, bleached in colour and inlaid with the arabesques and festoons of 1775-80. The inlaid figures are exceedingly graceful, and the large long lines of the design surrounding them are in the manner of Pergolesi. This artist accompanied Robert Adam to England on his return from Italy, and remained here until the end of the century, working for the celebrated Adelphi firm, designing and painting furniture with garlands of flowers, figures and landscapes. He published a book of

Fig. 849. *Inlaid Satinwood and Mahogany Commode*. Height, 2 feet 9 inches; length, 3 feet 6 inches; depth, 1 foot 6 inches. Property of A. Hall, Esq.

Fig. 850. *Inlaid Satinwood Commode.* Height, 2 feet 8 inches; length 3 feet 6 inches. Property of Basil Dighton, Esq.

designs, drawn between 1777 and 1801, and was largely responsible, in conjunction with Cipriani, Angelica Kauffmann and Zucchi, all members of our Royal Academy, for the introduction of painted furniture. These artists were of the greatest assistance to Robert Adam, not only for the introduction and carrying out of the colour schemes so necessary to his style, but, in the case of Pergolesi and Zucchi, actually designing architecture for the firm. This combination must have been rapid and industrious, for Angelica Kauffmann married Zucchi in 1781, returning with him to Italy in the following year. Cipriani, who came to England in 1755, is thus described by Fuseli: 'The fertility of his invention, the graces of his composition, and the seductive elegance of his forms, were only surpassed by the probity of his character, the simplicity of his manners, and the benevolence of his heart.'

Fig. 851. *Satinwood Inlaid and Painted Commode.* Height, 2 feet 11 inches; length, 3 feet 9 inches; depth, 1 foot 6 inches. Property of Messrs J. Mallett and Son.

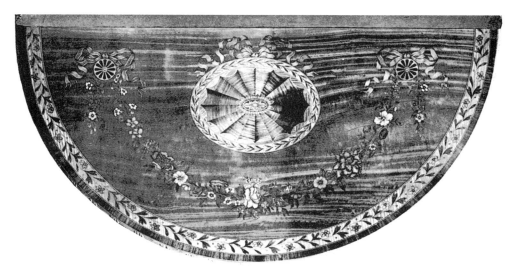

FIG. 852. *Top of Commode.*

His painting in connection with furniture was represented by graceful compositions of classical figures, painted with scholarly knowledge and a most refined sense of colour. As he died in 1785 and the Zucchis left London in 1781, and as painted furniture was not popular before 1775, it leaves but little time for its evolution at the hands of these particular artists.

In Fig. 851, inlay, painting and metal-mounting are combined in a beautiful and elaborate manner. It is semi-circular and veneered with West Indian satinwood, which is long in the figure. The top (Fig. 852) is inlaid with a framed patera of sycamore, and one large garland of flowers in coloured woods; this is headed by blue ribbon bows and wheel pateræ, the whole being surrounded by a flower border inlaid on a broad band of sycamore. A delicate inlay of urns and leaf sprays forms the frieze, the doors and sides being similarly treated with garlands and vases of flowers; a painting of Venus dressed in a Reynolds costume, by A. Kauffmann, accompanied by Cupid and doves, is enclosed in an inlaid ribbon border on the centre panel, the three marqueterie panels of the front are divided by stiles, headed by a

FIG. 853. *Inlaid and Painted Satinwood Commode.*

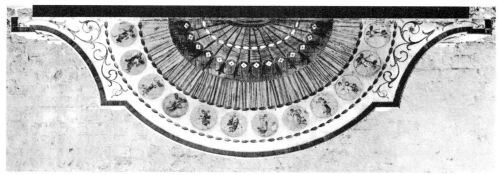

FIG. 854. *Top of same.*

FIG. 855. *Satinwood Inlaid and Painted Commode* Length, 5 feet 6 inches; height, 3 feet; depth, 1 foot 9 inches. Property of COLONEL FEARON TIPPING.

lion's mask and honeysuckle pendant. The brass mountings and feet are in the style of Louis XVI.

Fig. 853 is another of these important and decorative pieces of furniture with paintings by Angelica Kauffmann, and the elaborate metal mountings introduced into this country by Adam and Chippendale. Its shape is boldly serpentined, intersected by four flat pilasters. The front panel is of parqueterie in the French taste, framed in metal and sycamore, centring in a pastoral scene of nymphs making offerings to a statue of Pan. The frieze is of the same wood, closely festooned with flowers and pateræ in metal, and the pilasters are panelled in satin and rosewood, headed by large acanthus pateræ and classical trusses in metal, the side panels being inlaid with vases of flowers on a satinwood veneer. The top (Fig. 854) shows the bold curves of the commode, and is painted with twelve medallions of female figures on a delicate blue ground, representing the signs of the Zodiac, surrounded by sycamore veneer. Concentric borders of West India satinwood and sycamore, cut to resemble peacock's feathers, complete the semi-circle.

The metal-work has not the finish of the Harewood furniture, but the different veneers are admirably laid, and the general appearance of the piece suggests the work of Seddon.

Angelica Kauffmann, born in 1741, studied in Italy till she came to England in 1765, where she was received with great distinction, being created one of the original thirty-six members of the Royal Academy. She contributed eighty-two pictures to this institution between the years 1769 and 1797, and was largely employed by Adam and others for the painting of medallions and panels for ceilings, walls and furniture, until she married and returned to Italy. Very good specimens of her work can be seen on the ceiling of the entrance hall to Burlington House. They are graceful in composition, rich in colour, and are the best things of the kind produced by a woman in this country.

In the well-made commode (Fig. 855) of about 1785, the shape is semi-circular, supported on sideboard taper legs; the cupboard doors run through the frieze, which is of rosewood, painted with a festooning of tasselled pink drapery, and the four circles, which look as if originally intended for paintings, and by an afterthought filled with amboyna, are bordered with rosewood and framed in a fine mottled satinwood. The top is of the same wood, bordered and painted with a ribbon twist in rose and green.

The shape of the commode (Plate LVI) in some ways resembles the last specimen, but the origin in this instance is probably Irish, for the painting, although effective, wants finish, and the arrangement of the ornament on the legs is disconnected and without order. The colour and design of the piece is, however, most decorative, and possesses that individual distinction and attraction peculiar to the Irish and their work.

CHAPTER V

Mahogany, from its practical qualities, remained, and will always remain, the ideal wood for chairs, as the best results can be accomplished in a small space with this material; and to such an extent was its unchangeable quality appreciated that towards the end of the century even window frames were made of this wood; its powers were finally and most conclusively tested in the chairs made by Hepplewhite that accompanied and immediately succeeded those of Adam. The former designer introduced the heart-shaped and oval backs, fitted with slender curved ribs, and reduced their height from 1 foot 10 inches, as given by Chippendale, to an average of 1 foot 8 inches; he also adopted the rapid droop to the arms that was probably originated by Adam, Although perfect in execution, graceful and original in design, the proportions of Hepplewhite's chairs are seldom quite satisfactory, and they suggest the same feeling of disconnection that is observable in his marqueterie.

In Fig. 856, an early and transitional example by this maker, there are certain relics of the undulating lines of Chippendale in the frame of the back, which is filled with three splats looped and centred with large pateræ; the seat front serpentined in the manner of Adam, and the fluted legs headed with carved honeysuckle, are an attempt at originality, but quite disproportionate to the upper structure. The nailing and leather seat are not original, but accurate in design. In Fig. 857, another simple and early example, the back-rail and uprights are hoop-shaped, and the splat is divided into a double tier of fine ribs that amost suggests a reversion to the early mahogany chairs such as Fig. 546 ('The Age of Mahogany'). The seat is also sunk in a rabet, a fashion that disappeared after 1770, and the legs are straight and slightly fluted. A great many of these well-made and simple chairs are in existence, for, costing little, they formed the representative type in use amongst the middle classes. Fig. 858 shows another step in the Hepplewhite evolution, where the loopings of the back suggest the heart-shape; the three feathers, so favourite an ornament with this maker, being introduced as a cresting under the central loop. This royal cognisance was probably adopted from chairs made by Hepplewhite for George IV, when

FIG. 857. *Mahogany Chair.* Property of LORD ST OSWALD.

FIG. 856. *Mahogany Chair.*

FIG. 858. *Mahogany Chair.*

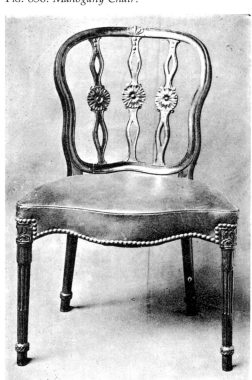

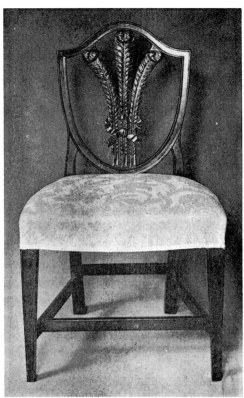

Fig. 859. *Mahogany Chair*. Property of ALFRED DAVIS, Esq.

Fig. 860. *Mahogany Chair*. Property of LADY RUSSELL.

Fig. 861. *Mahogany and Boxwood Chair*. Property of MESSRS WARING.

Prince of Wales, and obtained great fashion from 1770 to 1780. The beading on the inner side of these loops is most effective and refined; the arms are still straight, and their supports carved; the legs are of the Louis XVI type introduced by Adam.

In Fig. 859 a still further step in lightness is observable. The heart-shape is clearly shown and disconnected from the seat; the three feathers are again introduced in fine carving, and the loopings of the back are connected with slender festoons of drapery. The arms are still high, and undulate most gracefully; the legs are even lighter than in preceding examples, and the general proportion is in this instance perfect. In Fig. 860 the heart has become shield-shaped; the loopings are omitted, and the splat is entirely formed of the three feathers carved with solidity and boldness, the rest of the chair remaining plain. The taper legs are connected by stretchers and appear somewhat clumsy in the illustration, but in looking at all photographic representations of chairs it is well to remember that the front legs can never be focussed in exact proportion to the back.

Another interesting back in this series is shown in Fig. 861. Here a honeysuckle heading is inserted in boxwood and pateræ, with short pendants of the same wood, head the arms and shoulders of the shield-shaped back; the ribs of the splat are finely carved and tied horizontally by a bow-shaped attachment. The legs and stretchers appear coarse in the illustration, but these have again been exaggerated by photography. The shield, arms and seat-rail in Fig. 862 are guilloched in fine carving; the ribs of the back follow the shape of the shield, swelling with a slight entasis and finishing in acanthus cappings; the legs are exceedingly pure in style, and are headed with finely cut pateræ. This is a chair of great finish, and, if designed by Hepplewhite, unusually perfect in all its proportions, and so good are these that the design is more suggestive of Adam than this maker.

The introduction of wheat-ears into the carving was another favourite pattern. In Fig. 863 these head the outer ribs of the splat; the curves of the shield, the looping of the centre rib and the leafage, carved in low relief as a cresting, are Irish in treatment. The shield resting on the seat, and the straight legs, show that the date is early, being soon after 1770.

In Fig. 864 the point of the shield is sharp, resting upon the seat, the ribs are entirely formed of wheat-ears, their blades being rippled, so that a plaited effect is produced. Sets of these chairs are by no means common, but the pattern is most effective, its simplicity and good taste are more in

FIG. 862. *Mahogany Chair.* Property of F. SNOOK, Esq.

FIG. 863. *Mahogany Chair.*

FIG. 864. *Mahogany Chair.*

accordance with the designs of Chippendale and Haig. That this partnership existed in 1772 is proved by the heading of the Harewood bills of that date. The statement therefore that Haig entered the firm on the death of Thomas Chippendale in 1779 is incorrect. Haig left the firm in 1796, which was continued by Chippendale's son until 1821.

Fig. 865 is a well-known and effective design of Hepplewhite, in which the feather motive is represented by palm-leaves and forms the centre of the splat; this is surrounded by an oval rib, strengthened on either side of additional leaves. The seat and legs are in neat proportion, showing the reduction in size that had taken place in arm-chairs.

In Fig. 866, the beginning of the end is evident, and henceforward design in the backs of chairs was sacrificed to delicacy and eccentricity of line; real

FIG. 865. *Mahogany Chair.* Property of MESSRS WARING.

FIG. 866. *Mahogany Chair.* Height, 3 feet; width, 1 foot 10 inches.

FIG. 867. *Painted Mahogany Chair*. Property of Mrs FLEMING.

FIG. 868. *Upholstered Tub-chair*. Height, 3 feet 6 inches; width at ears, 2 feet 6 inches.

originality disappeared, and in the strengthless curves and fineness of the perpendicular ribs that take the form of slender columns, all sentiment of movement was lost; at times narrow festoons of drapery or wire-like sprays of acanthus are introduced, but the pattern of the splat is almost geometrical, and carving is often entirely omitted in favour of painted floral decoration, or japanning as it was then called; in the latter style, such as Fig. 867, the surface was entirely painted green, blue, black, buff or brown, and a painted design in colours was added. The seats often were caned to receive a loose squab in place of the usual stuffing, and in many instances chairs give the impression that they would break to pieces if sat upon, but in spite of this fragile appearance, the construction was so admirable, the wood so well chosen, that they have remained perfectly sound and practical. It would be difficult to say whether these two last examples are of the school of Hepplewhite or Sheraton. In *The Cabinet-maker's Book of Prices*, published 1788, there is so much resemblance in the designs of Hepplewhite and Shearer to those

FIG. 869. *Painted Beechwood Chairs*. Property of FRANK GREEN, Esq.

FIG. 870. *Mahogany Chair-back Settee.* Length, 7 feet. Property of MESSRS J. MALLETT AND SON.

of Sheraton, who published *The Cabinet-maker's and Upholsterer's Drawing-Book* in 1791-94, that the last-named designer must have been very greatly influenced by the drawings of the earlier London makers.

The grandfather or so-called tub-chairs of Hepplewhite and his contemporaries, such as Fig. 868, resembled in height those of the previous thirty years, but the backs and sides formed a complete half-circle, the arms running within the sides; the legs are always extremely simple during the latter part of the eighteenth century. Before leaving this section of chairs made between 1770 and 1788, it may be interesting to give an eccentric example of looping. Figs. 869 are made in beech, painted black, and of about the date 1768, for the dipped seat was introduced about that time. These are more ingenious than beautiful.

It is almost superfluous to say that varieties of the foregoing examples are almost numberless, for chairs of Hepplewhite and his followers exceed in number those of any other school; consequently it is only possible to select a few individual specimens that show evolution of style. It is also unnecessary to give more than one illustration of the chair-backed settees that accompanied this type, for they exactly resembled the chairs, varying in the number of their backs according to their length. Fig. 870 is five-backed and of the wheat-ear pattern already described, the backs at either end curve to meet the arms, which have a bold downward sweep. The back legs are confined to the ends.

CHAPTER VI

F chairs during the last quarter of the eighteenth century were not very decorative and sometimes monotonous, cabinets and book-cases gave great opportunities for the display of inlay and painting on satinwood. In Plate LVII, a writing-cabinet of about 1780, the construction and decoration are uncommon. The upper cupboard is surmounted by a shallow pediment, painted in grisaille on a turquoise ground, with imitations of the jasper Wedgwood plaques so often inserted on furniture, and in the centre of each door is inserted a mirror; the lower portion is composed of a writing-drawer, painted with a festoon of flowers, and a cupboard decorated to match the upper panels. The choice of subjects in these plaques is rather incongruous; the lower paintings representing Christ in the Garden of Gethsemane and Hagar and Ishmael, whilst those of the upper portion are devoted to dancing and other classical pursuits; the satinwood veneer is parqueted and bordered with tulip-wood.

Fig. 871 is a fine and simple book-case of the school of Hepplewhite. The motive is a double column framing each door, the upper order of the caps being Corinthian and the lower Ionic; the carving is limited to these and the headings of the glass framings; the lower doors are netted with copper wire backed by plaited silk, an opportunity for introducing colour that was greatly appreciated during the last quarter of the century.

Book-cases and china cupboards of all dimensions were veneered with satinwood, but the larger specimens are rare, not only on account of the cost

FIG. 871. *Mahogany Book-case*. Property of W. RAPHAEL, Esq.

FIG. 872. *Satinwood Book-case.* Length, 8 feet; height, 7 feet 9 inches. Property of Messrs J. Mallett and Son.

of material, but clearly such a mass of brilliant yellow, with the surrounding furniture of the same, would have been too much in a room. Fig. 872, of unusual size, was made for Queen Charlotte about 1780. It is surmounted by a swan-necked pediment and fluted frieze with mahogany mouldings, which give great relief and strength to the upper portion, which consists of a book-case of four glazed compartments, panelled in squares and octagons, for great variety was aimed at in the arrangement of this glazing. The lower portion is composed of two cupboards, veneered with satinwood and mouldings of mahogany, with drawers to match, containing an escritoire. The accurate proportions of this piece, and its former possession by royalty, would infer that it was made by the royal cabinet-makers, Chippendale the younger and Haig, who were then in partnership. Fig. 873 is a china cupboard or book-case, a few years later in date, made of solid satinwood, and probably by Hepplewhite. Here the pediment is depressed into two shallow scrolls, mounted with three small urns of the same wood. The upper portion is composed of a glazed cupboard, flanked by two narrow compartments with panelled doors banded in mahogany, a half patera being carved at their bases in the solid wood. The drawers in the lower portion are banded with mahogany, those at the top opening as an escritoire.

It should be noticed that at this time the structure of these pieces of furniture became more narrow, and that the lower part is higher in proportion to the upper, than in previous years. The feature is very characteristic of Sheraton, who arrived in London from Stockton-on-Tees in 1790, and published his first edition of *The Cabinet-maker's and Upholsterer's Drawing-Book* in 1791. Although expert and experienced as a cabinet-maker, he does not appear to have carried on this technical side of the work personally, for

Fig. 873. *Satinwood Cabinet and Escritoire.* Length, 3 feet 6 inches; height, 7 feet 2 inches. Property of Messrs Gill and Reigate.

Fig. 874. *Inlaid Mahogany Escritoire Book-case.* Height, 7 feet 6 inches; width, 3 feet 6 inches. Property of Robert Eastwood, Esq.

shortly after his arrival in London, he devoted himself to writing books of design for furniture and discourses on religion, differing from other cabinet-makers in becoming a designer more than an executant. It is extremely doubtful if Sheraton had at any time in London a well-established business for the manufacture of the furniture associated with his name, but probably he obtained a great many orders from his designs, employing other cabinet-makers to carry them out. In 1802-3 he published *The Cabinet Dictionary, containing An Explanation of all the Terms used in the Cabinet Chair and Uphol-stery branches, containing a display of useful pieces of furniture,* and died the following year while preparing a work in 125 numbers called *The Cabinet-maker, Upholsterer, and General Artist's Encyclopedia.* Sheraton's work was always delicate, the motives slender, vertical lines and long sweeping curves being characteristic of his taste. He advocated the use of solid satinwood in chairs, and was thereby enabled to introduce a little delicate carving in conjunction with inlay and painted decoration.

In Fig. 874 can be seen the usual type of book-case connected with Shera-ton's early designs, bearing the serpentine pediment, dentalled cornice and little vases that so frequently appear as finials on this kind of furniture. The writing part is faced by one deep drawer with cupboards beneath. A very great many book-cases of this exact type were made in mahogany, and occasionally in satinwood. Some of those which now follow are more

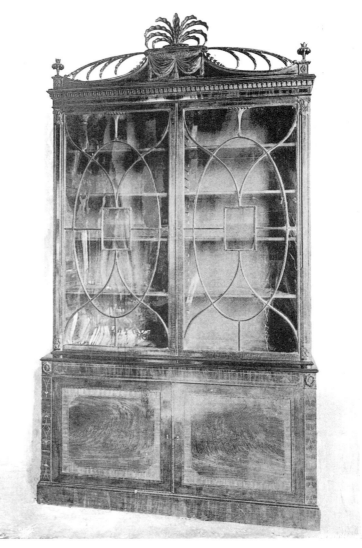

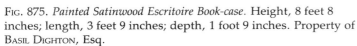

Fig. 875. *Painted Satinwood Escritoire Book-case.* Height, 8 feet 8 inches; length, 3 feet 9 inches; depth, 1 foot 9 inches. Property of Basil Dighton, Esq.

Fig. 876. *Mahogany and Satinwood Book-case.* Property of F. C. Hunter, Esq.

unusual in character, and consequently a little more interesting.

Fig. 875 is a satinwood book-case, made under Sheraton's influence, the form of the cornice is peculiar to his taste and the last ten years of the eighteenth century. The framings of the glass take the form of classical urns on bases, a fashion much affected in these glazings. The doors are headed by a painted frieze of flowers, repeated round the drawer facing the escritoire. Almost all these book-cases or chests of drawers contained an escritoire drawer, the flaps to bureau book-cases being out of fashion. The design for Fig. 876 is published in Sheraton's *Cabinet-maker,* and is most distinctive of his style; there is already a touch of Empire in the almost meretricious combination of palm branches and the festooned curtain forming the pediment, whilst all sense of order is lost in the treatment of the pilasters framing the doors, but much grace exists in the ovals and long sweeping curves of the glazing; the veneer is a mixture of the most carefully selected satin, mahogany and zebra-woods, and feet are discarded in favour of a plain plinth.

The design of the writing-drawer book-case in satinwood (Fig. 877) comes from the same source. The dentalled cornice finishing in sharp points on these two specimens was a particularly favourite feature of this master, and the broad bandings of inlay that have already been alluded to as identified with his work, are very noticeable in this graceful piece. The distribution of cupboards and drawers is a very distinct departure from any previous cabinet-maker's work, a sense of narrowness and elegance being preserved throughout. This is even more evident in the rare little Sheraton cabinet (Fig. 878), where the distribution of spacing to the drawers and cupbards is quite fresh, but the projection of the corners in columns, so characteristic of Sheraton, is not his invention, for occasional examples are found of this in Chippendale's work about 1765. The surface of this highly finished piece is principally satinwood, the heads and bases of the colonnettes being carved in this material; but the panels are veneered with the rare figured mahogany

FIG. 877. *Satinwood and Mahogany Escritoire Book-case*. Height, 7 feet; width, 3 feet 6 inches. Property of ALAN MACKINNON, Esq.

of the kind found on the clothes-press (Plate LIV), and the combination of the two woods is brilliant and beautiful. This carefully finished piece of furniture was originally one of a set of three pieces, the largest being headed by a clock, the other two with round Wedgwood plaques. It is interesting to realise the decoration of walls that formed the background to such brilliant examples. Little is left to use in contemporary description, and the silks which evidently often formed backgrounds, have long ago decayed or been replaced by other decorations. The stronger Genoa velvets of an earlier period still exist, even wall-papers dating from the middle of the eighteenth century are found upon the walls, but hangings of silk such as those described by Mary Frampton in her Journal, as belonging to Mrs Fitzherbert, have long ago disappeared. The arrangement of colour, even to the liveries of the footmen, must have formed a charming contrast to satinwood furniture, for she writes in 1786:

'A year or two after this, when Mrs. Fitzherbert was living in Pall Mall, within a few doors of Carlton House, we were at one of the assemblies she gave, which was altogether the most splendid I was ever at. Attendants in green and gold, besides the usual livery servants, were stationed in the rooms and up the staircase to announce the company, and carry about the refreshments, etc. The house was new and beautifully furnished. One room was hung with puckered blue satin, from which hangings the now common imitations in paper were taken.'

It must be remembered that this pretty and delicate furniture was used a

Fig. 879. *Painted and Inlaid Mahogany Escritoire*. Height, 5 feet 6 inches; length, 2 feet 4 inches; width, 1 foot 9 inches. Property of W. H. Lever, Esq.

Fig. 878 *(left)*. *Satinwood and Mahogany China Cupboard*. Height, 6 feet 6 inches; width, 3 feet 6 inches. Property of Lady Quilter.

great deal more at the time of its introduction than it is to-day, when these better pieces more or less form part of a collection, and that Sheraton designed such a piece as 'the ornamental ladies' secretary' (Fig. 879) for daily use. The painting of the ribband frieze and drapery, the inlaid lunette, with the arrangement and proportions of the drawers and cupboards, are most original and successful; but the semi-cabriole legs upon which this upper structure is mounted, although inlaid with exquisite work, are somewhat out of style, and too thick for perfect taste at their junction with the kneehole. Such furniture and the book-case (Fig. 880), equally delicate and refined in type, was doubtless made for such women as Lady Hamilton, Mrs Siddons, and Mrs Fitzherbert; its very colour and floral decoration suggest light and beautiful surroundings. In this fine example of Sheraton design the long lunette of the pediment is completed by the complementary curve of the wings, the framings of the doors are as light as possible, and the lower portion is varied by a tambour front, flanked on either side with small drawers most delicately painted with garlands of flowers; even the long brass handles help the flow of line that pervades the piece, and all severity is relieved by the scrolled and finely carved base of satinwood uniting the taper legs. The wood is most carefully chosen, small in figure, and exactly suited to the fine scale of the painting.

Fig. 881 is a highly finished small cabinet, evidently designed by the same

FIG. 880. *Satinwood Painted Book-case.* **Height, 7 feet 9 inches; length, 6 feet 6 inches.** Property of ALFRED LITTLETON, Esq.

hand. The frieze and cornice are unfortunately missing. The colonnettes in projection at the corners of the lower portion, the broad and simple bandings to the satinwood doors just sufficiently inlaid at their corners, and the beautiful drawing of the vases, all point to the work of Sheraton, and the introduction of silk behind what he called 'wire-worked doors' was a very favourite method with this master for obtaining an additional note of colour.

The last form of secretaire book-case (Fig. 882), and completing this series, is of about the year 1800. The doors here follow the lunette-shaped cornice, and the writing-desk opens with cylindrical movement; plain mahogany knobs take the place of brass handles, and the inlay is confined to an almost

FIG. 881. *Inlaid Satinwood Book-case Cupboard.* Height, 5 feet; length, 2 feet 6 inches; depth, 1 foot 3 inches. Property of T. Bassett, Esq.

FIG. 882. *Mahogany Book-case and Escritoire.* Property of Percy Macquoid, Esq.

FIG. 883. *Mahogany and Satinwood Curio Cupboard.* Height, 5 feet 8 inches; length, 3 feet 6 inches; width, 2 feet 2 inches. Property of W. H. Lever, Esq.

FIG. 884. *Satinwood and Mahogany Escritoire.* Property of Basil Dighton, Esq.

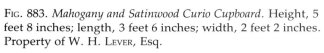

imperceptible line of ebony. This piece is signed W. B. White, and is almost Empire in feeling.

A very unusual, but genuine, specimen is given in Fig. 883. Although the framing of the glass to the upper portion may have undergone some alteration, the lower portion is untouched, the interest consisting in the circular openings, glazed and framed in brass for the display of curios, the front opening in two long doors; the upper portion is headed by a carefully painted frieze and a brass gallery, the whole standing upon a gilt table of about 1805. Besides these book- and china case escritoires, other forms of writing-cabinets were very numerous during the last ten years of the eighteenth century. Sheraton refers to one as 'a piece intended for a gentleman to write at, to keep his own accounts, and serve as a library, the style of furnishing it is neat, and sometimes approaching to elegance, being at times made of satinwood with japanned ornaments'. The latter have nothing whatever to do with lacquer or an oriental taste, but refer to the painting of floral wreaths and garlands found upon so much of this furniture.

Fig. 884 is a 'gentleman's secretary' in satinwood and mahogany, with the frieze painted or japanned in a ribbon and floral border; the bureau portion, mounted on taper legs, opens with the old-fashioned oblique flap supported by three slides. The very highly finished 'lady's secretary' (Fig. 885), with a

FIG. 885. *Inlaid Satinwood and Mahogany Escritoire.* Height, 4 feet 8 inches; width, 2 feet 8 inches; depth, 1 foot 10 inches. Property of BASIL DIGHTON, Esq.

FIG. 886. *Pollarded Oak and Rosewood Writing-table.* Length, 4 feet 4 inches; height, 2 feet 5 inches. Property of MISS SCHOLFIELD.

cylindrical front, is veneered in satinwood and mahogany; the arrangement of rectangular lines that border the cylinder are very distinctive of the beginning of the nineteenth century, and the high stops to the taper legs are indicative of Sheraton.

The shaped writing-table (Fig. 886) is also represented in *The Cabinet-maker's and Upholsterer's Drawing-book,* and described as 'a Kidney Table on account of its resemblance to that intestine part of animals so called'. It is veneered with pollarded oak and rosewood, extremely rich in the grain and beautiful in colour, a perforated brass gallery surrounds the table on three sides; the writing-chair in the early Louis XVI style, but of English make, is about fifteen years earlier in date than the table.

On Plate LVIII (a), is one of the numerous inlaid tea-caddies produced by the schools of Hepplewhite and Sheraton. This example is in choice satinwood inlaid with a large waved patera of green-stained wood and holly, repeated all round the box, on the lid, and covers to the inside boxes; these tea-caddies are often of most elaborate finish, for they succeeded the shagreen and mahogany case of Anne and the earlier Georges, containing silver tea-caddies made in the taste of these times. Knife-, fork- and spoon-cases were made with similar care, and Sheraton refers to them as follows:

'Of the knife-cases little need be said. It is only wanted to be observed that the corner pilasters of the left-hand case have small flutes of white holly or other coloured wood let in, and the middle pilasters have very narrow cross bands all round with the panels japanned in small flowers. The top is sometimes japanned

FIG. 887. *Painted Satinwood Table.* Height, 2 feet 5 inches.

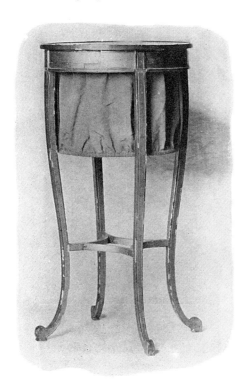

FIG. 888. *Painted Work-table*. Height, 2 feet 4 inches. Property of the MARQUESS OF CHOLMONDELEY.

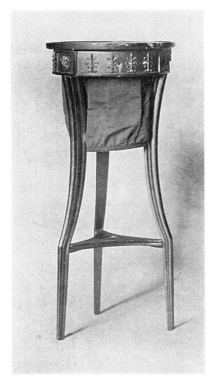

FIG. 889. *Painted Work-table*. Height, 2 feet 4 inches. Property of the MARQUESS OF CHOLMONDELEY.

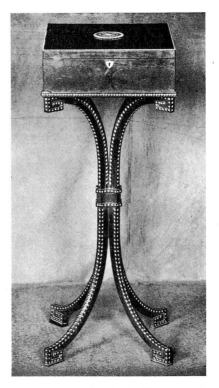

FIG, 890. *Work-box Table*. Property of BASIL DIGHTON, Esq.

and sometimes has only an inlaid patera. The half columns of the right-hand case are sometimes fluted out, and sometimes the flutes are let in. The feet may be turned and twisted, which will have a good effect.'

Fig. (b) on the same plate, is a variety of one of these knife-cases. A very great number of small pieces of furniture of plain-painted and inlaid satinwood such as ladies' work-tables, book-stands and cases for miniatures or other small objects of art, were made under Sheraton's direction, for the

FIG. 891. *Painted Satinwood Escritoire*.

FIG. 892. *Satinwood China Case*. Height, 2 feet 10 inches; length, 1 foot 9 inches. Property of ALFRED LITTLETON, Esq.

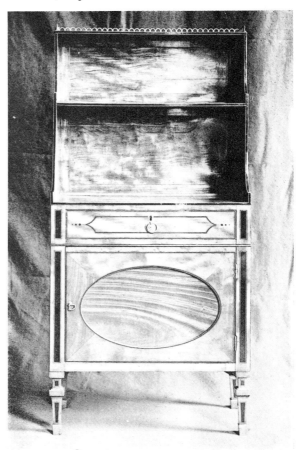

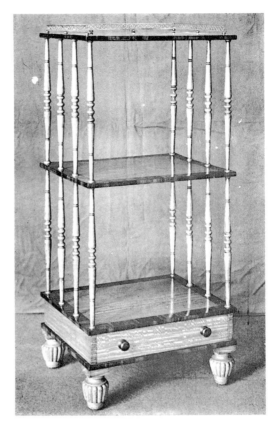

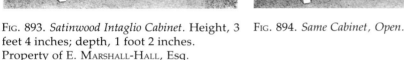

Fig. 893. *Satinwood Intaglio Cabinet.* Height, 3 feet 4 inches; depth, 1 foot 2 inches. Property of E. Marshall-Hall, Esq.

Fig. 894. *Same Cabinet, Open.*

Fig. 895. *Satinwood Folio-stand.* Height, 3 feet 6 inches; width, 1 foot 6 inches. Property of E. Marshall-Hall, Esq.

taste of this designer leant towards delicately finished work. These pieces distributed about a room gave an appearance of elegance that generally accompanies the *fin de siècle* taste, and although we were at war with France, and comparatively little furniture can have been produced there between 1789 and 1795 on account of the Revolution, French fashions were considered the height of good taste, and formed the guiding motives in dress and furniture. The little table (Fig. 887), of about 1795, is a specimen of Sheraton under French influence, and the delicate painting and treatment of the frame, with the almost Pompeian motive in the legs, show the ultra-classical feeling gradually pervading both countries. The same motives are shown in the little gilt pouch-tables (Fig. 888 and Fig. 889), with tops painted to imitate coloured marbles, much resembling some of the Roman bronze tables being found at Pompeii about that time, a taste that was fostered in this country by the investigations and interests of Sir William Hamilton, then ambassador at the Court of Naples. Another work-box table, of about 1800, is shown in Fig. 890, interesting for the cut-steel nails with which the box and legs are ornamented. This imitation of marble in paint, combined with satinwood and tinsel, is also used on the very small tambour writing-table (Fig. 891), another piece of fantastic classicism under Sheraton's influence

On Plate LIX (a) is a very delicate specimen of these work-tables in satin-wood painted with flowers, a handle of the same wood being attached to the box, the whole construction being so delicate that its existence of over one hundred years is surprising, but the condition of the veneer is perfect and the handle uninjured. On the same plate can be seen a dressing-table of earlier date. It is of plain satinwood, the ornament being etched in a fine black line, and when open, discloses a series of partitions to contain various washes and cosmetics. A folding looking-glass occupied the centre of the interior, the brushes, combs, etc., being kept in the lower drawer. This shape was also much made in mahogany, its fashion lasting from about 1780 till 1795.

Small cupboards, with china shelves of satinwood, such as Fig. 892, are often found surmounted by a brass gallery; the example given is inlaid with panels and lines of ebony, and is of the school of Hepplewhite.

Fig. 893 is a very highly finished coin- or intaglio-cabinet of West India satinwood, with panels of amboyna. The lid is coved and japanned with a bold palmated design in colours; the inside faced with rosewood, and shown in Fig. 894, opens in a series of shallow drawers. Larger cabinets for these collections, veneered and inlaid in an elaborate manner, were also made. In the journal and letters of Samuel Curwen, an American refugee, one of these is mentioned as follows:

'1783, *April 5th.* – Called at Mr. Jassey's to have a sight of the curious cabinet of satinwood, inlaid and decorated with many devices, figurative, etc., on front and sides. Its contents, rows of drawers containing impressions of intaglios, cameras, seals, etc., to the number of more than six thousand, duplicated, to be sent to the Empress of Russia. She is a great encourager of artists, particularly English ones.'

Stands to contain music and portfolios for the numerous engravings so fashionable at this time also became recognised as necessary pieces of furniture. Fig. 895, of about 1800, veneered with West India satinwood and bordered with rosewood, has satinwood balusters and feet, whilst the stand from the music-room at Harewood (Fig. 896) is of mahogany, finely fluted and lined with ebony, and about ten years later in date.

FIG. 896. *Mahogany Music-stand.* Length, 5 feet 4 inches; height, 2 feet 5 inches; depth, 2 feet 9 inches. Property of the EARL OF HAREWOOD.

CHAPTER VII

ABLES of all descriptions were made in great quantities during the last twenty-five years of the eighteenth century, the increase in the number of side-tables, apart from those used for cards, being especially noticeable. Dining-tables were for the first time made to extend by means of slides, and the taper legs to dining-tables, which had never really been satisfactory from a point of stability, gave place to a fluted leg of stronger construction soon after 1800; satinwood was occasionally employed as a border to these tables, but veneer and inlay were unpractical and seldom employed. Drinking after dinner was still a polite and recognised custom, and drunkenness was facilitated by the adoption of port in place of claret, which, until about 1770, had been the fashionable wine; the following paragraph, taken from the *Morning Post*, 26 July, 1800, shows that intemperance was not confined to the laity:

'At a village in Cheshire, last year, three clergymen, after dinner, ate fourteen quarts of nuts, and, during their sitting, drank six bottles of port wine, and No other liquor.'

Tables especially designed for drinking were made of narrow horseshoe shape, the open end being placed opposite the fire, where a bag of network kept the biscuits crisp. In the drinking-table (Fig. 897), of about 1790, adjustable circular fans rise as fire-screens on either side, whilst metal wells with brass covers sufficiently large to contain ice and bottles, are sunk in the tables to keep the wine cool. In Fig. 898, a later specimen of about 1810, the fans are replaced by a curtain hung upon a brass rail headed with Empire busts, the biscuit net is shown, but the wine was placed on the two trays that radiate from the centre; the double ridge on the surface of the table is to ensure the comparative safety of the glasses during drinking, and the fans and curtain to prevent apoplexy. In decoration, the legs and frame show the clumsy motives evolved from Empire furniture that eventually became celebrated as early Victorian.

Small tables during the last twenty years of the eighteenth century were often painted in beautiful taste. In Fig. 899 and Fig. 900 can be seen a

FIG. 897. *Mahogany Drinking-table*. Height, 2 feet; width, 1 foot 10 inches. Property of MISS TYNDALL.

FIG. 898. *Mahogany Drinking-table.* Property of F. BERENS, Esq.

FIG. 899. *Top of Painted Satinwood Table.* Length, 3 feet; width, 2 feet 4 inches.

FIG. 900. *Top of Painted Hairwood Card-table.* Length, 3 feet.

charming combination of hairwood veneer (sycamore) and painting. The edges of the Pembroke table are gracefully serpentined, and garlands of roses on a buff-painted border are edged with tulip-wood. The centre is occupied by a painting of Venus in the style of Zucchi, surrounded by garlands of flowers tied with bows of pink ribbon; these colours on the grey ground of the stained sycamore have a most refined effect.

The card-table to match, originally one of a pair, resembles the Pembroke in colour and arrangement; the legs of both are veneered with the same wood, painted with pendants of green garrya husks, and taper delicately in the style of 1785. Side-tables (such as Fig. 902) were often japanned entirely with cream white; the edges and carved portions gilded. The top (Fig. 901) is

FIG. 901. *Top of Table (Fig. 902).*

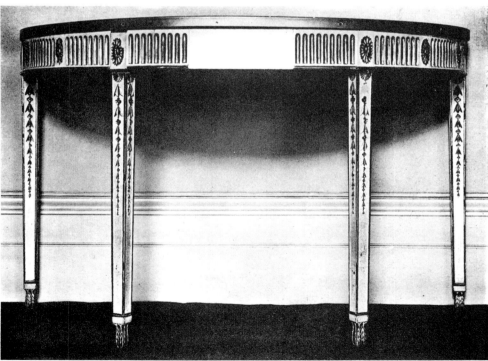

FIG. 902. *Painted Side-table.* Property of F. PARTRIDGE, Esq.

Fig. 903. *Top of Satinwood Painted Table.*

Fig. 904. *Gilt Side-table.* Length, 3 feet 6 inches. Property of F. Partridge, Esq.

elaborately painted with flowers and subjects on the cream ground, which afforded an opportunity for more delicate and brilliant results than the bare surface of the veneer; they were invariably made in pairs, and when joined together, formed an oval table of useful size; in Fig. 904 a pair are united in this manner. The sides and legs of these tables are entirely gilt, the latter showing the balustered development introduced by Pergolesi, who probably painted the satinwood top (Fig. 903), for the flowers and ribbons are touched in with consummate skill; the date being about 1790.

The finely executed piece from Hatfield (Fig. 905) is probably from an early design by Sheraton, as the curves are most unusual, the back being tub-shaped, and the cupboards and shelves that surmount the table are on the section of a circle; it no doubt was made for a semi-circular alcove, but now stands out in the room; the heart-shaped and honeysuckle inlaid frieze is of remarkable finish, and the very high stops to the feet, almost amounting to collars, show the date is about 1790.

After 1800, tables, like all other furniture, began to show signs of the coming dissolution, and the taper legs that for twenty-five years had been such a marked feature in all this furniture was replaced by a different structure. In the Empire round table (Fig. 906), with a yew top and black painted legs, traditional design of Adam is evident, but the palmated ornament on the legs is meaningless, and the relative proportion of the hoofs forming the feet, to the rams' heads, is ugly. Circular tables of this description with drawers are continually found mounted on a central support that branches into three or four curved legs, capped with brass lion paws' feet. These were accompanied by small oblong tables in satinwood and mahogany, supported at either end by central pilasters resting on yoke-shaped legs. The chess-table (Fig. 907 and Fig. 908) represents specimens of

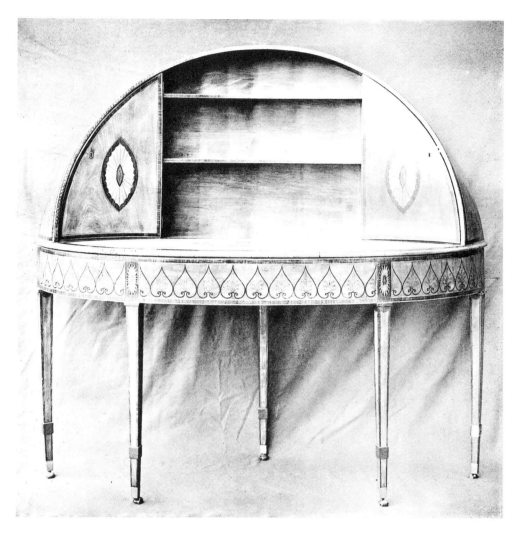

FIG. 905. *Satinwood Side-table*. Height, 4 feet 4 inches; length, 4 feet 4 inches. Property of the MARQUESS OF SALISBURY.

the period of Waterloo, but beyond their connection with these important times have but little interest.

Tall clocks continued to be made during the last twenty-five years of the eighteenth century very much on the same lines of those immediately preceding them. Fig. 909 is a handsome clock of about 1780, very simple and good in its proportions, and of finely selected mahogany and oak, but the demand for tall clocks was evidently small, for elaborately inlaid specimens

FIG. 906. *Yew Table*. Property of the EARL OF HAREWOOD.

FIG. 907. *Mahogany Chess-table.* Height, 2 feet 4 inches; length, 3 feet. Property of the EARL OF HAREWOOD.

FIG. 908 *Satinwood Table.* Length, 3 feet. Property of the EARL OF HAREWOOD.

FIG. 909. *Oak and Mahogany Clock.* Property of HERBERT CANAAN, Esq.

FIG. 910. *Inlaid Mahogany Clock.* Height, 6 feet 10 inches. Property of ALFRED DAVIS, Esq.

are not often found, nor are they even veneered with satinwood, which proves they were confined to the staircase, hall and passages, and no longer placed in sitting-rooms where the new furniture was all inlaid. Sometimes novelty was attempted, as in Fig. 910, where the heading is ballooned and surmounted by an inlaid hood supported on open pillars. The body in this instance tapers gracefully, the corners are inlaid with pendants of garrya and hairwood, and the design, probably by Sheraton, is homogeneous throughout.

Mirrors and wall lights presented no especial novelty until the advent of the convex mirrors, which were a revival from the fifteenth century. After 1795 these were surrounded by a circular and deeply moulded gilt frame, studded with balls, and generally surmounted by an eagle connected from the beak by chains to cut-glass candle-brackets. In Fig. 911, an unusually fine specimen, the heading is crowned by a dragon, disturbed by snakes who crawl from beneath a bed of acanthus; the foliage again being repeated at the base.

Wall lights towards the end of the century were generally of glass, but late specimens of the Adam type, approximating to Empire, and largely composed of wire and plaster gilt, are often found. Fig. 912 is from a house in Wells, and contemporary with the structural decoration of the room in

FIG. 911. *Gilt Convex Mirror*. Height, 4 feet 7 inches; width, 3 feet 4 inches. Property of ALFRED LITTLETON, Esq.

FIG. 912. *Painted Wall Light*. Property of CHARLES TUTWAY, Esq.

which it hangs, and is about 1785. Glass lustres on the walls are mentioned in Samuel Curwen's Journal, in his interesting description of the rather doubtful place of entertainment called Carlisle Hall:

'*May* 21st 1780 – Went to Carlisle Hall at a Sunday evening entertainment called the promenade; the employment of the company is simply walking through the rooms, being allowed tea, coffee, chocolate, lemonade, orgeat, negus, etc.; admission by ticket, three shillings; dress, decent, full not required; the ladies were rigged out in gaudy attire, attended by bucks, bloods, and macaronis, though it is also resorted to by persons of irreproachable character; among the wheat will be tares. The first room is of a moderate size covered with carpets, and furnished with wooden chairs and seats in the Chinese taste; passing through this you enter the

FIG. 913. *Gilt and Painted Settee*. Length, 7 feet; width, 2 feet 6 inches. Property of W. H. LEVER, Esq.

FIG. 914. *Mahogany Settee.* Length, 9 feet; width, 3 feet 4 inches.

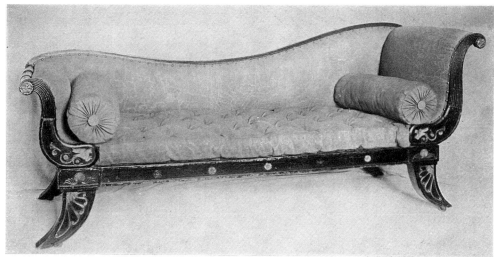

FIG. 915. *Rosewood Sofa.* Length, 7 feet. Property of the MARQUESS OF CHOLMONDELEY.

long room, about eighty feet by forty, lighted with glass chandeliers and branches fixed to side-walls, against which stand sofas covered with silk; the company usually resorting to these rooms was about 700; this evening the house was thronged with a good thousand.'

The sofas, covered with silk, were probably open back settees with upholstered seats, which were a very fashionable form of couch. The backs of these at times were very elaborate. Fig. 913 is from a set that is accompanied by chairs of similar design, their form being introduced at each end of the settee; the centre is occupied by a large oval, enclosed in the gilt reed and ribbon that forms the carved framing of the back and is painted in coloured flowers, and a classical figure subject on green and buff ground; small painted medallions also decorate the other splats.

To so great a degree of fineness were these long settees carried, that their practical stability would almost seem impossible. In Fig. 914. one of those made to accompany the chairs and tables introduced by Sheraton, the

FIG. 916. *Rosewood Sofa.* Length, 7 feet 6 inches; height, 3 feet. Property of the EARL OF HAREWOOD.

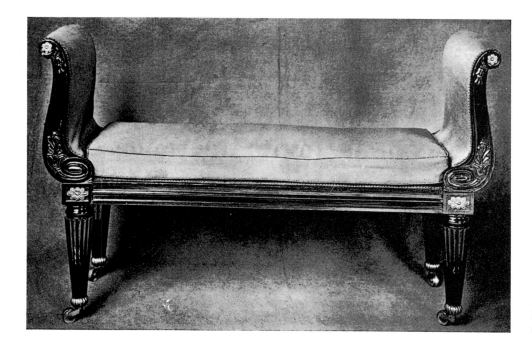

FIG. 917. *Rosewood Music-seat*. Length, 4 feet
6 inches. Property of the EARL OF HAREWOOD.

FIG. 918. *Mahogany Bed*. Length, 7 feet.
Property of the EARL OF HAREWOOD.

central arcade of the back is so delicate that it is difficult to understand how it
can withstand the weight of more than one occupant; but not a rail or a
column has cracked, and every piece of the seat is in perfect condition. A
series of cushions probably distributed the pressure, and the broad caned
seat was covered by a squab cushion, in depth almost touching the lower rail
of the back. Seats in this style, of shorter length, were more general, and
with the type of Hepplewhite already given, are representative of these seats
at the end of the century. A very great lapse in taste is perceptible between
Fig. 915 and the last specimen, yet only separated by a period of about fifteen
years. A totally different spirit pervades every line of its construction, for the
style known as Empire is but an adaptation of classical motives without any
of their original and natural charm. The curves are clumsy, and even where
the unsatisfactory-looking legs are made perpendicular, as in the long
rosewood sofa (Fig. 916) from the music-room at Harewood, the effect is not
much better. Fig. 917 is another seat from the same set, which is only a
clumsy evolution of the charming window-seats and settees designed by
Adam, with a thickness and solidity that is quite unnecessary. The monotonous scroll, that formed the principal feature in furniture after 1820, was
even introduced on beds, and very little difference is observable between the
bed (Fig. 918) and the sofas of the time; and it is somewhat of a relief to turn
from this cumbrous ugliness of the times of George IV to the pretty bird-cage
(Fig. 919) made towards the close of the previous century, and the charm-
ingly decorated commode, of about 1800, given on Plate LX.

FIG. 919. *Mahogany Inlaid Bird-cage*. Property
of C. EASTWICK FIELD, Esq.

CHAPTER VIII

T has been shown that, under the influence of Sheraton, chairs reached their limitations in delicacy of appearance. The most careful selection of wood and perfection of joinery was necessary to make these spidery constructions practical and permanent; where satinwood was employed, the hardness of the material was an advantage, but the appearance of a satinwood chair, unless painted, is never very satisfactory, and the majority of these very light examples were generally japanned in colour on mahogany or beech, for the waste entailed in chair-making precluded the general adoption of satinwood for this purpose. To look really well, this wood, when used in small pieces, requires to be very highly figured, and its value for veneer prevents it from being cut out in the solid: genuine satinwood chairs of the end of the eighteenth century are therefore rare, and before purchase should be most carefully inspected; a good many were made about thirty or forty years ago with other satinwood furniture, and even this ageing has considerably added to the difficulty of detection.

Fig. 920 is one of a set made for Harewood about 1790, and probably formed part of the state bedroom furniture, which was all of satinwood. The design is extremely simple, the splat being formed of three slender ribs carved with leafage, and the taper legs headed with small oval cabochons; the back rail is quite straight, and stretchers are of necessity introduced. The colour of the chair is a deep yellow, the satinwood having darkened very much in tone. The maker was probably Chippendale and Haig, as this firm was upholsterer to the Lascelles family, but the design is of Sheraton origin. The same master influenced the shape of the cherry-wood chairs (Figs. 921 and 922). The first example was originally painted; the wheel patterned treatment of the back, first introduced by Adam and Hepplewhite, was quickly appropriated by other and rather later designers. Fig. 922 shows the reintroduction of caning which took place after 1780, and is a very good specimen of this work on the curve. In Fig. 923 crossed diagonals take the place of perpendicular ribs, and the centre of the splat is filled in with caning headed with panels painted in grisaille; the legs and uprights being painted in colours on the satinwood. The surface in Plate LVIII (c), is entirely painted black, and on this coloured floral designs are added. These chairs are also of

FIG. 920. *Satinwood Chair*. Property of the EARL OF HAREWOOD.

FIG. 921. *Satinwood Chair*. Property of W. JAMES, Esq.

FIG. 922. *Cane and Satinwood Arm-chair*. Property of W. JAMES, Esq.

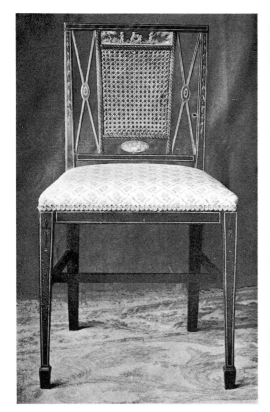

FIG. 923. *Painted Satinwood Chair*. Height, 2 feet 10 inches; width, 1 foot 5 inches. Property of MISS SCHOLFIELD.

FIG. 924. *Mahogany Chair*. Property of JAMES W. PIRIE, Esq.

FIG. 925. *White and Gold Chair, Covered in Spitalfields Silk*. Property of the MARQUESS OF CHOLMONDELEY.

the school of Sheraton, and shortly before the close of the century. Sometimes the whole of the splat was formed of crossed diagonal lines contained between two slender perpendiculars, as in Fig. 924; the legs and uprights being round and delicately fluted in the French directoire taste, and the panel of the cresting lightly carved in place of painting. A little later these lattice-worked splats were placed horizontally, the top rail being of baluster shape, slightly scrolling over and united to the splat by a flat entablature, which was at first painted but later ornamented with applied brass ornaments. The seats were caned as in Fig. 925, and a loose squab was generally added. The arm-chair, with mutilated feet (Fig. 926), which belongs to this set from Houghton, is of rather different design, but covered with the same Spitalfields silk, which was especially woven for the purpose. The woodwork of both is of white and gold, and the set, with their silk coverings, was presented to the Earl of Oxford by George IV when Prince Regent, early in the nineteenth century.

It is necessary to allude to the eccentricities that characterised the later designs of Sheraton, where in seeking for originality he lost all sense of tradition and propriety, and where griffins, eagles, lions' paws and cornucopia in combination with tortuous curves, replaced the simple, quiet and perfect lines of his earlier style. These fantastic motives, confined principally to designs for sofas, tables and chairs, were probably the effect of a mind worn out by the disappointment of losing influence on a public that was rapidly becoming meretricious in taste and insensible to simple beauty. In the chair, Fig. 927, one of a set of six, even the legs are tortured, and fail to give the impression of supports. The back is composed of crossed cornucopia, from which spring almost at right angles griffins' necks and heads, holding between them an umbrella-shaped canopy, with a foliated stem of trumpet flowers in false Chinese taste; the surface is painted in buff, red, green and blue, and although beautifully carved, is too eccentric. This example, although possessing certain points of resemblance to Empire furniture, in no way represents it, but the seat (Fig. 928) of about 1805 is very typical of this ultra-classical affectation. It is of 'X' form, with lion terminals of strong classical mannerism; in some instances these were brass, but here are gilt and carved, the rest is japanned black. Another and rather later example of this style made in mahogany can be seen in Fig. 929; here the shape more approximates early chairs of the sixteenth century, suggesting

FIG. 926. *White and Gold Arm-chair, Covered in Spitalfieds Silk.* Height, 3 feet; width, 2 feet 1 inch. Property of the MARQUES OF CHOLMONDELEY.

FIG. 927. *Painted Chair.* Property of H. FRANKLIN, Esq.

FIG. 928. *'X' Seat.* Height, 2 feet 6 inches; width, 2 feet 6 inches. Property of the EARL OF HAREWOOD.

FIG. 929. *Mahogany 'X' Chair.* Height, 3 feet 2 inches; width, 2 feet. Property of W. JAMES, Esq.

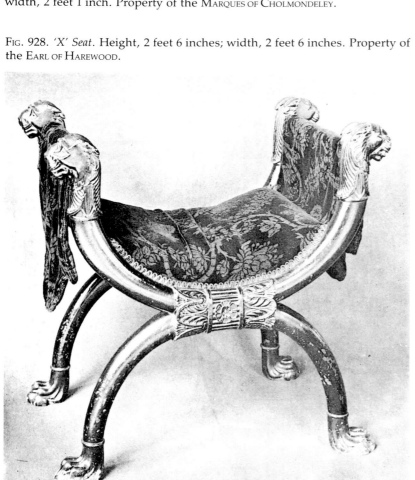

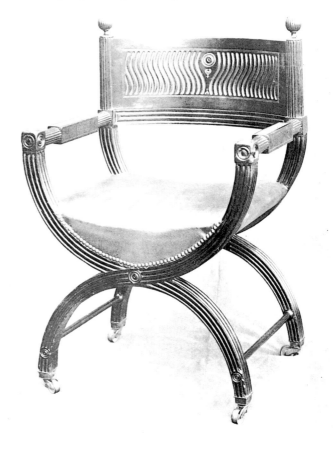

that the end of all evolutions is but a repetition of the beginning, for the movement in true furniture began in the classical taste and ended under the same inspiration, and nothing artistically original was produced after 1820. Fig. 930 is another classical shape much adopted for chairs without arms; the back is made of a flat piece bent round to form a semicircle; the taper legs curved backwards and forwards as in Greek and Roman chairs, and the surface is black, painted in buff and red with a few classical details; sometimes this shape was made in mahogany inlaid with similar patterns in ebony, often supported on dolphins, as in Fig. 931, and sometimes end in eagle or griffin heads, the seats being of cane, with the back-rail broad and flat; in this instance the back-rail has lost the painted decoration.

Fig. 932 is one from a set of fourteen, the broad, flat heading being of caning, with the top rail scrolled over and painted in gold and brown like the rest of the wood-work; the arm-supports rest upon lions' paws, which seem misplaced in this portion of the chair, and the legs show signs of the ugliness that was so soon to become universal. The chief interest in these chairs lies in the scroll over the back, a distinguishing and disagreeable feature adopted after 1820, for this clumsy detail, and the meaningless application of stamped brass ornament, was then as indicative of decadence and want of imagination as the tin hearts and hinges on the strange-looking boxes with railings that are called 'nouveau art' furniture in these times. To trace this decadence still further requires but little perception – the gap in taste between the chair, Fig. 925 and Fig. 933, separated by an interval of less than twenty years, shows so great a difference from all tradition of what was beautiful, that the mystery of this sudden change cannot be explained. The brass lines on the rosewood chair (Fig. 933) are better than the coarse brass pateræ of this metal on Fig. 934, and the curved classical legs more graceful than the thick rosewood and fluted horrors of later Guelphian times, but they are both without interest and imagination, belonging to a period of furniture that can only be described as commodious and commercial, made in that material age when the 'First Gentleman in Europe' was King of England.

With the close of the eighteenth century, originality and real beauty in English furniture ceased. Technically the work remained excellent, but as imagination and enthusiasm gradually disappeared, beautiful invention in domestic objects decayed and died; architecture, the parent of furniture, after the death of George III in 1820, became for the first time in England utterly ugly and uninteresting, textiles, plate, jewellery, as well as the

FIG. 930. *Painted Chair*. Height, 2 feet 8 inches; width, 1 foot 9 inches. Property of the EARL OF HAREWOOD.

FIG. 931. *Painted Chair*. Property of LORD ST OSWALD.

FIG. 932. *Gilt and Brown Caned Chair*. Height, 2 feet 8 inches. Property of MISS TYNDALL.

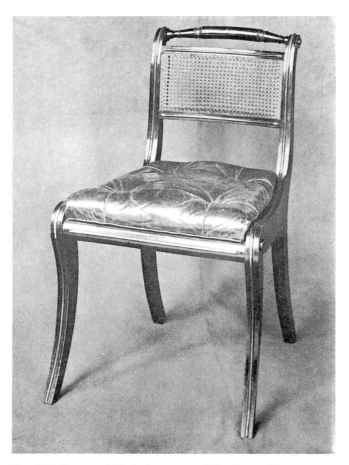

Fig. 933. *Rosewood Chair.* Property of the Earl of Harewood.

Fig. 934. *Rosewood Arm-chair.* Height, 3 feet 2 inches; width, 2 feet 2 inches. Property of the Earl of Harewood.

necessary accompaniments of everyday life, were but imitations of former periods, and invention was concentrated on science, finance and commercial enterprise in manufacture, little interest being taken in individual craftsmanship. Furniture no longer helped to carry out the decoration of houses, but became as ugly and uninteresting as its heavy and prosaic surroundings, for in some unexplained manner the long romance of beauty that had lasted in this country for eight centuries ceased suddenly, and was followed by a period, of forty years' duration, of the most appalling taste. Happily throughout this period, in many instances, the enthusiastic artist and collector survived, and in spite of being regarded as harmlessly eccentric during the dark age of early Victorian taste, they preserved, and were eventually the means of encouraging, the revival of the beautiful.

It is remarkable that so much furniture of the Age of Oak has survived to the present time, but its indestructible qualities have doubtless preserved it, though owing to its cumbrous construction, it was for a long time esteemed of little use and relegated to servants' quarters. In the Middle Ages all furniture was highly valued and scarce, a scarcity not altogether due to want of money, but induced by an out-of-door life that called for few luxuries. Even the most wealthy possessed but little furniture till the sixteenth century, when peaceful times were more conducive to domestic comfort. The individual requirements of woman, in spite of her indoor seclusion, apparently received little encouragement or attention from man, unless especially adding to her personal appearance, and it is not till about 1540 that we find furniture set apart exclusively for woman's use. Patronage of artistic skill was therefore chiefly concentrated upon architecture, armour, weapons, plate, jewellery and textiles. The treatment of early furniture resembled its stone surroundings, and was more or less comfortless in construction. About 1580 these architectural features began to be blended with new practical possibilities; such things already existing as small tables, long stools, settles, chairs, writing-desks, court-cupboards and buffets were added to early in the seventeenth century by luxurious upholstery, which took the place of loose cushions and draperies that had hitherto been the only means of giving colour and comfort to furniture. Cushions on the floor were gradually superseded by sets of chairs and small, comfortable settees, and the improvement proceeded rapidly until the time of the Rebellion, when for twenty years, artistic civilisation was arrested. With the restoration of the Monarchy, comfortable arm-chairs, with tall padded or cane backs, and with a sensible rake to the arms and back, were invented; also high-backed settees with padded arms, that quickly developed into the sofa of the end of the century; isolated specimens of day-beds and couches of the period of James I are in existence at Hardwick and Knole, but all sense of line and proportion is lacking in the examples of this period, and quite eighty years elapsed before such furniture became elegant or really decorative. In the same way the cumbrous posts and cornices to beds and the carved wooden headings were replaced by much taller and more spacious constructions entirely covered with silk or velvet. All the upholstered furniture made during the last twenty-five years of the seventeenth century was invested with true decorative sentiment; it was vigorous and original, practical in construction, and never artificial; full of colour in the happy combination of upholstery and marqueterie, or with just sufficient carving to emphasise its lines. The furniture of Charles II, William and Anne, may not be so suitable to the requirements of modern houses as the dainty and more delicate productions of the eighteenth century, but the largeness of style of the former period has pictorial qualities that always infer the work of the artist over and above the mere constructive cabinet-maker.

The fashion for gilding furniture had been sparingly adopted up till the end of the seventeenth century, but soon after that date it would be difficult to name any important article of furniture that was not to be found entirely gilt. In important houses like Blenheim, Houghton and Chatsworth, the furniture in the state-rooms was entirely gilt, even Chippendale a little later provided suites of gilt furniture for his clients, and the fashion for this gilding was continued by Adam through the last thirty years of the eighteenth century. Introduced for the sake of originality and ostentation, it was doubtless the means of bringing in new fantastic motives on the furniture.

Chippendale's rococo period was followed by his inlaid and painted satinwood, and this representation of gold colour was the culmination of the desire for brightness; but even Chippendale loses in dignity when he touches this satinwood style, so distinctly feminine in refinement, yet possessing a fascinating prettiness and brightness of its own that appeals to many, and for this reason and the excellence of its construction, will probably always remain popular. It is, in fact, the last original effort in our furniture, completing with great finish a long history of artistic taste, closely associated with our personality, and superior in straightforward simplicity and fascinating reticence to the furniture of other countries.

Foreign ideas and instruction no doubt at times greatly influenced our craftsmen, but such ideas and details were filtered through English minds, and during this process acquired the indescribable but distinct human interest found in all branches of our Art in which nothing is more nationally representative than English Furniture.

INDEX